Making FrontPage Work:

Essential Tips & Techniques

Konrad King

JAMSA PRESS
...a computer user's best friend®

ONWORD PRESS
THOMSON LEARNING™

Australia Canada Mexico Singapore Spain United Kingdom United States

ONWORD PRESS
THOMSON LEARNING

Making FrontPage Work: Essential Tips & Techniques
By Konrad King

Business Unit Director:
Alar Elken

Acquisitions Editor:
James Gish

Executive Editor:
Sandy Clark

Editorial Assistant:
Jaimie Wetzel

Executive Marketing Manager:
Maura Theriault

Executive Production Manager:
Mary Ellen Black

Project Editor:
W. K. Cheung

Senior Production Coordinator:
Toni Hansen

Art/Design Coordinator:
Rachel Baker

Cover Design:
Alan Giana
Venture Media Group

Printed in the United States
1 2 3 4 5 XXX 05 04 02 01

For more information contact
OnWord Press
an imprint of Thomson Learning,
PO Box 15015,
Albany, NY 12212-5015.

Or find us on the World Wide Web at
http://www.onwordpress.com

Library of Congress
Cataloging-in-Publication Data
ISBN 1-8841-3380-0

NOTICE TO THE READER

CONTENTS

INSTALLING FRONTPAGE

Installing FrontPage on your computer is a simple process. The most complicated task you face is making sure that your system meets the application's requirements—which you can review on the Microsoft Web site at *www.microsoft.com/frontpage*. Click your mouse pointer on the *FrontPage Tour* hyperlink on the Web page. Your Web browser, in turn, will display the first page of the FrontPage tour similar to that shown in Figure 1.1.

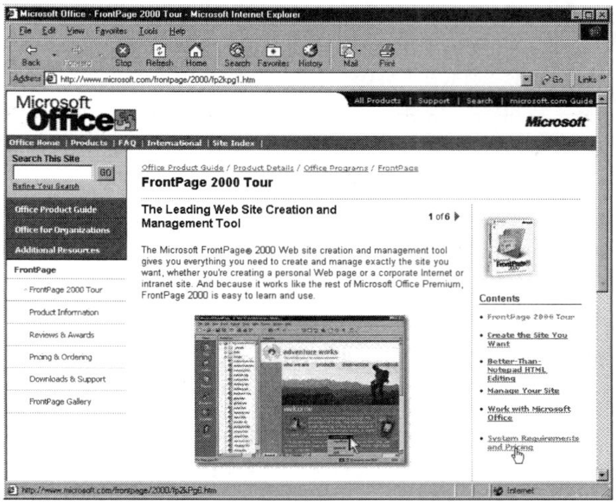

Figure 1.1 The first page of the FrontPage tour on the Microsoft Web site.

To see the list of requirements (and current product pricing), click your mouse pointer on the *System Requirements* hyperlink located along the lower right side of the Web page. Your Web browser, in turn, will display Microsoft's system requirements for running FrontPage. As of this writing the requirements for installing and running FrontPage are as shown in Table 1.1.

Requirements
✓ Personal Computer with a Pentium (75MHz) or Higher Processor
✓ Microsoft Windows 95/98 or Later Operating System, or Microsoft NT Workstation or Server 4.0 with Service Pack 3 or Later
✓ 24MB of RAM for Windows 95/98 or 40MB of RAM for Windows NT
✓ 167MB Available Hard Disk Space
✓ CD-ROM Drive
✓ VGA or Higher Resolution Monitor (Super VGA Recommended)
✓ Mouse or Compatible Pointing Device

Table 1.1 The FrontPage system requirements. *(Continued on next page)*

Optional:

- ✓ Sound Card—if you plan to record and playback sound during web site development
- ✓ An Internet Account with Rights to Save Your Web Pages
- ✓ An Internet Server Running FrontPage Server Extensions—if you want to use the FrontPage Web page publication Features
- ✓ Microsoft Mail, Microsoft Exchange, SMTP/POP3 Server, or Other MAPI-Compliant Software—if you want to use FrontPage e-mail features
- ✓ Microsoft Access or Another ODBC-Compliant Database—if you want to use the FrontPage database access features

Table 1.1 The FrontPage system requirements. (Continued from previous page)

Once you've met the minimum system requirements, you will of course need a copy of FrontPage. You can purchase FrontPage by itself or as part of the Microsoft Office XP Professional package. To install FrontPage, perform the following steps:

1. Exit any application programs currently running on your computer.
2. Insert the Microsoft Office XP Professional CD (or the FrontPage CD), into your CD-ROM drive. (Make sure that the CD label is facing up). Windows, in turn, will start the Setup program, which, in turn, will display a Customer Information dialog box similar to that shown in Figure 1.2.

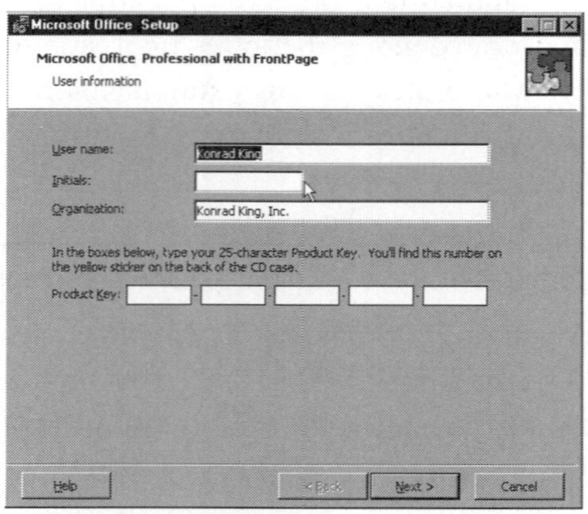

Figure 1.2 The Customer Information dialog box.

***Note:** If Windows does not display the first page of the setup application after you insert the CD, double-click your mouse pointer on the My Computer icon on your desktop. Windows, in turn, will display an icon for each of the drives on your system. Double-click your mouse pointer on the CD-ROM icon. Windows, in turn, will display the first screen of the Setup program.*

3. Enter your name in the User name field and your initials in the Initials field.
4. If your company owns the Microsoft Office or FrontPage software you are installing, enter the company name in the Organization field.
5. Enter the 25-character product key written on the sticker affixed to your CD case in the Product Key field. Then click your mouse pointer on the NEXT button. The Setup program, in turn, will display the End-User License Agreement.
6. After you've read the End-User License Agreement, click your mouse pointer on the radio button to the left of I accept the terms in the License Agreement. Then click your mouse pointer on the NEXT button. The Setup program, in turn, will display the Choose the Type of Installation You Need dialog box.

Note: *Before performing step 7, you must decide whether you want to perform the default or custom installation procedure. In general, you will want to use default installation procedure if this is a first time installation or if you have not customized your previous version of FrontPage. If you decide to use the custom installation procedure, finish the current installation process starting at Step 7 of the installation procedure shown in the next Tip. Otherwise, continue with Step 7 below to complete a default FrontPage installation.*

7. If the Setup program finds a previous version of FrontPage on your system, the you will be able to click select the Upgrade Now option on the Choose the Type of Installation You Need dialog box. Either select Upgrade Now (if available) or one of the other three installation options by clicking your mouse button on the radio button to the left of your choice. Then, click your mouse pointer on NEXT button.
8. The Setup program, in turn, will ask you which previous versions of the Microsoft Office programs (or FrontPage) you wish to keep. Either click your mouse pointer on the radio button to the left of Remove all previous versions or Remove only the following applications. If you choose the latter, click your mouse button on the check boxes to the left of the Office applications whose previous versions you want the setup program to remove.
9. Click your mouse pointer on the NEXT button, the Setup program, in turn, will display the Begin Installation dialog box.
10. Click your mouse pointer on the INSTALL button, and the Setup program will configure Microsoft Office (or FrontPage) and install the program(s) on your computer.

The setup process will take several minutes to complete. Windows will display a status bar to let you know it is still working and not "stuck." When the Setup program finishes copying files to your computer, it will display an Installer Information dialog box asking for permission to restart your computer.

When prompted, click your mouse pointer on the YES button to restart your computer and complete the installation process.

SELECTING FRONTPAGE INSTALLATION OPTIONS

If you followed the steps in the previous Tip, you used the Setup program to install the most commonly used (i.e., the default) FrontPage components into the C:\PROGRAM FILES\MICROSOFT OFFICE\OFFICE10 folder. One reason you might not use the default installation is if you want to keep your previous version of FrontPage intact. By installing FrontPage to a new folder (vs. replacing the existing files), you can continue to work with the original version while you learn the features of the new program. Moreover, if you made configuration changes to the previous version of the program, having both copies of the software available makes it easy to compare settings so that you get the new version of the program setup like you had the previous one.

Another reason for performing the custom installation procedure is to avoid having to stop working in FrontPage in order to install features not installed during the standard installation procedure. For example, FrontPage comes with several templates or themes that you can use to provide consistent background colors, text colors, and navigation buttons to the pages on your Web site. The default installation process does not copy all of the themes available on the CDROM onto your hard drive. If you are using FrontPage and select a theme not yet installed, FrontPage will prompt you with a dialog box similar to that shown in Figure 2.1.

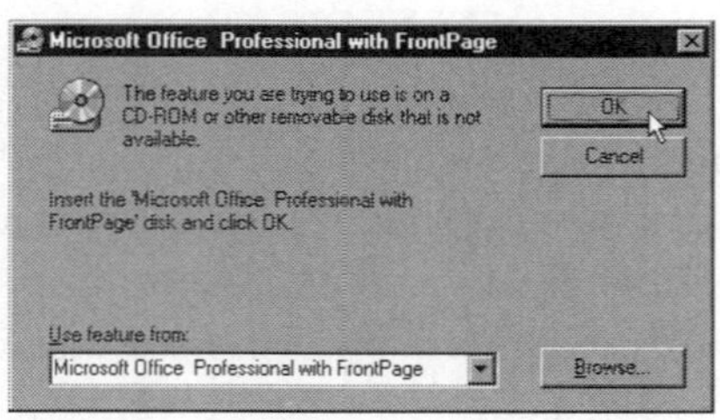

Figure 2.1 The Install On First Use install new feature dialog box.

While it only takes a few minutes to insert the installation CD-ROM and install the theme you want, doing so does interrupt your workflow and may not be possible if you are working on your laptop at home while your installation CD-ROM is on your desk at work.

To select the options during the FrontPage installation process perform the following steps:

1. Exit all application programs currently running on your computer.
2. Insert the Microsoft Office XP CD (or the FrontPage CD), into your CD-ROM drive. Make sure that the CD label is facing up). Windows, in turn, will start the Setup program, which in turn, will display the Customer Information dialog box.

Note: *If Windows does not display the first page of the setup application after you insert the CD, double-click your mouse pointer on the My Computer icon on your desktop. Windows, in turn, will display an icon for each of the drives on your computer. Double-click your mouse pointer on the icon of the CD-ROM drive into which you inserted the installation CD-ROM. Windows, in turn, will either start the Setup program or display the list of files and folders on the CD-ROM. If you see the list of files and folders, double-click your mouse pointer on the "Setup.exe" file.*

3. Enter your name in the User name field and your initials in the Initials field.
4. If your company owns the Microsoft Office or FrontPage software you are installing, enter the company name in the Organization field.
5. Enter the 25-character product key written on the sticker affixed to your CD case in the Product Key field. Then click your mouse pointer on the NEXT button. The Setup program, in turn, will display the End-User License Agreement.
6. After you've read the End-User License Agreement, click your mouse pointer on the radio button to the left of I accept the terms in the License Agreement. Then click your mouse pointer on the NEXT button. The Setup program, in turn, will display a Choose the Type of Installation You Need dialog box, similar to that shown in Figure 2.2.

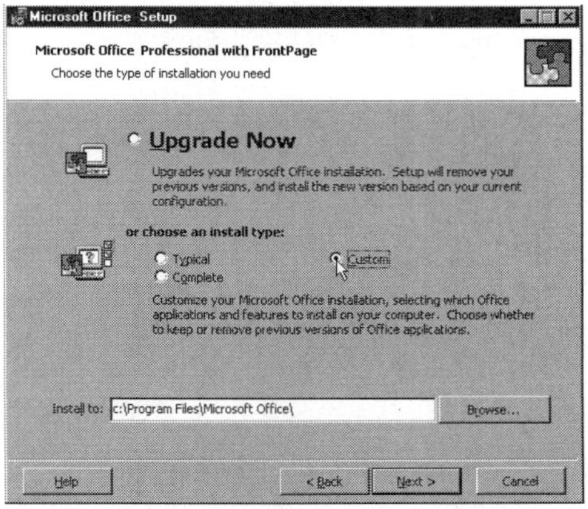

Figure 2.2 *The Microsoft Office Setup: Choose the Type of Installation You Need dialog box.*

7. Click your mouse pointer on the radio button to the left of the Custom option, and then click your mouse pointer on the NEXT button. The Setup program, in turn, will display a Choose Which Applications to Install dialog box similar to that shown in Figure 2.3.

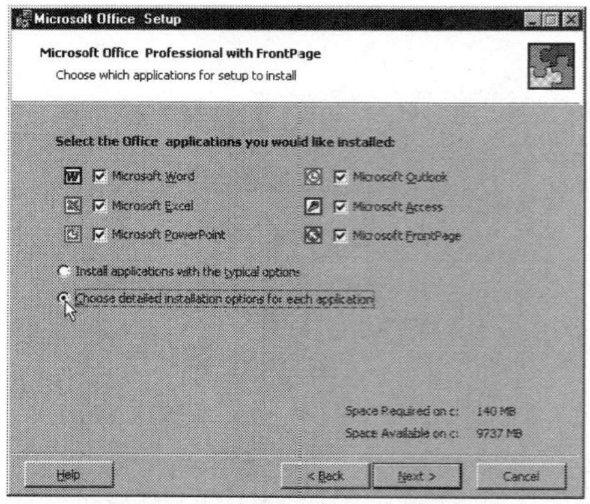

Figure 2.3 The Microsoft Office Setup: Choose Which Applications to Install dialog box.

8. Click your mouse pointer on the check boxes to the left of each application you want the Setup program to install until a check mark appears.
9. Click your mouse pointer on the radio button to the left of Choose detailed installation options for each application and then on the NEXT button. The Setup program, in turn, will display a Choose Installation Options dialog box.
10. To select specific FrontPage features to install, such as additional themes, click your mouse pointer on the plus to the left of the Microsoft FrontPage for Windows icon. The Setup program, in turn, will display the list of FrontPage features available and the default installation option for each feature, similar to that shown in Figure 2.4.

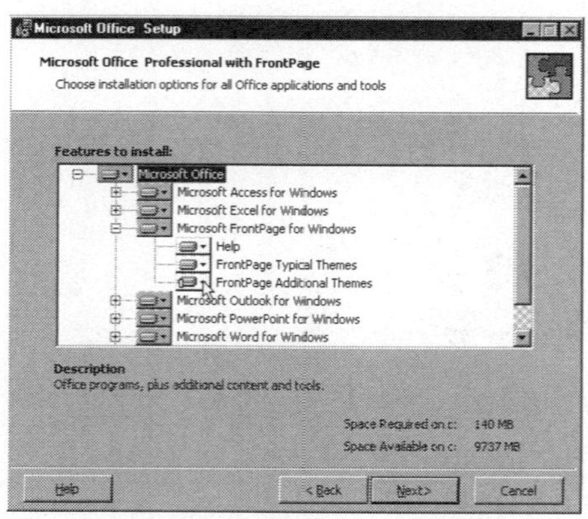

Figure 2.4 The Microsoft Office Setup: Choose Installation Options dialog box with Microsoft FrontPage features and installation options list.

11. To install additional FrontPage Themes during the installation process, click your mouse pointer on the icon to the left of Additional Themes. The Setup program, in turn, will display the installation option list shown in Figure 2.5.

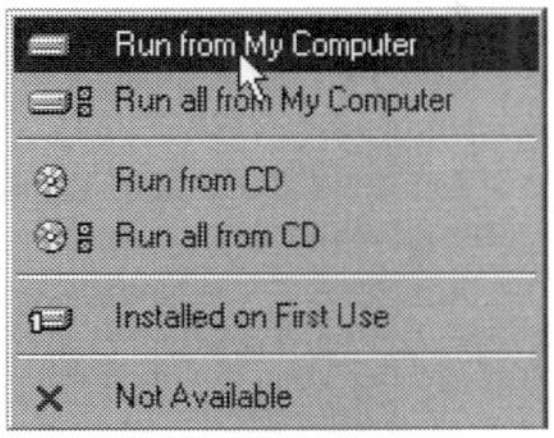

Figure 2.5 The FrontPage feature installation option list.

12. Click your mouse pointer on Run From My Computer to have the Setup program copy all FrontPage themes from the installation CD to your hard drive during installation. The Setup program, in turn, will change the icon to the left of Additional Themes to match the others that indicate those features that will be installed to disk during the installation option (vs. the icon with the "1" indicating the feature will be installed on first use—as shown in Figure 2.4).
13. Click your mouse pointer on the NEXT button. The Setup program, in turn, will display a Remove Previous Versions of Office Applications dialog box similar to that shown in Figure 2.6.

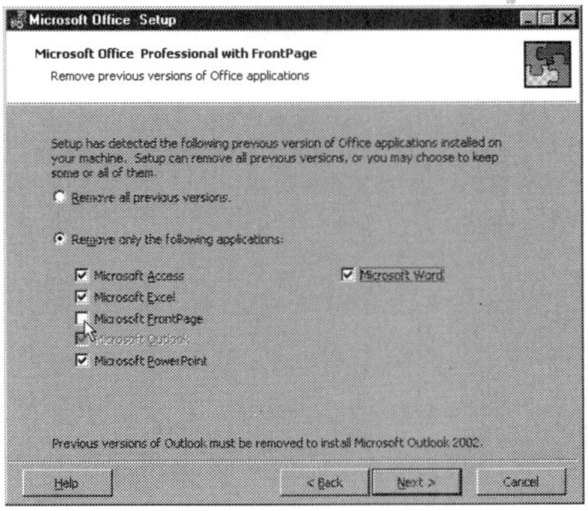

Figure 2.6 The Microsoft Office Setup: Remove Previous Versions of Office Applications dialog box.

14. If you want to keep previous versions of any of your Microsoft Office applications, click you mouse pointer on the radio button to the left of Remove only the following applications, and then on the check box to the left of each application you want the Setup program to leave unchanged on your system. For example, to leave the previous

version of FrontPage on your system, click your mouse pointer on the check box to the left of Microsoft FrontPage until the check mark disappears.

15. Click your mouse pointer on the NEXT button. The Setup program, in turn, will display a Begin Installation dialog box similar to that shown in Figure 2.7.

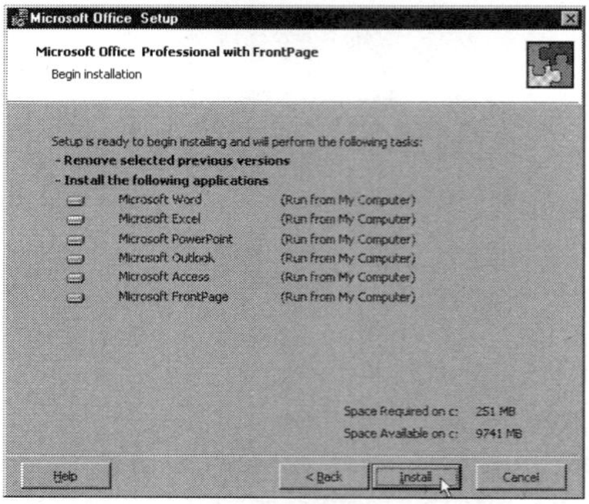

Figure 2.7 The Microsoft Office Setup: Begin Installation dialog box.

16. Click your mouse pointer on the INSTALL button. The Setup program, in turn, will install FrontPage (and other Office applications, if you are using the Microsoft Office CD-ROM) program(s) on your hard drive. Copying the files and registering the program(s) in the Windows registry will take several minutes. The Setup program will display a status bar to let you know it is still working and not "stuck." When the Setup program finishes copying files to your computer, it will display an Installer Information dialog box asking for permission to restart your computer.

When prompted, click your mouse pointer on the YES button to restart your computer and complete the installation process.

UNDERSTANDING WEB SITE DESIGN CHALLENGES

In conventional hardcopy layout design, such as specifying the layout for a magazine or a book, you can control exactly how each page will look. You specify the exact placement of text and pictures; you decide exactly how each character of text will look by selecting its font and color. In short, you have full control over the final product. Unfortunately, the same cannot be said about your control over how your Web pages will look to a Web site visitor. The beauty of the Web is that you use Hypertext Markup Language (HTML) to design Web pages without having to worry about the computer or Web browser a visitor will use to display them. Unfortunately, to gain the freedom of cross-platform compatibility, you have to give up some measure of control over how your Web page will look. We will discuss how to resolve specific color, font, and placement concerns and resolutions in Tips dealing specifically with these issues. For now, the important thing to know is that your Web pages may not look the same on a visitor's computer monitor as they look on your computer monitor.

Screen resolution is one issue you need to keep in mind. Most people browse the Web using a screen resolution of 800 x 600. If you scan a graphics image that can only be displayed at a resolution of 1024 x 768, your visitor will not be able to view your entire image at once. Moreover, if you are designing a Web site where you expect most of your visitors will be visiting via Web TV, you will want to design the site using a screen resolution of 640 x 480—which is the typical resolution of the current Web TV devices. The best advice when selecting a screen resolution is to determine what resolution your target audience will most likely use and design the site using that resolution on your system. Once you publish your Web pages, visit your Web site using various screen resolutions (e.g., 640x480, 800x600, 1024x768) to see what happens to the alignment of your graphics and text.

Also keep in mind that different browsers (and different versions of the same browser) have different capabilities. When a browser sees an HTML tag (or formatting command) it doesn't understand, the browser will ignore it. Therefore, if you use screen transition effects such has having text "fly" onto your Web pages one letter or word at a time, bear in mind that not all browsers will show the animation. Internet Explorer, for example, will display page transition effects. Netscape Navigator, on the other hand, ignores the page transition effects tags and just displays all the words on the Web page at once. The reason this happens is that Web page transition effects are not part of standard HTML. As a result some browsers do not understand the HTML tags (commands) that specify page transition effects. The best solution is to install several Web browsers on your development machine. You can then visit your Web site with each of the browsers to get a feel for the special effects your visitors will see based on the browser they are using. Currently, about 90% of the Web surfers use either Netscape Navigator or Microsoft Internet Explorer. As such, you will want to test your Web site with these two browsers, at a minimum. Other Web browsers you may want to include are Amaya, Arachne, HotJava, Lynx, Mosaic, NeoPlanet, Opera, and 1x Browser. To get more information on these browsers, enter the name of the Browser into the search field of your favorite search engine (such as Yahoo, Lycos, Netfind, etc.). Your Web browser, in turn, will give you a link to the browser's home page where you can get additional info about the browser and download it to your system.

Note: *As of this writing, you can download various versions of the most popular browses used on the Web at **www.browsers.com.***

One final issue to consider is connection speed. Although we live in the high speed Internet access world of ISDN, DSL, and cable modems, don't forget that some of your visitors will be using 28.8Kbps and 33.6Kbps modems. You can reduce the amount of time it takes to display a Web page by reducing the amount of data on the page. Use thumbnails in place of larger pictures—let the visitor click the mouse pointer on the thumbnail to view the original (large) picture. We'll discuss graphics images and optimizing them later. For now, the important thing to know is that your visitors may be using a much slower link than you have. As such, don't put large pictures of your company headquarters and staff on your main content pages. Visitors will tire quickly of waiting for the graphics to download to their computers each time they visit your site.

In addition to optimizing your graphic images, you can "speed up" a Web page by reducing the text on the page and by eliminating unnecessary Java applets and ActiveX components. Don't lose sight of the Web site's purpose as you add "bells and whistles". If you are designing a site where visitors can download sound and video, you can assume your audience will have a fast Internet connection and will probably expect a lot of exciting multimedia effects. On the other hand, if you are designing an order entry page or customer support site, assume your visitors will use a wide range of connection speeds. Customers looking for product information or installation instructions are more interested in a well laid out, easy to search and navigate site with plenty of two-dimensional pictures and drawings of the product—versus lots of distracting animations.

UNDERSTANDING STEPS IN PLANNING A WEB SITE

Although FrontPage makes it very easy to create Web pages and quickly link them together into a Web site, don't be tempted to skip the all-important planning process. There are five simple, but important, steps involved in planning a Web site:

1. Define the Web site's purpose and intent.
2. Understand the target audience.
3. Organize the Web site's content.
4. Create a "storyboard" for the Web site.
5. Apply a consistent look and feel to the Web site.

Don't worry if you are working on your first Web site. The following paragraphs will explain each of the five design steps in detail, and you'll find a list of Web sites you can review for additional examples at the end of the current Tip. Moreover, FrontPage comes with a set of Wizards and templates that guide you through the design process step by step.

The first step in planning your Web site is to define its purpose or intent. If your site's purpose is commercial, your visitors expect to find product descriptions, pictures, prices, and an order form. If you are creating a customer support site, visitors will expect to see installation and troubleshooting instructions, plenty of drawings and diagrams, and phone numbers to call for additional assistance. Finally, if you are creating a travel site, visitors will want to see descriptions of vacation destinations, travel package prices including itineraries and airfares, and an order form and phone numbers of a travel agent. Notice that a site's purpose determines its content. The better you understand what you are trying to accomplish, the more likely you'll be to include all of the "tools" a visitor will need to have a positive experience during a visit to your site.

Next, learn all you can about your target audience. For example, if you are creating a product support site for your customers, your technical writing will consist mainly of product installation instruction. Meanwhile, a Web site for your engineering or repair staff will have detailed circuit diagrams and component level repair information. While the overall purpose of the Web site is "product support," knowing the target audience tells you how to present the information. When defining your audience, consider your visitors' backgrounds and previous experiences. Try to discern their interests, tastes, and reason for visiting your site.

After you know what you are going to say and how you are going to say it, organize your Web site's content such that all significant information is within two or three mouse clicks of the home page. Properly linking a Web site with only a few pages is a relatively simple process. However, you can make even a large site easy to navigate if you organize it properly. Your home page should have links to the major "topics" on your Web site. One method of placing the necessary hyperlinks onto the home page is to present the site's table of contents as a button bar or menu along the sides or along the bottom of the page. Visitors will "drill down" into the Web site's structure—going from the general to the specific as they retrieve desired information. Later in this book you will learn how to place navigational bars on your Web pages so you can quickly reproduce your site's table of contents on each page and make it easy for visitors to jump among the topics on your Web site. At a minimum, you should provide a link back to your home page on every page of your Web site.

After organizing your site, decide what it will look like (i.e. create the storyboard). You must decide on both the structure (layout) and the graphic elements (pictures, background images, colors). Start with the structure and then work on the graphic elements. A well-structured site will be functional. Bear in mind that no matter how good a site looks, it will only be successful if its pages are well laid out and easy to use. Create a storyboard (a hand drawn sketch) of your Web pages. Ideally, you will storyboard your entire Web site. At a minimum draw the home page and each page to which the home page has a direct link. Don't worry if you're not an artist. Your goal is to organize your Web pages and not to finalize their design. Be sure to include text, graphics, buttons, and hyperlinks on your storyboards. While you don't need the exact graphic or text, you will want to make a basic sketch of the pictures and general outline of the text and decide on the specific placement of each element. Don't forget that your visitors are not going to read all the pages on your Web site, as they would a novel, by moving from page to page in a linear pattern. Instead, Web site visitors expect to jump quickly to specific items of interest, perhaps "drill down" for additional detail, and then quickly move on to another topic. Visitors may enter your site at any point from another site. As such, navigation elements are an essential part of each Web page. Make sure that visitors can easily find the navigation elements and that they are easy to use.

The final step in planning your Web site is to decide on the Web site's overall look and feel.

After planning the site's content and organization, give all of the Web pages a consistent combination of colors, graphics, fonts, and layout. FrontPage makes the process simple by supplying you with a set of templates and themes that place common elements such as navigation buttons, backgrounds, and layouts to all of the Web pages on the Web site.

FINDING DESIGN TIPS ON THE WEB

There are many sources of Web site design tips on the Internet. If you follow the basic design steps outlined in this Tip, you will create an outstanding Web site. However, if you want in-depth discussions by various authors and Web site creators on site design (and other related topics), check out the following Web sites:

- *www.builder.com* - C/Net Builder.com site for Web site builders has many articles on Web site design and Web technology. (As of this writing, visiting the *www.builder.com* Web site automatically redirects your browser to *home.cnet.com/webbuilding/0-3880.html.* If *www.builder.com* is no longer accessible as you read this text, go directly to the Web site *home.cnet.com* and look for a link on "Web Building" or "Web Design".)
- *communities.msn.com/webdesign* - click your mouse pointer on the "Web Design" link to find links to various discussion groups on all aspects of Web site design.
- *developer.netscape.com* – Netscape's online resources for building Web applications, more formally known as DevEdge Online. Find the link for "Web Building" to explore the site's Web site designing resources including "Site Central" which will let you select a type of Web site, personalize its content, add your own "cool stuff", and allow you to promote your site on America Online (AOL).
- *info.med.yale.edu/caim/manual/* - online version of the book "Web Style Guide: Basic Design Principles for Creating Web Sites" which covers both site and individual Web page design. You won't learn how to write HTML or how to import graphics from this book. However, you will find an in-depth discussion of navigation links, site structure, page structure, typography, graphics, tables, frames, editorial style, animations, and multimedia as they relate to good Web site design.
- *webdesign.about.com* - click your mouse pointer on the link for "Web Design Tips" to find articles and tutorials on Web site design. If you prefer to consult an expert, click your mouse pointer on the link for "The Web Designer Directory" to get contact information for professional Web site designers and to see examples of their work.

- *www.webreview.com* - click your mouse pointer on the "Design" section link to review the latest articles on Web site design and hints on how to make the most effective use of colors, fonts, page layout tools, and specific graphics programs such as Photoshop.

You can find other links to Web design information sites by typing "Web Design" into the search field of your favorite Web search engine such as *www.altavista.com*, *excite.com*, *infoseek.go.com*, *www.lycos.com*, and *www.yahoo.com* to name a few.

STARTING FRONTPAGE

After you install FrontPage (as discussed in the first two Tips in this book), perform the following steps to start FrontPage:

1. Click your mouse pointer on the START button. Windows, in turn, will display the Start menu.
2. Move your mouse pointer over Programs. Windows, in turn, will display a list of Start menu programs and folders, similar to that shown in Figure 5.1.

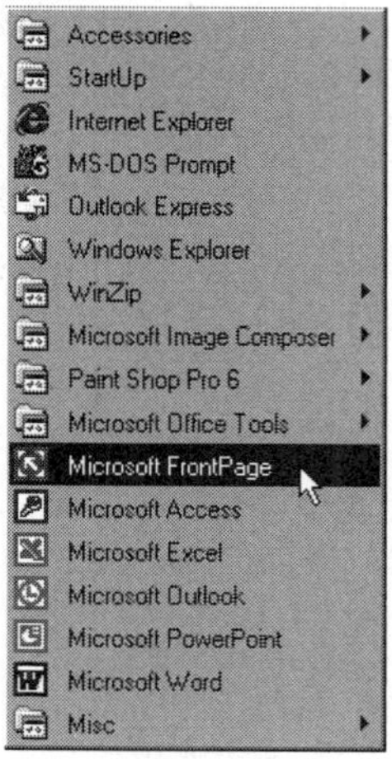

Figure 5.1 The Windows Start menu, Programs option.

3. Click your mouse pointer on Microsoft FrontPage. Windows, in turn, will start FrontPage, which, in turn, will display its main editing window similar to that shown in Figure 5.2.

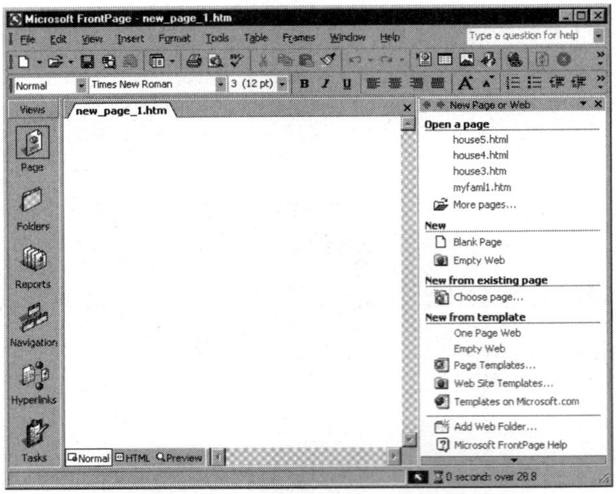

Figure 5.2 The FrontPage main editing window.

Note: *If you install a competing HTML editor such as Corel WordPerfect, after you install FrontPage, the program will display a dialog box similar to that shown in Figure 5.3 to let you know that it is not your default HTML editor.*

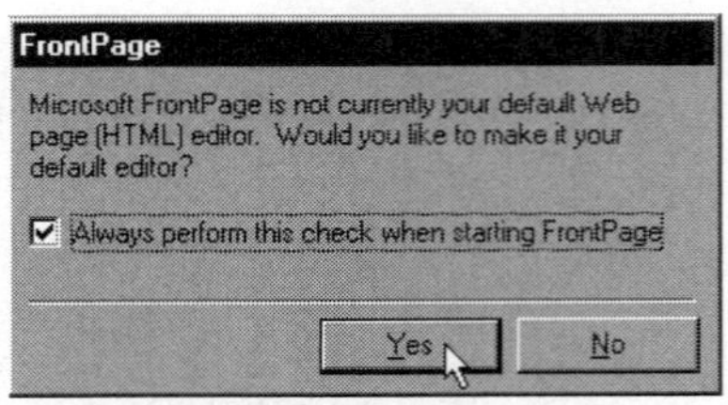

Figure 5.3 The FrontPage Default HTML Editor election dialog box.

To select FrontPage as your default HTML editor, click your mouse pointer on the YES *button. If you don't want to change the default HTML editor, click your mouse pointer on the check box to the left of Always perform this check when starting FrontPage until the check mark disappears. Then click your mouse pointer on the* NO *button. By clearing the Always perform this check box, you tell FrontPage not to ask you if you want to use FrontPage as the default HTML editor every time you start the program.*

If you are planning to use FrontPage often, create a shortcut on your desktop so you can start the program with a double-click of your mouse instead of having to navigate the Windows Start menu. To create a desktop shortcut to which starts FrontPage, perform the following steps:

1. Click your mouse pointer on the START button. Windows, in turn, will display the Start menu.

2. Move your mouse pointer over Programs. Windows, in turn, will display a list of Start menu programs and program folders.
3. Right click your mouse pointer on Microsoft FrontPage. Windows, in turn, will display a Properties menu similar to that shown in Figure 5.4.

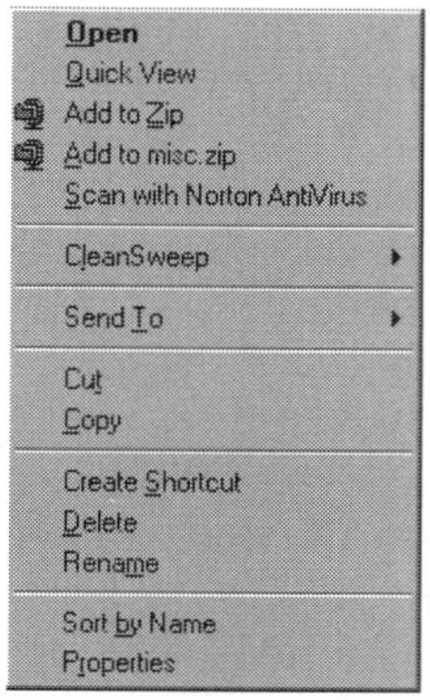

Figure 5.4 The Windows Start menu, Properties option menu.

4. Move your mouse pointer over Send To. Windows, in turn, will display a menu of Send To locations.
5. Click your mouse pointer on Desktop (create shortcut). Windows, in turn, will create a desktop shortcut to FrontPage similar to that shown in Figure 5.5.

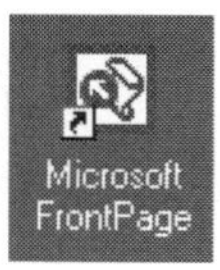

Figure 5.5 The FrontPage desktop shortcut.

6. Click your mouse pointer on any blank space on your desktop to tell Windows to remove the Start menu from your screen.

After you complete Step 6, find the FrontPage icon on your desktop. Note its location so that you can double-click your mouse pointer on the icon on your desktop the next time you want to start FrontPage.

USING A CONTENT TEMPLATE TO CREATE A PERSONAL WEB SITE

When you are ready to create a new Web site, you can use one of the three content templates included with FrontPage to get you started:

- **Customer Support Web** – Web site for companies to publish product help and information. Customers can find new product news, review answers to frequently asked questions (FAQ's), report problems, make suggestions, and participate in an on-line discussion with other customers. The template is designed to provide support services for software companies but can be easily adapted to provide customer support for other types of businesses.
- **Personal Web** – Web site to serve as a personal home page. You can enter a personal description and include areas of interest, photos, and links to your favorite Web sites.
- **Project Web** – Web site used to track the status of a project. You can enter team member information, a project completion schedule, current task status. The project site also includes a document archive and a discussion area for team members.

For example to create a Personal Web site, perform the following steps:

1. If FrontPage is not currently running on your computer, start the application now. Either double-click the FrontPage desktop icon you created in the preceding Tip and continue at Step 3, or click your mouse pointer on the START button (if you didn't create the desktop icon).
2. When Windows displays the Start menu, select Programs and then click your mouse pointer on Microsoft FrontPage on the Programs menu.
3. Click your mouse pointer on the drop-down list button to the right of the CREATE A NEW NORMAL PAGE button on the Standard toolbar. Then, select Web from the drop-down list. (The CREATE A NEW NORMAL PAGE button is the first button on the left on Standard Toolbar.) FrontPage, in turn, will display a New Web dialog box similar to that shown in Figure 6.

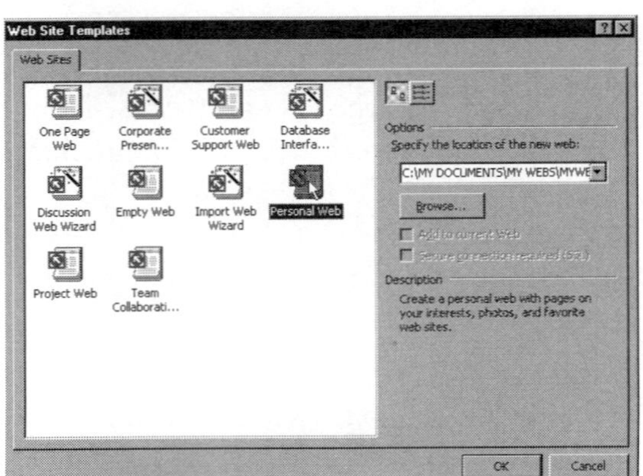

Figure 6 The FrontPage New Web dialog box.

4. Click your mouse pointer on the Web site template you want to use. For the current project, click your mouse pointer on the Personal Web template.
5. Enter the name of the folder in which you want FrontPage to create your Web site (Web pages and folders) in the Specify the location of the new web field. For the current project, accept the default directory of C:\MY DOCUMENTS\MY WEBS\MYWEB. (If the folder does not exist, FrontPage will create it.)

Note: *If you enter the name of an existing folder that does not contain a FrontPage Web, your existing files will not be affected. On the other hand, if you enter the pathname to a folder that already contains a FrontPage web, FrontPage will display a warning message stating that a FrontPage Web already exists in the folder you selected. After you click your mouse pointer on the OK button at the bottom of the warning message, FrontPage will return to the New dialog box so you can select another folder.*

6. Click your mouse pointer on the OK button. FrontPage, in turn, will generate the Web pages for the Personal Web site and return to the FrontPage main editing window.

To see what the generic FrontPage Personal Web site looks like, start your Web browser. Enter the full pathname to the Personal Web site's home page (INDEX.HTM) into the Web browser's Address field. To confirm the location of the FrontPage Web, look at the title bar at the top of the FrontPage window. For example, if you see that FrontPage shows that it created your Personal Web in the C:\MY DOCUMENTS\MYWEBS\MYWEB, enter C:\MY DOCUMENTS\MY WEBS\MY WEB\INDEX.HTM into your Web browser's Address field. After entering the address, press the ENTER key to have the Web browser display your Web site's home page. Previewing your Personal Web site's home page is covered more extensively in the Tip: Using Internet Explorer (IE) to View a FrontPage Web.

As you expand the portfolio of Web sites you've created, you will find that a certain set of Web pages will work well for more than one client. For example, once you get the background colors, Web page structure, and navigation buttons just right for a particular retailer's Web site, you need only change the title of the site, and the content of its pages in order to have an excellent site for second client. To make it easy for you to create Web sites quickly, FrontPage lets you create your own templates based on your Web site designs. After you create a template based on your Web site, you will be able to create similar Web sites (based on the saved template) as easily as you created the Personal Web in the current Tip.

UNDERSTANDING THE FRONTPAGE INTERFACE

FrontPage gives you the tools you need to create Web pages and manage Web sites in a single program. Figure 7 shows the integrated FrontPage Web site management and development environment in Navigation view of the MYWEB Web site you created in the preceding Tip (in the C:\MY DOCUMENTS\MY WEBS folder).

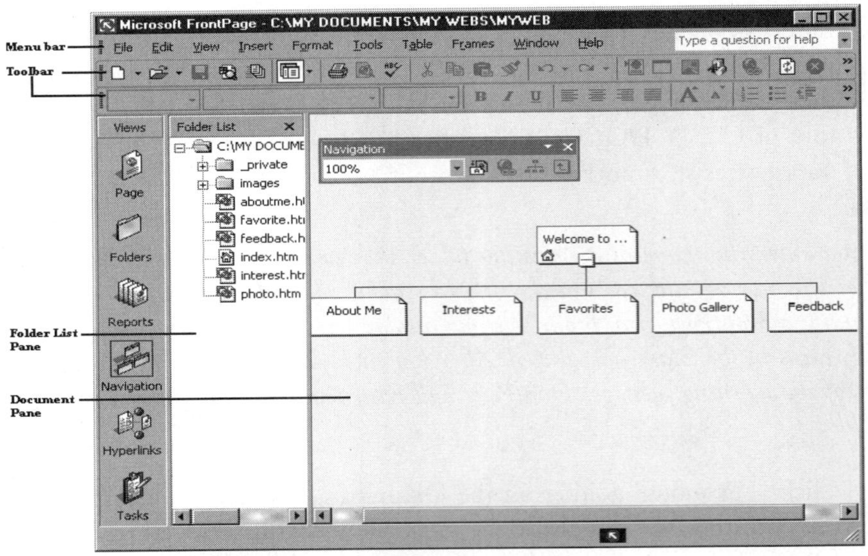

Figure 7 The FrontPage desktop in navigation view.

By default, you'll find the FrontPage menu system and toolbars along the top of the application window. You will learn how to customize the menu system later in this book. For now, the important thing to know is that the FrontPage menu system has all of the commands you need for creating and managing Web pages, and the toolbars have shortcuts (buttons) to the most often used functions. If you want, you can change the toolbars so that they have buttons for the commands you use most often. Moreover, you can drag the menu system bar and all toolbars to new locations anywhere on your screen—even outside the borders of the FrontPage application window.

FrontPage provides six views, or ways of displaying and working with your Web site. To select a view, click your mouse pointer on the icon of the view you want in the Views bar along the left side of the FrontPage application window (or select the View menu and click your mouse pointer on the name of the view you want to use). The six FrontPage views are:

- **Page** – Used to create and edit Web pages. When in Page view, FrontPage lists the Web site's Web pages in the Folder List pane and the Web page in the document pane to the right of the Folder List pane. You can change the Web page displayed in the document pane by double-clicking your mouse pointer on the Web page you want in the Folder List pane. If you want to create a new Web page, select the File menu New option and click your mouse pointer on Page (or click your mouse pointer on the NEW PAGE button on the Standard toolbar).

- **Folders** – Lists all of the files and folders associated with the current Web site. FrontPage will display the Web site's folders in the Folder List pane and will display subfolders and files in the document pane to the right of the Folder List pane. FrontPage shows the name, title, size, type, modified date, modified by, and comment information for each file and folder in the document pane. You can sort the list of files and folders in ascending or descending order by any one of the seven columns shown in the document pane.

- **Reports** – Lets you manage your Web and analyze its content through reports. After you click your mouse pointer on the Reports icon, you can select the report you want to see by using the floating Reporting toolbar or by selecting the View menu Reports option and clicking your mouse pointer on the desired report.

- **Navigation** – Gives you a hierarchical view of your Web site (such as that shown for the Personal Web in Figure 7), and helps you add navigation bars to your Web pages. In the Folder list pane, where you see a "+" in the site's tree structure, you can click your mouse pointer on it to expand that portion of the tree to see more detail. Where you see a "-" in the site tree, you can click your mouse pointer on it to hide detail for a higher level picture of the Web site.

- **Hyperlinks** – Shows the hyperlinks to and from the Web page you select in the Folder List pane. When you click your mouse pointer on a Web page in the Folder List pane, FrontPage will draw a graphical display of all links to and from the page in the document pane to the right of the Folder List pane.

- **Tasks** – Create and manage tasks for the development of the current Web site. FrontPage shows the status, task name, assigned to, priority, associated with, modified date, and description for each task. You can sort the task list in ascending or descending order by any of the fields displayed. To add a new task, either right-click in the document pane or select the Edit menu Task option, and click your mouse pointer on Add Task.

You will learn more about using each of the FrontPage views in subsequent tips. For now, the important thing to know is that FrontPage gives you a desktop with toolbars and menus you can use to create Web pages (and Web sites) in a what-you-see-is-what-you-get (WYSIWYG) environment. Moreover, in addition to making Web page editing easy, FrontPage also gives you a set of views you can use to manage the development of an entire Web site. If you still have the Personal Web you created in the preceding Tip open, go ahead and click each of the views to get familiar with the way in which they display the different aspects of the Web site.

USING FRONTPAGE WIZARDS TO CREATE A WEB SITE

In addition to content templates, FrontPage also comes with two Wizards you can use to create a Web site. Like the Wizards in other Microsoft Office products, the FrontPage wizards help to get you over the "blank page" hurdle when you start to setup a Web Site. The two wizards included with FrontPage are:

- **Corporate Presence Wizard** – Used to create a professional Internet presence for your business or organization. The Corporate Presence Web site is designed to publish corporate news and product and service information. The Wizard will also create a table of contents for the site and feedback and search pages.
- **Discussion Web Wizard** – Creates a site for a discussion group with threads, a table of contents, and full-text searching. A Discussion Web lets you create a site where your visitors discuss one or more topics by leaving notes for each other. Unlike e-mail, the notes are public and everyone that is a member of the discussion group is allowed to read the message(s) and post a reply.

To see how easy it is to use a Wizard to create a complex Web site, perform the following steps to create a Corporate Presence Web site:

1. Start FrontPage by clicking your mouse pointer on the START button, select Programs, and click your mouse pointer on Microsoft FrontPage.
2. Click your mouse pointer on the drop-down list button to the right of the CREATE A NEW NORMAL PAGE button (the first button on the left on the Standard toolbar) and select Web from the drop-down list. FrontPage, in turn, will display its New Web dialog box.
3. Enter the full pathname of the folder in which you want FrontPage to create the Corporate Presence Web into the Specify the location of the new web field. For the current project, accept the default—C:\MY DOCUMENTS\MY WEBS\MYWEB2.
4. Double-click your mouse pointer on the Corporate Presence Wizard icon in the list of templates and wizards in the left half of the dialog box. FrontPage, in turn, will display the first page of the Corporate Presence Web Wizard's introductory message.
5. After you've read the introductory message, click your mouse pointer on the NEXT button. FrontPage in turn will ask you to select the main pages you want to include on the Web site in addition to the home page, as shown in Figure 8.1. For the current project, accept the default additional page selections by leaving each of the Web page selection boxes checked.

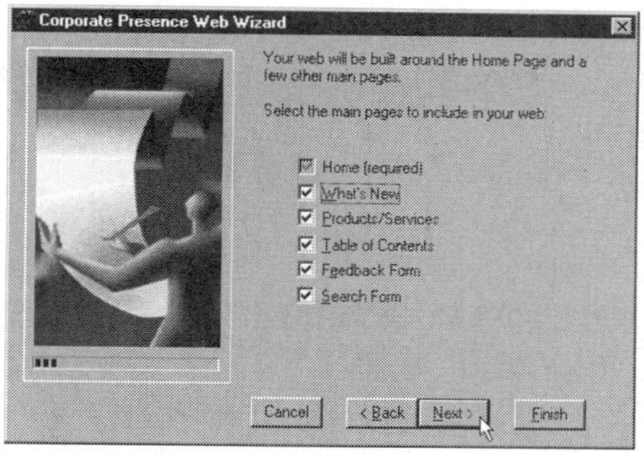

Figure 8.1 The Corporate Presence Web Wizard's main pages selection screen.

6. Click your mouse pointer on the NEXT button. FrontPage, in turn, will ask you to select the topics you want to publish on the Web site's home page as shown in Figure 8.2. For the current project, make sure all of the check boxes checked by clicking your mouse pointer on any empty check box until a check mark appears.

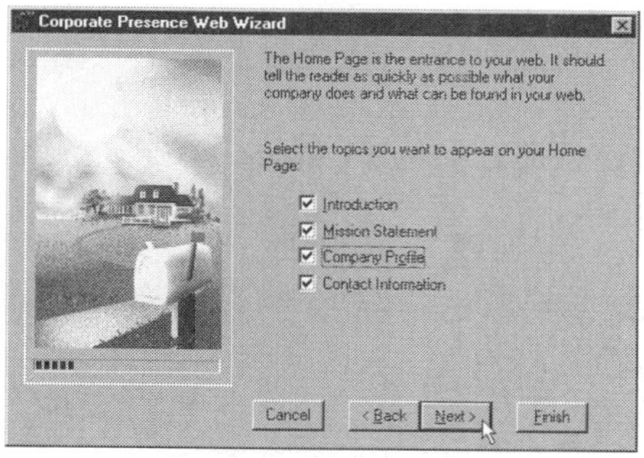

Figure 8.2 The Corporate Presence Web Wizard's Home Page topics selection screen.

7. Click your mouse pointer on the NEXT button. FrontPage, in turn, will ask you to select the topics you want to show on the "What's New Page," as shown in Figure 8.3. For the current project, accept the default and leave only the Web Changes box checked.

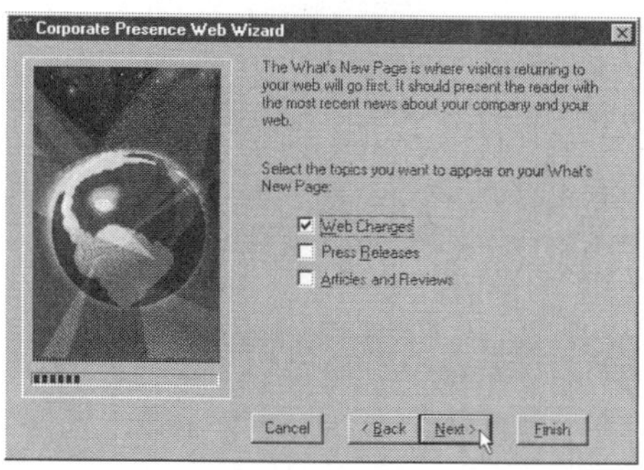

Figure 8.3 The Corporate Presence Web Wizard's What's New Page topics selection screen.

8. Click your mouse pointer on the NEXT button. FrontPage, in turn, will ask you to enter the number of products and the number of services you want to advertise on the Web site as shown in Figure 8.4. For the current project, accept the defaults of three products and three services.

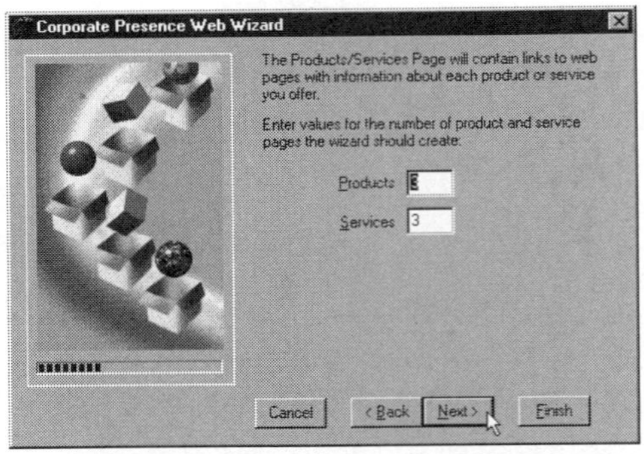

Figure 8.4 The Corporate Presence Web Wizard's Products/ServicesPage count screen.

9. Click your mouse pointer on the NEXT button. FrontPage, in turn, will let you select the items you want to include on each of the product and service pages as shown in Figure 8.5. For the current project, accept the defaults.

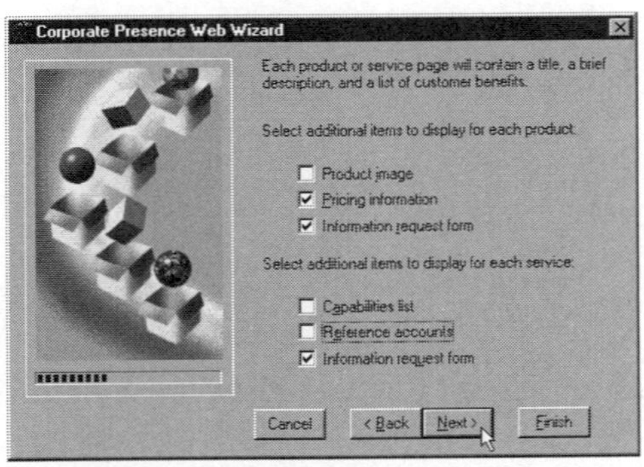

Figure 8.5 The Corporate Presence Web Wizard's product or service additional information items selection screen.

10. Click your mouse pointer on the NEXT button. FrontPage, in turn, will let you select the information you want visitors to enter when they submit comments about your Web site (or company) on the site's Feedback Form page as shown in Figure 8.6. (You told the Wizard to create a Web page with a feedback form as one of the default

pages you selected in Step 5.) For the current project, accept the default information item selections.

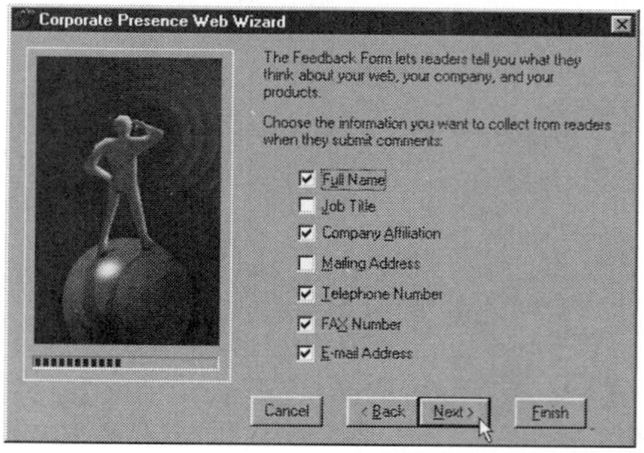

Figure 8.6 *The Corporate Presence Web Wizard's Feedback Form visitor information item selection screen.*

11. Click your mouse pointer on the NEXT button. FrontPage, in turn, will ask you how you want the information collected through the feedback form to be stored on your computer, as shown in Figure 8.7. For the current project, accept the default and store the feedback information in a tab-delimited format.

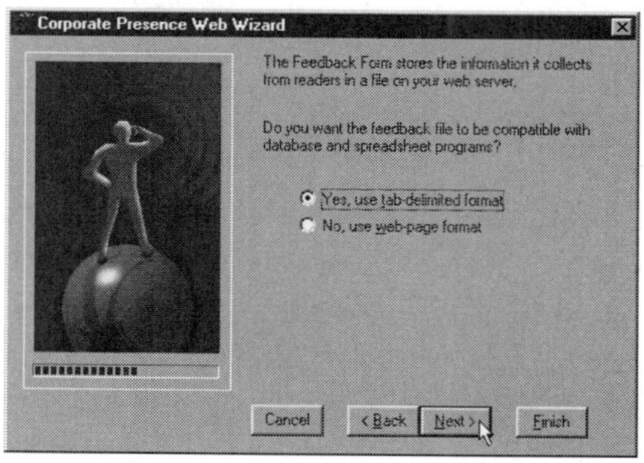

Figure 8.7 *The Corporate Presence Web Wizard's Feedback Form file format specification screen.*

12. Click your mouse pointer on the NEXT button. FrontPage, in turn, will ask you how you want the system to manage the Table of Contents Page as shown in Figure 8.8. (You told the Wizard to create the Table of Contents Page as one of the default Web page selections in Step 5.) For the current project, accept the default and have FrontPage create a site Table of Contents with bullets for each of the top-level pages.

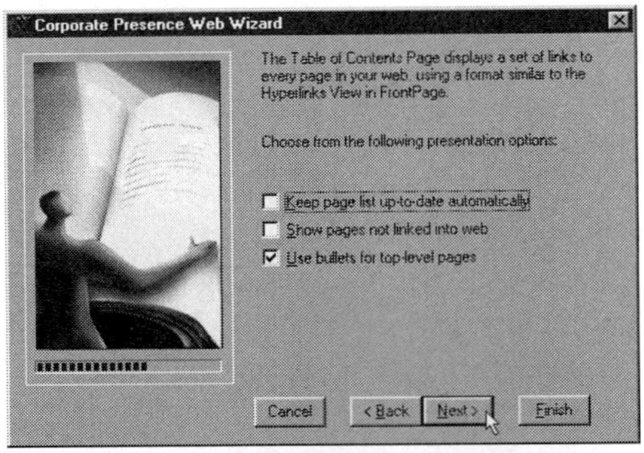

Figure 8.8 The Corporate Presence Web Wizard's Table of Contents Page presentation optons.

13. Click your mouse pointer on the NEXT button. FrontPage, in turn, will let you select the items you want to appear at the top and bottom of each Web page as shown in Figure 8.9. For the current project, accept the default items.

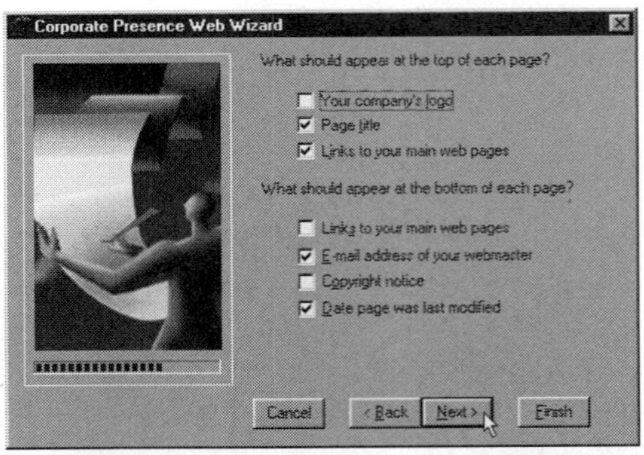

Figure 8.9 The Corporate Presence Web Wizard's Web page header and footer element specification screen.

14. Click your mouse pointer on the NEXT button. FrontPage, in turn, will ask you if you want to mark each unfinished page in the Web site with the Under Construction icon as shown in Figure 8.10. For the current project, accept the default answer of Yes.
15. Click your mouse pointer on the NEXT button. FrontPage, in turn, will ask you to enter your company name and address similar to that shown in Figure 8.11.

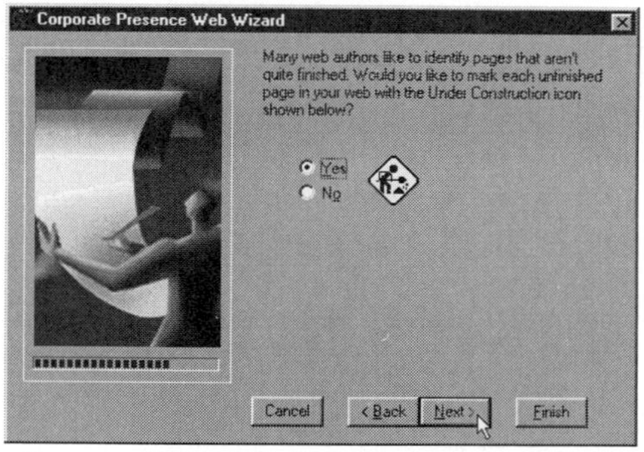

Figure 8.10 *The Corporate Presence Web Wizard's Under Construction icon election screen.*

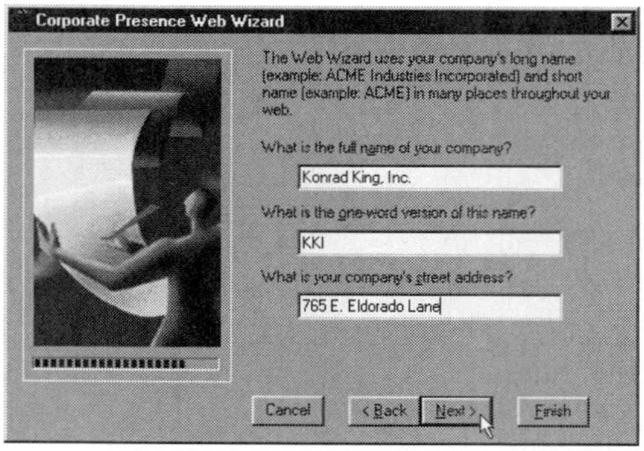

Figure 8.11 *The Corporate Presence Web Wizard's company name and address entry screen.*

16. For the current project, enter your company name in the What is the full name of your company? field (use your employer's company name if you don't have your own company). Enter an abbreviation for the company name in the What is the one word version of your company name? field. Finally, enter the company's address in the What is your company's address? field.
17. Click your mouse pointer on the NEXT button. FrontPage, in turn, will ask you for the company phone numbers and e-mail address similar to that shown in Figure 8.12.

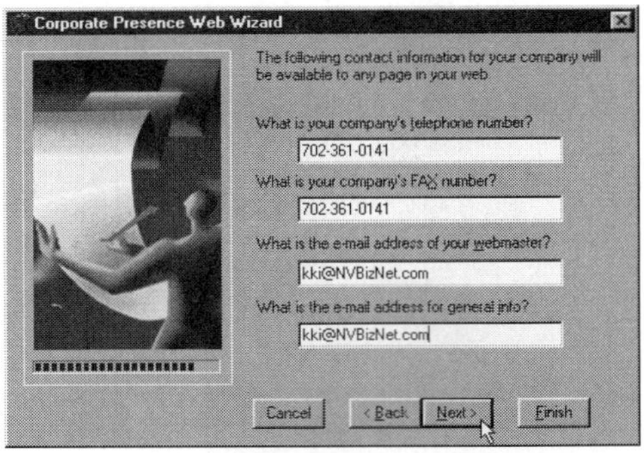

Figure 8.12 The Corporate Presence Web Wizard's company phone number and e-mail address entry screen.

18. For the current project, enter your company's (or your employer's company's) phone and FAX number in the first two fields on the page. Enter your e-mail address in the Web master and general info e-mail address fields at the bottom of the page.
19. Click your mouse pointer on the NEXT button. FrontPage, in turn, will let you select a theme by clicking your mouse pointer on the CHOOSE A WEB THEME button as shown in Figure 8.13. For the current project, skip the selection of a theme, and let the wizard apply the default Corporate theme to the Web site.

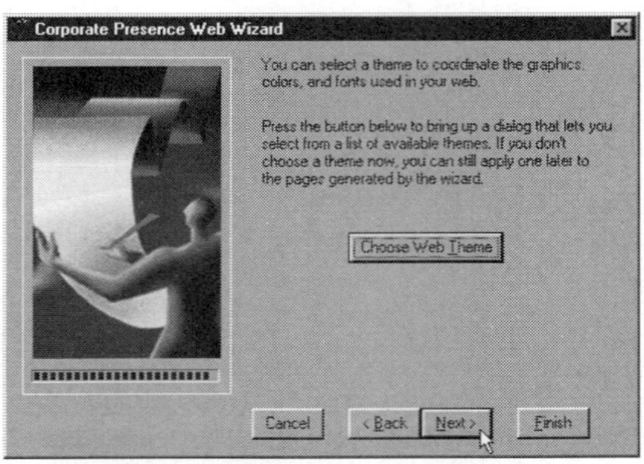

Figure 8.13 The Corporate Presence Web Wizard's Web theme selection screen.

20. Click your mouse pointer on the NEXT button. FrontPage, in turn, will display the final page of the Corporate Presence Web Wizard application as shown in Figure 8.14.
21. Click your mouse pointer on the FINISH button. FrontPage, in turn, will generate the Web pages for your Corporate Web Presence Web site and display the list of tasks required to make the site fully functional.

Click your mouse pointer on the Navigation view icon in the Views bar along the left side of the application Window. FrontPage, in turn, will display a wire diagram view of your Corporate Presence Web site similar to that shown in Figure 8.15.

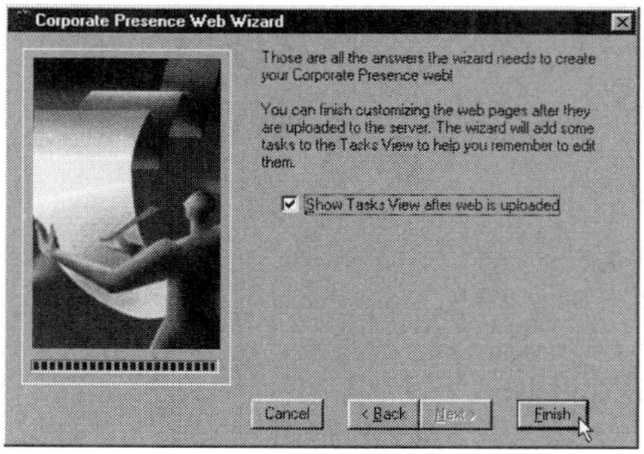

Figure 8.14 The Corporate Presence Web Wizard's final screen.

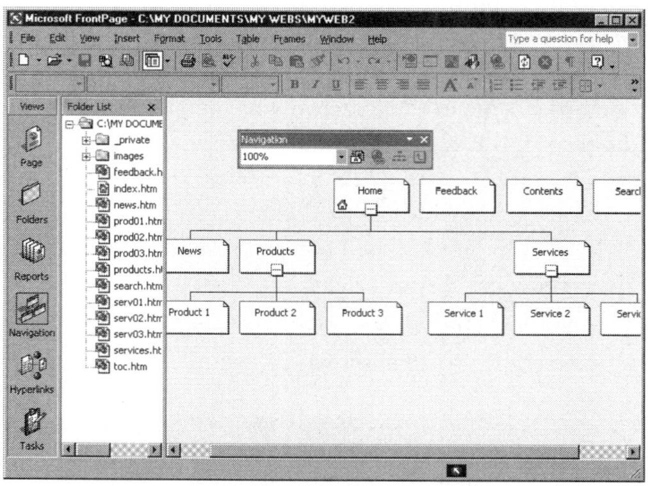

Figure 8.15 The Corporate Presence Web site shown in Navigation view.

Don't worry if you don't understand all of the features and choices you selected as defaults while using the Corporate Presence Web site wizard in this Tip. You will explore each screen in detail later. For now, the important thing to know is that FrontPage gives you a tool you can use to generate a large, complex Web site by having you make selections and answering a few questions. The next step in completing your Corporate Web Presence site is to customize the content of each Web page as specified in the task list you saw when you completed Step 21. (You can display the task list again by clicking your mouse pointer on the Tasks view icon in the Views bar on the left side of the application Window.)

USING INTERNET EXPLORER (IE) TO VIEW A FRONTPAGE WEB

If you worked the projects in the preceding Tips you now have two FrontPage webs on your hard drive. You already know that you can use a Web browser (such as Microsoft Internet Explorer) to view a Web site on the Internet by typing the site's Web address (or URL) into the Web browser's address field and then pressing the ENTER key. What you may not know is that you can use your Web browser to view Web pages and Web sites located on your computer system. To use Microsoft Internet Explorer (IE) to view a FrontPage Web on your computer system, perform the following steps:

1. Start the Internet Explorer (IE) by double-clicking your mouse pointer on the Internet Explorer icon (shown in Figure 9.1) on your desktop or on the task bar near the START button. (If you've removed the IE icon, click your mouse pointer on the START button, select Programs from the Start menu, and click your mouse pointer on Internet Explorer.)

Figure 9.1 The Internet Explorer icon.

2. Enter the full pathname to the folder in which you created the FrontPage Web followed by \INDEX.HTM in the Address field of your Web browser. For example, if you created the Corporate Web Presence web in the preceding Tip in the C:\MY DOCUMENTS\MY WEBS\MYWEB2 folder, enter C:\MY DOCUMENTS\MY WEBS\MYWEB2\INDEX.HTM into the Web browser's Address field.
3. Press the ENTER key. IE, in turn, will display the home page of the FrontPage web similar to that shown in Figure 9.2.

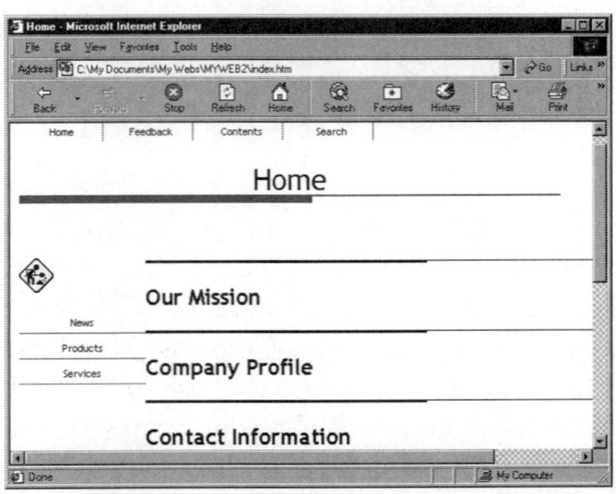

Figure 9.2 The home page for the Corporate Presence Web site generated by the Corporate Presence Web Wizard.

If you don't know the full pathname to your FrontPage web, enter the letter of the drive on which you think you created the FrontPage web followed by ":\". For example, if you know the FrontPage Web is located on your C: drive, enter C:\ into your Web browser's address field. When you press the ENTER key, your Web browser will display the list of folders and files in the C:\ folder similar to that shown in Figure 9.3.

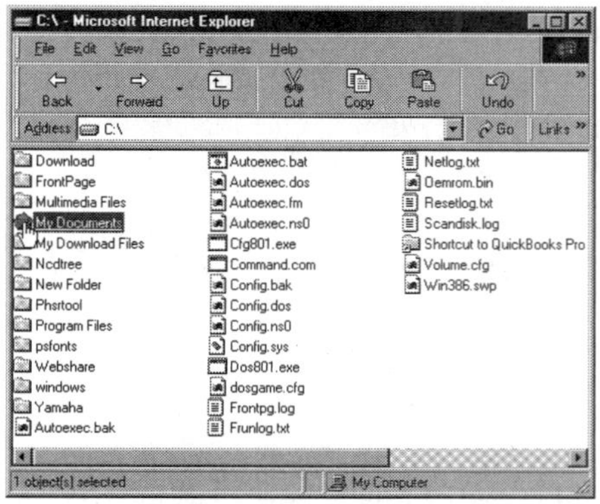

Figure 9.3 A hard drive file and folder list displayed by the Microsoft Internet Explorer.

Double-click your mouse pointer on one of the folders (such as MY DOCUMENTS) to display its contents. Continue double-clicking your mouse pointer on subfolders until you see the INDEX.HTM document. Double-click your mouse pointer on INDEX.HTM to display the FrontPage web's home page. You can move up one subfolder by clicking your mouse pointer on either the BACK button or the UP button on the Web browser's toolbar.

CREATING A BLANK OR EMPTY FRONTPAGE WEB

If you want to start a new FrontPage web but don't want FrontPage to generate Web pages for you, perform the following steps:

1. If FrontPage is not currently running on your computer, start the program by double-clicking your mouse pointer on the FrontPage icon on your desktop or by clicking your mouse pointer on the START button, selecting programs, and clicking your mouse pointer on Microsoft FrontPage.
2. Click your mouse pointer on the drop-down list button to the right of the CREATE A NEW NORMAL PAGE button (the first button on the left on the Standard toolbar), and select Web from the drop-down list. FrontPage, in turn, will display its New Web dialog box.
3. In the Specify the location of the new web field in the Options section of the New dialog box, enter the pathname of the folder in which you want FrontPage to create the web. For the current project, accept the default folder—C:\MY DOCUMENTS\MY WEBS\MYWEB3.

Note: *FrontPage will default the pathname in the Specify the location of the new web field to the "next" unused folder each time you select the File menu New option and click your mouse pointer on Web. If you install FrontPage using the default settings, FrontPage will place your first web in the C:\MY DOCUMENTS\MY WEBS\MYWEB folder. By default, FrontPage will place the next Web you create in the C:\MY DOCUMENTS\MY WEBS\MYWEB2 folder. The program will then place the third web you create in the C:\MY DOCUMENTS\MY WEBS\MYWEB3 folder, and so on. You can change the pathname of the folder in which FrontPage will create your web by changing the default pathname in the Specify the location of the new web field on the New dialog box. Once you change the pathname, FrontPage will use the new pathname as the default the next time you create a FrontPage web. For example, if you enter C:\WEB SITES\SITE1 as the location for the new FrontPage web, FrontPage will create any folders in the pathname that do not exist and generate your web in the SITE1 folder. The next time you create a new site, FrontPage will default the location of the web to C:\WEB SITES\SITE2.*

4. Double-click your mouse pointer on the One Page Web icon. FrontPage, in turn, will display a blank home page (INDEX.HTM) document and empty _PRIVATE and _IMAGES folders in the folder you entered in Step 3.

Note: *If you only want FrontPage to create the sub-directory structure without creating the INDEX.HTM document, double-click the Empty Web icon instead of the One Page Web icon in Step 4.*

After you complete Step 4, FrontPage will return to the main editing window. Click your mouse pointer on the Page view icon in the Views bar to have FrontPage display the editing pane to the right of Folder List pane. Notice that FrontPage defaults to creating a new Web page in the document pane—vs. defaulting to displaying the INDEX.HTM document you created in Step 4. As such, if you want to work with the Web site's home page (INDEX.HTM), double-click your mouse pointer on INDEX.HTM in the Folder List pane. FrontPage, in turn, will display the blank INDEX.HTM document in the editing pane and you can start entering the text and inserting the other items you want on your Web site's home page.

EXITING FRONTPAGE

When you double-click your mouse pointer on the FrontPage icon on your desktop (or start FrontPage by clicking your mouse pointer on the START button, selecting Programs, and clicking your mouse pointer on Microsoft FrontPage), Windows opens an application window and starts the FrontPage application in it. Moreover, each time you create a new FrontPage Web while in FrontPage, Windows opens up a new window and starts another copy of the FrontPage application. To exit FrontPage either click your mouse pointer on the CLOSE button (the X) in the upper right-hand corner of the application window or select the File menu Close option. FrontPage, in turn, will check to see if you've modified any of the pages in the current Web since the last time you saved them. If it finds any unsaved modifications, FrontPage will prompt you with a Save Changes dialog box similar to that shown in Figure 11 for each of the Web's unsaved pages.

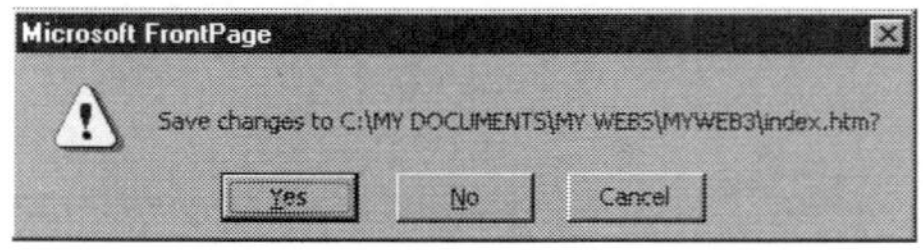

Figure 11 The FrontPage save Web page changes dialog box.

To save your changes, click your mouse pointer on the YES button. (If you have not previously saved the Web page, FrontPage will display the Save As dialog box so you can select a filename in which to save the document.) If you don't want to save your changes, click your mouse pointer on the NO button. Or, if you change your mind about exiting the FrontPage application, click your mouse pointer on the CANCEL button to cancel the exit operation and return to the FrontPage application window.

Once you've clicked the YES button or the NO button on the final Save Changes dialog box, Windows will exit the FrontPage program and close its application window. Exiting one copy of the FrontPage application has no effect on any other copies running on your system. As such, you will need to go through the exit process to close each open FrontPage application window.

OPENING AN EXISTING FRONTPAGE WEB

FrontPage lets you open Webs located on your system's hard drive, in a network directory to which you have access, or on a server on the Internet. To open a FrontPage Web on your hard drive or on a network drive, perform the following steps:

1. Select the File menu Open Web option. FrontPage, in turn, will display an Open Web dialog box similar to that shown in Figure 12.1.

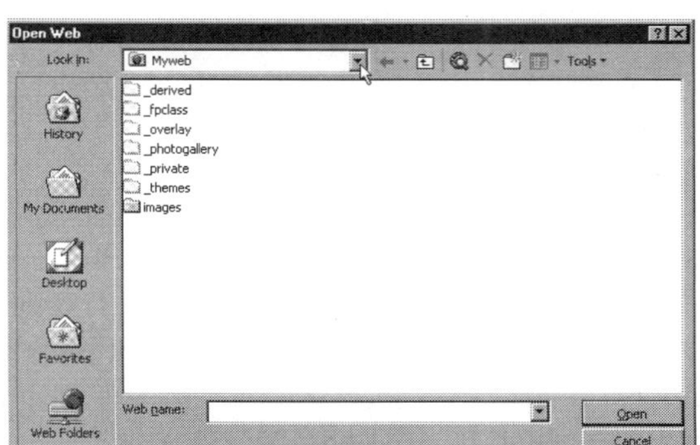

Figure 12.1 The Open Web dialog box.

2. Into the Web name field near the bottom of the Open Web dialog box enter the full pathname of the folder in which you created the FrontPage Web. For example, if you accepted the default location when you created the Personal Web site in a previous Tip, you would enter C:\MY DOCUMENTS\MY WEBS\MYWEB.

Note: *If you don't know the full pathname, click your mouse pointer on the drop-down list button to the right of the Look in field. FrontPage, in turn, will display a list of the drives and folders in the path to the current default folder. (The default folder is the most recent folder FrontPage used for a Save or Open operation.) Double-click your mouse pointer on the drive that contains the FrontPage Web you want to open. FrontPage, in turn, will display a list of folders on the drive you select. Continue double-clicking your mouse pointer on folder names until you reach the folder in which you created the FrontPage Web. (You will recognize a FrontPage Web folder because it will have a globe on top of the normal folder icon.) Once you see the FrontPage Web folder you want to open, click your mouse pointer on the folder to select it and then continue with Step 3.*

Note: *You can use the icons along the left side of the dialog box to locate the FrontPage Web you want to open. For example, if you know you recently worked with the FrontPage Web on the computer you are using now, click your mouse pointer on the History button. FrontPage, in turn, will display a list of Web pages and FrontPage Web folders. Either click your mouse pointer on the name of a Web page in the FrontPage Web you wish to open, or double-click your mouse pointer on the FrontPage Web folder that contains the FrontPage Web with which you want to work then continue with Step 3.*

3. Click your mouse pointer on the OPEN button. FrontPage, in turn, will open the Web it finds in the folder you selected in Step 2.

Although the preceding steps showed you how to open a FrontPage Web on your system's hard drive, you can use the same procedure to open a FrontPage Web located on another computer system on your network. For example, suppose a FrontPage Web is located in the folder C:\MY DOCUMENTS\MY WEBS\MYWEB on a workstation named NVBizNet with a C: drive is shared as "C-DRIVE". You can open the FrontPage Web from your computer by entering \\NVBIZNET\C-DRIVE\MY DOCUMENTS\MY WEBS\MYWEB in place of C:\MY DOCMUMENTS\MY WEBS\MYWEB in Step 2 of the procedure for opening an existing FrontPage Web.

If you are working with a Web server that has FrontPage server extensions installed, you can open a FrontPage Web directly on the server—without having the server physically connected to your local area network (LAN). To open a FrontPage Web on a Web server over the Internet, enter the Web site's address (URL) in the Web name field of the Open Web dialog box. You will need to enter the full URL including the HTTP:// in the Web name field. For example, to open the FrontPage Web at the Web site *WWW.OUTFRONT.NET*, you would enter HTTP://WWW.OUTFRONT.NET in the Web name field. When you click your mouse pointer on the

OPEN button, FrontPage will ask you to identify yourself by displaying an Enter Network Password dialog box similar to that shown in Figure 12.2.

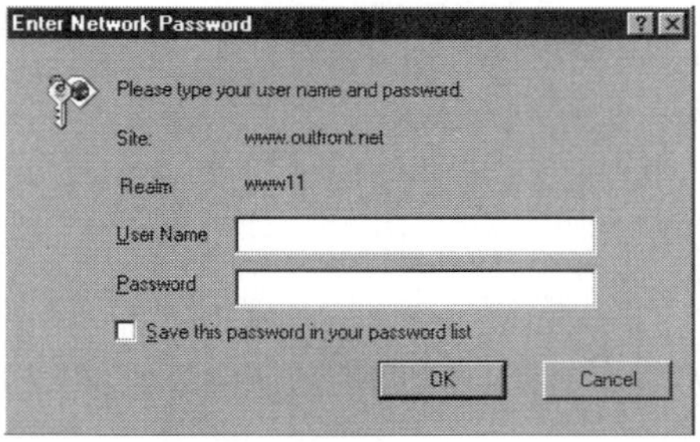

Figure 12.2 The Enter Network Password dialog box.

After the Web server validates your user name and password, you will be able to edit Web pages directly on the Web server. You will learn more about working with Web pages directly on a Web server later in this book.

USING THE IMPORT WEB WIZARD TO IMPORT AN EXISTING WEB SITE LOCATED ON A LOCAL OR NETWORK FOLDER

While you can use FrontPage to edit individual Web pages, the real power of the program is in its ability to manage entire Web sites. After all, if you only have a simple, single page Web, any text editor will do. You can even use Microsoft Word to generate the single page site by saving a Word document as a Web page. When you want FrontPage to manage a Web site, you must first import the site into FrontPage—thereby making it a FrontPage Web. To import an existing Web site located on your computer or on another network workstation, perform the following steps:

1. Select the File menu New option and click your mouse pointer on Page or Web. FrontPage, in turn, will display the New Page or Web menu along the right-hand side of the application window. Under the New from Template heading, click your mouse pointer on Web site templates. FrontPage, in turn, will display the Web Site Templates dialog box.
2. Into the Specify the location of the new web field, enter the pathname of the folder in which you want FrontPage to store the Web you are importing. Rather than accepting the default folder, change the name of the folder to correspond with the name of the Web site you are about to import. For example, if you were to import the QHFINC.COM Web site, change the pathname in the Location field to C:\MY DOCUMENTS\MY WEBS\QHFINC. While you could use the default MYWEBx folder (where "x" is a number generated by

FrontPage to make the new folder name unique), using a descriptive name will make it easier to know which folder to open the next time you start FrontPage and want to view or make changes to the Web you are importing.

3. Double-click your mouse pointer on the Import Web Wizard icon (or click your mouse pointer once on the Import Web Wizard icon and then click your mouse pointer on the OK button). FrontPage, in turn, will display an Import Web Wizard – Choose Source dialog box similar to that shown in Figure 13.1.

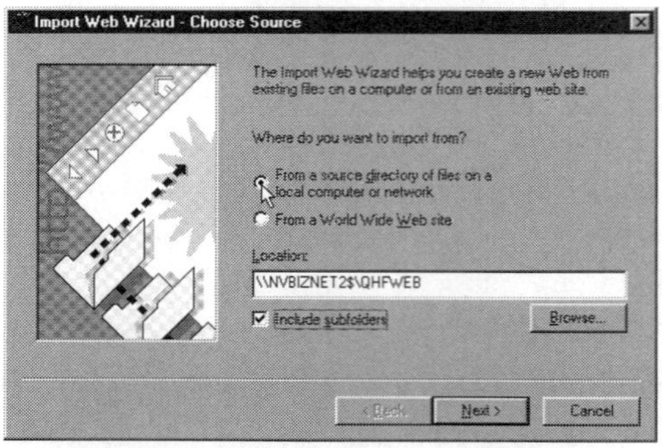

Figure 13.1 The Import Web Wizard - Choose Source dialog box.

4. Specify the source of the Web you are importing by clicking your mouse pointer on the appropriate radio button in the middle of the dialog box. To import a Web located on your hard drive or on another network workstation, click your mouse pointer on the From a source directory of files on a local computer or network radio button.
5. Enter the pathname of the folder that contains the Web site's pages in the Location field. For example, if the site you want to import is in a shared directory named QHFWEB on a workstation named NVBIZNET2$, you would enter \\NVBIZNET2$\QHFWEB in the Location field. If you don't know the pathname, click your mouse pointer on the BROWSE button. FrontPage, in turn, will display the File Open dialog box. If you don't see the folder with the Web you want to import, click your mouse pointer on the drop-down list button to the right of the Look in field. FrontPage, in turn, will display icons for local drives, the network neighborhood and FTP locations, similar to that shown in Figure 13.2. Notice that you can use the Browse for Folder dialog box to search for the Web site folder whether it is on your own computer or on a network workstation.

   If you are using the Look in drop-down list, click your mouse pointer on the icon for a drive, the network neighborhood, or FTP location with the Web site you want to import. Then, click your mouse pointer on the plus to the left of folder names to display subfolders until you see the folder you want. Click your mouse pointer on the name of the folder you want to open, and then click your mouse pointer on the OK button. FrontPage, in turn, will transfer the full pathname to the folder you selected to the Location field of the Import Web Wizard - Choose Source dialog box.

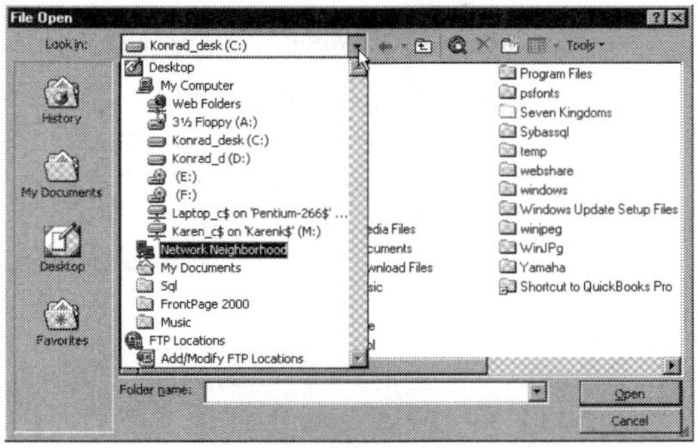

Figure 13.2 *The FrontPage File Open, Look in drop-down list.*

6. To have FrontPage reproduce the subfolder directory structure and contents in the folder you specified in Step 2, click your mouse pointer on the Include subfolders check box until the check mark appears. Retrieving the subfolders is important because many developers will put graphic images and scripts in their own subfolders rather than putting everything in the same folder as the Web documents. If you don't get the subfolder contents, any hyperlinks to subfolder contents will be broken on your FrontPage Web and you'll see a red "X" in place of the graphic images that you did not import.

7. Click your mouse pointer on the NEXT button. The Import Web Wizard, in turn, will display an Import Web Wizard - Edit File List dialog box similar to that shown in Figure 13.3.

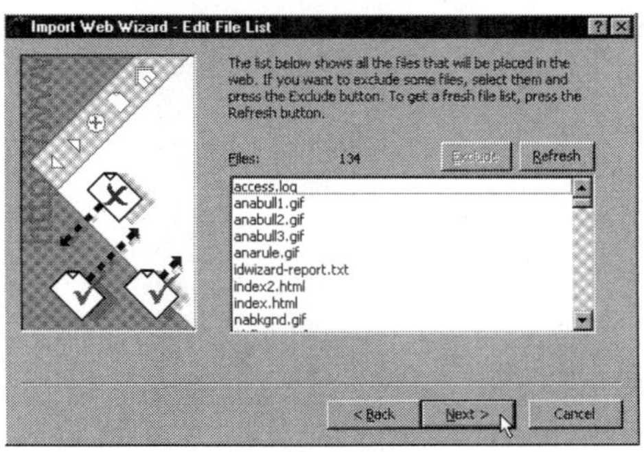

Figure 13.3 *The Import Web Wizard – Edit File List dialog box.*

Normally, you will want to import all of the Web site's files. However, if you want to avoid importing certain files to your computer (if you only want a site's graphic files or if only want a site's non-graphics, Web page source files, for example), click your mouse pointer on the names of the files you want to exclude and then click your mouse pointer on the EXCLUDE button. The Import Web Wizard, in turn, will remove the name of the file(s) you selected from the list of files to import and update the Files count above the file list.

Note: *After you select files you do not want to import and click your mouse pointer on the EXCLUDE button, the file names no longer appear in the list of files to import. If you change your mind about not importing a file, click your mouse pointer on the REFRESH button. The Import Web Wizard, in turn, will put all of the files you excluded back onto the list of files to import. Then you can start the exclude file selection process again.*

Note: *If you are trying to import a Web site located on a network workstation, and get an error message stating "The specified path is not a directory." when you click your mouse pointer on the NEXT button, click your mouse pointer on the OK button in the message box. Verify that you typed the workstation name and shared folder name into the Location field correctly. If it is correct, review the Tip entitled "Connecting to a Shared Folder on a Windows Network".*

8. Click your mouse pointer on the NEXT button. The Import Web Wizard, in turn, will display the Import Web Wizard - Finish dialog box.
9. If you want to change any options you entered on previous screens, click your mouse pointer on the BACK button until you're back on the page on which you want to make changes. When you are ready to complete the Web site import process, click your mouse pointer on the FINISH button. The Import Web Wizard, in turn, will build a FrontPage Web in the folder you specified in Step 2 using the contents of the Web site you selected in Step 4.

After the Import Web Wizard completes its tasks, FrontPage will return to the main edit screen. To edit one of the existing Web pages, double-click your mouse pointer on the name of the Web page in the Folder List area of the application window. When you are finished making changes to the FrontPage Web, the changed Web pages will only exist on your computer. If you want to update the Web site to reflect your modifications, you will have to "publish" your local FrontPage Web to the Web server.

Note: *The Import Web Wizard will correctly import a Web site if all of the Web documents for the site are located in either the site's main folder or in a subfolder of the main folder. If the Web site makes use of Web pages located in other folders, you'll need to import those pages into the FrontPage Web individually—you will learn how to do this in the Tip after the next one.*

USING THE IMPORT WEB WIZARD TO IMPORT ANY WEB SITE ON THE INTERNET

In the preceding Tip you learned how to import (or convert) a Web site located on your computer or on a network workstation into a FrontPage Web on your hard drive. You are not limited to importing Web sites you create—FrontPage lets you import any Web site on the Internet into a FrontPage Web on your computer. To import an Internet Web site perform the following steps:

1. If you don't have a permanent connection to the Internet, establish the dial-up connection with your Internet service provider (ISP).
2. In the FrontPage application window, select the File menu New Page or Web option. After FrontPage displays the New Page or Web menu, at the right side of the application window, click your mouse pointer on Web site templates (under the New from template heading). FrontPage, in turn, will display the Web site templates dialog box.
3. Enter the pathname to the folder in which you want FrontPage to build the Web site you are importing. Instead of accepting the default, use a name that corresponds to the imported Web site's name—this will make it easier to open the FrontPage Web the next time you start FrontPage. For example, if you are importing the *DesertRealtyLV.com* Web site, change the default pathname in the Specify the location of the new Web field to C:\MY DOCUMENTS\MY WEBS\DESERTREALTY.
4. Double-click your mouse pointer on the Import Web Wizard icon (or click your mouse pointer once on the Import Web Wizard icon and then click your mouse pointer on the OK button). FrontPage, in turn, will display an Import Web Wizard – Choose Source dialog box similar to that shown in Figure 14.1.

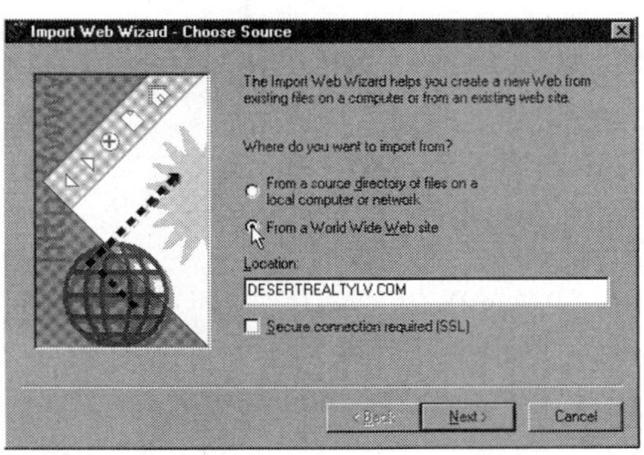

Figure 14.1 The Import Web Wizard - Choose Source dialog box.

5. Click your mouse pointer on the radio button to the left of From a World Wide Web site.
6. Enter the Web site address (URL) into the Location field. For example, to import the *DesertRealtyLV.com* Web site, enter DESERTREALTYLV.COM into the Location field.
7. Click your mouse pointer on the NEXT button. The Import Web Wizard, in turn, will display the Import Web Wizard – Choose Download Amount dialog box shown in Figure 14.2.

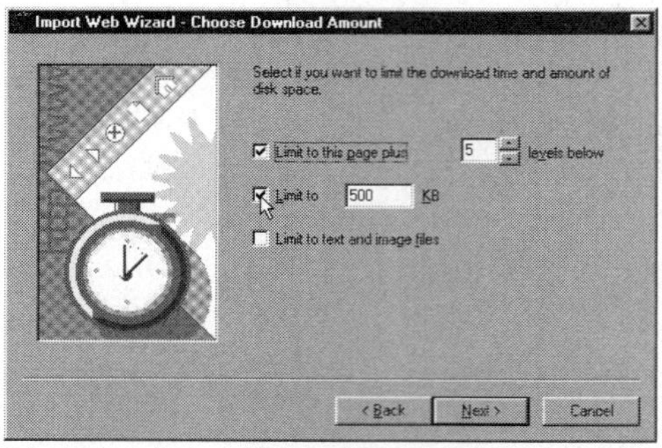

Figure 14.2 The Import Web Wizard – Choose Download Amount dialog box.

If you are importing a large Web site, you will have to increase the default amounts in the dialog box. For example, if the Web site has a lot of graphics images, you will need to increase the Limit to KB field to something larger than the default 500,000 bytes. Consider that a low-resolution full-page graphics file will be around 60,000 bytes—9 such files would exceed size limit and cause the Import Web Wizard to stop retrieving Web content. If you're not concerned about time and disk space, click your mouse pointer on the check boxes in the dialog box until the check marks disappear—this will tell the Import Web Wizard to retrieve all content without regard to the number of levels of links it must traverse or the total amount of data transferred to your system.

8. Click your mouse pointer on the NEXT button. The Import Web Wizard, in turn, will display the Import Web Wizard - Finish dialog box.
9. If you want to change any options you entered on previous screens, click your mouse pointer on the BACK button until you're back on the page on which you want to make changes. When you are ready to complete the Web site import process, click your mouse pointer on the FINISH button. The Import Web Wizard, in turn, will build a FrontPage Web in the folder you specified in Step 3 by connecting to

the Web site you selected in Step 6 and saving the Web pages, images, and scripts it finds. As you watch the operation of the Import Web Wizard, you will notice that it is following each of the hyperlinks in the Web pages on the Web site you are importing. Instead of displaying the pages as your Web browser does, the Import Web Wizard copies the content it receives from the site into the import folder you specified.

Note: *If FrontPage determines that you are importing a Web site which was created using FrontPage, you will see the dialog box shown in Figure 14.3.*

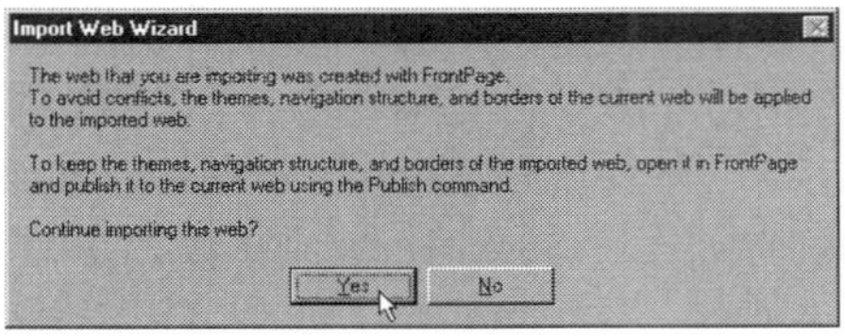

Figure 14.3 *The Import Web Wizard – continue importing FrontPage created Web dialog box.*

Click your mouse pointer on the YES button to continue with the import. The FrontPage Import Wizard will import the Web site as you see the site when you visit it with your Web browser—including its theme and navigation bars.

As was the case when you imported a Web site from a network workstation, FrontPage will return to the main edit screen and let you edit the contents of the Web pages you imported onto your local computer—you won't be making changes to the Internet site you imported. If you want the imported Web site to reflect the modifications you make to your locally stored copy of the site, you must have "write" or "author" access to the Web site on the Web server you want to update and *publish* the FrontPage Web on your computer to the Web server.

USING THE FILE MENU IMPORT OPTION TO IMPORT INDIVIDUAL WEB PAGES

While FrontPage gives you the ability to import entire Web sites from network workstations or Internet Web servers into FrontPage Webs on your hard drive, you may want to only import individual Web pages, for example, if you imported a Web page where all of the Web pages were not in the site's main folder or in a subfolder under the main folder. The Import Web Wizard will not import Web pages located in folders other than the main folder or a subfolder. As a result, your imported site may end up with a broken link—i.e., a link to a Web page that does not exist at the location specified in the hyperlink. To fix the "missing page" problem, import the individual "missing" Web pages individually by performing the following steps:

1. Open the FrontPage Web into which you wish to import the Web page.
2. Select the folder in the FrontPage Web into which you wish to import the Web page(s).

   If you are planning to import individual Web pages and supporting graphics files and you have a subfolder on your Web site for Web pages, click your mouse pointer on that folder in the Folder List area of the FrontPage application window to select it. The import program will then copy the files you select into the folder you selected without creating a new subfolder.

   Conversely, if you plan to import an entire folder (its contents and any subfolders and their contents), select the root folder of your FrontPage Web. The import program will create a folder with the same name as the one you are importing, and contents of the folder on the remote system into it. [If you only import individual Web pages (vs. an entire folder), FrontPage does not create a folder before copying them onto your system.]
3. Select the File menu Import option. FrontPage, in turn, will display the Import dialog box shown in Figure 15.1.

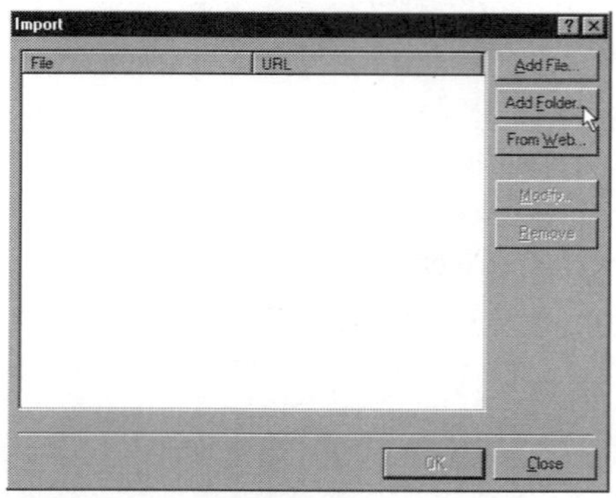

Figure 15.1 The FrontPage Import dialog box.

4. Select the files (and/or folders) you want to import into the folder you selected in Step 2. You can select more than one file (and/or multiple folders). If you want to select individual files to add to the list, click your mouse pointer on the ADD FILE button. FrontPage, in turn, will display an Add File to Import List dialog box similar to that shown in Figure 15.2.

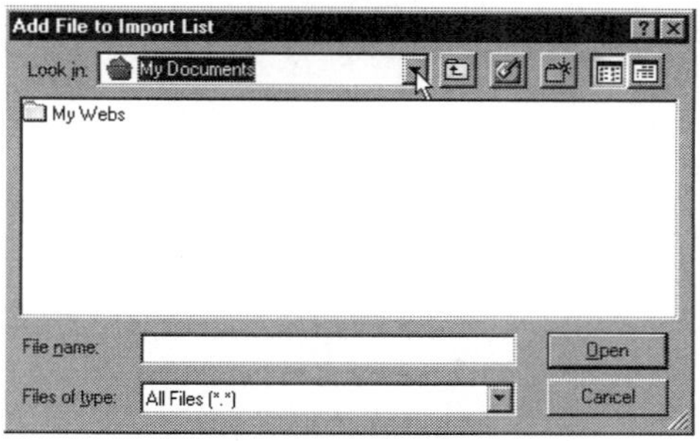

Figure 15.2 *The Add File to Import List dialog box.*

Use the drop-down list button to the right of the Look in field, to find the file you wish to import or enter the file's full pathname into the File name field. After you select the file you want to import (or enter its name in the File name field), click your mouse pointer on the OPEN button to add the file to the file to the list in the Import dialog box.

To import a folder, click your mouse pointer on the Import dialog box's ADD FOLDER button. If the folder you want is on a network workstation, click your mouse pointer on the drop-down list button to the right of the Look in field, and then double-click your mouse pointer on the Network Neighborhood icon on the drop-down list. FrontPage, in turn, will display the list of available network workstations in the File Open dialog box, similar to that shown in Figure 15.3.

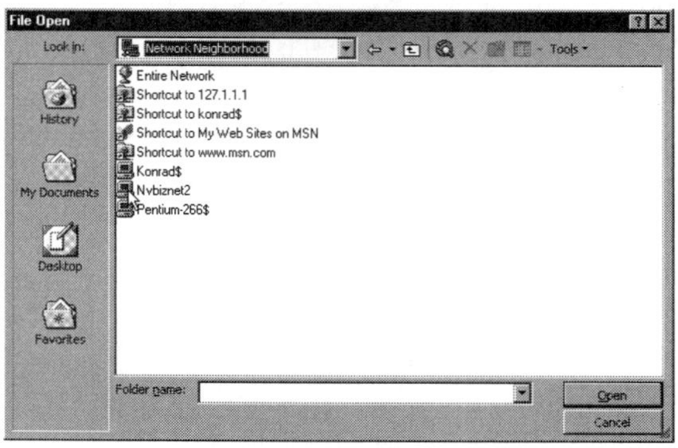

Figure 15.3 *The File Open Dialog box listing available network workstations.*

Double-click your mouse pointer on the workstation with the folder you want to import. Then, after FrontPage displays the list of shared folders on the workstation, click your mouse pointer on the folder you want to import. For example to import the shared EXECUTIVEWEB folder on the workstation NVBIZNET2, double-click your mouse pointer on the icon for NVBIZNET2 to the list of shared folders on the NVBIZNET2 workstation. Next, click your mouse pointer on the EXECUTIVEWEB folder to select it. Finally, click your mouse pointer on the OK button to transfer the list of files in the EXECUTIVEWEB folder to the file list area of the Import dialog box.

Note: If you click your mouse pointer on a password protected shared network folder for the first time or if the password has changed since your last access, Windows will display an Enter Network Password dialog box similar to that shown in Figure 15.4.

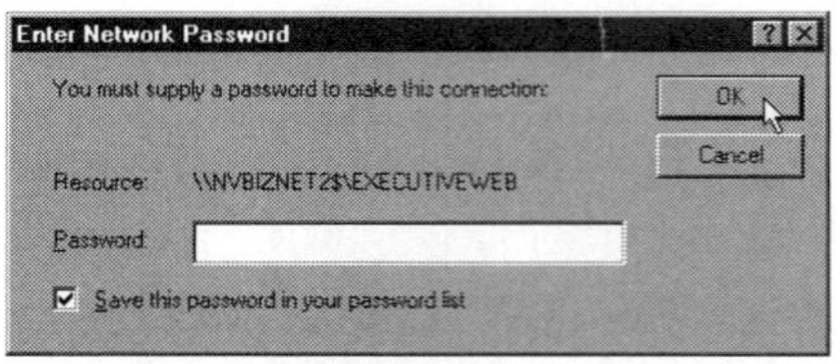

***Figure 15.4** The Windows Enter Network Password dialog box.*

Enter the password to access the contents of the folder and click your mouse pointer on the OK button to continue with the import procedure.

5. Click your mouse pointer on the OK button in the Import dialog box. If you selected individual files to import, FrontPage will copy the files in the folder you selected in Step 2. If you selected a folder to import, FrontPage will create the subfolder in the directory you selected in Step 2 and copy the files from the network workstation into the new subfolder.

Once you import the files and/or folders into your FrontPage Web, you still need to fix the broken hyperlinks by correcting the pathnames in the links to point to the new location of the files. If you are importing a new Web page or set of Web pages (in a folder), you will need to create one or more hyperlinks to the new page(s) on a Web page already in your FrontPage Web.

CONNECTING TO A SHARED FOLDER ON A WINDOWS NETWORK

When performing FrontPage functions such as opening existing Webs or importing Webs or folders, you are asked to enter the location (or pathname) of the folder you want to open or whose files you want to import. If the folder you specify is a password protected shared folder on a Windows network, Windows will prompt you to enter a password. Normally, you need only enter the password once if you click a check mark into the Save this password in your password list check box on the Enter Network Password dialog box. However, if the shared folder's owner later changes the password, Windows may not prompt you to enter the updated password. Instead, Windows will attempt to use the previously entered password for the shared folder and FrontPage will display an error message box stating: The specified path is not a directory.

When FrontPage displays the path is not a directory error message box, click your mouse pointer on the OK button (in the error message box) and verify that you entered the correct pathname for the shared folder. If the pathname is correct, you need to connect to the shared folder outside of FrontPage to gain access the folder's contents. To use the Network Neighborhood icon on your desktop to establish the connection to the shared directory, perform the following steps:

1. Minimize your current application so that you can see the Network Neighborhood icon on your desktop. (One way to do this is to click your mouse pointer on the Show Desktop button on the Windows Quick Launch toolbar just to the right of the Start button.)
2. Double-click your mouse pointer on the Network Neighborhood icon. Windows, in turn, will display the workstations on your network.
3. Double-click your mouse pointer on the workstation with the shared directory that contains the Web site you want to import. Windows, in turn, will display the list of shared folders on the workstation you selected.
4. Double-click your mouse pointer on the name of the shared folder that holds the Web site you want to import. Windows, in turn, will display the Enter Network Password dialog box.
5. Enter the shared folder's password and click your mouse pointer on the OK button. Windows, in turn, will display the list of files and subfolders in the folder.
6. Close file and Folder List pane by clicking on the "X" in the upper right-hand corner of the window.
7. Repeat Step 6 until you've closed all windows opened while searching for and connecting to the shared network folder.

FrontPage will not bypass the security system setup on your network. If the shared folder is not password protected, you can access it from FrontPage without first using Windows to establishing the connection. However, if the shared folder is password protected and you did not use your workstation to access it through the network prior to starting FrontPage, you will need to validate your access rights by entering the shared folder's password.

UNDERSTANDING FRONTPAGE

Earlier Tips showed you how to install FrontPage, create Web sites based on content templates and wizards, and how to import existing Web pages. None of these Tips, however, showed you the true nature of FrontPage as a Web authoring and Web publishing program. FrontPage lets you concentrate on the design of your Web site by generating the Web page Hypertext Markup Language (HTML) code for you. If you don't know what HTML tags are, don't worry—FrontPage lets you create stunning Web pages without writing a single line of HTML. When using FrontPage, you add and format text, pictures, and other page content using menus, and toolbars, all in a familiar word processor like application. You work in a What-You-See-Is-What-You-Get (WYSIWYG) environment, and, in the background, FrontPage generates the HTML needed to display your Web page on the Internet.

If you want to work with HTML, you will find several Tips that deal with HTML tags later in this book. While FrontPage generates HTML code for you, the program also makes it simple to display and edit any Web page's underlying code. Moreover, FrontPage gives you a way to add dynamic effects to your Web pages through animated graphics, animated text, and Web page transition effects. From the Tips in this book you will learn how FrontPage makes it possible to insert Components (such as Hit Counters, Hover Buttons, and Marquees) and Forms with the click of your mouse pointer on toolbar buttons. In addition, you will learn how FrontPage lets you handle cookies, database access, and build Web pages on the fly by inserting code from your favorite scripting language—whether it is Perl, VBScript, JavaScript, Java Applets, or Visual Basic. Don't worry if you haven't used any of these languages before. By the time you finish this book, you will know how to use all of them. Right now, the important thing to know is that FrontPage lets you create Web sites complete with forms, graphics, and animations without your having to write any code. In short, you design the site and FrontPage does the implementation.

In addition to creating individual Web pages, FrontPage also helps you manage an entire Web site (or group of Web sites). Normally, a Web site will consist of many Web pages that contain hyperlinks, tables, forms, buttons, and graphics. FrontPage has management reports that will tell you if any of the site's hyperlinks refer to Web pages that do not exist. (A visitor clicking his mouse pointer on one of the "broken" hyperlinks would receive an error message on his screen instead of desired Web page or picture.) After FrontPage ensures all hyperlink and graphics images are accessible on your local computer, it will then publish your entire Web site to a Web server. If you've ever published a Web site to a Web server using File Transfer Protocol (FTP), you know that doing so is a lot of work. You have to use FTP to login to your server. Then you have to make sure that you remember to put every picture, Web page, and style sheet into the proper folders (directories) on the server. FrontPage takes care of all file transfers for you. You tell FrontPage to "publish" the Web site, and the program will make sure that everything your site needs (graphics, style sheets, Web pages) is sent to the server for the world to see.

If you are developing the Web site as part of a team, you will want to use the FrontPage group collaboration management tools. Once you specify which of your team members are responsible for which portions of the Web site design, FrontPage will give you project status reports that show what has and has not been completed. When you have several people adding content to Web pages, it is easy for one person to save work only to have it overwritten by another person saving a different version of the same document. FrontPage prevents the loss of work through its document checkout system. If one author has a document "checked out," anyone else retrieving the same document will not be able to make any changes to it. Once the developer checks the document (Web page) back in, then another developer can check it out and work with it.

FrontPage is a comprehensive Web site development and management tool that lets you work in a word processor like environment as you create Web pages and entire Web sites. By the time you finish reading this book, you will be expert a using FrontPage to:

- Create individual Web pages either by importing existing pages and modifying them; using wizards or content templates to "get you started" with Web pages containing suggestions on text and graphics to add; or by entering new text on a blank Web page and formatting it using a familiar word processor like interface. (If you're at all familiar with Microsoft Word or Corel WordPerfect, you already know how to use FrontPage.)
- Use your mouse to draw tables you can use to position Web page items.
- Add pictures, animations, and other special effects to your Web pages with a few menu and toolbar selections.
- Apply "themes" which add background images, navigation buttons, and set Web page colors which not only give your Web site a consistent look and feel but also make it easy to navigate.
- Make changes to the Hypertext Markup Language (HTML) that FrontPage generates or add new HTML statements of your own.
- Add C, Visual Basic, Java, JavaScript, Perl Scripts, and VBScript code to your Web pages to give them dynamic content, e-commerce capability, and database access.
- Manage Web site creation in a collaborative environment by using built-in FrontPage functions that let you: manage who is allowed to make changes to Web pages, prevent one author from overwriting another's work through the document check-out and check-in system, and create, assign, and monitor the completion status of tasks necessary to create and publish a Web site.

- Publish (or send) your Web site to a Web server for the world to see on the Internet (World Wide Web) by clicking a single button on a toolbar or by using a simple, built-in file transfer program.

Don't worry if the list of what FrontPage lets you do seems long and complicated. In fact, the Tips in this book will show you that seemingly complex operations actually consists simple procedures that you can master easily. By the time you finish this book, you will be able to answer the question "How did they do that?" when you visit feature rich Web sites with a lot of special effects. Once you know how it's done, you'll be able to use FrontPage to create highly functional and exciting Web pages that will provide a memorable experience for visitors to your Web sites and keep them coming back.

USING A CONTENT WIZARD TO CREATE A ONE PAGE WEB

FrontPage provides templates that let you generate individual Web pages, as well as, multiple page Web sites. Most templates provide not only the layout, common page elements, and set the site's color scheme but also make suggestions as to the information (or content) you should include. If you want to create your own general-purpose Web from scratch, use the FrontPage One Page Web template. To have FrontPage create the folder structure for your Web site with a single, blank home page, perform the following steps:

1. Select the File menu New option and click your mouse pointer on Page or Web. After FrontPage displays the New Page or Web menu, click your mouse pointer on Web Site Templates. FrontPage, in turn, will display the Web Site Templates dialog box.
2. Enter the pathname of the folder in which you want FrontPage to create the Web into the Specify the location of the new Web field in the Options section of the dialog box. For the current project, enter C:\MY DOCUMENTS\MY WEBS\ONEPAGE.
3. Double-click your mouse pointer on the One Page Web icon. FrontPage, in turn, will generate a single page Web site and return to the main editing window, similar to that shown in Figure 18.1.

To see how easy it is to add content to your new Web site, edit the Web site's home page by performing the following steps:

1. Double-click your mouse pointer on the INDEX.HTM file in the Folder List pane of the main editing window. FrontPage, in turn, will display the INDEX.HTM document in the application window's document pane. (If you don't see the folder list, click your mouse pointer on the Toggle Pane button on the Standard toolbar.)

2. Enter the text you want visitors to your Web site to see. For the current project, enter the text shown in document pane (on the right-hand side) of the application window shown in Figure 18.2.

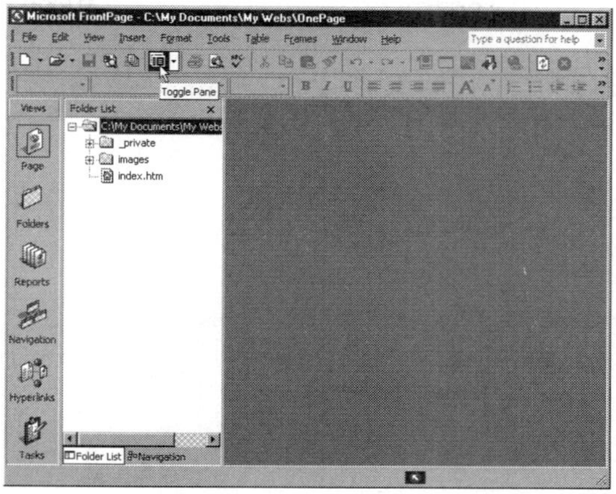

Figure 18.1 The FrontPage application window showing the folder structure for a One Page Web.

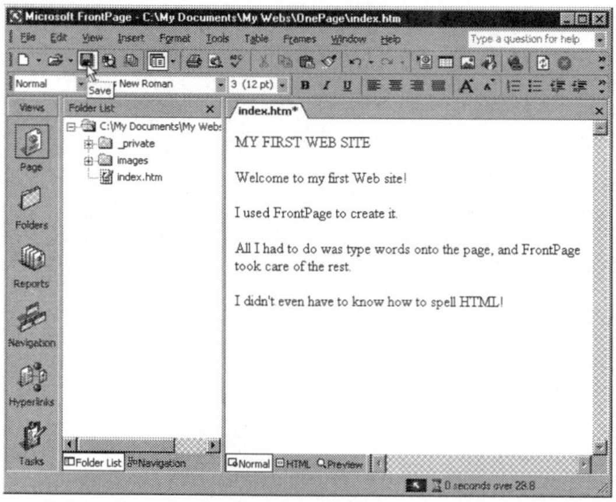

Figure 18.2 The One Page Web INDEX.HTM Web page displayed in the FrontPage application window's document pane.

3. Click your mouse pointer on the Save button on the Standard toolbar (or select the File menu Save option) to write the changes you made to INDEX.HTM to your hard drive.

That's all there is to it! To see what your Web page will look like to a Web site visitor, start your Web browser and enter the pathname of the INDEX.HTM file in the Web browser's Address field. For the current project, enter C:\MY DOCUMENTS\MY WEBS\ONEPAGE\INDEX.HTM, and then press the Enter key.

UNDERSTANDING FILES AND FOLDERS CREATED BY THE FILE MENU NEW WEB OPTION

When you import a Web site or use a FrontPage content template or Wizard to generate a FrontPage Web, FrontPage creates the directory structure it needs to manage your Web site's files. While individual files differ based on the type of Web created (Personal, Customer Support, Discussion, etc.), all FrontPage Webs have a common directory structure. For example, if you use the Project Web template to generate a Project Web in the C:\MY DOCUMENTS\MY WEBS\PROJECT folder, FrontPage will create a directory structure similar to that shown in Figure 19.

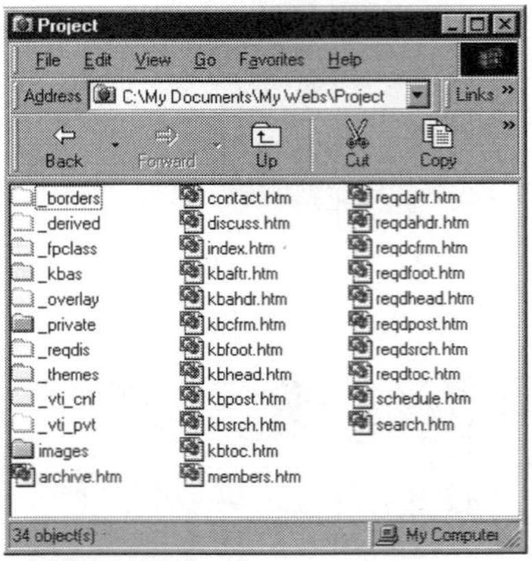

Figure 19 The FrontPage Web folder structure.

Refer to Table 19 for a description of the FrontPage Web's folders.

Folder	Description of Contents
_borders –	Web pages that contain the contents of the shared borders, or items that appear on each of the site's Web pages.
_cusudi –	unique to the Customer Services Web and contains files necessary for the discussion portion of the Customer Support Web.
_derived –	graphic (GIF) files that contain the text overlays in the _overlay directory combined with the graphic border elements. The files in the _derived folder are created when you apply a theme to a FrontPage Web.

Table 19 The folders in the FrontPage Web directory structure. *(Continued on next page)*

Folder	Description of Contents
_fpclass –	holds Java classes for hover and navigation buttons. FrontPage will automatically create Java applets in the _fpclass folder as you add hover and navigation buttons to your Web pages. You can use the folder to store Java applets you develop for the Web site as well.
_kbas –	unique to the Project Web and contains information needed for the Project Web's Knowledge Base articles.
_overlay –	text to be placed on top of Web page border graphics. The files in the _overlay directory are created when you apply a theme to a FrontPage Web.
_private –	holds files you want accessible for your Web pages but hidden from Web site visitors. If you add a Search component to your Web site, the pages in the _private folder will not be included in the index of Web pages.
_reqdis –	unique to the Project Web and contains files necessary for the discussion section of the Project Web.
_themes –	holds the cascading style sheets and graphics files necessary to display the FrontPage Web's theme (or themes). The _themes folder contains a subfolder for each of the Web site's themes. (You can apply a different theme (or no theme) to each of the pages in your Web site.)
_vti_cnf –	contains a Web page (with the same name) for each of the Web pages in your Web site. While your site's "public" Web pages contain content you want your visitors to see, the Web pages in _vti_cnf contain information about each page, such as: when the page was created, by whom, what program was used to create it, and so on.
_vti_pvt –	contains several files including the list of subWebs, the to-do list, and the to-do list history.
images –	storage place for pictures (GIF, JPG, and BMP files, for example).

Table 19 The folders in the FrontPage Web directory structure. (Continued from previous page)

Note: *The folders which start with an underscore (_) are hidden from Web site visitors and with the exception of the _private directory, from the FrontPage Folder List. If you want to see the "_" folders on the FrontPage Folder List, check the Show documents in hidden folders check box on the Advanced tab of the Tool menu Web Settings dialog box.*

USING A CONTENT TEMPLATE TO CREATE A PROJECT WEB SITE

As the name implies, the purpose of the Project Web is to track the status of a project. The Project Web content template will create a Web site that lets you enter team member information (including biographies, pictures, and a link to each member's home page), a project completion schedule, current task status, and upcoming events (such as project demonstrations and reviews). The Project Web site also includes a document archive, search page, and a discussion area for team members.

To use the Project Web content template to create a Project Web site, perform the following steps:

1. Select the File menu New option and click your mouse pointer on Page or Web. After FrontPage displays the New Page or Web menu, click your mouse pointer on Web Site Templates. FrontPage, in turn, will display the Web Site Templates dialog box.
2. Enter the pathname of the folder in which you want FrontPage to create the Project Web in the Specify the location of the new Web field on the right-hand side of the dialog box. For the current project, enter C:\MY DOCUMENTS\MY WEBS\PROJECT.
3. Click your mouse pointer on the Project Web icon on the left-hand side of the dialog box. Then click your mouse pointer on the OK button. FrontPage, in turn, will create the Project Web in the folder you specified in Step 2.

   If you were planning to use the Project Web as the outline for generating a Web site to monitor an actual project, you would now change the generic text on the Web pages to the specific content detailing your project. A good place to start is by editing the Web site's home page—INDEX.HTM. To edit the home page, double-click your mouse pointer on the INDEX.HTM file in the Folder List pane of the main editing window. FrontPage, in turn, will display the contents of the INDEX.HTM Web page in the document pane to the right of the Folder List, similar to that shown in Figure 20.

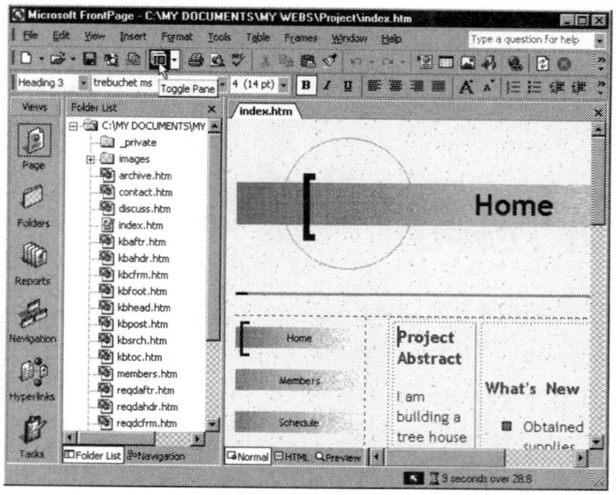

Figure 20 The FrontPage application window with the home page (INDEX.HTM) document for the Project Web in the document window.

To change the FrontPage generated text, use your mouse pointer to select what you want to change and start typing—just as if you were using a word processor like Microsoft Word or Corel WordPerfect.

Note: *If you want to expand the document editing pane by removing the Folder List pane, click your mouse pointer on the Toggle Pane button on the Standard toolbar. When you want to re-display the Folder List pane, just click your mouse pointer on the Toggle Pane button again.*

While you can click your mouse pointer on the Preview button at the bottom of the editing Window to see what the Web site will look like to your visitors, you will need to publish the site to a server with FrontPage Server Extensions installed to make use of all of the site's features such as the Search page and Knowledge Base. To avoid making an incomplete Web site publicly available, you can publish the site to a personal Web server running on your own computer.

USING A CONTENT TEMPLATE TO CREATE A CUSTOMER SUPPORT WEB SITE

A Customer Support Web site lets you publish product help and information. By visiting the site, customers can find new product news, review answers to frequently asked questions (FAQ's), report problems, download software updates, make suggestions, and participate in an on-line discussion with other customers. While the template is specifically designed to provide support services for software companies, you can easily modify the site's content to provide customer support for other types of businesses.

To use the Customer Support Web content template to create a Customer Support Web site, perform the following steps:

1. Select the File menu New option and click your mouse pointer on Page or Web. After FrontPage displays the New Page or Web menu, click your mouse pointer on Web Site Templates. FrontPage, in turn, will display the Web Site Templates dialog box.
2. Enter the pathname of the folder in which you want FrontPage to create the Customer Support Web in the Specify the location of the new Web field on the right-hand side of the dialog box. For the current project, enter C:\MY DOCUMENTS\MY WEBS\SUPPORT.
3. Click your mouse pointer on the Customer Support Web icon on the left-hand side of the dialog box. Then click your mouse pointer on the OK button. FrontPage, in turn, will create the Customer Support Web in the folder you specified in Step 2.

To replace the generic Web page content generated by FrontPage, look in the Folder List pane of the main edit window and double-click your mouse pointer on the page you want to change. For example, to change the content of the site's home page, double-click your mouse pointer on the INDEX.HTM file. FrontPage, in turn, will display the contents of INDEX.HTM in the document editing window to the right of the Folder List pane. Next, position your cursor where you want to insert text or use your mouse pointer to select text you want to replace—type the words you want to display in the Web page into the document editing pane as you would when using a word processor.

Although you can click your mouse pointer on the Preview tab at the bottom of the editing Window to display the site's Web pages and follow its hyperlinks by clicking your mouse pointer on them, you will need to publish the site to a server with FrontPage Server Extensions installed to make use of all of the site's features such as the Search page and the Bug Report form. You can publish your site to your Microsoft Personal Web Server running on your personal computer to prevent your customers from stumbling onto your support Web site before it's ready.

USING THE DISCUSSION WEB WIZARD TO CREATE A DISCUSSION WEB SITE

A Discussion Web site provides a means for visitors to have online conversations by leaving notes for each other on the Web site. Unlike e-mail, messages posted to a Discussion Web are public and everyone that is a member of the discussion group is allowed to read the message(s) and post a reply. While most Web sites provide a one-way flow of information from the author of the Web pages to the Web site's visitors, the Discussion Web requires that visitors be able to add to the Web content, as well as, read it.

In the past, the setup and maintenance of a Discussion Web was a difficult and time-consuming process. Due to the dynamic nature of the of the Web's content, the Webmaster had to spend a lot of time writing and modifying scripts to manage the two-way flow of information. Fortunately, FrontPage provides a simple wizard that will setup all of the components of a Discussion Web after you answer a few questions about how you want the site to look and whether you want to let anyone post messages or limit access to registered users. After that, Web site components automatically interact with the Web server and manage the flow of information among the site's visitors.

To generate a Discussion Web using the Discussion Web Wizard perform the following steps:

1. Select the File menu New option and click your mouse pointer on Page or Web. After FrontPage displays the New Page or Web menu, click your mouse pointer on Web Site Templates. FrontPage, in turn, will display the Web Site Templates dialog box.
2. Enter the pathname of the folder in which you want FrontPage to create the Discussion Web in the Specify the location of the new Web field on the right-hand side of the dialog box. Give some thought to the name of the folder in which you want FrontPage to create the Web. Unless your intention is to setup a Discussion Web Site where visitors will post messages about any topic that comes to mind, don't name the folder "DISCUSSION". Successful Discussion Webs are oriented around a specific topic, so a visitor knows what type of information to expect when entering the discussion. As such, if you need to discuss several diverse topics, setup a separate Discussion Web for each unique topic, and use a word or two that relates to the topic for the name of the folder in which FrontPage will create the Web. For the current project, assume that you want to setup a site for customers to exchange recipes. As such, enter C:\MY DOCUMENTS\MY WEBS\RECIPE in the Specify the location of the new Web field.
3. Click your mouse pointer on the Discussion Web Wizard icon on the left-hand side of the dialog box. Then click your mouse pointer on the OK button. FrontPage, in turn, will start the Discussion Web Wizard, which in turn, will display a screen describing the process of creating a Discussion Web in general terms.
4. Click your mouse pointer on the NEXT button. The Discussion Web Wizard, in turn, will display a dialog box asking you to select your Discussion Web's optional features similar to that shown in Figure 22.1.

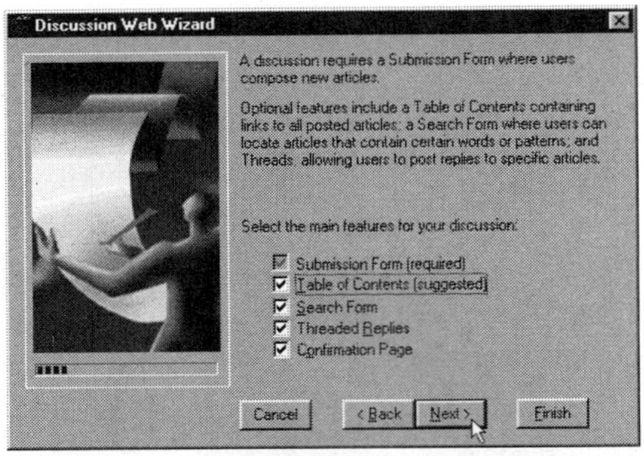

Figure 22.1 The Discussion Web Wizard optional features selection dialog box.

You will notice that the Submission Form check box is already checked—you have to provide a form for visitors to post messages to the Discussion Web. The optional features include:

- **Table of Contents** – provides a list of previously posted messages, sorted by subject. Visitors can view the list of postings and select those they want to read and those to which they wish to reply.
- **Search Form** – create a Search Form visitors can use to find messages in the Discussion Web that contain specified text strings in the message body or subject.
- **Threaded Replies** – link multiple messages on the same topic. Threads allow a visitor to go from one message to the next on a given subject. For example, if a visitor asks, "How do I cook a roast", people replying to the message would link the replies to the original message (using a thread). Someone looking for recipes for cooking roasts could then select the original message and move from one roast recipe to another.
- **Confirmation Page** – lets the visitor know whether a submitted message was successfully posted to the Discussion Web by displaying what the server received when the visitor clicked the SUBMIT button on the Submission Form.

For the current project, include all of the optional features by clicking your mouse pointer on each check box until the check mark appears.

5. Click your mouse pointer on the NEXT button. The Discussion Web Wizard, in turn, will ask you to enter a descriptive title for the Discussion Web by displaying a dialog box similar to that shown in Figure 22.2.

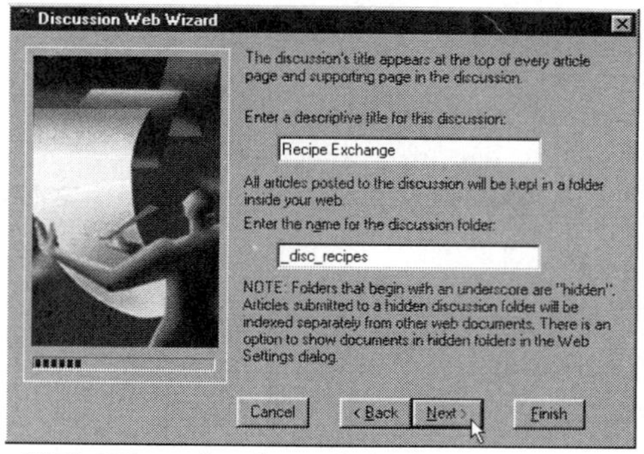

Figure 22.2 The Discussion Web Wizard title and folder name entry dialog box.

The title you enter in the Enter a descriptive title for this discussion field will appear on each page of the Discussion Web. As such, enter a title that will remind the visitors of the topic of the discussion. For the current project, enter "Recipe Exchange".

FrontPage needs a folder in which to place all of the discussion entries. You could accept the generic, default folder name supplied by the Discussion Web Wizard since the folder is hidden and will not appear in the Folder List pane of the FrontPage main editing window. However, if you later decide to run more than one discussion topic on the Discussion Web, using descriptive folder names will make it easy to determine which folder has which discussion group's messages. For the current project, enter "_disc_recipes" in the Enter the name for the discussion folder field.

6. Click your mouse pointer on the NEXT button. The Discussion Web Wizard, in turn, asks you to select the message submission form fields with a dialog box similar to that shown in Figure 22.3.

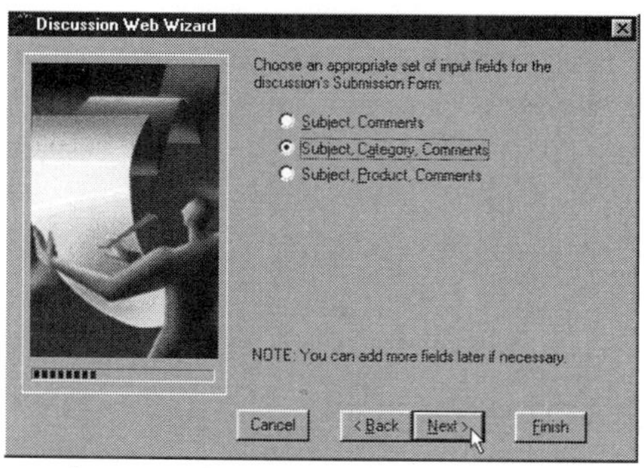

Figure 22.3 The Discussion Web Wizard submission form field selection dialog box.

When posting a message to the Discussion Web, the visitor will enter the topic the posting is about in the subject field and the actual message itself in the comments field. If you want to group messages by categories (or product, if your subjects are product based vs. category based), add Category (or Product) to the Submission Form by clicking your mouse pointer on the appropriate radio button. Assigning a message to a category (or product type) will allow the visitor to request a list of all messages pertaining to a category or product. For the current project, assume that you want to group recipes by category (such as meat, poultry, seafood). As such, click your mouse pointer on the radio button to the left of Subject, Category, Comments.

7. Click your mouse pointer on the Next button. The Discussion Web Wizard, in turn, allows you to decide if you want to force visitors to register with a username and password prior to reading and posting messages; or if you want to leave your Discussion Web open to everyone. This is accomplished by displaying the dialog box shown in Figure 22.4.

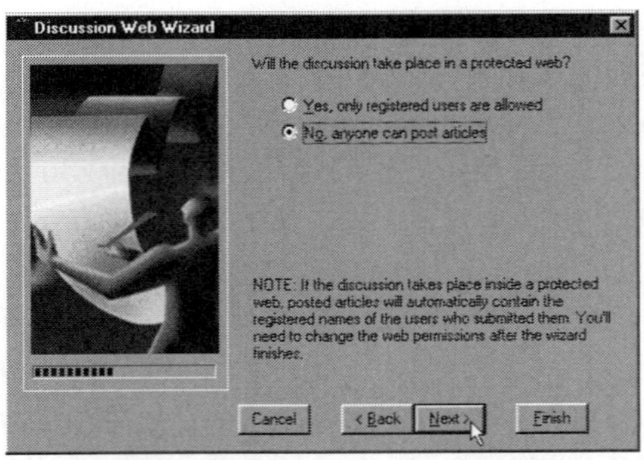

Figure 22.4 The Discussion Web Wizard protected Discussion Web election dialog box.

For the current project, leave the Recipe Exchange open to all by clicking your mouse pointer on the radio button to the left of No, anyone can post articles.

8. Click your mouse pointer on the Next button. The Discussion Web Wizard, in turn, will ask you to decide how the Table of Contents is to sort the list of articles by displaying a dialog box similar to that shown in Figure 22.5.

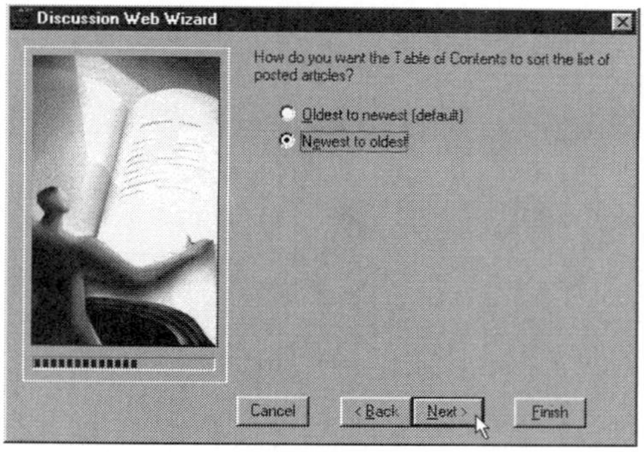

Figure 22.5 *The Discussion Web Wizard Table of Contents sort selection dialog box.*

Sorting from newest to oldest will put the most recent posting at the top of the Table of Contents. As a result, someone visiting the Discussion Web can quickly see what new messages (if any) were posted. If you sort the Table of Contents from oldest to newest, the visitor will have to scroll down to the end of the Table of Contents to see the latest postings. Having to scroll through a long list of messages only to find that there are no new messages will annoy your visitors. As such, newest to oldest is generally the preferred sort order. For the current project, click your mouse pointer on the radio button to the left of Newest to oldest.

9. Click your mouse pointer on the NEXT button. The Discussion Web Wizard, in turn, will ask if you want the Table of Contents page to be the Web Site's home page by displaying the dialog box shown in Figure 22.6.

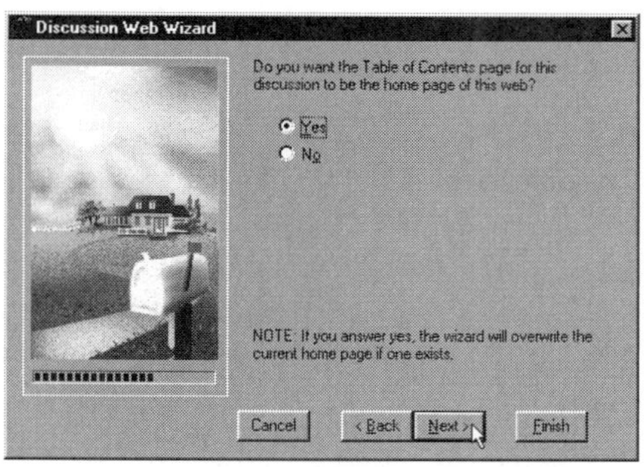

Figure 22.6 *The Discussion Web Wizard use Table of Contents as a home page election dialog box.*

If you are adding the Discussion Web to an existing Web site, select No. Otherwise, you will overwrite your current home page (INDEX.HTM). If you are creating a new Discussion Web site, select Yes. For the current project in which you are creating a new Web site for the Discussion Web, click your mouse pointer on the radio button to the left of Yes to use the Table of Contents as the Discussion Web's home page.

10. Click your mouse pointer on the NEXT button. The Discussion Web Wizard, in turn, will let you select the information to report for matching documents returned by the Search Form by displaying the dialog box shown in Figure 22.7.

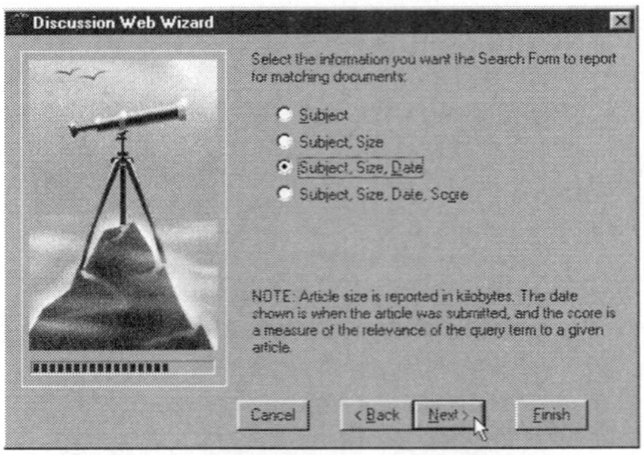

Figure 22.7 The Discussion Web Wizard Search form results selection dialog box.

For the current project, accept the default: Subject, Date, Size.

11. Click your mouse pointer on the NEXT button. The Discussion Web Wizard, in turn, will ask you if you want to apply a theme to the site by displaying the dialog box shown in Figure 22.8.

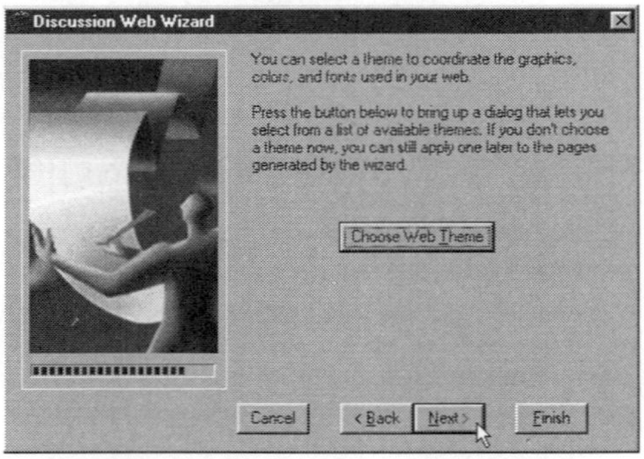

Figure 22.8 The Discussion Web Wizard theme selection dialog box.

If you are going to create a hyperlink from an existing Web site to the Discussion Web, apply the same theme to the Discussion Web as you did to the original Web site. As you know, the Web theme will set text and hyperlink colors, button styles, and background graphics and color. As such, selecting the same theme for the Discussion Web as you did for the Web that links to it, will give your Web site a consistent look and feel. Visitors will see the Discussion Web as an integral part of your main Web site—even though you created the Discussion Web as a separate FrontPage Web. To select a theme, click your mouse pointer on the CHOOSE WEB THEME button. The Discussion Web Wizard, in turn, will display the Choose Theme dialog box, so you can select the theme and click your mouse pointer on the OK button to return to the Discussion Web Wizard.

For the current project, accept the default (Cascade) theme.

12. Click your mouse pointer on the NEXT button. The Discussion Web Wizard, in turn, will ask you to select a Frame option by displaying the dialog box shown in Figure 22.9.

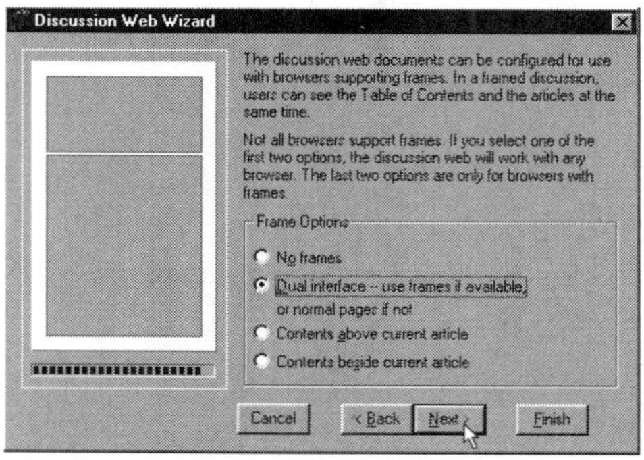

Figure 22.9 The Discussion Web Wizard page frame selection dialog box.

For the current project, click your mouse pointer on the radio button to the left of Dual interface — use frames if available so that your Discussion Web will be accessible both to browsers that support frames and to those that do not.

13. Click your mouse pointer on the NEXT button. The Discussion Web Wizard, in turn, will display the final page of the Discussion Web generation process as shown in Figure 22.10.

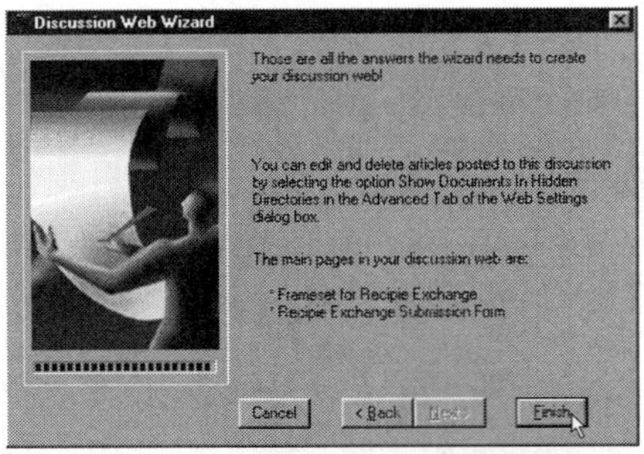

Figure 22.10 The final, wrap-up page of the Discussion Web Wizard.

If you need to change any information you supplied to the Discussion Web Wizard, click your mouse pointer on the BACK button until you reach the page whose information you want to change.

14. Click your mouse pointer on the FINISH button. The Discussion Web Wizard, in turn, will generate the Discussion Web and return to the FrontPage main editing window.

Once you've generated the Discussion Web's pages, visit each page and change the generic text with information specific to the discussion you want to host. You will learn more about setting up and managing Discussion Webs in Tips later in this book.

UNDERSTANDING FRONTPAGE VIEWS AND THE VIEWS TOOLBAR

After you open (or create) a FrontPage Web, you can select the view or the way in which you want FrontPage to display your Web site. Each of the six views gives you different types of information and editing capabilities. To select a view, click its icon on the Views toolbar located along the left side of the application window as displayed in Figure 23.

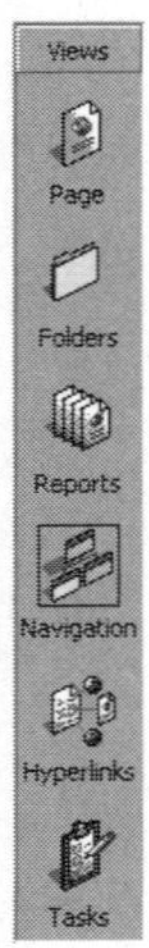

Figure 23 The FrontPage Views toolbar.

The six views available by clicking the buttons on the FrontPage Views toolbar are:

- **Page** – displays a list of the Web site's files and folders in the Folder List pane. Double-click your mouse pointer on the file you want to edit, and FrontPage will display the Web page you selected in the document pane on the right. Page View gives you a what-you-see-is-what-you-get (WYSIWYG) editor you can use to type what you want to see on your Web site and toolbars you can use to format text, insert pictures, draw tables, add hyperlinks, etc. In short, use Page View to put the content on your Web pages.
- **Folders** – shows you a list of the Web site's folders in the Folder List pane and a list of the folder's files and subfolders in the document pane. Folders View makes it easy for you to organize your Web site's files (Web pages and graphics images). While in Folders View, FrontPage will update your Web page hyperlinks as you create new folders and move files from one folder to another.
- **Reports** – hides the Folder List pane and lets you display any one of thirteen reports in the document pane.
- **Navigation** – displays a wire diagram showing the navigation structure of your Web site and lets you add navigation buttons (Back, Forward, Home, etc.) to your Web pages.
- **Hyperlinks** – displays the hyperlinks to and from each page in the FrontPage Web.
- **Tasks** – lists the tasks to be completed in order to make the Web site ready for publication. When you use a content template or wizard to create a Web site, FrontPage will generate a lists of tasks you need to perform before you make the Web site available to the world by publishing (or copying) the site to your Web server. Tasks view lets you review the to-do list, update the status of the tasks, and add new tasks as necessary.

If you previously removed the Views toolbar to give yourself a larger document editing pane, you can re-display the toolbar by selecting the View menu Views Bar option. FrontPage, in turn, will display the Views toolbar.

HIDING AND REDISPLAYING THE FOLDER LIST PANE AND VIEWS TOOLBAR

If you are editing a Web page, you may want to expand the size of the document pane so that it takes up the entire width of the screen. In so doing, you will be able to see how the Web page will look when displayed on a Web site Visitor's screen set to the same resolution as your screen. To expand the document pane to full screen width, you will need to hide both the Folder List pane and the Views toolbar.

To hide the Folder List pane, select the View menu Folder List option (or click your mouse pointer on the Toggle Pane button sixth button from the left on the Standard toolbar). FrontPage, in turn, will remove the Folder List from the application window and expand the size of the document pane.

To hide the Views Toolbar, select the View menu Views Bar option. FrontPage, in turn, will remove the Views Toolbar from the application window and increase the size of the document pane.

When you want to redisplay the Views toolbar, select the View menu Views Bar option. The menu selection acts as a toggle. If the Views toolbar is on the screen, selecting the Views Bar option hides it. Conversely, if the Views toolbar is not displayed, selecting the Views Bar option tells FrontPage to display it. The same holds true for the Folder List pane. If not displayed, select the View menu Folder List option to have FrontPage display the Folder List pane. If on the other hand, the Folder List pane is already displayed, selecting the View menu Folder List option will tell FrontPage to hide it.

UNDERSTANDING PAGE VIEW

When you click your mouse pointer on the Page view icon at the top of the Views toolbar (or select the View menu Page option), you tell FrontPage to go into its what-you-see-is-what-you-get (WYSWIG) editor mode. To see how Page View lets you work with a Web document, perform the following steps:

1. Select the File menu Open Web option. FrontPage, in turn, will display the Open Web dialog box.
2. Enter the pathname of the FrontPage Web you want to open in the Web name field. For the current project enter C:\MY DOCUMENTS\MY WEBS\RECIPE. (If you didn't create the Recipe Discussion Web in the Creating a Discussion Web Site Using a Content Template Tip, enter the pathname for any other FrontPage Web you've created.)
3. Click your mouse pointer on the OPEN button. FrontPage, in turn, will open the Web you entered in Step 2.
4. Click your mouse pointer on the Page button on the Views toolbar (or select the View menu Page option).
5. Double-click your mouse pointer on the name (or icon next to the name) of the page you want to display in the Folder List pane. (If you do not see the Folder List pane, select the View menu Folder List

option to display it.) For the current project, double-click your mouse pointer on DISC_RECIPIES_CFRM.HTM (the first Web page listed) in the Folder List pane. FrontPage, in turn, will display the site's first Web page (sorted alphabetically by name) in the document window similar to that shown in Figure 25.1.

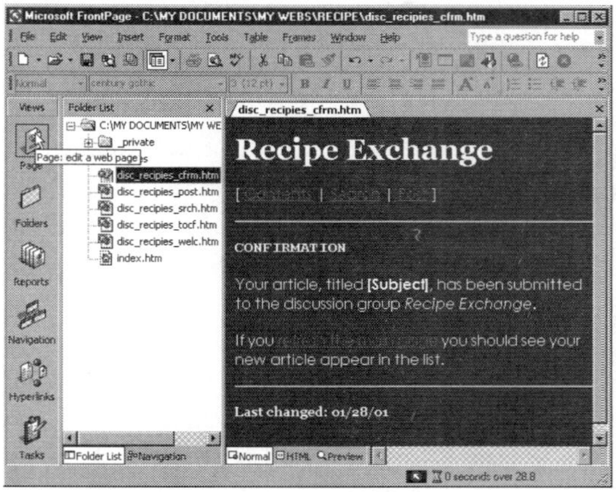

Figure 25.1. Page View with the DISC_RECIPES_CFRM.HTM Web page in the document pane.

While in Page view, you can double-click your mouse pointer on a Web page in the Folder List pane to display and make changes to that page in the document pane. For example, double-click your mouse pointer on DISC_RECIPES_POST.HTM, and FrontPage will display the disc_recipes_post.htm Web page (generated by the Discussion Web Wizard) similar to that shown in Figure 25.2.

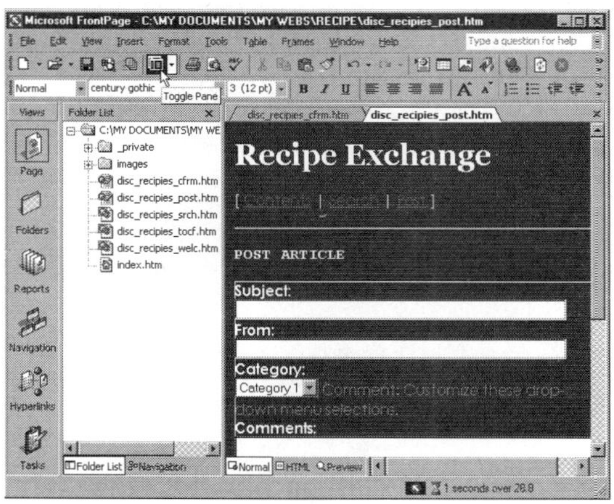

Figure 25.2. Page View with the Recipe Discussion Web message posting form displayed the document editing pane.

To make changes to the document, click your cursor into position in the document pane and begin typing. You can also select, cut-and-paste, and format text using toolbar buttons—as you would in any Windows compatible word processor.

Note: *You can hide the Folder List pane from view, so you can see more of the Web page in the document pane by clicking your mouse pointer on the Toggle Pane button (sixth button from the left on the Standard toolbar). The Folder List button acts as a toggle, so you can re-display the Folder List pane by clicking the Toggle Pane button again.*

There are three important tabs located at the bottom of the document pane—Normal, HTML, and Preview. When you click your mouse pointer on the Normal tab you tell FrontPage to display the Web page in the document pane in normal, editing mode. As such, you can work with the document in WYSIWYG editing mode. (The Web page displayed in the document pane of Figure 25.2 is displayed in Normal view.)

If you want to work directly with the hypertext markup language (HTML), the code that Web browsers receive when they request your Web page from the Web server, click your mouse pointer on the HTML tab. FrontPage, in turn, will display the HTML that defines the Web page similar to that shown in Figure 25.3.

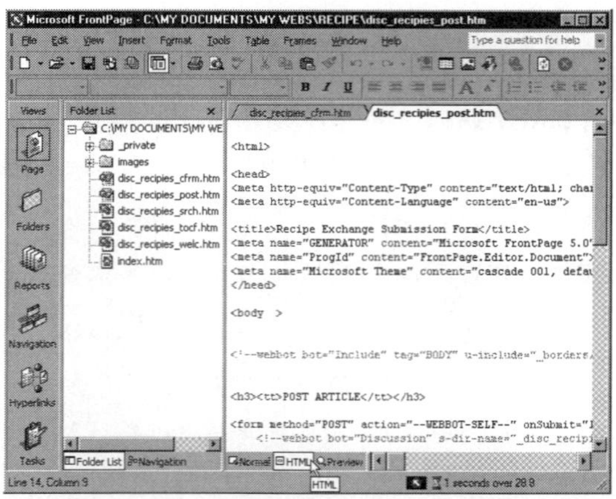

Figure 25.3. *Web page HTML as seen after clicking the mouse pointer on the Page View HTML button.*

To make changes to the HTML, just click your cursor into position in the document pane and begin typing.

Click your mouse pointer on the Preview button to display the Web page as it will look when displayed by a Web browser. If you click your mouse pointer on the Preview tab to display the disc_recipes_post.htm, FrontPage, in turn, will show the Web page in the document pane similar to that shown in Figure 25.4.

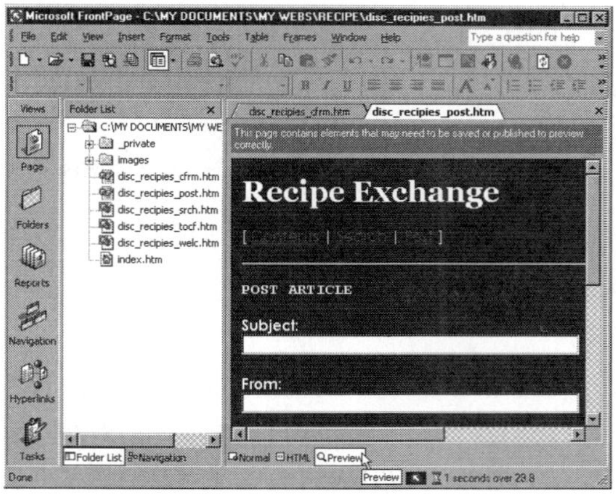

Figure 25.4. Page View of the Recipe Discussion Web with the message posting form displayed after clicking the mouse pointer on the Preview tab.

There are two important differences between the Normal view and Preview view. First, in Preview view, FrontPage displays your document without formatting marks. Notice that the line around the form in the lower half of the document in Figure 25.2 disappears when you display the Web page in Preview view. Second, clicking your mouse pointer on a hyperlink while in Preview view will cause FrontPage to display the linked document vs. positioning the cursor at the hyperlink (as FrontPage will do if you click your mouse pointer on a hyperlink while in Normal view).

UNDERSTANDING FOLDERS VIEW

When you click your mouse pointer on the Folders view button on the Views toolbar (or select the View menu Folders option), FrontPage, in turn, will display a hierarchical list of the Web site's folders in the Folder List pane and display a detailed list of the site's folders and Web pages in the document pane similar to that shown in Figure 26.

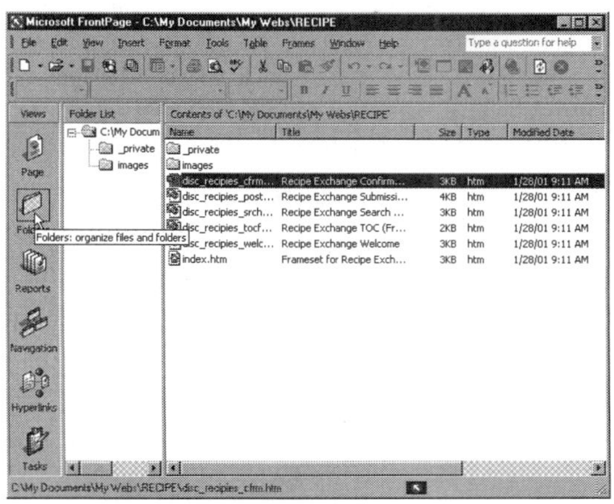

***Figure 26** Folders View of the Recipe FrontPage web.*

While in Folders view, you can:

- Create a new folder – by selecting the File menu New option and clicking your mouse pointer on Folder.
- Delete a file or folder – by right clicking your mouse pointer on the file or folder name and then selecting Delete on the pop-up menu.
- Display the contents of a folder – by clicking your mouse pointer on the folder name.
- Move a Web page into a folder – by moving your mouse pointer over the document icon, holding down the left mouse button as you move the pointer (and drag the document) over the folder into which you want to move it, and then releasing the left mouse button to drop the document into place. (When you move a Web page from one folder to another, FrontPage will automatically update hyperlinks to the document throughout the Web site.)
- Open a document in Page view – by double-clicking your mouse pointer on the document's icon.
- Rename documents or folders – by right clicking your mouse pointer on the name you want to change, selecting Rename on the pop-up menu and entering the new name for the document or folder. (When you change a document or folder name, FrontPage will automatically update Web site's hyperlinks to reflect the change.)
- Sort the file list – by clicking your mouse pointer on the column name. For example, to sort files by title, click your mouse pointer on the Title heading.
- View the properties of a document or folder – by right clicking your mouse pointer on the document or folder icon and selecting Properties on the pop-up menu.

UNDERSTANDING REPORTS VIEW

Reports View helps you manage the pages within your FrontPage web by displaying a wide range of information about each of the Web site's documents, hyperlinks, components, and tasks. To display your current FrontPage web in Reports View. Click your mouse pointer on the Reports button on the Views toolbar (or select the View menu Reports option and click your mouse pointer on Site Summary). FrontPage, in turn, will display a Site Summary report that gives you an overall view of the Web site's development and elements, similar to that shown in Figure 27.1.

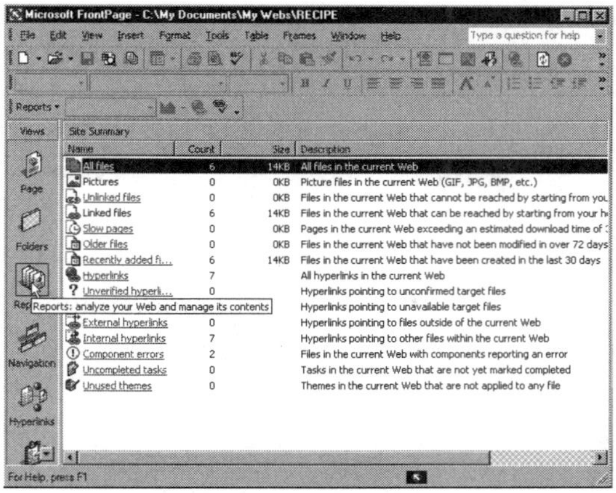

Figure 27.1 *Reports View displaying the Site Summary Report.*

To display the detail for a summary item on the Site Summary report, click your mouse pointer on the item. For example, if you want to display the detail for the Component Errors summary on the Site Summary report, click your mouse pointer on Component errors and FrontPage will display a Component Errors detail report similar to that shown in Figure 27.2.

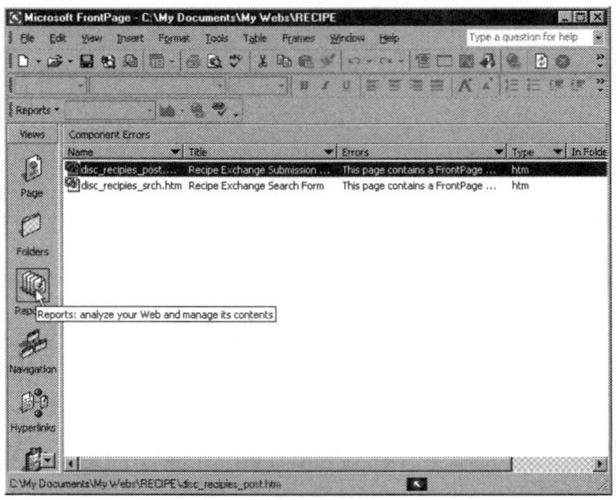

Figure 27.2 *Reports View displaying the Component Errors detail report.*

You can also tell FrontPage to display detail and other reports by selecting the View menu Reports option, moving your mouse pointer over the reports category, and then clicking your mouse pointer on the report you want to see. For example, to display the site's Daily Usage Summary report, select the View menu Reports option; move your mouse pointer over the Usage category and click your mouse pointer on Daily Summary, as show in Figure 27.3.

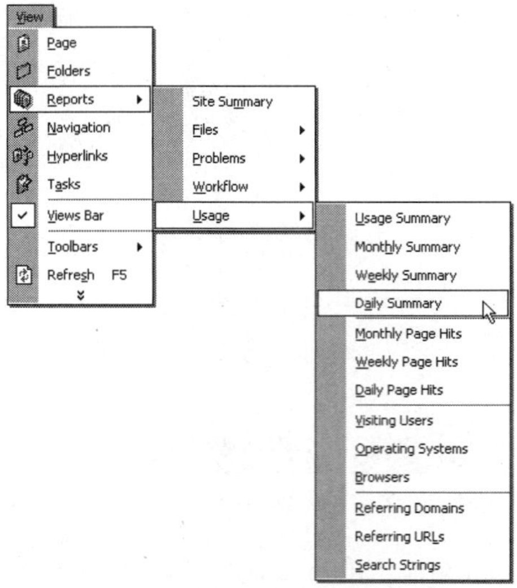

Figure 27.3 The FrontPage Reports menu Usage category reports list.

Table 27 displays the available FrontPage Web reports.

Category	Report
Site Summary	
Files	All Files, Recently Added Files, Recently Changed Files, Older Files
Problems	Unlinked Files, Show Pages, Broken Hyperlinks, Component Errors
Workflow	Review Status, Assigned To, Categories, Publish Status, Checkout Status
Usage	Usage Summary, Monthly Summary, Weekly Summary, Daily Summary, Monthly Page Hits, Weekly Page Hits, Daily Page Hits, Visiting Users, Operating Systems, Browsers, Referring Domains, Referring URL's, Search Strings

Table 27 Available FrontPage Web (site and page) reports.

You will learn all about the various FrontPage reports in later in this book.

UNDERSTANDING NAVIGATION VIEW

Navigation view shows you the hierarchical structure of your Web site. To see an example of Navigation View, perform the following steps:

1. Select the File menu Open Web option. FrontPage, in turn, will display the Open Web dialog box.

2. Enter the pathname of the FrontPage web you want to open in the Web name field. For the current project enter C:\MYDOCUMENTS\MY WEBS\MYWEB2. (If you didn't create the Corporate Presence Web when you worked the projects in the preceding Tips, enter the pathname for any other FrontPage web you've created.)
3. Click your mouse pointer on the OPEN button. FrontPage, in turn, will open the web you entered in Step 2.
4. Click your mouse pointer on the Navigation button on the Views toolbar (or select the View menu Navigation option), FrontPage, in turn, will generate a wire diagram of your Web site similar to that shown in Figure 28.

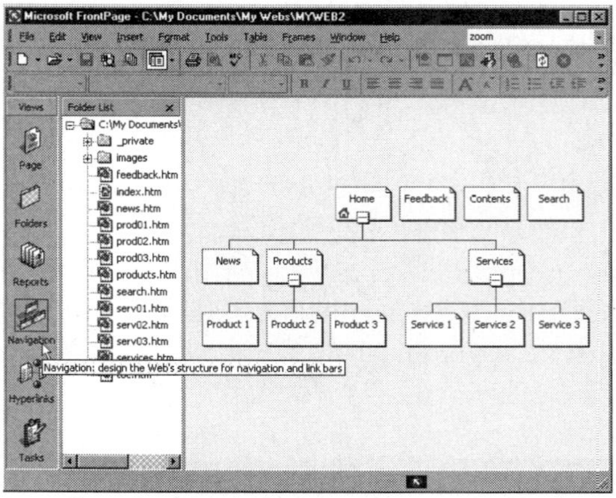

Figure 28 Navigation View of a Corporate Web Presence FrontPage Web.

Note: *If you cannot see all of the Web page icons shown in Figure 28, either change the resolution of your monitor, or you can tell FrontPage to size the Navigation view of the Web site to fit into the document pane. Right-click your mouse pointer on the background of the document pane (i.e. position the mouse pointer such that it is not on a page icon). FrontPage, in turn, will display a pop-up menu. Select the Zoom option and click your mouse pointer on Size to Fit.*

Upon review of the Navigation View of the Corporate Web Presence FrontPage Web shown in Figure 28, you can see that visitors would have to visit the Products Web page in order to continue on to pages with information on individual products (Web pages Product 1, Product 2, and Product 3). Similarly, to review detail on the company's services (Web pages Service 1, Service 2, and Service 3), the site visitor must first go to the Services Web page. Following this logic, you might think that the site has three inaccessible Web pages—Feedback, Contents, and Search which aren't shown as connected to other pages on the site. Actually, the *four* pages (Home, Feedback, Contents, and Search) are shown at the top of the hierarchy because they are accessible from anywhere on the site through the navigation menu at the top of each Web page. In addition, the Home page is shown wired to the rest of the pages below it because it has links to News, Products, and Services—Feedback, Contents, and Search are not attached because they only have links to each other and the Home page.

UNDERSTANDING HYPERLINKS VIEW

Hyperlinks View gives you a graphical display of all of the hyperlinks that point to and from the Web pages in your FrontPage web. To see an example of Hyperlinks View, perform the following steps:

1. Select the File menu Open Web option. FrontPage, in turn, will display the Open Web dialog box.
2. Enter the pathname of the FrontPage web you want to open in the Web name field. For the current project enter C:\MYDOCUMENT\MY WEBS\MYWEB2. (If you didn't create the Corporate Presence Web in when you worked the projects in preceding Tips, enter the pathname for any other FrontPage web you've created.)
3. Click your mouse pointer on the OPEN button. FrontPage, in turn, will open the web you entered in Step 2.
4. Click your mouse pointer on the Hyperlinks button on the Views toolbar (or select the View menu Hyperlinks option), FrontPage, in turn, will generate a graphical display of hyperlinks similar to that shown in Figure 29.1.

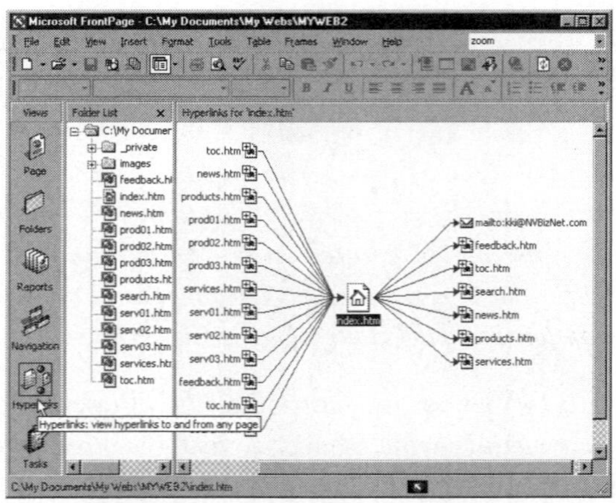

Figure 29.1 Hyperlinks View of the Corporate Web Presence web with the INDEX.HTM Web page selected.

Notice that FrontPage displays the selected Web page in the center of the document pane. (When you first open a FrontPage web and select Hyperlinks View, FrontPage will select the web's homepage, INDEX.HTM.) The Web pages to the left of the selected page contain links to that page. As such, the lines emerging FROM the Web pages to the left

INDEX.HTM in Figure 29.1 tell you that each of these Web pages contains at least one hyperlink TO INDEX.HTM. Conversely items to the right of the selected page represent the targets of hyperlinks found on that page. As such, Figure 29.1 shows that INDEX.HTM (the selected page) has hyperlinks that will take you to FEEDBACK.HTM, TOC.HTM, SEARCH.HTM, etc.

In addition to showing links to other Web pages, hyperlinks views also shows non-Web page hyperlinks. For example, if you look at Figure 29.1, you will see the first item in the hyperlink target list on the right-hand side of the document pane is MAILTO:KKI@NVBIZNET.COM with an envelope icon vs. the Web page icons shown for the remainder of the items in the list. The envelope icon and MAILTO: label tell you that there is a hyperlink on the INDEX.HTM page which when clicked will generate and e-mail message to KKI@NVBIZNET.COM—vs. taking you to another Web page.

To select the Web page whose hyperlinks you want to see, click your mouse pointer on the Web page icon in the application window's Folder List pane. For example, to display the hyperlinks from and to the site search page (SEARCH.HTM), click your mouse pointer on SEARCH.HTM in the folder list. FrontPage, in turn, will display the icon for SEARCH.HTM in the center of the document pane and show Web pages with hyperlinks to SEARCH.HTM to the left and the targets of hyperlinks on the SEARCH.HTM page to the right.

You can also display hyperlink targets found on Web pages shown as targets of the selected Web page. For example, look at Figure 29.1 and you will see that INDEX.HTM has a link to the search page (SEARCH.HTM). If you want to see the list of items that are targets of hyperlinks on the SEARCH.HTM page, click your mouse pointer on the SEARCH.HTM icon in the document pane of the Hyperlinks view. FrontPage, in turn, will change the plus (+) on the icon to a minus (-) and display the target items for the hyperlinks on SEARCH.HTM similar to that shown in Figure 29.2.

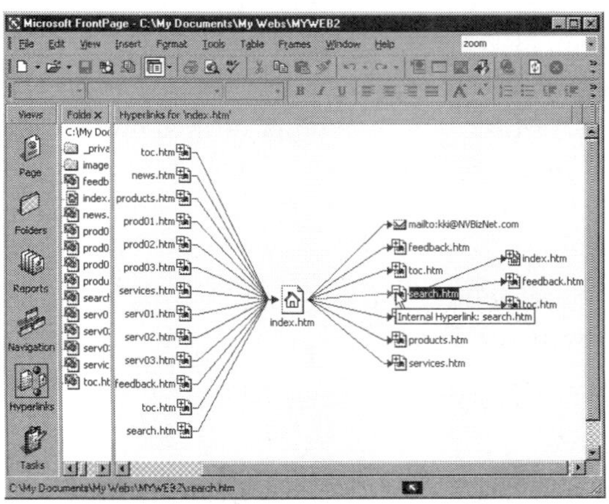

Figure 29.2 Extended Hyperlinks View showing the target of links on SEARCH.hTM in addition to links from and to the selected Web page (INDEX.HTM).

Similarly, if you click your mouse pointer on one of the Web pages on the left-hand side of the document pane (such as PROD01.HTM), FrontPage, in turn, will display a list of Web pages that have links TO that page. As such, clicking your mouse pointer on the PROD01.HTM icon on the left side of the document window will cause FrontPage to display those Web pages with hyperlinks to PROD01.HTM.

Note: *The plus (+) on file icon or folder icon indicates that you can "expand" the icon to show additional detail. A minus (-) on the file icon or icon folder icon indicates that you can "collapse" the detail into the icon so it is hidden from view. For example, if you click your mouse pointer on the plus (+) on a folder, FrontPage will change the plus (+) to a minus (-) and expand the icon to include a list of the files in the folder. If you no longer wish to see the folder's contents, click your mouse pointer on the icon again. FrontPage, in turn, will change the minus (-) on the folder icon to a plus (+) and collapse the list of files back into the folder icon—hiding them from view. Similarly, when you click an icon with a plus (+) in the document pane of the hyperlinks view, FrontPage will expand the icon to show the targets of hyperlinks on the Web page for pages on the right-hand side of the pane and expand the icon to show site hyperlinks to the page for pages on the left-hand side of the pane. Conversely, when you click your mouse pointer on an icon with a minus (-), FrontPage will collapse the hyperlinks list back into the icon.*

UNDERSTANDING TASKS VIEW

Tasks View helps you maintain an on-going to-do list of tasks that you (or other team members) need to perform in order to complete development of your Web site. To see an example of Tasks View, open the Corporate Web Presence web you created in the Tip entitled: "Using FrontPage Wizards to Create a Web Site", by performing the following steps:

1. Select the File menu Open Web option. FrontPage, in turn, will display the Open Web dialog box.
2. Enter the pathname of the FrontPage web you want to open in the Web name field. For the current project enter C:\MYDOCUMENTS\MY WEBS\MYWEB2. (If you didn't create the Corporate Presence Web in when you worked the project in previous Tips, enter the pathname for any web you created using a FrontPage content template, or wizard.)
3. Click your mouse pointer on the OPEN button. FrontPage, in turn, will open the web you entered in Step 2.
4. Click your mouse pointer on the Tasks button on the Views toolbar (or select the View menu Tasks option), FrontPage, in turn, will dis-

play the list of tasks that need to be completed similar to that shown in Figure 30.1.

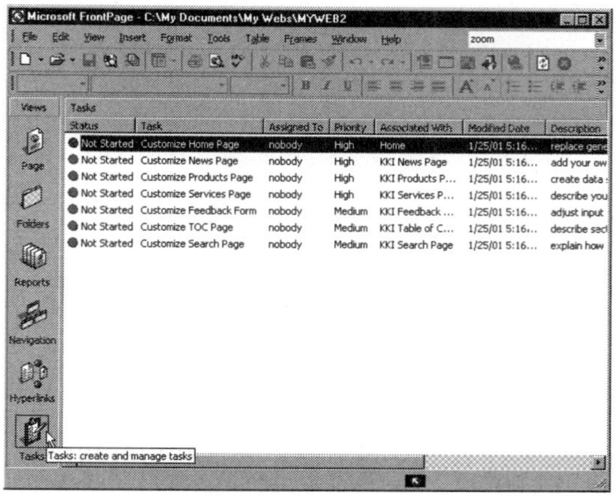

Figure 30.1 *Tasks View for the Corporate Web Presence FrontPage web.*

As was the case with Folders View, you can sort the items on the task list by clicking your mouse pointer on the headings. For example, to sort the task list by priority, click your mouse pointer on the Priority heading. FrontPage, in turn, will sort the task list in descending order by priority (i.e. HIGH, then MEDIUM, and then LOW). If you click your mouse pointer on the PRIORITY heading a second time, FrontPage will sort the task list in ascending order by priority (i.e. LOW, then MEDIUM, and then HIGH). To sort the task list by team member responsible for completing the task, click your mouse pointer on the Assigned To heading. Each time you click your mouse pointer on a new heading, FrontPage will sort the task list by that heading. If you click your mouse pointer on the same heading twice, FrontPage will reverse the order or the sort.

While useful as a reminder list of things to do if you are creating the Web site on your own, Tasks View is especially useful if you are managing a team of authors working on the site. By assigning tasks to team members, you make it possible for each author to generate a list of tasks that the author needs to perform. Conversely, as the authors perform the assigned tasks and change their status to completed, you will be able to review your team's progress toward having a fully functional Web site—without having to go through the hardship of scheduling a mutually agreeable group meeting time. You will learn more about using tasks to manage collaborative Web site development in future Tips.

To edit a task, double-click your mouse pointer on the task you want to change. FrontPage, in turn, will display a Task Details dialog box similar to that shown in Figure 30.2.

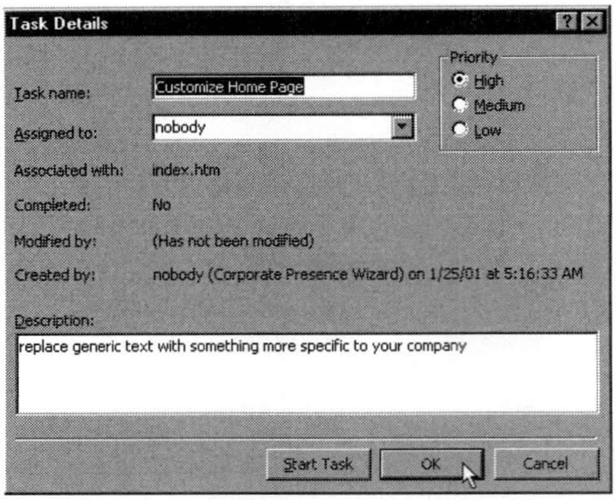

Figure 30.2 The Task Details dialog box.

Use the fields in the Tasks Details dialog box to enter the name of the task, select its priority, select the team member who is to complete the task, and enter a description of the work to be completed. After you've entered the information on the task, click your mouse pointer on the OK button to record your changes and return to the task list. You will learn more about editing tasks later in this book.

UNDERSTANDING FRONTPAGE ON-LINE RESOURCES AT MICROSOFT.COM

Microsoft provides product updates, add-in programs, technical support information, and hyperlinks to newsgroups and user group home pages for all MS-Office products (including FrontPage) on the company's Microsoft Office Products Update Web site (as of this writing, HTTP://OFFICEUPDATE.MICROSOFT.COM). The FrontPage area of the update site (like the areas for the other MS-Office products) contains three sections:

- **Welcome** – which has hyperlinks that let you display general information on FrontPage, download product upgrades, download add-in applications, read articles about HTML, and join the MS-Office on-line community.
- **Downloads** – which has hyperlinks to descriptions of available program updates, patches, additional Wizards, and other add-in products. In addition to letting you display information on the available software, the downloads page also has hyperlinks that let you download software to your computer.
- **Assistance** – which has hyperlinks to technical support documents and Knowledgebase articles, sources of additional FrontPage documentation, newsgroups, and user group home pages.

To access Microsoft FrontPage on-line resources, perform the following steps:

1. If your connection to the Internet is not currently active, establish a dial-up connection with your Internet service provider (ISP).
2. If you are not currently running FrontPage, start the program by clicking your mouse pointer on the START button. After Windows displays its Start menu, select Programs, and then click your mouse pointer on Microsoft FrontPage.
3. After Windows starts the FrontPage program, select the Help menu Office on the Web option. FrontPage, in turn, will have Windows start your Web browser, which in turn, will display the FrontPage Welcome page at the Microsoft Office Update site, similar to that shown in Figure 31.1

Note: *The first time you visit the Microsoft Office Update site, your Web browser will display a "Welcome to Office Update Worldwide" Web page that has hyperlinks to Microsoft Office Update Web servers running in various countries. Click your mouse pointer on the hyperlink link to the country nearest to your current location. Microsoft, in turn, will put a cookie on your computer that it can use to direct your Web browser to the same update server the next time you select the Office on the Web option on the FrontPage Help menu.*

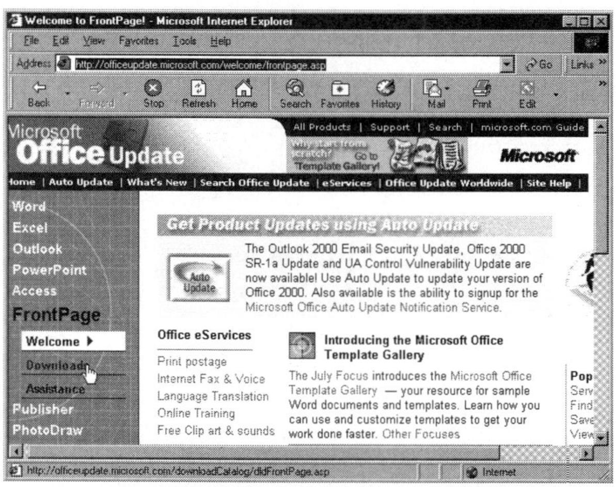

Figure 31.1 The FrontPage Welcome page at the MS-Office Update Web site.

4. Review the hyperlinks to Web sites and Web pages Microsoft feels would be of interest or helpful to FrontPage users. Feel free to click your mouse pointer on any of the hyperlinks on the page—you can always return to the Welcome page by clicking your mouse pointer on

your browser's BACK button repeatedly until you see the Welcome page again.

5. To display the Web page with download hyperlinks for FrontPage updates and Add-In programs, click your mouse pointer on the Downloads hyperlink (below the FrontPage heading along the left side of the current Web page). Your Web browser, in turn, will display a Downloads Web page similar to that shown in Figure 31.2.

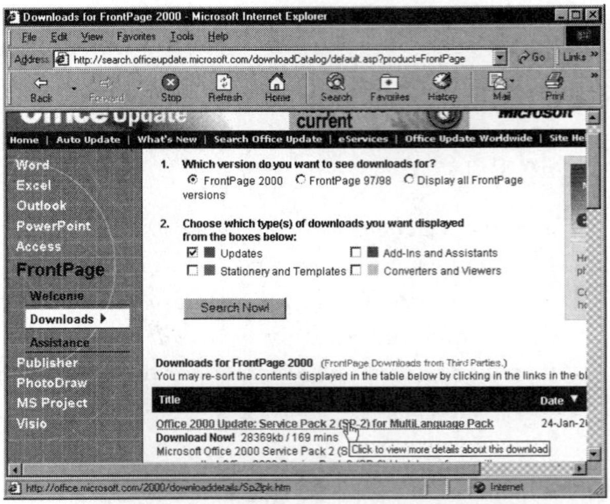

Figure 31.2 *The FrontPage Downloads page at the MS-Office Update Web site.*

6. To display a description of a particular download file, click your mouse pointer on its hyperlink (its title). When you are ready to have your Web browser copy the update or add-in onto your computer, click your mouse pointer on the Download Now hyperlink below the title of the download file you want. Your Web browser, in turn, will display a Web page with the set of instructions you must follow to download and install your selection.

7. To display a Web page with hyperlinks to on-line technical support resources, user groups, and additional FrontPage documentation, click your mouse pointer on the Assistance hyperlink. Your browser, in turn, will display a Web page similar to that shown in Figure 31.3.

When you finish using the resources on the Microsoft Office Update site, select your Web browser's File menu Exit option [or click your mouse pointer on the close button (the X) in the upper right-hand corner of the Web browser application window]. Windows, in turn, will exit the Web browser and return to the FrontPage application window.

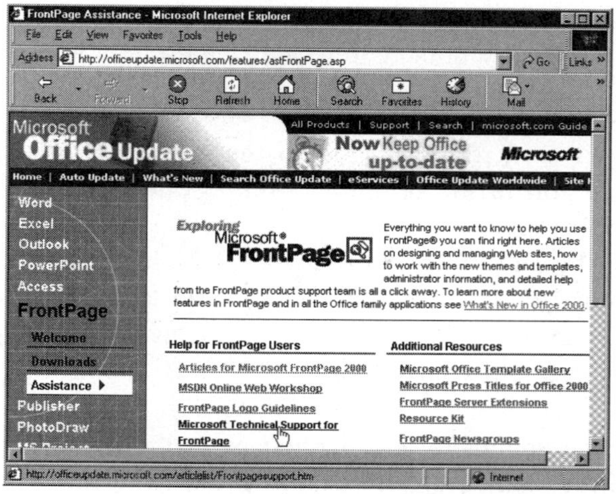

Figure 31.3 The FrontPage Assistance page at the MS-Office Update Web site.

UNDERSTANDING THE WEB CLIENT / SERVER RELATIONSHIP

The way in which the World Wide Web operates is really quite simple. An application [a Web browser like MS-Internet Explorer (IE)] running on one computer requests information from another application [a Web server such as MS-Internet Information Server (IIS)]. On the Internet, the Web browser (which requests information) is the *client* and the Web server (the application that sends the requested Web content to the client) is the *server*.

Assuming that both computers [the one on which the Web server is running and the one on which the Web browser (client) is running] are connected to the Internet or a local area network (LAN), passing information from server to client across the Web involves a four step communication process:

1. The client (browser) uses TCP/IP (Transmission Control Protocol/Internet Protocol) to establish a connection (either secured or unsecured) to the server over the Internet or LAN.
2. The client (browser) uses an HTTP (Hypertext Transfer Protocol) message to send a request to the Web server.
3. The Web server processes the request and uses an HTTP message to send the requested information (usually a Web page and its contents—text, graphics, sound files, etc.) across the Internet or LAN to the client (browser).
4. The client (browser) and Web server each terminates its own end of the TCP/IP connection.

Each time your browser connects to a Web Site and each time you click your mouse pointer on a hyperlink or on the send/submit button on a Web page, the client and server perform each of the four steps in the communication process.

One important thing to understand is that on the Internet, the client in a client/server relationship does not logon to the computer running the server application. Instead, the interaction between client and server is more like a phone call between yourself and your stock broker. Think of the TCP/IP as a program to establish a connection to the server much like the connection you establish when you dial your stock broker's phone number and the broker answers the phone. Like the Web browser, you make your request for information using a language both you and your broker understand—the browser and Web server use HTTP while the two of you use a language such as English, German, Dutch, etc., to communicate. After the broker responds to your request by giving you the stock quote, you both hang up to terminate the connection. If you then need more information from the broker, you will again go through the communications process—starting with the phone call.

When you publish a site on the Web, you put all of the site's content (i.e. its linked Web pages, graphics, sound files, etc.) in folders on a hard drive. The hard drive may be on the same computer that is running the Web server or on another machine to which the Web server has access. The Web server, for its part, runs in the background, waiting patiently for an information request. As soon as the server receives a request, it springs into action and sends the requested file(s), Web page, or other hyper linked object(s) to the Web browser. After satisfying the client's request, the server goes back to waiting for another request.

USING FRONTPAGE TO SETUP FOLDERS, CREATE FILES, AND DEFINE WEB SITE CREATION TASKS

After you design your Web site by deciding its purpose, organizing its content on paper, and creating a storyboard to depict the site's flow of information and layout, it is time to create the physical structure that will hold the site's Web pages, graphics, sound files, etc. With the physical structure in place, you can create a site map and a list of tasks that need to be completed in order to produce the Web you want to publish on the Internet.

To create the directory structure for a Web site, perform the following steps:

1. If you are not currently running FrontPage, start the program by clicking your mouse pointer on the START button. After Windows displays the Start menu, select Programs, and then click your mouse pointer on Microsoft FrontPage. Windows, in turn, will start the FrontPage program.
2. Select the File menu New option and click your mouse pointer on Page or Web. After FrontPage displays the New Page or Web menu, click your mouse pointer on Web Site Templates. FrontPage, in turn,

will display the Web Site Templates dialog box similar to that shown in Figure 33.1.

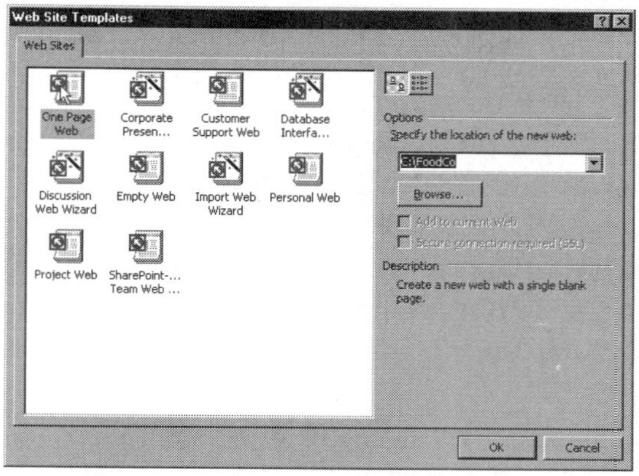

Figure 33.1 *The FrontPage Web Site Templates dialog box.*

3. Enter the name of the folder in which you want FrontPage to create the Web site in the Specify the location of the new web field in the Options section on the right-hand side of the New (Web) dialog box. For the current project, create a folder named FoodCo at the root of the C: drive by entering **C:\FoodCo** into the Specify the location of the new web field.
4. To have FrontPage create the Web's directory structure and a default homepage (INDEX.HTM), double-click your mouse pointer on the One Page Web icon in the Web Sites section of the New (Web) dialog box. FrontPage, in turn, will create the Web directories and display the single page Web site in Page View, similar to that shown in Figure 33.2.

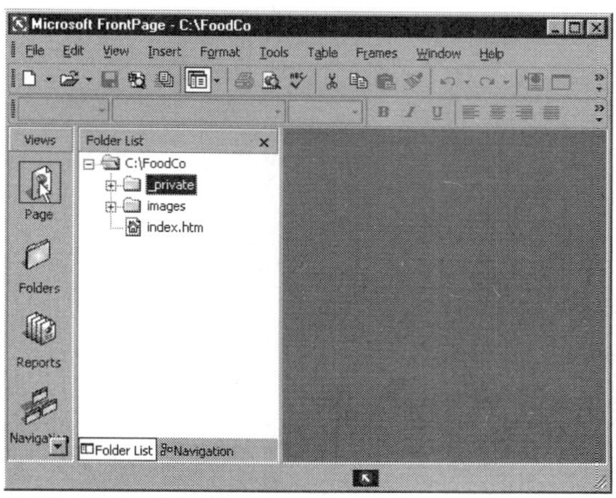

Figure 33.2 *A single page FrontPage Web in Page View.*

Note: *If your FrontPage window does not have the Views toolbar along its left-hand side, select the View menu and click your mouse pointer on Views Bar. Similarly, if you do not see the Folder List column in your FrontPage window, select the View menu and click your mouse pointer on Folder List.*

5. To create additional folders in the Web's root folder (C:\FoodCo, in the current example), click your mouse pointer on C:\FoodCo (at the top of the Folder List pane, and then right-click your mouse pointer on a blank area in the Folder List column. After FrontPage displays its pop-up menu, select the New option and click your mouse pointer on Folder. FrontPage, in turn, will create a new folder and prompt you to enter its name. For the current project, enter: **HTMLDocs** and then press the ENTER key.
6. Repeat Step 5 until you have created all of the folders needed to organize the site's content as decided during the site's design phase. When you want to create a subfolder (a folder within a folder), simply right-click your mouse pointer on the folder in which you wish to create another folder instead of the white space in the List Folders column. For the current project, create a NewsLetters subfolder in the HTMLDocs folder by right-clicking your mouse pointer on the HTMLDocs folder. After FrontPage displays its pop-op menu, select the New menu and click your mouse pointer on Folder. Then, when prompted for the new folder's name, enter: **NewsLetters** and press the ENTER key.
7. To create a Web page, select the File menu New option and click your mouse pointer on Page or Web. After FrontPage, in turn, displays the New Page or Web menu, click your mouse pointer on the Page Templates option. FrontPage, in turn, will display a Page Templates dialog box similar to that shown in Figure 33.3.

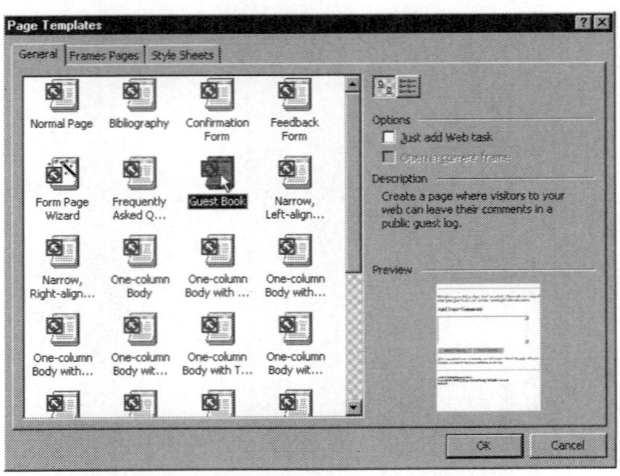

Figure 33.3 The FrontPage Page Templates dialog box.

8. Click your mouse pointer on the type or style of page you want to create. (Each time you click your mouse pointer on a page icon, FrontPage will display the page type's layout in the Preview Section of the New (page) dialog box. For the current project, click your mouse pointer on **GuestBook** and then on the OK button.
9. To save the new Web page to disk, select the File menu Save option. FrontPage, in turn, will display the Save As dialog box.
10. Double-click your mouse pointer on the icon of the folder in which FrontPage is to store the new Web page. If you do not see the folder you want, use the drop-down list button to the right of the Save in field at the top of the Save As dialog box to find the folder you want. For the current project: double-click your mouse pointer on the HTMLDocs folder.
11. To replace the new Web page's generic, default page title with one that describes the contents or purpose of the Web page, click your mouse pointer on the CHANGE TITLE button, near the bottom of the dialog box. FrontPage, in turn, will display the Set Page Title dialog box. Enter a title for the Web page. For the current project enter: **FoodCo Guestbook** and then click your mouse pointer on the OK button.
12. Enter the name of the Web page in the File name field near the bottom of the Save As dialog box. For the current project enter: **GuestBook** and then click your mouse pointer on the SAVE button near the lower right-hand corner of the Save As dialog box.
13. Repeat Steps 7 – 12 to create each of the Web pages you included in your site's storyboards.
14. To review and manage the list of tasks you and your team must accomplish before the Web site is ready for publication on the Net, click your mouse pointer on the Tasks button at the bottom of the Views toolbar. FrontPage, in turn, will display the Web production team's to-do list.
15. To add a new task, select the File menu New option and click your mouse pointer on Task. FrontPage, in turn, will display a New Task dialog box similar to that shown in Figure 33.4.
16. Enter a descriptive name for the task into the Task name field. For the current project enter: **Customize Guestbook Text**.
17. Set the priority of the task by clicking the appropriate radio button in the Priority section near the upper right-hand corner of the dialog box. For the current project, click your mouse pointer on the High priority radio button.

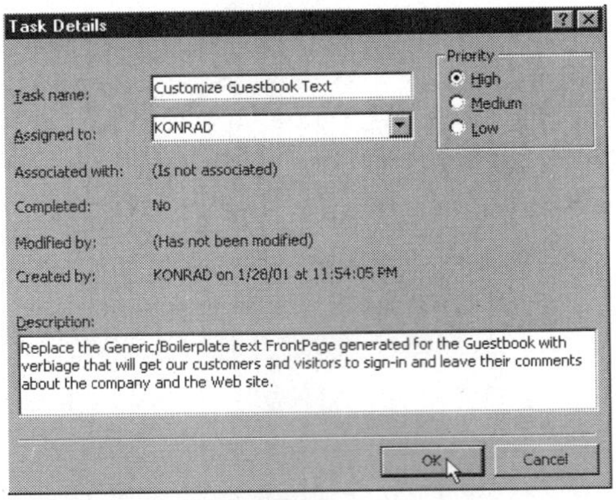

Figure 33.4 The FrontPage Task Details dialog box.

18. Use the drop-down list button to the right of the Assigned to field to list the usernames of your team members, and then click your mouse pointer on one of them to assign that team member the task you are creating. (You will learn how to manage the list of usernames later in this book.) For the current project, accept the default username shown on your screen.
19. Enter a brief description of the task in the Description scroll box near the bottom of the New Task dialog box. For the current project enter: **Replace the Generic/Boilerplate text FrontPage generated for the Guestbook with verbiage that will get our customers and visitors to sign-in and leave their comments about the company and the Web site.**
20. Click your mouse pointer on the OK button. FrontPage, in turn, will add the new task to the work schedule and return to Tasks view.
21. Repeat Steps 15 – 20 until you have created all of the tasks you and your team members need to accomplish in order to complete the production of the Web site.

Do not worry if you forget to create a folder, Web page, or task. You can always click your mouse pointer on the icon for the view you want (Page or Tasks), and then follow the steps in the preceding procedure to add additional folders, subfolders, Web pages, whenever you need to change the Web site's content or structure.

OPENING AND VIEWING AN EXISTING WEB IN PAGE VIEW

Working with FrontPage in Page View is very convenient in that (depending on the size of your monitor) you can display the Views Toolbar (which lets you switch between views), the Folder List (which shows the site's layout), and one of the site's Web pages (for viewing and/or editing)—all on one screen.

To open an existing FrontPage Web in Page View, perform the following steps:

1. If you are not currently running FrontPage, start the program by clicking your mouse pointer on the START button. After Windows displays the Start menu, select Programs, and then click your mouse pointer on Microsoft FrontPage.
2. In the FrontPage application window, select the File menu Open Web option. FrontPage, in turn, will display an Open Web dialog box, similar to that shown in Figure 34.

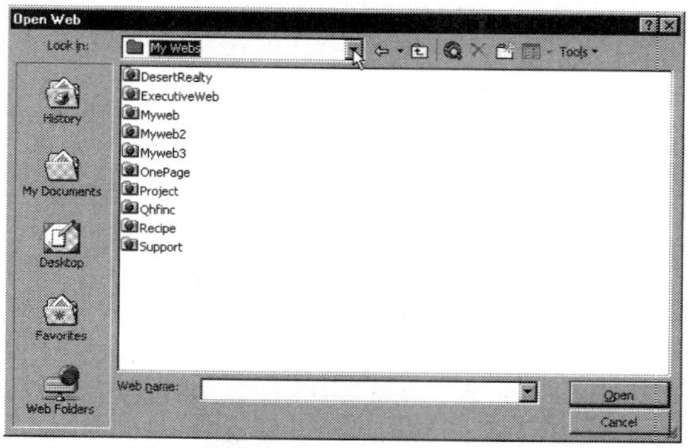

Figure 34 The FrontPage Open Web dialog box.

3. Look at the list of FrontPage Web folders in the list box below the Look in field, and double-click your mouse pointer on the folder that contains the FrontPage Web you want to open. If you do not see the folder you want, either enter the full pathname to the folder in the File name field at the bottom of the Open File dialog box and press the ENTER key, or use the drop-down list button to the right of the Look in field to find the folder you want. For the current project, double-click your mouse pointer on the SUPPORT folder. (You created a "customer support" Web site in the SUPPORT folder as a project in a previous Tip.) If you do not see the SUPPORT folder icon in the list box, enter the full pathname to the SUPPORT folder (C:\MY DOCUMENTS\MY WEBS\SUPPORT) in the File name field at the bottom of the dialog box and press the ENTER key. (If you did not create the Customer Support Web site as you worked the projects in the preceding Tips, double click your mouse pointer on any folder with a FrontPage Web you created in the past or are allowed to edit.)
4. For the current project, double-click your mouse pointer on INDEX.HTM—the default homepage for the Customer Support Web site. (If you do not see the folder list, select the View menu Folders

option.) FrontPage, in turn, will display the INDEX.HTM (home page) of the Customer Support web in the document editing pane.

As was mentioned the beginning of this Tip, one of the advantages of working in Page View is that you can display the Views toolbar, site Folder List, and one or more Web pages at the same time. FrontPage will automatically display one of the open Web site's pages when you are in Page View. However, if you do not see the Views toolbar, you can display it by selecting the View menu Views Bar option. Similarly, if you do not see the site's Folder List, you can display it by selecting the View menu Folder List option.

WORKING WITH AN EXISTING WEB PAGE WHILE IN PAGE VIEW

The FrontPage Page View lets you display and edit a Web site's pages using the FrontPage What-You-See-Is-What-You-Get (WYSIWYG) editor. Moreover, if you add the Folder List pane to the application window while in Page View, you can easily navigate a Web site's content to find a Web page which you can open with a double-click of your mouse pointer on its name.

If you do not have a FrontPage Web open, perform the steps in the preceding Tip to open the Customer Support web. (If you did not create the Customer Support Web as you worked the projects in previous Tips, perform the procedure in the preceding Tip to open a Web you created in the past or to which you have edit access.) Make sure FrontPage is in Page View either by clicking your mouse pointer on the Page View icon at the top of the Views toolbar or by selecting the View menu Page option.

To open a Web page in the Page view document pane, simply double-click your mouse pointer on the name of the Web page in the Folder List pane. For example, to open the Customer Support Web site's "Frequently Asked Questions (FAQ)" page, double-click your mouse pointer on FAQ.HTM in the Folder List pane. FrontPage, in turn, will open the Web page and display its content in the Page View document pane.

FrontPage does not close and store the page displayed in the document pane when you open another page. Instead, the program simply opens an additional page in memory each time you double-click your mouse pointer on the name of a page not yet open. In fact, FrontPage not only does not automatically close open pages as you open new ones, but the program also does not store any changes you make to those pages until you explicitly tell it to do so. You will learn more about editing Web pages in Page View and saving your work to disk later. For now, the important thing to know is that FrontPage lets you open more than one Web page at a time when you are working in Page View.

To return to an open page, either double-click your mouse pointer on the name of the page in the Folders List, or select the Window menu and click your mouse pointer on the name of the page you want to revisit. For example, if you opened the Customer Support Web as suggest for the current project, and then double-clicked on FAQ.HTM in the Folder List to open the

Frequently Asked Questions (FAQ) page, you now have two Web pages open—with the FAQ.HTM Web page displayed in the document pane. To return to the INDEX.HTM page, select the Window menu and click your mouse pointer on: 2 index.htm, or click your mouse pointer on the INDEX.HTM tag on the document editing pane. FrontPage, in turn, will replace the DOWNLOAD.HTM Web page with the INDEX.HTM Web page in the document window.

While in Page View, you can also open a Web page by following a hyperlink on the Web page currently displayed in the document pane. For example, to open the Customer Support Site's discussion page (DISCUSS.HTM), move your mouse pointer over the Discussion link on the navigation bar in the upper left-hand corner of the INDEX.HTM Web page. (The navigation bar is the menu just below the Welcome banner at the top of the page.) FrontPage will change your mouse pointer from an arrow to a finger pointing to a menu item as soon as you the mouse pointer across the navigation bar's border. When your "changed" cursor is over the FAQ hyperlink, hold down the your CTRL key on your keyboard and you click your left mouse button. FrontPage, in turn, will open the FAQ.HTM Web page and display its contents in the document window.

Note: *To open a Web page using a hyperlink that is not a part of navigation bar, right-click your mouse pointer on the hyperlink and then select the Follow Hyperlink option on the pop-up menu.*

CREATING A NEW WEB PAGE WHILE IN PAGE VIEW

Every Web site consists of Web pages. Without a doubt a site's graphics, animations, sound files, and video clips are what visitors think of when someone mentions the dot-com address of a popular site. However, in order for those objects to exist "on the Web", someone had create Web pages on which to put them.

Open the FoodCo Web by performing the following steps:

1. If you are not currently running FrontPage, start the program by clicking your mouse pointer on the Start button. After Windows displays the Start menu, select Programs, and then click your mouse pointer on Microsoft FrontPage.
2. In the FrontPage application window, select the File menu Open option. FrontPage, in turn, will display the Open File dialog box.
3. To open an existing FrontPage Web, either double-click your mouse pointer on the Web's name in the list box below the Look in field, or enter the full pathname of a Web page in the Web you want to open into the File name field. For the current project, open the FoodCo Web you created in a previous Tip entering: **C:\FoodCo\Index.htm** into the File name field and then click your mouse pointer on the

OPEN button. FrontPage, in turn, will open the FoodCo Web site and display the index.htm page in its document pane.

To create a new Web page while in Page View, perform the following steps:

1. To create a Web page, select the File menu New option and click your mouse pointer on Page or Web. After FrontPage, in turn, displays the New Page or Web menu, click your mouse pointer on the Page Templates option. FrontPage, in turn, will display a Page Templates dialog box similar to that shown in Figure 36.

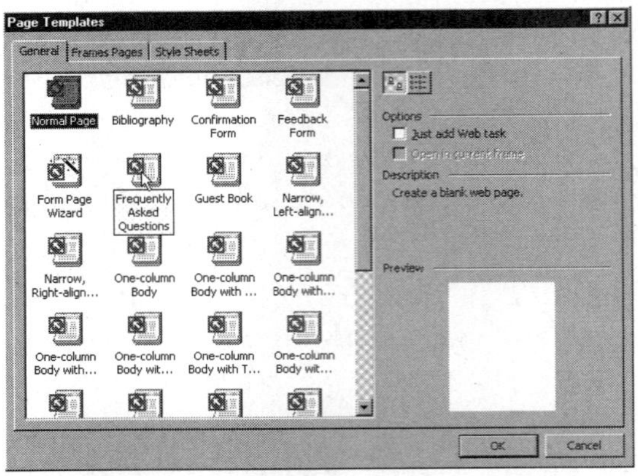

Figure 36 The FrontPage Page Templates dialog box.

2. Select the template that will create a page with the layout you want. (If you click your mouse pointer on the icon for a page type, FrontPage will display a brief description of the template in the Description area on the right-hand side of the dialog box and show the page layout just below the description, in the Preview area.) For the current project, click your mouse pointer the icon for Frequently Asked Questions to select the FAQ Web page template.
3. Click your mouse on the OK button to have FrontPage create a new Web page using the template you selected and return to Page View.

Look at Figure 36 again. Notice that the Page Templates dialog box has three tabs: General, Frame Pages, and Style Sheets. Although you only worked with templates on the General tab, the other two tabs have Web page templates on them as well. For example, to create a Web page with frames, you would click your mouse pointer on the Frames Pages tab and select one of the Web page templates on that tab in Step 2. (You will learn all about Frames and Style Sheets later in this book.)

Note: When you create a new Web page, FrontPage will use the first few words on the page as the title of the page. More often than not, this will not be the title you want. As such, change the page title by performing the following steps:

1. Right-click your mouse pointer on any white space in the newly created page, and select Page Properties from the pop-up menu.
2. FrontPage, in turn, will display the Page Properties dialog box.
3. Enter the page title into the Title field. For the current project enter: **Customer Frequently Asked Questions**.
4. Click your mouse pointer on the OK button.

ADDING TEXT TO A WEB PAGE WHILE IN PAGE VIEW

FrontPage Page View makes getting the words onto a Web page is as simple as typing text into an MS-Word (or your favorite word processing program) document. Simply position the cursor in the Web page on which you want the words to appear and start typing.

[If you are not currently running FrontPage, perform the procedures in the preceding Tip to open a FrontPage Web and create a Frequently Asked Questions (FAQ) Web page.]

To edit the contents of a Web page while in Page View, perform the following steps:

1. Click your mouse pointer where you want to insert new text. For the current project, click your mouse pointer after the question mark (?) after "How do I...?" just below the title Table of Contents.
2. Type the text you want to insert. For the current project, press the Enter key to add a new line and then type: How do I contact customer service?

That's it! Your Web page now has new words on it.

As you continue to use FrontPage, you will notice that it has many of the same functions as the word processor you already know how to use. For example, if you want to overwrite text instead of inserting, press the INSERT key on your keyboard before you type the text. Remember, the INSERT key is a toggle. As such, when you want FrontPage to go back to inserting text you type versus using it to replace text already on the page, simply press the INSERT key again.

Note: *Remember that FrontPage, unlike many word processors, does not automatically save work on new Web pages you create. As such, be sure to select the File menu Save option often—especially after* *you add new content. If you have not done so already, save the FAQ page you created in the preceding Tip and edited in this Tip.*

Select the File menu Save option. FrontPage, in turn, will display the Save As dialog box. Enter the full pathname for the new Web page in the File name field. For the current project enter: ***C:\FoodCo\HTMLDocs\FAQ.htm*** *into the File name field, and then click your mouse pointer on the SAVE button. If you did not create the FoodCo Web site at the root directory of your C: drive (C:\), insert the path to your FoodCo folder for C:\. For example, if you created the FoodCo Web in a \Data Files\My Webs folder on your C: drive, enter: C:\Data Files\My Webs\FoodCo\HTMLDocs\FAQ.htm in the File name field.*

In addition to typing text onto the Web page, you can also add content by copying (or cutting) and pasting text from other documents. For example, to copy text from a MS-Word document, perform the following steps:

1. Start MS-Word and open the document that has the content you want to place on the Web page.
2. Use your mouse pointer to select the text you want by holding down the left mouse button as you drag the mouse pointer across the text you want to copy to the Web site.
3. Select the Edit menu Copy option.
4. Switch back to the FrontPage application window and click your mouse pointer on the Web page at the location where you want to insert the text your are copying from the MS-Word document.
5. Select the Edit menu Paste option.

Bear in mind that text formatting instructions on a Web page are different than those in a word processing document. As such, use the copy-and-paste procedure to get the text on to the Web page and then use FrontPage text formatting tools (which will be discussed in future Tips) to make it look the way you want it to.

CREATING A TASK LINKED TO A WEB PAGE

As you learned previously, you can manage the workload involved in producing a "killer" Web site by keeping track of tasks and who is to accomplish them using the FrontPage to-do list. Some of the tasks on the to-do list will be general, such as "Spell check all Web pages." Other tasks will be specific to a particular Web page, such as "Meet with customer service manger and representatives, and put the questions customers ask most often onto the FAQ page."

To create a task linked to a particular Web page, perform the following steps:

1. Open the FrontPage Web in which you wish to create a Web page linked task and display the Web in Page View. For the current project, open the FoodCo Web (you used in each of the preceding two Tips). If your FrontPage is not currently in Page View, select the View menu Page option.
2. Look in the Folder List pane, and click your mouse pointer on the Web page to which you wish to link a task. (If you do not see the Folder List, select the View menu Folders option.) For the current project, click your mouse pointer on the plus (+) to the left of the HTMLDocs folder in the Folder List pane to display the list of Web pages in the HTMLDocs folder. Then, click your mouse pointer on FAQ.htm to select it.
3. Select the File menu New option and click your mouse pointer on Task. FrontPage, in turn, will display the New Task dialog box.
4. Give the task a descriptive name, so you will know what it involves when you see its name among the other tasks listed in Tasks View. For the current project enter: **Develop FAQ Page Content**.
5. Use the drop-down list button to the right of the Assigned field to select the user that is to accomplish the task. For the current project, accept the default (i.e., your user name).
6. Use the radio buttons in the upper right-hand corner of the New Task dialog box to set the task's priority. For the current project, click your mouse pointer on the High radio button to set the task as a "high priority" item on the to-do list.
7. Enter a description of the task in the Description area in the lower half of the dialog box. For the current project enter: **Meet with Customer Service department manager and reps. Find out what customers are asking and put the questions most often asked AND the answers on the FAQ page.**
8. Click your mouse pointer on the OK button.

After you complete Step 8, FrontPage will return to Page View. Do not be concerned that your task "disappeared." You will see it the next time you review the to-do list in Tasks View.

OPENING AN EXISTING WEB PAGE WHILE IN TASKS VIEW

As you learned in previous Tips, each of the FrontPage views has a different purpose. While Page View is designed to let you display and edit Web pages, Tasks View displays the items on the to-do list and their current completion status. Although Tasks View does not have a list of the site's Web pages (such as the one in the Folders List and in Folders View), you can open the Web page associated with (linked to) a task by performing the following steps:

1. Open a FrontPage Web and go to Tasks View. For the current project, open the FoodCo Web you created previously and select the View menu Tasks option.
2. Select the task on which you wish to work. (Notice that the Associated With column shows the title of the Web page to which a task is linked.) For the current project, click your mouse pointer on the Develop FAQ Page Content task.
3. Select the Edit menu Tasks option, and click your mouse pointer on Start Task. (Alternatively, you can right-click your mouse pointer on the task and select Start Task from the pop-up menu.)

After you finish working on the Web page in Page View, you can, of course, return to Tasks View by selecting the View menu Tasks option.

UNDERSTANDING THE SITE SUMMARY REPORT

The Site Summary report displays statistics for the FrontPage Web you currently have open. To view the Site Summary report, select the View menu Reports option and click your mouse pointer on Site Summary. FrontPage, in turn, will display a Site Summary report similar to that shown in Figure 40.

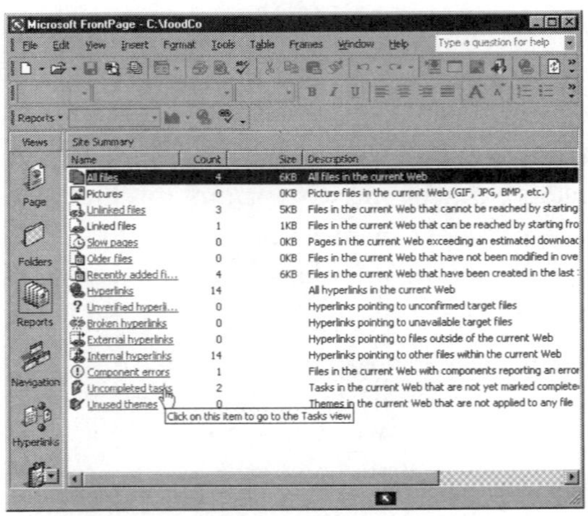

Figure 40 The FrontPage Site Summary report.

Some of the statistics available on the Site Summary report are:

- **All files** – the number of files that make up the Web site and the amount of disk storage space they use.

- **Pictures** - the number of graphics files (pictures) the site has and the amount of disk space it takes to store them.
- **Unlinked files** – the number and total size of the Web pages in the site's folders that are not linked to at least one other page on the site and the number and total size of graphics files that are not included on any of the site's pages.
- **Linked files** – the number and total size of Web pages with a hyperlink to at least one other Web page in the current Web and the number and total size of graphics files included on at least one page in the current Web.
- **Hyperlinks** – the number of hyperlinks on all of the Web pages in the current Web.
- **Broken Hyperlinks** – the number of hyperlinks that cannot be followed because they point to nonexistent target files (such as missing Web pages, graphics files, sound files, etc.)
- **External & Internal hyperlinks** – the number of *internal* hyperlinks that point to another page within the current Web and the number of *external* hyperlinks that point to pages outside the current Web.
- **Component Errors** – the number of Web pages that have FrontPage components that do not work. (You will learn about components in later in this book.)
- **Uncompleted Tasks** – the number uncompleted items on the current Web's to-do list.
- **Unused themes** – the number of FrontPage themes found in the current Web's folders but not applied to any of its pages. (You will learn how to use FrontPage themes to give a Web site a consistent look and feel later in this book.)

In addition to reviewing the various count and total size statistics, you can double-click your mouse pointer on several of the summary items to display a detailed report. For example, to display the Broken Hyperlinks (detail) report, double-click your mouse pointer on any one of the hyperlinks reports (All, Unverified, Broken, Internal, External).

UNDERSTANDING THE FILES REPORT

As its name implies, the All Files report gives a complete list of all files located in the root folder and all subfolders of the Web that FrontPage currently has open. To display the All Files report, select the View menu Reports option. Then, move your mouse pointer over the

Files category on the reports submenu and select the All Files option. FrontPage, in turn, will display an All Files report similar to that shown in Figure 41.

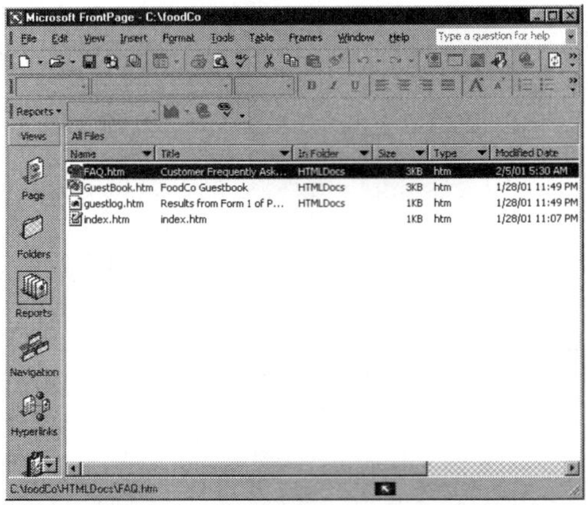

Figure 41 The FrontPage All Files report.

The All Files reports shows the name, title, size, and type of each file, the folder in which it is located, the date and time the file was last modified, and the username of the person who made the most recent change. Finally, the All Files report displays a portion of the comments attached to a file, if any.

Note: *To attach a comment to a file, right-click your mouse pointer on the name of the file. When FrontPage, in turn, displays a its pop-up menu, click your mouse pointer on Properties. After FrontPage displays the file Properties dialog box, click your mouse pointer on the Summary tab and enter the text you want into the Comments scroll box near the middle of the tab. When you are finished entering the comments, click your mouse pointer on the OK button to return to the All Files report.*

You can sort the All Files report by clicking your mouse pointer on the heading at the top of each column. For example, to sort the files by date and time last modified, click your mouse pointer on Modified Date. FrontPage, in turn, will sort the list of files in ascending order by date and time last modified. If you click your mouse pointer on the same heading a second time (i.e. twice in a row), FrontPage will reverse the sort from ascending to descending order (or vice versa).

Like the other reports, the All Files report also lets you edit any Web page on the report by double-clicking your mouse pointer on its name. In fact, on the All Files report, double-clicking your mouse pointer on any one of the report's items tells FrontPage (or Windows) to start the appropriate editor to work with the file based on its type. For example, if the file's type is HTM, double-clicking your mouse pointer on its name tells FrontPage to open the Web page in Page view. Similarly, double-clicking on a file of type GIF or JPG, tells Windows to start your system's graphics editing or display program (such as MS-Image Composer, or

WinJPeg, or Internet Explorer, etc.). In short, the All Files report gives you a convenient way to access every file on your Web—without having to look through every subfolder.

Note: *If your FrontPage Web contains hidden folders, the All Files report will not display the files they contain unless you tell FrontPage to include them. To have the All Files report display the files in hidden folders, select the Tools menu Web Settings option. FrontPage, in turn, will display the Web Settings dialog box. On the Advanced tab, click your mouse pointer in the Show hidden files and folders check box (in the Options section near the middle of the tab) until a check mark appears. Then, click your mouse pointer on the OK button to return to the All Files report.*

If you make any changes on any of the tabs in the Properties dialog box, FrontPage will prompt you to refresh the Web now. To update the report based on the settings you selected, click your mouse pointer on the YES button. FrontPage, in turn, will either add or remove files in hidden folders from the All Files report—depending on whether you left the box checked or cleared.

UNDERSTANDING THE SLOW PAGES REPORT

When visiting a Web site, no one likes to wait for content to download and display on the screen. Although the amount and type of content are only two of several factors that effect how fast a Web page shows up on visitor's screen, they are the only factors over which you have any control. The Slow Pages report gives you a list of those Web pages and files that will take longer than an acceptable amount of time to download to a user's computer. To view the Slow Pages report, select the View menu Reports. Then, move your mouse pointer over the Problems category on the reports submenu and select the Slow Pages option. FrontPage, in turn, will display a Slow Pages report similar to that shown in Figure 42.1.

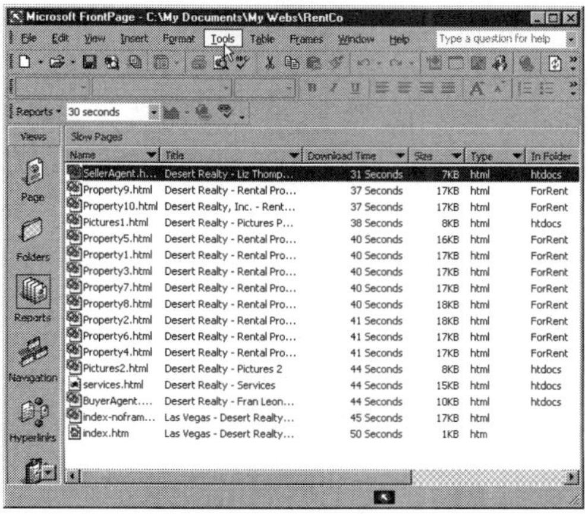

Figure 42.1 *The FrontPage Slow Pages report.*

The installation program sets the report's default "slow page" criteria to list any Web pages and pictures that will take longer than 30 seconds to download to a computer using a

28.8K connection to the Internet. To change the default "slow page" criteria, perform the following steps:

1. Select the Tools menu Options option. FrontPage, in turn, will display the Options dialog box.
2. Click your mouse pointer on the Reports View tab. FrontPage, in turn, will display a set of report inclusion criteria similar to those shown in Figure 42.2.

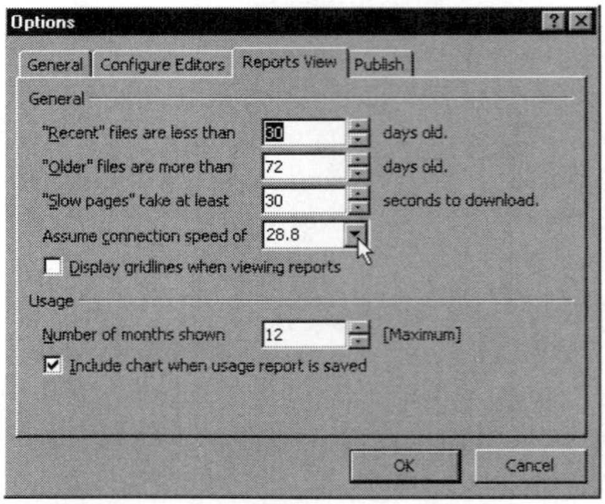

Figure 42.2 The FrontPage (Tools) Options dialog box.

3. To change the amount of time a page must take to download in order to be included on the report, type the number of seconds into the Slow Pages take at least field. Bear in mind the larger you make the number, the longer a page can take to download a page before FrontPage will warn you about its "slowness."
4. To change the default connection speed, click the drop-down list button to the right of the Assume connection speed of field and select a new connection speed. The faster the connection you assume visitors will use, the less time FrontPage will assume it will take to download a Web page. Do not be surprised if changing the default connection speed from 28.8 to 56.6 results in Web pages dropping off of the Slow Pages report. After all, doubling the connection speed means the same Web page will take half as long to download. Be sure to select the connection speed the majority of visitors to your site will be using.
5. Click your mouse pointer on the OK button to save your changes and return to the Slow Pages report.

To prevent your Web site from "feeling" sluggish to your visitors, consider splitting up the content of any Web pages listed on the Slow Pages report into more than one page. Given the same content, each of which will download more quickly, because the Web server has less data to send to the visitor's computer. Also, look at the graphics on the slow pages. Consider using thumbnails (which we will discuss later in this book) in place of full size pictures, and perhaps eliminate some graphics altogether. The less content (especially pictures) you have on a Web page, the faster the page will download.

UNDERSTANDING THE BROKEN HYPERLINKS REPORT

At some point during your travels on the Web, you have probably clicked your mouse pointer on a hyperlink only to have your Web browser inform you that "The page cannot be displayed." Or, perhaps you have seen Web pages that have boxes with a red X instead of the pictures that should be on them. Both of these errors are caused by broken hyperlinks—pointers to Web pages or files that are no longer accessible for one reason or another. The Broken Hyperlinks report helps you find and repair invalid links on your Web pages by listing any hyperlink whose status is either broken or unknown.

To display the Broken Hyperlinks report, select the View menu Reports option. Then, move your mouse pointer over the Problems category on the reports submenu and select the Broken Hyperlinks option. FrontPage, in turn, will display a Broken Hyperlinks report similar to that shown in Figure 43.1.

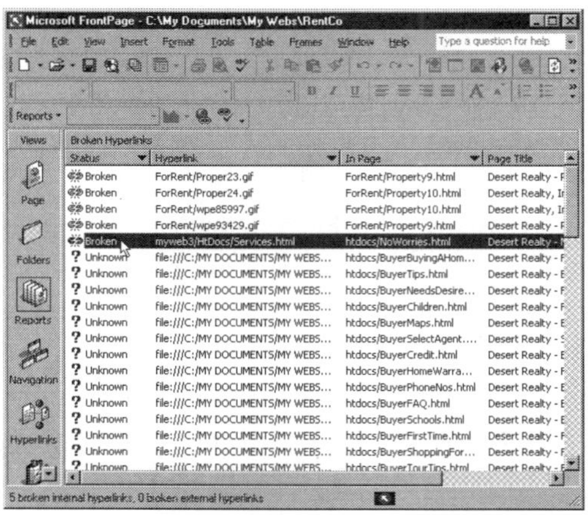

Figure 43.1 The FrontPage Broken Hyperlinks report.

After you open a FrontPage Web, the first time you select the Broken Hyperlinks report, most of the links will show a status of unknown (unverified). Unless you previously turned off the Verify Hyperlinks Now message box, FrontPage will ask you if you want it to verify the hyperlinks in the Web for you. To verify the hyperlinks, click your mouse pointer on the YES button. (Or, you can click your mouse pointer on the NO button on the message box and verify individual hyperlinks by right-clicking your mouse pointer on one of the items on the report and then selecting Verify Hyperlink from the pop-up menu.)

Note: *You can select an individual link by clicking your mouse pointer anywhere on the Broken Hyperlinks report line that lists the link you want to verify.*

To select more than one link, either hold down your SHIFT key as you click your mouse pointer on the first and last link—to select all links between the first and last (inclusive); or hold down the CTRL key on your keyboard as you click your mouse pointer on individual links to select them.

To repair a broken hyperlink, either double-click your mouse pointer on the link you want to edit, or right-click your mouse pointer on the link and select Edit Hyperlink from the pop-up menu. FrontPage, in turn, will display an Edit Hyperlink dialog box similar to that shown in Figure 43.2.

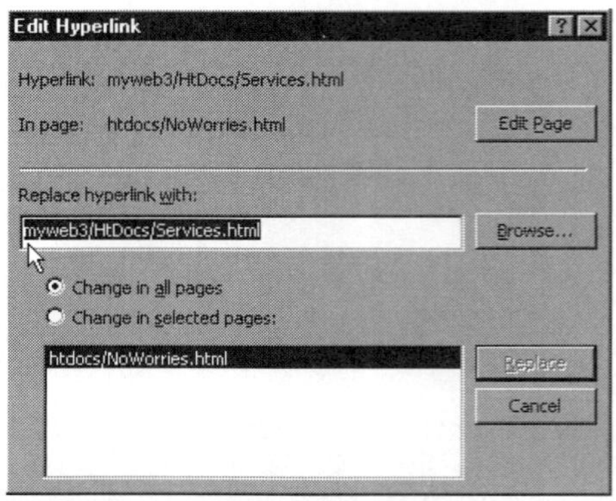

Figure 43.2 *The FrontPage Edit Hyperlink dialog box.*

Enter the new hyperlink in the Replace hyperlink with field, and then click your mouse pointer on the REPLACE button to replace the broken hyperlink with the one you entered on all of the Web site's pages that currently contain the old (broken) hyperlink. If you decide you want to remove the hyperlink altogether, click your mouse pointer on the EDIT PAGE button to display the Web page with the broken hyperlink. Next, look in the document pane, and find the broken hyperlink. To remove it, click your mouse pointer on the hyperlink and press the Delete key on your keyboard. We will discuss repairing and removing hyperlinks in more detail later.

UNDERSTANDING THE COMPONENT ERRORS REPORT

Components are small scripts that you can place on a Web page to provide such things as banners, hit counters, hover buttons, marquees, pictures that change periodically, etc. (You will learn about all of the components FrontPage provides and how to use them later in this book.) When a visitor goes to a Web page that has a component, either the Web server or the Web browser executes the script—depending on the type of component it is. In either case, the process is transparent to the visitor—the visitor just sees the Web page has an interesting interactive feature or content that seems to change all by itself. When you ask FrontPage to generate the Components Error report, the program checks the components (scripts) inserted onto the Web pages in the current Web site and reports those that are not functioning properly.

To generate the Component Errors report, select the View menu Reports option Then, move your mouse pointer over the Problems category on the reports submenu and select the Component Errors option. FrontPage, in turn, will check the components in the Web you currently have open and display any errors it finds on a Component Errors report similar to that shown in Figure 44.1.

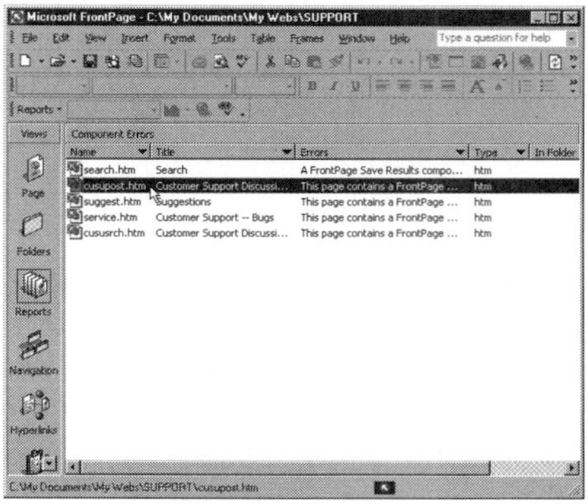

Figure 44.1 *The FrontPage Component Errors report.*

Do not worry if the report lists some components in need of repair. More often than not, the description of the component error in the Errors column will tell you how to fix the problem. If the description is truncated, right-click your mouse pointer on the line with the description you want to expand, and then select Properties from the pop-up menu. FrontPage, in turn, will display a (Web page) Properties dialog box similar to that shown in Figure 44.2.

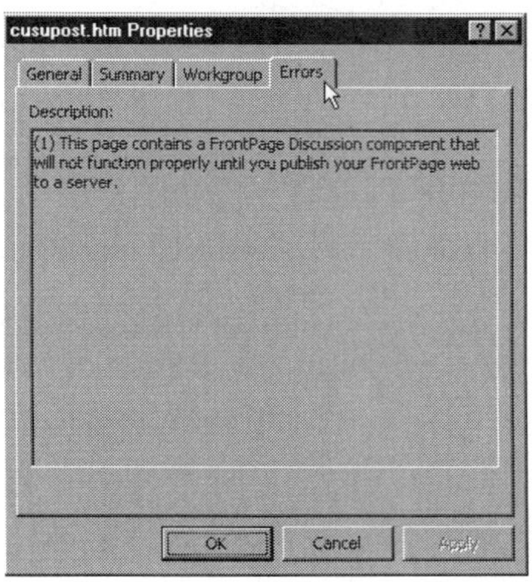

Figure 44.2 *The FrontPage (Web page) Properties dialog box, Errors tab.*

Click your mouse pointer on the Errors tab to see the full description of the Component Error. After you read the error message, click your mouse pointer on the OK button to return to the Component Errors report.

Some component "errors" are really just warnings—such as the one shown in Figure 44.2 that lets you know the component will not function properly until the Web is published to a Web server. Moreover, because FrontPage is not the only program that provides Web page components (scripts), the Component Errors report will sometimes list nonexistent errors—if FrontPage cannot interpret a script that is to be handled by another program (or the Web server), it assumes the script is improperly written and reports the component as inoperative on the Component Errors report. For each error on the report, relax, read the description of the error, and follow the instructions for fixing the problem.

To work on fixing a problem in a component, double-click your mouse pointer on the report line that lists the error you want to repair. FrontPage, in turn, will switch to Page View and display the Web page with the malfunctioning component in the document pane.

UNDERSTANDING THE REVIEW STATUS REPORT

When you develop a Web site as part of a team, the Review Status report helps you manage the collaborative effort. The report's Assigned To column is designed to keep track of who is assigned to work on each Web page (or item on a Web page, such as a graphic). Moreover, the person to whom the page is assigned can use the Review Status column to keep other team members abreast of their progress.

To display the Review Status report, select the View menu reports option. Then, move your mouse pointer over the Workflow category on the Reports submenu and select the Review Status option. FrontPage, in turn, will display a Review Status report similar to that shown in Figure 45.1.

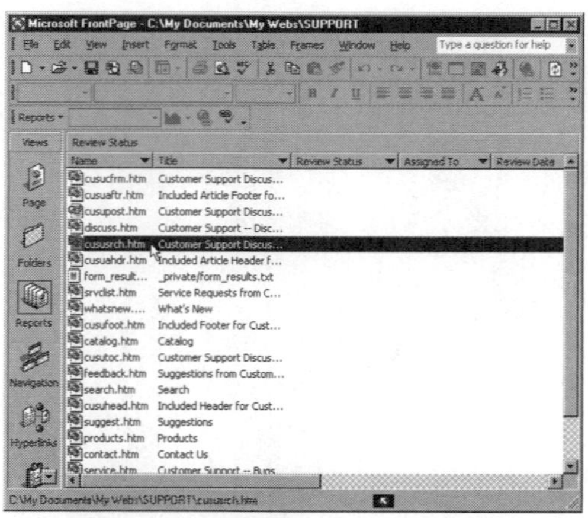

Figure 45.1 The FrontPage Review Status report.

To assign a Web page (or other Web object/file) listed on the report, perform the following steps:

1. Click your mouse pointer in any column of the line that lists the item you want to assign. FrontPage, in turn, will highlight the item you selected.
2. Click your mouse pointer in the selected item's Assigned To column. FrontPage, in turn, will display a drop-down list button.
3. Either type the username of the person to whom you wish to assign the Web site item and press the ENTER key, or click your mouse pointer on the drop-down list button to display the list of usernames in the FrontPage Usernames Master List. Then select the username you want from the list, and press the ENTER key. If the username you want is not on the list, either type it into the Assigned To field or continue at Step 4.
4. If you typed in the username or selected one of the usernames from the drop-down list, skip steps 5 - 10. Otherwise, click your mouse pointer on the drop-down list button to remove the drop-down list.
5. Right-click your mouse pointer in one of the other columns for the selected item on the report, and then select Properties from the popup menu. FrontPage, in turn, will display a (Web page) Properties dialog box similar to that shown in Figure 45.2.

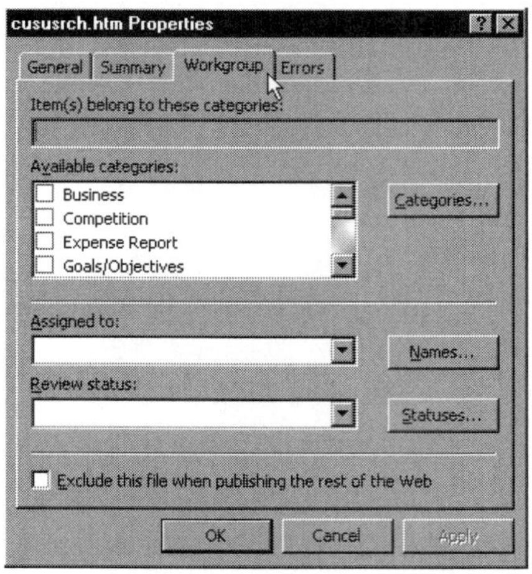

Figure 45.2 The FrontPage (Web page) Properties dialog box, Workgroup tab.

6. Click your mouse pointer on the Workgroup tab if it is not the one displayed in the dialog box.

7. Click your mouse pointer on the NAMES button. FrontPage, in turn, will display a Usernames Master List dialog box similar to that shown in Figure 45.3.

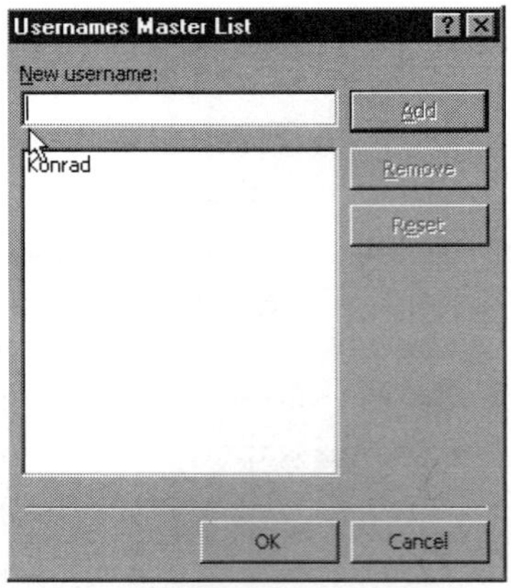

Figure 45.3 The FrontPage Usernames Master List dialog box.

8. To add a new name to the list, type the name into the New username field at the top of the dialog box. For the current project type: **Walter/Legal** into the New username field, and then click your mouse pointer on the ADD button.

Note: *Although the field only calls for the a Username, if you enter both a username and the type of review (or work) the user normally performs on pages assigned to him or her, you can keep track of both the assignment and why you made the assignment in the Assigned To field.*

9. Repeat Step 8 until you have added all of the usernames (and review types) you want and then click your mouse button on the OK button to return to the Workgroup tab.
10. Click your mouse pointer on the drop-down list button to the right of the Assigned to field (on the Web page Properties dialog box) and select the username to whom you wish to assign the item you selected in Step 1 from the drop-down list. For the current project, select Walter/Legal.

To exit the (Web page) Properties dialog box and return to the Review Status report, click your mouse pointer on the OK button at the bottom of the dialog box.

After you assign the Web page or file to a Web site development team member, the person to whom it is assigned should update the status of the work performed by executing the following steps:

1. Select the item with the status that needs updating by clicking the mouse pointer in one of its columns in the Review Status report. FrontPage, in turn, will highlight the item selected.
2. Click your mouse pointer in the selected item's Review Status column. FrontPage, in turn, will display a drop-down list button.
3. Either type the current status of the review to be performed and press the ENTER key, or click your mouse pointer on the drop-down list button to display the list of review statuses in the FrontPage Review Status Master List. Then select the current review status from the list, and then press the ENTER key. If the current review status not on the list, either type it into the Review Status field or continue at Step 4.
4. If you typed in the review status or selected one of the review statuses from the drop-down list, skip steps 5 - 11. Otherwise, click your mouse pointer on the drop-down list button to remove the drop-down list.
5. Right-click your mouse pointer in one of the other columns for the selected item on the report, and then select Properties from the pop-up menu. FrontPage, in turn, will display a (Web page) Properties dialog box similar to that shown in Figure 45.2 (of the previous procedure).
6. Click your mouse pointer on the Workgroup tab if it is not the one displayed in the dialog box.
7. Click your mouse pointer on the STATUSES button. FrontPage, in turn, will display a Review Status Master List dialog box (which is very similar to the Usernames Master List dialog box shown in Figure 45.3 of the previous procedure).
8. To add a new status to the list, type the status into the New review status field at the top of the dialog box. For the current project type: **In Progress** into the New review status field, and then click the mouse pointer on the ADD button.
9. Repeat Step 8 until all desired review statuses are on the Review Status Master List, and then click your mouse pointer on the OK button to return to the Workgroup tab.
10. Click your mouse pointer on the drop-down list button to the right of the Review status field (on the Web Page Properties dialog box) and select the review status to be assigned to the item selected in Step 1. For the current project select In Progress.
11. Click the mouse pointer on the OK button at the bottom of the (Web page) Properties dialog box to make the status assignment, and return to the Review Status report.

The reason you want the person to whom the item is assigned to update the status of the work performed is because FrontPage automatically puts the login name of the user changing the review status and the date and time of the change into the Reviewed By and Review Date columns of the Review Status report. FrontPage will not let you enter anything into either of these columns. As such, if you update the status yourself (vs. requiring the assigned team member to do so), FrontPage will put your login name (and not the reviewer's) into the Reviewed By column.

UNDERSTANDING THE ASSIGNED TO REPORT

The Assigned To report lists all of the Web site's files and tells you to whom each is assigned. The report also shows the username of the person that assigned each item in the FrontPage Web and the date the assignment was made. Unlike the Review Status report, which allows managers to assign items and the Web site developers to enter status updates, the Assigned To report only allows changes of the username to whom items are assigned.

To display the Assigned To report, select the View menu Reports option. Then, move your mouse pointer over the Workflow category on the reports submenu and select the Assigned To option. FrontPage, in turn, will display an Assigned To report similar to that shown in Figure 46 for the Support web previously created and stored at C:\My Documents\My Webs\SUPPORT.

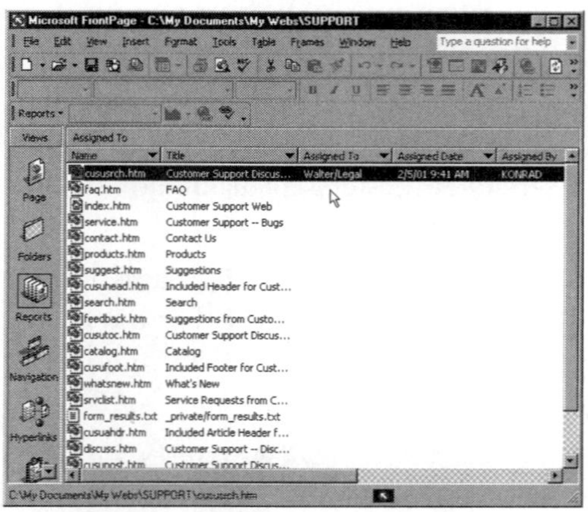

Figure 46 The FrontPage Assigned To report.

To assign a Web page (or other Web object/file) listed on the report to a member of the Web site development team, perform the following steps:

1. Click your mouse pointer in any column of the line that lists the item you want to assign. FrontPage, in turn, will highlight the item (line) you selected.

2. Click your mouse pointer in the selected item's Assigned To column. FrontPage, in turn, will display a drop-down list button.
3. Either type the username of the person to whom you wish to assign the Web site item and press the ENTER key, or click your mouse pointer on the drop-down list button to display the list of usernames in the FrontPage Usernames Master List. Then select the username you want from the list, and press the ENTER key. If the username you want is not on the list, either type a new name into the Assigned to Column or continue at Step 4.
4. If you typed in the username or selected one of the usernames from the drop-down list, skip steps 5 - 11. Otherwise, click your mouse pointer on the drop-down list button to remove the drop-down list.
5. Right-click your mouse pointer in a column other than the Assigned To column in the line (item) you selected in Step 1, and then select Properties from the pop-up menu. FrontPage, in turn, will display a (Web page) Properties dialog box similar to that shown in Figure 45.2 (in the previous Tip).
6. Click your mouse pointer on the Workgroup tab if it is not the one displayed in the dialog box.
7. Click your mouse pointer on the NAMES button. FrontPage, in turn, will display a Usernames Master List dialog box similar to that shown in Figure 45.3 (in the Previous Tip).
8. To add a new name to the list, type the name into the New username field at the top of the dialog box. For the current project type: **Konrad/Tech** into the New username field, and then click your mouse pointer on the ADD button.
9. Repeat Step 8 until you have added all of the usernames (and review types) you want and then click your mouse button on the OK button to return to the Workgroup tab.
10. Click your mouse pointer on the drop-down list button to the right of the Assigned to field (on the Web page Properties dialog box) and select the username to whom you wish to assign the item you selected in Step 1 from the drop-down list. For the current project, select Konrad/Tech.
11. To exit the (Web page) Properties dialog box and return to the Assigned To report, click your mouse pointer on the OK button at the bottom of the dialog box

When you assign a file to a user or remove an assignment by clearing the Assigned To column, FrontPage will automatically put the current date and time into the Assigned Date column and your login name in to the Assigned By column. As was the case with the Review Date and Reviewed By columns on the Review Status report, you cannot enter anything directly into the Assigned Date and Assigned By columns of the Assigned To report.

To remove an assignment (leaving the item unassigned), perform the following steps:

1. Click your mouse pointer in any column of the line that lists the item you want to show as unassigned. FrontPage, in turn, will highlight the item you selected.
2. Click your mouse pointer in the selected item's Assigned To column. FrontPage, in turn, will highlight the column's contents and display a drop-down list button.
3. Press the DELETE key on your keyboard to remove the name in the column.
4. Press your Enter key to exit edit mode on the Assigned To column.

As was mentioned previously, whenever you change the contents of the Assigned To column, FrontPage notes the date and time the change was made and your login name in the Assigned Date and Assigned By columns.

UNDERSTANDING THE CATEGORIES REPORT

FrontPage categories are subsets of information, or sub webs, within a Web site. Suppose, for example, that you are creating a company Web site with five sections: Company News, Products, Services, Technical Support, and Frequently Asked Questions. Given that the five categories are a comprehensive list of the types of information the Web site is to publish, almost all of the site's Web pages will "fit" into one or more of the five categories. Moreover, when a visitor comes to the site looking for a specific type (or category) of information, the visitor will want an easy way to review all of the Web pages the site has on the topic.

By inserting a FrontPage Categories component for each sub web (or category) on a Web site, you can create a self-maintaining index of the site's Web pages sorted by category. Each time an author adds a Web page to a category, FrontPage will automatically update the appropriate Categories component by adding a hyperlink a visitor can use to reach the new page. You will learn all about the Categories component in future Tips. For now, the important thing to know is that FrontPage uses *categories* to group a Web site's Web pages into sub webs of information. The Categories Report is a convenient way to list all of a site's categories. Moreover, you can also use the Categories Report to update the category assignment(s) of any of the files in the FrontPage Web.

To display the Categories Report, select the View menu Reports option. Then, move your mouse pointer over the Workflow category on the Reports submenu and select Categories.

FrontPage, in turn, will display a Categories report similar to that shown in Figure 47.1 created previously and stored at C:\MY DOCUMENTS\MY WEBS\Corp.

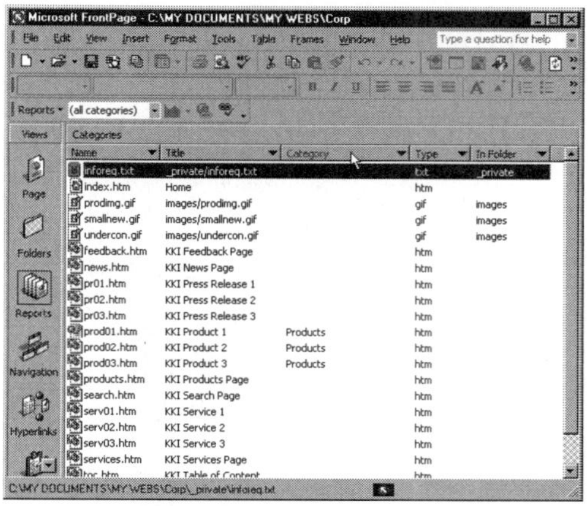

Figure 47.1 The FrontPage Categories report.

To assign a Web page to one or more categories, perform the following steps:

1. Right-click your mouse pointer on the Web page you want to assign to a category and select Properties on the pop-up menu.
2. Select the Workgroup tab. FrontPage, in turn, will display a (Web page) Properties dialog box similar to that shown in Figure 47.2.

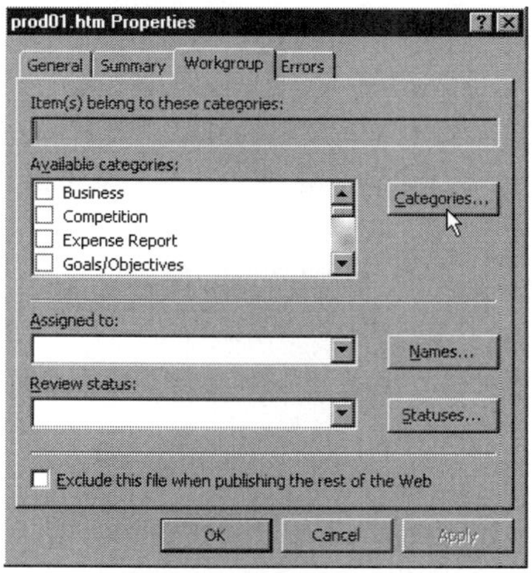

Figure 47.2 The FrontPage (Web page) Properties dialog box, Workgroup tab.

3. To assign the Web page to one or more categories, click your mouse pointer on the check box to the left of each category to which you want the Web page assigned. (Conversely, to take a Web page out of a

category, clear the category's check box.) If all of the categories to which you want to assign the file you selected in Step 1 are available, skip to the text following step 9.

4. To add a new category, click your mouse pointer on the CATEGORIES button. FrontPage, in turn, will display a Master Category List dialog box similar to that shown in Figure 47.3.

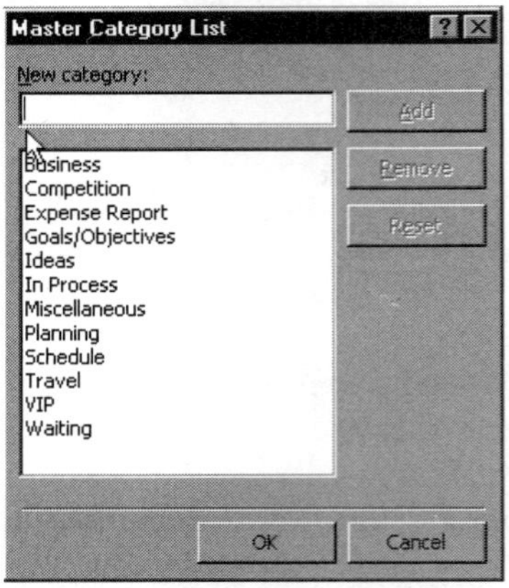

Figure 47.3 The FrontPage Master Category List dialog box.

5. Type the name of the new category into the New Category field at the top of the dialog box, and then click your mouse pointer on the ADD button.
6. Repeat Step 5 until you have added all of the new categories you want.
7. Click your mouse pointer on the OK button to return to the Workgroup tab.
8. If you added a new category and want to assign the Web page to it, continue at Step 3.
9. Click your mouse pointer on the OK button at the bottom center of the (Web page) Properties dialog box to return to the Categories report.

As is the case with the other FrontPage reports, you can sort the items on the Categories report by clicking your mouse pointer on one of the headings at the top of the report's columns. For example, if the report is not already sorted by category, click your mouse pointer on the heading, "Category", to sort the items on the report by the name of the category (or categories) to which each is assigned. If you click your mouse pointer on the same heading again, FrontPage will sort the report in reverse order. Thus, if the report is sorted in ascending order by category, clicking your mouse pointer on the heading at the top of the category column will tell FrontPage to sort the report in descending order by category, and vice versa.

UNDERSTANDING THE PUBLISH STATUS REPORT

When you tell FrontPage to publish (or copy) your Web site from the development machine to the Web server, FrontPage assumes that you want to send all of the files in the FrontPage Web on the development machine to the server. However, there are times when you may not want one or more of the Web's files sent to the Web server for the entire world to see on the Internet. The Publish Status report tells you which of the files FrontPage will publish to the server and which files you have flagged as not yet ready to be published.

To display the Publish Status report, select the View menu Reports option. Then, move your mouse pointer over the Workflow category on the Reports submenu and select the Publish Status option. FrontPage, in turn, will display a Publish Status report similar to that shown in Figure 48 for the previously created web page stored at C:\My Documents\My Webs\SUPPORT.

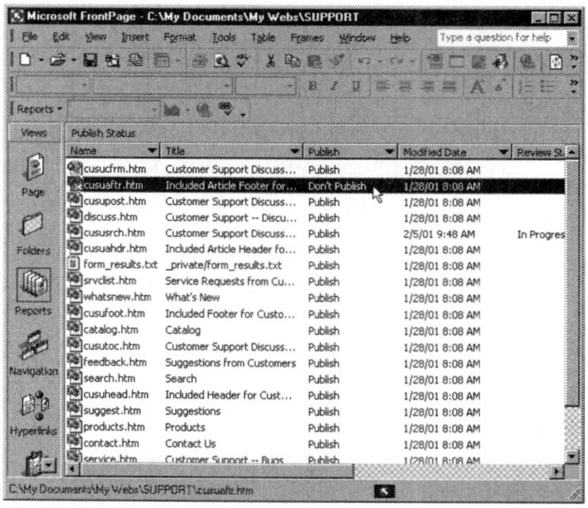

Figure 48 The FrontPage Publish Status report.

FrontPage will copy files with Publish in the Publish column to the Web server when you select the File menu Publish Web option. Conversely, FrontPage will not send any files marked Don't Publish to the Web server. To change the publication status of a file, perform the following steps.

1. Click your mouse pointer on the file whose publish status you want to change.
2. Click your mouse pointer in the Publish column of the item you selected in Step 1. FrontPage, in turn, will go into Edit mode and display a drop-down list button.
3. To tell FrontPage not to send the file you selected in Step 1 when publishing the remainder of the FrontPage Web to the Web server, press D on your keyboard. FrontPage, in turn, will change the

publish status of the item to Don't Publish. Conversely, if you want to include a previously excluded file, press P on your keyboard. FrontPage, in turn, will change the publish status of the item to Publish.

4. Press the Enter key to exit Edit mode.

You will learn how to use the File menu Publish Web option to copy a FrontPage Web to a Web server later in this book. For now, the important things to know are that you can exclude files from being sent to the Web server when publishing a FrontPage Web by changing the publish status to "Don't Publish", and the Publish Status report tells you the publish status for all of the files in the FrontPage Web.

UNDERSTANDING THE CHECKOUT STATUS REPORT

When creating a Web site as part of a team, each author needs a way to make sure that no one else updates a Web page on which the author is currently working. If two people work on the same file at the same time, the Web page will have only those changes made by the last person to save the file. The FrontPage Check-In/Check-Out feature lets an author *Check-Out* a Web page to prevent anyone else from editing or overwriting the page until the author relinquishes control by selecting *Check-In* from the File Properties pop-up menu. (FrontPage will display the File Properties pop-up menu when you right-click the mouse pointer on any file in the Folder List or item listed on one of the FrontPage reports.)

Note: *FrontPage will not display the Check-Out option on any pop-up menu or allow the selection of the Checkout Status report on the Reports menu until page-level Check-In/Check-Out is enabled. To enable FrontPage source control, select the Tool menu Web Settings option. FrontPage, in turn, will display the Web Settings dialog box. Click your mouse pointer on the check box to the left of Use document check-in and check-out at the bottom of the General tab until the check mark appears. Next click your mouse pointer on the OK button to apply the Web Settings update to the Web currently open in FrontPage, and exit the Web Settings dialog box.*

To display the Checkout Status report, select the View menu Reports option. Then, move your mouse pointer over the Workflow category on the Reports submenu, and select the Checkout Status option. FrontPage, in turn, will display a Checkout Status report similar to that show in Figure 49 for the Support Web page previously created and stored at C:\My Documents\My Webs\SUPPORT.

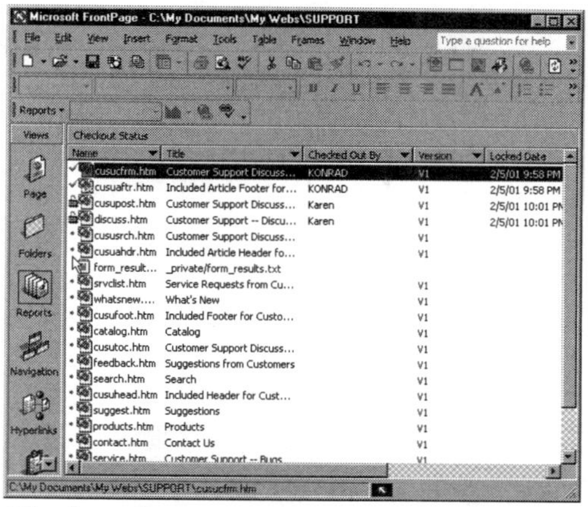

Figure 49 The FrontPage Checkout Status report.

The Checkout Status report shows the Check-In/Check-Out status of each file in the FrontPage Web. Refer to Figure 49 and you will see that there are three different icons to the left of the filenames in the report's Name column (first column on the left):

- **Red Checkmark** – indicates that your username (the name you used to login into the workstation running FrontPage) currently has the file checked out. As such, only your username can edit the file and save changes to it. You can also right-click your mouse pointer on the filename and select the Check In option from the pop-up menu to release your lock on the file and thereby let someone else Check-Out the file for editing.

- **Gray Padlock** – someone else (a username other than the one used to login to the workstation running FrontPage) has the file checked out. You can still open the file, but in "read-only" mode. As such, you can only save any changes made to the file by saving the changes to another filename.

- **Green Dot** – the file is available for Check-Out—i.e., no one currently has the file locked. As such, you can right-click your mouse pointer on the filename and select the Check Out option from the pop-up menu to prevent others from editing the file until you release your lock on the file by selecting Check In or Undo Check Out from the File Properties pop-up menu.

In addition to icons which give the Check-In/Check-Out status, the Checkout Status report also shows the login name of the person that has the file checked out, the version, and date and time checked out, for each file in the FrontPage Web.

USING THE OPTIONS DIALOG BOX, REPORTS VIEW TAB TO CHANGE DEFAULT REPORT PARAMETERS

The Reports View tab of the (Tools) Options dialog box lets you change four settings that effect the contents of three reports and one setting that effects the look of all reports available in Reports View. To display the (Tools) Options dialog box, Reports View tab, select the Tools menu Options option and click your mouse pointer on the Reports View tab to select it. FrontPage, in turn, will display a (Tool) Options dialog box similar to that shown in Figure 50.

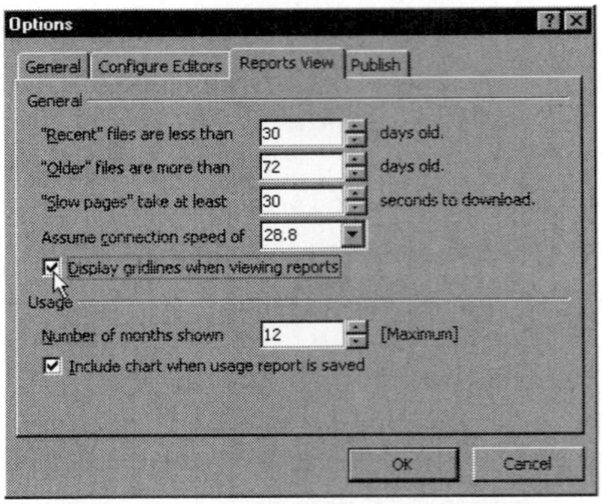

Figure 50 The FrontPage (Tools) Options dialog box, Reports View tab.

The four fields in the top half of the dialog box tell FrontPage the criteria to use in selecting the items it is to display on the Recently Added Files, Older Files, and Slow Pages reports, as follows:

- **"Recent" files are less than <number of days> days old.** – the value of <number of days> determines whether or not a file is to be included on the Recently Added Files report based on the number of days since the file was added to the FrontPage Web. For example, if the value of <number of days> is 30, then any files added to the Web more than 30 days ago will be excluded from the Recently Added Files report.
- **"Older" files are more than <number of days> days old.** – the value of <number of days> determines whether or not a file is to be include on the Older Files report based on the number of days since the file was last modified. For example, if the value of <number of days> is 72, then FrontPage will display on the Older Files report only those files last modified more than 72 days ago.
- **"Slow pages" take at least <number of seconds> seconds to download.** – value of <number of seconds> determines whether or not a file is to be included on the Slow Pages report based on the number of seconds

FrontPage estimates it will take to download the file to a visitor's computer given the file's size and the user's assumed connection speed (which is selectable from the drop-down list in the next field). For example, if the <number of seconds> is set to 30 and the connection speed is assumed to be 28.8, then FrontPage will display those files that will take more than 30 seconds to download to a visitor with a 28.8K modem connection.

- **Assume connection speed of <connection speed>.** – the <connection speed > selected tells FrontPage the transfer speed to assume when computing the amount of time it will take to send a file to a visitor's computer. The higher the speed, the less time it will take to send the same size file. To select a speed, click your mouse pointer on the drop-down list button to the right of the field and click your mouse pointer on one of the speeds listed: 14.4, 28.8, 56.6, ISDN, T1, or T3.

The next item on the Reports View tab, Display gridlines when viewing reports, tells FrontPage whether or not to display horizontal and vertical gridlines between the rows and columns on each report. To display gridlines, click your mouse pointer in the check box until a checkmark appears. To display all reports without gridlines, clear the check box by clicking your mouse pointer on the check box until the check mark disappears.

(You will learn about the Usage section of the Reports View tab when you read the Tips that deal with usage reports and statistics. Accept the defaults in the Usage section, for now.)

To exit the (Tools) Options dialog box either click your mouse pointer on the OK button to save any changes you made or click your mouse pointer on the CANCEL button to tell FrontPage to ignore any changes and revert the previously saved Reports View options settings.

CREATING A HOME PAGE IN NAVIGATION VIEW

If you create a wire diagram of the pages that make up a Web site, you will find that most (if not all) well organized sites can be represented by a hierarchical structure with the home page at the top of the hierarchy. (A site's home page is the default Web page the Web server sends when you visit the site by entering only its .com address, such as *www.NVBizNet.com*, into your Web browser's address field and pressing the ENTER key.) Pages directly accessible from a navigation bar on the home page represent the second level (or tier) of the hierarchy. These second level pages, in turn, have navigation bars with links to other pages on the site, which represent the third level (or tier) in the hierarchy. The navigation bars on third level pages link to fourth level pages, and so on.

To create a new Web (and home page) using Navigation View, start FrontPage and then perform the following steps:

1. Select the View menu Navigation option. FrontPage, in turn, will switch to Navigation view.
2. Select the File menu New option and then click your mouse pointer on Page or Web. When FrontPage, in turn, displays the New Page or Web menu, click your mouse pointer on the Web Site Templates option. FrontPage, in turn, will display the Web Site Templates dialog box.
3. Select the type of Web you want to create by clicking your mouse pointer on one of the Web creation Wizard icons (to have FrontPage generate an entire Web site); by clicking your mouse pointer on the One Page Web icon (to create a Web with only a home page); or by clicking your mouse pointer on the Empty Web icon (to create the folder structure for a Web, but none of its pages). For the current project, click your mouse pointer on the One Page Web icon in the Web Sites area on the left side of the Web Site Templates dialog box.
4. Enter the full pathname for the new Web site in the Specify the location of the new web field near the top right-hand side of the Web Site Templates dialog box. For the current project enter: **C:\MY DOCUMENTS\MY WEBS\MyWeb4**.
5. Click your mouse pointer on the OK button. FrontPage, in turn, will create the folder structure for a new Web site and one or more of its pages (depending on the icon you selected in Step 3). For the current project, FrontPage will create a Web site with only a home page and display the new Web in Navigation View, similar to that shown in Figure 51.

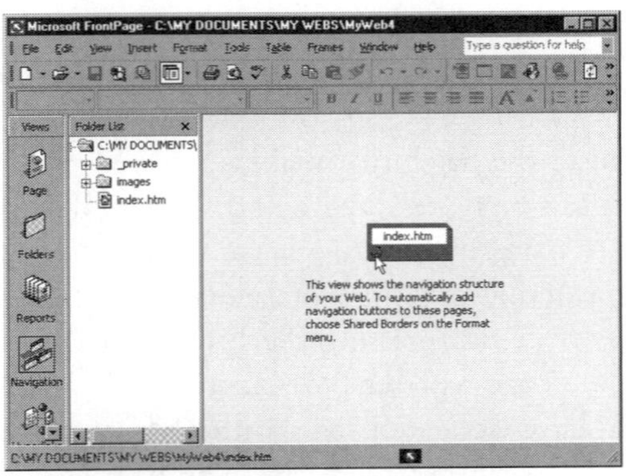

Figure 51 FrontPage Navigation View for a one page Web.

Notice that FrontPage uses index.htm as the title for the site's home page in Navigation View. Moreover, the home page item in the site's Navigation diagram has a small house (a *home*) in the lower left-hand corner to indicate that the page is indeed the site's home page.

Note: *The filename of the home page is very important. Visitors to your site may simply point their browser to the Web site's .com address (such as www.NVBizNet.com) without specifying a Web page. When a visitor fails to specify a Web page as part of the address entered into the Web browser's address field, the Web server will send the "default" Web page to the visitor's browser. Depending on which Web server software you are using to run the Web site, the Web site's default (home) page must be named: INDEX.HTM, INDEX.HTML, DEFAULT.HTM, or DEFAULT.HTML. If you do not name your Web site's (default) home page with the filename required by your Web server, the server will not be able to "find" the default home page and will report a Page Cannot Be Found (error 404) to the visitor's Web browser.*

Ask the Web server's administrator (or if you are the administrator, check your Web server's manual) for the filename required for a home page on your server. If FrontPage creates a home page using the wrong name, simply right-click your mouse pointer on the current filename of the home page in the Folder List pane of the application window, and select Rename from the pop-up menu. FrontPage, in turn, will prompt you to enter a new name for the site's home page. Enter the new filename and then press the ENTER key on your keyboard.

ADDING CHILD PAGES WHILE IN NAVIGATION VIEW

After creating a home page (which you learned to do in the preceding Tip), you can use Navigation View to create a hierarchical wire diagram of the site's layout. Setting up parent/child links between the pages in a Web site not only makes it easy to design the initial structure of the Web, but you can also tell FrontPage to place a self-maintaining Navigation Bar component on each Web page. Visitors will be able to use the hyperlinks on the Web site's navigation bars to move up and down the hierarchy between child and parent pages in the Web. (You will learn all about the Navigation Bar component later in this book.)

Start FrontPage, if the application is not currently running on your system. Open the FrontPage Web you created in the preceding Tip (MyWeb4). (If you did not create MyWeb4, either create a new one page Web now or open an existing Web on your system.) To create and link a new Web page (child) to an existing Web page (parent), perform the following steps:

1. Switch to Navigation View (if FrontPage is not already in Navigation View) by selecting the View menu Navigation option.
2. To create a Web page that is to be a *child* to the Home Page, right-click your mouse pointer on Home Page (parent) item in the Navigation diagram. Then, select New option from the pop-up menu and click your mouse pointer on Page. FrontPage, in turn, will add a new Web page (child) with a link to the Home Page (parent) icon, similar to that shown in Figure 52.1.

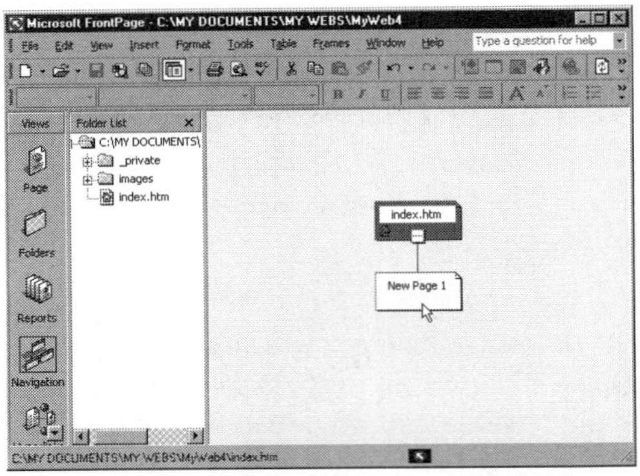

Figure 52.1 FrontPage Navigation View after adding a new child entry to a single page Web site.

3. Repeat Step 2 until you create all of the child Web pages you want to be accessible through the Navigation Bar component on the home page (parent). For the current project, add a second child to the home page by repeating Step 2, and then continue at Step 4.
4. To create add a Web page as a child of a page other than the Home Page, right-click your mouse pointer on the parent Web page. Then, select New from the pop-up menu and click your mouse pointer on Page.

   For the current project, create two child pages linked to New Page 1 (which you created in Step 2) by repeating Step 4 two times, right-clicking your mouse pointer on New Page 1 each time as the parent Web page.

That is all there is to it. For the current project, after you complete Step 4, your Web site (MyWeb4) will have five Web pages (counting the home page) similar to that shown in Figure 52.2.

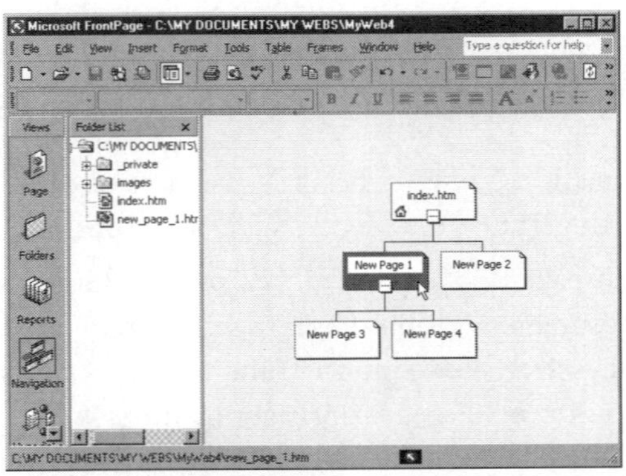

Figure 52.2 FrontPage Navigation View after adding child entries to the Home Page and New Page 1 entries.

After you add the Navigation Bar component to the current Web site, FrontPage will make New Page 1 and New Page 2 accessible from the home page by placing hyperlinks to both pages onto the navigation bar on the home page. Similarly, FrontPage will automatically place hyperlinks for New Page 3 and New Page 4 onto the navigation bar it places on New Page 1.

Notice that FrontPage does not add the new pages you created (in Navigation View) by following the preceding procedure, to the files listed in the Folder List pane. The reason for the omission is that the new pages are only Navigation view entries and not (yet) physical files. FrontPage will create and save blank Web pages for each new entry when you do any one of the following:

- Right-click your mouse pointer on a blank area in the Navigation pane and select Apply Changes from the pop-up menu.
- Switch to another view.
- Use FrontPage to edit a Web page by double-clicking your mouse pointer on the icon for an existing page or one of the new pages.
- Select the File menu Close Web option or the File menu Exit option.

You should change the name of the new pages you add to the Navigation diagram to something meaningful, before you tell FrontPage to create the Web pages and save them to disk. If you do not, FrontPage will use a filename based on the generic title (New Page X) it assigned to each of the new Navigation view entries you added. As a result, you will end up not only changing the title of the entry in the Navigation diagram but also renaming the file later.

To change the title of an entry in the Navigation diagram, perform the following steps:

1. Right-click your mouse pointer on the entry whose title you want to change. For the current project, right-click your mouse pointer on New Page 1.
2. Select Rename from the pop-up menu. FrontPage, in turn, will prompt you for the new Web page title.
3. Enter the new title for the entry and then press the ENTER key (or click your mouse pointer anywhere in the Navigation pane outside the entry you are changing). For the current project, enter: **Products** and then press the ENTER key. Next, repeat Steps 1 – 3 twice more, only right-click your mouse pointer on New Page 3 in Step 1 and enter: **Product 1** in Step 3, the second time through the procedure. Then, the third time through, right-click your mouse pointer on New Page 4 in Step 1 and enter: **Product 2** in Step 3.

Now, to tell FrontPage to save the files for the new (Web page) entries added to the site hierarchy, right-clicking your mouse pointer on the blank area outside the Web site hierarchy in the Navigation pane. Then, select Apply Changes from the pop-up menu. FrontPage, in turn, will create new Web pages using the filenames NEW_PAGE_2.HTM, PRODUCT_1.HTM, PRODUCT_2.HTM, and PRODUCTS.HTM, and add the filenames to the site's file (and folder) list in the Folder List pane.

Since the name "New Page 2" is not at all descriptive of the content the Web page will hold, repeat the preceding procedure to change the title, New Page 2 to Services by right-clicking your mouse pointer on New Page 2 in Step 1 and entering **Services** in Step 3.

Notice that FrontPage did not change the filename of the Services page (NEW_PAGE_2.HTM in the Folder List pane) when you changed its title in the Navigation diagram. Change the filename now by right-clicking your mouse pointer on NEW_PAGE_2.HTM in the Folders List pane. Then, select Rename from the pop-up menu. Next, type in the new filename: **services.htm** (for the current example), and press the ENTER key.

Note: *When you add the Navigation Bar component to the Web site, FrontPage uses the Title of the entries in the Navigation pane as the hyperlinks on the navigation bars. Therefore, you will want to use a short, yet descriptive, title for each Web page, so the visitor will have a good idea as to the content the server will send in response to a click of the mouse pointer on a parent or child hyperlink in a navigation bar.*

ADDING EXISTING WEB PAGES TO THE SITE HIERARCHY IN NAVIGATION VIEW

In addition to creating new pages for the Web in Navigation View, you can also attach already existing pages to the Web site diagram. (As you learned in the previous two Tips, FrontPage uses the parent/child relationships established on the site's Navigation diagram to create navigation bar hyperlinks.)

Start FrontPage, if the application is not currently running on your system. Open the FrontPage Web whose diagram you want to change. For the current project, open the Web on which you worked in the previous two Tips (MyWeb4). Next, switch to Navigation View by selecting the View menu Navigation option.

For the current project, if all of the existing pages in your FrontPage Web are already included in the Navigation diagram, (as is the case with MyWeb4), add three Web pages to the site by performing the following steps:

1. In the Folder List pane, click your mouse pointer on the icon of the folder in which you wish to create the new Web page. For the current project, click your mouse pointer on the folder icon at the top of the Folder List to create new pages in the Web site's root folder.
2. Click your mouse pointer on the New Page icon (the first icon on the left of the Standard Toolbar). FrontPage, in turn, will create a new Web page and prompt you to enter its filename. For the current project enter: **service_1.htm** as the filename.
3. Press the ENTER key to have FrontPage create and save a blank Web page in the folder selected in Step 1 using the filename entered in Step2.
4. Repeat Steps 1 through 3 until to for each new Web page you want to create. For the current project repeat Steps 1 through 3 twice more to create two additional pages. When you perform Step 2 for the second time, enter: **service_2.htm** as the filename, and when you perform Step 2 for the third time, enter: **comments.htm**.

After you complete Step 4, the MyWeb4 site will have eight Web pages—five included in the site's Navigation diagram and three which are not.

Note: *If your Web site already has existing Web pages which are not part of the Navigation diagram you would skip the preceding procedure.*

To attach existing Web pages to the site's Navigation diagram, perform the following steps:

1. Switch to Navigation View (if FrontPage is not already in Navigation View) by selecting the View menu Navigation option.
2. In the Folder List pane, move your mouse pointer over the icon of the Web page you want to add to the Navigation diagram. For the current project, move your mouse pointer over the icon to the left of service_1.htm.
3. Click and hold your left mouse button down as you drag your mouse pointer (and the Web page) toward its parent in the Navigation diagram. For the current project, make the service_1.htm Web page a child of the Services page by dragging it onto the Navigation diagram below and to the right of the Services item, similar to that shown in Figure 53.1. Notice that FrontPage draws a shaded line from a prospective parent on the diagram to the child you are dragging as you move the child page across the Navigation diagram.

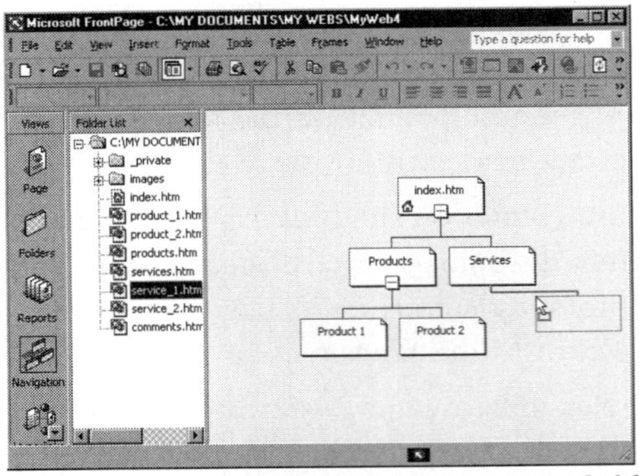

Figure 53.1 FrontPage Navigation View prior to "dropping" a child page onto the Navigation diagram.

4. Release the left mouse button after FrontPage draws a shaded line from the parent you want to the Web page you are dragging. For the current project, release the left mouse button when you see a shaded line from the Services item on the Navigation diagram to the icon under your mouse pointer (again similar to that shown in Figure 53.1).
5. Repeat Steps 2 through 4 for each of the existing Web pages you want to add to the Navigation diagram. For the current project, repeat Steps 2 – 4 once more. However, drag the icon to the left of service_2.htm in Step 2, so that it too will become a child of the Services Web page when you complete Step 4.

After you complete Step 4 for the current project, all of the existing Web pages in the MyWeb4 site will be a part of the site's Navigation diagram—with the exception of the Comments.htm page, which really does not fit into the site hierarchy. You might put the comments page as a child of the home page. However, if you think of the home page as a table of contents listing the first level topics available on the site, the comments page really is not a *content* page in that it provides a way for visitors to communicate with the company or site designers, and is not designed to provide information itself.

Fortunately, orphan Web pages, those that do not fit into the parent/child structure of the Web site are perfectly acceptable additions to the Navigation diagram. To add an orphan Web page to the Navigation diagram perform the following steps:

1. Switch to Navigation View (if FrontPage is not already in Navigation View) by selecting the View menu Navigation option.
2. Move your mouse pointer over the icon of the Web page you want to add to the Navigation diagram. For the current project, move your mouse pointer over the icon to the left of comments.htm.

3. Click and hold your left mouse button down as you drag your mouse pointer (and the Web page) to the right (or left) of the Home Page item until FrontPage draws a shaded line from the *top* of the Home Page item to Web page you are dragging onto the Navigation chart, similar to that shown in Figure 53.2. (If you see a shaded line from the *bottom* of the Home Page item on the Navigation diagram, drag your mouse pointer up, toward the top of the screen, until FrontPage draws the shaded line from the top of the Home Page.)

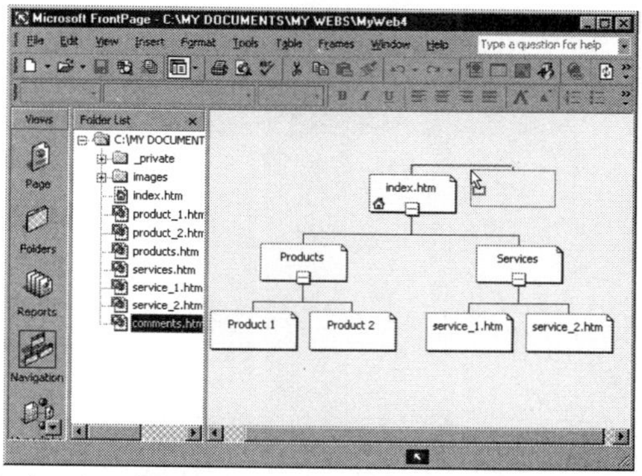

Figure 53.2 FrontPage Navigation View prior to "dropping" an orphan page onto the Navigation diagram.

4. Release the left mouse button after FrontPage draws a shaded line from the *top* of the home page item on the Navigation diagram to the Web page you are dragging. (If you release the left mouse button when FrontPage draws a shaded line from the *bottom* of the Home Page item, FrontPage will make Web page you are dragging a child of the Home Page instead of an orphan page on the diagram.)
5. Repeat Steps 2 through 4 for each of the existing Web pages you want to add to the Navigation diagram as orphan pages.

If you only plan to use the site's Navigation diagram to generate the hyperlinks on navigation bars, you need not add any orphan pages to it. However, if you plan to have FrontPage create a site map (as you will learn to do in a later Tip), or if you want to be able to see the structure of the *entire* Web site (including pages that do not fit into the Navigation View's parent/child hierarchical structure), you must include *all* of the site's Web pages (including orphans) on the Navigation diagram.

CUSTOMIZING THE NAVIGATION VIEW DISPLAY

As you add Web pages to the site's Navigation diagram, it may grow too large to fit all of its items on a single computer screen. As such, you may want to hide the portion of the diagram on which you are not currently working, so you have more room on the screen for the current area of interest.

To *collapse* or hide a portion of the Navigation diagram, click your mouse pointer on the minus (-) located at the center of the bottom of the parent item whose children you want to hide. For example, if you click your mouse pointer on the minus (-) at the bottom of the Products item (shown in Figure 53.2), FrontPage will collapse the Navigation tree below the Products item (hiding Product 1, Product 2, and any child items below) similar to that shown in Figure 54.1.

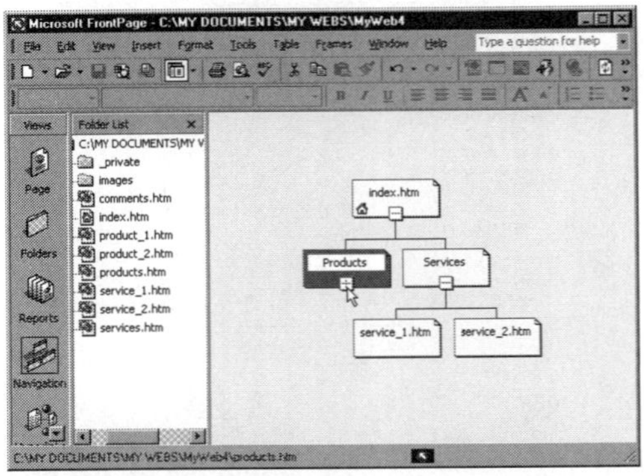

Figure 54.1 FrontPage Navigation View after collapsing (hiding) a portion (a subtree) of a Web.

Notice that FrontPage changes the minus (-) at the bottom of the parent to a plus (+) when it collapses (hides) the Web pages below an item on the Navigation diagram. To display the children again, click your mouse pointer on the plus (+) at the bottom of the parent whose children you want to see. FrontPage, in turn, will redisplay the parent's children (and the remainder of the hierarchical tree below the children, if any).

You can also tell FrontPage to collapse (hide) the parent and peers of any item in the Navigation diagram by right-clicking your mouse pointer on the item at the top of the subtree you want displayed and selecting View Subtree Only from the pop-up menu. For example, to view only the Services page and any child pages below Services in the MyWeb4 Navigation diagram, right-click your mouse pointer on Services and select View Subtree Only from the pop-up menu. FrontPage, in turn, will display only the Services subtree of the MyWeb4 Navigation diagram, similar to that shown in Figure 54.2.

To redisplay the remainder of the Navigation diagram, either right-click your mouse pointer on any of the items in the Services subtree and uncheck the View Subtree Only item on the pop-up menu, or click your mouse pointer on the VIEW ALL button above the at the top of the Navigation diagram (the button above Services in Figure 54.2 for the current example).

In addition to hiding a portion of the Navigation diagram, you can also rotate it 90 degrees. This feature is handy if you have a lot of Web pages at the same level, and you cannot display them all when viewing the site hierarchy from top-to-bottom on your screen. To display the Navigation diagram from left-to-right on the screen (instead of top-to-bottom), right-click your mouse pointer on a blank area in the background of the Navigation pane, and select Portrait/Landscape on the pop-up menu. FrontPage, in turn, will display the Navigation diagram from left-to-right similar to that shown in Figure 54.3.

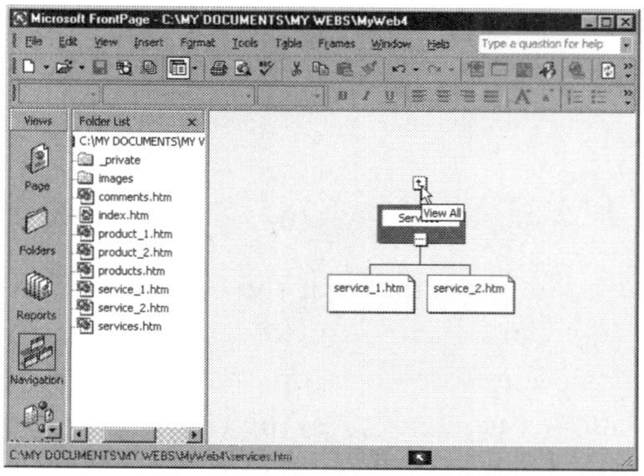

Figure 54.2 FrontPage Navigation View after collapsing (hiding) all but one subtree of a Web.

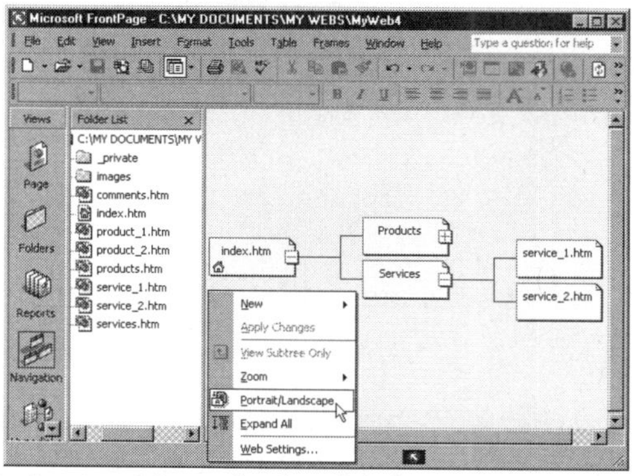

Figure 54.3 FrontPage Navigation View displayed left-to-right instead of top-to-bottom.

To change the display back to top-to-bottom, right-click your mouse pointer on a blank area in the Navigation pane again and select Rotate from the pop-up menu.

Finally, you can use the Navigation View's Zoom feature to control the degree of magnification of the items in the Navigation pane. For example, to have FrontPage change the magnification such that the entire Navigation diagram will fit on a single screen, click your mouse pointer on a blank area in the Navigation pane. After FrontPage displays its pop-up menu, move your mouse pointer to Zoom and then select Size To Fit.

If you increase the magnification (by selecting 150% vs. 100% on the Zoom menu, for example), you can enlarge the items on the Navigation diagram. This is handy if FrontPage is unable to display the full text of the item titles in the boxes on the Navigation diagram.

However, increasing the size of the Navigation diagram may force you to use scroll bars to see portions of the diagram FrontPage is no longer able to display on a single screen.

Conversely, you can use the Zoom feature to reduce the size of the Navigation diagram by selecting a lower percentage magnification (such as selecting 75% vs. 100% on the Zoom menu, for example). If you reduce the size of the items in the Navigation pane, to the point at which FrontPage cannot display the entire title of an object, the program display three dots (...) after the last letter in the portion of the title it is able to fit into the item's rectangle on the Navigation diagram.

DELETING A WEB PAGE

To remove a Web page you no longer want from the FrontPage Web you currently have open, switch to a view in which you can see the icon for the Web page you want to delete. Then, either right-click your mouse pointer on the icon and select Delete from the pop-up menu, or click your mouse pointer on the icon and press the DELETE key on your keyboard. FrontPage, in turn, will ask you to confirm your delete request by displaying a dialog box similar to that shown in Figure 55.

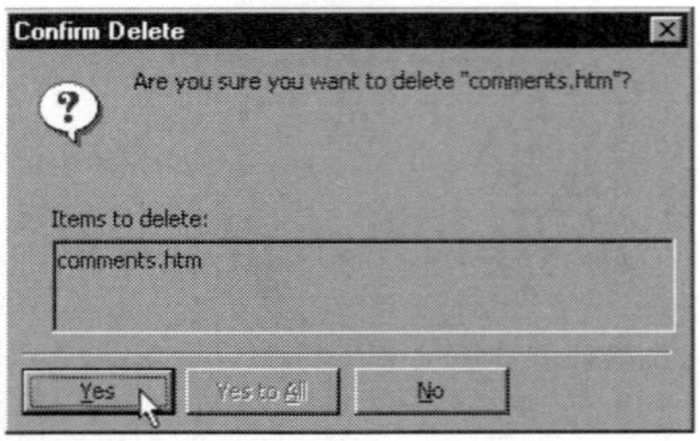

Figure 55 FrontPage Confirm Delete dialog box.

To confirm the deletion, and have FrontPage remove the Web page from the FrontPage Web and delete the file from your hard drive, click your mouse pointer on the YES button. If you change your mind and decide to keep the file, click your mouse pointer on the NO button instead.

Note: *The Folder List pane (which you can display by selecting the View menu Folder List option when in Page View, Navigation View, or Hyperlinks View) lists all of the site's Web pages (and folders). As such, the Folder List pane is the most convenient place to find the icon of the Web page you want to delete.*

USING THE FRONTPAGE SPELL CHECK AS YOU TYPE FEATURE

After you have labored long and hard getting the wording, screen colors, and graphics just right, the last thing you need is something as annoying as misspelled words to distract your visitors from fully appreciating your excellent work. Fortunately, FrontPage can check your spelling automatically as you type, and underline misspelled words with red squiggly lines, such as those shown under "Raskin", "teh", and "grocieres" in Figure 56.1.

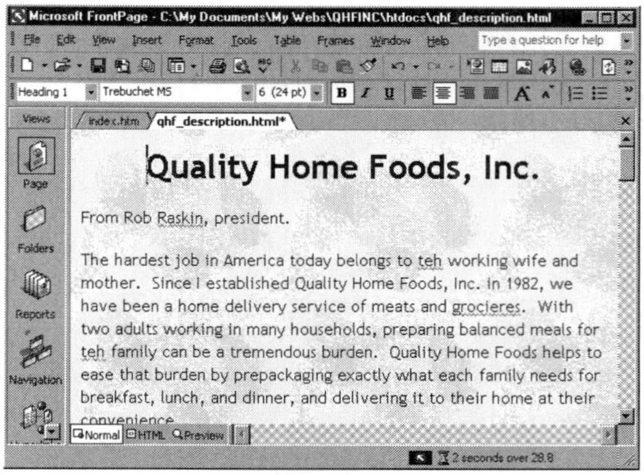

***Figure 56.1** FrontPage Page View of a document showing misspelled words underlined with red squiggly lines.*

When you see that FrontPage has marked a word as misspelled, you can correct the problem either by deleting the misspelled word and retyping it correctly, or by right-clicking your mouse pointer on the error to have FrontPage suggest possible corrections.

When you right-click your mouse pointer on a word that FrontPage has underlined as misspelled, the program will display a pop-up menu of suggested correct spellings, an Ignore All choice (which tells FrontPage to accept your spelling of the word as correct temporarily), and an Add choice (which tells FrontPage to add your spelling of the word to the spelling dictionary).

In the current example, the first *misspelling*, "Raskin", is a proper noun (the last name of the owner). To tell FrontPage that a word it "thinks" is misspelled is actually spelled correctly, right-click your mouse pointer on the "misspelling" ("Raskin", in the current example) and then select the Ignore All option from the pop-up menu. FrontPage, in turn, will accept the spelling of "Raskin" as correct and remove the red squiggly line used to underline misspellings. If you think you will be using the same, questionable spelling often, select the Add to Dictionary option on the pop-up menu to have FrontPage add the spelling of the word to the spelling dictionary. After you add a non-standard spelling to the dictionary, FrontPage will not mark the word as misspelled in the future.

The next misspelling in the current example, ("teh" instead of "the") needs to be corrected. As such, right-click your mouse pointer on "teh" and then select "the" from the pop-up menu. FrontPage, in turn, will replace the misspelled word on the Web page with the word you selected from the pop-up menu. When you select a correction from the spell check pop-up menu, FrontPage only fixes a single spelling error. Therefore, if the same word is misspelled in multiple places on the same page (or on different pages), you will have to either retype the word correctly at each location, or right-click your mouse pointer on each occurrence of the error and select the correct spelling from the pop-up menu.

Note: *If you find that the spell check while typing feature slows down your computer too much, or if the Web page uses a lot of nonstandard spellings or words not included in the spelling dictionary, you can turn off the spell check as you type feature by performing the following steps:*

1. Select the Tools menu Page Options option. FrontPage, in turn, will display a Page Options dialog box similar to that shown in Figure 56.2.

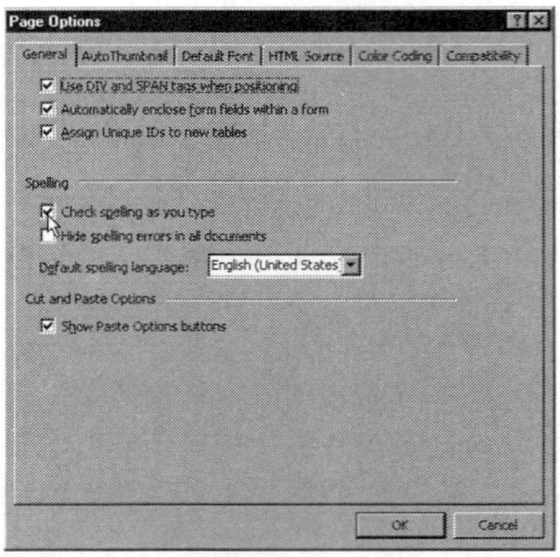

Figure 56.2 *The FrontPage Pages Options dialog box, General tab.*

2. Click your mouse pointer on the General tab.
3. Click your mouse pointer on the check box to the left of Check spelling as you type until the check mark disappears.
4. Exit the Page Options dialog box by clicking your mouse pointer on the OK button.

After you clear the Check spelling as you type check box, FrontPage will no longer draw red squiggles under your misspelled words, because the program will not spell check your Web pages until you tell it do so (as you will learn to do in the next Tip). If you later decide you want to re-enable the spell check as you type feature, simply repeat this procedure, except click your mouse pointer on the check box to the left of Check spelling as you type until the check mark appears (vs. disappears) in Step 3.

USING THE SPELL CHECKER TO CHECK THE SPELLING OF ALL WORDS IN A FRONTPAGE WEB

In addition to the spell check as you type feature you learned about in the preceding Tip, FrontPage also lets you spell check all of the Web pages in a FrontPage Web at once. As you may have noticed, correcting misspelled words one at a time is inconvenient when the same word is misspelled the same way multiple times—since you have to make the same correction repeatedly. Moreover, pulling up each Web page on a large site and visually scanning it for red squiggles is a tedious and error prone process.

Fortunately, FrontPage lets you spell check an entire Web site at once by performing the following steps:

1. Make sure the Web site you currently have open is displayed in a view other than Page View. For example, select the View menu Folders option to switch to Folders View. (If you perform Step 2 while in Page View, FrontPage will not display the menu shown in Figure 57.1 and will only spell check the page currently displayed in the application window.)
2. Select the Tools menu Spelling option. FrontPage, in turn, will display the Spelling dialog box shown in Figure 57.1.

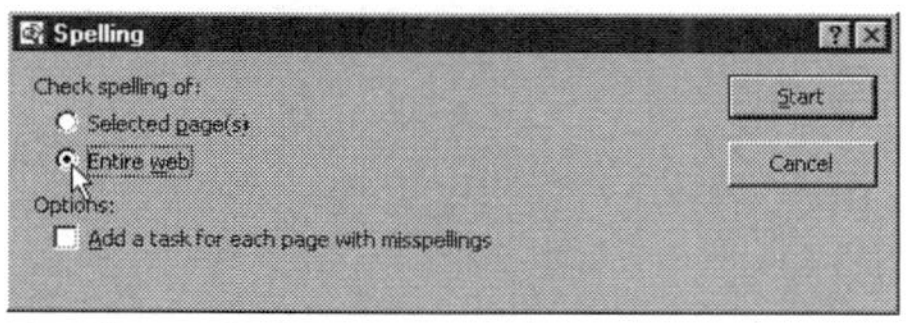

Figure 57.1 The FrontPage Spelling dialog box with spell check control options.

3. To have FrontPage check the spelling on all of the Web pages in the current FrontPage Web, click your mouse pointer on the radio button to the left of Entire web and then on the START button to start the spell check process. FrontPage, in turn, will check the Web for spelling errors and list the Web pages with misspelled words along with the misspellings in a scroll box at the bottom half of the Spelling dialog box similar to that shown in Figure 57.2.

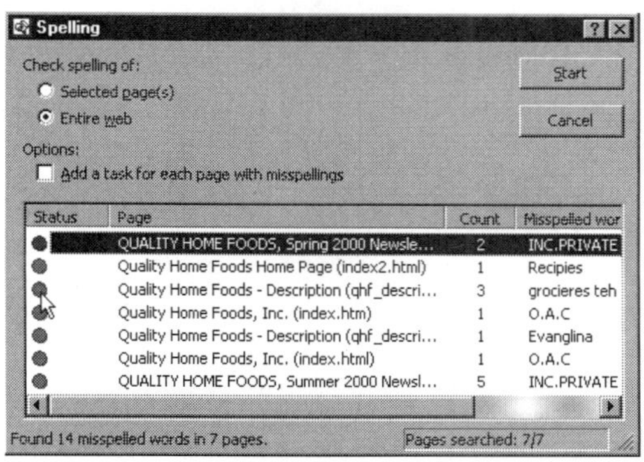

Figure 57.2 The FrontPage Spelling dialog box with a list of Web pages with questionably spelled words.

4. To correct misspellings, double-click your mouse pointer on one of the pages listed in the in the scroll box. FrontPage, in turn, will display the Web page in Page View, highlight the misspelled word on the page, and show you the incorrect word along with several suggested spellings in Spelling dialog box similar to that shown in Figure 57.3.

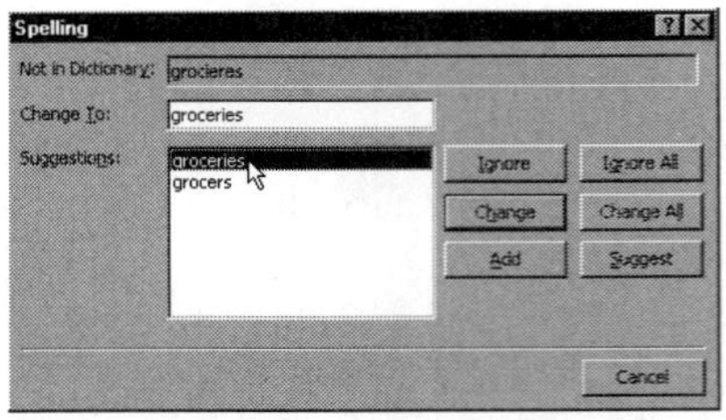

Figure 57.3 The FrontPage Spelling dialog box with a misspelled word and buttons to take the corrective course of action.

5. Tell FrontPage what you want done with about the questionable spelling by clicking your mouse pointer on one of the following Spelling dialog box buttons:

- IGNORE – accept the spelling of the current word and continue spell checking.
- IGNORE ALL – same as Ignore, however, accept all occurrences with the same spelling of the current word as correct.
- CHANGE – replace the spelling of the current word with the spelling entered in the Change To field. You can either click your mouse pointer on one of the suggested spellings shown in the Suggestions: area to display it in the Change To field, or you can type your own spelling of the misspelled word in the Change To field.
- CHANGE ALL – same as Change To, however change all occurrences in which the current word is spelled the same way to the entry shown in the Change To field.
- ADD – accept the spelling of the current word as correct and add it to the spelling dictionary. (Be careful if you select this choice, since adding a misspelled word to the spelling dictionary will prevent FrontPage from "catching" the same spelling error in the future.)
- SUGGEST – Check the spelling of a word you type into the Change To field and suggest alternatives.
- CANCEL – terminate the spell check.

6. Repeat Step 5 each time FrontPage displays a misspelled word on the Web page you selected in Step 4.
7. If FrontPage prompts you with a "Continue with the next page?" message box after you finishing spell checking a Web page, click your mouse pointer on the NEXT PAGE button to spell check the next page, and then continue at Step 5.
8. After FrontPage spell checks all Web pages indicated as having spelling errors in Step 3, the application will again display the Spelling dialog box you saw in Figure 57.2. This time, however, the status column will have a yellow dot and the word "Edited" next to each of the Web pages you spell checked.

To exit the spell check program, click your mouse pointer on the close button (the X) in the upper right-hand corner of the Spelling dialog box.

USING THE THESAURUS TO FIND THE "RIGHT" WORD

As you develop the content for a Web site's pages, you will sometimes run into a problem in finding just the "right" word you want to use. Perhaps you are looking for a word that "packs a punch" in order to drive home a point, or you may need a fresh word or another way to express a thought or concept. In either case, the FrontPage thesaurus can help by providing a list of synonyms for select words or phrases.

To use the thesaurus, perform the following steps:

1. While editing a Web page in Page View, highlight the phrase or click your mouse pointer on the word you want to look up in the thesaurus.
2. Select the Tools menu Thesaurus option. FrontPage, in turn, will display a Thesaurus dialog box similar to that shown in Figure 58 with the selected word or phrase in the Looked Up field.

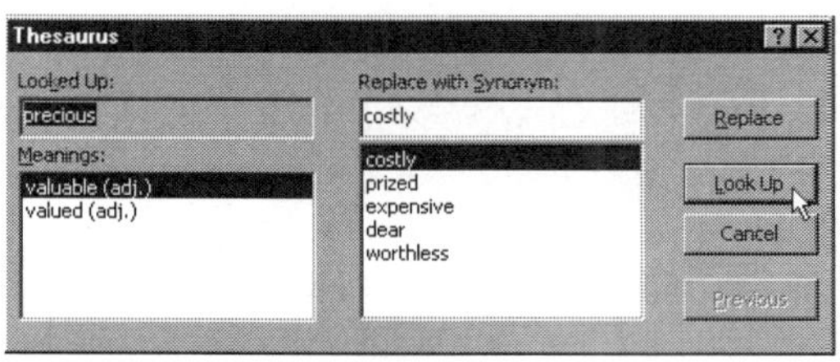

Figure 58 The FrontPage Thesaurus dialog box.

3. If the word or phrase has more than one meaning, FrontPage will list the various possible meanings in the Meanings list box. Click your mouse pointer on the meaning of the word or phrase based on the context in which you are using it. FrontPage, in turn, will display a list of synonyms in the list box below the Replace with synonym field.
4. Click your mouse pointer on the synonym you want to use in place of the word or phrase you selected in Step 1. FrontPage, in turn, will copy the synonym from the list box to the Replace with synonym field.
5. Click your mouse pointer on the REPLACE button to replace the word or phrase you selected in Step 1 with the contents of the Replace with synonym field. Or, if you change your mind about replacing the word or phrase you originally typed, click your mouse pointer on the CANCEL button to leave the Web page text unchanged.

After you complete Step 5, FrontPage will exit the Thesaurus dialog box and return to Page View edit mode, and you can continue editing the Web page contents.

Note: *If you see a word that is almost but not quite the one you want when FrontPage provides the list of synonyms in the synonym list box in Step 3, click your mouse pointer on the synonym that is "almost" acceptable, and then click your mouse pointer on the LOOK UP button. FrontPage, in turn, will copy the synonym you selected into the Looked Up field and display its meaning and synonyms (for the synonym) in the synonym list box.*

INSERTING PARAGRAPH BREAKS

As you type text onto a Web page, FrontPage automatically wraps your content from one line to the next. That is, when your typing reaches the right-hand margin, FrontPage automatically moves to the left-hand margin of the next line as you continue typing. However, if a Web page has a lot of text, you will want to block your sentences into paragraphs to make the content easier to read.

To insert a blank line on a Web page, press the ENTER key. FrontPage, in turn, will insert a paragraph break (which Web browsers will display as a blank line). For example, the Web page shown in Figure 59.1 has two paragraph breaks: one before the word "Key" in the phrase "Key practiced law in Georgetown", and one before the word "A" in the phrase "A deeply religious man."

If you switched to HTML View (by clicking your mouse pointer on the HTML tab near the lower left hand corner of the Page View pane), you would see HTML code similar to that shown in Figure 59.2 for the Web page shown in Figure 59.1.

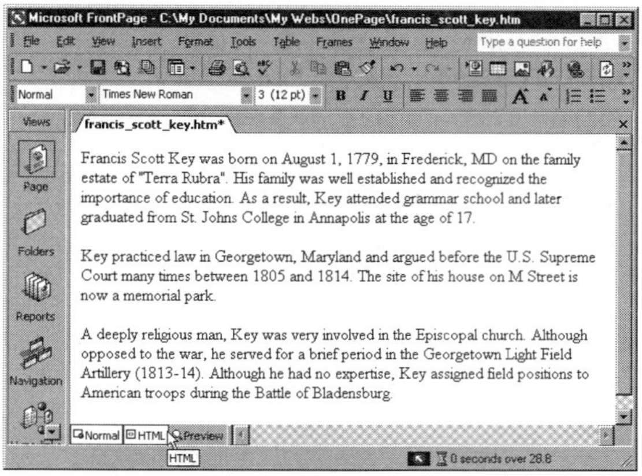

Figure 59.1 *Page View of a Web page with paragraph breaks used to group sentences into blocks.*

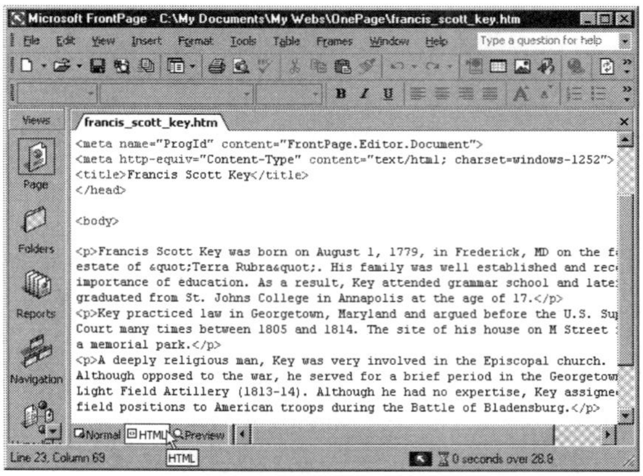

Figure 59.2 *HTML View of a Web page with paragraph breaks (<p> tags).*

Notice that FrontPage represents each paragraph break with the tag <p> in the HTML code that the Web server sends to the browser for display on the visitor's computer screen. Whenever a browser "sees" a paragraph tag (<p>) in the HTML code, then, it displays a blank line before showing the next Web page element on the screen. In the current example, the "next" element is more text. However, you can also use paragraph breaks to put one or more blank lines been graphic images, as shown in Figure 59.3.

In short, whenever you need a blank line to separate items on a Web page, press the ENTER key to have FrontPage insert a paragraph break (a <p> tag) into the HTML code it generates as you type.

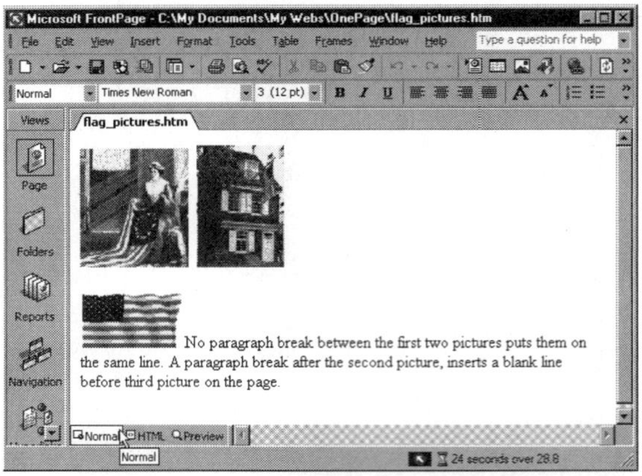

Figure 59.3 Page View of a Web page with a paragraph break used to insert a blank line between pictures.

INSERTING LINE BREAKS

In the previous Tip you learned how to format Web page content by using a paragraph breaks to insert one or more blank lines between blocks of text. However, there are times when you want to stop typing on one line (before you reach the right-hand margin), and continue on the next line—without inserting a blank line in between. For example, when you type a recipe, table of contents, or poem on a Web page, the lines of text will seldom stretch from margin to margin. Yet, you will want each item on a line by itself and no blank lines in between.

To insert a line break (which moves the cursor to the next line, without inserting a blank line), position your cursor at the end of the line in Page View and then hold down the SHIFT key and press ENTER. Figure 60.1, for example, shows the effects of using a paragraph break to terminate each line in the top half of the Web page, and then the same poem with line breaks used to end each line in the bottom half of the page.

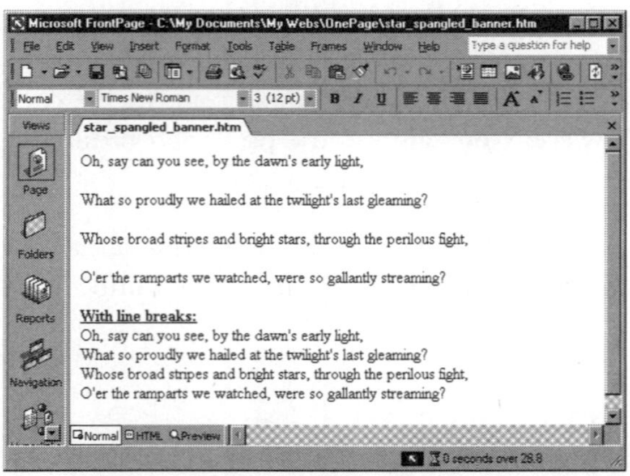

Figure 60.1 Page View of a Web page text separated by paragraph breaks in the top half and line breaks in the bottom half of the page.

In addition to pressing SHIFT+ENTER, you can also insert a line break by performing the following procedure:

1. Position your cursor at the end of the line.
2. Select the Insert menu Break option. FrontPage, in turn, will display the Break Properties dialog box shown in Figure 60.2.

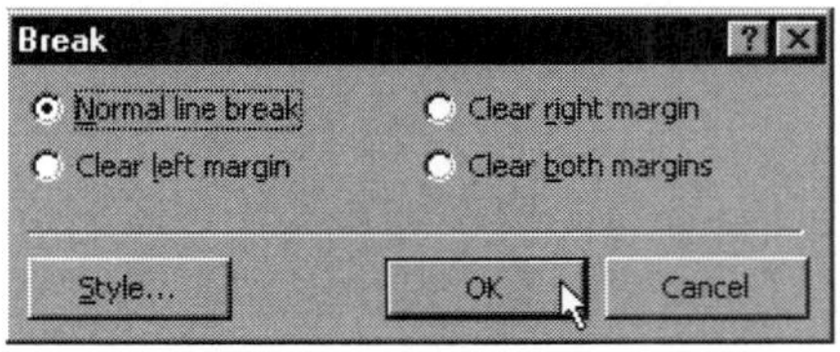

Figure 60.2 *The FrontPage (line) Break Properties dialog box.*

3. Click your mouse pointer on the radio button to the left of Normal line break and then on the OK button.

Note: *The Clear left margin, Clear right margin, and Clear both margins options on the Break Properties dialog box (shown in Figure 60.2) deal with the way text will float around an image when you insert a line break. However, the most reliable (and easiest) way to control the flow of text around in image is by setting the image properties and then using the SHIFT+ENTER key combination to insert line normal line breaks as necessary. You will learn all about controlling the flow of text around an image on a Web page later in this book.*

UNDERSTANDING THE NONBREAKING SPACE (HTML CODE)

On a Web page (as in other documents), a *space* (which you insert by pressing the SPACE BAR) is a character and not just a "space" between two words. If you use a text editor to create a Web page and insert multiple blank spaces, one after another, to format text into columns, you will find that the columns disappear (and the text appears scattered) when you view the page using a Web browser. Most Web browsers consider the second and subsequent spaces to be extraneous and display a single space for each group of spaces.

Fortunately, FrontPage, unlike a text editor, inserts *nonbreaking* spaces (HTML code:) when you repeatedly press the SPACE BAR for all but the (single) final space as you type text onto a Web page on the Page view Normal tab. Thus, if you use a text editor to add the line:

```
First Name     Last Name           Address       Phone Number
```

to the HTML for a Web page, a visitor's Web browser will display the line as:

```
First Name Last Name Address Phone Number
```

If, on the other hand, you type the same line onto a Web page using the Normal tab in FrontPage Page view, FrontPage will convert the spaces you type into the *nonbreaking* spaces shown in the HTML code:

```
First  Name      Last  Name  
         Address 
       Phone Number
```

As a result Web browsers will display the Web page with the column headings spaced as you typed them in Page view.

In addition to using a nonbreaking space for text spacing, you can also use it to prevent a Web browser from splitting an item with an embedded space character when it wraps text from one line to the next at the right-hand margin on a Web page or in a table cell. Suppose, for example, that you wanted to prevent a Web browser from displaying the area code portion of a phone number written as (702) 555-1212 on one line and wrapping the last seven digits (and dash) onto a second line. When typing the phone number onto the Web page on the Normal tab in Page view, press the Space Bar twice when after you type ")". FrontPage, in turn, will insert the code:

```
(702)  555-1212
```

onto the Web page. Click your mouse pointer on the HTML tab in Page view and delete the blank area (i.e., the space (" ") after the   that follows ")", so that the HTML reads:

```
(702) 555-1212
```

Then, click your mouse pointer on the Page view Normal tab. The phone number will appear as before (both on the Page view, Normal tab and when viewed in a Web browser). However, if the phone number happens to end up along the right-hand margin when displayed in a visitor's Web browser, the browser will wrap the entire phone number to the next line even if it could fit the first five characters "(702)" between the margins of the current line of the display.

ADJUSTING CHARACTER SPACING

Instead of using multiple successive nonbreaking space characters (HTML code:) to separate words and/or letters on a Web page, you can control the actual size of the space that separates characters (including the space and nonbreaking space characters) on a page. For example, to change the spacing between the characters in a text string such as: FoodCo Inc., perform the following steps:

1. In FrontPage Page view, Normal tab, select the text whose character spacing you want to change. (Either hold down the left mouse button as you drag your mouse pointer over the text you want to select, or double-click your mouse pointer at the left hand margin of a paragraph to select all of the text in the paragraph.)
2. Select the Format menu Font option. FrontPage, in turn, will display the Font dialog box.
3. Click your mouse pointer on the Character tab to display the current character spacing specification similar to that shown in Figure 62.

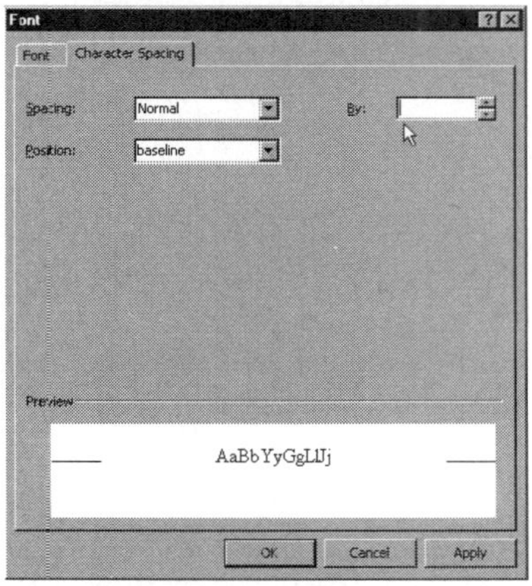

Figure 62 The FrontPage Font dialog box, Character Spacing tab.

4. In the By field, enter the number of pixels you want the Web browser to display between each character in the text you select in Step 1. Enter a positive number to increase the space between characters, or enter a negative number into the By field to decrease the space between characters. (After you enter a value into the By field and/or click your mouse pointer on the up or down buttons to the right of the By field to increase or decrease the value in the field, FrontPage will show you the new character spacing in the Preview area near the bottom of the dialog box.)

After you set the character spacing to the desired value, click your mouse pointer on the OK button (near the bottom center of the Font dialog box) to format the selected text and return to the Page view Normal tab.

ALIGNING TEXT

By default, FrontPage will align text in each paragraph flush with the left-hand margin of a Web page. This formatting style, called left-justification, results in the first letter of each line starting immediately below the first letter of the line above it. As a result, the left edge of the text on the page appears smooth while the right edge of the text is jagged, since the last letter of some lines will end closer to the right-hand margin than others.

While left-justification, such as that shown by the first paragraph in Figure 63.1, is the default, you can tell FrontPage to right-justify text (as shown by the second paragraph in Figure 63.1), center, or full-justify (both right-justify and left-justify) the text instead.

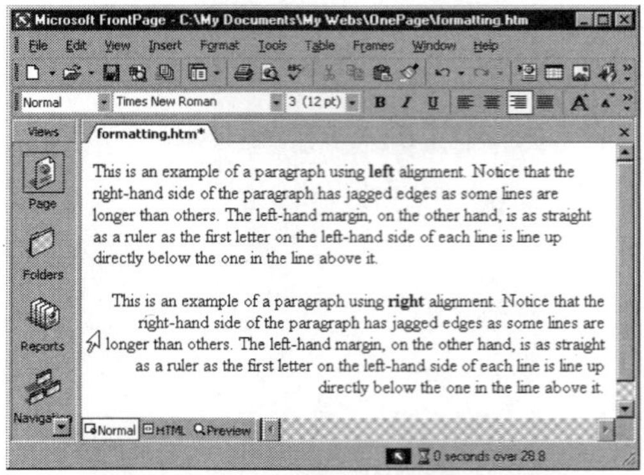

Figure 63.1 Web page with a left-justified paragraph followed by a right-justified paragraph.

To change the default (left) justification of text in a on a Web page, perform the following steps:

1. Click your mouse pointer into the paragraph you want to format or select multiple paragraphs by holding down your left mouse button as you drag your mouse pointer over the text you want to format.
2. Select the Format menu Paragraph option. FrontPage, in turn, will display a (format) Paragraph dialog box similar to that shown in Figure 63.2.

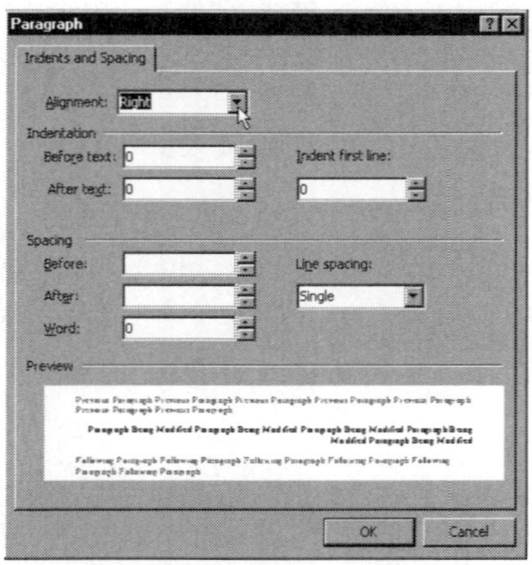

Figure 63.2 The FrontPage (format)Paragraph dialog box.

3. Click your mouse pointer on the drop-down list button to the right of the Alignment field, and then select the text formatting option you want from the drop-down list.
4. Click your mouse pointer on the OK button (near the lower right-hand corner of the dialog box) to format the text you selected in Step 1 and return to the Page view Normal tab.

Each time you select a justification option in Step 3, FrontPage will show you an example of how the text will look after it applies the new formatting in the Preview area near the bottom of the (format) Paragraph dialog box.

UNDERSTANDING FRONTPAGE TEXT ALIGNMENT BUTTONS

In addition to using the (format) Paragraph dialog box you learned about in the previous Tip, FrontPage also lets you change the alignment of paragraph text by clicking your mouse pointer on one of the four text alignment buttons on the Formatting Toolbar. (If you do not see the Formatting Toolbar, select the view menu Toolbars option and click your mouse pointer on Formatting.) The four text alignment buttons (shown in Figure 64) are from left to right: Align left, Center, Align right, and (full) Justify.

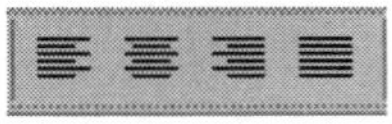

Figure 64 *The FrontPage Formatting Toolbar text alignment buttons.*

Notice that each of the buttons shows you how the text will look after you click your mouse pointer on the button to format a paragraph or selected block of text. For example, if you want your Web page text to have smooth left and right edges, select the paragraph(s) you want to format and then click your mouse pointer on the Justify button (i.e. the fourth button from the left). As shown, on the button, FrontPage, in turn, will increase the space between characters on each line such that the first character on each line lines up with the character on the line above it, and such that the last character on each line lines up with the last character on the line above it. Similarly, if you click your mouse pointer on the Align right button (third from the left), FrontPage will format that paragraph(s) you selected such that it has a smooth right-hand edge with a "jagged" left-hand edge. The last character on each line will line up with the last character of the line above it while some lines will extend further toward the left-hand margin than others.

Note: *Not all browsers support all of the text alignment options—especially* ***Justify*** *which makes each line of Web page text begin and end flush with both left and right margins on the page. When a Web browser encounters an alignment option it does not support, the visitor will see the Web page text left-justified.*

INDENTING PARAGRAPHS

To indent entire paragraphs in the manner shown in Figure 65, you could insert multiple nonbreaking space (HTML code:) characters before the first (non-blank) character on each line. (As you learned previously, when working in Page view on the Normal tab, FrontPage will insert nonbreaking space characters whenever you press the SPACE BAR to put more than two spaces in a row onto a line.)

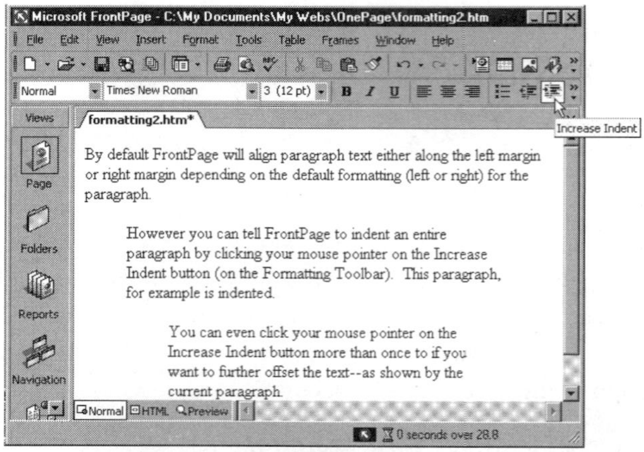

Figure 65 A Web page with paragraphs indented by the Increase Indent button on the Formatting Toolbar.

However, the Increase Indent button on the Formatting Toolbar gives you a more convenient way to indent the left margin for all of the lines in a paragraph. Simply click your mouse pointer anywhere within the paragraph you want to indent, and then click your mouse pointer on the Increase Indent button on the Formatting toolbar. FrontPage, in turn, will indent the left margin of the paragraph seven characters to the right of the left margin in the preceding paragraph.

Note: *If the paragraph text is left-justified (i.e. each line starts flush with the left margin), clicking your mouse pointer on the Increase Indent button moves the left margin seven characters to the right. Conversely, if the paragraph text is right-justified (i.e. each line ends with the last character flush with the right margin), clicking your mouse pointer on the Increase Indent button will move the right margin seven characters to the left.*

To reverse the process, click your mouse pointer on the paragraph whose indentation you want to change, and then click your mouse pointer on the Decrease Indent button (immediately to the left of the Increase Indent button) on the Formatting Toolbar.

As was the case when working with text alignment (which you learned about in the two preceding Tips), you can indent multiple paragraphs by holding down your left mouse button as you drag the mouse pointer over the Web page text you want to select. If you then click your mouse pointer on the Increase Indent button or the Decrease Indent button, FrontPage will change the indentation for all paragraphs which contain at least one character of the text you selected.

UNDERSTANDING FRONTPAGE PARAGRAPH STYLES

While you can apply text styles such as bold, underline, italics, Times New Roman font, and 24pt character size to sentences, words, or even individual letters, you must always apply paragraph styles to an entire paragraph. Unlike the four to five sentence paragraphs you learned about in composition class, a paragraph on a Web page may consist of single sentence or even a single word. Each time you press the ENTER key, FrontPage starts a new paragraph.

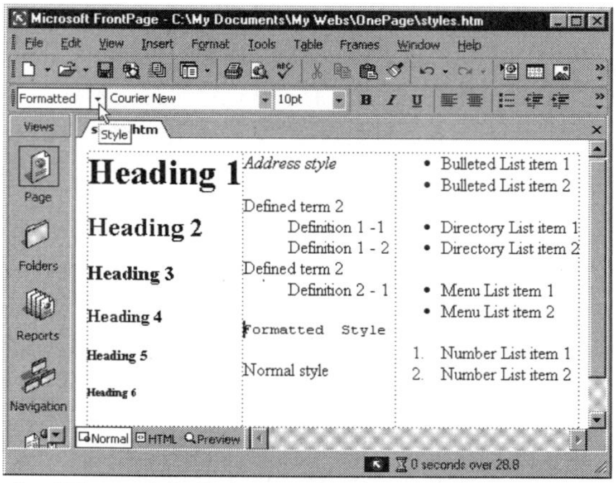

Figure 66 Examples of the fifteen default paragraph styles.

FrontPage lets you select one of fifteen paragraph styles shown in Figure 66 for each of the paragraphs on a Web page.

The paragraph styles are:

- **Heading** – the six heading styles (Heading 1 through Heading 6) are for successively lower-level titles. Heading 1 is the largest title and Heading 6 is the smallest. A paragraph formatted using Heading 4, for example, is considered subordinate to a Heading 2 paragraph, because the text in the paragraph formatted as Heading 2 is larger than the text in a paragraph formatted as Heading 4.
- **Defined Term** – is actually a list style—without the bullet character or number that precedes each item in a list. Defined Term and Definition are always used together. When you enter text in a paragraph formatted as Defined Term, FrontPage automatically changes the current format to Definition when you press the ENTER key to start a

new paragraph, so that you can enter one or more *definitions* for the *defined term*.

- **Definition** – used with the Defined Term style. Each Definition paragraph is indented to start to the right of the first column in the associated *Defined Term*. You can have more than one definition per Defined Term. The only difference between an ordered (numbered) or unordered (bulleted) list and a Defined Term is that each Defined Term and each Definition does not start with a number or bullet character.
- **Address** – was originally designed to identify Web addresses on a Web page and is now sometimes used to make e-mail hyperlinks stand out from other Web page text (and other non-e-mail hyperlinks). Most browsers display Address styled text in italics. Thus, formatting a paragraph using the Address style has the same effect as applying the italic format to the text in a paragraph. (As a result, the Address style has fallen into disuse but is still supported by almost all browsers.)
- **Normal** – most of the text on a Web page will be in *Normal* style. Normal style has no fixed line width, and the visitor's browser will display Normal text in the browser's default font and wrap one line of text onto the next at either the right or left margin depending on the paragraph's justification.
- **Formatted** – when you want to use a moonscape font (such as Courier) in which all letters have the same width and multiple spaces (both breaking and nonbreaking) are preserved, style the paragraph using the Formatted style. The Formatted style is especially usefully when you want to display an application code listing on a Web page, because the Formatted style tells the visitor's browser to preserve column and letter spacing and prevents it from wrapping lines within the browser window.
- **List** – there are three unordered (bulleted) list styles: Bulleted List, Directory List, and Menu List; and one ordered list style: Numbered List. Each bullet (line) in an unordered list begins with a bullet character while each line in an ordered list begins with a number. Although each of the three types of unordered lists starts with a bullet character in the visitor's browser, the browser may (or may not) display each style using a *different* bullet character and/or text font.

To format a paragraph using one of the fifteen default styles, click your mouse pointer on the paragraph you want to format. Then, click your mouse pointer on the drop-down list button to the right of the style column on the Formatting Toolbar, and select the paragraph style you want from the drop-down list. As was the case with text formatting and paragraph indentation, you can apply a paragraph style to multiple paragraphs at once by holding down your left mouse button as you drag your mouse pointer over the paragraphs you want to style. After you select the paragraph style you want from the drop-down list of styles, FrontPage will apply the style you selected to all paragraphs in which you selected at least one letter of text.

USING THE PARAGRAPH PROPERTIES DIALOG BOX TO ADJUST PARAGRAPH PROPERTIES

In addition to using the Increase Indent and Decrease Indent buttons to change the indentation of all lines in a paragraph, you can use the Paragraph (properties) dialog box to fine-tune the appearance of a paragraph. The Paragraph (properties) dialog box lets you set the indentation of the first line in a paragraph separately from the remaining lines, the amount of blank space before and after a paragraph, and the line spacing (single, 1.5, or double) of the lines within a paragraph.

To work with the Paragraph (properties) dialog box, right-click your mouse pointer on the paragraph whose properties you want to adjust, and then select Paragraph from the pop-up menu. FrontPage, in turn, will display a Paragraph (properties) dialog box similar to that shown in Figure 67.

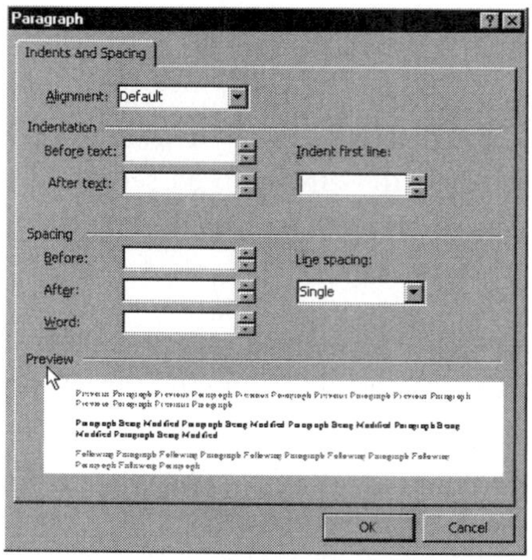

Figure 67 The FrontPage Paragraph (properties) dialog box.

The fields in the Indentation section of the dialog box let you adjust the indentation of the first line of the paragraph and set the number of pixels of blank space between the left-hand margin and the first character on a line and the right-hand margin and the last character on a line. For example, to have FrontPage indent the first line of the paragraph 36 pixels, enter a 36 into the Indent first line field. To have FrontPage insert blank space before the first character on a line, enter a positive number of pixels into the Before text field. Conversely, to have FrontPage leave white space between the last character on a line and the right-hand margin, enter the number of pixels into the After text field.

The fields in the Spacing section of the dialog box let you control the amount of space before and after the paragraph, as well as, between each line in the paragraph. For example, to increase the amount of space before the start of the paragraph, enter the number of pixels to leave blank into the Before field. Similarly, to increase the amount of blank space after the current paragraph and the start of the next, enter the number of pixels to leave blank into the After field. To control the spacing of the lines within the paragraph, click your mouse pointer on the drop-down list button to the right of the Line spacing field and then select Single, 1.5 lines, or Double from the drop-down list.

As you enter the number of pixels into the various Paragraph (properties) indentation and spacing fields, FrontPage will show you what the paragraph will look like if you choose to apply the changes in the Preview section near the bottom of the Paragraph (dialog) box.

When you are finished adjusting the paragraph spacing, click your mouse pointer on the OK button to have FrontPage format the paragraph, or on the CANCEL button to return to the Page View Normal tab without making any changes.

USING CUT-AND-PASTE AND DRAG-AND-DROP TO MOVE TEXT ON A WEB PAGE

As you work with Web page text on the FrontPage Page View Normal tab, you will see that the FrontPage editor (in Page View) has many of the same features found in word processors (such as MS-Word or WordPerfect). You already used several of the FrontPage *word processing* tools when you aligned (justified) paragraph text, changed fonts, and adjusted paragraph indentation and line spacing.

One of the important elements of Web site design, is to make each Web page easy to read and to move the most important (or interesting) items to the top of a page—so that the visitor will see them before moving on to other pages (or other sites). As a result, you will often find it necessary move text around on your Web pages as you add (or remove) pictures and adjust column counts and widths. Rather than retyping text you want to move, use the FrontPage drag-and-drop and cut-and-paste features.

For example, to *drag* text from one location on a Web page to another, perform the following steps:

1. Click and hold down your left mouse button as you move your mouse pointer over the Web page text you want to move. (If you want to

select an entire paragraph, double-click your mouse pointer in the margin immediately to the left of any line in the paragraph.)

2. Release the left mouse button after you have highlighted (selected) the text you want to drag. (If you need to adjust your selection, click your mouse pointer anywhere on the Web page outside of the selected area to deselect the text, and then repeat Step 1.)
3. Move your mouse pointer over any letter in the highlighted (selected) text.
4. Click and hold down your left mouse button as you move your mouse pointer to the location at which you want FrontPage to insert the text you selected in Step 1. FrontPage, in turn, will display a vertical gray line at the insertion point at which it will place the selected text.
5. After you move the insertion point indicator (the vertical gray line) to the location where you wish to move the selected text, release your left mouse button to *drop* the selected text into place.

The drag-and-drop method for moving text works best when you want to move text from one place to another on the same Web page and both the original location and the new location are visible at the same time on your computer screen. When you want to move text from one Web page to another, or if you have to scroll the contents of your screen to move from the text's current location to the point at which you want to move it, use cut-and-paste instead of drag-and-drop.

To cut selected text from a Web page and then paste it at another location on the same page or onto another page, perform the following steps:

1. To select the text you want to remove (cut) from its current location, click and hold down your left mouse button as you move your mouse pointer over the Web page text you want to select. (If you want to select an entire paragraph, double-click your mouse pointer in the margin immediately to the left of any line in the paragraph.)
2. Release the left mouse button after you have highlighted (selected) the text you want to cut. (If you need to adjust your selection, click your mouse pointer anywhere on the Web page outside of the selected area to deselect the text, and then repeat Step 1.)
3. Right-click your mouse pointer on any highlighted word in the text you selected in Step 1, and then select Cut from the pop-up menu. FrontPage, in turn, will remove the selected text from the Web page and save it in the Windows clipboard.
4. Right-click your mouse pointer at the point on the (same or different) Web page at which you want to insert the text you selected in Step 1,

and then select Paste from the pop-up menu. FrontPage, in turn, will insert the text from the Windows clipboard.

Note: *If you want to copy (vs. move) text from one location to another, either on the same page or different pages, select Copy from the pop-up menu instead of Cut in Step 3. (As you already now, when you cut or move text, you remove the text you select from the original location before you paste it at the new location; when you copy text, you end up with the same text in both the original location and the new location.)*

UNDERSTANDING THE FRONTPAGE STANDARD TOOLBAR

The FrontPage Standard Toolbar provides shortcut buttons that let you perform the tasks necessary to create a new Web site or open an existing one; add and edit text on one or more Web pages; insert (and/or remove) pictures on a Web page; print the site's pages, and save any changes you make to disk. The first nine buttons on the Standard Toolbar (shown in figure 69.1) deal with creating (or reopening), publishing, and saving Web pages.

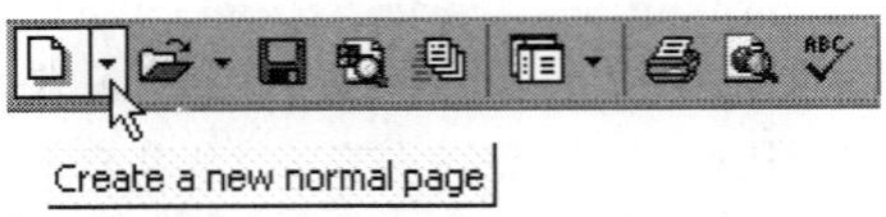

Figure 69.1 *The first nine buttons on the Standard Toolbar.*

Reviewing the function of each of the buttons from left to right:

- **Create a new normal page** – creates a new, blank Web page. Each time you click your mouse pointer on the first button (from the left) on the Standard Toolbar, FrontPage will add a new Web page as "new_page_1 .htm," "new_page_2.htm," "new_page_3.htm," etc. to the application's working area in memory. As you add content to the new Web pages, bear in mind that the FrontPage does not actually add a new Web page to the FrontPage Web you are editing until you select the File menu Save option (or click your mouse pointer on the Save button on the Standard Toolbar) and save the new page to disk. If you click your mouse pointer on the drop-down list button to the right of the Create a new normal page button on the Standard Toolbar, FrontPage will display a drop-down menu that lets you create a new Web page, create a new FrontPage Web, create a new Task, or if you are working in Folders View, create a new folder in the current FrontPage Web.
- **Open** – lets you open a Web page or FrontPage Web.
- **Save** – saves the current Web page to disk. If you previously saved the current Web page, FrontPage will overwrite the saved file's contents

with the content of the current Web page. Conversely, if you click your mouse pointer on the Save button to save the current Web page for the first time, FrontPage will display the Save As dialog box to prompt you for a filename before saving the current Web page to disk.

- **Search** – displays a search menu you can use to search for text strings in files stored on your computer or on another workstation on the network.

Note: *To search for text on the current Web page or text on any of the Web pages in the current FrontPage Web, select the Edit menu Find option, rather than clicking your mouse pointer on the Search button.*

- **Publish Web** – copies the current FrontPage web to the Web server that is hosting your Web site. When you *publish* your FrontPage web, you make its contents available to those that visit your Web site on the Internet.
- **Toggle Pane** – toggles (displays/removes) the Folder List pane in the FrontPage application window. If you click your mouse pointer on the drop-down list button to the right of the Toggle Pane button, you can select whether the Toggle Pane button toggles the display of the Navigation Pane or the Folder List pane. (By default, the Toggle Pane button toggles the display of the Folder List pane.)
- **Print** – sends the current Web page to the printer, if you are working in Page View, or sends the Navigation View of the current FrontPage Web to the printer if working in Navigation View.
- **Preview in Browser** – uses your default Web browser to display the current Web page.
- **Spelling** – checks the spelling of the words on the current Web page.

The next six buttons on the Standard Toolbar (shown in Figure 69.2) let you cut (remove), copy, and paste (insert) Web page objects as well as undo and redo work previously completed.

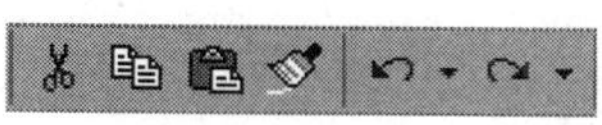

***Figure** 69.2 Buttons 10 – 15 on the Standard Toolbar.*

Reviewing the function of each of the buttons from left to right:

- **Cut** – remove the selected text or object from the current Web page and place it onto the Windows clipboard.

- **Copy** – make a copy of the selected text or object on the current Web page on the Windows clipboard.
- **Paste** – insert a copy of the Windows clipboard's contents at the insertion point on the current Web page.
- **Format Painter** – copy the formatting from one portion of a Web page onto another portion of the current Web page. To use format painter, first select the text with the format you want to copy. Then, click your mouse pointer on the Format Painter button. Move your mouse pointer over the first character of the text you want to format and then hold down your left mouse button as you *paint* (move) your mouse pointer across the text you want to format. Finally, release the left mouse button to format the text.
- **Undo** – reverse the most recent change made to a Web page. If you click your mouse pointer on the drop-down list button to the right of the Undo button, FrontPage will let you select the action you want to undo from a drop-down list of previously executed actions.
- **Redo** – reverses the most recent undo command. If you click your mouse pointer on the drop-down list button to the right of the Redo button, FrontPage will let you select the action you want to redo from a drop-down list of previously undone actions.

The next five buttons on the Standard Toolbar (shown in Figure 69.3) let you place non-text objects, tables, and hyperlinks onto the current Web page.

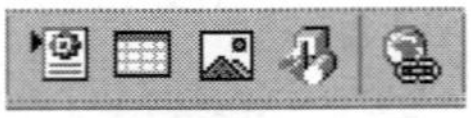

Figure 69.3 Buttons 16 – 20 on the Standard Toolbar.

Reviewing the function of each of the buttons from left to right:

- **Web Component** – displays the Insert Web Component dialog box which lets you select a component such as a hover button, marquee, spreadsheet, hit counter, table of contents, banner add, etc.
- **Insert Table** – creates a new table at the insertion point of the current Web page after you select the table's dimensions from the drop-down grid of table dimensions (which FrontPage will display after you click your mouse pointer on the Insert Table button).
- **Insert Picture From File** – lets you insert a picture stored on disk at the insertion point on the current Web page. When you click your mouse pointer on the Insert Picture From File button, FrontPage will display the Picture dialog box. The Picture dialog box lets you search

your computer, your network, or Internet to identify the picture you want to insert. The dialog box also lets you identify the types of picture files you want find.

- **Drawing** – toggles the display of the Drawing Toolbar in the application window.
- **Insert Hyperlink** – displays the Insert Hyperlink dialog box which lets you insert a hyperlink to a Web address (or disk file) and its label (the text you associate with the hyperlink's Web address or pathname) at the insertion point on the current Web page.

The final four buttons on the Standard Toolbar (shown in Figure 69.4) let you refresh the contents of the current Web page, toggle the display of normally invisible items, and access the FrontPage Help system.

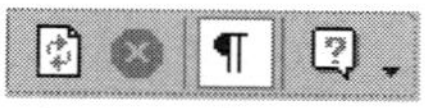

Figure 69.4 *The final four buttons on the Standard Toolbar.*

Reviewing the function of each of the buttons from left to right:

- **Refresh** – reload the current Web page and its objects (such as graphic images and multimedia files). If the current Web page has unsaved changes, FrontPage will prompt you to save your changes before overwriting the current Web page's contents with those stored on disk.
- **Stop** – tells FrontPage to stop loading the objects on a Web page accessed via a hyperlink.
- **Show All** – toggle the display of paragraph marks, hard-returns, bookmarks, and form outlines.
- **Microsoft FrontPage Help** – opens the FrontPage Help system window.

Note: *Each of the buttons on the Standard Toolbar (like each of the buttons on the other FrontPage toolbars) has an associated Tool Tip. If you move your mouse pointer over a button on the toolbar and wait a moment, FrontPage will display a yellow Tool Tip which tells you the button's name.*

UNDERSTANDING HYPERTEXT MARKUP LANGUAGE (HTML) TAGS

The FrontPage Web site generation wizards and the FrontPage Web page editor make it possible to build great Web sites without knowing anything about HTML. However, some site developers (myself included) simply cannot be happy without looking at and "tweaking" the HTML tags FrontPage generates when you create or edit a Web page.

Hypertext markup language (more commonly known as HTML) is a series of *tags* which consist of a tag name enclosed by a less than (<) greater (>) character pair—often referred to as "angle brackets." When reviewing the HTML in the body section of a Web page, anything inside <angle brackets> is an HTML tag, and everything else is content which the visitor's browser is to display.

The first word inside the <angle brackets> determines the tag's type, and the remaining items (if any) inside the tag specify either the attributes of the tag or the attributes of the page content that follows the tag. For example, the <HR WIDTH = 50%> is a Horizontal Rule (i.e. a horizontal line) whose "width" attribute tells the browser to draw the horizontal rule (line) such that it is 50% as wide as its container. (A Web page element's container is the Web browser application window, Web page frame, table cell, or other Web page object which surrounds the element and limits its size.)

Some HTML tags such as <HR> (horizontal rule),
 (line break), <IMG> (image), and <META> (meta tag) stand alone, while others occur in pairs. The first tag in a pair of tags such as <B> (bold), <I> (italic), <P> (paragraph), <TABLE>, <TITLE>, and <BODY> mark the beginning of an effect or object. Conversely, the second tag in a pair tags such as </B> (cancel bold), </I> (cancel italic), </P> (end paragraph), </TABLE> (end table), </TITLE> (end title), and </BODY> (end body) cancels the effect or marks the end of the item's contents. Notice that each "ending" or "cancel" tag has the same identifier as its matching "opening" tag preceded by a slash (/).

Finally, HTML tags are case-insensitive. As such the tag <p align = left> is equivalent to <P ALIGN = LEFT>. Moreover, the number of spaces, tab characters, and line endings you use to separate attributes within a tag is irrelevant, and therefore ignored by a Web browser that reads the tag and follows its instructions to display the Web page content.

Nearly all Web pages contain the following HTML tags:

```
<HTML>
  <HEAD>
  </HEAD>
  <BODY>
  </BODY>
</HTML>
```

in which:

- <HTML> and </HTML> - mark the beginning and end of the Web page HTML.
- <HEAD> and </HEAD> - mark the beginning and end of the Web page header section whose contents are not displayed by the visitor's Web browser. A Web page header includes items such as the page

title, style sheets with formatting attribute definitions, scripts the visitor's browser is to run, and <META> tags which define such things as the Web page description, keywords, and theme.

- <BODY> and </BODY> - mark the beginning and end of the Web page content the visitor's Web browser is to display.

Note: *For a complete list of HTML tags, visit HTTP://WWW.HTMLIB.COM and download a copy of Stephen Le Hunte's HTMLib. The HTMLib documents all of the HTML tags supported by Internet Explorer, Netscape Navigator, and NCSA Mosaic.*

UNDERSTANDING HTML COLOR TAGS

In addition to the <FONT> tag (which, among other things, lets you select the color of a portion of the text on a Web page), you can specify the color of five Web page elements:

- <TEXT> - specifies the color of Web page text which is not set to a specific color using the <FONT> tag.
- <BGCOLOR> - specifies the background color of a Web page or a specific element such as a table cell on a Web page.
- <ALINK> - specifies the color of the current, active hyperlink.
- <LINK> - specifies the color of unvisited (unused) hyperlinks.
- <VLINK> - specifies the color of visited (used) hyperlinks.

When specifying a color, you can either use the name of one of the 16 standard colors (black, white, green, maroon, olive, navy, purple, gray, yellow, lime, aqua, fuchsia, silver, red, blue, and teal), or the combination of three pairs of hexadecimal numbers which specify the Red, Green, and Blue (RGB) values that make up the composite color. For example, to set the background color of a Web page to yellow, you could include the <BGCOLOR> tag and attribute:

```
<BGCOLOR = yellow>
```

after the <BODY> tag on a Web page, or you can set the Web page background color to yellow by expressing the "yellow" attribute using its RGB value as in:

```
<BGCOLOR = "#FFFF00">
```

Don't worry. There is no need to memorize the RGB color codes for the more than 16 million composite color values you can specify—FrontPage lets you select the color you want from a palette of colors and will translate your color selection into its RGB value.

For example, to set the text color on a Web page to blue, perform the following steps:

1. Right-click your mouse pointer anywhere in the Web page on the Page View Normal tab and select Page Properties from the pop-up menu. FrontPage, in turn, will display the Page Properties dialog box.
2. Click your mouse pointer on the Background tab to display the Web page background properties similar to that shown in Figure 71.

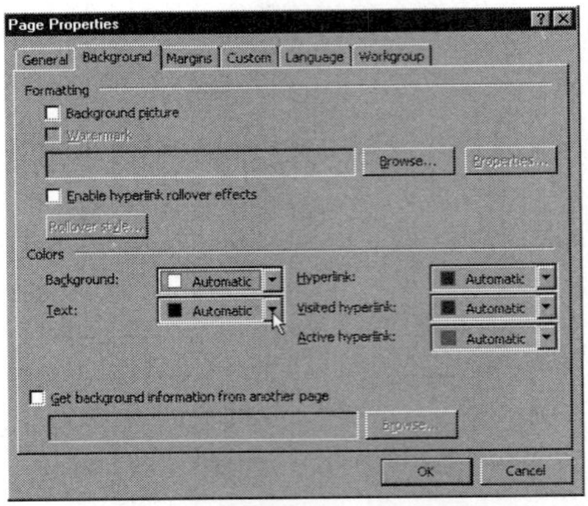

***Figure 71** The FrontPage Page Properties dialog box, Background tab.*

3. Click your mouse pointer on the drop-down list button to the right of the Text field and select the Web page background color you want from the drop-down display of color swatches. For the current project, click your mouse pointer on the blue swatch (second line, seventh swatch from the left). (In a future Tip, you will learn how to use the More Colors button on the drop-down display of color swatches to display the More Colors dialog box which lets you create custom colors.)
4. To exit the Page Properties dialog box, click your mouse pointer on the OK button.

After you complete Step 3, FrontPage will change the color of the text on the current Web page to the color you selected in Step 3 by setting attribute of the <TEXT> tag to the color's RGB value:

```
<TEXT = "#0000FF">
```

***Note:** In addition to the selecting the color of the Web page text (by adding a <TEXT> tag to the Web page HTML), you can also use the preceding procedure to set the color of the Web page background and unvisited, visited, and active hyperlinks. To set an element's color, simply click your* *mouse pointer on the drop-down list button to the right of the Background, Text, Hyperlink, Visited Hyperlink, or Active Hyperlink field in Step 3, and then on the color swatch of the color you want the element to be.*

UNDERSTANDING HTML PARAGRAPH STYLE TAGS

While *character* style tags (which you will learn about in the next Tip) set the characteristics of specific words (or perhaps characters) bracketed by style's begin/end tags, paragraph styles include tags which define comments, headings, horizontal lines, line breaks, lists, paragraphs, etc. The more commonly used paragraph style tags are:

- <!— —> - mark the beginning and end of a comment section (whose contents the Web browser are to ignore).
- **<ADDRESS>** and **</ADDRESS>** - mark the beginning and end of an address.
- **<BLOCKQUOTE>** and **</BLOCKQUOTE>** - mark the beginning and end of a paragraph the Web browser must indent from both the left and right margins
- **
** - tells the browser to display a line break—similar to pressing the SHIFT+ENTER key combination when editing the Web page text in Page View on the Normal tab.
- **<CENTER>** and **</CENTER>** - mark the beginning and end of text the Web browser is to center within its container.
- <COMMENT> and **</COMMENT>** - mark the beginning and end of a comment (which the Web browser is to ignore).
- <DL> and **</DL>** - mark the beginning and end of a definition list.
- <DD> - identifies the definition of the defined term (<DT>) that immediately precedes it.
- <DIV> and **</DIV>** - mark the beginning and end of a division (section) on a Web page. Each division can have its own alignment.
- <DT> - identifies a term to be defined (i.e. a defined term) in a definition list.
- <Hn> and **</Hn>** - (where n is a value 1 – 6, inclusive), mark the beginning and end of one of the six heading styles.
- <HR> - tells the browsers to draw a horizontal rule (i.e. a horizontal line) on the Web page.

- <LI> - identifies an item in an ordered (numbered) or unordered (bulleted) list
- <OL> and </OL> - mark the beginning and end of an ordered (numbered) list
- <P> and </P> - mark the beginning and end of a paragraph
- <PRE> and </PRE> - mark the beginning and end of formatted text
- <UL> and </UL> - mark the beginning and end of an unordered (bulleted) list

UNDERSTANDING HTML CHARACTER STYLE TAGS

Character style tags tell a Web browser how to display the words or characters enclosed between the pair of character style tags. The most commonly used character style tag pairs are:

- <B> and </B> - apply the bold character style to the enclosed characters
- <BIG> and </BIG> - display the enclosed characters one size larger than the standard (default) character size
- <CITE> and </CITE> - apply the "citation" logical character style to the enclosed characters
- <CODE> and </CODE> - apply the "code" logical character style to the enclosed characters. The typeface used for the code character style is normally one of the monospace (fixed-width) typefaces such as Courier.
- <DFN> and </DFN> - apply the "definition" logical character style to the enclosed characters. Definitions are normally written in italics.
- <EM> and </EM> - apply the "emphasis" logical character style to the enclosed characters. Emphasized characters are normally written in italics.
- <FONT> and </FONT> - apply the typeface, color, and size attributes specified along with the <FONT> tag to the enclosed characters.
- <I> and </I> - tells the browser to italicize the enclosed characters
- <KBD> and </KBD> - apply the "keyboard" logical character style. The typeface for the keyboard character style is normally one of the monospace (fixed-width) typefaces such as Courier.

- <S> and </S> - apply the strikethrough character style to the enclosed characters.
- <SAMP> and </SAMP> - apply the "sample" logical character style to the enclosed characters. The typeface for the sample character style is normally one of the monospace (fixed-width) typefaces such as Courier.
- <SMALL> and </SMALL> - display the enclosed characters one size smaller than the standard (default) character size.
- <STRONG> and </STRONG> - apply the "strong" logical character style to the enclosed characters. Strong characters are normally bold.
- _{and} - display the enclosed characters as a subscript (i.e. 1/2 of a line lower than the normal text).
- ^{and} - display the enclosed characters as a superscript (i.e.1/2 of a line above the normal text).
- <TT> and </TT> - display the enclosed text using the "typewriter text" character style. Typewriter text is normally written using one of the monospace (fixed-width) typefaces such as Courier.
- <U> and <U> - underlines the enclosed characters.

USING ESCAPE SEQUENCES TO DISPLAY SPECIAL CHARACTERS

One of the great things about FrontPage is that it is a What-You-See-Is-What-You-Get (WYSIWYG) Web page editor that lets you use the Page View Normal tab to create a Web page by simply typing the content you want to publish on the Web. If you look at the underlying HTML code that the Web server sends to the Web browser, you will find that most of the characters that make up the Web page content appear exactly as you typed them. There are however, a few keyboard characters that have a special meaning in HTML, and must therefore be encoded using *escape sequences.*

The angle brackets (<>) used to enclose HTML tags are actually greater than (<) and less than (>) symbols on your keyboard. Moreover, in HTML, the ampersand (&) is used to introduce an escape sequence. When you type one of these characters onto the Page View Normal tab, FrontPage automatically translates the "<", ">", or "&" character into the escape sequence that will tell the Web browser to display it.

- **less than** (<) – is represented as < or < in HTML.
- **greater than** (>) – is represented as > or > in HTML.

- **ampersand** (&) – is represented as & or & in HTML.

Notice that each of the escape sequences begins with an ampersand (&) and ends with a semicolon (;). Thus, the HTML code that displays the text: "This is a less than sign (<) and this is a greater than sign (>)" on the Web page reads:

```
This is a less than sign (&lt;) and this is a greater than sign
(&gt;)
```

on the Page View HTML tab.

Note: *Escape sequences, unlike other HTML tags, are case sensitive. As such, you cannot use < in place of < to represent the less than (<) symbol.*

To insert other special symbols such as the trade mark symbol (Ô), registered symbol (Ò), and copyright symbol (Ó) which are not found on standard keyboards, position your cursor where you want to insert the symbol, and then perform the following steps:

1. Select the Insert menu Symbol option. FrontPage, in turn, will display a Symbol dialog box similar to that shown in Figure 74 (you may have to scroll down a couple of lines to see the symbols shown).

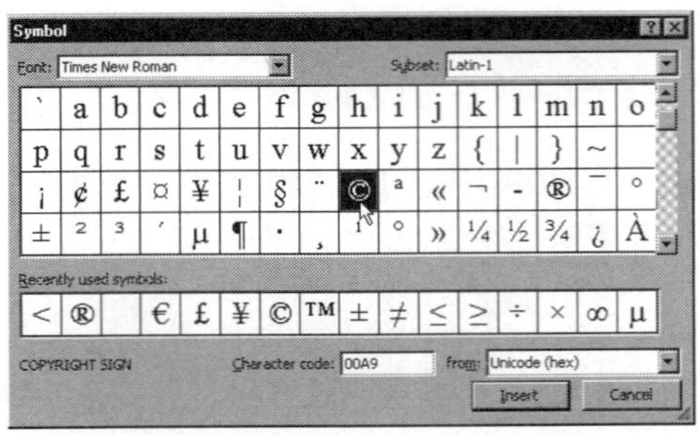

***Figure** 74 The FrontPage Symbol dialog box.*

2. Click your mouse pointer on the symbol you want to insert.
3. Click your mouse pointer on the INSERT button. FrontPage, in turn, will insert the symbol you selected in Step 2 at the insertion point on the current Web page, and changes the CANCEL button in the lower right-hand corner of the Symbol dialog box into a CLOSE button.
4. If you want to insert additional symbols, repeat Steps 2 and 3 until you have inserted all of the symbols you want.
5. Click your mouse pointer on the CLOSE button to exit the Symbol dialog box and return to the Page View Normal tab.

Note: *Like the greater than sign (>), less than sign (<), and ampersand (&), you can represent the trade mark symbol (™), registered symbol (®), and copyright symbol (©) as escape sequences on the HTML tab—instead of inserting them onto the Normal tab by selecting symbols from the Symbol dialog box.*

- **the trade mark symbol** (Ô) – can be written as ™ or ™ in HTML.
- **the registered symbol** (Ò) – can be written as ® or ® in HTML.
- **the copyright symbol** (Ó) – can be written as © or © in HTML.

UNDERSTANDING CASCADING STYLE SHEETS

A cascading style sheet (CSS) is a <STYLE></STYLE> section in the header (<HEAD></HEAD>) section of a Web page's HTML code which contains named sets of properties (styles) which you can later use as attributes in HTML tags in the Web page <BODY></BODY> section. For example, the <HEAD></HEAD> (header) section of the Web page HTML:

```
<html>
<head>
  <title>Web Page Title - Style Sheet</title>
  <style>
    h1.green {font-family: Arial black; font-weight: bold;
              color: green; font-size: 15}
    h1.red   {font-family: Arial black; font-weight: bold;
              color: red; font-size: 20}
    p.Courier    {font-family: Courier; font-size: 8}
    p.emphasized {font-family: impact; font-weight: bold;
                  color: red; font-size: 15}
  </style>
</head>

<body>
  <h1>Normal Heading 1 (24pt type)</h1>
  <h1 class=green>Green Heading 1 at 15pt type.</h1>
  <h1 class=red>Red Heading 1 with 20pt type.</h1>
  <p>Normal paragraph text (12pt type).</p>
  <p class=Courier>Paragraph using the Courier style (8pt).</
p>
  <p class=emphasized>paragraph using the emphasized style
(15pt).</p>
```

```
</body>

</html>
```

defines a "green" and "red" *class* for the <H1> (Heading 1) tag and a "Courier" and "emphasized" *class* for the <P> (paragraph tag). You can then use the classes as attributes for the tags in the <BODY></BODY> (content) section of the Web page HTML. For example, the Internet Explorer will display the Web page defined the preceding HTML code as shown in Figure 75.

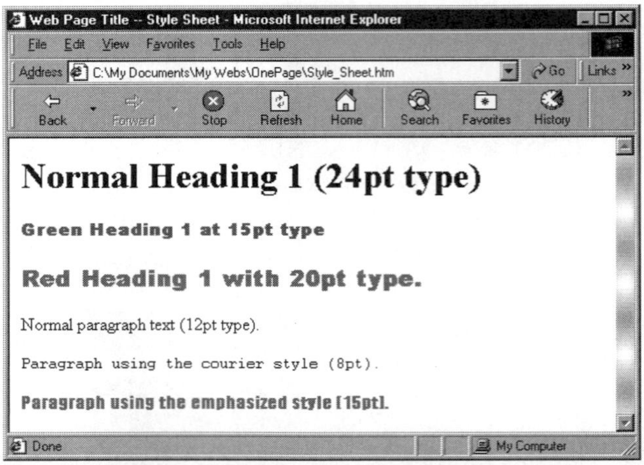

Figure 75 The Internet Explorer displaying a Web page whose text is formatted using a cascading style sheet (CSS).

You will learn all about cascading style sheets in future Tips. For now the important thing to understand is that you define the styles you want to use in the <HEAD></HEAD> (header) section of a Web page. Then, you use the styles you defined as attributes for tags in the <BODY></BODY> (content) section of the Web page to specify the appearance of the text governed by the HTML tag.

UNDERSTANDING THE <IMG> (IMAGE) TAG USED TO INSERT A PICTURE ON A WEB PAGE

If you have ever inserted a picture into a word processor document, you already know how to tell FrontPage to place a picture onto a Web page. Simply click your mouse pointer where you want to insert the image on the page. Then, select the Insert menu Picture option and click your mouse pointer on From File. FrontPage, in turn, will prompt you for the pathname of the picture you want to place onto the Web page by displaying the Picture dialog box. After you enter the full pathname of the picture into the File name field, and click your mouse pointer on the INSERT button, FrontPage will insert the picture on your Web page.

When you insert a picture into a word processor document, the program places a copy of the picture into the document. However, when you tell FrontPage to insert a picture onto a Web page, the program places an <IMG> (image) tag (and not a copy of the picture itself) in the Web page HTML code. The attributes of the <IMG> tag tell the Web browser where to find the picture at its current location on disk or out on the Web and how the browser is to display the picture relative to other elements (such as text) on the Web page.

For example, the <IMG> tag in the HTML:

```
<html>
<head><title>Betsy Ross</title></head>
<body>
<p>Betsy Ross is said to have sewn the first American Flag.

<img border="0" src="../images/betsy2.gif"
     alt="Picture of Betsy Ross" width="167" height="183">

</p>
<p>Click on the flag to see a gallery of flag pictures.<br>
Click on Betsy for the story of how she came to sew the
American Flag.<br>
Click on the room for a tour of Betsy's Home.</p>
</body>
</html>
```

tells a Web browser to display an "inserted" graphics image similar to that shown on the Normal tab of FrontPage Page View shown in Figure 76.

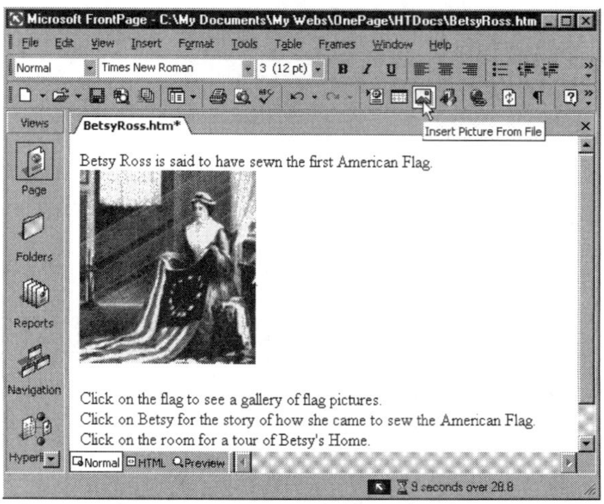

Figure 76 Web page with a graphic image inserted after the first line of text.

The attributes most commonly used in an <IMG> (image) tag are:

- **align** – tells the browser to position text in the same paragraph as the image at the TOP, MIDDLE, BOTTOM of the image, or to position the image to the LEFT or RIGHT of the text.
- **alt** – alternative text the browser is to display in the placeholder for the image if it cannot display the image itself.
- **border** – the number of pixels (often blank) to be drawn around the image.
- **height** – the height of the image in pixels.
- **hspace** – the number of pixels of blank space to leave on the left and right of the image.
- **src** – the file and path name (relative to the file location of the Web page itself) or the Web address (URL) at which the browser can find the image it is to display.
- **vspace** – the number of pixels of blank space to leave at the top and bottom of the image.
- **width** – the width of the image in pixels.

You will learn how to use a table to position pictures at specific locations on a Web page later in this book. For now, the important thing to understand is that the <IMG> (image) tag lets you insert a picture (a graphic image) on a Web page by telling the browser where to find the file.

UNDERSTANDING HTML TAGS USED TO DEFINE HYPERLINKS AND BOOKMARKS

A hyperlink is an element on a Web page on which you can click your mouse pointer to display the Web page at the address associated with the hyperlink, send an e-mail message, or download the file—depending on the attributes of the hyperlink's <A></A> (anchor) tag. You can anchor a hyperlink to Web page text, a graphic image, or (as you will learn in the next Tip), a portion of a graphic image.

For example, if you were to review the HTML for the Web page shown in Figure 77, you would see that each of the hyperlinks is actually an <A></A> (anchor) tag which is associated with either text or a graphic image on the page.

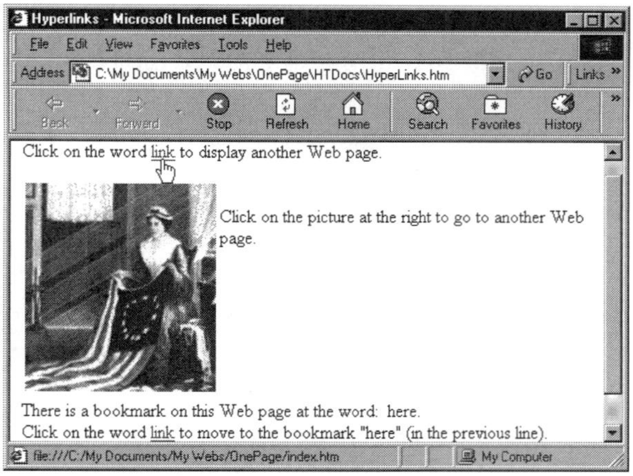

***Figure** 77 Web page with hyperlinks and a bookmark.*

The HTML for the first line in the Web page shown in Figure 77 is:

```
<p>Click on the word <a href="../index.htm">link</a> to display
another Web page.</p>
```

Notice that the text the Web browser displays as the *hyperlink*, the word "link" in the current example, is enclosed by the hyperlink's <A></A> (anchor) tags. The HREF attribute of the <A> (anchor) tag tells the browser what file (or Web page) to display when the visitor clicks the mouse pointer on the hyperlink text (which follows the tag).

If the hyperlink is a picture (instead of one or more letters or words of text), the <A> tag still uses the HREF attribute to tell the browser which Web page (or file) to display when the visitor clicks the mouse pointer on the hyperlink. However, instead of enclosing text between the <A></A> (anchor) tags, the anchor tags for a hyperlink based on a graphic image surround the <IMG> (image) tag of the picture on which the visitor is to click the mouse pointer to activate the hyperlink. For example, the HTML for the hyperlink based on the picture of Betsy Ross in Figure 77 is:

```
<p><a href="http://www.ushistory.org/betsy">
      <img border="0" src="../images/betsy2.gif"
           alt="Picture of Betsy Ross" align="left"
           width="167" height="183">
   </a></p>
```

When you use a hyperlink to reference a Web page either on the current Web site or on another Web site on the Internet, the Web browser will display Web page content starting at the top of the page to be displayed. Sometimes, however, you may want to use a hyperlink to jump to a location within a Web page rather than the top of the page. Suppose, for example, that you have a Web page with a list of terms at the top of the page followed by the definition of each of the terms on the remainder of the page. If you create an HTML *bookmark* at each definition and a hyperlink from each term (at the top of the page) to the bookmark associated with the term's definition further down in the body of the page. A person could display the Web page in a Web browser and click the mouse pointer on a term to jump to the definition of the term.

The HTML for the bookmark at the word "here" in the third sentence of the Web page shown in Figure 77 is:

```
<p>There is a bookmark on this Web page at the word:  <a
name="here">here</a>.<br>
```

Notice that the <A> (anchor) tag for the bookmark has a NAME attribute ("here" in the current example, and no HREF attribute. The HTML for a hyperlink which tells the browser to "jump" to the bookmark, such as the HTML for the fourth sentence in Figure 77:

```
Click on the word <a href="#here"\">link</a> to move to the
bookmark &quot;here&quot; (in the previous line).<br>
```

sets the value of its HREF attribute to the value of the bookmark's NAME attribute. The pound (#) sign in front of the bookmark's name (in the HREF attribute) tells the Web browser that it is to find a bookmark named "here" in the current Web page. If the value of the HREF attribute were set to "here" [without the leading pound (#) sign], the Web browser would look for a file named "here" in the same directory as the current Web page.

You will learn all about creating bookmarks and hyperlinks that reference images, text, files, e-mail addresses and book marks in future Tips. For now, the important things to know are that a hyperlink in HTML is formed by enclosing text or an <IMG> tag within <A></A> (anchor) tags, and the attributes of the <A> (anchor) tag are:

- **href** – identifies the destination universal resource locator (URL) which can be a Web address, bookmark, or pathname.
- **name** – used to provide a unique name for the <A> (anchor) tag when it is used as a bookmark vs. a hyperlink.
- **frame** – identifies a specific Web page frame to display when the hyperlinks destination is a Web page with frames. (You will learn all about Web page frames later in this book.)
- **title** – the text the browser is to display on its status line as the visitor moves the mouse pointer over the hyperlink. If the hyperlink has not TITLE attribute, the Web browser will display the value of the HREF attribute (the hyperlink's URL) on its status line.

UNDERSTANDING THE HTML USED TO DEFINE AN IMAGE MAP

As mentioned in the previous Tip, you can anchor a hyperlink either on an entire image or on a portion of an image. If you want to let the Web site visitor click the mouse pointer anywhere on a graphic image to activate a single hyperlink, anchor the hyperlink on the entire image. If, on the other hand, you want to use a single graphic image for multiple hyperlinks, you must establish *hot spots* on the picture, and then anchor each hyperlink to a different hot spot (or area).

For example, if you want to let the Web site visitor click the mouse pointer anywhere on the first flag on the Web page shown in Figure 78 to access the WWW.USFLAG.ORG Web site, use HTML such as:

```
<a href="http://www.usflag.org">
   <img border="0" src="flaganim.gif" width="100"
        height="55"></a>
```

to anchor the hyperlink to the entire image.

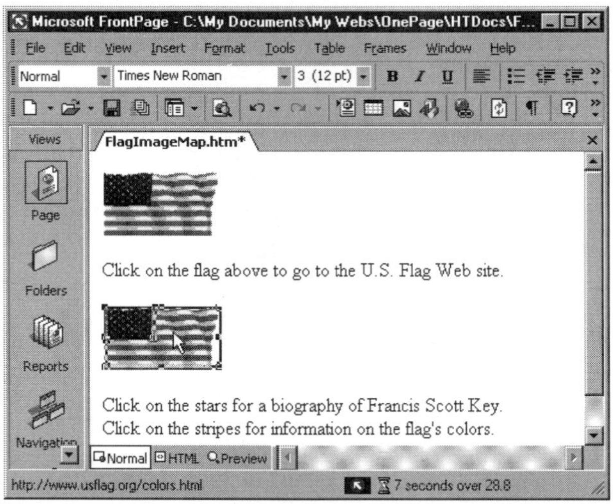

Figure 78 Web page with a graphic image which anchors a single hyperlink and a second picture showing the hot spots used to anchor multiple hyperlinks.

If, on the other hand, you want to let the visitor click the mouse pointer on the stars to display one Web page and on the stripes to display another, you must enclose your hyperlink definitions within <MAP></MAP> (image map) tags. Instead of the normal <A> (anchor) tag, each hyperlink in a <MAP> tag is specified using an <AREA> tag which contains the coordinates of the hot spot (or area) on the picture to which the hyperlink is anchored. For example, the HTML for the two hyperlinks on the second flag in Figure 78 is:

```
<map name="FPMap0">
   <area href="http://www.usflag.org/francis.scott.key.html"
         shape="rect" coords="3, 2, 43, 31">
   <area href="http://www.usflag.org/colors.html"
         shape="polygon" coords="45, 3, 99, 3, 99, 51, 4, 52,
4, 30, 43, 29"></map>

<img border="0" src="flaganim.gif" ismap usemap="#FPMap0"
     width="100" height="55"></p>
```

The hot spot for the first hyperlink (on the flag's stars) is a rectangle (SHAPE="RECT") with point coordinates as specified by the numbers assigned to the COORDS attribute of the <AREA> tag. Similarly, the hot spot for the second hyperlink (on the flag's stripes) is a polygon (SHAPE="POLYGON") with point coordinates as specified by the numbers assigned to the COORDS attribute in its <AREA> tag. Do not worry about how the coordinates are generated. As you will learn in a future Tip on creating hot spots for hyperlinks on a picture, FrontPage provides a toolbar with tools that let you "draw" the hot spot areas on the graphic image and will generate the HTML for the <AREA> tag (including its coordinates) for you.

Thus, the HTML tags and attributes associate with anchoring multiple hyperlinks to hot spots on a single graphic image are:

- **<area>** – gives the definition (including the associated hyperlink) for an image map (a hot spot) on a graphics image.
- **coords** – specifies the (x,y) coordinates needed to define the hot spot (area) on the picture in terms of image pixels for each point in the shape. (FrontPage will generate the necessary coordinates for the shape you draw on the graphic image.)
- **ismap** – specifies that the image [specified in the <IMG> (image) tag] has an image map.
- **<map></map>** - mark the beginning and end of an image map.
- **name** – specifies the name of the image map.
- **shape** – identifies the shape of the hot spot (the area to which the hyperlink is anchored).

- **usemap** – specifies the name of the image map that maps the hyperlink hot spots on the graphic image.

UNDERSTANDING THE UNIFORM RESOURCE LOCATOR (URL)

When you read about hyperlinks in the preceding Tips, you learned that each hyperlink has a target (specified by the HREF attribute) encoded as a *uniform resource locator* (URL). A URL is an address that specifies the protocol (such as FILE:, HTTP, FTP) and the location of a file, Web page, e-mail address, etc. For example, if the target of a hyperlink is the program file named "WINJPEG.EXE" in the WinJpg folder on the C: drive, the target's URL is:

```
file://C:/WinJpg/WINJPEG.EXE
```

where:

- **file://** - is the protocol.
- **/C:/WinJpg/** - is the pathname.
- **WINJPEG.EXE** – is the filename.

Similarly, if the target of a hyperlink is a Web page, the target's URL will include the name of the server in addition to the protocol, path, and filename to display. For example, the URL for the Delmar/Thomson Learning Catalog Web page is:

```
http://www.delmar.com/products/shop.html
```

where:

- **http://** - is the protocol.
- **www.delmar.com** - is the Web server.
- **/products/** – is the pathname of the Web page on the Web site.
- **shop.html** – is the filename.

Thus, a URL is nothing more than an extended filename, since it includes both the full pathname of the hyperlink's target file and the protocol (or method for accessing the file). (If you think about it, the name of the Web server could actually be considered to be part the target's *full* pathname (or location).)

UNDERSTANDING HTML TAGS USED TO CREATE TABLES

When authoring Web pages you will use tables for one of two purposes. First, as the name implies, you can use a *table* to display facts and figures in tabular form such, as shown by the table at the top of the Web page shown in Figure 80.

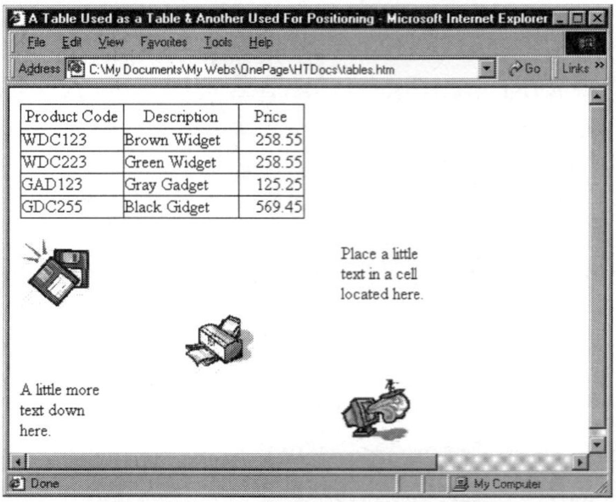

Figure 80 *Web page with a visible table at the top of the page and an "invisible" table with 0 width borders at the bottom of the page.*

The second use for a table is to position items on a Web page, as shown by the "invisible" table that holds the five items (three clip art images and two paragraphs of text) at the bottom of the Web page in Figure 80. Like the table at the top of the Web page, the table at the bottom of the page consists of a grid of cells in columns and rows (three rows of five columns each, to be exact). However, unlike the table at the top of the page, the table at the bottom has its cell border width set to 0 pixels (while each cell in the table at the top of the page has a black border with a 1 pixel width).

One of the first challenges you will encounter when you create your first real-life Web page with graphics and text is that HTML tags have no positioning attributes. As such, you cannot tell a browser to place text, images, or other objects at specific (x,y) coordinates on the page. However, when you visit Web sites, you see graphics (such as my personal favorites: banner ads) placed at strategic locations on the page—where they are guaranteed to catch your eye.

Web authors use tables with 0 width (hence invisible) borders (such as the one at the bottom of Figure 80) to establish a grid on the Web page. By adjusting the height and width of the cells in a table, you can establish a grid of cells that lets you place graphics, text, and other page content at specific locations. Instead of specifying an object's (x,y) coordinates (which

HTML does not yet support), you place the object in a table cell which happens (by design) to be at the location on the Web page where you want the item displayed by the visitor's Web browser.

Although the HTML for a table looks rather complex, FrontPage makes placing one or more tables on a Web page a simple process. Rather than forcing you to type the HTML tags and attributes that describe the table you want, FrontPage lets you turn your mouse pointer into a "pen" which you use to draw the table on the Web page. Then, as you will learn in future Tips, FrontPage lets you adjust the number of columns and cells in the table by using either your mouse pointer or by making a short a sequence of menu selections and dialog box entries.

The important thing to understand now, is that tables serve two functions—to display information in a tabular form and to provide a grid you can use to position objects at specific locations on a Web page. Whether you use a table as a table or as a positioning grid, the HTML is basically the same. For example, the HTML for the table at the top of Figure 80 is:

```
<table border="1" cellpadding="0" cellspacing="0"
   style="border-collapse: collapse" bordercolor="#111111"
   width="265" height="108" id="AutoNumber1">
   <tr>
      <td width="94" height="20" align="center">Product Code</
td>
      <td width="105" height=20" align="center">Description
</td>
      <td width="59" height="20" align="center">Price</td>
   </tr>
   <tr>
      <td width="94" height="7">WDC123</td>
      <td width="105" height="7">Brown Widget</td>
      <td width="59" height="7" align="right">258.55</td>
   </tr>
   <tr>
      <td width="94" height="7">WDC223</td>
      <td width="105" height="7">Green Widget</td>
      <td width="59" height="7" align="right">258.55</td>
   </tr>
   <tr>
      <td width="94" height="7">GAD123</td>
      <td width="105" height="7">Gray Gadget </td>
      <td width="59" height="7" align="right">125.25</td>
   </tr>
   <tr>
```

```
    <td width="94" height="7">GDC255</td>
    <td width="105" height="7">Black Gidget </td>
    <td width="59" height="7" align="right">569.45</td>
  </tr>
</table>
```

and the HTML for the table at the bottom of the page contains the same HTML tags (albeit more of them) and has its BORDER attribute set to "0".

The most commonly use table tags and attributes are:

- **align** – has one of several meanings, depending on the tag in which the attribute appears:
  - when used as an attribute of the <TABLE> tag, ALIGN specifies whether the browser is to place the table flush with LEFT margin, flush with the RIGHT margin, or CENTER it between the left and right margins of the Web page
  - when used as an attribute of the <TR> (table row) tag, ALIGN specifies whether the text in each of the cells in a specific row of cells is to be aligned LEFT, RIGHT, or CENTER of each cell's vertical borders;
  - when used as an attribute of the <TD> (table data/cell) tag, ALIGN specifies whether the text in a specific cell is to be aligned LEFT, RIGHT, or CENTER of the cell's vertical borders; and
  - when used as an attribute of the <CAPTION> tag, ALIGN specifies whether the table's caption (its title) is to be aligned LEFT, RIGHT, or centered between the table's left and right hand margins.
- **background** – has one of several meanings, depending on the tag in which the attribute appears:
  - when specified as an attribute in the <TABLE> tag, BACKGROUND specifies the uniform resource locator (URL) of a graphic image to be used as the background for the table;
  - when specified as an attribute in a <TR> (table row) tag, BACKGROUND specifies the URL of the image to be used as the background for all of the cells in a specific row in the table; and
  - when specified as an attribute in a <TD> (table data/cell) tag, BACKGROUND specifies the URL of the image to be used as the background for a specific cell.

- **bgcolor** – has one of several meanings, depending on the tag in which the attribute appears:
    - when used as an attribute in the <TABLE> tag, BGCOLOR specifies the background color for all of the cells in the table;
    - when used as an attribute in a <TR> (table row) tag, BGCOLOR specifies the background color for all of the cells in a specific row in the table; and
    - when used as an attribute in a <TD> (table data/cell) tag, BGCOLOR specifies the background color of a specific cell in the table.
- **border** – specifies the width, in pixels, of the border to be drawn around all of the cells in the table.
- **bordercolor** – has one of several meanings, depending on the tag in which the attribute appears:
    - when used as an attribute in the <TABLE> tag, BORDERCOLOR specifies the color of the border to be drawn around all of the cells in the table;
    - when used as an attribute in the <TR> (table row) tag, BORDERCOLOR specifies the color of the border to be drawn around all of the cells in a specific row in the table; and
    - when used as an attribute in the <TD> (table data/cell) tag, BORDERCOLOR specifies the color of the border to be drawn around a specific cell.
- **bordercolordark** – applicable only to tables with 3-D borders.
    - When used as an attribute in a <TABLE> tag, BORDERCOLORDARK specifies the color of the "dark" (shadowed) portion of all cell borders in the table;
    - when used as an attribute in a <TR> (table row) tag, BORDERCOLORDARK specifies the color of the "dark" portion of the border for a specific row of cells in the table; and
    - when used as an attribute in a <TD> (table data/cell) tag, BORDERCOLORDARK specifies the color of the "dark" portion of the border for a specific cell.
- **bordercolorlight** – applicable only to tables with 3-D borders.
    - When used as an attribute in a <TABLE> tag, BORDERCOLORLIGHT specifies the color of the "light" (non-shadowed) portion of all cell borders in the table;

  - o when used as an attribute in a <TR> (table row) tag, BORDERCOLORLIGHT specifies the color of the "light" portion of the border for a specific row of cells in the table; and
  - o when used as an attribute in a <TD> (table data/cell) tag, BORDERCOLORLIGHT specifies the color of the "light" portion of the border for a specific cell.

- **<caption></caption>** - mark the beginning and end of a table's caption (title).

- **cellpadding** – specifies the amount of blank space, in pixels, to be left between the borders (the walls) of each cell and the contents within the cell.

- **cellspacing** – specifies the amount of blank space, in pixels, to be left between the cells in a table.

- **cols** – specifies the number of columns in a table.

- **colspan** – when specified as an attribute of the <TD> (table data/cell) tag, COLSPAN specifies the number of columns in the table a cell should span.

- **height** – has one of several meanings, depending on the tag in which the attribute appears:

  - o when used as an attribute in the <TABLE> tag, HEIGHT specifies the height of a table either in pixels or as a percentage of the area in the container in which the table is displayed;
  - o when used as an attribute in the <TR> (table row) tag, HEIGHT specifies the height of all of the cells in a specific row of the table in either pixels or as a percentage of the total height of the table's container; and
  - o when used as an attribute in the <TD> (table data/cell) tag, HEIGHT specifies the height of a specific cell in the table in either pixels or as a percentage of the total height of the table's container.

- **nowrap** – when specified as an attribute of the <TD> (table data/cell) tag), NOWRAP specifies that the text in the cell cannot be wrapped onto the net line in the cell at the right-hand margin, thus forcing the width of the cell to expand such that it will accommodate the longest line of text.

- **rowspan** – when specified as an attribute of the <TD> (table data/ cell) tag), ROWSPAN specifies the number of rows in the table a cell should span.

- **style** – has one of several meanings, depending on the tag in which the attribute appears:
    - o when used as an attribute in the <TABLE> tag, STYLE specifies a style sheet to use to format the text content of all cells in the table;
    - o when used as an attribute in the <TR> (table row) tag, STYLE specifies the style sheet to use to format the contents of each of the cells in a specific row in the table; and
    - o when used as an attribute in the <TD> (table data/cell) tag, STYLE specifies the style sheet to use to format the contents of a specific cell in the table.
- **<table></table>** - mark the beginning and end of a table definition.
- **<td></td>** - mark the beginning and end of each cell in the table.
- **<tr></tr>** - mark the beginning and end of a row of cells in a table.
- **valign** – has one of several meanings, depending on the tag in which the attribute appears:
    - o when used as an attribute of the <TABLE> tag, VALIGN specifies whether table's caption (i.e. its title) is to appear at the TOP or at the BOTTOM of the table;
    - o when used as an attribute of the <TR> (table row) tag, VALIGN specifies whether the text in each of the cells in a specific row of cells is to be aligned with the TOP, BASELINE, BOTTOM, or CENTER between the horizontal borders of each cell; ; and
    - o when used as an attribute of the <TD> (table data/cell) tag, VALIGN specifies whether the text in a specific cell is to be aligned with the TOP, BASELINE, BOTTOM, or CENTER between the cell's horizontal borders.
- **width** – has one of several meanings, depending on the tag in which the attribute appears:
    - o when used as an attribute in the <TABLE> tag, WIDTH specifies the width of a table either in pixels or as a percentage of the area in the container in which the table is displayed; and
    - o when used as an attribute in the <TD> (table data/cell) tag, WIDTH specifies the width of a specific cell in the table in either pixels or as a percentage of the total width of the table's container.

UNDERSTANDING HTML TAGS USED TO DEFINE FORMS

Adding forms to Web pages lets you establish two-way communications with your Web site's visitors. While Web page graphics and text let you send information, a form's fields give you a way to retrieve data from your Web site visitors. The HTML used to implement a form describes the length of each field and the type of data the visitor is to enter into it. In addition to data entry fields, every form includes a button on which the site visitor clicks the mouse pointer to send the form's data to the Web server for processing.

At first glance, the HTML for a form looks complex, and the process of typing the descriptions and default values for its fields and menu selections appears tedious at best. However, FrontPage makes the forms creation process "quick and painless" by letting you place labels, fields, radio buttons, check books, drop-down list buttons, and push buttons on a form by selecting the items you want from menus displayed when you select the Insert menu Forms option.

For example, Figure 81 shows a form created by making selections from the menu displayed by the Insert menu Form option. (You can find the Web page shown in Figure 81 on the companion CD as **D:\MyWebs\OnePage\HTDocs\InfoRequest.htm**—substitute the drive letter of your CD ROM drive for "D".)

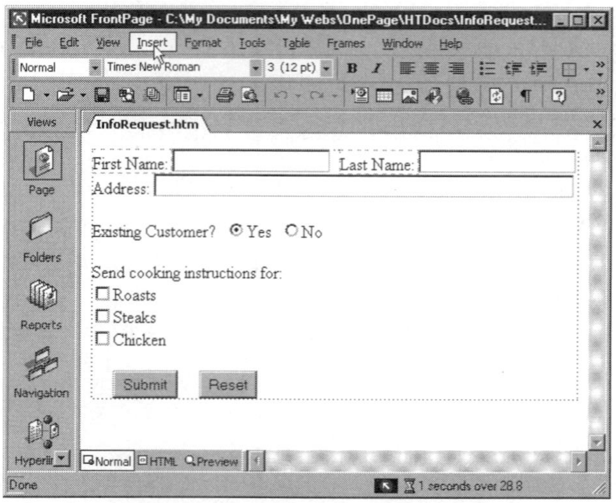

Figure 81 Page view of a form created using the FrontPage Insert menu Form option.

FrontPage, in turn, generated the form's HTML:

```
<html>
  <head><title>Information Request</title></head>
  <body>
    <form method="POST"
      action="—WEBBOT-SELF—" onSubmit=""><!—webbot
      bot="SaveResults" startspan u-
        file="../_private/form_results.csv"
        s-format="TEXT/CSV" s-label-fields="TRUE" —>
        <input TYPE="hidden" NAME="VTI-GROUP" VALUE="0">
        <!—webbot
      bot="SaveResults" endspan —><p>
      <label for="fp1">First Name: </label>
      <input type="text" name="fname" size="20"
        id="fp1"> 
      <label for="fp2">Last Name: </label>
      <input type="text" name="lname" size="20"
        id="fp2"><br>
      Address: <input type="text" name="address"
        size="55"><br><br>
      Existing Customer? 
      <input type="radio" value="V3" checked
        name="R1">Yes 
      <input type="radio" name="R1" value="V2">No<br><br>
      Send cooking instructions for: <br>
      <input type="checkbox" name="C1" value="ON">Roasts<br>
      <input type="checkbox" name="C2" value="ON">Steaks<br>
      <input type="checkbox" name="C3"
        value="ON">Chicken<br><br>
           <input type="submit"
        value="Submit" name="B1">    
      <input type="reset" value="Reset" name="B2"></p>
    </form>
  </body>
</html>
```

In future Tips, you will learn all about creating forms and processing data entered into the forms. For now, the two things to understand are that a form gives you a way to retrieve data from a Web site visitor, and that the elements on a form are described using the HTML tags and attributes.

The tags and attributes commonly used on a forms page are:

- **<button></button>** - mark the beginning and end of a push button definition.
- **<fieldset></fieldset>** - mark the beginning and end of a set of fields.
- **<form></form>** - mark the beginning and end of a form.
- **align** – specifies the position of the (text) label on a field of type "image."
- **checked** – specifies whether a field of type "checkbox" or "radio" defaults to selected (TRUE) or unselected (FALSE).
- **cols** – specifies the number of columns in a text area.
- **hidden** – specifies that a form field is not to be displayed but its contents are to be sent to the server when the form is submitted.
- **<input>** - identifies the beginning of an input field.
- **name** – identifies the name of a field or menu selection.
- **maxlength** – specifies the maximum number of characters a site visitor can enter into a text field.
- **multiple** – indicates that multiple items (options) can be selected from a drop-down list (menu).
- **<option></option>** - mark the beginning and end of a menu item in a drop-down list (menu) box.
- **rows** – specifies the number of rows of text to be displayed in a text area.
- **<select></select>** - mark the beginning and end of a drop-down list (menu) box.
- **selected** – specifies that a drop-down list (menu) item is initially selected.
- **size** – specifies the width, in characters, of an input field or the number of rows displayed at once on a drop-down list (menu).
- **src** – specifies the URL of the picture for an input field of type "image."
- **<textarea></textarea>** - mark the beginning and end of a textbox.
- **<value>** - specifies the default value for a textbox, input field, or drop-down list (menu) item.
- **type** – specifies the input field's type as "checkbox", "file", "hidden", "image", "password", "radio", "reset", "submit", or "text."

UNDERSTANDING HTML TAGS USED TO SETUP PAGE FRAMES

HTML frames let you setup independently scrollable areas on a Web page. In a Web browser an HTML frame functions like a pane in a Windows application. While <BODY></BODY> tags enclose the content of a Web page without frames, <FRAMESET></FRAMESET> tags enclose HTML for each set of vertical and/or horizontal frames (i.e. the framesets) on the home page the browser is to display.

For example, Figure 82 shows a home page with four frames: Top, Bottom, Contents, and Main.

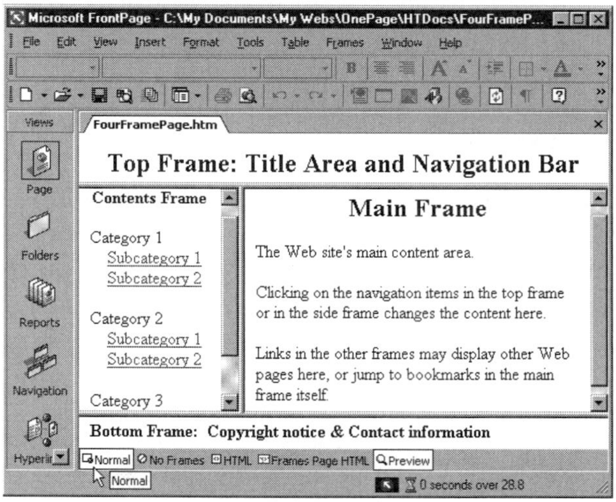

Figure 82 Page view of a Web page with four frames.

The HTML that defines the frames page for the Web page shown in Figure 82 is:

```
<html>
  <head><title>Web Page With Four Frames</title></head>
  <frameset rows="48,*,31">
    <frame name="top" scrolling="no" noresize
         target="contents" src="FourFrameWeb_Top_Frame.htm">
    <frameset cols="150,*">
      <frame name="contents" target="main"
             src="FourFrameWeb_Contents_Frame.htm">
      <frame name="main" src="FourFrameWeb_Main_Frame.htm">
    </frameset>
    <frame name="bottom" scrolling="no" noresize
      target="contents" src="FourFrameWeb_Bottom_Frame.htm">
```

```
    <noframes>
      <body>
        <p>This page uses frames, but your browser doesn't
support them.</p>
      </body>
    </noframes>
  </frameset>
</html>
```

Each <FRAME> tag enclosed within <FRAMESET></FRAMESET> tags, identifies the name of the frame and specifies the Web page the browser is to display in the frame. As shown in the HTML for the frames page in the current example, a well designed frames page includes a <NOFRAME></NOFRAME> section with a <BODY></BODY> section that provides content for browsers that cannot handle frames to display. (Often the <NOFRAMES></NOFRAME> content consists of a simple message such as: "This page uses frames, but your browser doesn't support them.")

As you will learn in future Tips, FrontPage lets you create Web sites with page frames by selecting the layout of the frames page from the examples shown on the Frames Pages tab of the Page Templates dialog box. (To display the Page Templates dialog box, select the File menu New option, click your mouse pointer on Page or Web, and then select Page Templates from the New Page or Web menu.) After you select the frames page style you want, FrontPage will generate the HTML for the frames page and prompt you to for the Web page to be displayed in each frame or let you create new Web page content for it.

The tags and attributes commonly used on the frames page are:

- **<frame></frame>** - marks the beginning end of a frame on the frames page.
- **<frameset></frameset>** - marks the beginning end of a set of vertical and/or a set of horizontal frames.
- **bordercolor** – has one of two possible meanings, depending on the tag in which the attribute appears:
    - when used as an attribute in the <FRAMESET> tag, BORDERCOLOR specifies the color of the border around all of the frames in a set of vertical or horizontal frames in the frameset; and
    - when used as an attribute in a <FRAME> tag, BORDERCOLOR specifies the color of the border around an individual frame.
- **cols** – specifies the number of vertical frames (columns) in the frameset.

- **frameborder** – has one of two possible meanings, depending on the tag in which the attribute appears:
    - when used as an attribute in the <FRAMESET> tag, FRAMEBORDER specifies whether or not the browser is to draw a border around all of the frames in the set of vertical or horizontal frames in the frameset;
    - when used as an attribute in a <FRAME> tag, FRAMEBORDER specifies whether or not the browser is to draw a frame around a specific frame. FRAMEBORDER="yes" or FRAMEBORDER="1" tells the browser to draw a border; FRAMEBORDER="no" or FRAMEBORDER="0" tells the browser that there is to be no border.
- **framespacing** – specifies the amount of blank space, in pixels, the browser is to insert between frames.
- **<iframe></iframe>** - marks the beginning and end of the specification for a "floating" frame. A *floating* frame is a scrollable area within a Web page other than the frames page, around which text may flow as it does around a graphic image inserted on the page.
- **marginheight** – specifies the amount of blank space, in pixels, the browser is to lave between the Web page content and the top and bottom margins in a frame.
- **marginwidth** – specifies the amount of blank space, in pixels, the browser is to leave between the Web page content and the left and right margins in a frame.
- **name** – identifies the name of a frame so that the frame can be referred to by TARGET attributes.
- **<noframes></noframes>** - marks the beginning and end of the HTML to be displayed by browsers without the ability to work with frames. The HTML in the <NOFRAMES></NOFRAMES> section of the Web page is ignored by browsers that are able to display frames.
- **noresize** – prevents the user from changing the size of the frame when displayed by the Web browser.
- **rows** – specifies the number of horizontal frames (rows) in the frameset.
- **src** – identifies the filename of the Web page to be displayed in either the current frame being defined or its target frame.
- **scrolling** – specifies whether or not the frame is to display scrollbars that let the visitor scroll the contents of the Web page in a frame, if the

Web page is too large to fit into the frame all at once. The possible values for the SCROLLING attribute are: "no", "yes", and "auto". The *automatic* (SCROLLING="auto") display of scroll bars when the Web page content does not fit in the frame is the default.

- **target** – specifies the NAME of the frame in which the browser is to display the Web page specified as the URL value of the SRC attribute SRC that follows the TARGET=:"<name>" specification in the <FRAME> tag.

UNDERSTANDING HTML TAGS USED TO ADD MULTIMEDIA ELEMENTS TO A WEB PAGE

A *multimedia* element is an audio file, video clip, or other animation displayed on a Web page. You can either offer the multimedia file for download and display on the visitor's computer, or you can place the multimedia element (inline) within the HTML code and have it start automatically when the visitor's browser retrieves the Web page or moves the mouse pointer across the element.

For example, to have a visitor's browser play a sound file in the background when it retrieves the Web page, perform the following steps:

1. Right-click your mouse pointer on a blank area of the Web page on the Page view Normal tab, and select Page Properties from the pop-up menu. FrontPage, in turn, will display a Page Properties dialog box similar to that shown in Figure 83.

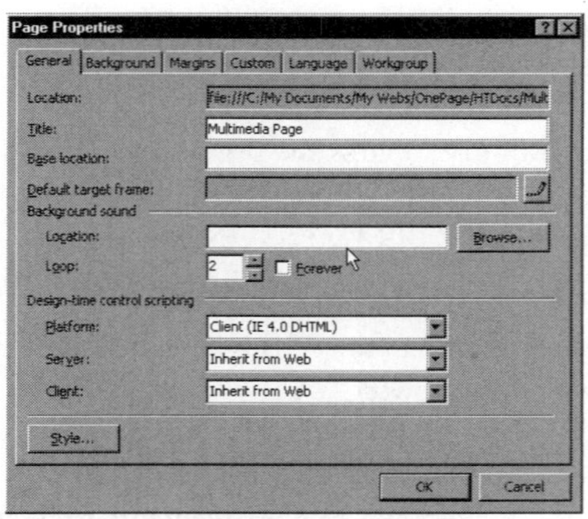

Figure 83 The FrontPage Page Properties, General tab.

2. Enter the pathname of the sound file you want the browser to play into the Location field on the General tab of the Page Properties dialog box. The contents of the Location field shown in Figure 83 specify the Web browser is to play the MIDI (music) file: "america.mid" which is located in the in the "../multimedia/" folder. (You can find the file america.mid on the companion CD as **D:\MyWebs\OnePage\MultiMedia\amreica.mid**—substitute the letter of your CD ROM drive for "D".)
3. Either check the Forever check box to have the browser play the sound file until it goes on to load another Web page, or clear the Forever check box and enter the number of times you want the browser to play the background sound file into the Loop field. The Page Properties dialog box in Figure 83 specifies that the browser it to play the sound file specified in the Location field two times.
4. Click your mouse pointer on the OK button.

After you complete Step 4, FrontPage will insert a <BGSOUND> tag similar to:

```
<bgsound src="../MultiMedia/america.mid" loop="2">
```

into the Web page HTML.

Similarly, if you want the visitor's browser to replay a video clip when the user moves the mouse pointer over a graphic image, double-click your mouse pointer on the picture on the Page view Normal tab. FrontPage, in turn, will display the Picture Properties dialog box. Into the Video source field on the Video tab, enter the pathname of the video clip you want the browser to replay and click your mouse pointer on the On mouse over radio button. After you click your mouse pointer on the OK button near the bottom of the Picture Properties dialog box, FrontPage will add DYNSRC and START attributes similar to:

```
<IMG border="0" src="../images/kowloon.jpg"
     dynsrce="../MultiMedia/kowloon.avi" start="mouseover">
```

to the <IMG> tag used to place the graphic image on the Web Page. (You can find the file kowloon.avi on the companion CD as **D:\MyWebs\OnePage\MultiMedia\kowloon.avi,**— substitute the appropriate letter of your CD ROM drive for "D".)

You will learn all about working with video clips, sound files, and text animations later in this book. For now, the important thing to understand is that FrontPage will generate the HTML tags you need when you want to add multimedia elements to Web pages.

The most common multimedia control tags and attributes are:

- **<bgsound>** - specifies a sound file the browser is to play in the background when it retrieves a Web page and displays its contents. While Internet Explorer uses the <BGSOUND> tag, the Netscape Navigator uses the <EMBED> tag to perform the same function.
- **controls** – specifies whether or not the video player's controls should be displayed when it plays the video clip.
- **dynsrc** – specifies the URL of the video clip to be played.
- <IMG> - specifies the video clip or animation to be played.
- **loop** – specifies the number of times the browser is to replay the sound file or video clip. A LOOP value of –1 indicates the music or video clip is to be played indefinitely (i.e. forever).
- **loopdelay** – specifies the amount of time, in milliseconds, to wait between repetitions of the video clip.
- **src** – when used with a <BGSOUND> tag, the SRC attribute identifies the sound file to be played; when used with an <IMG> (image) tag, the SRC attribute identifies the picture to display until the browser displays the first frame of the video clip.
- **start** – specifies when the video clip or animation specified as the value of the DYNSRC attribute is to start playing. START="fileopen" means the video or animation is to start when the Web browser opens the Web page; START="mouseover" (the default) tells the Web browser to start the clip or animation when the visitor moves the mouse pointer over its location on the Web page.

USING THE PAGE VIEW HTML TAB TO DISPLAY THE HTML THAT DEFINES A WEB PAGE

As mentioned previously, you do not have to know HTML tags and attributes to create dynamic Web pages that include multimedia events such as video clips and background sounds. However, the more involved you are with publishing great looking, fully functional Web sites, the more you will find that HTML is a dynamic/evolving language with new tags being added to the language more quickly than they can be included for automatic generation in the latest version of FrontPage.

To view and perhaps modify the HTML that defines a Web page, perform the following steps:

1. Start FrontPage and select the File menu Open option, or click your mouse pointer on the Open button (second button from the left) on the Standard Toolbar. FrontPage, in turn, will display the Open File dialog box.
2. Enter the pathname of the Web page you want to work on into the File name field near the bottom of the Open File dialog box. If you do not know the pathname of the Web page you want to open, click your mouse pointer on the drop-down list button to the right of the Look in field and use the list box below the Look in field to open folders and select the file you want. For the current project, either open any Web page you created previously, or enter the pathname of the MultimediaPage.htm Web page on the companion **CD: D:\MyWebs\OnePage\MultiMediaPage.htm**—substitute the drive letter of your CD ROM drive for "D".
3. Click your mouse pointer on the OPEN button to tell FrontPage to open the Web page you selected in Step 2 in Page view. Similar to that shown in Figure 84.1. (If your FrontPage application is not in Page view, select the View menu Page option, or click your mouse pointer on the Page view button at the top of the Views Bar along the right-hand side of the FrontPage application window.)

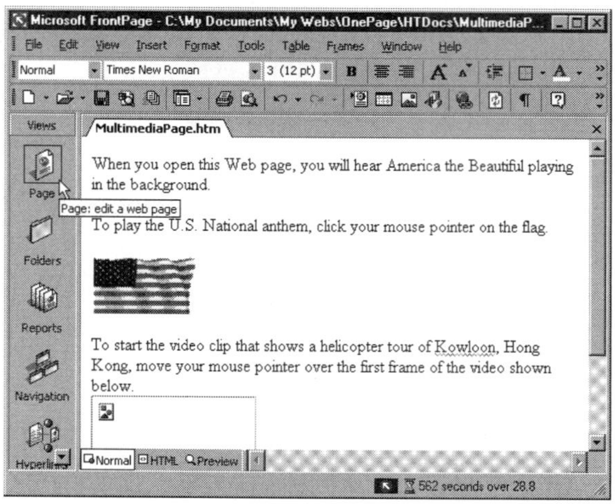

Figure 84.1 The MutliMediaPage.htm displayed on the Page view Normal tab.

4. To view the HTML for the Web page you opened in Step 3, click your mouse pointer on the HTML tab near the bottom left-hand corner of the Document pane in the FrontPage application window. FrontPage, in turn, will display the Web page HTML similar to that shown in figure 84.2.

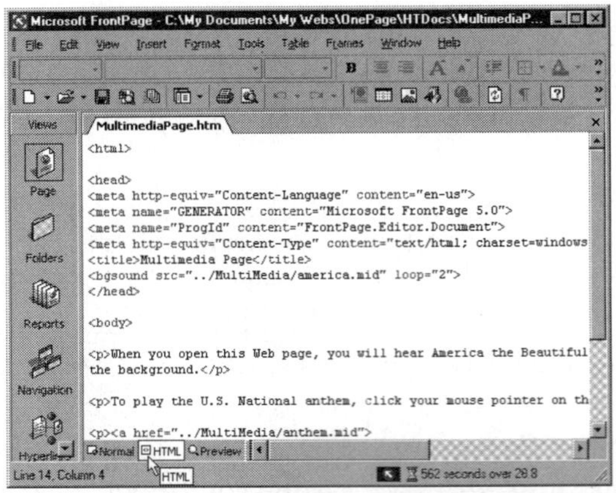

Figure 84.2 The MutliMediaPage.htm displayed by the Page view HTML tab.

To return to what-you-see-is-what-you-get (WYSIWYG) edit mode, click your mouse pointer on the Normal tag.

REVEALING HTML TAGS IN PAGE VIEW

In the preceding Tip you learned how to use the Page view HTML tab display the all of the HTML that defines the current Web page. When you want to see most of the tags used in the body of a Web page and not all of the HTML code that defines the page, select the View menu Page option and click your mouse pointer on the Normal tab. Then, select the View menu Reveal Tags option (or press CTRL+/ on your keyboard). FrontPage, in turn, will display HTML tags in Page view similar to that shown in Figure 85.

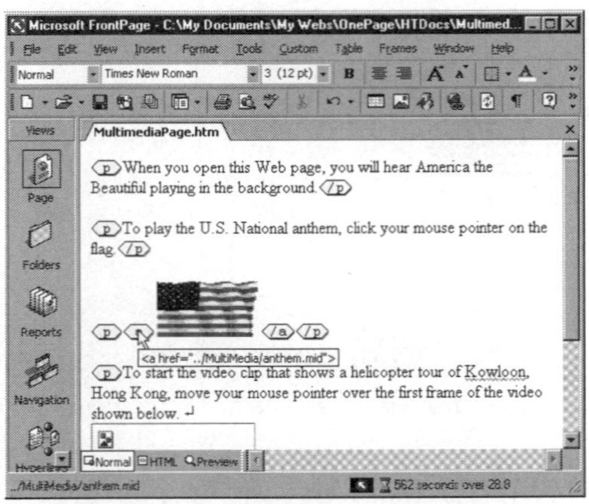

Figure 85 HTML tags revealed on the Page view Normal tab.

To remove the tags from the Page view Normal tab display, press CTRL+/ or select the View menu Reveal Tags option again.

Revealing HTML tags on the Page view Normal tab does not give you any extra editing capability beyond that which FrontPage provides on the Page view HTML tab. Although displaying HTML tags on the Page view Normal tab will let you locate and remove HTML with no visible appearance on the web page (such as paragraphs with nothing in them), you will have to use the Page view HTML tab make any significant changes to the HTML that describes the current Web. Moreover, the View menu Reveal Tags option does cause all HTML tags to become visible (and therefore accessible) on the Page view Normal tab.

For example, while FrontPage will display the <TABLE> tag before the contents of the cell in the upper left-hand corner of a table and the </TABLE> tag after the contents of the cell in the lower right-hand corner of a table, FrontPage will not display any of the <TR></TR> tags which surround a table row or <TD></TD> tags which enclose each cell in the table.

Note: *To reveal additional information on the HTML tags displayed on the Page view Normal tab, move your mouse pointer over the tab and wait a moment. FrontPage, in turn, will display a Screen Tip (such as the HREF information for the <A></A> anchor tags) about the tag.*

MODIFYING FRONTPAGE HTML TO CHANGE A TABLE'S APPEARANCE

The FrontPage Table Properties dialog box and Cell Properties dialog box give you an easy way to adjust a table's appearance—including the width and color of the border around the table (the table's frame) and the width and color of the borders around individual cells in the table. However, when you want to remove the frame around a table while leaving the borders around the cells in place, you will find it more convenient to work with the table's HTML directly—rather than working with the FrontPage table and cell properties dialog boxes.

For example, if your Web page has a table such as the one shown at the bottom of the Web page in Figure 86.1.

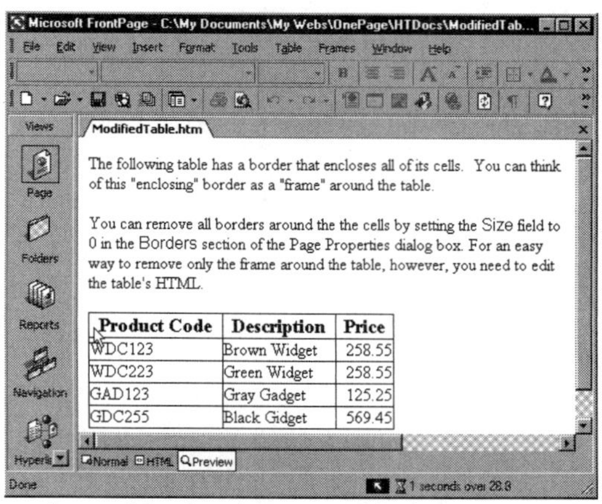

Figure 86.1 A Web page with a table that has a visible frame around its cells.

you can remove the table's frame by performing the following steps:

1. Display the current Web page in Page view and click your mouse pointer on the Normal tab.
2. Click your mouse pointer on the object in the cell at the top left-hand corner of the table to select the object, or double click your mouse pointer on the text in the cell to select the text.
3. Click your mouse pointer on the Page view HTML tab. FrontPage, in turn, will display the Web page HTML with the tag and attributes of the object or the text you selected in Step 1 highlighted.
4. Find the first <TABLE> tag that precedes the highlighted HTML code.
5. Click your mouse pointer just after the initial "<table" that starts the table's HTML, and insert a FRAME attribute whose value is set to "void" such that the table's (updated) definition starts as:

```
<table frame="void"
```

6. To see how the table looks without the enclosing frame, click your mouse pointer on the Preview tab.

After you complete Step 6, FrontPage will display the table with cell borders and no enclosing frame similar to that shown in Figure 86.2.

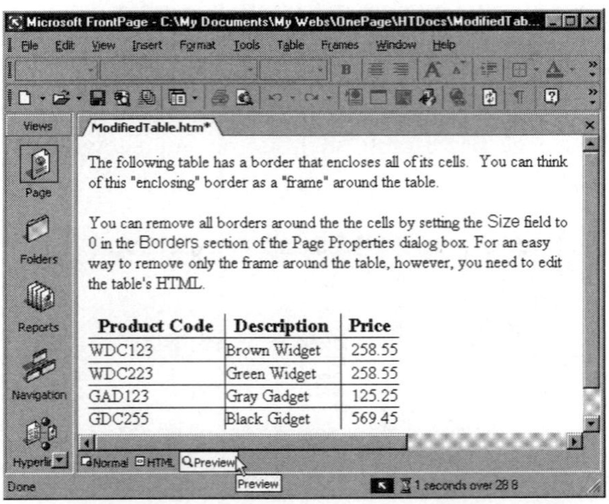

Figure 86.2 The Web page (show in Figure 86.1) with the table's FRAME attribute set to "void".

USING THE INSERT HTML FRONTPAGE COMPONENT TO INSERT HTML CODE WHICH FRONTPAGE WILL NOT REFORMAT OR VALIDATE

If you enter HTML directly onto the Page view HTML tab, FrontPage will validate and reformat what you typed before the program saves the Web page HTML to disk or displays on the Page view Normal or Preview tab. Sometimes, however, you want FrontPage to leave the HTML you insert onto a Web page untouched.

For example, if you insert HTML with a tag for a newly supported feature or an attribute that FrontPage does not understand, you do not want the program to comment out what it considers to be *invalid* HTML. Similarly, if you need to use HTML for an obsolete feature still supported by a Web browser but no longer allowed by FrontPage, you can insert HTML code FrontPage will not inspect by performing the following steps:

1. Open the Web page on which you wish to insert the HTML code unchanged, and display the page on the Page view Normal tab.
2. Click your mouse pointer at the location on the Web page where you want to insert the HTML.
3. Select the Insert menu Web Component option. FrontPage, in turn, will display the Insert Web Component dialog box.
4. Click your mouse pointer on Advanced Controls in the left-hand, "Component type" pane.
5. Double-click your mouse pointer on HTML in the right-hand, "Choose a control" pane. FrontPage, in turn, will display an HTML Markup textbox similar to that shown in Figure 87. (Unlike the textbox shown in Figure 87, which contains example HTML code that defines a "floating" frame, FrontPage will display an empty textbox when you complete Step 5.)

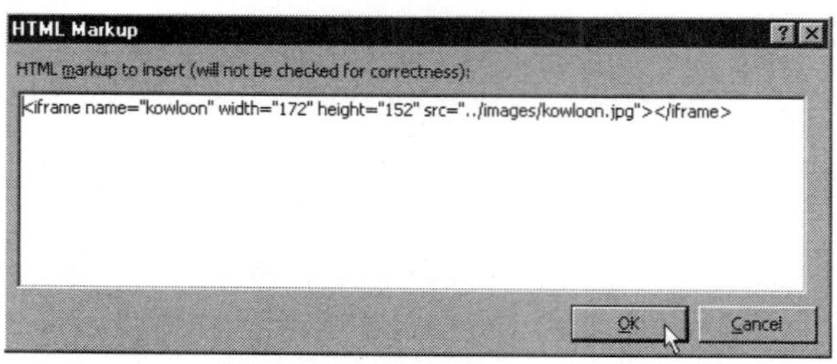

Figure 87 The FrontPage HTML Markup textbox.

6. Into the HTML Markup textbox, enter the HTML you want placed unchanged on the Web page.
7. Click your mouse pointer on the OK button.

After you complete Step 7, the inserted component (complete and unchecked HTML code fragment you entered in Step 6) will appear as a question mark icon on the Page view Normal tag at the insertion point on the Web page (which you selected in Step 2). To interpret and display the results of processing the HTML tags and attributes you entered in Step 6, either display the Web page using a Web browser or click your mouse pointer on the Page view Preview tab.

To redisplay the HTML you entered, double-click your mouse pointer on its question mark icon on the Page view Normal tab. FrontPage, in turn, will display the HTML in the HTML Markup textbox. You can then make any changes you want and write the updated HTML to the Web page (replacing the previous code fragment) by clicking your mouse pointer on the OK button.

If you want to remove a previously inserted HTML component, click your mouse pointer on its question mark icon, and then press the DELETE button on your keyboard.

UNDERSTANDING WEB PAGE METADATA

Metadata is the set of <META> tags in the <HEAD></HEAD> (header) section of the Web page HTML that provides information and instructions to search engine intelligent agents (bots)/Web crawlers and Web browsers. Although a Web browser will not display the metadata itself, it does use certain tags to govern its behavior. For example, if the current Web page includes the <META> tag:

```
<meta http-equiv="refresh" CONTENT="10;url=http://
www.NVBizNet.com/index.html">
```

then 10 seconds after the Web browser loads and displays the current Web page, it will retrieve and display the Web page at the Web address (URL): http://www.NVBizNet.com/index.html.

Some of the most commonly used <META> tags are:

- **author** – identifies the name of the Web page author.
- **bulletin date** – specifies the date for the associated BULLETIN TEXT <META> tag.
- **bulletin text** – the text of the announcement you want to make.

- **classification** – used by some search engines to list the Web page in the correct category. Yahoo, for example, uses classifications such as: Advertising, Agriculture, Arts and Crafts, Business Supplies, Catalogs, Christmas, Family, General Hardware, Hobbies, Medical, Software, Sports, Web hosting, etc.
- **copyright** – states the owner of the copyright of the Web site content and design.
- **distribution** – used for content control. Web servers that adhere to the HTTP 1.1 specification will not send LOCAL web pages to Web visitors. Values: LOCAL, GLOBAL.
- **description** – gives the search bot/Web crawler or Web page visitor a brief synopsis of what the Web site is all about. Some search engines display the contents of the description tag when presenting the hyperlink to a Web site in response to a keyword search.
- **expires** – tells the browser that caches Web pages when it should fetch a fresh copy of the Web page vs. displaying the one stored in the cache. For example: **<meta http-equiv="Expires" CONTENT="Mon, 02 Feb 2000 08:00:001 GMT">.**
- **generator** – identifies the tool you last used to create/update the HTML file. Some Web bots (intelligent agents) search the Web for all sites developed by a particular Web page creation tool.
- **keywords** – list of words that the search bot/Web crawler is to place in its search engine database to identify the content of your Web page. In order for a search engine (such as Yahoo, AOL NetFind, AltaVista, Lycos, etc.) to present your Web page as a choice for a user to visit, the keyword the user enters into the search engine's Search field must match one of the words in your Web page's keywords list.
- **language** – identifies the language of the Web page content. FrontPage will generate the language code (en-us, af, ar-ae, ar-bh, etc.) for the language you select from the Page language drop-down list on the Language tag of the Page Properties dialog box.
- **pragma** – tells the Web browser to reload the Web page every time it visits the page vs. using a copy of the page it has stored in a local memory/disk cache.
- **rating** – the Web site's target audience—values such as: 14 YEARS, GENERAL, MATURE, RESTRICTED, SAFE FOR KIDS.

- **refresh** – tells the Web browser to load the Web page specified in the URL after “n” seconds. For example: **<meta http-equiv=“refresh” CONTENT=“5;url=http://www.NVBizNet.com/index.html”>.**
- **reply to** – provides the e-mail address to which the Web site visitor is to send comments about the site.
- **revisit** – tells the search bot/Web crawler when it should return to the site for new keywords or descriptions, because the site’s content will most likely have changed.
- **robots** – instruct a search bot/Web crawler on how to index the Web page:
- ALL – index and follow, i.e. index the current page and follow its hyperlinks to other pages and index those, as well.
- INDEX – index only the current page (i.e. do not follow its hyperlinks to index other pages).
- FOLLOW – follow the hyperlinks on the page and index the hyperlinked pages.
- NOINDEX—follow the hyperlinks on the page to index the linked pages, but do not index the current page.
- NOFOLLOW – follow the hyperlinks on the current page and index those pages. However, do not follow the hyperlinks on the hyperlinked pages—i.e. only index hyperlinked pages one level deep.

When you use FrontPage to create a Web page, the program will automatically place the following metadata in the Web page <HEAD></HEAD> (header) section:

```
<meta name="GENERATOR" content="Microsoft FrontPage 5.0">
<meta name="ProgId" content="FrontPage.Editor.Document">
<meta http-equiv="Content-Type" content="text/html;
     charset=windows-1252">
```

The most convenient way to add additional <META> tags is to use a tool such as the Hiawatha Island Software Company’s TagGen program. Although you can type the <META> tags you want onto the Page view HTML tab, using third party software to generate the tags will save you some typing, and you will not have to remember the syntax of the <META> tags you want to use.

DOWNLOADING AND INSTALLING HIAWATHA ISLAND'S TAGGEN PROGRAM WHICH INSERTS METADATA INTO FRONTPAGE WEB PAGES

As mentioned in the preceding Tip, a third party program such as Hiawatha Island's TagGen simplifies the generation and insertion of <META> tags into the <HEAD></HEAD> (header) section of your Web pages. TagGen, for example, lets you generate all of the metadata you want by filling in the fields on three dialog box tabs. Moreover, TagGen provides drop-down lists that let you select the value for the CLASSIFICATION, DISTRIBUTION, LANGUAGE, ROBOTS, RATING, REVISIT, and USE PRAGMA <META> tags. Furthermore, the program retains text you enter for the AUTHOR, COPYRIGHT, and REPLY-TO <META> tag fields, so that you can reuse the values again on future Web pages by selecting them from drop-down lists.

To download a free, 15-day trial version of TagGen and/or other third party Web page generation products/add-ins for FrontPage from download area of the Microsoft Office Update Web site by performing the following steps:

1. If you do not have an active (open) connection to the Internet, establish a dial-up connection with your Internet service provider (ISP).
2. Start the Microsoft Internet explorer or the Web browser you normally use.
3. Into the Address field of your Web browser, enter the URL:

   http://OfficeUpdate.Microsoft.com/DownloadCatalog/DldFrontPage.asp
4. Press the ENTER key on your keyboard.
5. Click your mouse pointer on the hyperlink: **Downloads for FrontPage (FrontPage Downloads from Third Parties)** locate somewhere in the top half of the Web page your browser will display after you complete Step 4. Your Web browser, in turn, will display a third-party software add-ins for FrontPage download page similar to that shown in Figure 89.
6. Review the descriptions of the downloadable FrontPage add-ins as you scroll (down) the Web page until you see the hyperlink for: **HISC TagGen**, and then click your mouse pointer the hyperlink. Your Web browser, in turn, will display the Microsoft Office add-in Web page on the Hiawatha Island Software Company Web site: **http://www.HiSoftware.com/OfficeUpdate/**.

7. Click your mouse pointer on the "Download Now" hyperlink for the latest version of HiSoftware TagGen for FrontPage (release 4.5, as of this writing). Windows, in turn, will display the File Download dialog box.

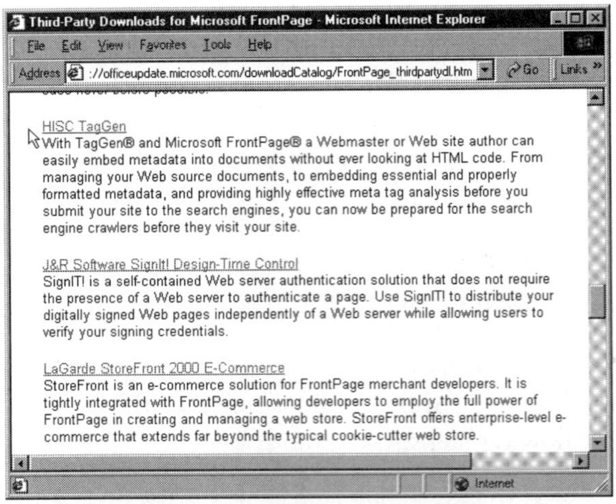

Figure 89 A portion of a Microsoft Office Update Web page with download hyperlinks for third party software add-ins for FrontPage.

8. Click your mouse pointer on the Save this program to disk radio button, and then on the OK button near the bottom of the File Download dialog box. Windows, in turn, will display the Save As dialog box.
9. Use the drop-down list button to the right of the Save in field to select the folder in which you wish to store the file: **TGFP4.exe**, and then click your mouse pointer on the SAVE button. Windows, in turn, will start to download a copy of the file and display a status message box that gives you an estimated time to completion. (Depending on the speed of your Internet connection, the download process may take several minutes since the TagGen installation file is almost 6 megabytes in size.)
10. After Windows finishes retrieving and storing the TGFP4.exe on your computer, use the Windows explorer to display the files in the folder you selected in Step 9, and then click your mouse pointer on TGFP4.exe. TagGen, in turn, will start the InstallShield Wizard and prompt you with several screens on which you should simply accept the defaults by clicking your mouse pointer on the NEXT button.
11. On the InstallShield Wizard's next to last screen, click your mouse pointer on the INSTALL button and then on the FINISH button on the final screen.

After you install the program, click your mouse pointer on the Windows start button, and then move your mouse pointer to programs on the Windows Start menu. After Windows displays the Start menu of programs and program groups on your system, move your mouse pointer to the HiSoftware TagGen for FrontPage program group, and click your mouse pointer on TagGen for FrontPage.

TagGen's screens and data entry fields are self-explanatory. Moreover, the program has an extensive help system that explains all <META> tags, their attributes, and provides suggestions for many of the <META> tags such as the KEYWORDS and DESCRIPTION <META> tags (for example). To insert the metadata into the <HEAD></HEAD> (header) section of your Web pages, click your mouse pointer on the BATCH button on the program's "Step 3 – Validate & Update Meta Tags" tab. TagGen, in turn, will display the list of Web pages in the FrontPage Web you currently have open in FrontPage, so you can click your mouse pointer on the check box for each Web page in which you want the program to insert the metadata you described with field entries and menu selections.

USING FOLDERS VIEW TO CREATE OR RENAME A FOLDER IN THE CURRENT FRONTPAGE WEB

FrontPage Folders view lets you manage the files in a FrontPage Web by creating, deleting, and renaming folders, so you can organize the site's Web page, script, graphics, and multimedia files by moving them into appropriately named folders. Although the Web visitor will not notice if you leave all Web pages and other files in a single folder or if you organize your files by placing pictures in one folder, Web pages in another, and multimedia files in a third. After all, when the site visitor clicks the mouse pointer on a hyperlink, the Web server will send the corresponding Web page or page element to the visitor in the same way, no matter where the Web page or page element is physically located on disk. However, if you have a large site with a lot of files, grouping like types of files and like types of Web pages will make it easier to find the Web page you want to edit as you maintain the Web site by updating its content to keep it accurate and to provide new features that keep visitors coming back to see "what's new".

To create new folders in Folders view, perform the following steps:

1. Open the FrontPage Web whose folders and files you want to mange.
2. Select the View menu Folders option, or click your mouse pointer on the Folders button (second from the top) on the View Bar along the right-hand side of the FrontPage application window. FrontPage, in turn, will display the files and folders in the current Web site in Folders view, similar to that shown in Figure 90.

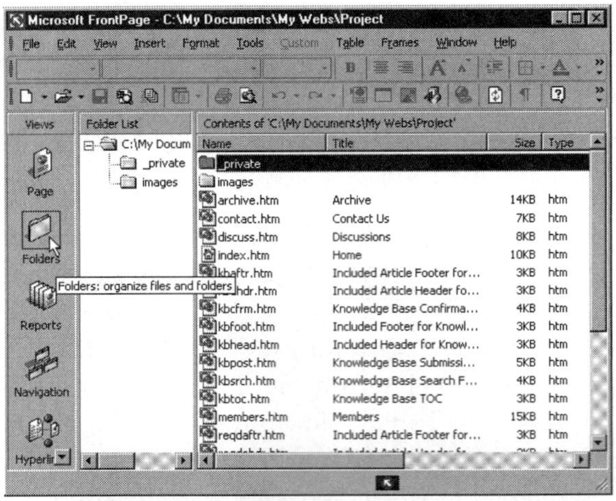

Figure 90 *A FrontPage web displayed in Folders view.*

3. To create a new folder, right-click your mouse pointer on the folder in which you wish to create it. For example, to create a new folder at the root of the current FrontPage web, right-click your mouse pointer on the folder at the top of the Folder List pane.
4. From the FrontPage pop-up menu, select the New option and click your mouse pointer on Folder. FrontPage, in turn, will create a new folder named New_Folder.
5. Enter the name of the folder in the field to the right of the New_Folder icon, and then press the ENTER key. For example, to create a folder for HTML documents, you might enter: **HTML** to replace New_Folder in the field to the right of the New_Folder icon in the (folder) Contents pane to the right of the Folder List pane.
6. Repeat Steps 3 – 5 until you have created all of the folders you need to organize the Web site's content.

To move files into folders, perform the following steps:

1. Hold down the CTRL button on your keyboard as you click your mouse pointer on the files (listed in the Contents pane) that you want to move to a particular folder.
2. Release the CTRL button and right-click your mouse pointer on one of the filenames you select in Step 1.
3. Select Cut from the pop-up menu.
4. Right-click your mouse pointer on the icon of the folder into which you wish to move the files, and then select Paste from the pop-up menu.

After you complete Step 4, FrontPage will move the files you selected in Step 1 into the folder you selected in Step 4. As it moves each file, FrontPage goes through the current FrontPage web's Web pages and updates the HREF and SRC tags that refer to the file being moved to reflect pathname of the file's new location.

If you want to rename a folder in a FrontPage web, perform the following steps:

1. Open the FrontPage Web whose folders and files and folders you want to mange.
2. Select the View menu Folders option, or click your mouse pointer on the Folders button (second from the top) on the View Bar along the right-hand side of the FrontPage application window. FrontPage, in turn, will display the files and folders in the current Web site in Folders view, similar to that you saw in Figure 90.
3. Right-click your mouse pointer on the folder you want to rename (either in the Folder List pane or in the Contents pane), and then select the Rename option on the pop-up menu. FrontPage, in turn, will open an edit field with the folder's current name next to the folder's icon.
4. Enter the folder's new name and then press the ENTER key.
5. Repeat Steps 3 and 4 until you have change the names of all of the folders you want to rename.

As you complete Step 4 for each folder, FrontPage will go through the current FrontPage web's Web pages and update any HREF or SRC references to files in the folder you just renamed to reflect the target file's new pathname.

USING FOLDERS VIEW TO IMPORT IMAGE FILES INTO YOUR IMAGES DIRECTORY

In previous Tips you learned that organizing your FrontPage web content, graphic images, and multimedia files into folders simplifies the process of finding the Web pages on which you wish to work and the pictures, animations, movie clips and sound files you want to place on them. Moreover, by copying the pictures you want to use on your Web pages to an IMAGES folder in your FrontPage web directory, you can make sure that the pictures are available for your Web pages—even if a someone renames the original files or removes them from their original locations. The FrontPage Folders view makes it easy to copy pictures (or other files) into a folder in your FrontPage web.

For example, to import (copy) a graphic image (picture) into the IMAGES folder of your current FrontPage web, perform the following steps:

1. Display the FrontPage web you currently have open in Folders view by clicking your mouse pointer on the Folders icon (second from the top) in the Views Bar along the left-hand side of the FrontPage application window, or by selecting the View menu Folders option.
2. Click your mouse pointer on the icon for the folder into which you wish to import the picture. For example, to import pictures into the IMAGES folder, double click your mouse pointer on the IMAGES folder. FrontPage, in turn, will display the current contents of the IMAGES folder.

Note: *If you do not have an IMAGES folder, you can create it (or any other new folders you want) while in Folder view. Just right-click your mouse pointer on the folder in which you wish to create the new folder. Then, select New from the pop-up menu and click your mouse pointer on Folder. After FrontPage creates the new folder, change its name from "New Folder" to IMAGES (or whatever name you want), and press the* ENTER *key on your keyboard.*

3. Select the File menu Import option. FrontPage, in turn, will display an Import dialog box similar to that shown in Figure 91.

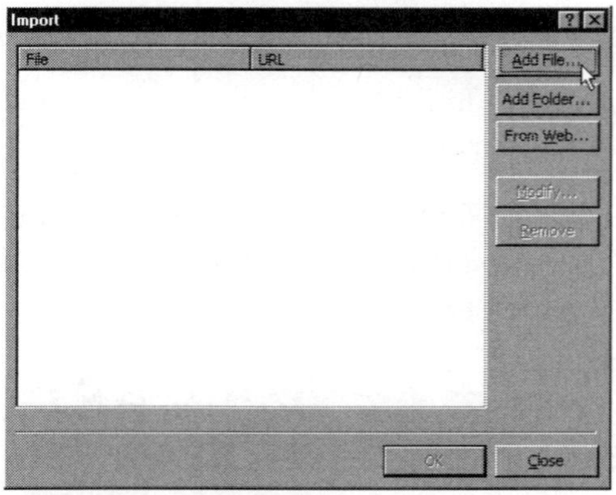

Figure 91 *The FrontPage (file) Import dialog box.*

4. To add individual files from your computer or from another computer on your network, click your mouse pointer on the ADD FILE button. FrontPage, in turn, will display the add File to Import List dialog box—which is very similar in function to the File Open and File Save (and File Save As) dialog boxes you have used in previous Tips.
5. Use the drop-down list button to the right of the Look in field to display the list of folders accessible from your computer, and then select the folder in which the picture you want to import is located by clicking your mouse pointer on the folder's name in the drop-down list. FrontPage, in turn, will display the folder's contents in the list

box below the Look in field. (If you prefer, you can enter the folder's full pathname into the File name field, and then click your mouse pointer on the OPEN button, instead of using the drop-down list to select the target folder.)

6. Click your mouse pointer on the filename of the picture you want to import. (To import more than one picture, hold down the CTRL key on your keyboard as you click your mouse pointer on the filenames of the pictures you want to import.)
7. Click your mouse pointer on the OPEN button. FrontPage, in turn, will write the filename(s) you selected in Step 6 and each file's URL in list box in the Import dialog box.
8. If you want to import additional files from other folders repeat Steps 4 - 7 for each set of files you want to import.
9. To copy the files you selected (in Steps 4 – 8) to the folder you selected in Step 2, click your mouse pointer on the OK button near the bottom right-hand corner of the Import dialog box.

Take another look at the Import dialog box in Figure 91. Notice that you can also choose to import entire folders (by clicking your mouse pointer on the ADD FOLDER button), or files from the Web sites on the Internet (by clicking your mouse pointer on the FROM WEB button). If you click your mouse pointer on the ADD FOLDER button, FrontPage will display its File Open dialog box, so that you can specify the folder you want to import (copy) into the folder you selected in Step 2 of the import procedure. Similarly, if you click your mouse pointer on the FROM WEB button (in Step 4 of the preceding procedure), FrontPage will display the first page of the Import Web Wizard which will guide you through the process of locating and retrieving pictures on the Web.

USING FRONTPAGE WEB SITE CREATION WIZARDS TO GENERATE TASKS

When you are working on a large Web site, you want to be able to concentrate on the content of its numerous Web pages without also trying to keep track of all of the millions of other things you need to accomplish in order to finish the project. FrontPage *tasks* let you stay focused on producing Web pages by helping you manage the efforts of your team—if you are fortunate enough to have help in creating the site. Alternatively, if you are working alone (as is often the case), you can use FrontPage tasks as a "To Do" list to make sure you do not forget something critical—such as spell checking your Web pages or testing the scripts that let your site's visitors make purchases online.

In addition to adding tasks manually (as you will learn To Do in each of the next five Tips), FrontPage Wizards used to generate Web sites, may also create tasks you need to perform to finish the work started by the Wizard. For example, the Corporate Presence Wizard (which you used to generate the FoodCo Web site earlier in this book), will generate a tasks list of seven things To Do before you put the corporate presence Web site online.

If you created the FoodCo Web site earlier, open it now by selecting the File menu Open Web option, entering the pathname of the FoodCo web into the Web name field of the Open Web dialog box, and clicking your mouse pointer on the OPEN button. Alternatively, if you did not create the FoodCo web, or if you want to use the Corporate Presence Wizard (again) to create a Web site and its To Do list of tasks, perform the following Steps:

1. With FrontPage running, select the File menu New option and click your mouse pointer on Page or Web. FrontPage, in turn, will display the New Page or Web menu along the right-hand side of the application window.
2. Click your mouse pointer on Web Site Templates on the New Page or Web menu. FrontPage, in turn, will display the Web Site Templates dialog box.
3. Into the Specify the location of the new Web field (on the right-hand side of the dialog box), enter the pathname of the folder in which you want the FrontPage Wizard to create the new Web. (When FrontPage invokes the Wizard, FrontPage will provide a default pathname for the new folder the Wizard is to create, such as: **C:\MYDOCUMENTS\MY WEBS\MYWEB5**. Be sure to the change default pathname if you want to create the new FrontPage web in another folder.)
4. Double-click your mouse pointer on the icon for the Corporate Presence Wizard. FrontPage, in turn, will create the folder specified in Step 3 and display the first page of the Corporate Presence Wizard.
5. When using the Wizard to generate an actual Corporate Presence Web site, you will fill in the fields on each of the Wizard's screens to customize the Web site for your company. If you are just using the Wizard to see how it generates the tasks list (for the current project) click your mouse pointer on the FINISH button on Wizard's first screen (or on any subsequent screen) to skip the remaining screens and generate a generic Web site.

After you complete Step 5, the Corporate Presence Wizard will create a Web site and return to the FrontPage application window displaying the current FrontPage web in Tasks view similar to that shown in Figure 92. If the Wizard did not finish in a Tasks view, you can display the list of tasks generated by the Wizard, by clicking your mouse pointer on the Tasks icon at the bottom of the Views Bar (along the left-hand side of the application window) or selecting the View menu Tasks option. FrontPage, in turn, will display the current FrontPage web in Tasks view similar to that shown in Figure 92.

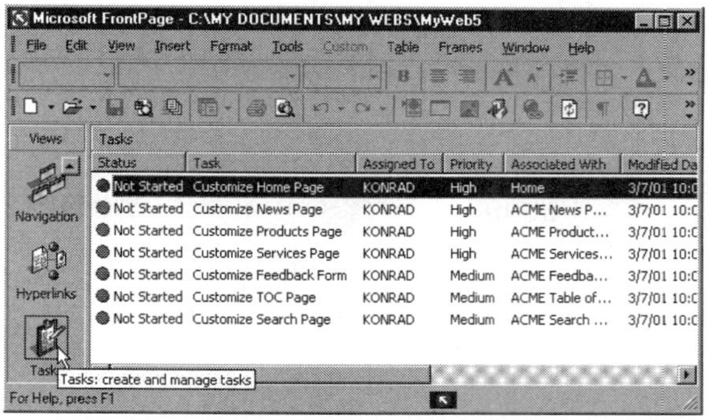

Figure 92 *The FrontPage Tasks view of the Wizard generated Corporate Presence Web site.*

After you learn how to add additional tasks in the next five Tips you will learn how to Edit tasks and how to use them to manage team collaboration.

CREATING A TASK WHILE IN PAGE VIEW

While working on your Web site, you will spend the majority of your time in Page view. After all, creating the site's content is your main objective, and the FrontPage what-you-see-is-what-you-get (WYSIWYG) editor (in Page view) lets you add hyperlinks, text, and multimedia objects to your Web pages quickly and easily. If you are working with others to develop a site, or even when you are working alone, you will sometimes need to put a placeholder on a page where you want to place content or some other object that is not currently available. Suppose, for example, that you are working on your company's Web site and want to include a picture of the employees as a group on the home page. If the picture is not yet available, you could insert another graphic temporarily (as a placeholder) for page layout purposes. Whenever you place a temporary placeholder on a Web page, you should create a task that reminds you to replace the placeholder with the actual content or other object before you put the Web site on-line.

To associate a task with the current Web page displayed in Page view, perform the following steps:

1. Select the Edit menu Tasks option, and click your mouse pointer on Add Task.
2. FrontPage, in turn, will display a New Task dialog box similar to that shown in Figure 93.
3. Enter a descriptive name for the task into the Task name field. Limit the name to three or four words, so that FrontPage will be able to display the entire name in the Task column when you display the site's To Do list in Tasks view. For example, if you need to add a company photo to the home page, you might enter: **Add Company Photo** into the Task name field.

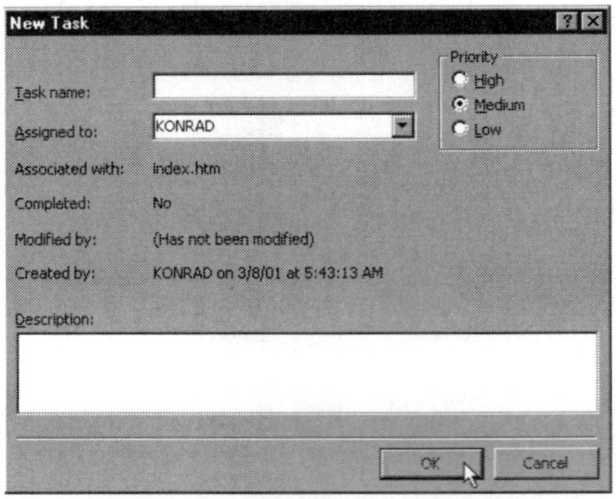

Figure 93 The FrontPage New Task dialog box.

4. Set the task's priority by clicking your mouse pointer on the radio button to the left of High, Medium, or Low in the Priority section near the upper right-hand corner of the New Task dialog box.
5. Enter the name of the person who is supposed to perform the task into the Assigned to field. By default, FrontPage will enter the name you used to login to the network. (On a non-networked PC, FrontPage will enter the name under which you registered Windows during the Windows installation process into the Assigned to field.) If you previously assigned other tasks to the user to whom you want to assign the current task, you can click your mouse pointer on the drop-down list button to the right of the Assigned to field, and then assign the current task by clicking your mouse pointer on the assignee's name among those listed in the drop-down list box.
6. Enter the full description of the work to be done into the Description field near the bottom of the New Task dialog box.
7. Click your mouse pointer on the OK button.

Notice that when you create a new task, FrontPage automatically fills in the Associated with, Completed, Modified by, and Created by fields on the New Task dialog box.

CREATING A TASK WHILE IN FOLDERS VIEW

In addition to adding new tasks while in Page view (as you learned To Do in the preceding Tip), you can add tasks associated with specific Web pages while in Folders view. Remember, Folders view gives you a directory like list of the folders and files located in the current FrontPage web. As such, Folders view makes it possible to associate a task with any Web page, graphic image, video clip, sound file, or file of any other type (for that matter). Moreover, you do not have to open a file in order to link a task to it.

To link a task to a file in Folders view, perform the following steps:

1. With the FrontPage web displayed in Folders view, select the file with which you want to associate a task by clicking your mouse pointer on the file's name.
2. Select the Edit menu Tasks option and select Add Task. FrontPage, in turn, will display a New Task dialog box similar the one you saw in Figure 93.
3. Enter a descriptive name for the task into the Task name field. Limit the title to three or four words so that FrontPage will be able to display the entire title in the Task column when you display the site's To Do list in Tasks view. For example, if you need to add a company photo to the home page, you might enter: **Add Company Photo** into the Task name field.
4. Set the task's priority by clicking your mouse pointer on the radio button to the left of High, Medium, or Low in the Priority section near the upper right-hand corner of the New Task dialog box.
5. Enter the name of the person who is supposed to perform the task into the Assigned to field. (If you previously assigned another task to the user to whom you wish to assign the current task, you can click your mouse pointer on the drop-down list button to the right of the Assigned to field, and then assign the task by clicking your mouse pointer on the assignee's name among those listed in the drop-down list box.)
6. Into the Description field near the bottom of the New Task dialog box, enter the full description of the work to be accomplished when performing the task.
7. Click your mouse pointer on the OK button.

After you complete Step 7, FrontPage will save the task to disk, close the New Task dialog box, and return to the application window with the FrontPage web displayed in Folders view.

CREATING TASKS TO MANAGE THE CREATION OF NEW WEB PAGES

The previous two Tips dealt with associating a task with an existing Web page. However, FrontPage also lets you create a task that reminds you to create the Web page associated with the task at a later time. Suppose for example that you want to create frequently asked questions (FAQ) page for your Web site. If the FAQ page is not a mission critical part of the site, and you are on the (normal) short deadline for getting the site up and running, you might decide to create the FAQ page after you publish the Web site to the Internet. Once the rest of the site is on-line the pressure will be off (for a short while anyway), and you will have time to add additional support pages such as the FAQ page and perhaps a feedback page and a guest book, as well.

To generate a task that will remind you to create a Web page later, perform the following steps:

1. Display the New Page or Web menu by selecting the File menu New option and clicking your mouse pointer on Page or Web.
2. Select Page Templates near the bottom of the New Page or Web menu. FrontPage, in turn, will display the Page Templates dialog box.
3. Click your mouse pointer on the icon of the template for the type of page you want to create later. For example, if you want to create a task that reminds you to work on an FAQ page later, click your mouse pointer on the icon labeled Frequently Asked Questions.
4. Click your mouse pointer on the Just add Web task check box near the top right-hand side of the Page Templates dialog box until a check mark appears
5. Click your mouse pointer on the OK button. FrontPage, in turn, will display the Save As dialog box.
6. Click your mouse pointer on the folder in which you want FrontPage to create the new Web page. For example, to save the Web page in the HTDOCS folder, click your mouse pointer on HTDOCS in the list box below the Save in field. (If you do not see the folder you want, use the drop-down list button to the right of the Save in field to navigate to the desired folder in which you want to store the new Web page.)
7. Enter the name of the new Web page into the File name field. For example, if you are creating an FAQ page, you would (most likely) enter FAQ as the new page's filename into the File name field.
8. Click your mouser pointer on the CHANGE TITLE button (above the right-hand corner of the File name field). FrontPage, in turn, will display the Set Page Title dialog box.
9. Enter a title for the new page into the Page title field. For example, if you are creating an FAQ page, you might enter a title similar to: **Frequently Asked Questions**.
10. Click your mouse pointer on the OK button near the bottom of the Set Page Title dialog box.
11. Click your mouse pointer on the SAVE button near the bottom right-hand corner of the Save as dialog box.

After you complete Step 12, FrontPage will save the template for the new page you selected in Step 3 into the folder you selected in Step 6, and create a task named "Finish FAQ.HTM".

(If you entered a filename other than FAQ into File name field in Step 7, FrontPage will replace the FAQ portion of the finish task's name with the name you entered in Step 7.) Because the description of the new task is a generic "Added by the FrontPage New Page dialog", you may want to edit the task (as you will learn To Do in the next Tip) to enter a more detailed description.

When you are ready to develop the new Web page, perform the following steps to start editing the Web page from Tasks view:

1. Display the current FrontPage web in Tasks view by clicking your mouse pointer on the Tasks icon near the bottom of the Views bar (along the left-hand side of the application window) or by selecting the View menu Tasks option.
2. Right-click your mouse pointer on the Finish task associated with the page on which you wish to work. For example, if you created a task to remind you to create a page you named FAQ.HTM, right-click your mouse pointer on the task named Finish FAQ.HTM in the list of tasks.
3. Select Start Task from the pop-up menu.

After you complete Step 3, FrontPage will switch to Page view so you can use the what-you-see-is-what-you-get (WYSIWYG Page view) editor to enter content and/or insert objects onto the Web page you selected in Step 2.

EDITING TASKS WHILE IN TASK VIEW

At some point after you create a task, you may want to change its priority, assign it to another development team member, or update the description of the work that remains to be accomplished.

To edit the fields that define a task, perform the following steps:

1. Switch to Tasks view by clicking or mouse pointer on the Tasks button at the bottom of the Views Bar along the left-hand side of the FrontPage application window (or, select the View menu Tasks option).
2. Double-click your mouse pointer on the task you want to change. FrontPage, in turn, will display the Task Details dialog box. (Instead of double-clicking your mouse pointer on the task, you can right-click your mouse pointer on the task you want to modify, and then select Edit Task from the pop-up menu.)
3. Make the changes you want to the contents of the Task name, Assigned to, and/or Description fields. To change the task's priority, click your mouse pointer on the High, Medium, or Low radio button in

the Priority section (at the upper right-hand corner) of the Task Details dialog box.

4. To save your change(s) and return to Tasks view, click your mouse pointer on the OK button at the bottom of the dialog box. (If you want FrontPage to ignore any changes you made, click your mouse pointer on the CANCEL button instead.)

You can also modify task details directly on the tasks list instead of making the changes by using the Task Details dialog box. For example, if you want to change the person to whom you have assigned a task, click your mouse pointer on the Assigned to column of the task (row) you want to change. FrontPage, in turn, will change the Assigned to column in the task's row from *display* to *edit* mode. Enter the new username to which the task is to be assigned, and then press the ENTER key on your keyboard.

CREATING A TASK NOT LINKED TO A WEB PAGE

Thus far, each of the task creation Tips showed you how to create a task linked to a particular Web page. Sometimes, however, you need to create a task associated with work to be performed on the current FrontPage web (or a portion of the site) vs. on a particular Web page or object. For example, you may need for the company's owner to review the overall look-and-feel of the Web site before you publish it to the Web; or you may need the office/production manager to review the products and services sections of the FrontPage web to make sure the products and services described on the Web site are actually still offered as advertised.

To create a task not associated with a particular Web page or object on a Web page in the current FrontPage web, perform the following steps:

1. Switch to a view other than Page or Folders view. Or, if in Page view, close any open pages (by selecting the File menu Close option until no page is displayed); if in Folders view, click your mouse pointer on one of the current FrontPage web's folders to select the folder (vs. leaving one of the Web pages or other files selected).
2. Select the File menu New option, and click your mouse pointer on Tasks. FrontPage, in turn, will display the New Task dialog box.
3. Enter a descriptive name for the task into the Task name field. Limit the name to three or four words so that FrontPage will be able to display the entire name in the Task column when you display the site's To Do list in Tasks view. For example, if you want the company's human resources (HR) director to review the job listings and benefits sections of the site, you might enter: **HR Content Review** into the Task name field.

4. Set the task's priority by clicking your mouse pointer on the radio button to the left of High, Medium, or Low in the Priority section near the upper right-hand corner of the New Task dialog box.
5. Enter the name of the person who is supposed to perform the task into the Assigned to field. (If you previously assigned another task to the username to which you want to assign the current task, you can click your mouse pointer on the drop-down list button to the right of the Assigned to field and assign the task by clicking your mouse pointer on the assignee's name among those listed in the drop-down list box.)
6. Enter the full description of the work to be done into the Description field near the bottom of the New Task dialog box.
7. Click your mouse pointer on the OK button.

In general, the procedure for adding an *unlinked* (or unassociated) task is the same as adding a task linked to a specific Web page or other file used on the Web site. The important thing to understand is that if you have a Web page open in Page view or a non-folder item selected (highlighted) in Folders view, FrontPage will associated the task you are creating with the Web page displayed in page view or the Web page (or other file) highlighted in Folders view.

When trying to add an unlinked (unassociated) task, review the contents of the Associated with field in the New Task dialog box. The value of the Associated with field for an unlinked task will read: "Is not associated". Therefore, if you see a filename in the Associated with field, click your mouse pointer on the CANCEL button (in the lower right-hand corner of the New Task dialog box), deselect the item you have selected (by selecting the File menu Close option in Page view or by clicking your mouse pointer on a folder name in Folders view), and then repeat the steps of the procedure in the current Tip.

CREATING A TASK TO MANAGE SPELL CHECKING

Before you make a Web site accessible to those connected to the Internet by publishing the Web site to your Web server, be sure to check all of the site's Web pages for spelling errors. Although you can have FrontPage check spelling as you type, some members of your development team may have turned off this feature or may have ignored the red "squiggly" line FrontPage uses to mark misspellings it cannot correct.

Ignoring spelling errors during site development is not necessarily a character flaw. Sometimes you just need to get your thoughts down on paper when your creative juices are flowing. You can always check your grammar and spelling later, since both are somewhat mechanical processes. Bursts of creativity, on the other hand, happen sporadically (for most of us), and you would hate to miss out on using a great idea or phrasing a thought in a memorable way because you did not type it in as it came to mind.

When you tell FrontPage to check the spelling of the words on all of the pages on your Web site, the program will present a summary showing the number of spelling errors on each page. You can then either go to each Web page and correct the typographical errors immediately, or you can tell FrontPage to create a "Fix misspelled words" task for each Web page that contains one or more misspellings. After you generate the spell check tasks, you can divide up the tedious work of correcting spelling errors by assigning some of the tasks to different members of your site development team.

To have FrontPage create spell check tasks for misspellings across the Web pages in the current FrontPage web, perform the following steps:

1. Switch to a view other than Page view, or if you want to remain in Page view, close all currently open Web pages.
2. Click your mouse pointer on the Spelling button (with the ABC and check mark) on the Standard Toolbar, or select the Tools menu Spelling option. FrontPage, in turn, will display the Spelling dialog box shown in Figure 98.1.

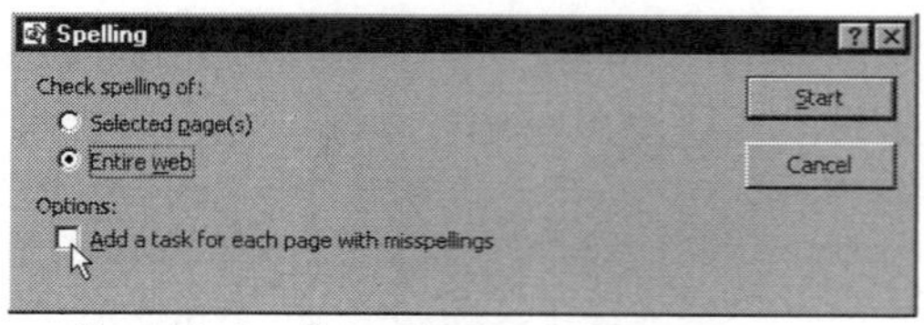

Figure 98.1 The FrontPage (batch) Spelling dialog box.

3. To have FrontPage check the spelling for all of the pages in the current FrontPage web, click your mouse pointer on the Entire web radio button.
4. To tell FrontPage to create a spell check task for each page on which it finds a spelling error, click your mouse pointer on the check box to the left of Add a task for each page with misspellings until a check mark appears.
5. Start the spell check by clicking your mouse pointer on the Start button near the top right-hand corner of the Spelling dialog box. FrontPage, in turn, will add a list box to the Spelling dialog box and display a list of Web pages (in the current FrontPage web) which have one or more spelling errors as it adds a task titled "Fix misspelled words" for each page with at least on misspelling to the current FrontPage web's tasks list.
6. To exit the spell check, click your mouse pointer on the close button (the "X") in the upper right-hand corner of the Spelling dialog box.

When you are ready to perform one or more of the spell check tasks, switch to Tasks view, right-click your mouse pointer on one of the "Fix misspelled words" tasks, and select Start Task from the pop-up menu. FrontPage will then display a spelling dialog box similar to that shown in Figure 98.2 for each of the misspellings on the page, in turn. After you have corrected all of the spelling mistakes on a page, FrontPage will display the Spelling Check complete message box and leave you in Page view on the page for which you just completed the spell check task after you click your mouse pointer on the OK button at the bottom of the message box.

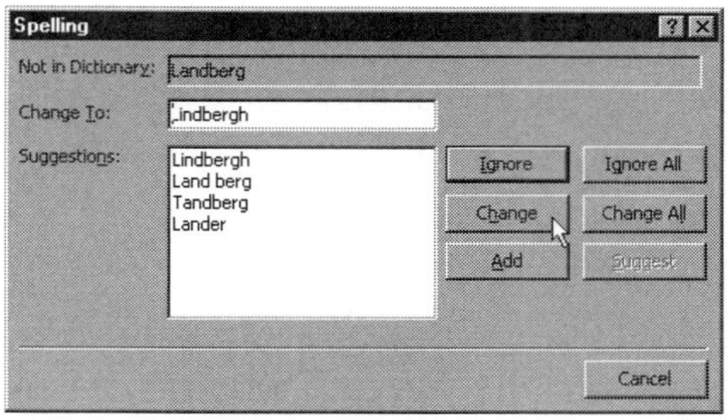

Figure 98.2 The FrontPage (correct individual error) Spelling dialog box.

Unfortunately, FrontPage will not mark the "Fix misspelled words" task complete automatically after you fix all of the spelling errors on the Web page. As such, you must manually mark the spell check task as complete by returning to Task view, right-clicking your mouse pointer on the currently highlighted task, and then selecting Mark Complete from the pop-up menu.

MANAGING TEAM COLLABORATION WHILE IN TASK VIEW

FrontPage automatically keeps track of the username of the person that created a task (as well as when it was created), and the username of the last person that modified the Web page linked to the task (as well as the date and time of the last change). Moreover, in a multi-user (networked) environment, FrontPage uses the login name to verify the user's rights to make the modification any time a user attempts to make a change to the current Web, and then stores the username in the associated task's Modified by field. Therefore, in order to use FrontPage tasks to manage a team's collaborative efforts, you must make sure that each team member logs onto the network using his or her own unique username.

As you may have noticed when you created the tasks in the preceding Tips, FrontPage automatically assigns each task it creates to the username under which you logged into the network. (If you are running FrontPage on a personal computer, the program uses the name you entered when you installed the Windows operating system.) Therefore, be sure to change the default entry in the Assigned to field of the Task Details dialog box to the username of the team member who is to complete the task.

Note: *Although you may assign a task to a specific username, anyone (any username) with enough privilege can complete the task and then change its status to completed. While FrontPage does not force the username to whom the task is assigned to complete it, the program does keep track of the username of the user that made the most recent change to Web page to which the task is linked.*

To view the tasks and the completion status of each task for the current FrontPage web, select the View menu Tasks option. The Tasks view Assigned To column shows you the username to which each task is assigned and the Modified Date column shows you the last date and time that the task's associated Web page was changed.

You can sort the lists of tasks by clicking your mouse pointer on any of the column headings on the Task view display. For example, if you want to sort the list of tasks by the username to which each is assigned, click your mouse pointer on the heading at the top of the Assigned To column. If you click your mouse pointer on the heading a second time, FrontPage will re-sort the tasks in descending (vs. ascending) order by Assigned To username.

If you want to reassign a task to another username, you can do so right on the Tasks view display (i.e. you do not have to use the Tasks Details dialog box). To change a task's assignment, click your mouse pointer on the task's Assigned To column. After FrontPage opens an edit field, enter the new username to which you want the task assigned, and then press the ENTER key on your keyboard.

In short, FrontPage tasks view provides you an easy way to assign different Web site generation jobs (tasks) to different usernames. In addition, Tasks view lets you quickly review who is assigned what tasks, whether each task is not started, in progress, or completed and the date and time of the last modification made to the Web page (or other object) associated with a task.

The FrontPage task management system works as long as the team members login using their own usernames, work on each task by right-clicking the mouse pointer on the task, and then selecting Start Task from the pop-up menu. If you display a Web page in Page view by right-clicking your mouse pointer on the Web page's associated task in Tasks view and selecting Start Task from the pop-up menu, FrontPage will ask you whether or not you want to mark the task as completed when you tell the program to save your changes. If you click your mouse pointer on the YES button when asked if you want the task marked as completed, FrontPage will change the value in the task's Status column to Completed. If you click your mouse pointer on the NO button, FrontPage will change the value in the Task's Status column to In Progress.

USING THE TASK HISTORY TO DISPLAY COMPLETED TASKS

When you mark a task as having been completed, FrontPage will remove the task from the Tasks view the next time you select the View menu Refresh option or the next time you open the current FrontPage web and switch to Tasks view. Although FrontPage removes completed tasks from the Tasks view display, the program does not permanently delete the tasks until you tell it to do so.

To display completed tasks that FrontPage has removed from the Tasks view display, perform the following steps:

1. Select the View menu Tasks option. FrontPage, in turn, will display the list of all uncompleted (not yet started and in progress) tasks.
2. Select the Edit menu Tasks option and click your mouse pointer on Show History. FrontPage, in turn, will display the completed tasks on the Task view display along with the list of uncompleted tasks.

Bear in mind that the Show History selection on the Tasks submenu is a toggle. As such, FrontPage will continue to show the completed tasks on the current FrontPage web's Tasks view display until you repeat the preceding procedure. (If you open another FrontPage web, or close and then reopen the current FrontPage web, FrontPage will uncheck the Show History toggle on the Tasks submenu and will only display the uncompleted tasks in Tasks view—unless you repeat the preceding procedure.)

Note: *To permanently remove a task you no longer want displayed, switch to Tasks view and right-click your mouse pointer on the task you want to remove. Then, select Delete from the pop-up menu.*

PUBLISHING A FRONTPAGE WEB TO A WEB SERVER WITH FRONTPAGE EXTENSIONS

When you *publish* a Web site, you copy the Web pages and other files from your computer into the Web site's root folder on a computer running a Web server. The computer running the Web server (and hosting your Web site) has a permanent connection to the Internet and sends your site's Web pages whenever they are requested across the Internet to the Web site visitor's Web browser for display. Although we refer to someone that requests a Web site's Web pages and activates its hyperlinks as a site *visitor*, a Web site *visitor* really does not "visit" the Web site at all. Instead, the site visitor's Web browser runs on their local computer and sends Web page requests to the Web server across the Internet.

For example, when you enter the URL **HTTP://NVBizNet2.com/index.html** into your Web browser's Address field and press the ENTER key, your Web browsers sends a request to the Web server hosting the NVBizNet2.com Web site, which in turn sends the Web page, INDEX.HTML, back to your Web browser for display.

Before you can use FrontPage to publish your Web site to a Web server, you must, of course, have the appropriate permissions from the Internet Service Provider (ISP) that runs the Web server. If the ISP hosting your Web site is using the Microsoft Internet Information Server (IIS) or some other Web server (such as Apache or Website) on which the ISP has installed FrontPage Server Extensions, you can use FrontPage to publish your Web site to the server by performing the following steps:

1. After using FrontPage to open the FrontPage web you wish to publish, select the File menu Publish Web option. FrontPage, in turn, will display a Publish Destination dialog box similar to that shown in Figure 101.1.

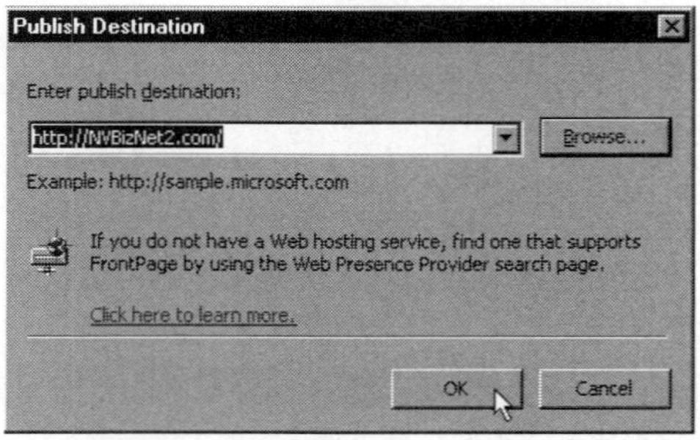

Figure 101.1 The FrontPage Publish Destination dialog box.

2. Into the Enter publish destination field enter the .com address of your Web site or its Internet Protocol (IP) address. For example, if the .com address of your Web site were NVBIZNET2.COM, you would enter **HTTP://NVBIZNET2.COM/** or **HTTP://24.234.49.5/** into the Enter publish destination field.

Note: *If you are publishing your Web site on your ISP's Web server for free, the ISP may require that your Web be a "subweb" of one of his existing Web sites. If this is the case, you will need to enter the ISP's .com address in front of the Web address for your Web site. For example, to publish the FoodCo*

Web site (which you created in a previous Tip in this book) as a subweb of NVBizNet2.com Web site, you would enter: ***HTTP://NVBizNet2.com/FoodCo/*** *into the Enter publish destination field. If your ISP lets you publish your Web site on the Web server as a top-level (root) web, your Web site visitors need only type your .com address into the Web browser's Address field in order to display your home page, such as:* ***HTTP://FoodCo.com.*** *On the other hand, if you publish your FrontPage web as a subweb of another site, the visitor must enter the .com address of the main Web followed by the root directory of the subweb, such as:* ***HTTP://NVBizNet2.com/FoodCo/.***

3. Click your mouse pointer on the OK button. FrontPage, in turn, will prompt you to enter your username and password on the Web server with an Enter Network Password dialog box similar to that shown in Figure 101.2.

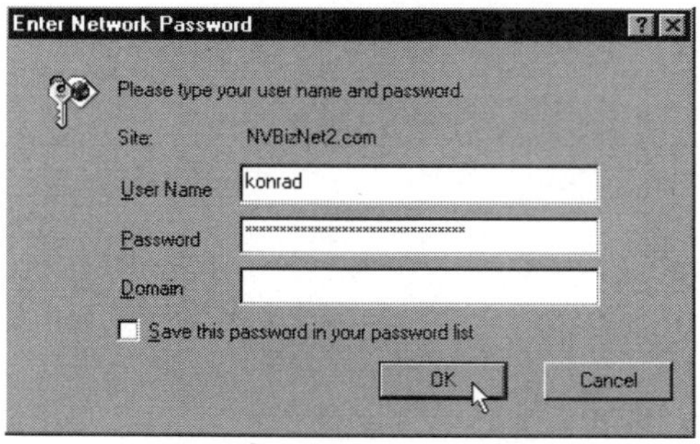

Figure 101.2 *The FrontPage Enter Network Password dialog box.*

Note: *The first time you publish the FrontPage web or subweb to the Web server, FrontPage will prompt you with a message box asking if you want to create the web's folders on the server. If FrontPage displays the message box, click your mouse pointer on the OK button to have the Web server create your site's directory (folder) structure and continue with the publication process.*

4. Enter the information provide by your ISP into the User Name, Password, and Domain fields on the Enter Network Password dialog box. Then, click your mouse pointer on the OK button to login to the Web server.
5. FrontPage, in turn, will display a Publish Web dialog box similar to that shown in Figure 101.3.

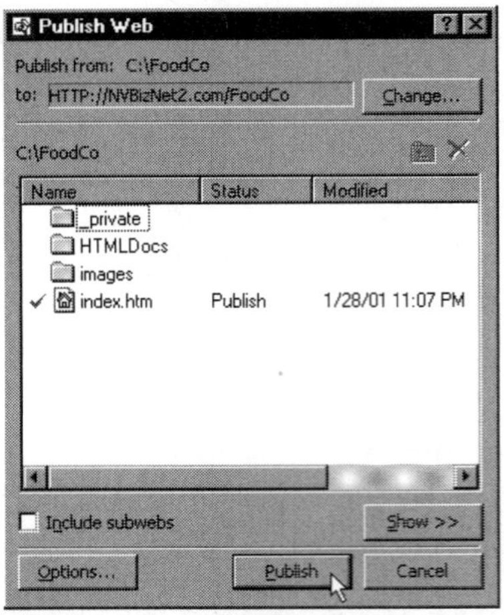

Figure 101.3 The FrontPage Publish Web dialog box.

6. Click your mouse pointer on the OK button near the bottom of the Publish Web dialog box.

After you complete Step 6, FrontPage will contact the Web server and send the files in the current FrontPage web, one file at a time, to the Web server for storage on the Web server's hard drive. If FrontPage successfully completes the publication process, the application will display the success message box shown in Figure 101.4.

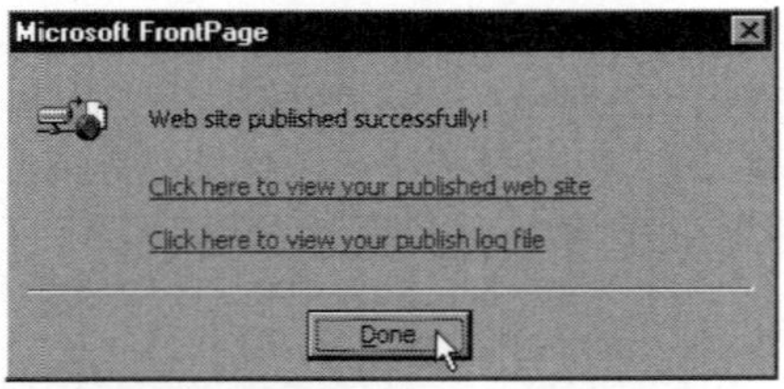

Figure 101.4 The Microsoft FrontPage Publish Success message box.

If you want to use your Web browser to see what your Web site looks like, click your mouse pointer on the Click here to view your published web site hyperlink. Otherwise, click your mouse pointer on DONE button at the bottom of the message box.

Note: *FrontPage Server Extensions are a set of programs and scripts installed on a Web server which extend the server's functionality to support FrontPage authoring tools and security. To find an ISP with FrontPage Server Extensions installed on its Web server, use your Web browser to display the Web page at:* ***HTTP://www.Microsoftwpp.com/wppsearch/****. If Microsoft has moved the Web page by the time you read this book, click your mouse pointer on the Click here to learn more hyperlink near the bottom of the Publish Destination dialog box (which you saw in Figure 101.1) and follow the hyperlink to the new location of the ISP search page.*

UNDERSTANDING AND SETTING WEB SITE DEVELOPMENT PERMISSIONS

After you publish a FrontPage web to a Web server that has FrontPage Server Extensions installed, you can use the FrontPage Tools menu Server option to set the access available to different members of the Web site development team. FrontPage provides for three levels of development permissions:

- **Administer** – usernames granted Administer access can create, delete, and edit Web sites and Web pages. Moreover, a username with Administer permission can adjust the permissions assigned to other usernames.
- **Author** – usernames given Author access can create, delete, and edit Web pages but cannot create or delete Web sites. Moreover, usernames with Author access cannot adjust permissions assigned to other usernames.
- **Browse** – usernames allowed Browse access can only view the Web site with a Web browser. Moreover, usernames with only Browse access cannot use FrontPage to open the Web site on the Web server.

To work with a site's permissions, you must open the FrontPage web on the Web server. As such, you cannot adjust the development permissions on the current FrontPage web until you publish the web to the Web server. After you have published a FrontPage web to the Web server, perform the following steps to set the site's development permissions:

1. Select the File menu Open Web option. FrontPage, in turn, will display the Open Web dialog box.
2. Enter the Web site's .com address or Internet Protocol (IP) address in the Web name field. For example, to open a Web site you published to the IP address 24.234.49.5, enter: **HTTP://24.234.49.5** into the Web name field. Then, click your mouse pointer on the OPEN button. FrontPage, in turn, display the Enter Network Password dialog box (you saw in Figure 101.2, in Tip 101).
3. Enter your username and password for the Web server into the User Name and Password fields of the Enter Network Password dialog box. Then, click your mouse pointer on the OK button.
4. Click your mouse pointer on the OPEN button near the lower right-hand corner of the Open Web dialog box.
5. Select the Tools menu Server option and click your mouse pointer on Permissions. If you entered a .com address (or IP address) only in Step 2, you are opening a main (root) Web, and FrontPage will display a

Permissions dialog box with a Group and a Users tab similar to that shown in Figure 102.1.

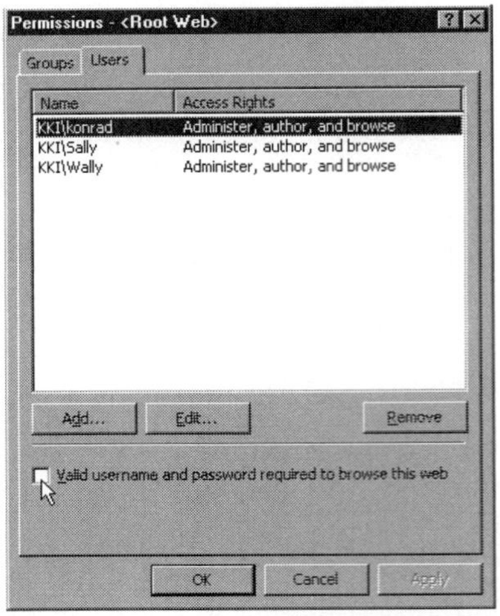

Figure 102.1 The Microsoft FrontPage (root web) Permissions dialog box.

If you entered a .com address (or IP address) followed by a folder name in Step 2, you are opening a subweb, and FrontPage will display a Permissions dialog box with a Settings, Group, and Users tab similar to that shown in Figure 102.2.

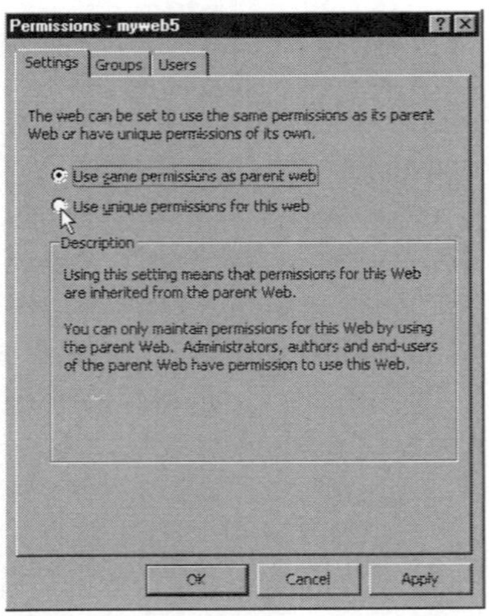

Figure 102.2 The Microsoft FrontPage (subweb) Permissions dialog box.

6. If you are working with a subweb and you want to maintain a separate set of permissions for the subweb, click your mouse pointer on the Use unique permissions for this web radio button. (If you click your

mouse pointer on the Use same permissions as parent web radio button, you will only be able to add usernames and adjust their permissions on the main (root) web because the subweb will inherit its usernames and their permissions from the root web.) Then, click your mouse pointer on the APPLY button.

7. Click your mouse pointer on the Users tab.
8. To add a new user, click your mouse pointer on the ADD button. FrontPage, in turn, will display an Add Users dialog box similar to that shown in Figure 102.3.

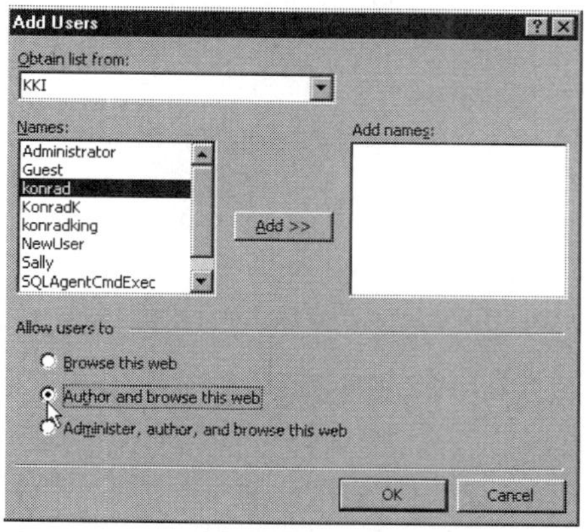

Figure 102.3 The Microsoft FrontPage Add Users dialog box.

9. Double-click your mouse pointer on each username in the Names list box that should have the same set of privileges. After you double-click your mouse pointer on a username, FrontPage will copy the username from the Names list box on the left into the Add names list box on the right.
10. Click your mouse pointer on the Browse, Author, or Administer radio button to set the permissions you want to grant each of the users listed in the Add names list box.
11. Click your mouse pointer on the OK button. FrontPage, in turn, will update the FrontPage web's username/permissions list and return to the Permissions (either root or subweb) dialog box.
12. If you want to restrict browser access to the Web site's pages so that only users to whom you have granted Browse permission or above can access the Web site, click your mouse pointer on the check box to the left of Valid username and password required to browse this web" until a check mark appears. If you leave the check box cleared, anyone with a Web browser can view the Web site's pages.

13. Click your mouse pointer on the OK button near the bottom of the Permissions dialog box.

After you complete Step 13, FrontPage will update the usernames and their permissions on the Web server and return to the FrontPage application window.

UPDATING WEB SITE DEVELOPMENT PERMISSIONS

In addition to using the Permissions dialog box to add usernames and their privileges, you can use it to change previously granted privileges or to remove a username's development privileges altogether. For example, the Permission's dialog box lets you upgrade a username's Author permissions to Administer or to downgrade a username's Administer access to Browse. The most important thing to remember is that like adding new usernames and their privileges, changing permissions and/or removing usernames requires that you open the FrontPage web whose development permissions you want to change directly on the Web server. If you open a FrontPage web by using something other than its hypertext transport protocol (HTTP) universal resource locator (URL), FrontPage will disable the Tools menu Server option that lets you update a Web site's development permissions.

To update a Web site's development permissions, perform the following steps:

1. Open the FrontPage Web whose development permissions you want to change by selecting the File menu Open Web option.
2. After FrontPage displays the Open Web dialog box, enter the Web site's .com address or Internet Protocol (IP) address into the Web name field. For example, to open a Web site you published to the IP address 24.234.49.5, enter: **HTTP://24.234.49.5** into the Web name field. Then, click your mouse pointer on the OPEN button. FrontPage, in turn, will prompt you to enter your username and password for the Web server hosting the Web site into the fields of the Enter Network Password dialog box (you saw in Figure 101.2, in Tip 101).
3. Enter your username and password for the Web server into the User Name and Password fields of the Enter Network Password dialog box. Then, click your mouse pointer on the OK button.
4. Click your mouse pointer on the OPEN button near the lower right-hand corner of the Open Web dialog box.
5. Select the Tools menu Server option and click your mouse pointer on Permissions. FrontPage, in turn, will display the Permissions dialog box.
6. Click your mouse pointer on the Users tab.
7. Click your mouse pointer on the username whose Web development permissions you want to change, and then click your mouse pointer

on the EDIT button. FrontPage, in turn, will display an Edit Users dialog box similar to that shown in Figure 103.

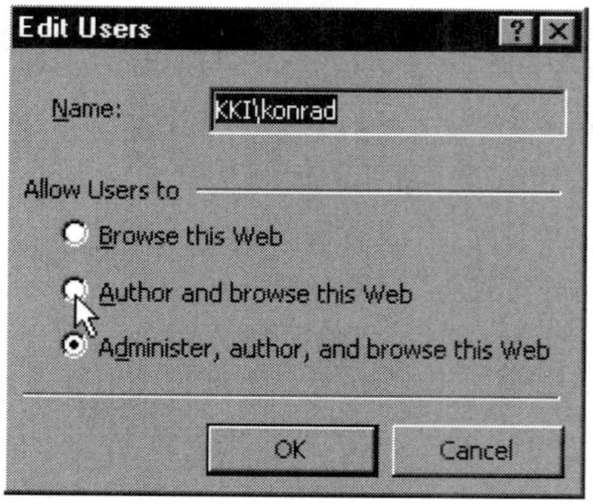

Figure 103 The Microsoft FrontPage Edit Users dialog box.

8. To change the development privileges for the username you selected in Step 7, click your mouse pointer on the radio button (Browse, Author, or Administer) of the new permission level, and then on the OK button near the bottom center of the Edit Users dialog box. FrontPage, in turn, will change the username's permission level and return to the Users tab of the Permissions dialog box.
9. If you want to remove a username, click your mouse pointer on the username you want to remove to select it, and then on the Remove button to remove the username from the Web site developers list.

Repeat Steps 7 - 9 until you have adjusted all of the development permissions and/or removed the usernames that should no longer have development access to the site from the Web site's developers list. Then, click your mouse pointer on the OK button near the bottom center or of the Edit Users dialog box to return to the FrontPage application window.

USING THE PAGE PROPERTIES, WORKGROUP TAB TO MANAGE THE MASTER STATUS LIST

Before you publish a Web page in your company's Web site on the Internet, the Web page may have to go through several levels of review. After all, the Web content you place on the Web site paints a picture of your company for all of the potential customers that visit the site before deciding to do business with your company. A Web page may, for example, be required to go from Content Development status (by the author) to Content Review status (by the department head) and then to Legal Review status (by the firm's lawyers) before you are allowed to publish it on the company's Web site.

While FrontPage does not have a built-in routing facility that will send a Web page (via e-mail or other electronic means) from one level of review to the next, FrontPage does have the ability to store the description of the most recent level of review, who did it, and when it was done. However, the default review levels that come with the program are meant as a guideline as to the types of reviews your Web pages might go through before you publish them. Fortunately, FrontPage provides an easy way to customize the Master Review Status list so that it satisfies the particular needs of your organization.

To customize the Review Status Master List, perform the following steps:

1. Open an existing FrontPage web or use one of the FrontPage Wizards to create a new FrontPage web.

Note: *The Review Status Master List is global to all FrontPage webs, as such, it does not matter which FrontPage web you open (or create) in order to customize the Review Status Master List.*

2. Select the View menu Folders option to display the current FrontPage web in Folders view.
3. Right-click your mouse pointer on the name or icon of one of the Web pages listed in Folders view and select Properties from the pop-up menu. FrontPage, in turn, will display the (Page) Properties dialog box.
4. Click your mouse pointer on the Workgroup tab.
5. On the (Page) Properties dialog box Workgroup tab, click your mouse pointer on the STATUSES button. FrontPage, in turn, will display a Review Status Master List dialog box similar to that shown in Figure 104.

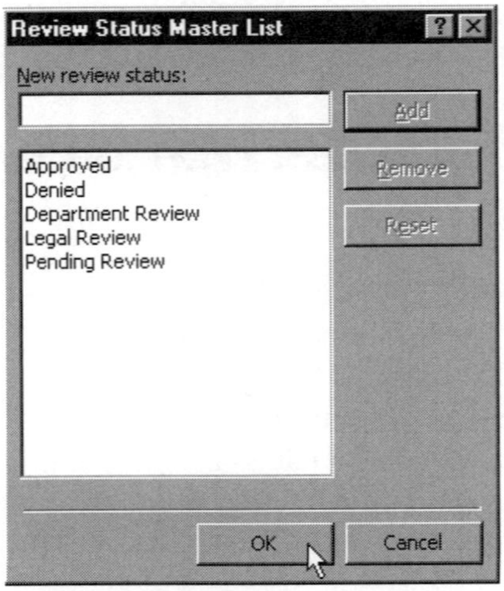

Figure 104 *The FrontPage Review Status Master List dialog box.*

6. To add a new review status to the master list, type the review status you want to add into the New review status field at the top of the dialog box, and then click your mouse pointer on the ADD button to the right of the New review status field. For example, if your company requires that the manager of the marketing department must review web content before it is published, type: **Marketing Manager Review** into the New review status field, and then click your mouse pointer on the ADD button.
7. Repeat Step 6 until you have added all of the review status descriptions you need.
8. If the Review Status Master List has any review status description you do not need, click your mouse pointer on the review status you want to delete (to select it) and then on the REMOVE button to the right of the review status list box to remove the Review Status you selected.
9. Repeat Step 8 until you have removed all Review Status descriptions your organization does not use.
10. To exit the Review Status Master List dialog box, click your mouse pointer on the OK button near the bottom of the dialog box. FrontPage, in turn, will return to the (Page) Properties dialog box.
11. To exit the (Page) Properties dialog box and return to the FrontPage application window, click your mouse pointer the OK button near the bottom center of the dialog box.

As you remove unneeded Review Status descriptions in Step 8, remember that FrontPage uses the same Review Status Master List for all FrontPage webs. Therefore, only remove a Review Status description if you do not plan to use it in *any* of the FrontPage webs you plan to use the program to maintain—i.e. do not remove a Review Status description just because you do not need it for the current FrontPage web.

USING THE PAGE PROPERTIES, WORKGROUP TAB TO MANAGE THE USERNAMES LIST

Any time you assign a Web page to a username for review or assign a task to a username for completion, you can either type the username or (if you previously added the username to the Usernames Master List), you can use the drop-down list button to the right of the User name field and click your mouse pointer on the username you want in the drop-down list of usernames. Unlike the Review Status Master List (which is global across all FrontPage webs), the Usernames Master List is unique to each FrontPage web.

To add a username to the drop-down list of usernames displayed when you click your mouse pointer on the drop-down list button to the right of a User name field, perform the following steps:

1. Open the FrontPage web shows Usernames Master List you want to change.
2. Select the View menu Folders option to display the current FrontPage web in Folders view.
3. Right-click your mouse pointer on the name or icon of one of the Web pages listed in Folders view, and then select Properties from the pop-up menu. FrontPage, in turn, will display the (Page) Properties dialog box.
4. Click your mouse pointer on the Workgroup tab.
5. On the (Page) Properties dialog box Workgroup tab, click your mouse pointer on the NAMES button. FrontPage, in turn, will display a Usernames Master List dialog box similar to that shown in Figure 105.

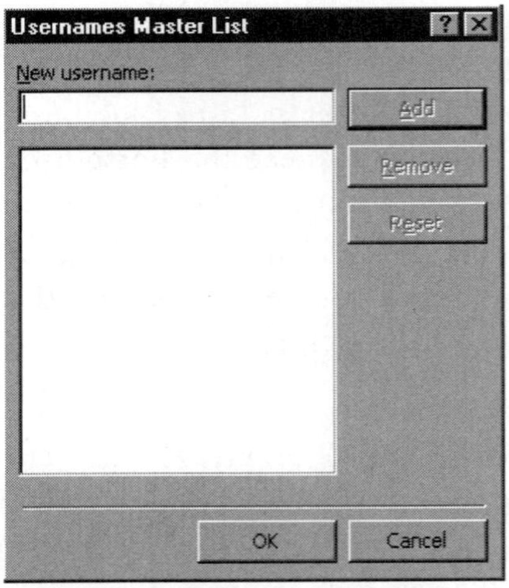

Figure 105 The FrontPage Usernames Master List dialog box.

6. To add a new username, enter it into the New username field at the top of the dialog box, and then click your mouse pointer on the ADD button to the right of the New username field. For example, if "Konrad" needs to review one or more Web pages or complete a task or two, type: **Konrad** into the New username field and then click your mouse pointer on the ADD button.
7. Repeat Step 6 until you have added all of the usernames you need for the current FrontPage web.
8. If the Usernames Master List contains usernames you do not need, click your mouse pointer on the username you want to delete (to select it) and then on the REMOVE button to the right of the username list box to remove the username you selected.

9. Repeat Step 8 until you have removed all usernames you do not need for the current FrontPage web.
10. To exit the Usernames Master List dialog box, click your mouse pointer on the OK button near the bottom of the dialog box. FrontPage, in turn, will return to the (Page) Properties dialog box.
11. To exit the (Page) Properties dialog box and return to the FrontPage application window, click your mouse pointer the OK button near the bottom center of the dialog box.

The usernames you enter into the New username field of the Usernames Master List dialog box do not have to be actual network users. As such, you can add *usernames* such as Marketing, Sales, Office, Service, or Collections, as well as the actual names of individual users such as Konrad, Karen, Amber, etc.

ENABLING FRONTPAGE SOURCE CODE CONTROL

When two or more people work on Web pages for the same Web site, there is a distinct possibility that more than one of them will be making changes to the same file at the same time. Unfortunately, FrontPage is not able to merge each person's changes into a new composite Web page when this happens. As a result, the last person to save (or publish) the Web page "wins"—overwriting (and thereby erasing) the changes made to the Web page by other users who were editing it at the same time. Having a site developer overwrite another's work causes frustration due to having one's work erased and adversely affects the development team's productivity.

To prevent one Web page author from undoing another's work inadvertently, you can turn on FrontPage source control for a particular FrontPage web (or subweb). After you activate source control for a web or subweb, FrontPage will require an author to *check-out* a Web page before allowing the author to modify it. If another author already has a page checked-out, then FrontPage will let the author open the Web page for read-only access, but will not allow the author to make changes to the page. Since only one person can check-out a Web page at a time, only one site developer will be able to make changes to a Web page—the developer who has the paged checked-out. All others must wait until the author checks-in before FrontPage will allow one of them to check-out the Web page again for further modification.

Because the majority of the people that purchase FrontPage work on a Web site alone, FrontPage initially turns off source control in each new FrontPage web you create. To activate source control, perform the following steps:

1. Open the FrontPage web whose source control you want to activate.
2. Select the Tools menu Web option. FrontPage, in turn, will display a Web settings dialog box similar to that shown in Figure 106.

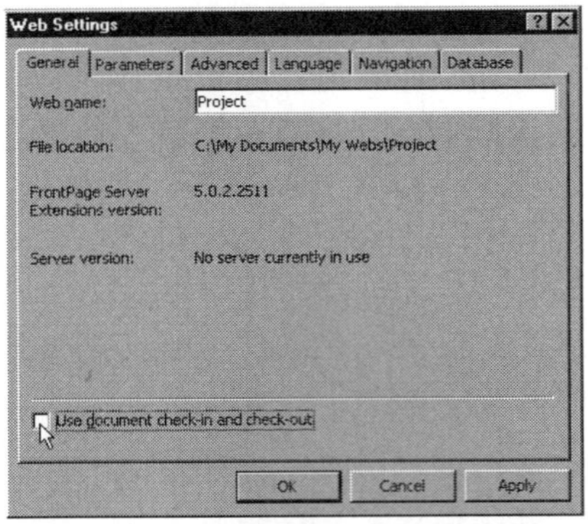

Figure 106 The FrontPage Web Settings dialog box, General tab.

3. If it is not displayed, click your mouse pointer on the General tab.
4. Click your mouse pointer on the Use document check-in and check-out check box (near the bottom of the Web Settings dialog box,), until a check mark appears.
5. Click your mouse button on the OK button.

After you complete Step 5, FrontPage will prompt you with a message box stating that it must recalculate the current FrontPage web since you changed its source control status. When you see the message box, click your mouse pointer on the YES button to finish activating the web's source control.

The next Tip will explain how to check-out and check-in files in a FrontPage Web with source control. For now, the important thing to understand is that FrontPage source control (once activated) prevents one developer from overwriting another developer's work by allowing only one developer at a time to check-out a file for modification. The FrontPage Checkout Status report shows you who has a file checked-out, the file's current version number (which indicates how often the file has been modified), and when the file was checked-out.

UNDERSTANDING THE FILE CHECK-IN AND CHECK-OUT PROCEDURES

As you learned in the preceding Tip, turning on FrontPage source code control prevents one developer from unknowingly erasing another's work by allowing only one developer at a time make changes to a particular file used in a FrontPage web. While FrontPage allows more than one developer to open a Web page at the same time, the program only lets one of them open the Web page for update access. After one person opens the Web page with update access rights, FrontPage grants only read only rights to anyone else that opens the same Web page.

When source control is active for a particular FrontPage web, FrontPage displays a file's check-out status next to the file's icon in the Folder List pane, in Folders view, and in Reports view. Figure 107 shows the Folder List pane for a FrontPage web with its files under source control.

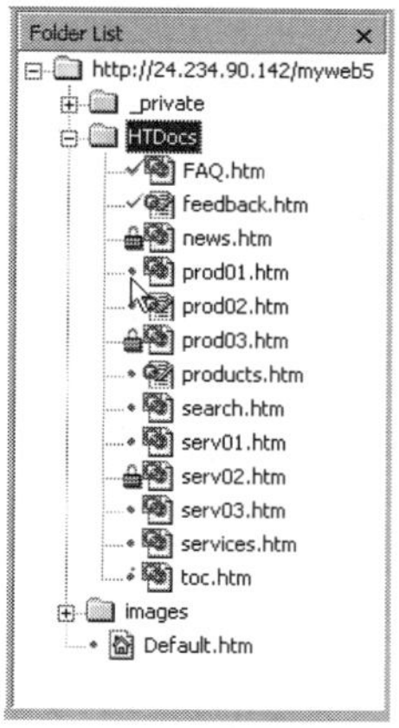

Figure 107 *The FrontPage Folder List pane with source control activated.*

A red checkmark to the left of a file's icon indicates that current FrontPage user has the file checked-out; a green dot to the left of a file's icon indicates that a file is not checked-out; and a padlock to the left of a file's icon indicates that another user has the file-checked out.

To check-out a file, right-click your mouse pointer on the file's name (or the icon to the left of the file's name), and then select Check Out from the pop-up menu. FrontPage, in turn, will change the green dot to the left of the icon to a red checkmark to indicate that you (the current FrontPage user) have the file checked-out. (Each red check mark to the left of a file's icon in your FrontPage application window will appear as a padlock to the left of the file's icon in another user's FrontPage application.) You can open and modify any file preceded by either a green dot (indicating it has not been checked-out) or a red check mark (indicating that the file is checked-out to your username). If you attempt to open a file with a padlock to the left of its icon, FrontPage will prompt you with a warning message that lets you know the name of the user who has the file checked-out and asks if you want to open a read-only copy of the file.

Note: *When you try to open a file that is not currently checked-out, FrontPage will ask you if you want to check-out the file. If you click your mouse pointer on the NO button when asked if you want to check-out the file, FrontPage will still allow you to edit the file, but will not change the file's check-out status. As a result, any changes you make could be overwritten by another developer that saves his changes to the file's original contents after you save any changes you make. Conversely, if you click your mouse pointer on the YES button at the bottom of the message box, FrontPage will check-out the file to your username, and no one else can change the file until you check-in the file again.*

When you save changes to disk, FrontPage does not automatically change the file's check-out status to from checked-out to checked-in. This allows you to save changes periodically as you are working without having to worry about another user checking-out the file you are modifying before you are finished with the changes you want to make.

To check-in a file (and thereby make it available for modification to another user), right-click your mouse pointer on the file's icon, and then select Check In from the pop-up menu. FrontPage, in turn, will change the red check mark to the left of the file's icon back to a green dot. (You can only check-in files that you previously checked-out, i.e. the files with a red check mark to the left of the file's icons in your FrontPage application window.)

UNDERSTANDING FRONTPAGE WEBS

As you already know, Microsoft FrontPage is a program that lets you create and manage Web sites. In general, a Web site consists of a set of folders and subfolders which contain HTML documents (Web pages) and other support files (such as pictures, video clips, sound files, command scripts, and executable programs) displayed on or activated by hyperlinks on the Web pages.

In addition to acting as a what-you-see-is-what-you-get (WYSIWYG) editor you can use to generate Web page HTML as you type and format the site's text, FrontPage provides wizards that will automatically generate Web pages that you can use as a template to create a custom Web site and a directory structure that makes it easy to keep the HTML documents and the Web site's other files organized. If FrontPage stopped right there—with Web page and directory (folder) structure generation—you would have a Web site and not a *FrontPage web*. What differentiates a FrontPage web from a Web site is the availability of management tools and reports.

As you learned from the previous Tips in this book, FrontPage lets you create a To Do (or task) list, and provides tools to assign tasks to various users. The program also gives users the ability to update the status of the task they are assigned as they complete their work and provides management reports so you can make sure the project remains on track. In addition to task management, you can activate a FrontPage web's source control to prevent one author from inadvertently overwriting another's work.

A FrontPage web also includes various reports that tell you which Web pages will take too long to transfer to a Web visitor's browser, reports that alert you to broken links and component errors you need to repair before you put the Web site online, and reports that show you the Web site's layout including all hyperlinks to and from each of the FrontPage web's pages.

In short, a FrontPage web includes Web pages and other support files organized in folders—just like any other non-FrontPage web. However, unlike non-FrontPage webs, a FrontPage web also includes management tools, publishing tools, and reports that help you create and maintain the Web site.

UNDERSTANDING FRONTPAGE SUBWEBS

A *subweb* is a FrontPage web within another FrontPage web. Although a subweb's main (or root) folder is a subfolder within the main (or top-level) FrontPage web, a subweb is more than just another folder in a FrontPage web's directory (folder) structure. In fact, each subweb of a FrontPage web has its own set of files organized in folders within the subweb's main (root) folder, management tools, reports, tasks lists, and usernames.

When you publish a FrontPage web, FrontPage copies all of the web's folders and their contents to the Web server. However, FrontPage will not publish any of the current FrontPage web's subwebs [the folders within the FrontPage web's main (root) folder that themselves contain FrontPage webs], unless you tell it to do so by clicking a check mark into the Include Subwebs check box near the bottom left-hand side of the of the Publish Web dialog box.

Although a subweb is a FrontPage web within another FrontPage web, it is up to the Web site administrator to decide whether a Web site's FrontPage web and its subwebs (if any) appear as a single "Web site", or if the main (the top-level) FrontPage web and some or all of its subwebs have the look and feel of multiple, individual Web sites—accessible by hyperlink(s) from one web (or subweb) to another.

Suppose, for example, that you create a Corporate Presence Web site as the main (top-level) FrontPage web. You might use another FrontPage Wizard to create a Customer Support subweb for the Corporate Presence web (by creating the Customer Support web in a folder subordinate to the Corporate Presence site's main folder). In this scenario, you want the Customer Support subweb to appear as if it were just another part of the company's Web site. Therefore, you would apply the same FrontPage theme (the same colors and text styles) to both the main FrontPage web and the subweb.

Now, suppose your company allowed its employees to create their own (very tasteful, of course) personal Web sites as subwebs of the main (Corporate Presence) web. Although accessible from the company's main Web site, you would want a clear distinction between the company's Web content and the employee created subwebs. In addition, you would use the FrontPage web's development permissions to let each employee have author privilege on his or her own subweb and to publish their personal Web sites (FrontPage subwebs) at will.

OPENING A FRONTPAGE WEB ON A LOCAL COMPUTER

If you worked the projects in the previous Tips in this book, you already know how to open a FrontPage web. However, don't worry if you haven't worked the projects, opening an existing FrontPage web is a simple process:

1. After you start the FrontPage application, select the File menu Open Web option. FrontPage, in turn, will display an Open Web dialog box similar to that shown in Figure 110.

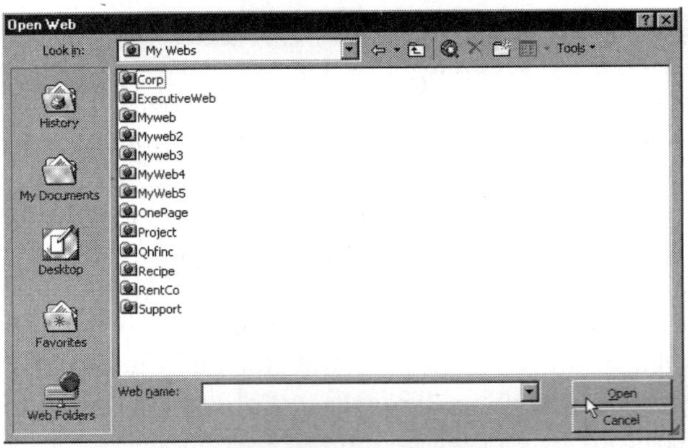

Figure 110 The Microsoft FrontPage Open Web dialog box.

2. Use the drop-down list button to the right of the Look in field to navigate to the folder which contains the FrontPage web you want to open.

Note: *By default, FrontPage will place FrontPage webs you create and save to disk into the folder: C:\My Documents\My Webs. You can navigate your computer to the C:\My Document folder by clicking your mouse pointer on the My Documents icon (second from the top) on the icon bar along the left-hand side of the Open Web dialog box. After you click your mouse pointer on the My Documents icon, look for and double-click your mouse pointer on* ***My Webs*** *in the list box below the Look in field. FrontPage, in turn, will navigate to the C:\My Documents\My Webs folder and display its contents (the FrontPage webs you saved to the default folder), in the list box below the Look in field.*

3. In the list box below the Look in field, click your mouse pointer on the folder with the FrontPage web you want to open.
4. Click your mouse pointer on the OPEN button in the lower right-hand corner of the Open Web dialog box.

Instead of navigating to the folder which contains the FrontPage web folders in Step 2 and then selecting the folder with the FrontPage web you want to open in Step 3, you can skip Steps 2 and 3 if you enter the full pathname of the FrontPage web you want to open into the Web name field at the bottom of the Open Web dialog box instead. For example, if you stored the FrontPage web you want to open in the FoodCo folder at the root of your C: drive, you would perform Step 1 of the procedure, enter C:\FoodCo into the Web name field (instead of performing Steps 2 and 3), and then click your mouse pointer on the OPEN button as specified in Step 4.

Note: *If you recently saved the FrontPage web you want to open, select the File menu Recent Webs option (instead of the File menu Open Web option). FrontPage, in turn, will display its Recent*

Webs list. If you see the name of the FrontPage web you want to open in the Recent Webs list, click your mouse pointer on its name, or press the number next to the name. FrontPage, in turn, will open the web.

After you open a web, FrontPage will display it in the view the program was in before you opened the web. For example, if you were in Tasks view before you performed the procedure to open an existing FrontPage web, FrontPage will display the web in Tasks view. Do not worry if you are in Page view and see an empty document pane after you open a FrontPage web. FrontPage does not automatically open a Web page in the current web for you. To display one the Web pages in the FrontPage web you just opened, select the View menu Folders option to switch to Folders view, and then double-click your mouse button on the Web page you want to display in Page view.

OPENING A FRONTPAGE WEB ON A WEB SITE

In addition to opening an existing FrontPage web stored on your computer or on a hard drive accessible on your local area network (LAN), FrontPage also lets you open (and edit) FrontPage webs on a Web site. However, in order to open the FrontPage web on a Web site, the site's Web server must have FrontPage Server Extensions installed, and you must know a username/password pair that gives you access rights to modify the site's Web pages.

Bear in mind that any changes you make to the Web pages on the Web server will be seen immediately by anyone visiting the Web site—so be careful. Normally, you should work on the copy of the FrontPage web stored on your computer (or network), and then use the File menu Publish option to send your finished (checked and rechecked) product to the Web server. However, FrontPage does not require that you make changes to the Web site offline. In fact, opening a FrontPage web on a Web server across the Internet is almost as easy an opening the same FrontPage web on a local computer.

To open a FrontPage web on a Web site, perform the following steps:

1. If you do not have an "always on" (i.e. permanent) connection to the Internet, use your modem to establish a dial-up connection to your Internet Service Provider (ISP).
2. After you start the FrontPage application, select the File menu Open Web option. FrontPage, in turn, will display an Open Web dialog box similar to the one you saw in Figure 109.
3. Into the Web name field (near the bottom of the Open Web dialog box) enter the Web address (URL) of the Web site that contains the FrontPage web you want to open. You can enter either a .com address or the Internet Protocol (IP) address. For example, if you want to open the FrontPage web at NVBiznet2.com (IP address: 24.234.90.142),

you could type either **HTTP://NVBizNet2.com/** or **HTTP://24.234.49.5/** into the Web name field.

4. Click your mouse pointer on the OPEN button near the bottom right-hand corner of the Open Web dialog box. FrontPage, in turn, will contact the Web server and display an Enter Network Password dialog box similar to that shown in Figure 111 if you are not already logged into the Web server.

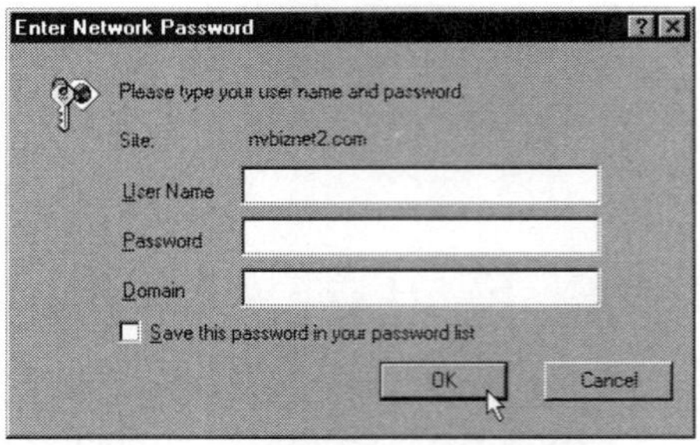

***Figure 111** The FrontPage Enter Network Password dialog box.*

5. Enter your username and password into the User name and Password fields of the Enter Network Password dialog box, and then click your mouse pointer on the OK button near the bottom right-hand side of the dialog box.

After you perform Step 5, FrontPage will again contact the Web server and send the username and password you entered into the fields of the Enter Network Password dialog box. If the Web server validates the username/password pair you entered as valid for update access to the Web site, FrontPage will open the FrontPage web on the Web site and display it using the current view. If you select the File menu Folders view, FrontPage will display the Web site's directory (folder) structure, and you can double-click your mouse pointer on name (or icon) of the Web page you want to edit in Page view.

To write the changes you make to the Web site, select the File menu Save option or click your mouse pointer on the Save button (third button from the left) on the Standard Toolbar. Because FrontPage will save the file(s) directly to the Web server, anyone that visits the Web site and requests the Web page(s) you modified after you tell FrontPage to save your changes will see the updated (and not the original) Web page(s).

CLOSING A WEB SITE

Each instance of FrontPage running on your computer will only let you open one FrontPage web at a time. However, unlike previous versions of the program, FrontPage no longer forces you to close the current FrontPage web when you select the File menu Open Web option or attempt to edit a Web page in a web other than the current FrontPage web. Instead, FrontPage now automatically tells Windows to start another copy of itself, and the new running copy (or instance) of the program opens the other FrontPage web.

You can switch between the multiple instances of FrontPage running on your system by clicking your mouse pointer on the Microsoft FrontPage buttons on the Windows task bar. Moreover, you can use the Windows clipboard, cut-and-paste, and copy-and-paste operations to move or copy text, entire Web pages, and other support files from one FrontPage web to another.

When you are finished working with a FrontPage web and want to work on another without starting another copy of FrontPage, select the File menu Close Web to close the current FrontPage web. FrontPage, in turn, will prompt you to save any unsaved changes to currently open Web pages. When prompted, click your mouse pointer on the message box YES button to save a modified page.

Note: *If you created a new Web page in the current FrontPage web and close the web before saving the Web page to a disk file for the first time, FrontPage will prompt you with a Save As dialog box instead of a message box. To save a new Web page, enter its file name into the File name field near the bottom of the Save As dialog box, and then press the ENTER key on your keyboard.*

After FrontPage is finished saving modified and newly created Web pages, the program will close the current FrontPage web and wait for you to either create a new FrontPage web or open an existing one.

DELETING A FRONTPAGE WEB

Although a Web site's Web pages only take up a small amount of disk space, the graphics images, movie clips, animations, and sound files stored in a Web site's folders can consume a huge chunk of your computer's hard drive. As such, you should look through the FrontPage webs on your system periodically and remove the Web sites you no longer need. For example, perhaps you created some Web sites for practice—to see what one or more of the FrontPage site generation Wizards could do. Or, perhaps you previously used FrontPage to retrieve a Web site from the Internet onto your computer, so you could "look under the hood" to see how some of the site's more interesting features were implemented. Whatever the reason, FrontPage gives you an easy way to delete Web sites from your computer and free up the disk space they occupy.

To delete a FrontPage web, perform the following steps:

1. Open the FrontPage web you want to remove (by executing the procedure in the earlier Tip entitled "Opening a FrontPage Web on a Local Computer" or "Opening a FrontPage Web on a Web

site"—depending on whether the FrontPage Web you want to remove is on your local computer or on a Web site).

2. Select the View menu Folders option to switch to Folders view.
3. To delete the current FrontPage web, right-click your mouse pointer on its root folder (i.e. the first folder listed at the top of the Folders List pane, and select Delete from the pop-up menu. FrontPage, in turn, will display a Confirm Delete message box similar to the one shown in Figure 113.

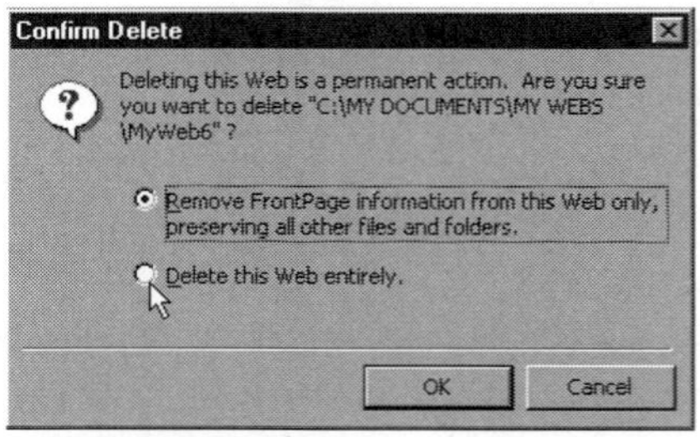

Figure 113 The Microsoft FrontPage Confirm (web) Delete message box.

4. If you want to remove the FrontPage web including all of its folders, subfolders, and the files in those folders, click your mouse pointer on the radio button to the left of Delete this Web entirely. Alternatively, if you want to keep the FrontPage web's content files (Web pages, sound files, movie clips, etc.) and maintain its directory (folder) structure, click your mouse pointer on the radio button to the left of Remove FrontPage information from this Web only, preserving all other files and folders. Bear in mind that only the first option actually deletes files and folders to free up disk space on your computer. Conversely, the second option, to remove FrontPage information only, will free up a small amount of space because FrontPage will leave the web's files and folders on your computer, and remove only such things as the FrontPage web's task list, file check-in/check-out status data, its publication status, etc.
5. Click your mouse pointer on the OK button at the bottom of the Confirm Delete message box.

After you complete Step 5, FrontPage will either delete the Web sites file's and folders from your hard drive or will leave the site's files and folders in place while removing only the sites FrontPage web specific information—depending on the option you selected in Step 4.

If you chose to delete the FrontPage web entirely (in Step 4), the folder that contained the web [and its subweb(s), if any] will not appear among the list of FrontPage web folders the next time you select the File menu Open Web option. After all, FrontPage will have removed the folder (and its subfolders) from your hard drive. Conversely, if you chose to remove only the FrontPage information, the web's folder structure (and files) will remain intact, and you will see a folder without a globe (indicating a non-FrontPage web folder) among the list of folders when you select the File menu Open Web option.

Note: *If you remove FrontPage information from a FrontPage web, and later change your mind, you can convert the (now) non-FrontPage web back into the FrontPage web by performing the following steps:*

1. Select the File menu Open web option and open the FrontPage web folder that contains the non-FrontPage web you want to convert. For example, if you have been using the default directory structure created when you installed FrontPage to save your FrontPage webs to the default FrontPage web folder, you will find your FrontPage webs are actually subwebs of the FrontPage web C:\MY DOCUMENTS\MY WEBS on your hard drive. Therefore, to convert a non-FrontPage web in the C:\MY DOCUMENTS\MY WEBS folder, enter **C:\MY DOCUMENTS\MY WEBS** into the Web name field at the bottom of the Open Web dialog box and then click your mouse pointer on the OPEN button.
2. Display the current FrontPage web in Folders view by selecting the View menu Folders option.
3. Right-click your mouse pointer on the non-FrontPage web folder you want to convert, and then select Convert to Web from the pop-up menu.
4. When FrontPage asks you to confirm your desire to convert a folder to a FrontPage web, click your mouse pointer on the YES button near the bottom center of the confirmation message box.

If the folder you converted into a FrontPage web has any subfolders that should be subwebs (i.e. FrontPage webs within the newly converted FrontPage web), you will need to open the converted FrontPage web and repeat Steps 2 – 4 of this procedure for each of the subfolders you want to convert into a subweb.

SAVING A FRONTPAGE WEB TO DISK

When using FrontPage to create a Web site, you should save your work to disk at frequent intervals. Because FrontPage does not automatically save new pages you create, the content on these pages resides only in your computer's memory until you save the page to your hard drive. As such, if your computer locks up before you save your work, you will have to recreate any pages not previously saved. Conversely, if you save your FrontPage web to disk periodically and your computer locks up, you need only redo the work you performed since the last time you saved your work to disk.

You have two choices when you want to save your work to disk. You can either save Web pages to disk one page at a time, or you can tell FrontPage to save all new (previously unsaved) and modified Web pages at once by selecting the File menu Save All option. If you used the Insert menu Picture option to insert graphics or other multimedia files on one or more of the Web pages, FrontPage will display a Save Embedded Files dialog box similar to that shown in Figure 114.1 for each Web page with one or more embedded files.

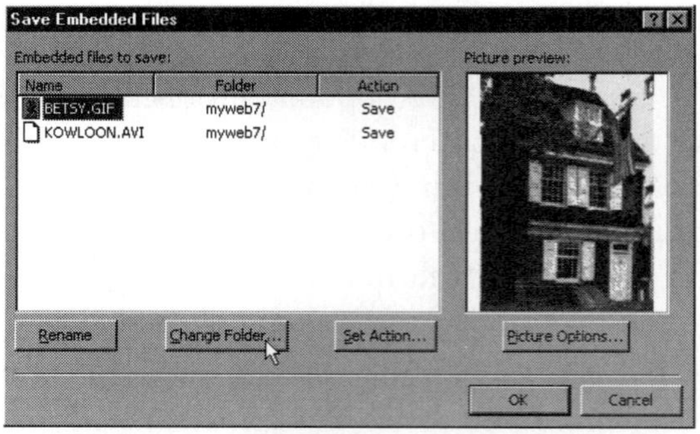

Figure 114.1 *The Microsoft FrontPage Save Embedded Files dialog box.*

If you click your mouse pointer on the OK button near the bottom of the Save Embedded Files dialog box—without changing any options in the dialog box—FrontPage will save a copy of the embedded file in the same folder as the Web page on which it is embedded. However, as discussed in previous Tips, you may want to keep your Web site's files organized in subfolders by file type. As such, store embedded files in a folder other than the one you are using for your HTML documents.

To save an embedded file in a folder other than the HTML documents folder, perform the following steps:

1. Click your mouse pointer on the name of the embedded file in the Embedded files to save list box on the Save Embedded Files dialog box. If you have more than one embedded file of the same type, hold down the CTRL button on your keyboard as you click your mouse pointer on all of the embedded files of the same type to select multiple files.
2. Click your mouse pointer on the CHANGE FOLDER button. FrontPage, in turn, will display a Change Folder dialog box similar to that shown in Figure 114.2.

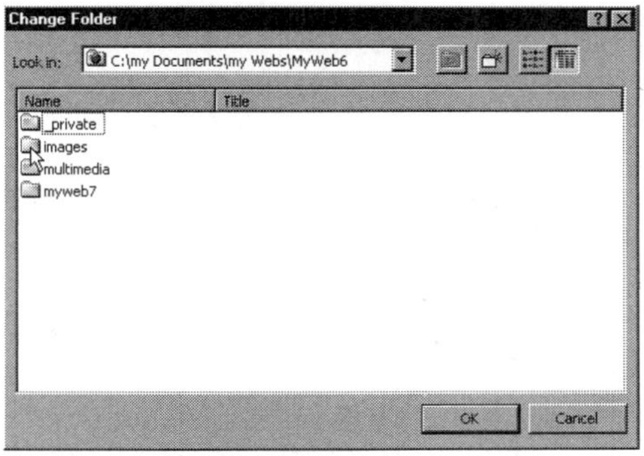

Figure 114.2 The Microsoft FrontPage Change Folder dialog box.

3. Use the drop-down list button to the right of the Look in field to navigate to the folder which contains the folder in which you want to save the embedded file(s) you selected in Step 1.

Note: *If the folder you want does not yet exist, click your mouse pointer on the Create New Folder button (second button to the right of the Look in field). When prompted, enter the new folder's name and then press the ENTER key on your keyboard.*

4. In the folder list box below the Look in field, double-click your mouse pointer on the destination folder (i.e., the folder in which FrontPage is to save the embedded file). Then, click your mouse pointer on the OK button near the bottom right-hand side corner the Change Folder dialog box. FrontPage, in turn, will change the embedded file's destination folder and display the folder's name in the Folder column of the dialog box.
5. To save the embedded file(s) to the folder(s) you specified in Step 1, click your mouse pointer on the OK button near the bottom right-hand corner of the Save Embedded Files dialog box.

Note: *If you embedded the same file on more than one Web page, FrontPage will only prompt you with the Save Embedded Files dialog box once for any one file. After you specify a particular embedded file's destination folder once, FrontPage will save one copy of the file in the folder you specified and change the references on the remaining Web pages that use the file to point to the file's new location.*

SAVING A WEB PAGE TO A "LIVE" WEB SITE

After you make changes to a FrontPage web's pages or add new ones, you can use the File menu Save All option to save all of your work at once, or you can save one (modified or newly created) page at a time by selecting the File menu Save option repeatedly.

Normally, when you are ready to update the content of the Web site on the Web server, you will use the File menu Publish option. However, when you *publish* a FrontPage web stored on your computer to the Web server, FrontPage not only sends any new or modified Web pages and support files to the server, but the program also deletes any files and folders from the server that you previously removed from the locally stored FrontPage web. In short, when you publish a FrontPage web to the Web server, the program makes the folders and folder contents on the Web site look exactly like the FrontPage web on your computer (or on some other workstation on your local area network). Sometimes, however, you only want to update the Web site to reflect some (and not all) of the changes you have made to the FrontPage web. Fortunately, the File menu Save As option lets you update the Web site's content on the Web server one page at a time.

To save a new or modified Web page to the "live" Web site on a Web server, perform the following steps:

1. If you do not have an "always on" (i.e. permanent) connection to the Internet, use your modem to establish a dial-up connection to your Internet Service Provider (ISP).
2. Display the Web page you want to save to the Web server in Page view. If you have more than one Web page open in the Page view document pane, click your mouse pointer on the tab at the top of the Web page you want to save to the Web server.

Note: *If the Web page you want to send to the Web server is not currently open in your FrontPage application window, select the View menu Folders option to switch to Folders view. Click your mouse pointer on the folder that contains the Web page you want to send, and then double-click your mouse pointer on the its filename to display the Web page in the Page view document pane.*

3. Select the File menu Save as option. FrontPage, in turn, will display the Save As dialog box.
4. Into the File name field (near the bottom of the Save As dialog box) enter the Web address (the URL) where you want FrontPage to store the Web page on the Internet. For example, if you want to store the Web page, PRODUCTS.HTM, into the HTDOCS folder on the FOODCO.COM Web site, you would type: **HTTP://FOODCO.COM/HTDOCS/PRODUCTS.HTM** into the File name field.

5. Click your mouse pointer on the SAVE button near the bottom right-hand corner of the Save As dialog box. FrontPage, in turn, will contact the Web server and (if you are not already logged into the Web server) display an Enter Network Password dialog box (similar to the one you saw in Figure 111).
6. Enter your username and password into the User name and Password fields of the Enter Network Password dialog box, and then click your mouse pointer on the OK button near the bottom right-hand corner of the dialog box.
7. If FrontPage displays the Save Embedded Files dialog box because the Web page you are saving to the Web server has one or more embedded files (such as pictures, sound files, video clips), use the Save Embedded Files dialog box to tell FrontPage where to store the embedded files—as you learned to do in the preceding Tip entitled, "Saving a FrontPage Web to Disk".

After you complete Step 6 (if the Web page you are saving has no embedded files) or Step 7 (if it does), FrontPage will again contact the Web server and tell the server to store the Web page you selected in Step 2 at the URL you specified in Step 4. In addition, FrontPage will copy to the folder(s) you specified in Step 7 any files embedded on the Web page you saved to the server.

Note: *If you create a new Web page or modify an existing one and save your work directly to the Web server, the FrontPage web on your local computer will no longer match the Web site's content on the "live" Web site. Therefore, be sure to use the File menu Save as option to store any modified or new Web pages to your local FrontPage web either immediately before or after you save your work to the Web server.*

SAVING WEB PAGES WITH IMAGES

Each of the two preceding Tips mentioned that when you insert an external file (such as picture, video clip, or sound file, for example) into a Web page, FrontPage will display the Save Embedded Files dialog box. However, as you work with FrontPage and save your Web pages to disk, you will find that FrontPage only displays the Save Embedded Files dialog box when the Web page you are saving uses a file that is not stored in the current FrontPage web's folders. After you use the Save Embedded File dialog box to store a copy of the embedded (inserted) file(s) to a folder in the current FrontPage Web, FrontPage no longer presents the Save Embedded File dialog box when you tell the program to save your work to disk—unless you modify an embedded file's contents.

The Save Embedded Files dialog box gives you a convenient way to import a file from its current location in a folder outside the current FrontPage web into a folder within the current web. When you use the Save Embedded Files dialog box to import a file, keep in mind that you are only copying the file and not moving it. Moreover, if you use FrontPage to edit a picture by cropping, annotating, or changing its orientation, for example, FrontPage will again present a Save Embedded Files dialog box (such as the one shown in Figure 116.1) when you save the Web page which contains the modified file.

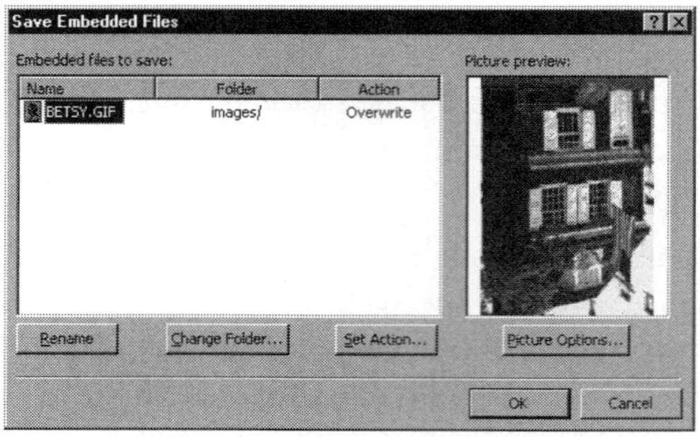

Figure 116.1 *The Microsoft FrontPage Save Embedded Files dialog box.*

If you only want to use the modified picture in your current FrontPage web, click your mouse pointer on the OK button in the lower right-hand corner of the Save Embedded Files dialog box. FrontPage, in turn, will replace the current file on disk with the modified file because the *action* specified in the Action column is "overwrite" by default.

Conversely, if you want to use the modified picture (on the current page) and the original image elsewhere, click your mouse pointer on the RENAME button at the bottom of the Save Embedded Files dialog box. FrontPage, in turn, will prompt you to change a new filename in the file's Name column. After you change the name, press the ENTER key on your keyboard. FrontPage, in turn, will change the *action* of the OK button (as shown in the Action column) to Save. As a result, when you click your mouse pointer on the OK button, FrontPage will save the modified graphic image to a new filename, and both the original and the modified picture will be available for your use.

More often than not, you will want to save a copy of embedded files into a folder within your current FrontPage web. In so doing, you avoid losing the embedded file when the file's owner moves the embedded file to a new folder or deletes it altogether. In either case, your Web page will no longer be able to display the picture, play the background music, or show the video clip—depending on how the Web page is trying to use the (now) no longer accessible embedded file.

However, there are times when you do not want to save a copy of an embedded file to a folder in your current FrontPage web. Suppose, for example, that you are creating a Web page to serve as a table of contents for your company's video clips library. Rather than make a second copy of each video clip in a folder in the current FrontPage web (which can take up several hundred megabytes or gigabytes of disk space), tell FrontPage to create a hyperlink that retrieves the file from its current location when activated. Remember, so long as a file is accessible at its original location, there is no difference in using the file in its original location or a copy of the file located in a folder in the current FrontPage web as far the visitor's browser is concerned.

By default, FrontPage will save a copy of the embedded file in the same folder as the Web page when you click your mouse pointer on the OK button on the Save Embedded Files dialog box without changing any of the options on the dialog box. To tell FrontPage not to save a copy of the file you embed on the Web page, perform the following steps:

1. After FrontPage displays the Save Embedded Files dialog box, click your mouse pointer on its SET ACTION button. FrontPage, in turn, will display the Set Action dialog box shown in Figure 116.2.

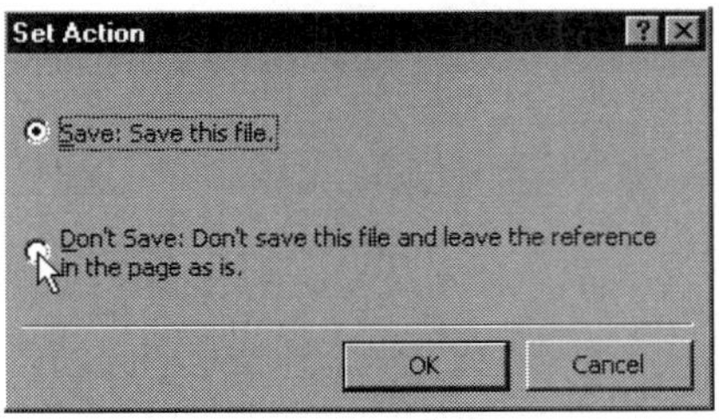

***Figure 116.2** The Microsoft FrontPage Set Action dialog box.*

2. Click your mouse pointer on the radio button to the left of "Don't Save: Don't save this file and leave the reference in the page as is.", and then on the OK button at the bottom of the Set Action dialog box. FrontPage, in turn, will change the action in the Action column to "Don't Save" when it returns to the Save Embedded Files dialog box.
3. Click your mouse pointer on the OK button at the bottom of the Save Embedded File dialog box to have FrontPage insert the embedded file by creating a hyperlink that tells the Web server to send the file from its original location to the Web browser that requests the Web page.

***Note:** If you select "Don't Save" option on the Save File Names dialog box, when saving a Web page, FrontPage will display the Save Embedded Files dialog box each time you save the Web page with the embedded file (that you have elected not to copy to a folder in the current FrontPage web). Be sure to click your mouse pointer on the SET ACTION button and change select the "Don't Save" option each time you see the Save Embedded Files dialog box. Otherwise, FrontPage, by default, will make a copy of the file in the same folder in which it saves the Web page that contains a hyperlink to the embedded file.*

Although the example in the current Tip showed only a single file in the Save Embedded Files dialog box, if you embed multiple files on the same Web page, FrontPage will list all of the files you have inserted and have not saved in a folder within the current FrontPage web. You can rename each file, change the folder in which you want FrontPage to save it, and/or set the action you want FrontPage to take on each file independently. Just click your mouse pointer on the filename of the file whose settings you want to change, and then use the buttons below the Embedded files to save list box to set the selected file's save options. After you set the options as desired for each file listed in the Embedded files to save list box, click your mouse pointer on the OK button near the bottom right-hand corner of the Save Embedded Files dialog box.

UNDOING CHANGES MADE TO A WEB PAGE

FrontPage only saves the changes you make to Web pages when you tell it to do so by clicking your mouse pointer on the Save button (third from the left, with the floppy disk icon) on the Standard Toolbar, or by selecting the File menu Save, Save As, or Save All option. (FrontPage will also prompt you to save changes by clicking your mouse pointer on a YES button if you select the File menu Close option to close a modified and (as yet) unsaved Web page or if you attempt to exit the program before saving your work.)

As is the case with the other Microsoft Office applications, FrontPage lets you use the Edit menu Undo option to reverse changes you have made to a Web page, in reverse order, one action at a time. For example, if you insert text, remove text, insert a picture, and then resize the picture. Selecting the Edit menu Undo option will return the picture to its original size. Selecting the Edit menu Undo option again, will remove the picture from the Web page by undoing the Insert. Selecting the Edit menu Undo option a third time will "bring back" the text you deleted from the page, and so on. Moreover, if you have multiple Web pages open at the same time, FrontPage maintains a separate modification list for each of them. As such, you can undo changes, one at a time on each page independently by clicking on the tab for the modified page in Page view, and selecting the Edit menu Undo option to undo a change you made to that page.

In addition to the Edit menu Undo option, which lets you undo work both before and after you save changes to disk, FrontPage lets you undo all changes made since you last time you saved the current Web page by performing the following steps:

1. Select the View menu Page option to display the current FrontPage web in Page view.
2. Click your mouse pointer on the tab at the top of the Web page with the work you want to undo to make it the current Web page in Page view.
3. Select the View menu Refresh option. FrontPage, in turn, will display a message box to let you know that you have changed the current Web page and ask you if you want to revert to the saved version of the file.

4. Click your mouse pointer on the YES button at the bottom of the message box to have FrontPage discard all changes you made to the Web page since the last save by retrieve the previous saved version of the page from disk.

FrontPage indicates the Web pages with modifications you have not yet saved to disk by placing an asterisk (*) after the filename on the tab at the top of each page in Page view. You can also determine the list of open pages with unsaved changes by selecting the Windows menu. Each page with changes you have not yet saved to disk has an asterisk (*) after its filename on the Windows drop-down menu.

IMPORTING TEXT ONTO A WEB PAGE

When developing Web pages, you often want to include text from other documents. Although you could just retype the text you want to include, FrontPage includes several file converters that let you import files created by other programs directly onto your Web page. Instead of placing a file you are including on a Web page as a graphic image or other object, FrontPage uses a file converter to change the format of the file to HTML.

For example, to import a Microsoft Word document into a Web page, perform the following steps:

1. Open the Web page onto which you want to place the file's contents in Page view.
2. Move the insertion point (the FrontPage vertical blinking cursor) to the place on the page where you want the text you are importing to start.
3. Select the Insert menu File option. FrontPage, in turn, will display a Select File dialog box similar to that shown in Figure 118.1.

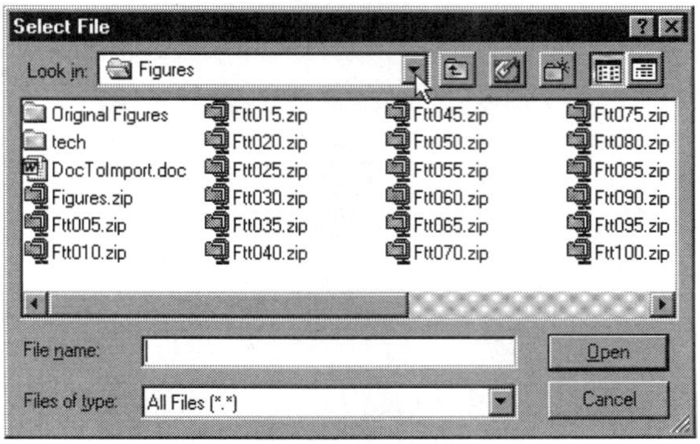

Figure 118.1 The Microsoft FrontPage Select File dialog box.

4. Use the drop-down list button to the right of the Look in field and the folders in the list box below the field to navigate to the folder that contains the file whose contents you want to import, and then click your mouse pointer on the file's name in the list box below the Look in field. Alternatively, you can enter the full pathname of the file you want to import into the File name field, and then click your mouse pointer on the OPEN button near the bottom right-hand corner of the Select File dialog box.

Note: If you use the drop-down list button to the right of the Look in field to navigate to the folder which contains the file you want to import and you do not see its filename in the list box below the Look in field, use the drop-down list button the right of the Files of type field to select the "All Files (.*)".*

5. If this is the first time you are importing a file of a type for which you have not yet installed the converter FrontPage needs to change the file's contents to HTML, FrontPage will display a message box similar to that shown in Figure 118.2. Click your mouse pointer on the YES button to have FrontPage install the converter from the Microsoft Office installation CD-ROM.

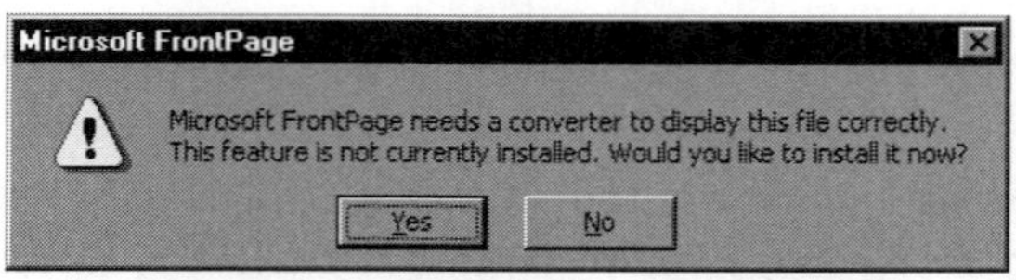

Figure 118.2 The Microsoft FrontPage Converter Not Yet Installed message box.

FrontPage, in turn, will check your drives for the file it needs to install and display the message box shown in Figure 118.3 to prompt you to insert the Microsoft Office CD into your CD-ROM drive.

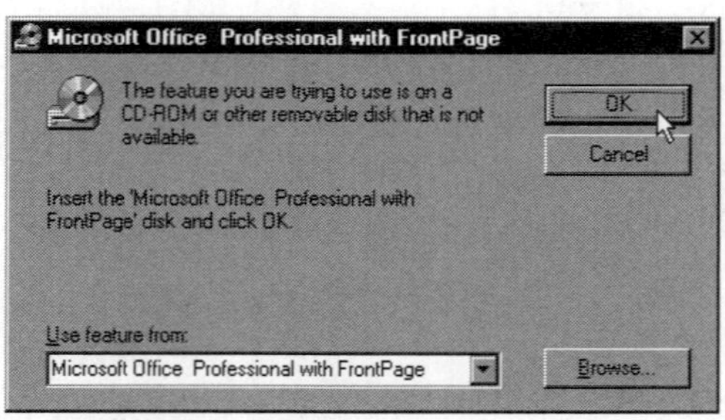

Figure 118.3 The Microsoft FrontPage Insert Microsoft Office Installation CD message box.

6. If prompted, with the message box in Figure 118.3, insert the Microsoft Office CD-ROM and then click your mouse pointer on the OK button.

After you complete Step 4 (or, if you have to install the converter, after you complete Step 6), FrontPage will convert the contents of the file you selected in Step 4 to HTML and insert the HTML into the current Web page at the insertion point.

If you only want to insert a portion of the text from a file or from a Web page on the Internet, use the Windows clipboard by performing the following steps:

1. Open the Web page onto which you want to place the file's contents in Page view.
2. Open the file with the text you want to insert using the program used to create the file, or using your Web browser if the content you want is from a Web page on a Web site.
3. To select the text you want to import, click and hold down the left-hand button on your mouse as you drag the mouse pointer over the text you want.
4. Select the Edit menu Copy option to copy the text you selected (in Step 3) onto the Windows clipboard.
5. Switch back to the FrontPage application and click your mouse pointer at the point on the current Web page where you want FrontPage to insert the selected text you copied to the Windows clipboard in Step 4.
6. Select the Edit menu Paste option.

After you complete Step 6, FrontPage will copy the contents of the Windows clipboard onto the current Web page, starting at the insertion point you set in Step 5.

USING THE EDIT MENU FIND OPTION TO FIND TEXT ON ONE OR MORE WEB PAGES

While developing or maintaining a Web site, you sometimes need to find (and perhaps change a piece of information) on several Web pages. For example, if the company relocates or if a key employee moves on to another opportunity, you may need to change the company's contact information throughout the site. Similarly, you may need to change the description of products, list of services, or the prices listed on the site from time to time. Fortunately, FrontPage provides a global Find option that simplifies the process of locating text on and opening Web pages you need to modify in Page view.

To search for text in the current FrontPage web, perform the following steps:

1. If you only want to find a text string on a single Web page, open the page you want to search and select the View menu Page option to display the Web page in Page view.
2. Select the Edit menu Find option. FrontPage, in turn, will display a Find and Replace dialog box similar to that shown in Figure 119.1.

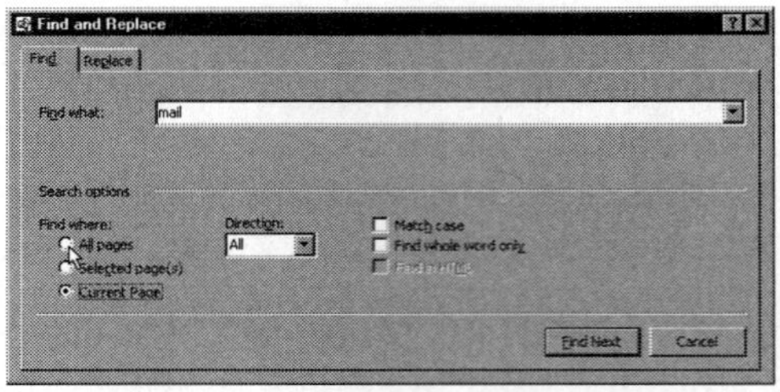

Figure 119.1 The Microsoft FrontPage Find and Replace dialog box.

3. Into the Find what field, enter the text you want to find.
4. Click your mouse pointer on the radio button that specifies the location(s) where you want FrontPage to search for the text you entered into the Find what field. For example, to search all of the pages in the current FrontPage web click your mouse pointer on the radio button to the left of All pages. Alternatively, if you displayed the current FrontPage Web in folder's view and used your mouse pointer to select one or more pages, you can click your mouse pointer on the radio button to the left of Selected page(s) to have FrontPage search for occurrences of the text string on those pages. Finally, if you opened a Web page in Page view, you can click your mouse pointer on the radio button to the left of Current Page to search for the text string in the Find what field only on the single, current Web page.
5. To start the text search, click your mouse pointer on the FIND NEXT button near the bottom right-hand corner of the Find and Replace dialog box.

Note: *If you are not in Page view when you select the Edit menu Find option, FrontPage will display a FIND IN WEB button instead of the FIND NEXT button at the bottom of the Find and Replace dialog box. As such, click your mouse pointer on the FIND IN WEB button if you see it instead of the FIND NEXT button in Step 5.*

6. If you told FrontPage to search for the text string on either All pages or Selected page(s), the program will expand the Find and Replace dialog box to display the search results, similar to that shown in Figure 119.2. Otherwise, continue at Step 8.

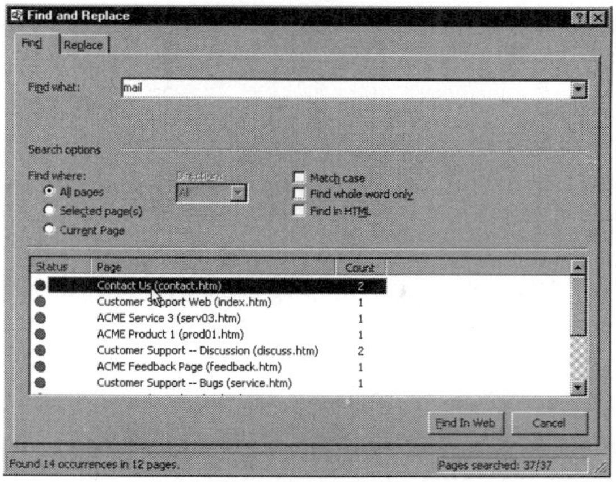

Figure 119.2 *The Microsoft FrontPage Find and Replace dialog box expanded to include search results.*

7. To open a Web page which contains the text string you told FrontPage to find, double-click your mouse pointer on the title of the Web Page in the Page column of the search results list box. FrontPage, in turn, will open and display the Web page in Page view and highlight the first occurrence of the text string it finds on the page. (You may have to drag the Find and Replace dialog box out of the way to see the highlighted text.)
8. Click your mouse pointer on the FIND NEXT button near the bottom right-hand corner of the Find and Replace dialog box repeatedly to move one at a time through the occurrences of the text string on the Web page.
9. If you told FrontPage to search multiple pages in Step 5, the program will prompt you with the "Continue with next page?" dialog box shown in Figure 119.3 after you click your mouse pointer on the FIND NEXT button and there are no more occurrences of the text on the page. Otherwise, FrontPage will display a Finished Searching message box and return to the Find and Replace dialog box when you click your mouse pointer on its OK button.

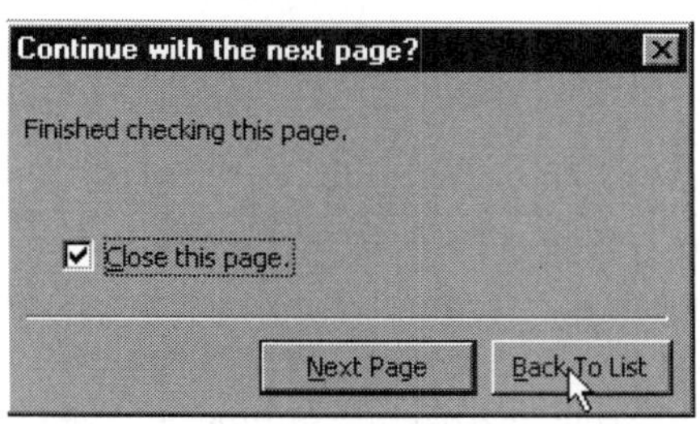

Figure 119.3 *The Microsoft FrontPage "Continue with next page?" dialog box.*

10. If you see the "Continue with next page?" dialog box (shown in Figure 119.3), click your mouse pointer on the NEXT PAGE button to search the next Web page shown in the search results list box and continue at Step 8. Otherwise, click your mouse pointer to the BACK TO LIST button to display the list of Web pages returned by the search and continue at Step 7.

You can quit searching for text and return to Page view at any time by clicking your mouse pointer on the close button (the "X") in the upper right-hand corner of the Find and Replace dialog box.

USING THE EDIT MENU FIND OPTION TO REPLACE TEXT ON ONE OR MORE WEB PAGES

In the preceding Tip, you learned how to use the Edit menu Find option to search for text on one or more Web pages. When you want FrontPage to replace the text it finds, perform the following steps:

1. To replace text on a single Web page, open the page you want to search and select the View menu Page option to display it in Page view.
2. Select the Edit menu Find option. FrontPage, in turn, will display a Find and Replace dialog box similar to the one you saw in Figure 119.1.
3. Click your mouse pointer on the Replace tab. FrontPage, in turn, will display the Replace tab on the Find and Replace dialog box similar to that shown in Figure 120.1.

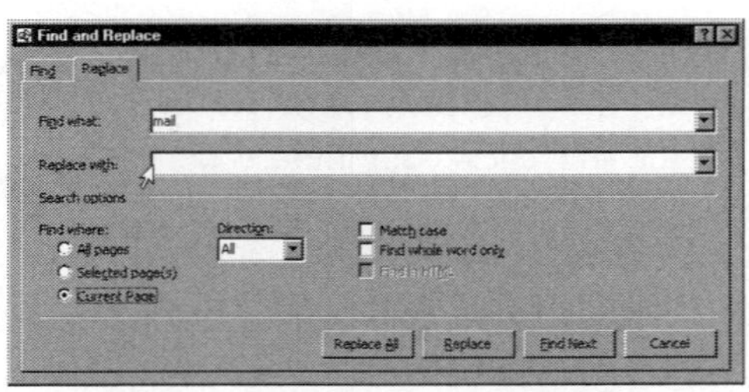

Figure 120.1 The Microsoft FrontPage Find and Replace dialog box, Replace tab.

4. Into the Find what field, enter the text you want to find.
5. Into the Replace with field, enter the text you want FrontPage to put in place of the text string you entered into the Find what field.
6. Click your mouse pointer on the radio button that specifies the location(s) where you want FrontPage to search for the text you entered into the Find what field. For example, to search all of the pages

in the current FrontPage web click your mouse pointer on the radio button to the left of All pages. Alternatively, if you displayed the current FrontPage Web in folder's view and used your mouse pointer to select one or more pages, you can click your mouse pointer on the radio button to the left of Selected page(s) to have FrontPage search for occurrences of the text string on those pages. Finally, if you opened a Web page in Page view, you can click your mouse pointer on the radio button to the left of Current Page to search for the text string in the Find what field only on the single, current Web page.

7. To start the text search, click your mouse pointer on the FIND NEXT button near the bottom right-hand corner of the Find and Replace dialog box.

Note: *If you are not in Page view when you select the Edit menu Find option, FrontPage will display a FIND IN WEB button instead of the FIND NEXT button at the bottom of the Find and Replace dialog box. As such, click your mouse pointer on the FIND IN WEB button if you see it instead of the FIND NEXT button in Step 5.*

8. If you told FrontPage to search for the text string on either All pages or Selected page(s), the program will expand the Find and Replace dialog box to display the search results, similar to that shown in Figure 120.2. Otherwise, continue at Step 10.

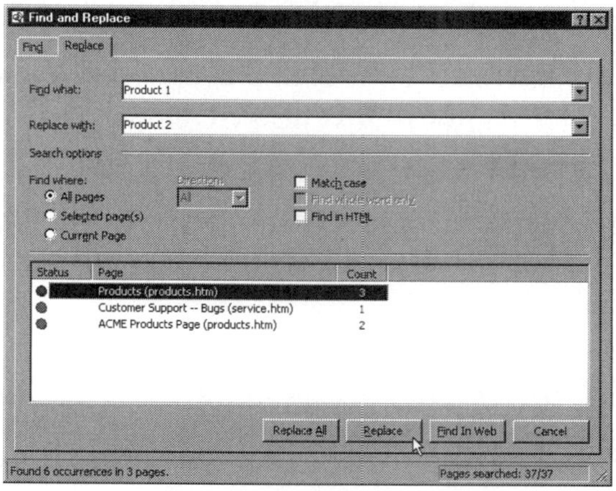

***Figure 120.2** The Microsoft FrontPage Find and Replace dialog box, Replace tab, expanded to include search results.*

9. To open a Web page which contains the text string you told FrontPage to find, double-click your mouse pointer on the title of the Web Page in the Page column of the search results list box. FrontPage, in turn, will open and display the Web page in Page view and highlight the

first occurrence of the text string it finds on the page. (You may have to drag the Find and Replace dialog box out of the way to see the highlighted text.)

10. To replace one occurrence of the text you entered into the Find what field with the text you entered into the Replace with field, click your mouse pointer on the REPLACE button. Alternatively, if you want FrontPage to replace all occurrences of the target txt on the Web page at once, click your mouse pointer on the REPLACE ALL button. If you simply want to move on to the next occurrence of the target text without changing anything, click your mouse pointer on the FIND NEXT button.
11. If you told FrontPage to search multiple pages in Step 6, the program will prompt you with the "Continue with next page?" dialog box you saw in Figure 119.3 if click your mouse pointer on the FIND NEXT, REPLACE, or REPLACE ALL button when there are no more occurrences of the target text on the current Web page. Conversely, if you told FrontPage to search a single page in Step 6, the program will display a Finished Searching message box when there are no more occurrences of the target text on the current Web page. If you see the Finished Searching message box, click your mouse pointer on its OK button to return to the Find and Replace dialog.
12. If you see the "Continue with next page?" dialog box (shown in Figure 119.3), click your mouse pointer on the NEXT PAGE button to search the next Web page shown in the search results list box and continue at Step 10. Otherwise, click your mouse pointer to the BACK TO LIST button to display the list of Web pages returned by the search and continue at Step 9.

You can quit searching for and replacing text and return to the Page view at any time by clicking your mouse pointer on the close button (the "X") in the upper right-hand corner of the Find and Replace dialog box.

USING THE FILE MENU SAVE OPTION OR FILE MENU SAVE AS OPTION TO SAVE A WEB PAGE

When using FrontPage to create or edit a Web page, you should save your work periodically. If your computer experiences a lockup or FrontPage ends abnormally for some reason before you save your work, you will lose any changes you made since the last save. Remember, FrontPage does not write the modifications you make on a Web page to disk as you make them. Instead, FrontPage only stores the changes you make to Web pages in your computer's memory until you tell the program to make your changes permanent by saving them to disk.

To save the current Web page to disk, perform the following steps:

1. Display the Web page you want to save in Page view by selecting the View menu Page option and then clicking your mouse pointer on the tab (with the Web page filename) at the top of the Web page you want to save. As an alternative, you can select the View menu Folders option to display the current FrontPage web in Folders view, and then double-click your mouse pointer on the filename of the Web page you want to save. FrontPage, in turn, will display the page on which you double-clicked your mouse pointer as the current Web page in Page view.
2. To save the current Web page to disk by overwriting the disk file's current contents, select the File menu Save option. If you want to keep the original Web page as is and save the current Web page to a new filename, select the File menu Save as option instead of the File menu Save option.
3. If this is the first time you are saving a new Web page to disk, or if you selected the File menu Save As option in Step 2, FrontPage will display the Save As dialog box. Use the drop-down list button to the right of the Save in field to navigate to the folder in which you wish to save the current Web page. Then, enter the filename into the File name field, and click your mouse pointer on the SAVE button in the lower right-hand corner of the Save As dialog box.

Note: *In Page view, FrontPage indicates the Web pages with unsaved changes by placing an asterisk after the filename on the tab at the top of each page. In Folders view, FrontPage indicates the Web pages with changes you need to save by changing the icon to the left of the filename to include a pencil and lines that represent text.*

CHOOSING A FILENAME FOR A WEB PAGE

With the exception of the Web site's homepage, there are few restrictions as to the filename you choose for a Web page. A Web site's homepage is the (default) Web page that the Web server sends to the Web browser when the site visitor only specifies the site's .com (or IP) address in the browser's Address field. For example, if you enter a Web address (i.e, a universal resource locator (URL)) such as HTTP://NVBIZNET.COM into the browser's Address field, the Web server will send the site's homepage to the browser for display, even though the browser did not request a specific Web page as part of the URL.

Whenever the URL (the Web address) entered into the Web browser's Address field specifies only a .com (or IP) address and no Web page filename, the Web server assumes the browser wants the Web site's default Web page. Most Web servers assume (and therefore require that the site's default page (i.e. the site's homepage) has the filename INDEX.HTM, INDEX.HTML, DEFAULT.HTM, or DEFAULT.HTML. (Check your Web server's documentation for the filename it requires you to use for the Web site's homepage.)

The best rule to follow when deciding on the filename for a Web page (other than the site's homepage) is to use a short, one-word name. By keeping the filename short, you save your Web site visitors from having to type a long URL into the Web browser's Address field when they request the page from the Web server. True, a site visitor could avoid entering the Web page name by adding the page to the Web browser's Favorites. However, I know that I (like most people) prefer to keep my list of Favorites as short as possible, so I can find the sites I visit often without having to scroll through a long list of sites that does not fit on a single computer screen.

Although you may be tempted to use a long filename that describes the contents of the Web page, bear in mind that the visitor's browser displays the title of Web page (and not its filename) prominently in the upper left-hand corner of the browser's application window. Moreover, FrontPage displays the title of each Web page next to its filename when you display the FrontPage web in Folders view. As such, a descriptive multi-word title (which you can enter when you save the Web page to disk by clicking your mouse pointer on the CHANGE TITLE button on the Save As dialog box) is better suited for use in describing the Web page content than its filename.

Note: *While FrontPage lets you save Web pages to files with multi-word filenames that include spaces between words in the filename—don't do it. If you feel that you must separate the words in a filename, use an underscore (_) between the words instead of a space. When a filename includes spaces, the site visitor must represent each space in the file name with "%20" in the URL entered into the browser's Address field. Similarly, to create a hyperlink to the Web page, you will have to replace each space in the target filename with "%20" in the hyperlink's HREF attribute. For example, the URL for the Web page stored in the file named:* ***THIS IS A WEB PAGE.HTM*** *on the NVBizNet.com Web site must be typed as:* ***HTTP://NVBIZNET.COM/THIS%20IS%20A%20WEB%20PAGE*** *when entered into the Web browser's Address field. Arguably, the visitor will find it easier to enter* ***HTTP://NVBIZNET.COM/THIS_IS_A_WEB_PAGE*** *to display the Web page—if you use an underscore (_) instead of a space between each word in the filename. (My suggestion, save the site's Web pages to files with short, single-word filenames.)*

USING A WEB BROWSER TO PREVIEW A WEB PAGE

As a final test before you release your Web site on the Internet, you should review the site's Web pages using various browsers and at different screen resolution in each browser. When you select the View menu Page option and click your mouse pointer on the Preview tab, FrontPage gives you an approximate idea of how the current Web page will look when displayed by the Microsoft Internet Explorer at your screen's current resolution. However, the Internet Explorer's application window does not have all of the toolbars that surround the preview pane in the FrontPage application window. Therefore, to see exactly how a Web page will look when displayed by the Internet Explorer, you need to open the page using the Internet Explorer itself instead of previewing the Web page on the FrontPage Page view Preview tab.

FrontPage makes it easy to use various Web browsers to display the current Web page at different screen resolutions when you perform the following steps:

1. Either display the current Web page in page view, or select the Web page you want to preview by double-clicking your mouse pointer on its filename in Folders view.
2. Select the File menu Preview in Browser option. FrontPage, in turn, will display a Preview in Browser dialog box similar to that shown in Figure 123.

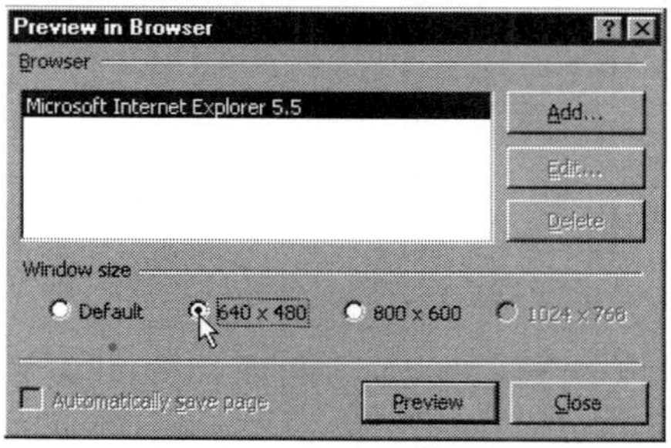

Figure 123 *The Microsoft FrontPage Preview in Browser dialog box.*

3. Click your mouse pointer on the Web browser in which you want to preview the Web page you selected in Step 1.

Note: *After you install FrontPage, the Browser list box in the Preview in Browser dialog box lists all of the Web browsers installed on your computer before you installed the program. Figure 123 show the results of installing FrontPage on a computer with only the Microsoft Internet Explorer installed. In the next Tip, you will learn how to add additional browsers to those listed in the Browser list box on the Preview in Browser dialog box. At a minimum you should install and preview your Web page with Internet Explorer, NCSA Mosaic, and Netscape Navigator Web browsers.*

4. Click your mouse pointer on the radio button to the left of the screen resolution you want the Web browser to use when displaying the Web page.
5. Click your mouse pointer on PREVIEW button near the lower right-hand corner of the Preview in Browser dialog box. FrontPage, in turn, will tell Windows to start the Web browser you selected in Step 3 in an application window set to the screen resolution you selected in

Step 4. (Depending on the speed of your computer, there may be a several second lag between the time you click your mouse pointer on the PREVIEW button and when the Web browser displays the current Web page.)

6. After you finish the preview of the current Web page in the Web browser, select the browser's File menu Exit option, or click your mouse pointer on the close button (the "X") in the upper right-hand corner of the browser's application window to return to the FrontPage application window.

Before publishing a new Web site or updated Web page to the Web server, be sure to repeat the preceding procedure several times—once for each browser set to each of the available screen resolutions.

ADDING BROWSERS TO THE FRONTPAGE PREVIEW IN BROWSER DIALOG BOX

Every Web developer must face an important fact of life—while you can control your Web site's content, you have little control over the way it will look when viewed by the site's visitors. You can, however, view the site's pages using various browsers to experience the Web site from the visitor's point of view and adjust its content to use only features supported by the browsers used by the majority of your site's visitors. (If you need features available only in the latest version of a specific browser, you will at least know about it beforehand and provide a hyperlink the visitor can use to download the browser on the site's homepage.)

The Netscape Navigator and the Microsoft Internet Explorer are by far the most commonly used Web browsers. Therefore, at a minimum, you should preview your Web site using each of them to make sure the site's content looks great in both. In addition, you may also want to test your site using the NCSA Mosaic browser to see what your Web pages look like when viewed using a program that adheres more closely to the HTML standard than the feature rich offerings from Netscape (now owned by America Online (AOL)) and Microsoft.

As you learned in the preceding Tip, FrontPage makes it easy to preview your Web pages in the browsers installed on your system when you installed the program. (When you install FrontPage on your computer, the installation program detects the Web browsers already installed on your computer and adds them to Browser list box on the Preview in Browser dialog box.) However, more likely than not, you only had a single Web browser on your computer when you installed FrontPage. As a result, your Preview in Browser dialog box, like the one you saw in Figure 123, will only let you select the one browser.

Fortunately, FrontPage lets you add additional Web browsers to the Browser list box on Preview in Browser dialog box by performing the following steps:

1. Download and install the Web browser you want to use to preview your Web site's pages.

***Note:** The steps in this Tip detail how to add browsers already installed on your computer to the FronPage Preview in Browser dialog box. The next Tip will show you how to find Web browsers available for you to download for free on the Internet. After you retrieve a Web browser from the Internet onto your computer, follow its installation instructions and make a note of the folder into which you install it. You will need the pathname of the browser's executable (.EXE) file in Step 6.*

2. If FrontPage is not currently running on your computer, start the program now, and use it to open an existing FrontPage web.
3. Select the File menu Preview in Browser option. FrontPage, in turn, will display a Preview in Browser dialog box, similar to the one you saw in Figure 123.
4. Click your mouse pointer on the ADD button. FrontPage, in turn, will display the Add Browser dialog box shown in Figure 124.1.

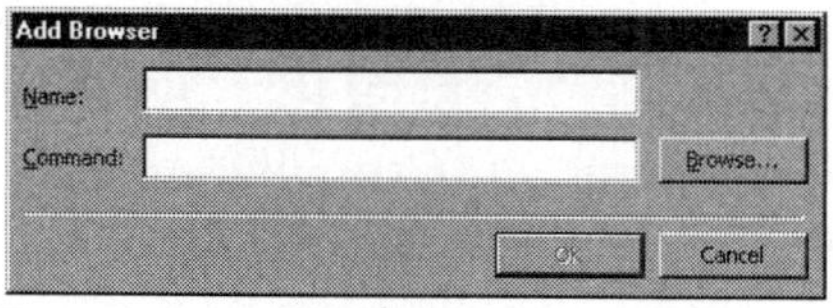

***Figure 124.1** The Microsoft FrontPage Add Browser dialog box.*

5. Into the Name field, enter the text you want to see as the name of the browser in the Browser list box of the Preview on Browser dialog box. For example, if you are adding the NCSA Mosaic browser to the Preview in Browser dialog box, you would enter a name similar to **NCSA Mosaic Version 3.0** into the Name field.
6. Into the Command field, enter the pathname of the browser's executable (.EXE or .COM) file. If you do not know the pathname of the browser's executable file, click your mouse pointer on the BROWSE button to the right of the Command field. FrontPage, in turn, will display an Add Browser (Open) dialog box similar to that shown in Figure 124.2. Use the drop-down list button to the right of the Look in field to navigate to the folder into which you installed the Web browser in Step 1.

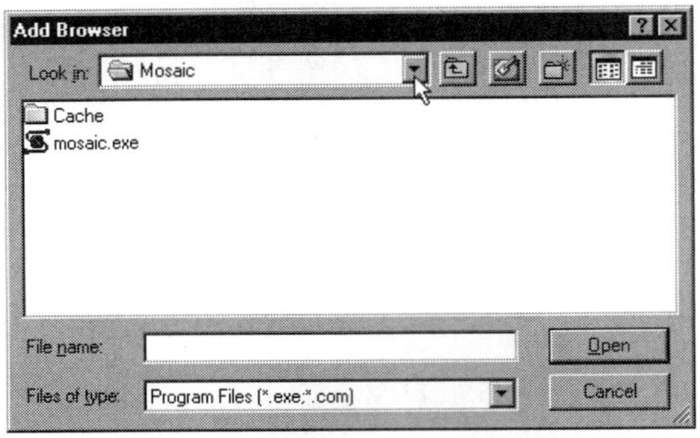

Figure 124.2 The Microsoft FrontPage Add Browser (Open) dialog box.

Next, click your mouse pointer on the browser's filename (the one with the .EXE or .COM extension) and then on the OPEN button near the bottom right-hand corner of the Add Browser (Open) dialog box. FrontPage, in turn, will close the Add Browser (Open) dialog box, return to the Add Browser dialog box (you saw in Figure 124.1), and enter pathname of the Web browser's executable file into its Name field.

7. Click your mouse on the OK button. FrontPage, in turn, will return to the Preview in Browser dialog box with the name of the browser (which you entered in Step 5) among those listed in Browser list box.
8. Click your mouse pointer on the CLOSE button near the bottom right-hand corner of the Preview in Browser list box.

If you recently installed more than one browser on your computer, repeat Steps 4 – 7 of the preceding procedure for each additional Web browser you want to add to those already listed in the Preview in Browser dialog box. Do not be surprised when some Web browsers, like the Netscape Navigator, automatically add themselves to the Browser list box when you install them.

FINDING WEB BROWSERS ON THE INTERNET

If you are operating your computer under Windows you already have the Microsoft Internet Explorer installed on your system. To search for other Web browsers available for you to download from the Internet, perform the following steps:

1. If you do not have a permanent (always on) connection to the Internet, use your modem to establish a dial-up connection to the Internet through your Internet Service Provider (ISP).
2. Start your current Web browser, and then click your mouse pointer on the "search" button on the browser's Standard Toolbar.

3. Into the keyword search field of the Web browser's search pane, enter "Web browsers" and press the ENTER key on your keyboard. (Be sure to include the quote marks ("") around the two keywords.) Your Web browser, in turn, will display a list of the Web sites with one or more Web browsers available for you to download and install on your computer.
4. Click your mouse pointer on the hyperlink for one of the Web sites returned by your Web browser's search feature to visit the site with the browser(s) you can download, and then follow Web site's instructions for retrieving and installing the browser(s) you want on your computer.

If you plan to download and install more than one Web browser, bear in mind that many installation programs require that you let them reset your computer to complete the installation process. As such, you can save yourself some time by retrieving all of the Web browsers you plan to install into a folder (such as C:\MY DOWNLOAD FILES) on your computer prior to installing any of them. After you have them all on your system, double-click the My Computer icon on your Windows desktop and use the Windows explorer to navigate to the folder in which you stored the Web browser download files. To install a browser, double-click your mouse pointer on its download file's name and follow the installer's onscreen instructions.

Be sure to visit the CNET Download.Com Web site (**HTTP://DOWNLOAD.CNET.COM**) when you are ready to retrieve and install either additional Web browsers or updates to the one(s) you are currently using. Find the **Internet** section on the site's homepage, and click your mouse pointer on either the **Internet** or on the **Browsers** hyperlink. The CNET site, in turn, will display hyperlinks you can activate to display a list of alternative browsers, browser plug-ins, and browser companion programs. (The CNET site's Free Downloads page also has hyperlinks that let you download the latest version of the Microsoft Internet Explorer, the Netscape Navigator, and the most popular software applications, based on the number of downloads, available on the site.)

Click your mouse pointer on the **Alternative Browsers** hyperlink to display a list of Web browsers you can download to your computer. You can sort the list of Web browsers by name, purchase price (most are free), date the browser was added to the list, user rating, total downloads, or the size of the download file. To download one of the Web browsers available on the DOWNLOAD.CNET.COM Web site, click your mouse pointer on the browsers name. The CNET site, in turn, will display a Web page that lets you read the browser's specifications and user comments about the browser, submit your opinion on the browser, and download the browser to your computer. Click your mouse pointer on the **Download Now** hyperlink, and then follow the instructions given by the Windows dialog boxes that will take you through the Internet file download process.

USING THE FILE MENU PRINT OPTION TO PRINT A WEB PAGE

The FrontPage File menu Print option lets you generate a hardcopy (a printed copy) of your Web site, one Web page at a time. Do not confuse a Web *page* with a *printed* page. When sent to a printer, the content on a single Web page may generate several pages of printed output. Although your computer screen (like a piece of paper) has physical boundaries, the Web browser, unlike the printer, is able to "extend" the screen with scroll bars that let you move the screen's focus (or frame) around to different parts of a single Web page. As a result, you need to think of a Web page as a mass (or chunk) of information that may require several physical pages to print.

If you want to see how the current Web page will look on paper and determine the number of printed pages printing the Web page will produce, display the current Web page in Page view. Then, select the File menu Print Preview option to display a representation of a printed page onscreen similar to that shown in Figure 126.1.

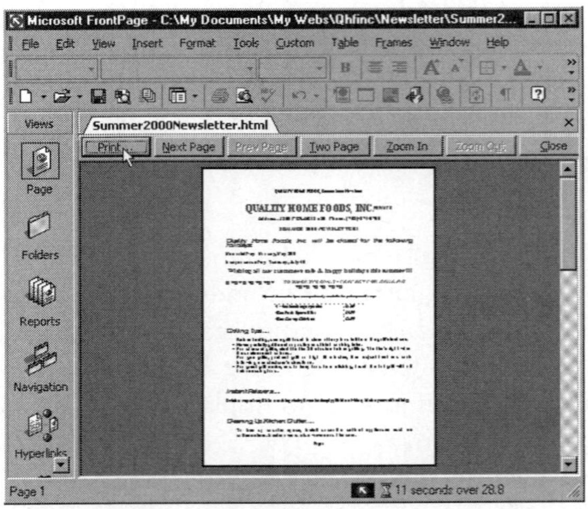

Figure 126.1 A Web page displayed using the File menu Print Preview option.

The initial display of the print preview of a Web page is designed to show you the layout of the Web page content on a physical piece of paper. As such, the content on the page may be too small to read (and its pictures, if any, to small too see). To display a portion of the printed page onscreen in a larger size, click your mouse pointer on the ZOOM IN button. Then use the scroll bars that FrontPage adds to the application window to move the screen's focus around on the onscreen representation of the page to be printed. After you "zoom in", FrontPage will enable the ZOOM OUT button, so you can click your mouse pointer on it to decrease the size of the page content, and see more (or all) of the page to print at once.

To scroll forward and backward through the onscreen display of the pages to print, click your mouse pointer on the NEXT PAGE button and the PREVIOUS PAGE button, respectively.

When you are finished with the print preview, either click your mouse pointer on the CLOSE button to return to Page view without printing, or click your mouse pointer on the PRINT button to display the Print dialog box and continue at Step 3 of the following procedure.

To print a Web page on paper, perform the following steps:

1. Open the Web page you want to print and display it in Page view by selecting the View menu Page option. If you have not yet opened the Web page you want to print, you can select and open it in Page view by selecting the View menu Folders option and then double-clicking on its filename.

Note: *FrontPage only lets you print the current Web page, and not the entire Web site at once. As such, you must open each Web page you want to print in turn. Moreover, you must display the current Web page in Page view before FrontPage will enable Print and Print Preview options on the File menu.*

2. Select the File menu Print option. FrontPage, in turn, will display a Print dialog box similar to that shown in Figure 126.2.

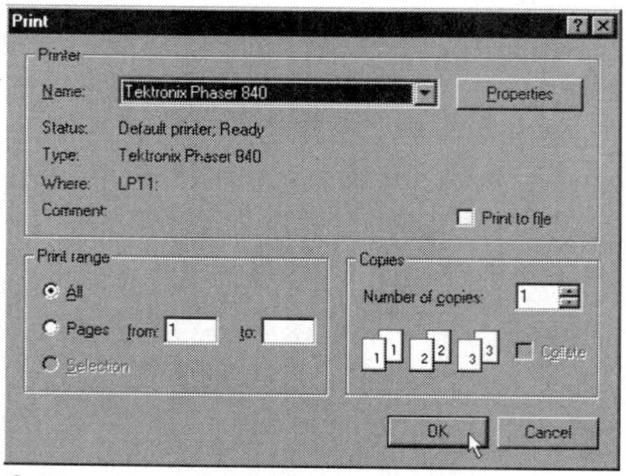

Figure 126.2 *The Microsoft FrontPage Print dialog box.*

3. Use the drop-down list button to the right of the Name field to select the printer you want to use.
4. If printing the Web page will require more than one physical piece of paper and you want to print the entire content of the page, click your mouse pointer on the All radio button. Conversely, if you only want to print a portion of the content on the current Web page, click your mouse pointer on the Pages radio button, and enter the page numbers of the pages that contain the content you want to print into the from and to fields to the right of the Pages field.

5. Enter the number of copies of the current Web page you want to print into the Number of copies field. (The default is to print a single copy of the current Web page.)
6. Click your mouse pointer on the OK button near the lower right-hand corner of the Print dialog box.

As mentioned at the beginning of this Tip, FrontPage only lets you print one Web page at a time. Therefore, you will need to repeat the preceding procedure for each Web page you want to print on paper.

USING THE FILE MENU PROPERTIES OPTION TO SET THE WEB PAGE TITLE

Unlike the title of a book or one of its chapters, the title of a Web page is not text that appears on the page itself. Instead, the title of the current Web page is displayed in the Web browser's menu bar and the browser application window button on the Windows taskbar. In addition, Internet search engines index the words in the Web page title (along with the words in the KEYWORDS attribute in the <META> tag) and use the title as a hyperlink you can activate to retrieve the Web page when its keywords or words in its title match the search conditions you specified. Your Web browser also adds the titles of the Web pages you visit as hyperlinks in its History list (of sites you have visited) and as the default hyperlink for the Web page when you tell the Web browser to add the current Web page to its list of Favorites.

To change the title of a Web page, perform the following steps:

1. Open the Web page whose title you want to change and display it in Page view. If the current FrontPage web contains the Web page whose title you want to change, select the View menu Folders option and double-click your mouse pointer on the filename of the Web page to display it in page view. Otherwise, select the File menu Open option and use the Open File dialog box to open the Web page you want. Then, select the View menu Page option to display to display it in Page view.
2. Select the File menu Properties option or right-click your mouse pointer on any blank area on the current Web page and select Page Properties from the pop-up menu. FrontPage, in turn, will display a Page Properties dialog box similar to that shown in Figure 127.

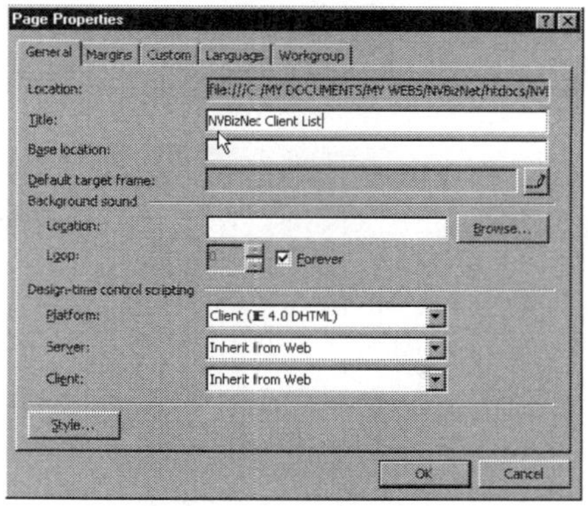

Figure 127 The Microsoft FrontPage Page Properties dialog box.

3. Enter the title of the Web page into the Title field.
4. Click your mouse pointer on the OK button near the bottom right-hand corner of the Page Properties dialog box.

After you complete Step 4, FrontPage will insert the text you entered into the Title field between <TITLE></TITLE> tags in the header section of the current Web page and return to Page view. Be sure to select the File menu Save option to write the updated Web page HTML to disk. Remember, FrontPage does not save any changes you make in Page view to disk until you tell it to do so.

INSERTING SPECIAL CHARACTERS ON A WEB PAGE

As you know, when you display a Web page in Page view, FrontPage functions like a what-you-see-is-what-you-get (WYSIWYG) text editor by letting you use your keyboard to type the content you want to see on the Web page. Sometimes, however, you want to use special characters (or symbols) that do not appear your keyboard. You can insert special characters on a Web page by entering special codes (called escape character sequences) onto the Page view HTML tab. However, the Insert menu Symbol option lets you insert special characters (and symbols) by selecting them with your mouse pointer instead of having to memorize and type a complex set of escape characters that will generate the symbol.

To insert a special character (or symbol) on a Web page, perform the following steps:

1. With the current Web page displayed in Page view, move your cursor (the blinking vertical line) to the location on the Web page at which you want to insert the special character (or symbol).

2. Select the Insert menu Symbol option. FrontPage, in turn, will display a Symbol dialog box similar to that shown in Figure 128.

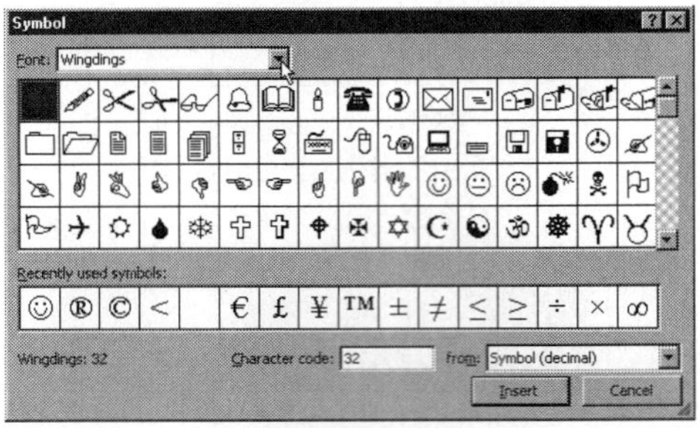

Figure 128 *The Microsoft FrontPage Symbol dialog box.*

3. If the symbol you want to use is not in the font displayed, use the drop-down list button to the right of the Font field to select the font that has the special character you want to insert on the Web page.
4. Click your mouse pointer on the special character (the symbol) you want to insert, and then on the INSERT button near the lower right-hand corner of the Symbol dialog box.
5. If you want to insert additional symbols, repeat Steps 3 and 4 for each special character you want to place on the Web page.
6. Click you mouse pointer on the CLOSE button in the lower right-hand corner of the Symbol dialog box to close the dialog box and return to the Page view Normal tab.

When you insert special characters onto a Web page, keep in mind that some browsers may not be able to display certain symbols. Moreover, if the site visitor's computer does not have the font (i.e. the character set) which contains the symbol you inserted, the special character will not appear on the Web page when it is displayed by the visitor's Web browser.

INSERTING IMAGES FROM THE CLIP GALLERY

When you install FrontPage on your computer, the installation program installs not only the FrontPage application but also a set of support files including a large gallery of media clips. The clip gallery is a set of royalty free digital images of backgrounds, buttons, icons, lines, caricatures and other multimedia clips (sound files, animations, video clips) you can insert on your Web pages.

To insert a clip from the clip gallery on your hard drive onto a Web page, perform the following steps:

1. Open the Web page on which you want to place a clip art image and then select the View menu Page option to display the page on the Page view Normal tab.
2. Click your mouse pointer at the location on the current Web page where you want to insert the clip art. (As an alternative, you can use the arrow keys on your keyboard to move the insertion point, shown by a blinking vertical line, to the point on the Web page at which you want to insert the digital image.)
3. Select the Insert menu Picture option and click your mouse pointer on Clip Art. FrontPage, in turn, will display the Insert Clip Art menu along the right-hand side of the FrontPage application window.

Note: *The first time you tell FrontPage to select an image from the clip gallery on your computer (in any Microsoft Office application, including FrontPage), the Microsoft Clip Organizer will prompt you to let it catalog and categorize the multimedia files, clip art and other graphic images stored on your hard drive. If you have five to ten minutes when presented with the message box shown in Figure 129.1, click your mouse pointer on the NOW button to let the Clip Organizer do its job. On the other hand, if you are in a hurry click your mouse pointer on the LATER button. However, until you let it update your clip gallery, the Clip Organizer will prompt you with the message box in Figure 129.1 each time you try access the gallery. To avoid running the Clip Organizer altogether (without being prompted to run it in the future), click your mouse pointer on the check box to the left of "Don't show this message again" until a check mark appears and then on the LATER button.*

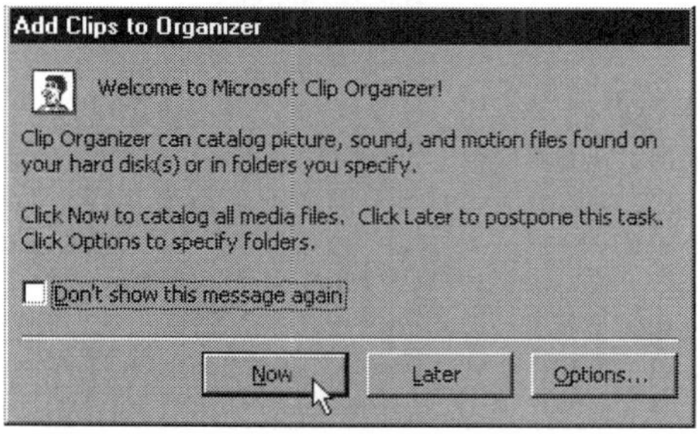

Figure 129.1 *The Add Clips to Organizer message box.*

4. Into the Search text field at the top of the Insert Clip Art menu (along the right-hand side of the FrontPage application window), enter one or more keywords you want FrontPage to use when searching the clip gallery for the clip you want. For example, if you want to insert a clip art image of a car, enter **CAR** into Search text field. (If you want FrontPage to display the thumbnails for all of the clips available in the clip gallery, leave the Search text field blank.)

5. Click your mouse pointer on the SEARCH button below the Search text field. FrontPage, in turn, the search results as display thumbnails of the media clips whose keywords satisfy your search conditions in a list box on the Insert Clip Art menu, similar to that shown in Figure 129.2. (You can expand the size of the list box to display more thumbnails at once by clicking your mouse pointer on the "expand" icon above the upper left-hand corner of the list box.)

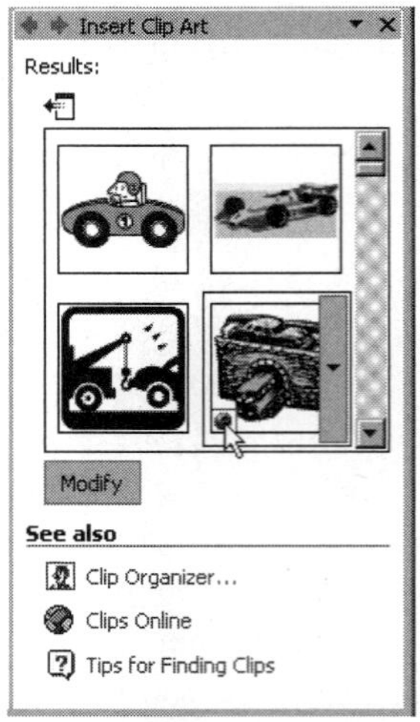

Figure 129.2 The Microsoft FrontPage Insert Clip Art menu with the list box showing clipart gallery search results.

Note: *If your computer is connected to the Internet when you search the clip gallery, FrontPage will include thumbnails for clip art available on the Microsoft clip art download site. Each of the thumbnails for clip art on the Internet has a globe in its lower right-hand corner. (The mouse pointer is pointing at the globe in Figure 129.2.)*

6. To insert a clip art image onto the Web page, click your mouse pointer on its thumbnail in the clip gallery search results list box.
7. To remove the Insert Clip Art menu from the FrontPage application window, click your mouse pointer on the close button (the "X") at the right-hand end of the Insert Clip Art menu's title bar.

Unless you leave the Search text field blank, the keywords associated with each clip in the clip gallery determine which thumbnails the Clip Organizer presents to you in the search results list box. The next Tip will show you how to edit the keywords associated with clips in the clip gallery.

Finding the clip art you want to use is much easier when you know the keywords associated with the type of clip you want—rather than having to leave the Search text field blank and scrolling through the entire gallery's contents to find an image.

SETTING KEYWORDS ON CLIPS IN THE CLIP GALLERY

Depending on the amount of clip art and number of pictures, sound files, and video clips stored on your hard drive, the number of media clip thumbnails in your clip gallery can grow rather large—especially as you continue to download and add clips you find on the Internet. Without the proper keywords attached to the thumbnails, searching the clip gallery for clips you want to use is tedious at best. Fortunately, the Microsoft Clip Organizer makes it easy to organize, categorize, and attach keywords to media clips in the clip gallery.

To use the Microsoft Clip Organizer to attach keywords to a clip in the clip gallery, perform the following steps:

1. Open an existing Web page and select the View menu Page option to display the page in Page view. Since the current procedure does involve making changes to the Web page you open, you can create a new page by clicking your mouse pointer on the Create a new normal page button (the first button on the left on the Standard Toolbar) to create a new, blank page instead of opening an existing one.
2. Select the Insert menu Picture option and click your mouse pointer on Clip Art. FrontPage, in turn, will display the Insert Clip Art menu along the right-hand side of the FrontPage application window.
3. Click your mouse pointer on the Clip Organizer option in the "See also" section at the bottom of the Insert Clip Art menu. Windows, in turn, will start the Microsoft Clip Organizer in a new application window, similar to the one you shown in Figure 130.1.

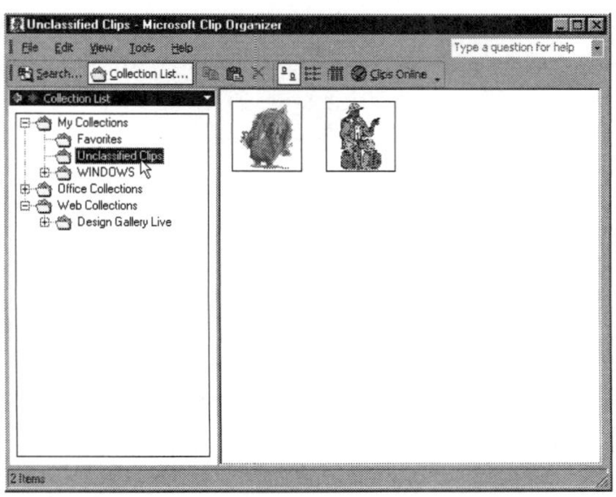

Figure 130.1 The Microsoft Clip Organizer application Window.

4. Click your mouse pointer on the Collection folder with the clip whose keywords you want to edit. If you see a plus (+) next to a Collection folder, you can click your mouse pointer on the plus (+) to display the Collection subfolders it contains.

Note: *You can only edit the keywords of clips you add to the clip gallery. If you want to change the keywords on a clip installed from the Microsoft Office CD (in the Office Collections) or downloadable from the Internet (in the Web Collections), you will need to copy the clip's shortcut to another Collection folder. Then, you can edit the keywords on the shortcut you copied.*

5. Click your mouse pointer on the thumbnail for the clip whose keywords you want to edit.
6. Right-click your mouse pointer on the thumbnail you selected in Step 5, and then select Edit Keywords from the pop-up menu. The Microsoft Clip Organizer, in turn, will display a Keywords dialog box, similar to that shown in Figure 130.2.

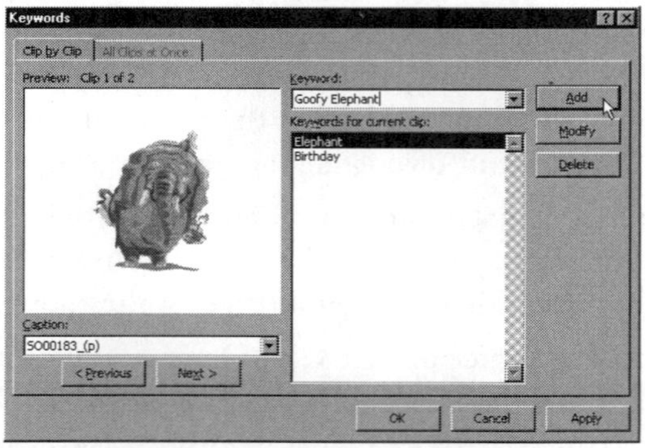

Figure 130.2 The Microsoft Clip Organizer Keywords dialog box.

7. Into the Keyword field, enter the words you want to use when searching for the clip. For example, to find the clip shown in Figure 130.2 when searching for clips with the keyword "Goofy" or "Elephant", or the phrase "Goofy Elephant", enter "Goofy Elephant" into the Keyword field.
8. Click your mouse pointer on the ADD button. The Clip Organizer, in turn, will add the text you entered into the Keyword field to the list of keywords in the Keywords for current clip list box.
9. Repeat Steps 7 and 8 until you have entered all of the keywords you want to associate with the clip you selected in Step 5.

10. If you want to remove one of the keywords currently associated with the clip, click your mouse pointer on the one you want to remove in the Keywords for current clip list box and then on the DELETE button.
11. Click your mouse pointer on the OK button near the bottom of the Keywords dialog box to exit the dialog box and return to the Microsoft Clip Organizer application window.

To exit the Clip Organizer (and return to the FrontPage application window) select the File menu Exit option or click your mouse pointer on the Close button (the "X") in the upper right-hand corner of the Microsoft Clip Organizer application window.

USING THE MICROSOFT CLIP ORGANIZER TO RETRIEVE CLIP ART FROM THE INTERNET

In addition to the clip art installed from the Microsoft Office CD-ROM, the Microsoft Clip Organizer lets you preview and download clip art from the Microsoft clip art gallery on the Internet. By including the thumbnails for Internet based clip art images, Microsoft lets you execute a keyword search for media clips on its Web site and lets you limit the clips on your hard drive to those you want to use—which saves disk space and reduces the number of undesired clips you have to search through to find the ones you want.

To use the Clip Organizer to retrieve media clips from the Microsoft Web site, perform the following steps:

1. If you do not have a permanent (always on) connection to the Internet, use your modem to establish a connection to the Internet through your Internet Service Provider (ISP).
2. If FrontPage is not currently running on your system, start it now by clicking your mouse pointer on the Windows START button. After Windows displays its start menu, move your mouse pointer to Programs and select Microsoft FrontPage.
3. Open an existing Web page and select the View menu Page option to display the page in Page view. Since the current procedure does involve making changes to the Web page you open, you can create a new page by clicking your mouse pointer on the Create a new normal page button (the first button on the left on the Standard Toolbar) to create a new, blank page instead of opening an existing one.
4. Select the Insert menu Picture option and click your mouse pointer on Clip Art. FrontPage, in turn, will display the Insert Clip Art menu along the right-hand side of the FrontPage application window.

5. Click your mouse pointer on the Clip Organizer option in the "See also" section at the bottom of the Insert Clip Art menu. Windows, in turn, will start the Microsoft Clip Organizer in a new application window similar to the one you saw in Figure 130.1.
6. Find the Web Collections folder near the bottom of the Collection List pane (along the left-hand side of the Clip Organizer application window). If there is a plus (+) to the left of your Web Collections folder, click your mouse pointer on the plus (+) to display the Collection subfolders it contains.
7. Find the Design Gallery Live Collection subfolder in the Web Collections folder. If there is a plus (+) to the left of the Design Gallery Live folder on your computer, click your mouse pointer on the plus (+) to display the Collection subfolders it contains. The Clip Organizer, in turn, will display an alphabetized list of Collection folders whose names indicate the category of clips each contains.
8. Click your mouse pointer Collection folder for the category of clips you want to retrieve from the Microsoft Web site. The Clip Organizer, in turn, will display the thumbnails for the Collection's clips in the Clip Organizer application window to the right of the Collection List pane, similar to that shown in Figure 131.1.

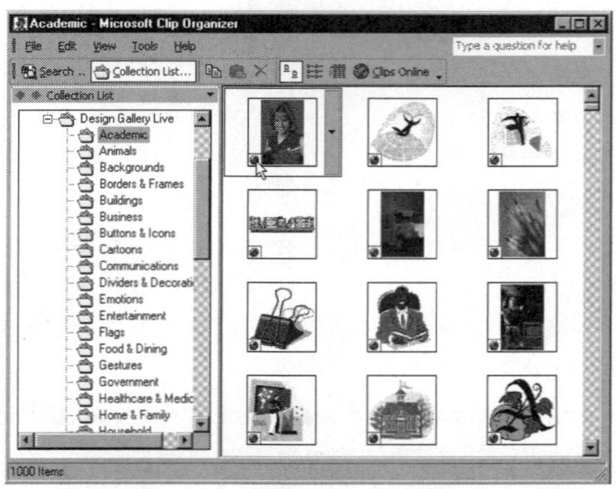

Figure 131.1 The Microsoft Clip Organizer with thumbnails for clip art images available for download from the Microsoft Web site.

9. Click your mouse pointer on the thumbnail for the clip you want to retrieve from the Microsoft Web site to select the thumbnail.
10. Right-click your mouse pointer on the thumbnail you selected in Step 9, and then select the Copy to Collection option on the pop-up menu. The Microsoft Clip Organizer, in turn, will display a Copy to Collection dialog box similar to that shown in Figure 131.2.

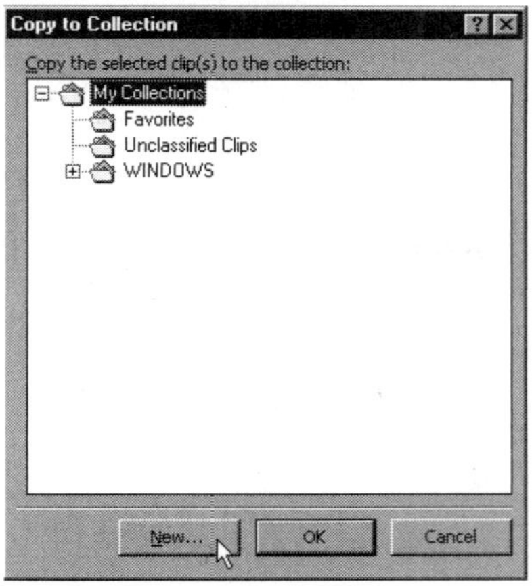

Figure 131.2 *The Microsoft Clip Organizer Copy to Collection dialog box.*

11. Click your mouse pointer on the Collection folder into which you want to download the clip from the Microsoft Web site.

Note: *After downloading a few clips from the Microsoft Web site, you will see that Microsoft has done a good job of categorizing the clips you retrieve to make them easy to find. As such, if you have not done so already, I suggest you create a Collection subfolder in the My Collections folder that has a filename that matches the one with the thumbnail for the clip you want to download from the Internet.*

*For example, if you are downloading a clip from the Academic subfolder, click your mouse pointer on the NEW button near the bottom of the Copy to Collection dialog box. The Clip Organizer, in turn, will display the New Folder Dialog box. Enter the name of the new Collection folder into the Name field (**Academic**, in the current example). Next, click your mouse pointer on the OK button near the bottom of the New Collection dialog box. Then, continue at Step 11.*

12. Click your mouse pointer on the OK button near the bottom of the Copy to Collection dialog box. The Clip Organizer, in turn, stores a copy of the Internet based clip on your hard drive and creates a shortcut to the local copy of the clip into the Collection folder you selected in Step 11.
13. Repeat Steps 8 – 12 until you have retrieved all of the clip art you want (for now) from the Microsoft Web site.

To exit the Clip Organizer (and return to the FrontPage application window) select the File menu Exit option or click your mouse pointer on the Close button (the "X") in the upper right-hand corner of the Microsoft Clip Organizer application window.

The main advantage of downloading media clips from the Web site and storing them on your computer is that you will be able to search your clip gallery and insert artwork on your Web pages without an active connection to the Internet during the site development process. This allows you the freedom to complete your work at locations that do not have Internet access and lets you avoid the per-minute cost of wireless Internet access time by letting you retrieve the art you need beforehand through less expensive (if not free) Internet connections.

DOWNLOADING CLIPS FROM THE MICROSOFT DESIGN GALLERY LIVE WEB SITE

In the preceding Tip you learned how to use the Microsoft Clip Organizer to retrieve clip art from the Microsoft clip art archive on the Internet. However, the Microsoft Clip Organizer only lets you retrieve a clip art image from the Web site if the Clip Organizer has a shortcut referencing the clip in the clip gallery. Because, Microsoft developers are constantly adding new clip art to the Microsoft Design Gallery Live, you need to visit the site periodically to download additional, new artwork for which there are no shortcuts in the clip library on your computer.

To visit Microsoft clip gallery (Microsoft Design Gallery Live, at HTTP://MGN.MICROSOFT.COM) and retrieve digital images perform the following steps:

1. If you do not have a permanent (i.e., always on) connection to the Internet, use your modem to establish a connection to the Internet through your Internet Service Provider (ISP).
2. To start the Microsoft Clip Organizer click your mouse pointer on the Windows START button. After windows displays the Start menu, move your mouse pointer to Programs, and then to Microsoft Office Tools on the Programs submenu. Finally, select Microsoft Clip Organizer in the Microsoft Office Tools group.
3. Click your mouse pointer on the Clips Online button on the right-hand end of the Microsoft Clip Organizer's Standard toolbar. Windows, in turn, will start your default Internet browser. The Web browser, in turn, will display the opening page of the Microsoft Design Gallery Live Web site—a portion of which is shown in Figure 132.1.
4. Either use the search fields along the left-hand side of the Web page or the hyperlinks to groups of featured clips (near the center of the Web page) to find the clip art you want to download to your computer. For example, to select clip art from a set of St. Patrick's Day artwork recently available on the site (as shown in Figure 132.1), click your mouse pointer on the St. Patrick's Day hyperlink (in the March Featured Clips section of the Web page). Your Web browser, in turn, will display a set of hyperlinks similar to those shown in the right-hand half of Figure 132.2.

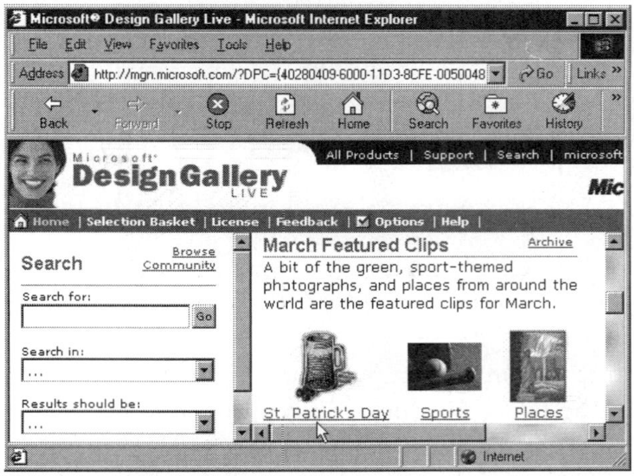

Figure 132.1 A portion of the Web page recently displayed as the opening page of Microsoft Design Gallery Live subweb on the HTTP://MGN.MICROSOFT.COM Web site.

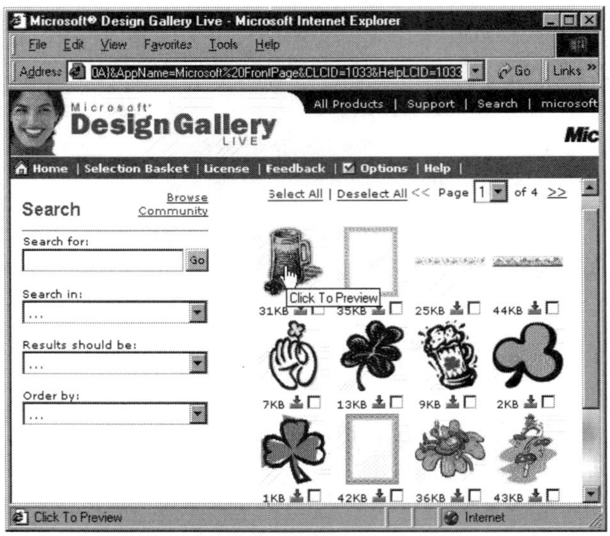

Figure 132.2 A set of hyperlinks (with thumbnails) for St. Patrick's Day related clip art images recently found on the Microsoft Design Gallery Live Web site.

5. To start the download process, click your mouse pointer on the thumbnail (or hyperlink) of the clip art you want to retrieve. Your Web browser, in turn, will open a separate window and display a preview of the clip art associated with the thumbnail.
6. Right-click your mouse pointer on the clip art in the preview window, and then select Save Picture As from the pop-up menu. Windows, in turn, will display a Save Picture dialog box similar to that shown in Figure 132.3.

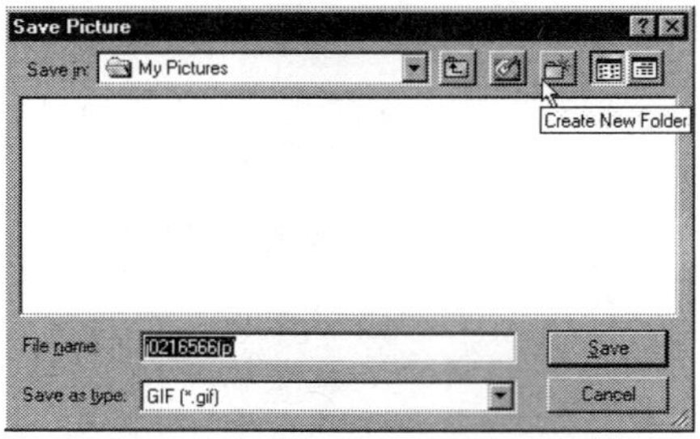

Figure 132.3 The Windows Save Picture dialog box.

7. Use the drop-down list button to the right of the Save in field to navigate to the folder in which you want to store the clip art on your computer. Be sure to make a note of the folder you use, so you can find the new clip art when you want to use it on a Web page or when you are ready to add it to the clip gallery (which you will learn how to do in the next Tip).

Note: *Unless you previously used the Save Picture dialog box to store a picture in another directory, Windows will default to saving pictures into the C:\MY DOCUMENTS\MY PICTURES folder on your hard drive. I suggest that you create a "Clip Art" subfolder in the MY PICTURES folder and use it to store clip art you download from the Internet.*

To create a new folder, first use the drop-down list button to the right of the Save in field to navigate to the folder in which you wish to create the new folder—C:\MY DOCUMENTS\MY PICTURES, in the current example. Then, click your mouse pointer on the on the Create New Folder Button, and enter the name of the new folder when prompted—for the current project, enter ***Clip Art*** *and then press the* ENTER *key on your keyboard.*

After you create the new folder, open it by double-clicking your mouse pointer on its name. For the current project, double-click your mouse pointer on the CLIP ART folder to select: C:\MY DOCUMENTS\MY PICTURES\CLIP ART as the folder in which to store the clip art you are about to retrieve from the Internet.

8. Click your mouse pointer on the SAVE button near the lower right-hand corner of the Save Picture dialog box.
9. Click your mouse pointer on the close button (the "X") in the upper right-hand corner of the clip art preview window to close the preview window and return to the Web browser's application window.
10. Repeat Steps 6 – 12 to download any additional clip art images you want to retrieve from the Web site and store on your computer.
11. Select the File menu Exit option or click your mouse pointer on the close button (the "X") in the upper right-hand corner of your Web

browser's application window to exit your browser, close its application window, and return to the Microsoft Clip Organizer application window.

Before you can use the Microsoft Clip Organizer to search for and insert the clip art you download onto your computer, you need to add the digital images to the Clip Organizer's Collections—which you will learn how to do in the next Tip.

ADDING NEW SEARCHABLE CLIP ART IMAGES TO THE CLIP GALLERY

Because the Microsoft Clip Organizer only searches the keywords associated with shortcuts to clips in the clip gallery on your computer, you must add a shortcut to any clip art files you download to the gallery before you can use the Clip Organizer to find the digital images and insert them on your Web pages. In the preceding Tip you learned how to download a clip art image from the Microsoft Design Gallery Live on the Internet. If you only intend to use the clip art on a single Web site, simply move the clip art file to the Web site's IMAGES subfolder and then execute the Insert Picture procedure you will learn about in the next Tip. However, if you are involved in designing multiple Web sites, you should add the clip art you download to your clip gallery because you will most likely use it on Web pages in more than one Web site.

To add new clip art (or other media clips) to the clip gallery, perform the following steps:

1. If the Microsoft Clip Organizer is not running on your computer, start it now by clicking your mouse pointer on the Windows START button. After windows displays the Start menu, move your mouse pointer to Programs, and then to Microsoft Office Tools on the Programs submenu. Finally, select Microsoft Clip Organizer in the Microsoft Office Tools group.
2. In the Microsoft Clip Organizer application window, select the File menu Add Clips to Organizer option, and then click your mouse pointer on "On My Own". The Clip Organizer, in turn, will display the Add Clips to Organizer dialog box (which is similar in form and function to the Open dialog boxes you have seen throughout this book).
3. Use the drop-down list button to the right of the Look in field to navigate to the folder in which you stored the clip art (or other media clip) you want to add to the clip gallery.
4. Click your mouse pointer on the ADD TO button near the bottom of the Add Clips to Organizer dialog box. The Clip Organizer, in turn, will display an Import to Collection dialog box similar to that shown in Figure 133.

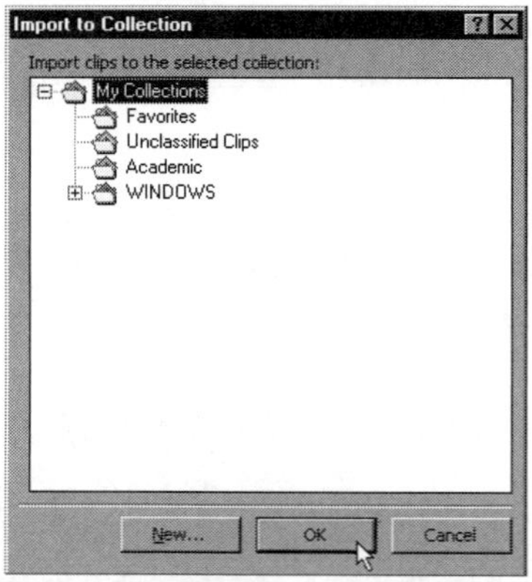

Figure 133 *The Microsoft Clip Organizer Import to Collection dialog box.*

5. Click your mouse pointer on the name of the Collection folder to which you want to add a shortcut to the clip art image. If the Collection folder you want is a subfolder in another Collection folder, click your mouse pointer on the plus (+) to the left of the Collection folder which contains the subfolder you want. Then, click your mouse pointer on the desired Collection subfolder to select it.

Note: *Organizing the clips you add to the clip gallery into Collection folders by type makes it possible for you to display all of the thumbnails in your clip gallery for clips of a specific type (like Holiday, Birthday, Sports, Business, etc.) at once. If you do not have a Collection folder for the category of clip you are adding, click your mouse pointer on the NEW button near the bottom left-hand corner of the Import to Collection dialog box, and perform Steps 3 and 4 of the procedure in the next Tip. Then, continue at Step 5 of the procedure in the current Tip.*

6. Click your mouse pointer on the OK button near the bottom center of the Import to Collection dialog box. The Clip Organizer, in turn, will return to the Add Clips to Organizer dialog box and display the name of the Collection folder you selected on the left-hand end of the title bar at the top of the dialog box.
7. Click your mouse pointer on the name of the clip art file you want to add to the Collection in the list box below the Look in field. (If you want to add multiple clips to the same folder, hold down the CTRL key on your keyboard as you click your mouse pointer on the filename of each of the clip art images you want to add to the Collection.)
8. Click your mouse pointer on the ADD button near the lower right-hand corner of the Add Clips to Organizer dialog box. The Clip Organizer, in turn, will insert a shortcut to the clip art file into the Collection folder and then exit and close the Add Clips to Organizer dialog box.

After you add a clip art image to a Collection, be sure to edit the clip art's keywords (as you learned how to do in a previous Tip entitled: "Setting Keywords on Clips in the Clip Gallery". Otherwise, you will only be able to use the Clip Organizer to retrieve the clip (and insert it on your Web page) by browsing the contents of the Collection folder in which you placed its shortcut. As mentioned previously, associating keywords that describe the clip with the shortcut to the clip will make it easier to find the clip when you are ready to use it.

Note: *Adding a clip to the clip gallery does not create a physical copy of the clip art file inside a Collection folder. Instead, when you add a clip to a Collection folder, you are actually adding a shortcut that points to the clip art file at its current location on your hard drive. As such, if you delete the clip from the folder in which it is saved, removes the clip from your computer completely and makes it unavailable to the Clip Organizer.*

ADDING A NEW COLLECTION FOLDER TO THE CLIP GALLERY

More often than not, you will search for clips in the clip gallery by keyword. However, placing similar clips in a Collection folder whose name indicates the type of clips it holds lets you display thumbnails for clips of a specific type when you are undecided as to the exact clip you want to use. For example, if you retrieve St Patrick's Day related clip art, add the clips to a Collection folder with a name such as Holiday. Then, add clips related to Thanksgiving, Christmas, Memorial Day, and other holidays the HOLIDAY Collection. With all your holiday related clips in a single Collection, you will be able to display all of your holiday related clip art by clicking your mouse pointer on one Collection folder (HOLIDAY) in the Collection List pane of the Clip Organizer application window. Being able to see all of the holiday clip art at once is especially convenient when you want to add clip art to a Web page (such as your home page) to spruce it up for a particular holiday.

To add a new Collection folder to the clip gallery, perform the following steps:

1. If the Microsoft Clip Organizer is not running on your computer, start it now by clicking your mouse pointer on the Windows START button. After windows displays the Start menu, move your mouse pointer to Programs, and then to Microsoft Office Tools on the Programs submenu. Finally, select Microsoft Clip Organizer in the Microsoft Office Tools group.
2. Right-click your mouse pointer on the existing Collection folder in which you wish to create a new Collection, and then select New Collection from the pop-up menu. For example, to create a new Collection folder in the "My Collections" Collection, click your mouse pointer on MY COLLECTIONS, and then select New Collection from the pop-up menu. The Clip Organizer, in turn, will display a New Collection dialog box, similar to that shown in Figure 134.

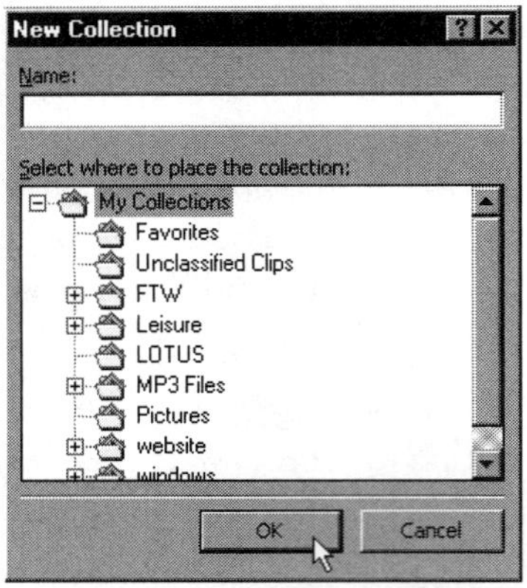

Figure 134 The Microsoft Clip Organizer New Collection dialog box.

3. Into the Name field at the top of the New Collection dialog box, enter the name of the new Collection. For example, if you are planning place holiday-type clips to the Collection, you would enter **Holiday** into the Name field.
4. Click your mouse pointer on the OK button near the bottom center of the New Collection dialog box. The Clip Organizer, in turn, will add the new Collection folder and close the New Collection dialog box.

Note: *In addition to organizing the clips you add to the clip gallery by placing similar clips (by category) into the same Collection folder, be sure to add the name of the Collection folder to the clip's keyword list. If you use the Collection folder's name as one of the keywords for the clips you add to the Collection, you will be able to display all of the clips in a Collection by executing a keyword search for the name of the Collection.*

USING THE INSERT MENU PICTURE OPTION TO INSERT A PICTURE ON A WEB PAGE

If you ever add a picture to a document while working with a word processor (such as Microsoft Word or WordPerfect, for example), you already know how to insert a picture onto a Web page.

To place a picture on the current Web page while using FrontPage, perform the following steps:

1. Select the View menu Page option to display the current Web page in Page view.

2. Use the arrow keys on your keyboard to move the cursor to the location on the Web page where you want to insert the picture. (If you do not see the FrontPage blinking vertical line cursor, click your mouse pointer on the Normal tab—you cannot modify the current Web page on the Page view Preview tab.)
3. Select the Insert menu Picture option and click your mouse pointer on From File. FrontPage, in turn, will display a Picture dialog box similar to that shown in Figure 135.

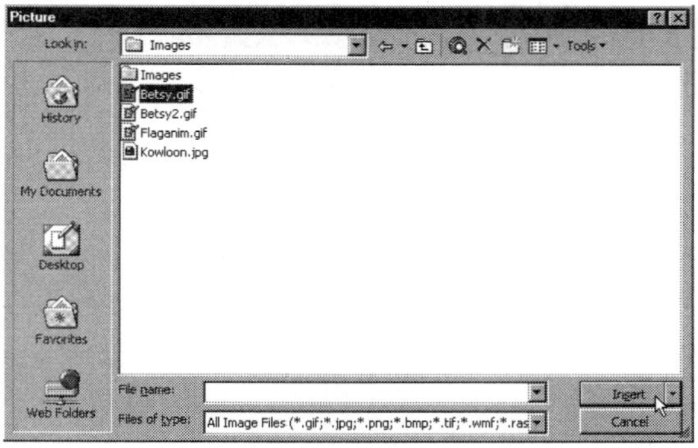

Figure 135 The Microsoft FrontPage Picture dialog box.

4. Use the drop-down list button to the right of the Look in field to navigate to the folder that contains the picture you want to place on the Web page, and then click your mouse pointer on the picture's filename in the list box below the Look in field. By the way, instead of navigating to the folder with the picture you want, you can enter the file's full pathname into the File name field at the bottom of the Picture dialog box. (If the file is in the current folder, i.e. the folder in the Look in field, you need only enter the file's name, without the directory path, into the File name field.)

Note: *If you want to insert multiple pictures at once, hold down the* CTRL *button on your keyboard as you click your mouse pointer on the filenames of the pictures you want to insert. FrontPage, in turn, will highlight the filename of each image file you select for insertion. To undo a selection, simply click your mouse pointer on a highlighted (selected) filename.*

5. Click your mouse pointer on the INSERT button near the lower right-hand corner of the Picture dialog box. FrontPage, in turn, will insert the picture(s) on the Web page at the insertion point you specified in Step 2 and return to Page view.

As you can see now, the procedure for placing a picture on a Web page is similar to inserting a picture into the document you are editing in a word processor. However, unlike the word processor document which contains an actual copy of the picture you insert, when you look at a picture on a Web page, you are actually looking at two files—the Web page and the file which contains the picture. Instead of inserting the picture directly into the Web page document (like a word processor), FrontPage inserts an <IMG> (image) tag into the Web page HTML. The <IMG> tag's attributes tell the Web browser where to retrieve the graphic image (the picture) file and specify its dimensions.

USING THE DRAG-AND-DROP METHOD TO INSERT A PICTURE ON A WEB PAGE

In addition to using the Insert menu Picture (From File) option you learned about in the preceding Tip, FrontPage also lets you insert a picture on a Web page by dragging the image file from the folder in which it is stored and drop it onto the current Web page in Page view. While the drag-and-drop method is simple to use, it does have one (perhaps severe) limitation—you can only drag-and-drop picture files stored in folders that are a part of a FrontPage web. (The Insert menu Picture (From File) option you learned about in the preceding Tip lets you insert a picture stored in any folder to which you have access—whether that folder part of a FrontPage web or not.)

To insert a picture on a Web page using the drag-and-drop method, perform the following steps:

1. Select the View menu Page option to display the current Web page in Page view.
2. If you do not see the Folder List pane in the FrontPage application window, select the View menu Folder List option to display it.
3. To display the contents of the folder with the picture(s) you want to place on the Web page, click your mouse pointer on the plus to the left of the folder's name in the Folder List pane. For example, if the pictures for the FrontPage web are stored in the IMAGES folder, click your mouse pointer on the plus to the left of IMAGES to display the folder's contents.
4. In the Folder List pane, move your mouse pointer onto the filename of the picture you want to insert on the Web page.
5. Click and hold down your left mouse button as you move your mouse pointer (and *drag* the picture) from the Folder List pane to the insertion point on the Web page. As shown in Figure 136, FrontPage shows you where it will *drop* the picture with a gray vertical line. (As such, the example in Figure 136 indicates that FrontPage will insert the picture between "here:" and "for" in the third line of the second paragraph.)

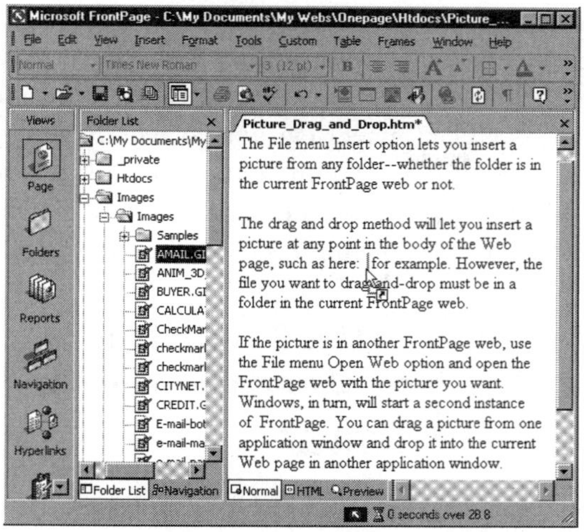

Figure 136 *A Web page in Page view just before releasing the left mouse button to drop a file between the fifth and sixth words in the second paragraph.*

6. When you have the insertion point (the gray vertical line) positioned where you want to insert the picture, release the left mouse button to drop the picture into place on the Web page.

If you want to insert a picture from a folder in a web other than the current FrontPage web, execute the first step in the preceding procedure on the current FrontPage web. Then, without closing the current FrontPage web, use the File menu Open Web option to open the web that has the picture you want. Windows, in turn, will start another instance (copy) of FrontPage on your computer in a new application window. Perform Steps 2 and 3 of the preceding procedure in the new application window. Then, in Step 5, drag the file from the Folder List pane in the new application window, and drop it onto the current Web page in the original application window in Step 6.

Note: *When you drag-and-drop a picture from a folder onto a Web page, you are not actually moving the graphic image file around. FrontPage simply inserts an <IMG> (image) tag at the insertion point in the current Web page and sets the <IMG> tag's SRC attribute to the pathname of the graphic image.*

REMOVING A PICTURE FROM A WEB PAGE

Removing a picture from a Web page is a simple two-step process. First, select the picture you want to remove by clicking your mouse pointer anywhere on the image. FrontPage, in turn, will display the Pictures (editing) toolbar and place sizing handles at each corner of the picture and at the center of each of its four sides. Second, delete the picture you selected by pressing either the DELETE or BACKSPACE key on your keyboard. FrontPage, in turn, will remove the picture from the Web page without prompting you for confirmation.

If you change your mind about removing the picture, you can undo the delete by selecting the Edit menu Undo Clear option (or by pressing CTRL-Z on your keyboard). Moreover, when you remove a picture from a Web page, FrontPage does not delete a file on disk. The program only removes the <IMG> (image) tag (which tells browsers to display the picture) from the Web page HTML. Therefore, since the image file itself remains in its folder after you delete the picture from the Web page, you can perform either of the procedures you learned in the two preceding Tips to put the picture back on the Web page later.

UNDERSTANDING WHY PICTURES INSERTED FROM OUTSIDE A FRONTPAGE WEB DO NOT APPEAR ON WEB PAGES PUBLISHED TO THE WEB SERVER

Without regard as to how it got there, a picture is "in" the FrontPage web so long as the image file is located in either the web's root folder or in one of the root's subfolders. Therefore, inserting a picture "in" a FrontPage web means that you are inserting a picture stored in the FrontPage web's root (i.e. its top-level) folder or in a subfolder in the web's root folder. FrontPage makes no distinction between pictures you import into a web subfolder or its root folder using the import procedure you learned in the previous Tip titled: "Using Folders View to Import Image Files Into Your Images Directory" and those you copy or move using the Windows Explorer, other Windows programs, or even the DOS COPY or MOVE command.

Whether the image file you insert on a Web page is from a folder "in" or from a folder "outside" of a FrontPage web becomes important when you publish the web to a Web server. As you learned in previous Tips, when you tell FrontPage to insert a picture on a Web page, the program inserts an <IMG> (image) tag and not the picture itself into the Web page HTML. The value of the <IMG> tag's "src" (source) attribute tells the Web browser where to find the picture it is to display.

When you use the File menu Publish option to publish a FrontPage web to a Web server, FrontPage creates a copy of the web's directory (folder) structure on the Web server and copies the contents of the web's root folder and subfolders to the corresponding folders on the server. As such, the <IMG> tag "src" references to files of pictures "in" the FrontPage web will work properly after you publish the web to the Web server because the Web browser will be able to retrieve the pictures from folders on the Web server. Conversely, "src" attributes that reference files of pictures "outside" the FrontPage web will appear as Missing Picture icons similar to the one shown in Figure 138, when the Web browser encounters an <IMG> tag and is not able to retrieve the picture from the location specified in the tag's "src" attribute.

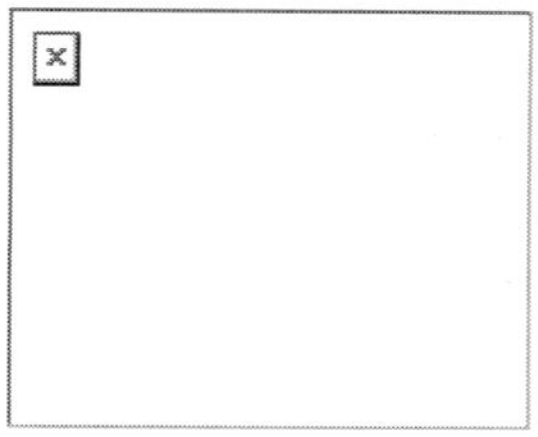

Figure 138 The Web browser Missing Picture icon.

The reason "src" references to image files inserted from outside the FrontPage web fail after you publish the web to the Web server is because FrontPage does not automatically create on the Web server the folder structure and copy the contents of folders and subfolders that are outside the FrontPage web when you publish the web. As such, "src" references to pictures outside the FrontPage web will only work if you manually create (i.e. create apart from the web publishing process) on the server the folders (and subfolder(s)) used to store the picture files outside the FrontPage web on your computer, and then copy the image files themselves into their corresponding folders (which you created) on the Web server.

SAFELY INSERTING PICTURES FROM OUTSIDE A FRONTPAGE WEB

As you learned in the preceding Tip, pictures you insert onto a Web page from outside the current FrontPage web may look fine when you use a browser to display the Web page on your computer but appear as Missing Picture icons when you display the published Web page on the Web server. The problem with inserting pictures from outside the FrontPage web is that FrontPage does not automatically copy them to the Web server when you select the File menu Publish Web option to publish (i.e., copy) the FrontPage web to the Web server. The easiest way to insure that Web browsers will be able to display all of the pictures you insert on your Web pages, is to import (into the current FrontPage web) any pictures you insert from outside the current web when you save the current FrontPage web to your hard drive.

For example, to insert a picture from outside the current FrontPage web, perform the following steps:

1. Display the Web page on which you wish to insert the picture in Page view. (If necessary, select the View menu Page option to display the current Web page in Page view.)
2. Move the cursor (the flashing vertical line) to the place on the Web page where you want to insert the image.

3. Select the Insert menu Picture option and click your mouse pointer on From File. FrontPage, in turn, will display the Picture dialog box.
4. Use the drop-down button to the right of the Look in field to and the contents of the list box below the Look in field navigate to the folder which contains the picture you want to insert.
5. In the list box below the Look in field, click your mouse pointer on filename of the picture you want to insert. Or, if you prefer, you can type the picture's full pathname into the File name field.
6. Click your mouse pointer on the INSERT button near the bottom right-hand corner of the Picture dialog box.

If you insert an image from a file on your computer, FrontPage will insert an <IMG> (image) tag with a "src" (source) attribute that contains the location of the image file in relation to the Web page on which you have inserted it. For example, given the folder structure:

```
PICTURES
MYWEB
  IMAGES
  HTMLDOCS
```

if you used the preceding procedure to insert PICTURE1.JPG stored in the PICTURES folder onto a Web page in the MYWEB folder, FrontPage will generate an <IMG> tag similar to:

```
<img border="0" src="../pictures/picture1.jpg" width="152"
height="122"
```

Similarly, if you insert PICTURE1.JPG on a Web page stored in the MYWEB\HTMLDOCS folder, FrontPage will generate an <IMG> tag similar to:

```
<img border="0" src="../../pictures/picture1.jpg" width="152"
height="122"
```

Finally, if you use the preceding procedure to insert a picture located on another workstation on your local area network (LAN), the <IMG> tag's "src" attribute will contain the file's absolute (vs. its relative) file location, as in:

```
<img border="0" src="file:///M:/pictures/picture1.jpg"
width="152" height="122"
```

(where M: is a drive mapped to the workstation on which the image being inserted is stored).

To have FrontPage import pictures you insert on a Web page from outside the FrontPage web, perform the following steps:

1. Select the File menu Save option (or the File menu Save As option) to save the Web page with the image you inserted from outside the FrontPage web to disk. (If you are saving a newly created Web page for the first time or if you select the File menu Save As option, FrontPage will display the Save As dialog box to prompt you to enter a name for the Web page and the folder in which you want to save it.)
2. If the Web page HTML has <IMG> tags whose "src" attributes specify files in folders outside the current FrontPage web, FrontPage will display a Save Embedded Files dialog box, similar that shown in Figure 139.1 which lists all of the images inserted from outside the current FrontPage web onto the Web page you are saving to disk.

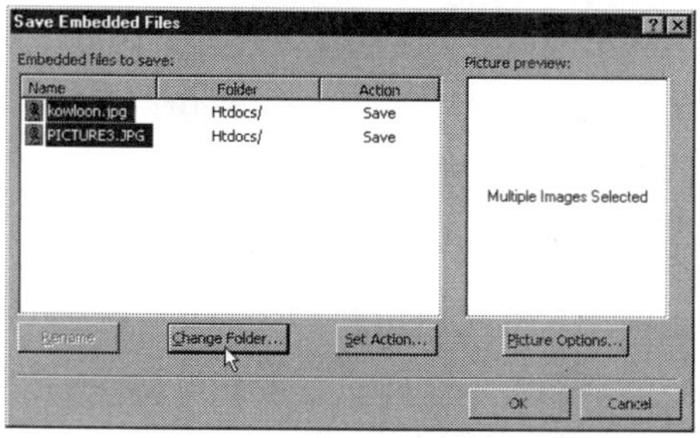

Figure 139.1 The Microsoft FrontPage Save Embedded Files dialog box.

3. Click your mouse pointer on the Change Folder button near the bottom center of the dialog box. FrontPage, in turn, will display a Change Folder dialog box similar to that shown in Figure 139.2.

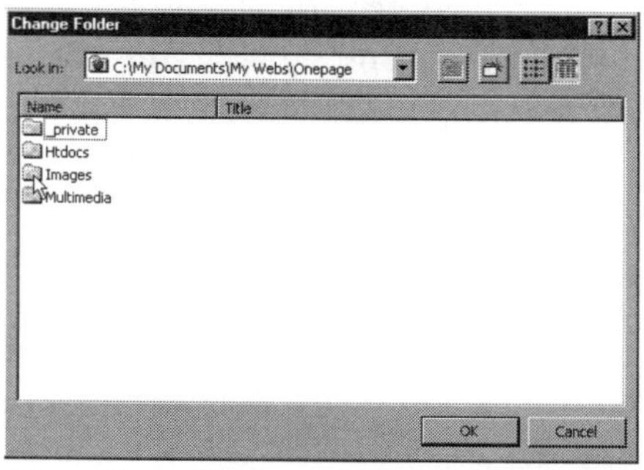

Figure 139.2 The Microsoft FrontPage Change Folder dialog box.

4. Click your mouse pointer on the folder into which you wish to import the image(s) in the folder list box below the Look in field, and then click your mouse pointer on the OK button at the bottom of the dialog box. If the Web page you are editing is being saved in a subfolder (vs. the current web's root folder), you may need to use the

drop-down list button to the right of the Look in field and the folders shown in the list box below the Look in field to navigate to the folder which contains the subfolder in which you want to store the image files.

5. Click your mouse pointer on the OK button near the bottom right-hand corner of the Save Embedded Files dialog box.

After you complete Step 5, FrontPage will save copies of the images you inserted onto the Web page from outside the current FrontPage web in the folder you selected in Step 4. In addition, before writing the Web page disk, FrontPage changes all of the "src" attributes of the <IMG> tags on the Web page it is saving to reference the copies of the images you imported into the root folder or into a subfolder in the FrontPage web.

In short, importing images inserted from outside a FrontPage web when you save the Web page, makes the page "safe" for publication, because FrontPage makes copies of the image files in a folder within the web and changes the <IMG> tag "src" attributes to reference the copies of the images within the current FrontPage web. Remember, when you use the File menu Publish web option to publish the FrontPage web to the Web server, FrontPage duplicates the web's directory structure and folder contents on the server. As such, all pictures inserted from folders in the FrontPage web on your computer will end up in the same relative location to the Web page after you publish the site to the Web server.

USING PICTURES AND DRAWINGS FROM OTHER WEB SITES ON YOUR WEB PAGES

When you tell FrontPage to insert a picture on a Web page, the program inserts an <IMG> (image) tag whose "src" (source) attribute tells the Web browser where to retrieve the picture it is to display. The previous Tips in this book showed you how to insert a picture stored in a folder within the current FrontPage web, in a folder at another location on the local computer's hard drive, and in a folder on the hard drive in another workstation on the local area network (LAN). However, you are not limited to using only pictures stored on the hard drive in the local computer or the hard drive on a workstation on the LAN. You can also insert pictures being displayed at Web sites on the Internet.

To insert on a Web page in the current FrontPage web an image displayed at a Web site on the Internet, perform the following steps:

1. If you do not have a permanent (always on) connection to the Internet, use your modem to connect to the Internet through your Internet Service Provider (ISP).
2. In the FrontPage application window, display the Web page on which you wish to insert the picture in Page view. (If necessary, select the View menu Page option to display the current Web page in Page view.)

3. Move the cursor (the flashing vertical line) to the place on the Web page where you want to insert the image.
4. Select the Insert menu Picture option and click your mouse pointer on From File. FrontPage, in turn, will display the Picture dialog box.
5. Into the File name field near the bottom of the dialog box, enter the URL (the Web address) of the picture you want to insert. For example, to insert the picture of the briefcase near the top of the NVBizNet.com homepage, you would enter **HTTP://NVBIZNET.COM/IMAGES/NVBIZNET1.JPG** into the File name field.

Note: *If you don't know the URL of the picture you want to insert, start your favorite Web browser and visit the page with the image you want. Right-click your mouse pointer on the picture, and then select Properties from the pop-up menu. (If you are using the Netscape Navigator instead of the Internet Explorer, select View Info from the pop-up menu.)*

6. Click your mouse pointer on the INSERT button near the bottom right-hand corner of the Picture dialog box.

After you complete Step 6, FrontPage will insert an <IMG> tag similar to:

```
<img border="0" src="http://nvbiznet.com/images/nvbiznet1.jpg"
width="265" height="223"
```

into the Web page HTML, and display the image from the Web site on the normal tab of the current Web page in Page view.

If you publish the FrontPage web to the Web server without importing the picture into the FrontPage web first, Web browsers will correctly display the image on your Web at the Web server—unless the site's owner changes the filename or location of the image file referenced in the "src" attribute of the <IMG> tag, or if the site itself is down. In short, if you use the picture's Web address to insert it on a Web page, a Web browser will display your Web page correctly as long as the picture remains accessible at its current location and filename on the Web site. If the site is down or if the site's owner removes the file, moves the file to another folder, or renames the file, the Web browser will display the image as a Missing Picture icon.

Thus, to be safe, have FrontPage import any pictures you insert onto a Web page from their current locations on the Internet by performing the following steps:

1. Select the File menu Save option (or the File menu Save As option) to save the current Web page to disk. (If you are saving a newly created Web page for the first time or if you select the File menu Save As option, FrontPage will prompt you to enter the name for the Web page and the folder in which you want to save it by displaying the Save As dialog box.)

2. After FrontPage displays a Save Embedded Files dialog box (similar to the one you saw in Figure 139.1), click your mouse pointer on the CHANGE FOLDER button near the bottom center of the dialog box. FrontPage, in turn, will display the Change Folder dialog box.
3. Click your mouse pointer on the folder into which you wish to import the image(s) in the folder list box below the Look in field, and then click your mouse pointer on the OK button at the bottom of the dialog box. If the Web page you are editing is being saved in a subfolder (vs. the current web's root folder), you may need to use the drop-down list button to the right of the Look in field and the folders in the list box below the Look in field to navigate to the folder which contains the subfolder in which you want to store the image files.
4. Click your mouse pointer on the OK button near the bottom right-hand corner of the Save Embedded Files dialog box.

After you complete Step 4, FrontPage will contact the Web server hosting the Web site with the picture you want to import, retrieve a copy of the picture from the site, and save the copy in the folder you selected in Step 3. Before saving the Web page, the FrontPage will change "src" attribute of the <IMG> tag on the current Web page to reference the copy of the image you told the program to import into a folder in the FrontPage web.

IMPORTING A PICTURE FROM A WEB SITE ON THE INTERNET INTO THE CURRENT FRONTPAGE WEB

Near the end of the text of the preceding Tip, you learned how to let FrontPage import a picture you inserted from a Web site into a folder in the current FrontPage web. You can also use your Web browser to import a picture manually from the Web site into a folder in the FrontPage web.

To import or download a picture from a Web site on the Internet into a folder on your computer, perform the following steps:

1. If you do not have a permanent (always on) connection to the Internet, use your modem to connect to the Internet through your Internet Service Provider (ISP).
2. Start your Web browser.
3. Into the browser's Address (or Location) field, enter the .com (Web) address of the Web page with the image you want to retrieve, and press the ENTER key on your keyboard.
4. After your Web browser displays the Web page with the picture you want to retrieve, right-click your mouse pointer on the image and select Save Picture As from the pop-up menu. (If you are using the

Netscape Navigator instead of the Microsoft Internet Explorer, select Save Image As from the pop-up menu.) Windows, in turn, will display the Save Picture dialog box.

5. Use the drop-down list button to the right of the Save in field and the folders shown in the list box below the Save in field to navigate to the folder in which you wish to store the picture from the Web page, and then click your mouse pointer on the SAVE button near the lower right-hand corner of the Save Picture dialog box.

Note: *While browsing the Web, you will find many pictures that you can download and use free of charge. However, some Web pages and their images are copyrighted and you must have the author's or Web site owner's permission to use the pictures on your Web pages. Look for a copyright footnote at the bottom of the site's pages. If you see the copyright symbol or are unsure as to whether or not a picture is copyrighted, contact the site's owner to ask permission before downloading and using the pictures from the site.*

UNDERSTANDING PICTURE/TEXT ALIGNMENT OPTIONS

Since most Web pages contain both text and graphics, you often need to specify how you want the text to flow around the graphics. By default, FrontPage aligns the bottom of the pictures with the bottom of any text that surrounds it, similar to that shown in Figure 142.1. However, the drop-down list button to the right of the Alignment field on the Picture Properties dialog box lets you select one of eleven text alignment options:

- **Default** – tells the Web browser to use its default alignment when displaying the Web page. By default, Web browsers align text along the bottom edge an embedded image.

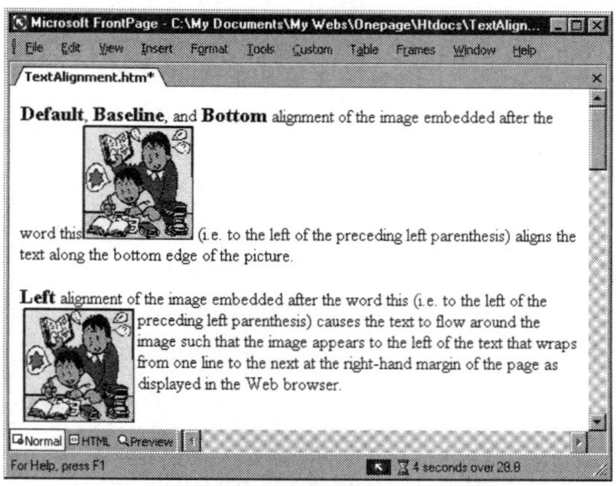

Figure 142.1 A Web page showing Default, Baseline, and Bottom alignment of text with an embedded image in the first paragraph and Left alignment of text with an embedded image in the second paragraph.

- **Left** – aligns the graphic with the left-hand margin of the Web page and displays the remaining text in the paragraph to the right of the image.
- **Right** – aligns the graphic with the right-hand margin of the Web page and displays the remaining text in to the left of the image.

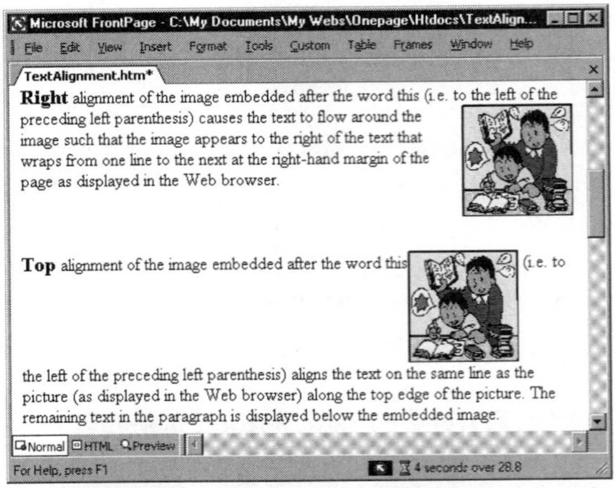

Figure 142.2 A Web page showing Right alignment of text with an embedded image in the first paragraph and Top alignment of text with an embedded image in the second paragraph.

- **Top** – aligns text in the same line as the image along the top edge of the picture. Text in subsequent lines is displayed below the bottom edge of the picture.
- **Texttop** - aligns text on the same line as the image such that the top edge of the picture is aligned with the top of the tallest character in the line of text. Text in subsequent lines is displayed below the bottom edge of the picture. Texttop alignment is usually, but not always, the same as Top alignment.
- **Middle** - aligns text on the same line as the image such that the baseline of the text is aligned with the middle of the image. Text in subsequent lines is displayed below the bottom edge of the picture. Middle alignment causes a slight off-center alignment of the text in relation to the middle of the picture. The baseline of the text is an imaginary line drawn along the bottom of the lines letters such as “abcdefhiklmnorstuvwxz” whose “tails” to do not extend below the baseline such as those on the letters “gjpqy”.
- **Absmiddle** - aligns text on the same line as the image such that an imaginary line drawn through the middle of the letters of text on the line will go through the horizontal middle of the image. Text on subsequent lines is displayed below the bottom edge of the picture.

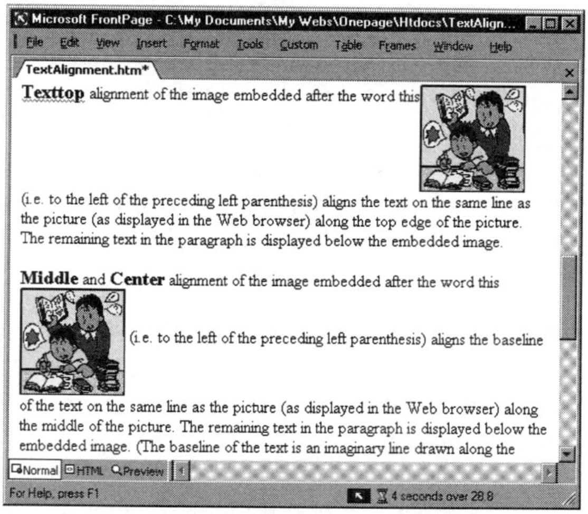

Figure 142.3 A Web page showing Texttop alignment of text with an embedded image in the first paragraph and Middle and Center alignment of text with an embedded image in the second paragraph.

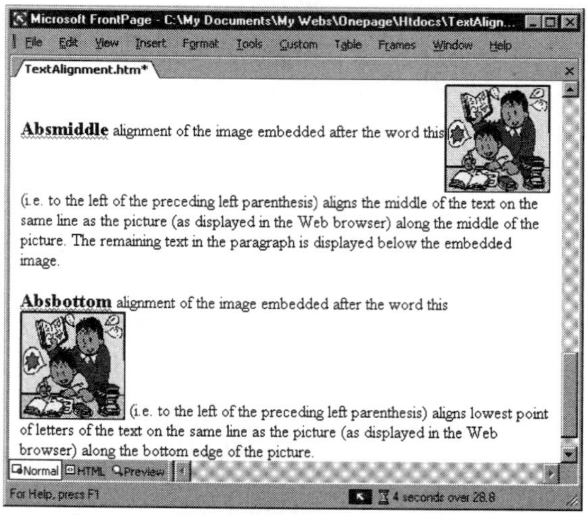

Figure 142.4 A Web page showing Absmiddle alignment of text with an embedded image in the first paragraph and Absbottom alignment of text with an embedded image in the second paragraph.

- **Baseline** - aligns text on the same line as the image such that the baseline of the text is aligned with the bottom of the image. Baseline and Bottom alignment produce the same effect

- **Bottom** - aligns text on the same line as the image such that the baseline of the text is aligned with the bottom of the image.

- **Absbottom** - aligns text on the same line as the image such that the bottom of the text is aligned with the bottom of the image. While Baseline and Bottom alignment align text along the baseline (the imaginary line drawn along the bottom of letters such as "abcdefhiklmnorstuvwxz" whose "tails" to do not extend below the baseline), Absbottom alignment aligns the bottom of the image with the lowest point of all letters on the line—including "gjpqy" whose tails extend below the baseline.
- **Center** - aligns text on the same line as the image such that the baseline of the text is aligned with the middle of the image. Text in subsequent lines is displayed below the bottom edge of the picture. Center and Middle alignment produce the same effect.

The following Tip will show you how to use the Picture Properties dialog box to set a picture's alignment with the text in which it is embedded.

SETTING PICTURE/TEXT ALIGNMENT OPTIONS

The Figures in the preceding Tip showed you the effect of selecting each of the eleven specifications for how text aligns with an embedded image. In general, the alignment options govern the way text on the same line as the picture will line up with the top, bottom, or center of the imbedded image. The resolution and size of the browser's application window determines the number of (and in effect which) words of text appear on the same line as the picture.

To set a picture's text alignment options, perform the following steps:

1. Use the Page view Normal tab to display the Web page with the embedded image whose picture/text alignment you want to set.
2. Right-click your mouse pointer on the picture, and select Picture Properties from the pop-up menu. FrontPage, in turn, will display the Picture Properties dialog box.
3. If not displayed already, click your mouse pointer on the Appearance tab.
4. Click your mouse pointer on the drop-down list box to the right of the Alignment field. FrontPage, in turn, will display a list of text/picture alignment options similar to that shown in the middle of the Picture Properties dialog box in Figure 143.

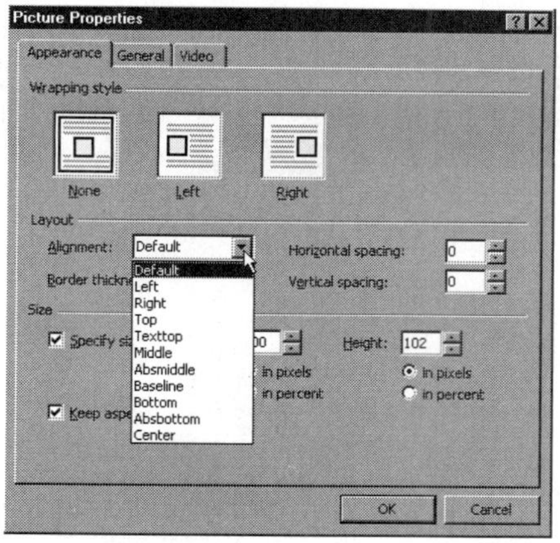

Figure 143 The Microsoft FrontPage Picture Properties dialog box with the picture/text alignment option drop-down list displayed.

5. Click your mouse pointer on the alignment option you want the Web browser to use when displaying text on the same line as the picture.
6. Click your mouse pointer on the OK button near the bottom right-hand corner of the Picture Properties dialog box.

After you complete Step 6, FrontPage will close the Picture Properties dialog box, return to the Page view Normal tab, and apply the alignment option you selected in Step 5 to the text that aligns with the picture you selected in Step 2.

SETTING THE DISPLAY DIMENSIONS OF A GRAPHICS IMAGE

In addition to the buttons on the Pictures toolbar that let you annotate, rotate, crop, bevel, and change the brightness, colors, and contrast of a picture, FrontPage also lets you tell the Web browser the height and width (i.e., the dimensions) it is to use when displaying the image. Specifying the dimensions of the picture has no effect on the image file itself. Instead, the Web server sends the unmodified picture to the browser, and the Web browser changes the way the picture looks in the browser application window per the dimensioning instructions in the Web page HTML.

FrontPage lets you adjust the dimensions of a picture either in terms of pixels or as a percentage of the size of the browser's application window. The first picture shown in Figure 144, show a clip art image in its original dimensions. In a moment, you will learn how to adjust the number of pixels in a picture's height and/or width to increase the picture's size as shown by the second picture in Figure 144, and how to specify the picture's height and/ or width as a percentage of the application window's size as shown by the third picture at the bottom of Figure 144.

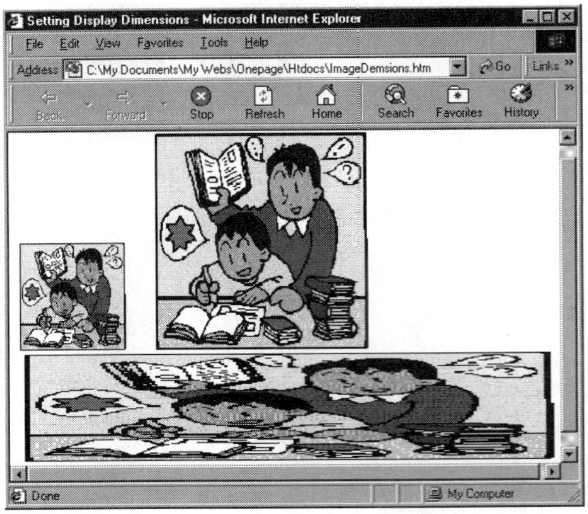

Figure 144 A Web page with the a single image file displayed in its original dimensions, after doubling the number of pixels in the picture's length and width, and after setting the width to 100%.

To specify a picture's dimensions to the Web browser by setting the number of pixels in its width and height, perform the following steps:

1. Right-click your mouse pointer on the picture whose dimensions you want to adjust, and select Picture Properties from the pop-up menu. FrontPage, in turn, will display a Picture Properties dialog box, similar to the one you saw in Figure 143 in the preceding Tip.
2. If not displayed already, click your mouse pointer on the Appearance tab.
3. Review the contents of the Specify size check box in the Size section in the bottom half of the dialog box. If the check box is empty, click your mouse pointer on the Specify size check box until a check mark appears. (By default, FrontPage checks the Specify size check box for you, so you only need to click a check mark into it if you previously cleared the check box to display the picture using its original dimensions.)
4. Click your mouse pointer on the in pixels radio button beneath the Width field and then on the in pixels radio button beneath the Height field.
5. Review the contents of the Keep aspect ratio check box. If the check box is empty, click your mouse pointer on the Keep aspect ratio check box until a check mark appears to tell FrontPage to keep the picture's width and height in the correct proportions when you change either its width or its height.

Note: *Unless you want to distort the picture by increasing (or decreasing) its size in one dimension more than the other, click a check mark into the Keep aspect ratio check box. FrontPage, in turn, will keep the ratio of the picture's width to its height (i.e., its aspect ratio) constant as you adjust the picture's width and/or its height. Conversely, if you clear the Keep aspect ratio check box, FrontPage will let you change the picture's width and height independently. If you increase the width without increasing the height, for example, you can create a squashed image such as that shown by the third picture (near the bottom) in Figure 144.*

6. To make the displayed image larger than the one in the image file, increase the number of pixels in the Width field either by entering a number into the field or by clicking your mouse pointer on the increase button at upper right-hand corner of the Width field. Conversely, to make the displayed image smaller than the one in the image file, decrease the number of pixels in the Width field either by entering a number into the field or by clicking your mouse pointer on the decrease button at the lower right-hand corner of the Width field.

Note: *When you clicked a check mark into the Keep aspect ratio check box in Step 5, you told FrontPage to make sure that the ratio of the picture's width to its height (and vice versa) remains constant. As a result, when you adjust the value in the Width field, FrontPage automatically changes the value in the Height field to keep the picture's aspect ratio (the ratio of width to height) constant. Although Step 6 has you adjust the value in the Width field, you can also change the displayed size of the picture by adjusting the value in the Height field instead. As is the case when you change the value in the Width field, when you change the value in the Height field, FrontPage will automatically change the value of the Width field as necessary to keep the picture's aspect ratio constant.*

7. Click your mouse pointer on the OK button near the lower right-hand corner of the dialog box.

To adjust the picture's dimensions by percentage (vs. by pixel count), click your mouse pointer on the in percent radio button beneath the Width field and on the in percent radio button beneath the Height field in Step 4. Then, continue at Step 6.

Note: *If you choose the set the picture's dimensions by percentage, FrontPage cannot maintain the picture's aspect ratio.*

In Step 6, enter the percentage of the width of the Web browser application window's width the picture is to take up into the Width field, and enter the percentage of the Web browser application window's height the picture is to take up into Height field.

Note: *You do not have to change both the width and height by percent or by pixel. For example, if you want to keep the original height of the picture while adjusting the width such that the picture* *stretches the full width (100%) of the browser's application window, click your mouse pointer on the in percent radio button below the Width field, and enter 100 into the Width field. Leave the value in the Height field and the selection of the in pixels radio button below the Height field unchanged.*

CONTROLLING THE SIZE OF THE WHITE SPACE AROUND AN IMAGE

When you combine pictures and text on a Web page, the page content will appear crowded unless you set the pictures off from the text. Notice the way the first and last letters of some of the words almost get lost in the pictures on the Web page in Figure 145.1.

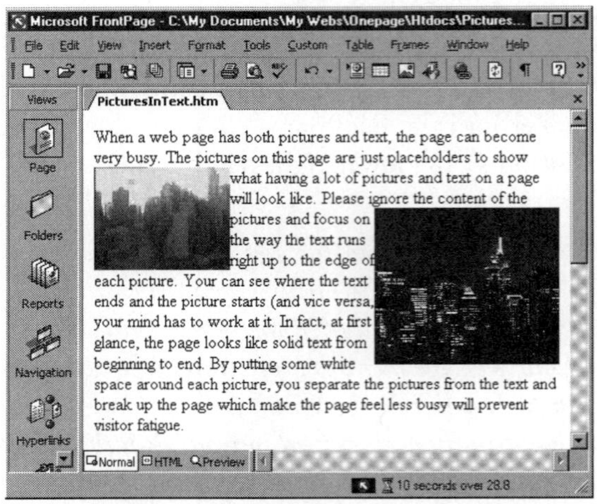

Figure 145.1 A Web page with both pictures and text.

Although you could put a border around the pictures, borders sometimes make the page look cluttered or clash with the colors in the picture. Another option is to increase the white space around the picture by performing the following steps:

1. With the Web page displayed on the Page view Normal tab, right-click your mouse pointer on the picture that you want to set off from the surrounding text and select Picture Properties from the pop-up menu. FrontPage, in turn, will display the Picture Properties dialog box.
2. If not displayed already, click your mouse pointer on the Appearance tab.
3. Into the Horizontal spacing field near the right-hand side of the Layout section at the center of the dialog box, enter the number of pixels of white space you want to leave between the left and right sides of the picture and the text on the Web page.

4. Into the Vertical spacing field near the right-hand side of the Layout section at the center of the dialog box, enter the number of pixels of white space you want to leave between the top and bottom of the picture and the text on the Web page.
5. Click your mouse pointer on the OK button near the bottom right-hand corner of the Picture Properties dialog box.

Repeat the procedure for each of the pictures on the Web page. Figure 145.2, for example, shows how the Web page in Figure 145.1 would look if you set the Horizontal spacing to 15 pixels and the Vertical spacing to 5 pixels for the first picture; and both the Horizontal spacing and Vertical spacing to 10 for the second picture.

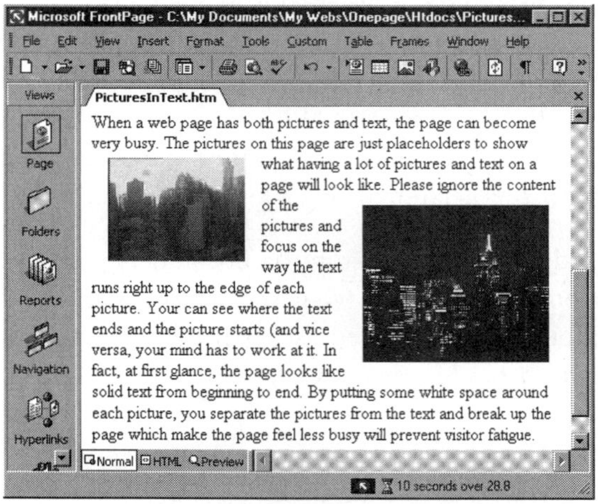

Figure 145.2 *A Web page with pictures separated from its text by white space borders.*

Notice that the increased white space around the pictures has the effect of putting a white border around each of them. The white border sets the picture off from the text without cluttering up the page or clashing with the colors in the picture.

WORKING WITH THE BORDER AROUND A PICTURE

In the preceding Tip, you learned that white space around a picture, when wide enough, acts like a border by separating the picture from text and other elements on the Web page without adding clutter to the page. Conversely, when you want to draw the visitor's attention to a picture, FrontPage lets you tell the Web browser to draw a border around it.

To draw a border around a picture, perform the following steps:

1. With the Web page displayed on the Page view Normal tag, right-click your mouse pointer on the picture that you want the browser to

enclose with a border. FrontPage, in turn, will display the Picture Properties dialog box.

2. If not displayed already, click your mouse pointer on the Appearance tab.
3. Into the Border thickness field enter the width (in pixels) of the border you want the browser to draw around the picture. (To display the picture without a border, enter a zero into the Border thickness field.)
4. Click your mouse pointer on the OK button near the lower right-hand corner of the Picture Properties dialog box.

After you complete Step 4, FrontPage will close the Picture Properties dialog box. If you entered a non-zero value into the Border thickness field in Step 3, FrontPage will show a border around the picture you selected in Step 1. The border around the picture will be black if the picture is not a hyperlink. Conversely, if the image is a hyperlink, the color of the border around the image will be the same as the default color of an unvisited hyperlink. After the Web visitor activates the hyperlink, by clicking the mouse pointer on the picture, the border color will change to the default color of a visited hyperlink.

Whether you draw a border around a picture or not and if you chose to draw a border, its width is a matter of personal preference. I suggest that if you draw borders around pictures at all, only draw borders around pictures used as hyperlinks. Figure 146, for example, shows a Web page with 2 pixel width borders around the hyperlink images in the bottom half of the Web page.

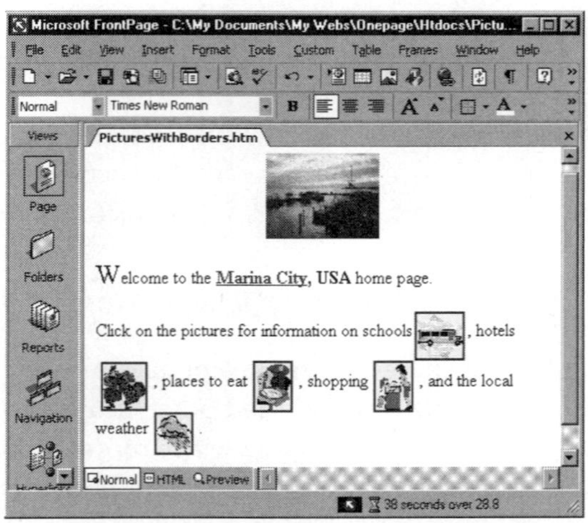

Figure 146 A Web page with 2 pixel borders drawn around clipart used as hyperlinks.

The advantages of drawing a border around an image you are using as a hyperlink are that the border draws the visitor's attention to the hyperlink and clearly indicates where to click the mouse pointer to activate the hyperlink. Moreover, because the border changes color (from the default unvisited hyperlink color to the default visited hyperlink color) after the visitor activates the hyperlink, borders around hyperlinks make it easy for Web site visitors to keep track of which image based hyperlinks they have and which hyperlinks they have not yet activated.

SPECIFYING TEXT TO DISPLAY AS AN ALTERNATIVE TO DISPLAYING A GRAPHICS IMAGE

In the early days of the Internet, text-only Web browsers were the norm. Nowadays, browsers can handle not only pictures, but also animations, and even full motion video. There is, however, a significant disabled population, a large number of people in remote areas with restricted bandwidth, many people using older computer systems and a growing number of people using wireless and handheld devices with small screens that want to access Web sites on the Internet. What they all have in common is that they turn off the Web browser's graphics capability either out of necessity or to increase the speed of their access to information (text) on the Web pages they access. Although you could simply ignore those who choose not to display the graphics you painstakingly selected to enhance the visitor's experience on your Web site, a better option is to provide a text alternative (i.e., ALT text) for their browsers to display in place of the images.

Whenever a browser is unable to or told not to display an image on a Web page, the browser draws a placeholder where the picture would have been displayed. When you provide alternative text (i.e., ALT text) for a graphics image, the browser will display as much of the ALT text as will fit within the borders of the image's placeholder. Moreover, most browsers display the ALT text as a "Tool Tip" just below the mouse pointer if the visitor holds the mouse pointer on the image (or its placeholder) for a few seconds.

For example, Figure 147 shows how the Web page in Figure 146 would look if the Web browser (Microsoft's Internet Explorer, in the current example) were told not to display pictures.

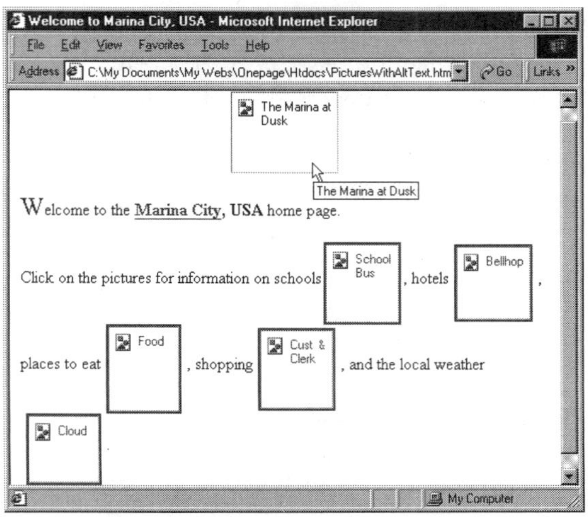

Figure 147 The Microsoft Internet Explorer displaying a Web page after turning off the "Show pictures" option on the Advanced tab of the Internet Options dialog box.

In general, when supplying ALT text for a picture, use one or more words that describe the graphics image. Site visitors with text-only browsers will then be able to infer the picture's purpose from the ALT text displayed in its placeholder on the Web page.

To provide ALT text for a picture, perform the following steps:

1. Display the Web page with the picture whose ALT (alternative) text you want to enter or modify.
2. Right-click your mouse pointer on the picture, and select Picture Properties from the pop-up menu. FrontPage, in turn, will display the Picture Properties dialog box.
3. Click your mouse pointer on the General tab.
4. Into the Text field in the Alternative representations section near the center of the dialog box, enter the ALT (alternative) text you want displayed in the missing picture's placeholder (and as a Tool Tip when the visitor holds the mouse pointer over the picture for a few seconds).
5. Click your mouse pointer on the OK button near the bottom right-hand corner of the Picture Properties dialog box.

Note: *Make sure the ALT (alternative text) will fit into the placeholder for the graphics image. While the Web browser will wrap multiple words from one line to the next, it will not split (hyphenate) a single word onto multiple lines. If an entire word of ALT text does not fit on a single line within the placeholder, the browser will truncate the word to the letters that will fit.*

ADDING A BACKGROUND IMAGE TO A WEB PAGE

A background image, as its name implies, is a picture you tell FrontPage to use as the background on a Web page. If you think of a Web page as a white wall in a room, then a background image works like wallpaper—it covers the wall, and any pictures or writing goes on top of the wallpaper.

Although you can use any picture you want as the background for a Web page, some images work better than others. The key to selecting a background that adds pizzazz is to choose one that does not interfere with the readability of the text on the page. To assist you in finding a suitable background for your Web page, the Microsoft includes several backgrounds you can use in the Clip Gallery.

If you already have an image file you want to use as a background skip the following procedure. Otherwise, if you want to search the Clip Gallery for a background, perform the following steps:

1. Display the Web page whose background you want to change on the Page view Normal tab.
2. Select the Insert menu Picture option and click your mouse pointer on Clip Art. FrontPage, in turn, will display the Insert Clip Art pane along the right-hand side of the FrontPage application window.
3. Into the Search text field enter **Background**, and then click your mouse pointer on the SEARCH button below the Search text field. FrontPage, in turn, will display thumbnails for clips identified (by keyword) as backgrounds in a results scroll box at the top of the Insert Clip Art pane.
4. Use the vertical scrollbar on the right-hand side of the results scroll box to scroll through the clip thumbnails. When you see the thumbnail for a clip art image you want to use as a background image, click your mouse pointer on it. FrontPage, in turn, will insert the clip art image on your Web page.

Note: *If the search yields no results, click your use pointer on the MODIFY button below the search results list box. FrontPage, in turn, will the search specification fields. Make sure that the selection in the Search in field is "All Collections". If it is not, click your mouse pointer on the drop-down list button to the right of the Search in field and click a check mark in to each of the checkboxes in the drop down list of search locations. Then, continue at Step 3.*

5. To close the Insert Clip Art Pane, click your mouse pointer on its close button (the "X") in the pane's upper right-hand corner.
6. Select the File menu Save option. FrontPage, in turn, will display the Save Embedded Files dialog box.
7. Make a note of the name of the file (shown in the Name column) and the name of the folder (shown in the Folder column) in which FrontPage is planning to save the image. You will need to know the pathname of the image file when you use the Page Properties dialog box to select the picture to use as the page background in the next procedure. [If you see three dots (…) as part of the filename or folder name, use your mouse pointer to drag the right-hand side of the Name and/or Folder column heading to the right to expand the column, so you can see the entire text in the column.]
8. Click your mouse pointer on the OK button near the lower right-hand side of the Save Embedded Files dialog box.

9. Click your mouse pointer on the clip art image you inserted in Step 4 to select it, and then press the DELETE key to remove the picture from the Web page. (You only inserted the clip art image and saved the page so FrontPage would import the image from the Clip Gallery into a folder in the current FrontPage web.)
10. Select the File menu Save option to save the current Web page as it was before you temporarily inserted the clip art image you plan to use for the page background.

To specify a background for a Web page, perform the following steps:

1. Display the Web page whose background you want to change on the Page view Normal tab.
2. Right-click your mouse pointer on a blank area on the Web page and select Page Properties from the pop-up menu. FrontPage, in turn, will display the Page Properties dialog box.
3. Click your mouse pointer on the Background tab.
4. Click your mouse pointer on the Background picture check box (in the Formatting section at the top of the Background tab) until a check mark appears.
5. Into the field below the Watermark check box, enter the pathname of the picture you want to use as the background for the Web page. (If you prefer, click your mouse pointer on the BROWSE button to the right of the field and then use the Select Background Picture dialog box to search for and select the image file with the picture you want to use.)
6. Click your mouse pointer on the OK button near the lower right-hand corner of the Page Properties dialog box. FrontPage, in turn, will close the dialog box and display the image you specified in Step 5 as the Web page background behind the text and images inserted on the Web page.

If you select a clip art image which is smaller than the size of the maximized Web browser's application window, the browser will tile the image (i.e. duplicate it as many times as necessary) to fill the background of the Web page.

UNDERSTANDING THE FRONTPAGE PICTURES TOOLBAR

FrontPage is a tool that makes it easy for you to create and maintain Web sites—either alone or in a collaborative environment with other authors. The program has Wizards that will generate the structure for several types of Web sites and a what-you-see-is-what-you-get

(WYSIWYG) editor that makes creating individual Web pages as simple as using a Word processor. In short, FrontPage is designed to let you concentrate on the site's content and its overall look and feel by freeing you from the drudgery of memorizing and typing the HTML tags necessary to create Web pages, insert multimedia objects, and generate animation effects.

While the program lets you set the dimensions of the pictures on your Web page and specify how text is to flow around them, FrontPage is not a full featured image editor. As such, do not plan on using FrontPage as the primary tool you will use to create and edit images. If you need to create or make extensive changes to artwork for a Web site, use such high-end tools as Adobe Illustrator, Freehand, or Photoshop.

The FrontPage Pictures toolbar does, however, provide a few basic image editing tools.

Unless you previously closed the toolbar by clicking your mouse pointer on its close button (the "X") in its upper right-hand corner, FrontPage will display the Pictures toolbar whenever you click your mouse pointer on a picture displayed on the Page view Normal tab. (If you click your mouse pointer on a picture and FrontPage does not display the Pictures toolbar, or if you want to display the toolbar without clicking your mouse pointer on an image, select the View menu Toolbars option and click your mouse pointer on Pictures.)

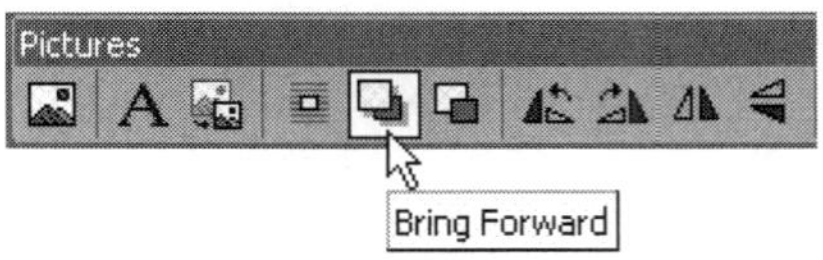

***Figure 149.1** The first ten buttons on the left-hand end of the Microsoft FrontPage Pictures toolbar.*

Working left to right, the first ten buttons on the Pictures toolbar, shown in Figure 149.1, perform the following functions:

- **Insert Picture From File** – displays the Pictures dialog box you can use to add an image to the Web page from a folder on the local hard drive, from a folder on a local area network (LAN) accessible hard drive, from the Microsoft Clip Gallery, or from a site on the Web.
- **Text** – lets you superimpose text on a GIF image—a graphics image stored in a file using the graphic interchange format.
- **Auto Thumbnail** – inserts a reduced size copy a graphics image (i.e. a thumbnail) on the Web page in place of the full size image and creates a hyperlink that lets a Web page visitor click the mouse pointer on the thumbnail to display the original, full size image.
- **Position Absolutely** – sets the image's position property such that a Web browser will display the image at specific *x-y* coordinates in relative to the browser's upper left-hand corner.

- **Bring Forward** – moves the selected object to top of the stack (i.e. to the front of the picture) when a GIF or clip art image is composed of multiple objects (called sprites) stacked one on top of another.
- **Send Backward** – moves the selected object to bottom of the stack (i.e. to the back of the picture) when a GIF or clip art image is composed of multiple objects (called sprites) stacked one on top of another.
- **Rotate Left** – rotates the selected image ninety degrees counterclockwise .
- **Rotate Right** – rotates the selected image ninety degrees clockwise.
- **Flip Horizontal** – reverses the selected image left to right.
- **Flip Vertical** – reverses the selected image top to bottom.

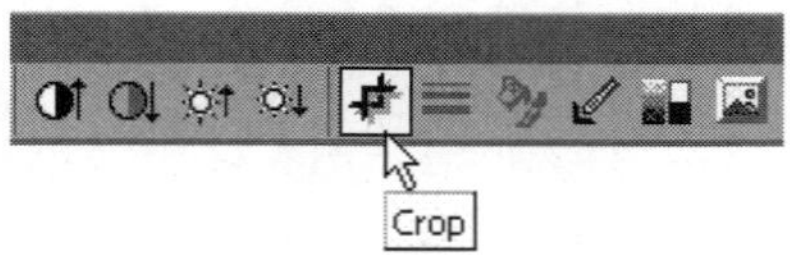

Figure 149.2 The ten buttons at the center of the Microsoft FrontPage Pictures toolbar.

Again working from left to right, the next set of ten buttons on the Pictures toolbar, shown in Figure 149.2, perform the following functions:

- **More Contrast** – increases the contrast of the colors in an image by darkening its darker colors and lightening its lighter colors.
- **Less Contrast** – decreases the contrast of the colors in an image by lightening its darker colors and darkening its lighter colors.
- **More Brightness** – increases the brightness of an image by brightening its dark colors.
- **Less Brightness** – decreases the brightness of an image by darkening its light colors.
- **Crop** – lets you use the mouse pointer as a cropping tool you can use to remove the portion of the image that falls outside of a rectangular square you draw by dragging your mouse pointer diagonally across the image.
- **Line Style** – (not yet implemented and therefore grayed out on the toolbar as unavailable).
- **Format Picture** – (not yet implemented and therefore grayed out on the toolbar as unavailable).
- **Set Transparent Color** – lets you select a color in the current image and make all of the pixels of that color transparent.

- **Color** – displays a menu that lets you washout the colors in a picture or reduce the colors in a picture to black and white, or use a grayscale to represent the colors in a picture.
- **Bevel** – adds a three-dimensional, beveled border around an image.

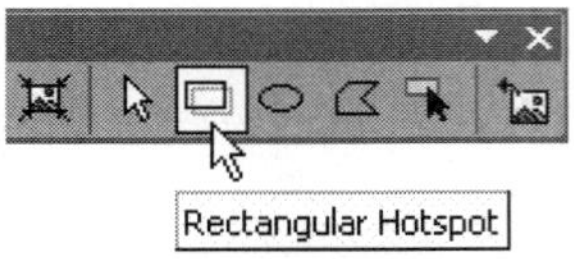

Figure 149.3 The final seven buttons on the right-hand end of the Microsoft FrontPage Pictures toolbar.

Finally, working from left to right once more, the last seven buttons on the right-hand end of the Pictures toolbar, shown in Figure 149.3, perform the following functions:

- **Resample** – creates a new image file for the current image to match the new dimensions set by dragging the image's sizing handles.
- **Select** – tells FrontPage to use the mouse pointer as a selection tool that lets you select an image by clicking the mouse pointer on it. (After you used the Crop button to turn the mouse pointer into a cropping tool, use the Select button to return the mouse pointer to its default behavior as a selection tool.)
- **Rectangular Hotspot** – lets you use the mouse pointer to draw a rectangular hotspot on an image. (When you use a Web browser to display the Web page with the image, clicking your mouse pointer on any pixel within the rectangular hotspot will activate the hyperlink associated with the hotspot.)
- **Circular Hotspot** – lets you use the mouse pointer to draw a circular hotspot on an image.
- **Polygonal Hotspot** – lets you use the mouse pointer to mark an irregular shaped, straight-sided area on an image.
- **Highlight Hotspots** – displays all of the current hotspots on an image.
- **Restore** – reverses all unsaved changes you made to an image since the last time you saved the picture to a disk file.

If you display the Pictures toolbar by clicking your mouse pointer on a graphics image on the Page view Normal tab, you can remove the toolbar from the application window by clicking your mouse pointer on the Web page, anywhere outside the borders of the picture(s) inserted on the page, or by clicking your mouse pointer on the close button (the "X") at the upper right-hand corner of the Pictures toolbar.

PLACING TEXT ON TOP OF A GRAPHICS IMAGE

The Text button (second from the left on the Pictures toolbar) lets you type text on a graphics image. You often need to add text to an image you plan to use as a button on the Web page. Figure 150, for example, shows how adding text to a clip art lets you use the same image for multiple buttons with different functions.

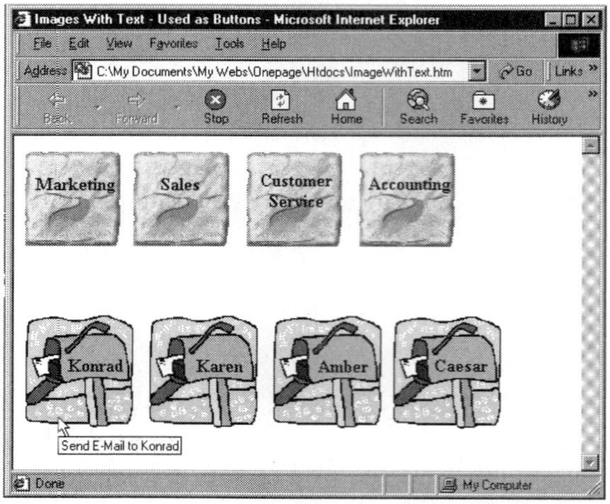

Figure 150 A Web page showing an image on the left and its washed-out version on the right.

While a single clip art image repeats four times in the first row of Figure 150, the text on the clip art (button) tells the site visitor on which button to click the mouse pointer to jump to the subweb for a particular department. Similarly, the text on the four clip art mail boxes at the bottom of the Figure tells the visitor which button to click in order to send an e-mail message to one of the four e-mail accounts.

To add text to a graphics image, perform the following steps:

1. Use the Page view Normal tab to display the Web page with the embedded image(s) you want to edit.
2. Click your mouse pointer on a picture you want to label. FrontPage, in turn, will place sizing handles on the picture's borders and display the Pictures toolbar. (If FrontPage does not display the Pictures toolbar, select the View menu Toolbars option and click your mouse pointer on Pictures.)
3. Click your mouse pointer on the Text button (the "A", second from the left) on the Pictures toolbar. FrontPage, in turn, will create a text area (with sizing handles on its borders) inside the picture you selected in Step 2.

Note: *You can only add text to a graphic interchange format image—better know as a GIF file. (GIF filenames have a .GIF extension). If you click your mouse pointer on the Text button after selecting an image in another format, such as JPG, for example, FrontPage will prompt you to let it convert the image file's contents to the GIF format. If you see the prompt, click your mouse pointer on the OK button near the bottom center of the message box.*

4. Use the buttons on the Formatting toolbar to select the text's color, font, and point size. Then, enter the text (label) into the text area that the Text button opened on the image. Use the sizing handles on the text area's borders to increase (or decrease) its size as necessary. (Remember, you can press SHIFT-ENTER to move to insert a line break if you want to create a multi-line label.)
5. When you are done entering text, click your mouse pointer on the Web page somewhere outside the borders of the graphics image. FrontPage, in turn, will exit picture edit mode, removing the sizing handles (from the picture and text), and will close the Pictures toolbar.

If you need to change the position of the text on the graphics image, click your mouse pointer on the text. After FrontPage displays the sizing handles on the borders of the picture, the sizing handle on the borders of the text area(s), and the Pictures toolbar, click and hold down your left mouse button as you drag the mouse pointer and the text area beneath it to its new position on the image. After you drag the text to the desired location on the image, release the left mouse button to drop the text into place.

To change the text you previously added to an image, click your mouse pointer on the text. After FrontPage displays the sizing handles around the image and the text of the existing label, click your mouse pointer on the text again. FrontPage, in turn, will display the vertical cursor in the text field and you can begin editing its contents. When you are done, click your mouse pointer somewhere on the Web page outside the borders of the image.

If you want to remove a text label from an image, click your mouse pointer on the text, and then press the DELETE or BACKSPACE key on your keyboard.

APPLYING THE WASHOUT EFFECT TO AN IMAGE

When selecting a background image for a Web page, you need to use a picture that will not interfere with the Web visitor's ability to read the text on the page. The washout effect lets you use images would normally be unacceptable as Web page backgrounds. For example, the washout effect applied to the picture on the left in Figure 151 both increases the picture's brightness and lowers its contrast to produce the picture shown on the right.

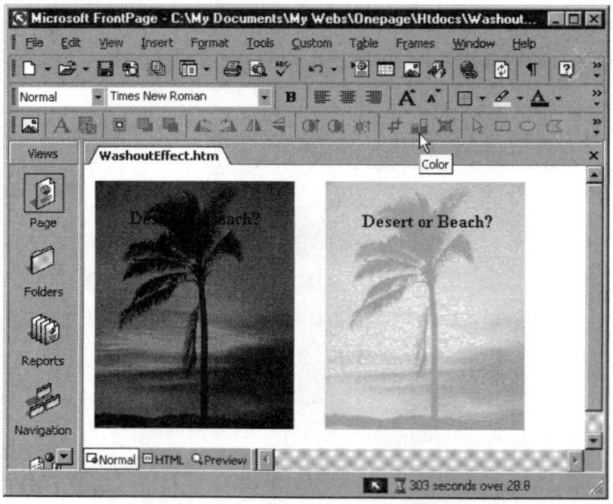

Figure 151 A Web page with the image on the right showing how the image on the left will look after applying the washout effect.

Notice that the text typed on top of the original image (on the left) is unreadable, while you have no difficulty in reading text type on top of the same image (shown in the right) after applying the washout effect.

To apply the washout effect to an image, perform the following steps:

1. Display the Web page with the image you want washed-out on the Page view Normal tab.
2. Click your mouse pointer on the image you want to washout. FrontPage, in turn, will display the Pictures toolbar and sizing handles on the borders of the image. (If FrontPage does not display the Pictures toolbar, select the View menu Toolbars option and click your mouse pointer on Pictures.)
3. Click your mouse pointer on the Color button on the Pictures toolbar. (The Color button is the ninth button from the right on the Pictures toolbar and is marked with the grayscale icon.) FrontPage, in turn, will display the Color button menu.
4. Select Wash Out from the Color button menu. FrontPage, in turn, will washout the image by increasing its brightness and lowering its contrast.
5. Click your mouse pointer on the Web page outside of its picture(s) to exit picture edit mode.

Because applying the washout effect changes the image, FrontPage will prompt you with the Save Embedded Files dialog box when you tell the program to save the Web page. The default action is for FrontPage to overwrite the original image with its washed-out version. If you want to keep both the original and washed-out versions of the image, click your mouse pointer on the RENAME button near the bottom left-hand side of the Save Embedded Files dialog box, and enter a new filename for the picture file. For example, if the filename of the original picture file is **PalmTree.GIF**, you may want to enter a name like **PalmTreeWO.GIF** as the filename its washed-out version.

To use the washed-out image as a background, delete the washed-out image from the Web page, and then perform the steps in the second procedure in the previous Tip entitled "Adding a Background Image to a Web Page." Enter the pathname of the washed-out image file into the field below the Watermark check box on the Page Properties dialog box in Step 5 of the procedure.

CREATING A TRANSPARENT GIF

Clip art images you insert on a Web page often have a postage stamp like appearance. While the artwork in the image has an irregular shape, it is displayed on a rectangular, white background whose sides extend beyond some portion of the art in each of the four directions. As a result, if you insert the clip art on a Web page with a (nonwhite) color background or on a page with a background image, the picture is set off in a rectangular box, such as the image on the left in Figure 152.

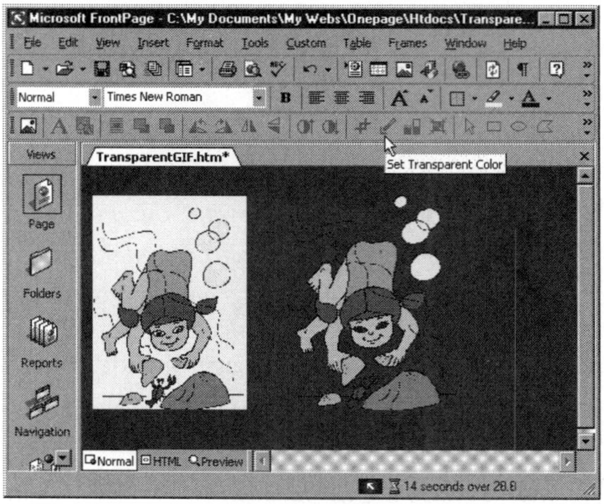

Figure 152 A Web page with a clip art image displayed with a normal and then a transparent background.

To make the background of an image transparent, such as the background of the image at the right in Figure 152, perform the following steps:

1. Display the Web page with the image whose background you want to make transparent on the Page view Normal tab.

2. Click your mouse pointer on the image you want to edit. FrontPage, in turn, will display the Pictures toolbar. (If FrontPage does not display the Pictures toolbar, select the View menu Toolbars option and click your mouse pointer on Pictures.)
3. Click your mouse pointer on the Set Transparent Color button (the button with the picture of the pencil, eraser end down) on the Pictures toolbar. FrontPage, in turn, will change the arrow mouse pointer into a pencil with a small, black arrow attached to the eraser when you move the mouse pointer onto the image you are editing.

Note: *You can only set a transparent color in images stored as GIF and Portable Network Graphics (PNG) files. If the image you selected in Step 2 is of another file type such as JPEG, FrontPage will prompt you with a message box asking if you want to convert the image to GIF format. Before you click your mouse pointer on the OK button to continue, bear in mind that a GIF image can have at most 256 colors. As such, a high resolution picture (with several thousand colors) may look little like the original when FrontPage maps the colors in the JPEG file to the maximum of 256 colors allowed in the GIF file.*

4. Click the arrow at the top of the pencil mouse pointer on a pixel of the color that you want to make transparent in the GIF. For example, to make its white background transparent, click the pencil mouse pointer anywhere on the GIF's background.

Note: *You can only select a single color in the GIF image as the transparent color. If you repeat Step 3 – 4—clicking the pencil mouse pointer on a color other than the transparent background color in Step 4, the new color will become the transparent color and the white background will return. You can also make the white background non-transparent without making another color transparent by repeating Steps 3 – 4—clicking the pencil mouse pointer on the transparent background in Step 4.*

5. Click your mouse pointer on the Web page outside of its picture(s) to exit picture edit mode.

Note: *Notice that the girl's eyes in the image at the right in Figure 152 are blue—just like the Web page background. The whites of the eyes are now blue because they were the same color as the white background made transparent by applying the transparent color effect. (Making a color transparent makes ALL pixels of that color transparent—whether the pixels are in the background or a part of the artwork.) To prevent "holes" from appearing in the artwork where the background shows through, you must first use a program such as Paintshop to change the colors in the artwork such that none of them is the same as the color of the background (or vice versa).*

Because making a color in a GIF transparent changes the image, FrontPage will prompt you with the Save Embedded Files dialog box when you save the Web page. The default action is for FrontPage to overwrite the original image with the modified version. If you want to keep both the original and the edited version of the image, click your mouse pointer on the RENAME button near the bottom left-hand side of the Save Embedded Files dialog box and enter a new filename for the picture. For example, if the filename of the original picture file is **Diver.GIF**, you may want to enter a name such as **DiverTB.GIF** for the filename of the picture with the transparent background.

USING THE CROPPING TOOL TO REMOVE A PORTION OF A GRAPHICS IMAGE

Cropping a picture means removing the parts of the image you do not want. When using the FrontPage cropping tool, draw a rectangle around the part of the picture you want to keep and then tell FrontPage to remove the rest. For example, to crop a picture such as the one the left in Figure 153 such that only the lion's head remains,

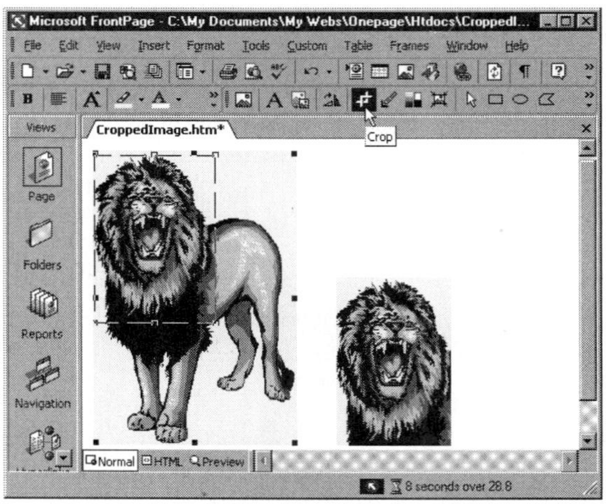

Figure 153 *A Web page with a clip art lion on the left and the cropped lion head on the right.*

perform the following steps:

1. Display the Web page with the image you want to edit on the Page view Normal tab.
2. Click your mouse pointer on the image you want to crop. FrontPage, in turn, will display the Pictures toolbar. (If FrontPage does not display the Pictures toolbar, select the View menu Toolbars option and click your mouse pointer on Pictures.)
3. Click your mouse pointer on the Crop button (the button with the picture of the overlapping corners of a picture frame) on the Pictures toolbar. FrontPage, in turn, will draw a dashed rectangle around a portion of the image you selected in Step 2, and will display the mouse

pointer as a plus (+) instead of an arrow when you move the mouse pointer onto the image you plan to crop.

4. Move the mouse pointer just above and to the left of the portion of the picture you want to keep.
5. Click and hold the left mouse button as you drag the plus mouse pointer to just below and to the right of the portion of the image you want to keep. FrontPage, in turn, will draw a rectangle with its upper left-hand corner at the point you started in Step 5 and its lower right-hand corner at the center of the plus (+) mouse pointer as you drag the mouse pointer diagonally across the area of the picture you want to keep.
6. When the cropping rectangle's dashed borders enclose the portion of the picture you want to keep, release the left mouse button.
7. If you made a mistake when you positioned the upper-left hand corner of the rectangle in Step 4 and/or the lower right-hand corner of the rectangle in Step 6, and the area of the picture you want to keep is not within the dashed borders of the rectangle, simply draw it again by continuing at Step 4. Or, if you prefer, you can change the dimensions of the cropping rectangle by using your mouse pointer to drag the sizing handles at the corners and middle of each side of the rectangle to change its dimensions.
8. To remove the portion of the picture that lies outside the dashed (cropping) rectangle, click your mouse pointer on the Crop button on the Pictures toolbar.
9. Click your mouse pointer on the Web page outside of its picture(s) to exit picture edit mode.

Because cropping changes an image, FrontPage will prompt you with the Save Embedded Files dialog box when you save the Web page. The default action is for FrontPage to overwrite the original image with the cropped version. If you want to keep both the original and the cropped version of the image, click your mouse pointer on the RENAME button near the bottom left-hand side of the Save Embedded Files dialog box, and enter a new filename for the cropped picture. For example, if the filename of the original picture file is **Lion.GIF**, you may want to enter a name such as **LionHead.GIF** for the filename of the picture from which you cropped all but the lion's head.

PLACING A THUMBNAIL ON A WEB PAGE

As you know, a thumbnail is a small, preview image of a larger picture. The main reason for using thumbnails on a Web page is to decrease the amount of time it takes for the visitor's Web browser to receive the page and display its contents. Even in these days of broadband (cable modem, DSL, ISDN) access to the Internet, many Web surfers still use dial-up accounts at work, on the road, and in the many areas where broadband access is not yet available. Since dial-up access to the Internet usually occurs at speeds of 28.8K – 44K (vs. 128K – 1.1MB+ for broadband access), you need to limit the number of pictures on a page to reduce your visitors' annoyance level at having to wait for graphics they have already seen or do not need to download over a slow connection.

Thumbnails provide a way for you to build Web pages that rely on pictures, (e.g. a picture gallery, an online store, or a catalog), and still load in an acceptable amount of time. Because a thumbnail is a smaller version of the larger picture, the Web server can download it to the visitor's browser more quickly. As such you can insert several thumbnails on your Web page while still keeping its load time low.

To view the full size picture, the visitor simply clicks the mouse pointer on its thumbnail. It will take the same amount of time to download the larger picture whether you include it on the Web page or send it in response to a visitor's request. However, your Web visitors will be willing to wait a few moments to see pictures they request by clicking the mouse pointers on thumbnails. Most visitors, like me, only get annoyed at having to wait for pictures they do not want each time they visit the Web site.

To insert a thumbnail on a Web page, perform the following steps:

1. Use the Page view Normal tab to display the Web page on which you wish to insert the thumbnail.
2. If you have not done so already, use the Insert menu Picture option and select From File or From Scanner or Camera to place the full size picture you want to change into a thumbnail onto the Web page.
3. Click your mouse pointer on the picture you want to replace with a thumbnail. FrontPage, in turn, will display the Pictures toolbar. (If you do not see the Pictures toolbar, select the View menu Toolbars option and click your mouse pointer on Pictures.)
4. Click your mouse pointer on the Auto Thumbnail button (third from the left) on the Pictures toolbar.

After you complete Step 4, FrontPage will replace the full size picture on the Web page with a thumbnail of the picture and create a hyperlink from the thumbnail to the original, full size picture.

When you save the Web page, FrontPage will display the Save Embedded Files dialog box so you can decide where to store the thumbnail image file. By default, FrontPage will store the thumbnail in the same folder as the original image file. For example, if the original picture is stored in the IMAGES folder as HOTEL.JPG, FrontPage will save the thumbnail in the

IMAGES folder as HOTEL_SMALL.JPG. Unless you want to store the thumbnail in a different folder or want to use another filename, simply click your mouse pointer on the OK button near the lower right-hand corner of the Save Embedded Files dialog box.

The reduction in Web page load time when using thumbnails in place of full size pictures can be rather dramatic. While a browser can download and display the nine thumbnails on the Web page shown in Figure 154 over a 28.8K line in just 9 seconds, a Web page with the nine full size pictures will take over three minutes to retrieve and display at the same connection speed.

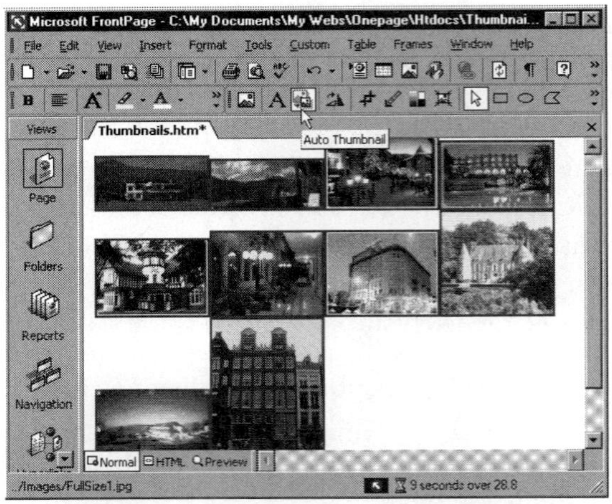

Figure 154 A Web page with a picture gallery of nine thumbnails.

Note: *As you work on a Web page in Page view, FrontPage shows you the page load time near the lower right-hand corner of the application window. If the load time gets too high (over one minute, for example) either split the Web page content onto multiple pages, or if the page has several full size pictures, try replacing them with thumbnails. You can change the connection speed used to compute the load time by selecting the Tools menu Options option, and choosing the value you want for the Assume connection speed of field on the Reports View tab.*

WORKING WITH THUMBNAIL SETTINGS

In the preceding Tip, you leaned how to replace an image on a Web page with a smaller, preview copy of the picture called a thumbnail. Since the thumbnail is itself a picture, you can change its dimensions, the width of its border, and/or add a bevel to make it look more like a button. Rather than make the same changes to each thumbnail you create, you can change the FrontPage default thumbnail settings.

To specify the dimensions, border width, and bevel setting FrontPage is to use when generating thumbnails, perform the following steps:

1. Select the Tools menu Page Options option. FrontPage, in turn, will display the Page Options dialog box.
2. Click your mouse pointer on the Auto Thumbnail tab to display the current thumbnail default settings, similar to that shown in Figure 155.

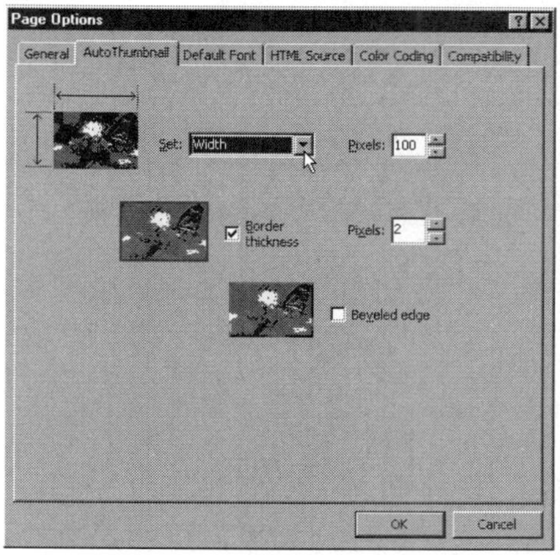

Figure 155 The Microsoft FrontPage Page Options dialog box, Auto Thumbnail tab.

3. Click your mouse pointer on the drop-down list button to the right of the Set field to choose the thumbnail dimension you wish to control. You can choose to control the width, height, shortest side, or longest side. For example, if you want all thumbnails to be at least a certain height or width, select shortest side.
4. Into the Pixels field to the right of the Set field, enter the number of pixels you want for the dimension you selected in Step 3. For example, if you want all thumbnails to be at most 100 pixels in width or height, enter 100 into the Pixels field after selecting longest side for the Set field to the left of the Pixels field. Conversely, if you want all thumbnails to be at least 100 pixels in width or height, enter 100 into the Pixels field and select shortest side in the Set field.
5. If you want FrontPage to create thumbnails without borders, click your mouse pointer on the Border thickness checkbox until it is empty. Otherwise, click your pointer on the Border thickness checkbox until a check mark appears.
6. Into the Pixels field to the right of the Border thickness field, enter the number of pixels wide you want the border around each thumbnail to be.
7. If you want thumbnails to have beveled edges, click your mouse pointer on the Beveled edge checkbox until a check mark appears. (Creating a

thumbnail with a beveled and no border will make the miniature picture look more like a button.)

8. Click your mouse pointer on the OK button near the lower right-hand corner of the Page Options dialog box.

While existing thumbnails will remain unchanged, FrontPage will create future thumbnails according to your new specifications after you complete Step 8.

USING INTERLACED GIF IMAGES (PROGRESSIVE RENDERING) TO REDUCE WEB PAGE LOAD TIME

Using an interlaced GIF does not really reduce Web page load time; it just appears to do so. If the visitor's Web browser supports interlaced GIF's, the browser will display interlaced pictures on the screen gradually. The pictures will at first appear blurry and be displayed along with the Web page text content and hyperlinks. While the pictures continue to load, the visitor can start reading text or activate a hyperlink to go on to another Web page. As the Web browser receives additional pixels for the GIF image from the server and displays them as part of the GIF, the image will become clearer. At some point, the browser will have received all of the GIF's pixels, and the image on the Web page will look exactly like the original.

Note: *You can only interlace images stored in the GIF file format. If you have a picture stored using the JPEG format, use the procedure in the next Tip entitled: "Using Progressive JPEG Images to Reduce Web Page Display Time."*

To turn a non-interlaced GIF into an interlaced image that will appear grainy at first and then clear up as its pixels are loaded, perform the following steps:

1. Display the Web page with the image you want to convert to an interlaced GIF on the Page view Normal tab.
2. Click your mouse pointer on the picture whose interlaced setting you want to change. FrontPage, in turn, will display the Pictures toolbar. (If you do not see the Pictures toolbar, select the View menu Pictures option to display it.)

Note: *In order to change the GIF's interlaced setting, you need FrontPage to display the Save Embedded Files dialog box. By changing the picture in the following Step, you ensure that FrontPage will display the dialog box when you tell the program to save the Web page.*

3. To have FrontPage display the Save Embedded Files dialog box when you save the Web page, make a change to the picture you selected in Step 2. For example, click your mouse pointer on the Rotate Left

button on the Pictures toolbar. Then, click your mouse pointer on the toolbar's Rotate Right button to undo the change.

4. Select the File menu Save option. FrontPage, in turn, will display the Save Embedded Files dialog box.
5. Click your mouse pointer on the PICTURE OPTIONS button below the Picture preview area at the right-hand side of the dialog box. FrontPage, in turn, will display a Picture Options dialog box, similar to that shown in Figure 156.

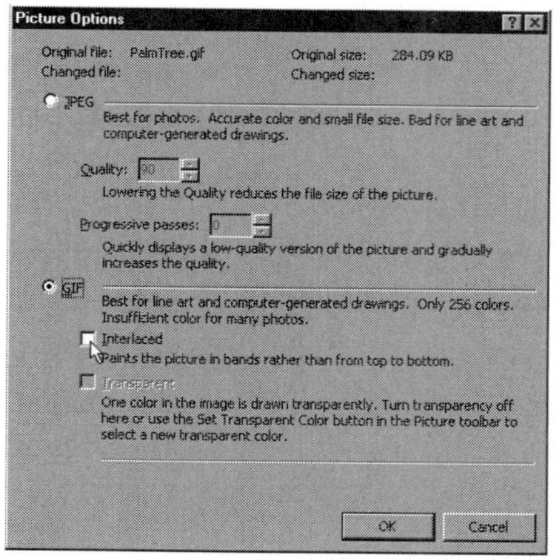

Figure 156 The Microsoft FrontPage Picture Options dialog box.

6. Click your mouse pointer on the Interlaced checkbox in the GIF area in the half of the dialog box until a check mark appears. FrontPage, in turn, will generate an interlaced GIF image for the current picture and display new image's filename and size above the JPEG area at the top of the dialog box.
7. Click your mouse pointer on the OK button near the lower right-hand corner of the Picture Options dialog box to return to the Save Embedded Files dialog box.
8. By default, FrontPage will overwrite the original GIF with the interlaced GIF image. If you want to keep both the interlaced and non-interlaced files, click your mouse pointer on the RENAME button below the lower left-hand corner of the Embedded files to save list box, and enter a new filename for the interlaced GIF file. For example, if the original GIF is stored in a file named **PalmTree.GIF**, you may want use the filename **PalmTreeI.GIF** for the filename of the interlaced GIF file.
9. Click your mouse pointer on the OK button near the lower right-hand corner of the Save Embedded Files dialog box.

After you complete Step 9, FrontPage will save the interlaced GIF to a file with the name you specified in Step 8. The picture will not look any different when displayed in the FrontPage application window. To see the interlacing effect in action, display the Web page with the interlaced image using a Web browser which supports interlaced GIF's.

USING PROGRESSIVE JPEG IMAGES TO REDUCE WEB PAGE DISPLAY TIME

As you learned in the preceding Tip, you can make a Web page with GIF images appear to load more quickly by using interlaced GIF images. A Web page with interlaced GIF's seems to load more quickly because the Web browser only has to download some of the pixels in each interlaced GIF images before starting to display the pictures on the screen. The visitor then has something at which to look (the fuzzy pictures) and the Web page text to read while waiting for the browser to finish loading the GIF file. Having something on the screen to read while waiting gives the viewer the feeling that it takes less time to load the GIF's and therefore, the entire Web page—even though it does not.

The same concept of phased refinement of pictures when applied to Joint Photographic Experts Group (JPEG) encoded images is called partial rendering. Instead of displaying more and more pixels to bring the interlaced GIF into focus, progressive rendering involves filling rectangular areas of color that define a JPEG image with more and more information. As a result, progressively rendered JPEG files appear both blocky and blurry at first. Then as the rectangles receive more data, they take on their final colors and the image comes into focus.

To turn a JPEG into a progressively rendered JPEG, perform the following steps:

1. Display the Web page with the image you want to convert to a progressively rendered JPEG on the Page view Normal tab.
2. Click your mouse pointer on the picture whose rendering you want to change. FrontPage, in turn, will display the Pictures toolbar. (If you do not see the Pictures toolbar, select the View menu Pictures option to display it.)

Note: *In order to change the JPEG's progressive rendering setting, you need for FrontPage to display the Save Embedded Files dialog box. By changing the picture in the following Step, you ensure that FrontPage will display the dialog box when you tell the program to save the Web page.*

3. To have FrontPage display the Save Embedded Files dialog box when you save the Web page, make a change to the picture you selected in Step 2. For example, click your mouse pointer on the Rotate Left button on the Pictures toolbar. Then, click your mouse pointer on the toolbar's Rotate Right button to undo the change.

4. Select the File menu Save option. FrontPage, in turn, will display the Save Embedded Files dialog box.
5. Click your mouse pointer on the PICTURE OPTIONS button below the Picture preview area at the right-hand side of the dialog box. FrontPage, in turn, will display a Picture Options dialog box, similar to the one you saw in Figure 156 in the preceding Tip.
6. Into the Progressive passes field in the JPEG section at the top half of the dialog box, enter the number of passes you want the browser to make in rendering the picture. For example, if the JPEG takes 60 seconds to download on the Web page and you want the page displayed in 6 seconds, enter a 10 into the Progressive passes field. The browser will then receive 1/10 of the picture's data during each of the ten passes. As such the first pass will take 1/10 of the time it takes the entire picture to load, i.e. 6 seconds.
7. Click your mouse pointer on the OK button near the lower right-hand corner of the Picture Options dialog box to return to the Save Embedded Files dialog box.
8. By default, FrontPage will overwrite the original JPEG with the progressively rendered JPEG image. If you want to keep both the original JPEG and the progressively rendered JPEG images, click your mouse pointer on the RENAME button below the lower left-hand corner of the Embedded files to save list box, and enter a new filename for the progressively rendered JPEG file. For example, if the original JPEG is stored in a file named **Hotel.JPG**, you may want use the file name **HotelPR.JPG** for the filename of the progressively rendered JPEG file.
9. Click your mouse pointer on the OK button near the lower right-hand corner of the Save Embedded Files dialog box.

After you complete Step 9, FrontPage will save the progressively rendered JPEG image to a file with the name you specified in Step 8. The picture will not look any different when displayed in the FrontPage application window. To see the progressive rendering take place, display the Web page with the JPEG file using a Web browser which supports progressively rendered JPEG's.

PLACING A HORIZONTAL LINE ON A WEB PAGE

When you need to separate parts of a Web page visually, HTML provides a <HR> (horizontal rule) tag you can use to draw a horizontal line across the width of the page. By default a *horizontal rule* (short for ruled horizontal line) looks as if you used a ruler and a pencil to draw a (straight) horizontal gray line from a point on the left margin across the Web page to a point the same distance from the top of the page on the right margin. Moreover, a horizontal rule (i.e. a horizontal line), like the one shown below the first paragraph of text in Figure 158, normally includes a line of white space both above and below the line.

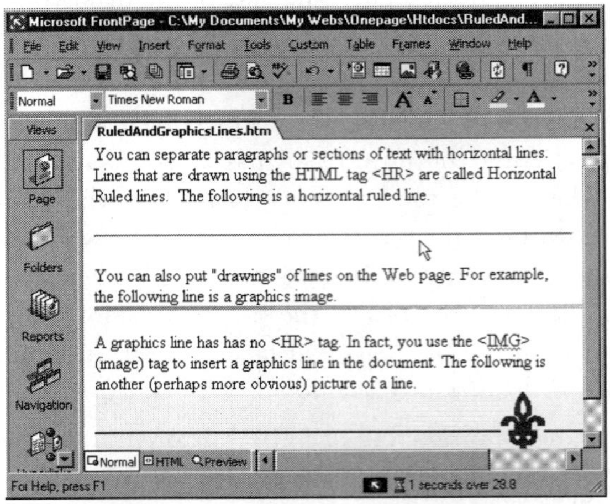

Figure 158 A Web page with one horizontal rule at the top of the page and two graphic lines separating sections of text at the middle and bottom of the page.

Many of the more elaborate horizontal lines you see on Web pages (such as the one that follows the second paragraph of text in Figure 158 and the one at the bottom of the Figure) are actually graphics images. You will learn more about inserting and working with the properties of graphical lines later in this book.

To insert an HTML horizontal rule (horizontal line) on a Web page, perform the following steps:

1. In the Web page displayed on the Page view Normal tab, place the cursor where you want FrontPage to draw the horizontal line.
2. Select the Insert menu Horizontal Line option. FrontPage, in turn, will insert horizontal line both preceded and followed by a blank line at the insertion point at which you placed the cursor in Step 1.

Now that you know how to draw a horizontal line across a Web page, you can use the procedure in the next Tip to adjust the line's width, thickness, color, and shading.

UNDERSTANDING AND WORKING WITH RULED LINE PROPERTIES

More often than not, when you need a horizontal line to set off a section of text from other text or images on a Web page, you will want to change the horizontal rule's default length, thickness, and/or color. Fortunately, FrontPage makes changing a horizontal rule's properties as simple as performing the steps in the following procedure:

1. Display the Web page with the horizontal rule (i.e. the horizontal line) whose properties you want to change on the Page view Normal tab.
2. Double-click your mouse pointer on the horizontal line whose properties you want to change. (Or, right-click your mouse pointer on the horizontal line and select Horizontal Line Properties from the pop-up menu.) FrontPage, in turn, will display a Horizontal Line Properties dialog box similar to that shown in Figure 159.

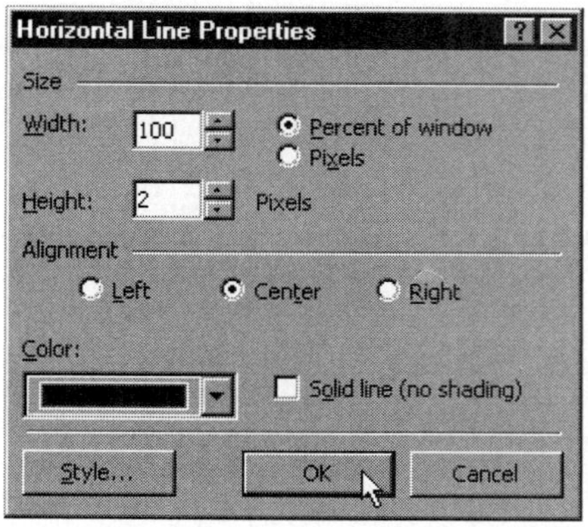

***Figure 159.1** The Microsoft FrontPage Horizontal Line Properties dialog box.*

3. Select the unit of measurement you want to use in specifying the line's width by clicking your mouse pointer on either the Percentage of window or on the Pixels radio button on the right-hand side of the Size area at the top of the dialog box. If you want the line to occupy a certain percentage of the width of the Web page as displayed in the browser's application window, click your mouse pointer on the Percentage of window radio button. On the other hand, if you want the line to be a certain length without regard to the width of the browser's application window, click your mouse pointer on the Pixels radio button.

***Note:** Expressing the line as a percentage of the width of the application window works best if you are using the horizontal rule to separate paragraphs of text or a heading. If you are trying to draw a line that spans the width of a fixed width element (such as a graphics image), specify the length of the line in terms of pixels to guarantee that it will be the same length regardless of the width of the browser's application window.*

4. Into the Width field, enter the length of the horizontal rule either as a percentage of the browser's application window or as a number of pixels—depending on the radio button you selected in Step 3. For

example, to draw a line that runs half way across a Web page, click your mouse pointer on the Percentage of window radio button in Step 3, and enter 50 into the Width field.

5. Into the Height field, enter the line's height, i.e. its thickness, as a number of pixels. For example, to draw a line 10 pixels tall (or thick), enter 10 into the Height field.
6. If you specified a line with a length other than 100% of the width of the browser's application window (in Steps 3 and 4), click your mouse pointer on one of the radio buttons in the alignment section in the bottom half of the dialog box. To have the browser start the line at the left margin of the Web page, click your mouse pointer on the Left radio button; to have the browser draw the line such that it ends at the right margin of the Web page, click your mouse pointer on the Right radio button; or to have the browser center the line between the left and right margins, click your mouse pointer on the Center radio button.
7. To select line color other than the default (usually gray or black), click your mouse pointer on the drop-down button to the right of the Color field near the bottom of the dialog box. Then, click your mouse pointer on one of the standard color swatches on the drop-down palette of colors, or select the More Colors option at the bottom of the palette to create and apply a custom color to the line.
8. If you want the browser to draw the line without a 3-D shading effect, click your mouse pointer on the Solid line (no shading) checkbox until a check mark appears. Conversely, to apply shading that gives the line a 3-D appearance, clear the Solid line (no shading) checkbox.
9. Click your mouse pointer on the OK button near the bottom center of the Horizontal Line Properties dialog box. FrontPage, in turn, will apply the settings you entered to the line you selected in Step 2 and return to the application window.

Please refer to Figure 159.2 for examples of horizontal rules (i.e. horizontal lines) with various length, thickness, and alignment properties.

Note: *After you use the Horizontal Line Properties dialog box to set the properties of a line, FrontPage will apply the properties you specified to the line whose properties you are changing and to future lines you insert until you change the values in the dialog box again.*

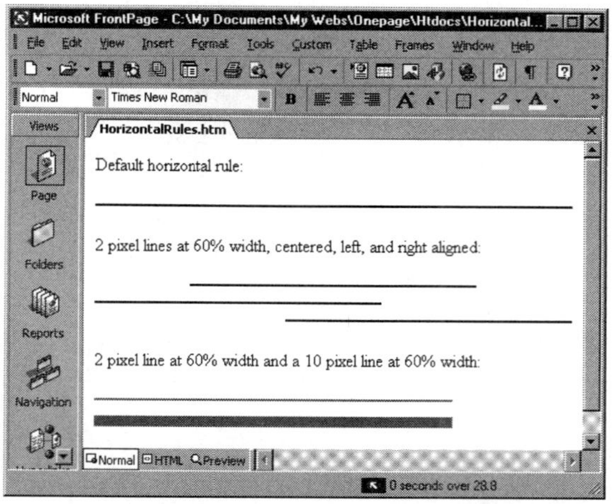

Figure 159.2 A Web page with lines of different widths and thicknesses and margin alignments.

INSERTING GRAPHICAL LINES ON A WEB PAGE

The horizontal lines you learned to insert in the preceding two Tips are rather plain. A horizontal rule (i.e. a horizontal line) as defined by the attributes of the <HR> (horizontal rule) tag in HMTL consists of a single height (thickness) and a single color. So, what about all of those fancy lines you see on pages at Web sites on the Internet? As it turns out, those multi-colored, variable thickness, pastel and textured lines are not horizontal rules at all—they are graphics images masquerading as horizontal lines.

In general, you can convert any graphics image into a line by telling the Web browser to adjust the picture's dimensions to the length you want and a height of two to ten pixels, or so. However, stretching an image that is not long and narrow into a line will distort the picture beyond recognition. Fortunately the Clip Gallery has a large assortment of images intended to be used as lines.

To insert a graphical line from the Clip Gallery, perform the following steps:

1. In the Web page displayed on the Page view Normal tab, place the cursor where you want to insert the horizontal line clip art.
2. Select the Insert menu Picture option, and click your mouse pointer on Clip Art. FrontPage, in turn, will display the Insert Clip Art search pane along the right-hand side of the application window.
3. Into the Search text field enter a keyword such as: **decorations**, **dividers**, **lines**, **patterns**, **frames**, or **borders**.

4. Click your mouse pointer on the SEARCH button below the Search text field. FrontPage, in turn, will display the thumbnails for some of the graphical line clip art images available in the Clip Gallery.
5. Use the scroll buttons to the right of the search results list box to move through the thumbnails, and click your mouse pointer on thumbnail for the "fancy line" you want to use. FrontPage, in turn, will insert the graphical line on your Web page at the insertion point you set in Step 1.
6. Click your mouse pointer on the close button (the "X") in the upper right-hand corner of the Insert Clip Art pane to remove it from the application window.

After you insert a clip art line on your Web page, you can adjust its thickness (height) and length by clicking your mouse pointer on the graphics image, and then dragging the sizing handles FrontPage displays on the picture. (Alternatively, you can perform the steps in the procedure you learned in the previous Tip entitled "Setting the Display Dimensions of a Graphics Image.")

If your web page has a background image or a nonwhite background color, perform the procedure in the previous Tip entitled: "Creating a Transparent GIF" to remove the clip art's white background and so only the line artwork is displayed on the Web page.

RETRIEVING GRAPHICAL LINES FROM WEB PAGES ON THE INTERNET

While surfing the Web, keep your eyes open for "interesting" lines you find separating sections of text or images on Web pages. As you learned in the two preceding Tips, "fancy" lines are really long, thin graphics images of artwork used to serve as a horizontal (or vertical) line on the page. To use one of these lines on your own Web pages, first retrieve it from the Web page onto your hard drive, and then add the line to the Clip Gallery to make it easy to find when you need it.

To download a graphical line from a Web page on the Internet, perform the following steps:

1. With the Web page displayed by your Web browser, right-click your mouse pointer on the horizontal (or vertical) line you want to retrieve.
2. Select Save Picture As from the pop-up menu (if you are using the Netscape Navigator, vs. the Internet Explorer, select Save Image As from the pop-menu). Windows, in turn, will display the Save As dialog box.

3. Use the drop-down list button to the right of the Save in field and the folders in the list box below the field to navigate to the folder in which you wish to save the graphics image.
4. Into the File name field near the bottom of the dialog box, enter a filename for the file in which to store the graphical line. For example, you may want to enter a name such as **HR_BLUE** for a blue line (i.e., a blue horizontal rule). Alternatively, you can enter the full pathname in which to save the graphical line into the File name field instead of navigating to a folder in which to save the graphics image in Step 3. For example, to save the image of a blue line into the **MY DOWNLOAD FILES** folder at the root of the C: drive, you might enter a pathname such as: **C:\MY DOWNLOAD FILES\HR_BLUE** into the File name field.
5. To tell windows to copy the graphics image (the fancy line) to your computer, click your mouse pointer on the SAVE button near the lower right-hand corner of the Save As dialog box.

After saving the graphics image to a folder (such as C:\MY DOWNLOAD FILES) on your computer, add the graphics image of the horizontal line to the Clip Gallery by performing the procedure in the previous Tip entitled: "Adding New Searchable Clip Art Images to the FrontPage Clip Gallery." Be sure to associate keywords such as lines, dividers, and decorations with the graphics image when you save it to a collection in the Clip Gallery.

Note: *As is the case with all other graphics images you find on the Internet, make sure that you observe all copyright restrictions applicable to the horizontal line artwork. If you see a copyright notice on the Web site, contact the site's owner and get permission before downloading any of the site's graphics images—including the graphics images used as lines on its Web pages.*

CREATING A HYPERLINK TO A WEB PAGE ON THE INTERNET

The most difficult part of creating a hyperlink to a page on a Web site is deciding on the text to use as the hyperlink's anchor. Although you can anchor a hyperlink to any text on a Web page, try to make the hyperlink's anchor text something meaningful. If you anchor the hyperlink to text that describes the hyperlink's target, the site visitor will know what lies at the end of the hyperlink before activating it. For example, instead of using the words "Click here" as the hyperlink to Microsoft's online clip gallery, use something like "Microsoft Design Gallery Live" (the Web page title), as the hyperlink's anchor text.

To create a hyperlink based on text typed on the current Web page, perform the following steps:

1. Display the Web page in which you wish to create the hyperlink on the Page view Normal tab.
2. To select the hyperlink's anchor text, click and hold down your left mouse button as you drag your mouse pointer across the words you want to use. Then, release the left mouse button.
3. Click your mouse pointer on the Insert Hyperlink button (with the picture of the globe and link of chain, fifth from the right) on the Standard toolbar. (Or, right-click your mouse pointer anywhere on the text you selected in Step 2, and select Hyperlink from the pop-up menu.) FrontPage, in turn, will display an Insert Hyperlink dialog box similar to that shown in Figure 162.

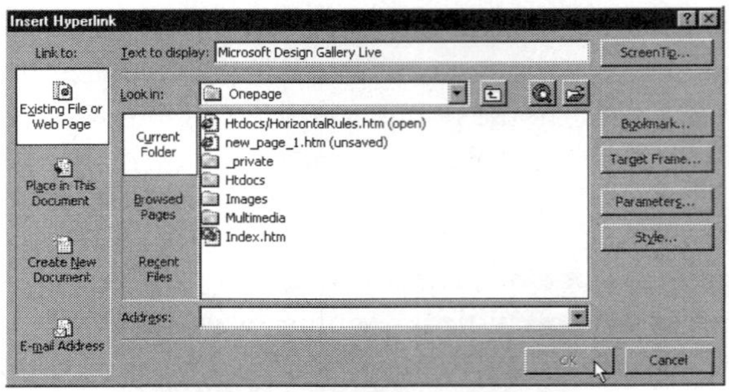

Figure 162 *The Microsoft FrontPage Insert Hyperlink dialog box.*

4. Into the Address field near the bottom of the dialog box, enter the Web address [i.e. the uniform resource locator (URL)] of the Web page you want the activated hyperlink to retrieve. For example, to create a hyperlink to the Microsoft Design Gallery, enter **HTTP://MGN.MICROSOFT.COM** into the Address field.

Note: *If you do not remember the URL for the Web page to which you wish to create the hyperlink, clear the contents of the Address field near the bottom of the Insert Hyperlink dialog box. With FrontPage running in the background on the same system, use a Web browser to visit the Web page to which you wish to create the hyperlink. When you have the target Web page displayed in your Web browser, click your mouse pointer on Microsoft FrontPage button on your Windows task bar to return to the FrontPage application window. FrontPage, in turn, will copy the URL from the Web browser's Address field into the Address field on the Insert Hyperlink dialog box.*

5. Click your mouse pointer on the OK button near the lower right-hand corner of the Insert Hyperlink dialog box.

After you complete Step 5, FrontPage will close the Insert Hyperlink dialog box, underline the hyperlink text you selected in Step 2, and insert <A></A> (anchor) tags around the hyperlink (anchor) text in the Web page HTML. For example, if you selected the text: "Microsoft Design Gallery Live" in Step 2 and entered the URL: **HTTP://MGN.MICROSOFT.COM** in Step 4 of the preceding procedure, FrontPage will modify the Web page HTML to include the hyperlink defined by:

```
<a href="HTTP://MGN.MICROSOFT.COM/">Microsoft Design Gallery
Live</a>
```

CREATING A HYPERLINK BY TYPING ITS URL ONTO THE CURRENT WEB PAGE

The preceding Tip showed you how to anchor a hyperlink to existing words on a Web page. You can also created a hyperlink by entering the Web address of the target page directly onto the Page view Normal tab. For example, if you want to create a hyperlink to the Web site NVBizNet.com, type **HTTP://NvBizNet.com** onto the current Web page on the Page view Normal tab. FrontPage, in turn, will recognize the "HTTP://" portion of the what you typed as signifying the subsequent text up to the next space, line, or paragraph mark is a Web address [i.e. a Uniform Resource Locator (URL)]. As such, FrontPage will underline the text as a hyperlink and will place the hyperlink <A> (anchor) tag:

```
<a href="HTTP://NVBIZNET.COM">HTTP://NVBIZNET.COM</a>
```

on the Page view HTML tab.

To replace the hyperlink anchor text, **HTTP://NvBizNet.com**, with words that better describe the hyperlink's destination, perform the following steps:

1. Double-click your mouse pointer on the anchoring text you want to change.
2. Right-click your mouse pointer anywhere on the text you selected in Step 1, and select Hyperlink Properties from the pop-up menu. FrontPage, in turn, will display an Edit Hyperlink dialog box (similar to the Insert Hyperlink dialog box you saw in Figure 162).
3. Replace the text in the Text to display field at the top of the dialog box with the descriptive text for the hyperlink that you want to see on the Web page. For example, you might replace **HTTP://NVBIZNET.COM** in the Text to display field with: **Homepage – Konrad King, Inc.**
4. Click your mouse pointer on the OK button near the bottom right-hand corner of the Edit Hyperlink dialog box.

After you complete Step 4, FrontPage will replace the hyperlink (anchor) text you selected in Step 1 on the Web page with the text you entered into the Text to display field.

Before testing the hyperlink to a Web page at a site on the Internet, you will need to connect your computer to the Internet. Therefore, if you do not have a permanent (always on) connection to the Net, use your modem to establish a dial-up connection.

To test the hyperlink, click your mouse pointer on the Preview tab at the lower left-hand corner of the Page view pane. Then, click your mouse pointer on the underlined, hyperlink (anchor) text. FrontPage, in turn, will replace the current Web page with the target Web page on the Page view Preview tab.

Note: If you try to follow a hyperlink on the Page view Preview pane while not connected to the Internet, will display a Web page unavailable while offline message box. To clear this message box either click your mouse pointer on the CONNECT *button on the* STAY OFFLINE *button. If you want to see the Web page the hyperlink tried to retrieve, click your mouse pointer on the* CONNECT *button and follow your normal procedure to connect to the Internet.*

To return to the original page you edited, click your mouse pointer on the Normal tab below the lower left-hand corner of the Page view pane.

CREATING HYPERLINKS TO BOOKMARKS WITHIN A WEB PAGE

Bookmarks let you specify points within a Web page that you can use as targets of hyperlinks on the same Web page and on other Web pages. You might use bookmarks to create a Web page with a table of contents or a list of terms at the top of the page that anchor hyperlinks to bookmarked section titles or definitions further down in the body of the page. Creating internal hyperlinks that let you jump from one place within a Web page to another, is a simple two step process: 1) create a bookmark, and then 2) create a hyperlink to the bookmark.

To create a bookmark, perform the following steps:

1. Display the Web page on which you wish to create the bookmark on the Page view Normal tab.
2. Click and hold down the left mouse button as you drag your mouse pointer across the text you want to bookmark. Or, if you want to create a bookmark without selecting any text, simply click your mouse pointer on the point in the Web page at which you want to create the bookmark.
3. Select the Insert menu Bookmark option. FrontPage, in turn, will display a Bookmark dialog box similar to that shown in Figure 164.1.

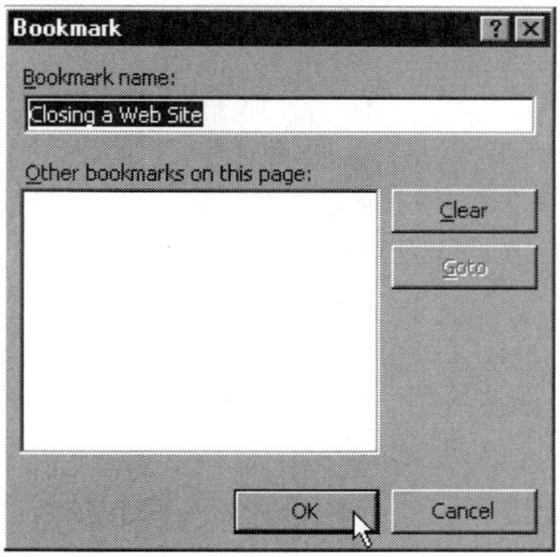

Figure 164.1 *The Microsoft FrontPage Bookmark dialog box.*

4. Into the Bookmark name field at the top of the dialog box, enter a descriptive name for the bookmark. FrontPage does not write the text you enter into the Bookmark name field on the Web page itself. You can enter a single letter, a single word, or multiple words as the bookmark's name. However, each bookmark must have a name that is unique among all of the other bookmark names on the same Web page.

   Since you will be using the bookmark's name as the target for one or more hyperlinks, use a name that somehow describes the bookmark's location. If you do so, the name will be easy to remember when you need to select it while creating a hyperlink to the bookmark (as you will learn to do in the next procedure). Moreover, if the bookmark's name is descriptive of its location, you will be able to look at the hyperlink to the bookmark later and have some idea as to where activating the hyperlink will take you.

Note: *If you selected Web page text to bookmark in Step 3, FrontPage copies the text to the Bookmark name field as the default name for the bookmark. You can either accept the selected text for the bookmark name or replace it with other, more descriptive text. Changing the text in the Bookmark name field does not change any text on the Web page.*

5. Click your mouse pointer on the OK button near the lower right-hand corner of the Bookmark dialog box.

After you complete Step 5, FrontPage will return to the application window and mark the location of the bookmark on the Web page. If you selected text to bookmark in Step 2 of the preceding procedure, FrontPage will mark the bookmark's location by placing a dashed line under the text you selected. On the other hand, if you simply clicked your mouse pointer at a location on the current Web page without selecting text to bookmark, FrontPage will show the bookmark's location as a small flag, underlined with a dashed line.

Note: *You will only see the bookmark locations on the Page view Normal tab, and the Web page will appear as if it has no bookmarks when viewed on the Page view Preview tab or in a Web browser.*

Repeat the preceding procedure for each bookmark you want to create on the Web page. Then, create a hyperlink to each bookmark on the page by performing the following steps:

1. Display the Web page on which you wish to create the hyperlink to a bookmark on the Page view Normal tab.
2. Click and hold down the left mouse button as you drag the mouse pointer across the text you want to use as the hyperlink (anchor) text. For example, if you want to link an entry in the table of contents at the top of a Web page to the bookmarked section on the Web page to which it pertains, click and hold down the left mouse button as you drag your mouse pointer across the entry in the table of contents.
3. After selecting the hyperlink's anchor text, release the left mouse button, and select the Insert menu Hyperlink option. FrontPage, in turn, will display an Insert Hyperlink dialog box, similar to that shown in Figure 164.2.

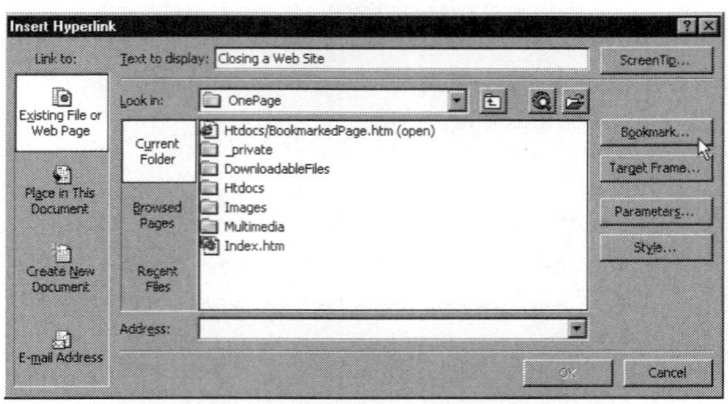

Figure 164.2 The Microsoft FrontPage Insert Hyperlink dialog box.

4. Click your mouse pointer on the BOOKMARK button to the right of the upper right-hand corner of the list box below the Look in field.

FrontPage, in turn, will display a Select Place in Document dialog box, similar to that shown in Figure 164.3.

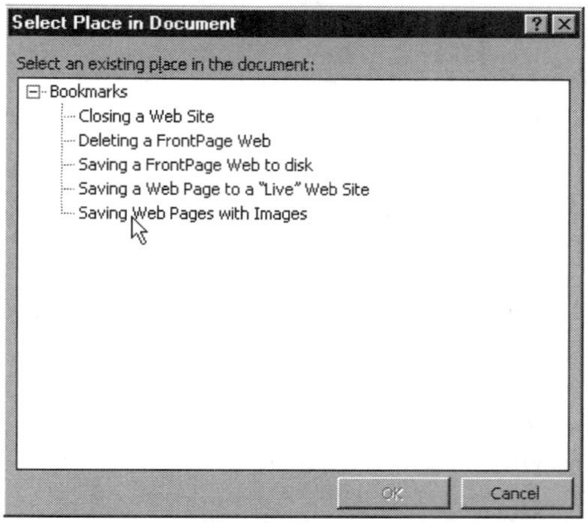

Figure 164.3 *The Microsoft FrontPage Select Place in Document dialog box.*

5. Click your mouse pointer on the name of the bookmark at the point in the Web page to which you wish to jump when the hyperlink is activated.
6. Click your mouse pointer on the OK button near the lower right-hand corner of the Select Place in Document dialog box. FrontPage, in turn, will return to the Insert Hyperlink dialog box, and enter a pound sign (#) followed by the bookmark's name into the Address field near the bottom of the dialog box.
7. Click your mouse pointer on the OK button near the lower right-hand corner of the Insert Hyperlink dialog box.

After you complete Step 7, FrontPage will return to the Page view Normal tab and underline the hyperlink (anchor) text you selected in Step 2.

The HTML for a hyperlink to a bookmark is an <A> (anchor) tag with the same syntax as the hyperlink to a Web page. The only difference between a hyperlink to a bookmark and a hyperlink to a Web page is that the HREF attribute of the <A> (anchor) tag for a hyperlink to a bookmark contains a pound sign (#) followed by the bookmark's name instead of the relative path to the Web page. For example, the <A> (anchor) tag for a hyperlink created from the hyperlink (anchor) text "Closing a Web Site" to a bookmark named: "Closing a Web Site" on the same Web page would read:

```
<a href="#Closing a Web Site">Closing a Web Site</a>
```

CREATING HYPERLINKS TO BOOKMARKS ON ANOTHER WEB PAGE

When you click your mouse pointer on a hyperlink on one Web page that takes your Web browser to another Web page, the browser, by default, will display the content of the page to which it moved starting at the top of the page. Sometimes, however, you want to jump to a point within a hyperlinked page and have the Web browser display the page content from that point forward—vs. starring at the top of the page. You can use the bookmarks you learned about in the preceding Tip to do just that.

To create a hyperlink from one Web page to a bookmark in another Web page, perform the following steps:

1. If you have not done so already, create the bookmark in the target Web page by performing the steps in the first procedure in the preceding Tip.
2. Use FrontPage to open the Web page on which you wish to create the hyperlink to the bookmark in another page, and select the View menu Page option to display the page on the Page view Normal tab.
3. Click and hold down the left mouse button as you drag your mouse pointer over the hyperlink's (anchor) text.
4. Right-click your mouse pointer at any point within the anchor text you selected in Step 3, and select Hyperlink from the pop-up menu. (Or, select the Insert menu Hyperlink option.)
5. Use the drop-down list button to the right of the Look in field and the folders in the list box below the field to navigate to the folder with the Web page that has the target bookmark. Then, click your mouse pointer on the filename of the Web page with the bookmark. FrontPage, in turn, will insert into the Address field, the bookmark's address relative to the current Web page. (Rather than navigating to the folder with the target Web page and clicking your mouse pointer on its filename, you can enter the address of the Web page relative to the current page into the Address field near the bottom of the dialog box.)
6. Click your mouse pointer on the BOOKMARK button on the right-hand side of the Insert Hyperlink dialog box. FrontPage, in turn, will display a Select Place in Document dialog box, similar to the one you saw in Figure 164.3.
7. Click your mouse pointer on the name of the bookmark at the point in the Web page to which you wish to jump when the hyperlink is activated.

8. Click your mouse pointer on the OK button near the lower right-hand corner of the Select Place in Document dialog box. FrontPage, in turn, will return to the Insert Hyperlink dialog box, and append a pound sign (#) followed by the bookmark's name to the relative address of the Web page in the Address field near the bottom of the dialog box.
9. Click your mouse pointer on the OK button near the lower right-hand corner of the Insert Hyperlink dialog box.

After you complete Step 9, FrontPage will return to the Page view Normal tab and underline the hyperlink (anchor) text.

The HTML for a hyperlink to a bookmark in another Web page is an <A> (anchor) tag with an HREF attribute that contains not only the relative path to the other Web page, but also a pound sign (#) followed by the name of the target bookmark on that page. For example, selecting "How to Close a Web Site" as the anchor text on a document in a FrontPage web's root folder and creating a hyperlink to a bookmarked named "Closing a Web Site" in a document named BOOKMARKEDPAGE.HTM in the HTDOCS subfolder will create the <A> (anchor) tag:

```
<a href="HTDOCS/BOOKMARKEDPAGE.HTM#Closing a Web Site">How to
Close a Web Site</a>
```

on the Page view HTML tab for the current Web page.

CREATING A HYPERLINK TO A DOWNLOADABLE FILE

In addition to creating hyperlinks that move the visitor's Web browser to Web pages or bookmarks when activated, you can also create hyperlinks that Web site visitors can activate to download files from your Web site (or other Web sites on the internet) to a folder on a local or local area network (LAN) hard drive. The procedure you follow to create a hyperlink to a downloadable file is the same as the one you execute to create a hyperlink to a Web page or bookmark. Moreover, the HTML <A> (anchor) tag for a "file download" hyperlink uses the same syntax as the hyperlinks used to tell the Web browser to move to a Web page and display its contents.

What makes a Web browser execute a file download operation instead of displaying the contents of the hyperlink's target is the file type of the target file as specified in the HREF attribute of the hyperlink's <A> (anchor) tag.

If the Web browser recognizes the target file type in the hyperlink's HREF attribute as a Web page or image, the browser will display the page content or image in its application window.

Conversely, if the extension on the target filename is not one of the extensions the browser recognizes as an image or HTML document (i.e. a Web page), the browser will display a File Download dialog box similar to that shown in Figure 166.

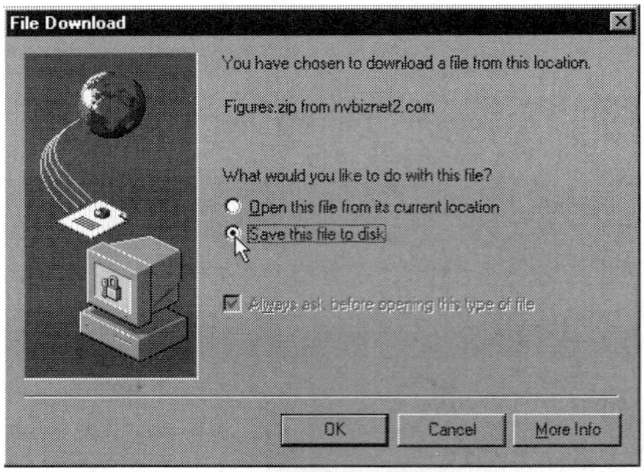

Figure 166 The Microsoft Internet Explorer File Download dialog box.

The visitor can then either click the mouse pointer on the OK button near the bottom center of the dialog box to have the Web server send a copy of the hyperlink's target file for storage in a folder on the local or LAN hard drive.

To create a hyperlink that lets site visitors download a file from your Web site, perform the following steps:

1. Move the file (or a copy of the file) that you want to let site visitors download into a subfolder within the site's FrontPage web. Keep the Web site's files organized by placing all downloadable files in a single subfolder with a name like DownloadableFiles.

Note: *Since Web browsers recognize files with .HTM and .HTML extensions as Web pages and files with .JPG, GIF, and (sometimes) .PNG extensions as image files, you will need to use a program such as WinZip to compress files of these types into files with a .ZIP extension if you want to create a hyperlink that allows the visitor to download Web pages and image files. If you execute the following steps without converting a targeted Web page or image file to another file type, the Web browser will simply display the Web page or image instead of prompting the visitor with the File Download dialog box when the visitor activates the hyperlink.*

2. Use FrontPage to open the Web page on which you wish to create the file download hyperlink, and select the View menu Page option to display the page on the Page view Normal tab.

3. Click and hold your left mouse button as you drag your mouse pointer over the hyperlink's (anchor) text.
4. Right-click your mouse pointer at any point within the anchor text you selected in Step 3, and select Hyperlink from the pop-up menu. (Or, select the Insert menu Hyperlink option.)
5. Use the drop-down list button to the right of the Look in field and the folders in the list box below the field to navigate to the folder with the file you want to make available for download. Then, click your mouse pointer on the target file's name in the list box. FrontPage, in turn, will insert into the Address field, the file's address relative to the current Web page. (Rather than navigating to the folder with the downloadable file, and clicking your mouse pointer on its filename, you can enter the file's name and location relative to the current Web page into the Address field near the bottom of the dialog box.)
6. Click your mouse pointer on the OK button near the lower right-hand corner of the Insert Hyperlink dialog box.

After you complete Step 6, FrontPage will create a hyperlink that, when activated, targets the file you selected in Step 5. For example, if you selected the anchor text "FrontPage Tips Figures" on a Web page in the HTDOCS subfolder in Step 3; and then selected a file named Figures.zip from the contents of DownloadableFiles subfolder in Step 5, FrontPage will generate the download file hyperlink:

```
<a href="../DownloadableFiles/Figures.zip">FrontPage Tips Fig-
ures</a>
```

on the Page view HTML tab for the current Web page.

To create a hyperlink for a downloadable file on another Web site, enter the file's uniform resource locator (URL) into the Address field in Step 5 of the preceding procedure. For example, if you are working on the **NVBizNet2.com** Web site and want to let site visitors download the **Figures.zip** file from the **DownloadableFiles** folder on the **NVBizNet.com** Web site, enter **HTTP://NVBizNet.com/DownloadableFiles/Figures.zip** into the Address field in Step 5. FrontPage, in turn, will generate the hyperlink:

```
<a  href=  "HTTP://NVBizNet.com/DownloadableFiles/
Figures.zip">FrontPage Tips Figures</a>
```

on the Page view HTML tab for the current Web page after you complete Step 6 of the preceding procedure.

CREATING A HYPERLINK TO A WEB PAGE IN THE CURRENT FRONTPAGE WEB

While external hyperlinks (i.e. hyperlinks to Web pages outside the current FrontPage web) connect the Web site to the rest of the world via the Internet, internal hyperlinks (i.e. hyperlinks between Web pages within the current FrontPage web) transform folders full of documents into a Web site. Although HTML encoded documents may reside in the same folder on a Web server, there is no way to get from one document to another without at least one hyperlink in a document that gives the Web browser the address of another document in the folder. A hyperlink then, is the Web page element that binds one page to another to produce the interconnecting "web" of documents that defines a Web site.

To create a link from one Web page in the current FrontPage web to another, perform the following steps:

1. Use FrontPage to open the Web page on which you wish to create a hyperlink, and select the View menu Page option to display the page on the Page view Normal tab.
2. Click and hold down the left mouse button as you drag your mouse pointer over the hyperlink's (anchor) text.
3. Right-click your mouse pointer at any point within the anchor text you selected in Step 2, and select Hyperlink from the pop-up menu. (Or, select the Insert menu Hyperlink option.)
4. Use the drop-down list button to the right of the Look in field and the folders in the list box below the field to navigate to the folder in which you stored the site's Web pages. Then, click your mouse pointer on the filename of the target Web page. FrontPage, in turn, will insert into the Address field, the address of the (soon to be) hyperlinked Web page relative to the current Web page. (Rather than navigating to the folder with the Web site's HTML documents, you can enter the address of the Web page you want to hyperlink relative to the current Web page into the Address field near the bottom of the dialog box.)
5. Click your mouse pointer on the OK button near the lower right-hand corner of the Insert Hyperlink dialog box.

After you complete Step 5, FrontPage will create a hyperlink that, when activated, will retrieve and display another Web page in the current FrontPage web.

Storing all of the Web site's pages, with the exception of its homepage, in a single subfolder such as HTDOCS, greatly simplifies entering the relative address of the page that you want to hyperlink in Step 4 of the preceding procedure. For example, to create a hyperlink from the homepage (stored in the Web site's root folder) to a Web page named **PAGE1.HTM** stored in the HTDOCS subfolder, enter **HTDOCS\PAGE1.HTM** into the Address field on the Insert Hyperlink dialog box. Then, to hyperlink two Web pages in the HTDOCS folder, simply enter the filename (including the extension) of the hyperlinked Web page into the Address field. Finally, to create a hyperlink from a Web page in the HTDOCS subfolder to the homepage (in the root folder), enter **\INDEX.HTM** into the Address field.

Rather than using the Insert Hyperlink dialog box, you can also create a hyperlink to a Web page by dragging its hyperlink from in the Folder List pane onto a Web page displayed on the Page view Normal tab—which you will learn about in the next Tip.

USING DRAG-AND-DROP (OR COPY-AND-PASTE) TO CREATE A HYPERLINK

The previous Tips in this book showed you how to create hyperlinks from one Web page to another and from a Web page to a bookmark on the same or on another Web page by selecting the anchoring text and then entering the hyperlink's target into the Address field at the bottom of the Insert Hyperlink dialog box. Sometimes, however, you may need a quick way to create several hyperlinks on a Web page without first entering the anchoring text.

Suppose, for example, that you want to create a Web page which lists your company's products and lets a site visitor click the mouse pointer on any product in the list to jump to and display a Web page with a picture or diagram and full page description of the product. If you already have the individual product description pages, you can use the drag-and-drop or the copy-and-paste method to quickly create the hyperlinks on the Item List Web page that let you jump to the Product Description Web pages.

To create a hyperlink by dragging-and-dropping a Web page from the Folder List pane onto a Web page, perform the following steps:

1. Open the Web page on which you wish to create the hyperlinks on the Page view Normal tab.
2. If the Folder List pane is not displayed in the FrontPage application window (similar to that shown in Figure 168), select the View menu Folder List option.

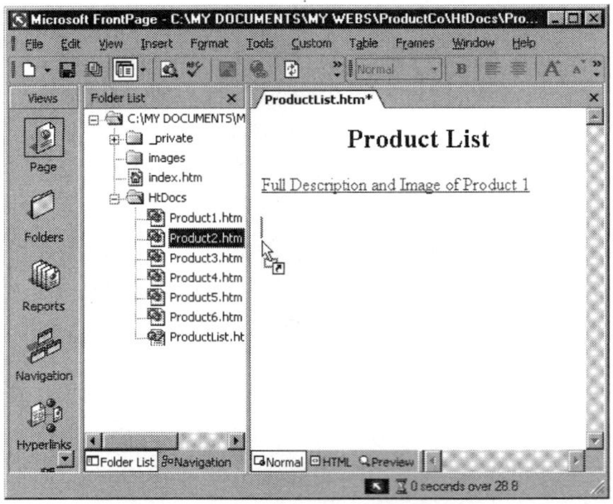

Figure 168 The Microsoft FrontPage application window in Page view with the Folder List pane displayed while dragging a Web page icon from the Folder List pane onto a Web Page on the Page view Normal tab.

3. If the target Web page for the hyperlink is "hidden" in a closed subfolder in the Folder List pane, click your mouse pointer on the plus (+) to the left of the subfolder's icon in the site's folder tree to open the subfolder and display its contents.
4. Move your mouse pointer over the icon in the Folder List pane to the left of the Web page to which you wish to create a hyperlink (i.e. move your mouse pointer over the icon of the target Web page).
5. Click and hold down the left mouse button as you drag the mouse pointer (and the icon of the page to which you wish to create the hyperlink) onto the current Web page on the Page view Normal tab. FrontPage, in turn, will display a shortcut icon below the mouse pointer and show the insertion point as a squiggly vertical line (similar to that shown in Figure 168) as you drag the mouse pointer onto the Web page.
6. When you see the insertion point (indicated by the squiggly vertical line) where you want to create the hyperlink, release the left mouse pointer.

After you complete Step 6, FrontPage will create a hyperlink at the insertion point in the Web page on the Page view Normal tab to the Web page whose icon you dragged onto the page in Steps 4 – 5. Moreover, FrontPage will display the title (i.e., the text in the <TITLE> ta— which may or may not be the same as the filename) of the Web page you dragged as the hyperlink's anchor text on the current Web page. In Figure 168, for example, the first hyperlink on the PRODUCTLIST.HTM Web page is anchored to the text: "Full Description and Image of Product 1"—the title of the Web page stored in the file: PRODUCT1.HTM.

Note: *If you prefer to use copy-and-paste instead of drag-and-drop, right-click your mouse pointer on the page to which you want to create the hyperlink in Step 4, and select Copy from the pop-up menu. Then, in place of Steps 5 and 6, right-click your mouse pointer on the point in the Web page on the Page view Normal tab where you want to insert the hyperlink, and select the Paste option from the pop-up menu.*

More often than not, you will want to use anchor text other than the title of the hyperlinked Web. The next Tip will show you how to edit a hyperlink's anchor text and/ or its target/destination.

EDITING A HYPERLINK'S ANCHOR TEXT AND/OR ITS DESTINATION

As you learned from the previous Tips on hyperlinks, the hyperlink *anchor text* is the underlined text on which you click the mouse pointer to activate the hyperlink. Since you want its anchor text to tell the Web site visitor something about the hyperlink's target, you may need to change the hyperlink's anchor text after you change the content of the hyperlink's target. Suppose, for example, that clicking the mouse pointer on the text "Spring Newsletter" tells the browser to display the company's seasonal newsletter stored in the file NEWSLETTER.HTM. When you update the content in NEWSLETTER.HTM at the start of the summer, you will need to change the hyperlink's anchor text to "Summer Newsletter."

To change only the hyperlink's anchor text (and not its destination), perform the following steps:

1. Open the Web page with the hyperlink anchor text you want to change on the Page view Normal tab.
2. Click and hold down the left mouse button as you drag the mouse pointer across the hyperlink you want to change, and then release the left mouse button. Or, to insert text, click your mouse pointer on the point in the existing anchor text at which you want to insert the additional text.
3. Enter the new or additional anchor text.

Changing its anchor text does not change the hyperlink's destination/target. Therefore, if you use the text "Fall Newsletter" to anchor a hyperlink which targets the Web page in FALLNEWSLETTER.HTM, the Web browser will still display the same content when you activate the hyperlink after changing its anchor text to "Winter Newsletter."

When you need to change a hyperlink's destination (i.e. its target), or when you need to change both a hyperlink's anchor text and its destination, perform the following steps:

1. Display the Web page with the hyperlink you want to edit on the Page view Normal tab.
2. Right-click your mouse pointer on the hyperlink whose anchor text or destination you want to change, and select Hyperlink Properties from the pop-up menu. FrontPage, in turn, will display an Edit Hyperlink dialog box similar to that shown in Figure 169.

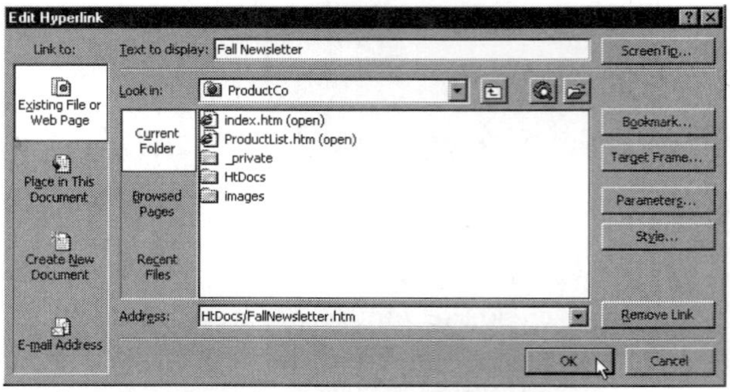

Figure 169 The Microsoft FrontPage Edit Hyperlink dialog box.

3. To change the hyperlink's anchor text, edit the contents of the Text to display field at the top of the dialog box. For example, if you want the hyperlink anchor text displayed on the Web page to read "Winter Newsletter," change the contents of the Text to display field to read: Winter Newsletter.
4. Into the Address field near the bottom of the dialog box, enter the hyperlink's new destination/target. For example, if you are working on a Web page in the web's root folder and you want the Web browser to display the contents of WINTERNEWSLETTER.HTM stored in the HTDOCS subfolder, enter **HtDocs/WinterNewsletter.htm** into the Address field.
5. Click your mouse pointer on the OK button near the lower right-hand corner of the Edit Hyperlink dialog box.

After you complete Step 5, FrontPage will return to the Page view Normal tab, change the hyperlink anchor text to read "Winter Newsletter," and replace the hyperlink <A> (anchor) tag:

```
<a href="HtDocs/FallNewsletter.htm">Fall Newsletter</a>
```

with the <A> (anchor) tag:

```
<a href="HtDocs/WinterNewsletter.htm">Winter Newsletter</a>
```

on the Page view HTML tab for the current Web page.

Note: *When creating a new hyperlink which targets the file whose relative address you entered into the Address field at the bottom of the Edit Hyperlink dialog box, FrontPage does not verify the target file's existence. As such, if the target is not available at the address you entered, FrontPage will create a broken hyperlink (i.e. a hyperlink that will fail to display a document when activated) without warning. Therefore, before you publish a Web page to the Web site on the Internet, be sure to execute the procedures to verify (and if necessary, repair) the site's hyperlinks, which you will learn about later in this book.*

CREATING A HYPERLINK TO AN E-MAIL ADDRESS

A hyperlink to an e-mail address is often called a *mailto* hyperlink because the hyperlink's HREF attribute contains the word "mailto." and when activated, the hyperlink tells the Web browser to start the default e-mail program on the visitor's system and send e-mail to the hyperlink's target address.

While many mailto hyperlinks are anchored to graphics images, FrontPage will generate a text anchored mailto hyperlink whenever you type an e-mail address on the current Web page on the Page view Normal tab. For example, if you type two text strings separated by an at sign (@) such as **kki@NVBizNet.com**, FrontPage will underline what you typed as hyperlink anchor text and generate the mailto hyperlink:

```
<a href="mailto:kki@NVBizNet.com">kki@NVBizNet.com</a>
```

on the Page view HTML tab for the current Web page. If you want to change the mailto hyperlink's anchor text to something like "Contact the Author" (instead of showing the actual e-mail address on the Web page), execute the first procedure in the preceding Tip.

Rather than typing an e-mail address onto a Web page and letting FrontPage convert it into a hyperlink to an e-mail address, you can create a mailto hyperlink anchored to any Web page text (or graphics image) by performing the following steps:

1. Click and hold your left mouse button as you drag your mouse pointer over the text you want to use as the anchor for the mailto hyperlink. If you want to anchor the mailto hyperlink to a graphic, click your mouse pointer on the image.
2. Right-click your mouse pointer at any point within the anchor text or image you selected in Step 1, and select Hyperlink from the pop-up menu. (Or, select the Insert menu Hyperlink option.) FrontPage, in turn, will display the Insert Hyperlink dialog box.
3. Click your mouse pointer on the E-mail Address button near the lower left-hand corner of the dialog box. FrontPage, in turn, will change the fields below the anchor text in the Text to display field to those shown in Figure 170.

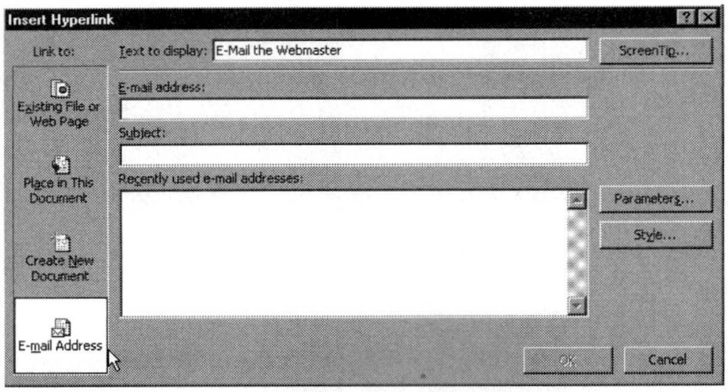

Figure 170 *The Microsoft FrontPage Insert Hyperlink dialog box with E-mail Address fields displayed.*

Note: *After you change its fields by clicking your mouse pointer on the E-mail Address button, the Insert Hyperlink dialog box will display the e-mail address fields again each time you tell FrontPage to insert a hyperlink. As such, when you want to create a hyperlink to a downloadable file or Web page after creating a hyperlink to an e-mail address, click your mouse pointer on the Existing File or Web Page button near the upper right-hand corner of the dialog box to replace the e-mail address fields with the (non-e-mail) Look in and (Web page or file) Address fields.*

4. Into the E-mail address field, enter the e-mail address to which you want the Web visitor's e-mail program to send an e-mail message after the visitor activates the hyperlink. FrontPage will automatically insert the text "mailto:" to the left of the first letter you type into the field. (Or, if you see the e-mail address you want in the Recently used e-mail addresses scroll box in the bottom half of the dialog box, click your mouse pointer on the e-mail address, and FrontPage will copy the address into the E-mail address field.)
5. Into the Subject field, enter the text you would like to see in the subject line of the e-mail message. You can use the text in the Subject field to remind the visitor of the mailto hyperlink's purpose by supplying a subject such as "Comments Regarding the ProductCo Web Site" for the e-mail generated by activating the "E-mail the Webmaster" hyperlink.
6. Click your mouse pointer on the OK button near the lower right-hand corner of the Insert Hyperlink dialog box.

After you complete Step 6, FrontPage will underline the hyperlink anchor text you selected in Step 1, and use the e-mail address and subject you entered in Steps 5 and 6 to create a mailto hyperlink such as:

```
<a href="mailto:kki@NVBizNet.com?subject=Comments Regarding the
ProductCo Web Site">E-mail the Webmaster</a>
```

on the Page view HTML tab for the current Web page.

Every Web site should have at least one mailto hyperlink. Even if you use Web page forms (which you will learn about later in this book) to accept customer orders and queries on-line, visitor friendly Web sites always provide a way to send comments and suggestions about the site to its author(s) and/or to the webmaster. The Tip titled "Modifying the Contents of a Shared Border" (which you will find later in this book), shows you how to create a mailto hyperlink such as "E-Mail the Webmaster" once and then have the Web browser replicate the hyperlink at the bottom of each of the site's Web pages for you.

CUSTOMIZING HYPERLINK COLORS

On a Web page, hyperlinks (that is, the text used to anchor the hyperlinks) stand out from the remaining, non-hyperlink text content on the page because hyperlink anchor text is underlined and displayed in a different color. While the default color for non-hyperlink Web page text is black, hyperlink anchor text is displayed in one of three colors:

- **(unvisited) hyperlink** – the hyperlink's color before the visitor has activated the hyperlink (by clicking the mouse pointer on it)—the default is blue. The Web browser displays the hyperlinks in the unvisited color when you first display a Web page—except those hyperlinks whose target addresses appear in your Web browser's recently viewed pages (history) list.
- **visited hyperlink** – the hyperlink's color after you have activated the hyperlink by clicking your mouse pointer on the hyperlink's anchor text—the default is purple. The Web browser displays any hyperlink whose target appears on its recently viewed pages (history) list in the visited hyperlink color.
- **active hyperlink** – the color of the hyperlink in mid-click—the default is red. Clicking your mouse pointer on a hyperlink link means you move your mouse pointer over the hyperlink, press down and then release the left mouse button. A Web browser such as the Internet Explorer, for example, will change the color of the hyperlink anchor text to the *active* color when you depress the left mouse button while the mouse pointer is over the hyperlink. The Web browser does not actually activate the hyperlink until you complete the "click" by releasing the left mouse button. As such, when you depress the left mouse button with the mouse pointer over a hyperlink, you are in mid-click, and the Web browser will use the active hyperlink color to display the hyperlink anchor text.

Note: *When using the Microsoft Internet Explorer, if you move your mouse pointer over a hyperlink, depress the left mouse button, and then move the mouse pointer off of the hyperlink, the Web browser will not activate the hyperlink.*

If the default (blue, purple, red) hyperlink colors clash with the color scheme of your Web page (or if you just want to change one or all three of them for some other reason), perform the following Steps:

1. Display the Web page whose default hyperlink colors you want to change on the Page view Normal tab.
2. Right-click your mouse pointer anywhere on the Web page and select Page Properties from the pop-up menu. FrontPage, in turn, will display the Page Properties dialog box.
3. Click your mouse pointer on the Background tab to expose the current background, text, and hyperlink color settings, similar to those shown in the Colors section of the Page Properties dialog box in Figure 171.

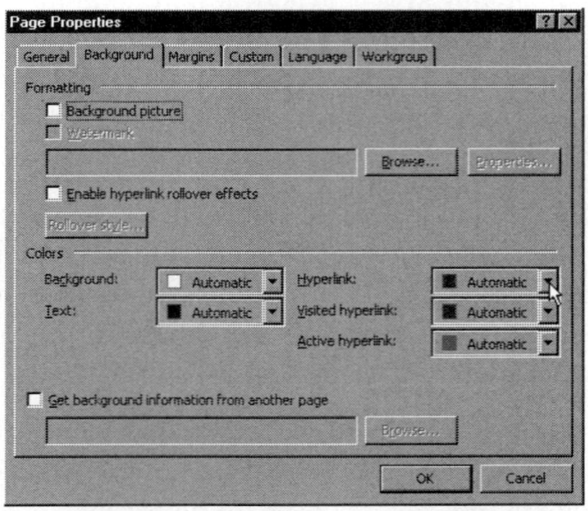

Figure 171 *The Microsoft FrontPage Page Properties dialog box, Background tab.*

4. To change the color of unvisited hyperlinks, click your mouse pointer on the drop-down list button to the right of the Hyperlink field. Then, select the color you want unvisited hyperlinks to be on the current Web page by clicking your mouse pointer on one of the 16 color swatches, or to create a custom color, select the More Colors option at the bottom of the drop-down color pallet.
5. To change the color of visited (i.e. previously activated) hyperlinks, click your mouse pointer on the drop-down list button to the right

of the Visited hyperlink field. Then, select the color you want unvisited hyperlinks to be on the current Web page by clicking your mouse pointer on one of the 16 color swatches, or to create a custom color, select the More Colors option at the bottom of the drop-down color pallet.

6. To change the color of the active hyperlink (i.e. the hyperlink under the mouse pointer after you have depressed and not yet released the left mouse button), click your mouse pointer on the drop-down list button to the right of the Active hyperlink field. Then, select the color you want active hyperlinks to be on the current Web page by clicking your mouse pointer on one of the 16 color swatches, or to create a custom color, select the More Colors option at the bottom of the drop-down color pallet.
7. Click your mouse pointer on the OK button near the lower right-hand corner of the Page Properties dialog box.

After you complete Step 7, FrontPage will close the Page Properties dialog box, store the hyperlink color settings you changed (from Automatic) into the <BODY> tag's LINK (unvisited hyperlink), VLINK (visited hyperlink), and ALINK (active hyperlink) attributes, and then redisplay the Web page on the Page view Normal tab using the unvisited hyperlink (LINK attribute) color setting you selected in Step 4.

If you change any one (or all three) of the hyperlink anchor text color settings, you can switch the color(s) back to the default by executing the preceding procedure and selecting the Automatic option at the top of the drop-down pallet when performing Steps 4 – 6.

ENHANCING A HYPERLINK WITH A ROLLOVER EFFECT

As you learned in the previous Tip, hyperlinks are displayed underlined and in a different color to set them off from the other (non-hyperlinked) text on a Web page. Some browsers, such as the Microsoft Internet Explorer and the Netscape Navigator (version 4 and above), support Dynamic HTML, which lets you further enhance the uniqueness of the hyperlinks on a Web page by applying a *rollover* effect.

A rollover effect is a change in the appearance of the hyperlink anchor text produced by the Web browser whenever the visitor rolls the mouse pointer over the hyperlink. For a rollover effect, you can have the Web browser change the hyperlink text's size, color, character font, and/or its alignment with other text on the line whenever the visitor passes the mouse pointer over or places it on the hyperlink.

To create a rollover effect for the hyperlinks on a Web page, perform the following steps:

1. Display the Web page with the hyperlinks to which you want to add a rollover effect on the Page view Normal tab.
2. Select the Format menu Background option to display the Background tab for the Page Properties dialog box (similar to what you saw in Figure 171).
3. Click your mouse pointer on the Enable hyperlink rollover effects checkbox just above Colors section at the center of the Background tab until a check mark appears. FrontPage, in turn, will enable the (grayed out) ROLLOVER STYLE button immediately below the Enable hyperlink rollover effects checkbox.
4. Click your mouse pointer on the ROLLOVER STYLE button. FrontPage, in turn, will display a Font Dialog box, similar to that shown in Figure 172.1.

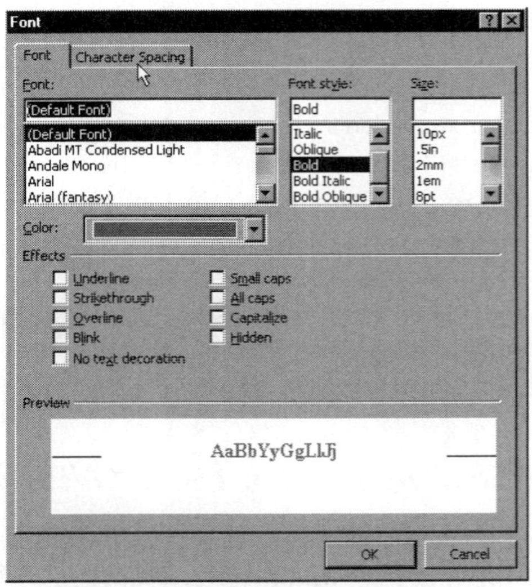

Figure 172.1 The Microsoft FrontPage Page Font dialog box, Font tab.

5. Use the Font, Font style, and Size drop-down list boxes across the top of the Font tab to select rollover effect's character font, style, and size. As you make your selections, FrontPage will use the Preview area at the bottom of the Font tab to show you what the hyperlink anchor text will look like when the visitor rolls the mouse pointer over or onto the hyperlink.
6. If you want the browser to change the color of the hyperlink's anchor text as part of the rollover effect, click your mouse pointer on the

drop-down list button to the right of the Color field. Then, click your mouse pointer on one of the 16 default color swatches, or create a custom color by selecting More Colors at the bottom of the drop-down color pallet.

7. To apply one or more of the text effects listed in the Effects area near the middle of the background tab, click your mouse pointer on the checkbox to the left of each effect you want until a checkmark appears. Conversely, to remove an effect, click your mouse pointer on the check mark in the effect's checkbox to clear it.
8. Click your mouse pointer on the Character Spacing tab. FrontPage, in turn, will display the Font dialog box Spacing tab, similar to that shown in Figure 172.2.

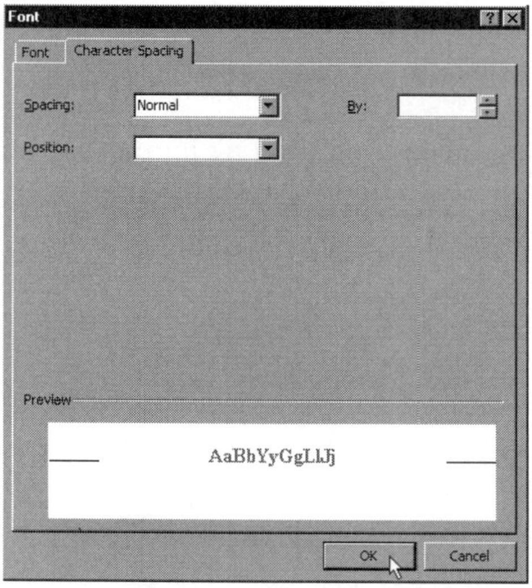

***Figure** 172.2 The Microsoft FrontPage Page Font dialog box, Character Spacing tab.*

9. Use the drop-down list button to the right of the Spacing field to select Normal, Expanded, or Condensed spacing. Select Normal spacing if you do not want to change the character spacing as part of the rollover effect. To have the browser display the characters in the hyperlink anchor text further apart, select Expanded spacing. Conversely, to have the Web browser display the characters closer together, select Condensed.
10. If you select either Expanded or Condensed spacing in Step 9, enter the change in the number of points of blank space between the letters in the anchor text you want the Web browser to make when applying

the rollover effect. For example, if you select Expanded in Step 9 and enter a positive number into the By field, the Web browser will display the characters of text further apart; enter a negative number into the field to display the hyperlink's letters closer together. Conversely, if you select Condensed in Step 9, a positive value in the By field tells the Web browser to display the letters closer together, while a negative value tells the browser to spread them out.

11. If you want the Web browser to change the position of the hyperlink anchor text as compared with the rest of the text on the line when applying the rollover effect, click your mouse pointer on the drop-down list button to the right of the Position field, and select one of the alignment options from the drop-down list.
12. Click your mouse pointer on the OK button near the lower right-hand corner of the Font dialog box. FrontPage, in turn, will close the Font dialog box and return to the Background tab of the Page Properties dialog box.
13. Click your mouse pointer on the OK button near the lower right-hand corner of the Page Properties dialog box.

After you complete step 13, FrontPage will close the Page Properties dialog box, return to the Page view Normal tab in the application window, and write a Dynamic HTML <STYLE> tag similar to:

```
<style fprolloverstyle>A:hover {color: #FF0000;
      font-family: Jokerman; font-size: 24pt;
      letter-spacing: -5; vertical-align: super;
      font-style: oblique; font-weight: bold}</style>
```

into the <HEAD> tag enclosed header section on the Page view HTML tab for the current Web page.

Note: *Standard hypertext markup language (HTML) tags tell the Web browser how to format and where to display text and images on a Web page. Dynamic HTML is an additional set of tags that extend standard HTML to include tags that tell the Web browser how to change the standard (static) appearance of Web page content when certain events occur. You will learn more about Dynamic HTML effects later in this book.*

To see the rollover effects you added in action, click your mouse pointer on the Preview tab near the lower left-hand corner of the Page view pane in the FrontPage application window. Then, move your mouse over the hyperlinks on the Web page displayed on the Preview tab.

USING A GRAPHICS IMAGE AS A HYPERLINK

The previous Tips showed you how to create hyperlinks anchored to text on the current Web page. You used the Insert Hyperlink dialog box to create the hyperlinks manually, and you saw how FrontPage created hyperlinks automatically for the .com and e-mail addresses you typed on the Page view Normal tab. In addition to text hyperlinks (i.e. hyperlinks anchored on Web page text), you can also create hyperlinks anchored on graphics images.

One of the most often used image based hyperlinks is a mailto hyperlink anchored to a picture of a mail box. For example, to create a mailto hyperlink anchored to one of the mailboxes shown at the bottom of Figure 173,

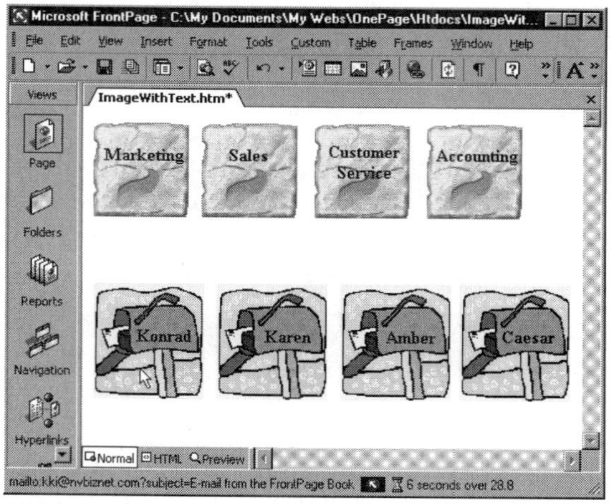

Figure 173 A Web page with examples of graphics images you can convert to buttons by using them as anchors for hyperlinks.

perform the following steps:

1. Use the Page view Normal tab to display the Web page with the image to which you wish to anchor the hyperlink.
2. Right-click your mouse pointer on the picture (on the mailbox, in the current example), and select hyperlink from the pop-up menu. FrontPage, in turn, will display the Insert Hyperlink dialog box.
3. Click your mouse pointer on the E-mail Address button near the lower left-hand corner of the dialog box. FrontPage, in turn, will display the E-mail address and Subject fields along with the Recently used e-mail addresses list box.
4. Into the E-mail address field, enter the e-mail address to which you want the Web browser to send an e-mail message when the site visitor

clicks the mouse pointer on the picture selected in Step 2. FrontPage will automatically insert "mailto:" to the left of the first letter you type into the field. (Or, if you see the e-mail address you want in the Recently used e-mail addresses scroll box in the bottom half of the dialog box, click your mouse pointer on the e-mail address to have FrontPage copy it into the E-mail address field.)

5. Into the Subject field enter the text you would like to see in the subject line of the e-mail message.
6. Click your mouse pointer on the OK button near the lower right-hand corner of the Insert Hyperlink dialog box.

Similarly, to use a graphics image, such as the ones shown at top of the Web page in Figure 173, to anchor a hyperlink that retrieves and displays a Web page, perform the following steps:

1. Display the Web page containing the graphics image on which you want to anchor a hyperlink using the Page view Normal tab, right-click your mouse pointer on the picture you want to use as the anchor for a hyperlink, and select hyperlink from the pop-up menu. FrontPage, in turn, will display the Insert Hyperlink dialog box.
2. Click your mouse pointer on the Existing File or Web Page button near the upper left-hand corner of the dialog box. FrontPage, in turn, will display the Look in and Address fields along with a list box (which lists files and folders in the current folder) below the Look in field.
3. To retrieve a Web page from the Internet when the hyperlink is activated, enter the Web address (i.e., the URL, the HTTP:// address) of the Web page into the Address field at the bottom of the Insert Hyperlink dialog box, and continue at Step 5. Otherwise, use the drop-down list button to the right of the Look in field and the folders in the list box below the field to navigate to the folder with the Web page or file to which you want to create the hyperlink.
4. Click your mouse pointer on the filename of the Web page or downloadable file the Web browser is to retrieve when the visitor clicks the mouse pointer on the hyperlink to activate it.

Note: *Instead of navigating to its folder and clicking your mouse pointer on the hyperlink's target in Steps 3 - 4, you can enter the relative address of the file the Web browser is to retrieve from a folder in the current FrontPage Web into the Address field near the bottom of the dialog box.*

5. Click your mouse pointer on the OK button near the lower right-hand corner of the Insert Hyperlink dialog box.

Later in this book you will learn how to divide a single graphics image into multiple areas called hotspots—each of which can serve as the anchor for a hyperlink. For now, the important thing to understand is that like text hyperlinks, image hyperlinks are activated by clicking the mouse pointer on the hyperlink's anchor—i.e. by clicking the mouse pointer on the *anchor* text for a text based hyperlink or on the graphics image for an image based hyperlink.

RECALCULATING AND VERIFYING HYPERLINKS

A hyperlink that tells your browser to move to a new Web page or to download a file is considered *broken* if its target is inaccessible when the hyperlink is activated. As mentioned previously, FrontPage does not verify that it can retrieve the file whose address you enter into the Address field at the bottom of the Insert Hyperlink dialog box. Therefore, for example, if you mistype the address of a Web page, FrontPage will store the invalid address without warning you that the address is invalid. When the Web visitor clicks the mouse pointer on the hyperlink, however, the Web server will send an error message stating that "The page cannot be displayed" instead of the target Web page.

Fortunately, FrontPage automatically prevents the greatest cause of broken hyperlinks—the renaming or relocating of a Web site's pages without updating the hyperlinks that weave (link) those pages into the web. When you rename a file or move it from one folder to another while working within the FrontPage application window, the program automatically updates the web's hyperlinks to reflect the target file's new address and/or filename. Unfortunately, several other causes of broken links are beyond the program's control:

- someone renames, moves, or deletes a target file while working outside the FrontPage application window.
- the hyperlink targets an external file (i.e. a file not in one of the folders in the current FrontPage web) and the file is no longer available because someone moved, deleted, or renamed it.
- the hyperlink targets a file on an external Web site that is currently down or unavailable for some other reason.
- the hyperlink targets a file that is no longer available on an external Web site because someone moved, renamed, or deleted the file.
- you import an existing Web site into a FrontPage web, but halt the import process before it is done or set the import Wizard's maximum level or maximum bytes to import count too low and the program does not import all of the Web site's documents and images.

Whatever their cause, broken hyperlinks can ruin the site visitor's experience on your Web site. As such, periodically (i.e. every two weeks or so) perform the steps in the following procedure to validate the hyperlinks to files within the current FrontPage web and verify the hyperlinks to external files:

1. If the FrontPage web has hyperlinks to external Web sites and you do not have a permanent (always on) connection to the Internet, use your modem to establish a dial-up connection with your internet service provider (ISP).

Note: *If the FrontPage web has hyperlinks to Web pages and downloadable files on the Internet and you attempt to verity the web's hyperlinks without first establishing a connection to the Net, FrontPage will report these external hyperlinks as broken. After all, without an active connection to the Internet, any hyperlinked pages and files on other Web sites will be inaccessible to FrontPage running in an application window on your computer.*

2. Open the FrontPage web whose hyperlinks you want to recalculate and verify. Or, if you already have one or more Web pages in the FrontPage web open, select the File menu Save All option to save any changes you have made to disk.
3. Select the View menu Reports option. Click your mouse pointer on Problems and select Broken Hyperlinks. FrontPage, in turn, will recalculate (check) and report the current status of internal hyperlinks and will show the status of external hyperlinks as Unknown on the Broken Hyperlinks report.
4. If prompted by FrontPage with the Reports View message box shown in Figure 174.1, click your mouse pointer on the YES button near the bottom center of the message box, to have FrontPage verify the web's external hyperlinks, and skip the remaining Steps (5 and 6) in the current procedure.

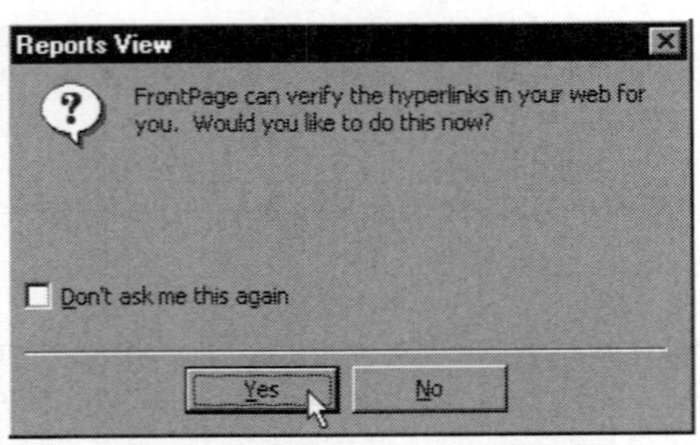

Figure 174.1 The Microsoft FrontPage Reports View, verify the hyperlinks message box.

5. If not prompted with the Reports View message box (or if you accidentally clicked your mouse pointer on the NO button near the bottom center if the message box), click your mouse pointer on the Verify Hyperlinks button on the right-hand end of the Reporting toolbar (shown in Figure 174.2).

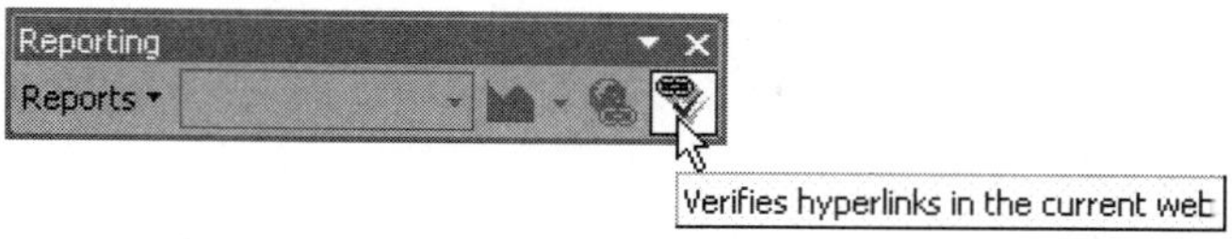

Figure 174.2 The Microsoft FrontPage Reporting toolbar.

FrontPage, in turn, will display the Verify Hyperlinks dialog box shown in Figure 174.3. (If FrontPage did not display the Reporting toolbar when you selected the Broken Hyperlinks report in Step 2, select the View menu Toolbars option and click your mouse pointer on Reporting.)

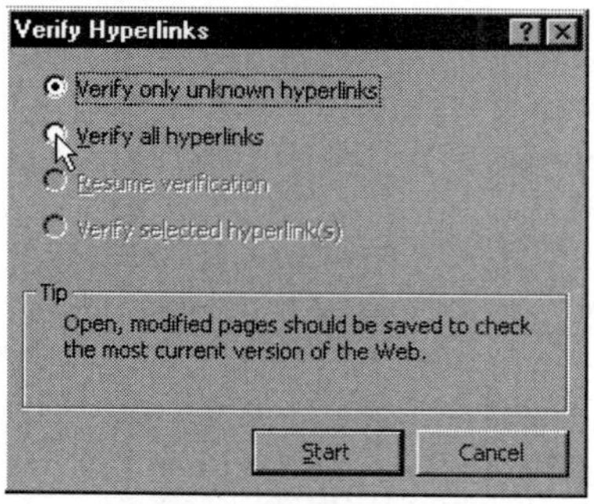

Figure 174.3 The Microsoft FrontPage Verify Hyperlinks dialog box.

6. Click your mouse pointer on the START button near the bottom center of the Verify Hyperlinks dialog box.

After you click your mouse pointer on the YES button near the bottom center of the Reports View verify hyperlinks message box (in Step 4) or complete Step 6 of the preceding procedure, FrontPage will attempt to access the target of each of the current web's external hyperlinks. Depending on the number of external hyperlinks and the speed of your Internet connection, this process may take quite some time. Fortunately, FrontPage can execute its external hyperlinks check in the background—which lets you work with the program to complete other tasks, if you like. FrontPage tells you which hyperlink it is checking and the verification processes' percentage of completion along the bottom of the application window as it completes the external hyperlink check.

As the program checks the status of the web's external hyperlinks, FrontPage will update the status column on the Broken Hyperlinks report. The possible statuses are:

- **OK** – FrontPage was able to access the hyperlink's target.
- **Broken** – the hyperlink's target is not accessible.
- **Verifying** – FrontPage is currently verifying the hyperlink.
- **Unknown** – the hyperlink has not yet been verified.

You will, of course, want to fix or delete any broken hyperlinks. Fortunately, FrontPage lets you select the broken hyperlink and start the Edit Hyperlink dialog box to repair the hyperlink right on the Broken Hyperlinks report. As a result, you do not have to search for broken hyperlinks on your Web pages before you can fix them. The next Tip will show you how to select and repair broken hyperlinks while in Reports view.

REPAIRING BROKEN HYPERLINKS WSHILE IN REPORTS VIEW

If you have not done so already, execute the procedure in the preceding Tip to generate the Broken Hyperlinks report based on the results of checking the current web's external links. Or, to display a previously generated Broken Hyperlinks report for the current FrontPage web, select the View menu Reports option. Click your mouse pointer on Problems and select Broken Hyperlinks. FrontPage, in turn, will switch to Reports view and display a Broken Hyperlinks report similar to that shown in Figure 175.1.

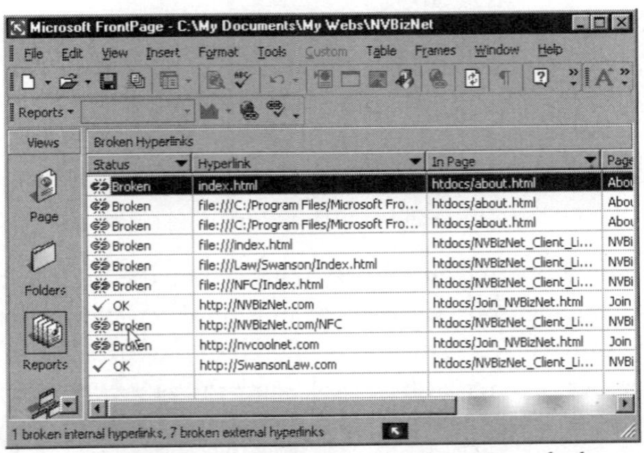

Figure 175.1 The Microsoft FrontPage Reports view Broken Hyperlinks report.

To repair a broken hyperlink, perform the following steps:

1. Double click your mouse pointer on the contents of any column in a line on the Broken Hyperlinks report that has Broken in its Status column. (Or, right-click your mouse pointer in any column of a broken hyperlink's line on the report and select Edit Hyperlink from the pop-up menu.) FrontPage, in turn, will display an Edit Hyperlink dialog box similar to that shown in Figure 175.2.

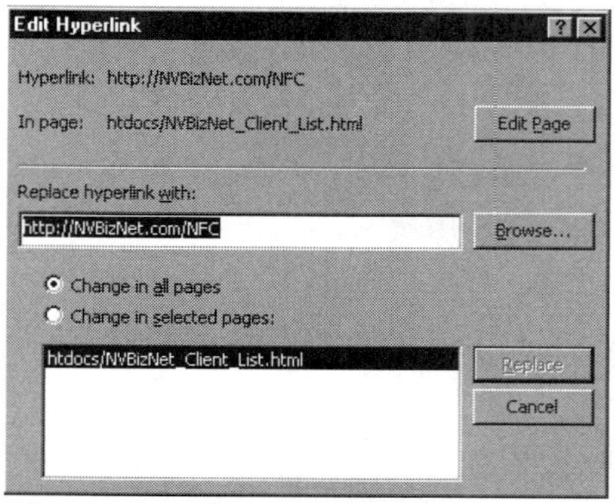

***Figure 175.2** The Microsoft FrontPage Edit Hyperlink dialog box.*

2. If you want to modify the hyperlink directly on the Web page in which it was inserted, click your mouse pointer on the EDIT PAGE button near the top of the Edit Hyperlink dialog box. FrontPage, in turn, will display the Web page with the broken hyperlink on the Page view Normal tab. Modify the broken hyperlink (as described in the Tip entitled "Editing a Hyperlink's Anchor Text and/or Its Destination," then select the File menu Save option to store the updated Web page onto the hard drive. Finally, click your mouse pointer on the Reports button (third from the top) on the Views Bar along the left-hand side of the FrontPage application window to return to the Reports view. (If you do not see the Views Bar, select the View menu Views Bar option.)

   If you want to modify the hyperlink using the fields in the Edit Hyperlink dialog box, enter the correct relative address or the correct URL of the hyperlink's target in the Replace hyperlink with field. As you change the field's contents, FrontPage will enable the REPLACE button near the bottom right-hand side of the Edit Hyperlink dialog box.

***Note:** If you do not know the hyperlink target's address, click your mouse pointer on the BROWSE button to the right of the Replace hyperlink with field. FrontPage, in turn, will display the Edit*

Hyperlink dialog box shown in the Tip entitled "Editing a Hyperlink's Anchor Text and/or Its Destination." Use the drop-down list button to the right of the Look in field (near the top of the new Edit Hyperlink dialog box) and the folders in the list box below the field to navigate to the folder that contains the hyperlink's target. Then, click your mouse pointer on the target's filename in the list box below the Look in field. FrontPage, in turn, will write the target file's address relative to the current Web page into the Address field at the bottom of the dialog box.

Or, if the hyperlink's target is an external Web page on the Internet, click your mouse pointer on the Browse the Web button (with the globe and magnifying glass) two buttons to the right of the Look in field. FrontPage, in turn, will start your Web browser. Use the Web browser to display the hyperlink's target Web page, and then click your mouse pointer on the FrontPage button on your Windows task bar. When windows returns to the FrontPage application window, FrontPage will copy the contents of your Web browser's Address field into the Address field near the bottom of the Edit Hyperlink dialog box.

Once you have the hyperlink target's address in the Address field, click your mouse pointer on the OK button near the lower right-hand corner of the new (second) Edit Hyperlink dialog box. FrontPage, in turn, will return to the original (first) Edit Hyperlink dialog box (you saw in Figure 175.2) and copy the contents of the Address field from the second Edit Hyperlink dialog box to the Replace hyperlink with field near the middle of the first Edit Hyperlink dialog box.

After you have made the corrections you need to make to the hyperlink target's address, click your mouse pointer on the Change in all pages radio button to tell FrontPage to make the same repair to the hyperlink on all pages on which the identical, broken hyperlink appears. Finally, click your mouse pointer on the REPLACE button near the bottom right-hand corner of the Edit Hyperlink dialog box. FrontPage, in turn, will change the hyperlink's target to the address you entered into the Replace hyperlink with field on all of the pages listed in the scroll box to the left of the REPLACE button, and then return to the Reports view

3. After FrontPage returns to the Page view Broken Hyperlinks report and changes the status of the hyperlink(s) it changed to "Edited", repeat Steps 1 and 2 for each of the hyperlinks whose status column indicates the hyperlink is still "Broken".

After you change all of the hyperlinks that were initially reported as broken, the Status column of the Broken Hyperlinks report will contain only two statuses: "OK" and "Edited". Before leaving the Reports view, click your mouse pointer on the Verify Hyperlinks button (with the link of chain and the check mark) on the right-hand end of the Reporting toolbar, and have FrontPage verify the hyperlinks in the current FrontPage web one last time. If

FrontPage changes the status of any of the hyperlinks to Broken during the re-check, repeat the preceding procedure until you see an OK in the status column next to each hyperlink on the Broken Hyperlink report.

REMOVING A HYPERLINK

When you no longer need a hyperlink, FrontPage gives you two ways to remove the hyperlink from the Web page. If you want to remove the hyperlink *and* the text or image to which it is anchored on the Web page, perform the following steps:

1. Display the Web page with the hyperlink you want to remove on the Page view Normal tab.
2. Double-click your mouse pointer on the hyperlink's anchor text or image (if the hyperlink is anchored to a picture) to select it.
3. Press the DELETE or BACKSPACE key on your keyboard to delete both the hyperlink and its anchor text or image.

On the other hand, if you want to remove only the hyperlink and leave the anchor text or image on the Web page, perform the following Steps:

1. Display the Web page with the hyperlink you want to remove on the Page view Normal tab.
2. Right-click your mouse pointer on the hyperlink's anchor text or image, and select Hyperlink Properties from the pop-up menu. FrontPage, in turn, will display the Edit Hyperlink dialog box.
3. Click your mouse pointer on the REMOVE LINK button near the lower right-hand corner of the Edit Hyperlink dialog box.

After you complete Step 3, FrontPage will leave the text or image used to anchor the hyperlink in place, but the visitor will no longer be able to click the mouse pointer on the text or image to activate a hyperlink, since the "link/target" portion of the hyperlink is no longer there.

REMOVING A BOOKMARK

When done correctly, removing a bookmark from a Web page requires that you perform the steps in two procedures: 1) remove the bookmark, and 2) delete the hyperlinks that target the bookmark. Because FrontPage does not automatically remove the hyperlinks that point to a bookmark when you delete the bookmark, performing only the first procedure will leave one or more hyperlinks that do nothing when activated. (Unlike a broken hyperlink to an unavailable Web page or file, the Web server will not generate an error message when the site visitor clicks the mouse pointer on a hyperlink that targets a nonexistent bookmark.)

To remove a bookmark from a Web page, perform the following steps:

1. Display the Web page with the bookmark you want to remove on the Page view Normal tab.
2. Select the Insert menu Bookmark option. FrontPage, in turn, will display the Bookmark dialog box.
3. Double-click your mouse pointer on the bookmark you want to delete in the Other bookmarks on this page scroll box. (Or, click your mouse pointer on the bookmark you want to delete and then on the GOTO button to the right of the Other bookmarks on this page scroll box.) FrontPage, in turn, will jump to and select the bookmark on the current Web page in the Page view Normal tab.
4. Make a note of the bookmark's name before you delete the bookmark. You will need the bookmark's name to search for all of the hyperlinks that target the bookmark, so that you can delete those hyperlinks after you remove the bookmark from the Web page.
5. To delete the bookmark you selected in Step 3, click your mouse on the CLEAR button to the right of the upper right-hand corner of the Other bookmarks on this page scroll box.

As mentioned previously, FrontPage does not delete the hyperlinks that target a bookmark when you remove the bookmark from a Web page. Moreover, the broken hyperlinks report will not alert you to hyperlinks that point to bookmarks you have cleared (i.e., deleted). Therefore, after you remove a bookmark, edit each of the pages with a hyperlink to the bookmark and perform the procedure to you learned in the preceding Tip to delete the hyperlink from the Web page.

The next Tip shows how to search for and delete hyperlinks that target a bookmark. Execute the procedure in the next Tip if you do not know which of the web's pages have hyperlinks to the bookmark you just removed or when you want to make sure that you have indeed deleted all of the hyperlinks that target the bookmark you cleared.

FINDING AND DELETING HYPERLINKS THAT TARGET A BOOKMARK

While FrontPage reports hyperlinks that target deleted or otherwise unavailable Web pages on the Broken Hyperlinks report, the program does not report hyperlinks to bookmarks on the report at all. Therefore, if you remove a bookmark from a Web page, FrontPage will not give you a list of (now broken) hyperlinks that target the deleted bookmark.

Unfortunately the hyperlinks to deleted bookmarks do not just "disappear." Instead, when the site visitor clicks the mouse pointer on a "broken" hyperlink to a nonexistent bookmark, nothing happens—no error message and no movement to another point on the same page or on another page. Because hyperlinks to deleted bookmarks do nothing but obscure other, functioning hyperlinks on the page, you will want to eliminate them.

To find and delete hyperlinks that target a bookmark, perform the following steps:

1. Start FrontPage and use the File menu Open Web option to open the FrontPage web whose pages you want to search for hyperlinks to the bookmark.
2. Select the Edit menu Find option. FrontPage, in turn, will display a Find and Replace dialog box similar to that shown in Figure 178.1.

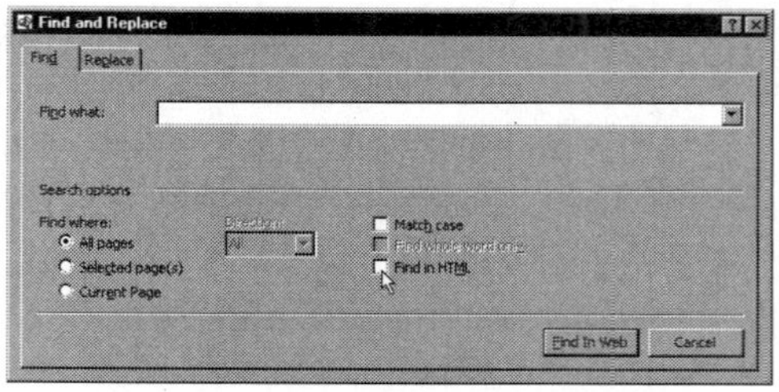

Figure 178.1 The Microsoft FrontPage Find and Replace dialog box, Find tab.

3. Into the Find what at the top of the Find and Replace dialog box Find tab, enter a pound sign (#) followed by the name of the bookmark. For example, if you want to delete hyperlinks that target the bookmark "Saving a FrontPage web to disk," into the Find what field, enter **#Saving a FrontPage web to disk.**
4. Click your mouse pointer on the All Pages radio button in the Find Where section of the Search options Section in the lower half of the dialog box. (You want FrontPage to search all Web pages in the current FrontPage web.)
5. Click your mouse pointer on the Find in HTML checkbox until a check mark appears. (You want FrontPage to find the hyperlink itself, which is in the Web page HTML, and not the hyperlink's anchor text, which is on the Web page.)
6. Click your mouse pointer on the FIND IN WEB button near the bottom right-hand corner of the dialog box. FrontPage, in turn, will search the HTML for all Web pages in the current FrontPage web and add a scroll box with the search results to the bottom of the Find and Replace dialog box.
7. If the search results scroll box has no entries, skip the remaining Steps in this procedure. Otherwise, double-click your mouse pointer on the first entry in the search results scroll box. FrontPage, in turn, will

display the Web page with the hyperlink to the bookmark on the Page view HTML tab behind the dialog box.

8. On the Page view HTML tab, click your mouse pointer just left of the less than sign (<) in the <a> (anchor tag) of the hyperlink you want to delete. [FrontPage highlighted the hyperlink's text for you when you performed Step 7; look to the left of the highlighted text to find the less than sign (<) that starts the <a> (anchor) tag.]
9. Press and hold down the Delete key until you have removed the HTML code starting with the less than sign (<) that starts the <a> (anchor) tag and ending with the greater than sign (>) that follows the quoted bookmark name.
10. If you want to delete the hyperlink's anchor text (i.e. the text to which the hyperlink is anchored on the Web page), press and hold down the Delete key until you have deleted all of the text up to the </a> (end anchor) tag. Otherwise, use the right-arrow key on your keyboard to move the cursor past the anchor text.
11. Press and hold down the Delete key until you have removed the hyperlink's </a> (end anchor) tag.
12. Click your mouse pointer on the Find Next button near the lower right-hand corner of the Find and Replace dialog box. FrontPage, in turn, will search for another hyperlink to the bookmark on the current Web page. If FrontPage finds another hyperlink on the current Web page, continue at Step 8. Conversely, if there are no additional hyperlinks to the bookmark on the current Web page, FrontPage will prompt you with a Continue with next page dialog box such as that shown in Figure 178.2.

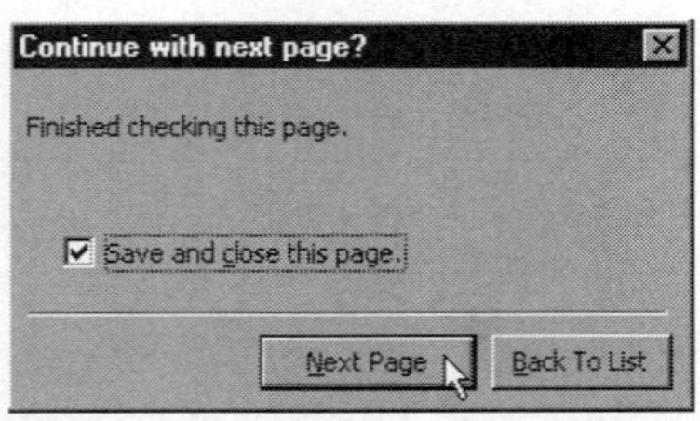

Figure 178.2 The Microsoft FrontPage search function's Continue with the next page dialog box.

13. If displayed, click your mouse pointer on the Next Page button near the bottom center of the dialog box. FrontPage, in turn, will close the Web from which you deleted the hyperlink(s) and save your changes

to disk—as long as you do not clear the Save and close this page checkbox. If there are additional Web pages on the search results list (returned in Step 6), continue at Step 8.

14. When there are no more Web pages on the search results list (returned in Step 6), FrontPage will display the a Finished checking pages dialog box. Click your mouse pointer on the BACK TO LIST button in the lower right-hand corner of the dialog box. FrontPage, in turn, will save the changes you made to the current Web page, close the Web page, and return to the Find and Replace dialog box.
15. Click your mouse pointer on the close button (the "X") in the upper right-hand corner of the Find and Replace dialog box.

Although it goes without saying, be careful as you are deleting the hyperlink <A> (anchor) tag in Steps 8 – 9. Make sure that you start deleting at the less than sign (<) that precedes the bookmark's name and stop deleting when you reach the greater than sign (>) that follows the quote mark (") after the bookmark's name. Also, do not forget to delete the </a> (end anchor) tag that follows the hyperlink's anchor text.

Whether or not you delete the hyperlink's anchor text (in Step 10) depends on the Web page content. For example, if the anchor text is a term and the bookmark you deleted was the definition of the term, then you will want to delete the anchor text, since the term is no longer a bookmarked definition. Conversely, if the anchor text is the name of a product in a list of products sold by your company, you may want to keep the anchor text and add: "(Discontinued)", so that you have a complete product list of all items the company ever sold—including those that are now discontinued (and marked as such).

USING THE FILE MENU SAVE AS OPTION TO SAVE A WEB PAGE AS A TEMPLATE

FrontPage templates save you time and effort by letting you create new Web pages with a standard layout and text and graphics images you want to appear on every page. To create a new Web page based on a template, perform the following steps:

1. Select the File menu New option and click your mouse pointer on Page or Web. FrontPage, in turn, will display the New Page or Web menu pane along the right-hand side of the application window.
2. Click your mouse pointer on Page Templates in the bottom half of the menu. FrontPage, in turn, will display the Page Templates dialog box.
3. Click your mouse pointer on the template you want to use for the new Web page. (After you click your mouse pointer on a template, FrontPage

shows you what a Web page based on the template will look like in the Preview area in the lower right-hand corner of the dialog box.) For the current project, click your mouse pointer on **One-column Body with Contents on Left**—the twelfth standard template.

4. Click your mouse pointer on the OK button near the lower right-hand corner of the Page Templates dialog box. FrontPage, in turn, will display a new Web page based on the template on the Page view Normal tab.

The new Web page created using the template "One-column Body with Contents on Left" has a banner and a graphics image at the top of the page, a table of contents (for the Web page) along the left-hand side of the page, and the content in a single column to the right of the table of contents. To use a Web page created from the template, you replace each of its placeholder elements (banner, graphics image, table of contents, and content, in the current example) with your own graphics and text content. While the content (on the right) and the table of contents (on the left) will be different for each Web page you create from the "One-column Body with Contents on Left" template, you might use the same banner and graphics image at the top of each page, if you use the company name as the banner text and substitute the its logo for the graphics image, for example.

If you find yourself making the same changes to the FrontPage templates you use for your Web pages, create custom templates to save yourself some work. For example, to customize the template you used to create a new Web page in the preceding procedure, perform the following steps:

1. Display the Web page created from the template on the Page view Normal tab. For the current project, display the page created using the template "One-column Body with Contents on Left".
2. On the document in the Page view Normal tab, make the changes you "always" make to the standard template. Suppose, for example, that you always substitute the company's name for "Your Heading Goes Here." Delete the fish photo and its caption, and put your name as a mailto hyperlink at the bottom of each page. Go ahead and make those changes now. (For the current project, replace "Your Heading Goes Here" with your own name if you cannot think of a company name to use.)

   To create the mailto hyperlink at the bottom of the page, click your mouse pointer on the HTML tab to display the Web page HTML. Use the vertical scroll bar along the right-hand side of the Page view pane to move to the bottom of the Web page. Click your mouse pointer at a point to the left of the less than sign (<) on the **</body>** tag, and type **Webmaster:** followed by a space and your name. Then, click your mouse pointer on the Normal tab to work with the current Web page on the Page view Normal tab. Next, click and hold down your left mouse button as you drag the mouse pointer across the text you typed on the HTML tab (i.e. Webmaster: and your name), and then follow the procedure in a previous Tip entitled "Creating a Hyperlink to an E-Mail Address."

3. To save the current Web page as a custom template, select the File menu Save As option. FrontPage, in turn, will display the Save As dialog box.
4. Click the drop-down list button to the right of the Save as type field at the bottom of the dialog box, and select **FrontPage Template (*.tem)** from the drop-down list.
5. Into the File name field (above the Save as type field), enter the name you want to use for the template file. For example, if you are creating a template for "standard" Web pages in your FrontPage web(s), enter a name such as **WebPageTemplate** into the File name field.
6. Click your mouse pointer on the SAVE button near the lower right-hand corner of the Save As dialog box. FrontPage, in turn, will display a Save As Template dialog box similar to that shown in Figure 179.

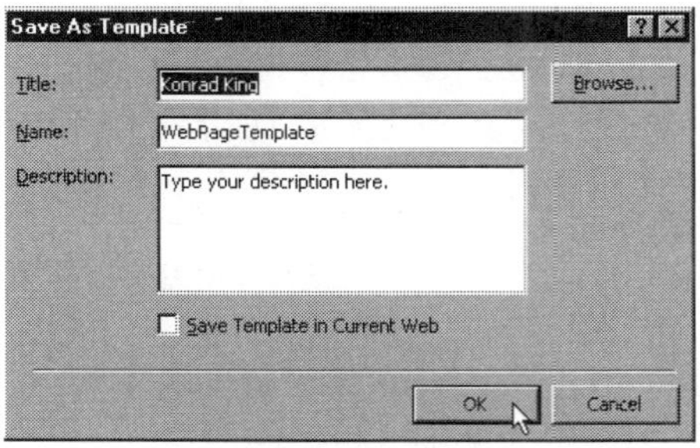

***Figure 179** The Microsoft FrontPage Save As Template dialog box.*

7. Into the Title field, enter the text you want FrontPage to display below the icon for your custom template in the Page Templates dialog box. For the current project, enter **Custom Web Page Template** into the Title field.
8. Into the Description field, enter a brief description of the template's layout or function. For the current project enter **Standard Web page with table of contents on the left and content on the right** into the Description field. (FrontPage will display the description you enter in the Description area of the Page Templates dialog box when you click your mouse pointer on the icon for your custom template.)

9. Click your mouse pointer on the OK button near the lower right-hand corner of the Save As Template dialog box.
10. Select the File menu Close option.

The next time you perform the Steps in the first procedure in this Tip to create a new Web page based on a template, you will find the icons for any custom templates you previously created and saved listed alphabetically by title after the last standard Template that comes with FrontPage.

Although the procedure in this Tip showed you how to create a new template by modifying an existing template, you can create a template based on any Web page. Simply open the Web page whose layout and content you want to use as a template in the future. Then, execute the Steps in the preceding procedure starting with Step 3.

APPLYING A FRONTPAGE THEME TO A WEB SITE

A FrontPage theme lets you set (or change) the look and feel of a Web site by using a consistent set of fonts for the site's text elements, applying a color scheme to the site's pages, text, and graphics, and supplying a Web page background image and a set of graphics images for bullets, banners, and menu bars. In short, applying a FrontPage theme will make an ordinary Web site look extraordinary. Moreover, each of the many FrontPage themes included in a standard installation of the program can give your Web site a very different look if applied.

To apply a FrontPage theme to a Web site, perform the following steps:

1. Use the File menu Open Web option to open the FrontPage Web to which you want to apply a theme. For example, to apply a theme to the Personal Web **MyWeb** (which you created earlier in this book), select the File menu Open Web option. FrontPage, in turn, will display the Open Web dialog box. Into the Web name field at the bottom of the Open Web dialog box enter **C:\MY DOCUMENTS\MY WEBS\MYWEB**, and click your mouse pointer on the OPEN button in the lower right-hand corner of the dialog box.
2. Select the Format menu Theme option. FrontPage, in turn, will display the Themes dialog box shown in Figure 180.1.
3. Select the theme you want FrontPage to apply to the current web (you opened in Step 1) by clicking your mouse pointer on the theme's title in the scroll box on the left-hand side of the dialog box. Before making a final selection, feel free to "experience" the themes FrontPage has to offer. Each time you click your mouse pointer on a theme title,

FrontPage will show you the theme's color scheme, fonts, and graphics on a Web page in the Sample of Theme scroll box. For the current project, click your mouse pointer on **Expedition** to select a theme that gives your personal Web site a safari-like appearance. (The themes in the theme scroll box are listed alphabetically by title.)

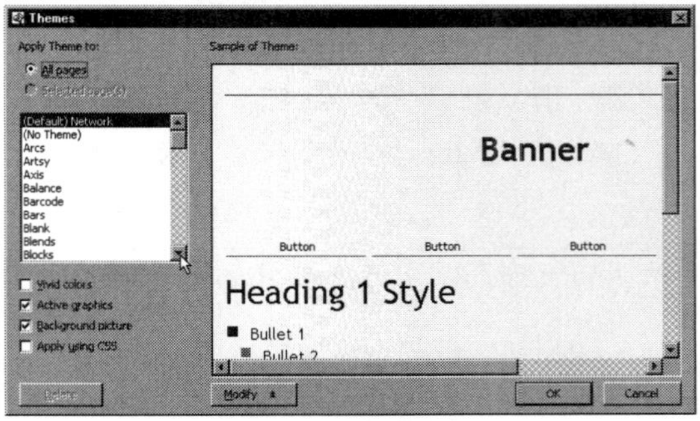

Figure 180.1 *The Microsoft FrontPage Themes dialog box.*

4. Decide whether or not you want to use a theme's brighter or darker set of colors. To use brighter (lighter) colors, click your mouse pointer on the Vivid colors checkbox until a checkmark appears. Conversely, to use the theme's darker color set, clear the Vivid colors checkbox. For the current project, clear the Vivid colors checkbox.
5. To use animated bullets and navigation bar buttons that change shape or color when activated, click your mouse pointer on the Active graphics checkbox until a checkmark appears. Conversely, to use static images and no dynamic-HTML effects, clear the Active graphics checkbox. For the current project click your mouse pointer on the Active graphics checkbox until a checkmark appears.
6. To give the Web site's pages a textured background, click your mouse pointer on the Background picture checkbox until a checkmark appears. Conversely, to use a white background (i.e. Web pages with no background picture), clear the Background picture checkbox. For the current project, click your mouse pointer on the Background picture checkbox until a checkmark appears.
7. To have FrontPage apply the theme using cascading style sheet (CSS) commands, click your mouse pointer on the Apply using CSS checkbox until a checkmark appears. To apply the theme using standard HTML tags, clear the Apply using CSS checkbox. For the current project, clear the Apply using CSS checkbox. (You will learn all about using CSS later in this book.)

8. Click your mouse pointer on the OK button near the lower right-hand corner of the Themes dialog box.

After you complete Step 8, FrontPage will apply the theme you selected in Step 3 to the current FrontPage web (you opened in Step 1). If the current web already has some formatting information, FrontPage will prompt you with the Continue to Apply Theme message box shown in Figure 180.2.

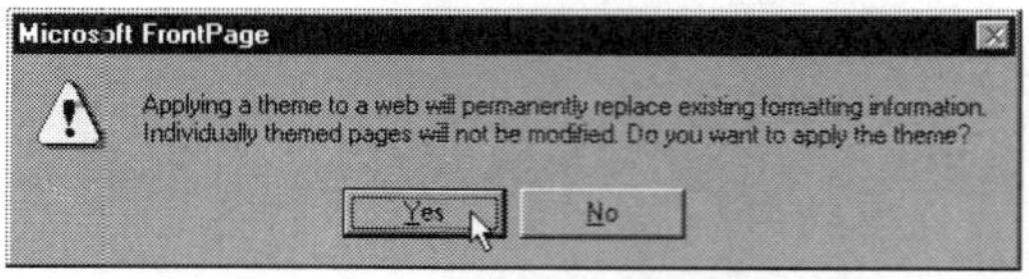

Figure 180.2 The Microsoft FrontPage, Continue to Apply Theme message box.

Click your mouse pointer on the YES button near the bottom center of the message box to finish applying the theme to the current FrontPage web.

To see how applying the FrontPage theme has changed the site's homepage, click your mouse pointer on the Folders button (second from the top) in the Views Bar along the left-hand side of the application window. (Or, select the View menu Folders option.) Double-click your mouse pointer on the Web site's homepage, INDEX.HTM (or DEFAULT.HTM). FrontPage, in turn, will display the site's homepage on the Page view Normal tab.

VARYING THE THEME ON INDIVIDUAL WEB PAGES

As you learned in the preceding Tip, you normally apply a theme to an entire Web site so that all of the site's pages use the same color scheme, fonts, and graphics for text, buttons, bullets, and banners. However, there are times when you want one or more pages to stand out from the others in the web. For example, you might to change the theme used on bibliography, legal disclaimer, or feedback pages to show that these Web pages provide information that is not integral to the Web site's overall message.

To apply a theme to individual Web pages or to remove a theme from some pages and not others:

1. Open the FrontPage web whose theme you want to change.
2. Select the View menu Folders Option to display the Web in Folders view.
3. Click your mouse pointer on the Web page whose theme you want to change. (To change the theme on multiple (but not all) pages, hold down the CTRL key on your keyboard as you click your mouse pointer on the filenames of the Web pages with themes you want to change.)

4. Select the Format menu Theme option. FrontPage, in turn, will display a Themes dialog box similar to the one you saw in Figure 180.1. However, Selected page(s) will be selected in the current Themes dialog box, whereas the selection is grayed out as unavailable in the Figure 180.1. (The difference between the two is that you selected one or more Web pages before selecting the Format menu Themes option in the current instance.)
5. Click your mouse pointer on the title of the theme you want to apply to the page(s) you selected in Step 2. Or, to remove the theme previously applied to the page(s), click your mouse pointer on the "(No Theme)" entry in the themes list box.
6. Click your mouse pointer on the OK button near the lower right-hand corner of the Themes dialog box.

After you complete Step 6, FrontPage will apply the theme you selected in Step 4 to the Web page(s) you selected in Step 3 and return to Folders view. To see how a Web page looks after applying a theme, double-click your mouse pointer on the filename of the Web page in Folders view to display the page on the Page view Normal tab.

MODIFYING THE COLORS OF A FRONTPAGE THEME

Although Microsoft's "crack team" of graphics artists and Web page designers created the themes included with the latest version of FrontPage, the theme colors, graphics, and text styles are not "set in stone." Therefore, if you like the colors in one theme and the graphics in another, you can use the color scheme from one on the graphics and text elements of the other. Or, if you just want to tweak the colors in a theme—just a little—well, you can do too.

When working with a theme's color scheme, keep in mind that the theme must coordinate the colors used for each of the Web page elements. As such, if you want to change a theme's colors, either select the color scheme used in another scheme, or if you change the color of individual elements, make sure the colors you choose appropriate colors for all of the elements, which include:

- **Background** – the normal and vivid colors selected for the background of Web pages without a graphics image background.
- **Banner Text** – the color of the text in the banner at the top of the page.
- **Body** – the default normal and vivid colors selected for normal (non-hyperlink and non-heading) text in the body of the Web page.
- **Heading** (1 – 6) – the default normal and vivid colors selected for each of the six levels of headings.
- **Hyperlink** (Active) – the default normal and vivid colors selected for a hyperlink in mid-click.

- **Hyperlinks (Followed)** – the default normal and vivid colors selected for visited hyperlinks.
- **Hyperlinks** – the default normal and vivid colors selected for unvisited hyperlinks.
- **Navigation Text** – the default color of the text labels on the theme's navigation buttons.
- **Table Border** – the default normal and vivid colors selected for the color of table borders.

Because FrontPage will not let you create a theme "from scratch," you must start with one of the themes already on your system and modify it to create a custom theme. Although not required, if you currently have a FrontPage web open, you may want to select the File menu Close option to close it—so you do not inadvertently apply your custom theme to the web until you have the theme's colors "just right." (While you must start with an existing theme to create a new one, you do not have to have a FrontPage web open to modify a theme.)

To create a theme with a custom set of colors, perform the following steps:

1. Select the Format menu theme option. FrontPage, in turn, will display the Themes dialog box.
2. Select the theme you want to modify by clicking your mouse pointer on the theme's title in the scroll box on the left-hand side of the dialog box. For example, if you like the graphics and font styles used in the Axis theme, but want to change its colors, click your mouse pointer on **Axis** in the themes title scroll box on the left-hand side of the Themes dialog box. FrontPage, in turn, will display samples of the theme's graphics, text, and colors in the Sample of Theme display area of the Themes dialog box.
3. Click your mouse pointer on the MODIFY button below the lower left-hand corner of the Sample of Theme display area in the Themes dialog box to expose the additional buttons (shown below the Sample of Theme display area in Figure 182.1) that let you modify the theme's colors, graphics, and text.
4. Click your mouse pointer on the COLORS button. FrontPage, in turn, will display the color modification tabs to the left of the Sample of Theme display area of a Modify Theme dialog box, similar to that shown in Figure 182.2.

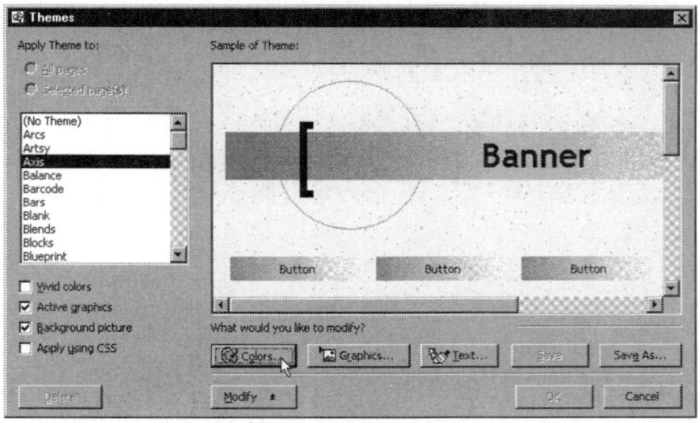

Figure 182.1 The Microsoft FrontPage Themes dialog box with theme modification buttons exposed.

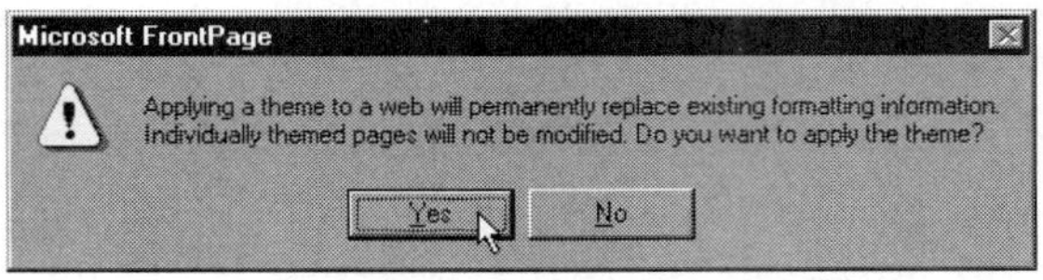

Figure 182.2 The Microsoft FrontPage Modify Theme dialog box, Color Schemes tab.

5. If you want to apply the color scheme from another theme to the theme you selected in Step 2, on the Color Schemes tab, click your mouse pointer on the title of the theme whose color scheme you want to apply. Each time you click your mouse pointer on a color scheme, FrontPage will use the Sample of Theme display area of the Modify Theme dialog box to show you how the theme's graphics, background, and text elements will look after applying the new color scheme.

   After you select the color scheme for the theme's *Normal colors*, click your mouse pointer on the Vivid colors radio button, in the center at the bottom of the dialog box, and select the color scheme for the theme's *Vivid colors*. (As mentioned in the preceding Tip, a theme normally has two sets of colors: normal and vivid. Colors in the normal color set are usually darker, more subdued than those in the theme's vivid color set.)

6. To adjust a theme's colors based on the selection of the Hue, Saturation and Brightness of the primary colors (Red, Green, and Blue), click your mouse pointer on the Color Wheel tab to expose the Color Wheel shown on the left-hand side of the Modify Theme dialog box in Figure 182.3.

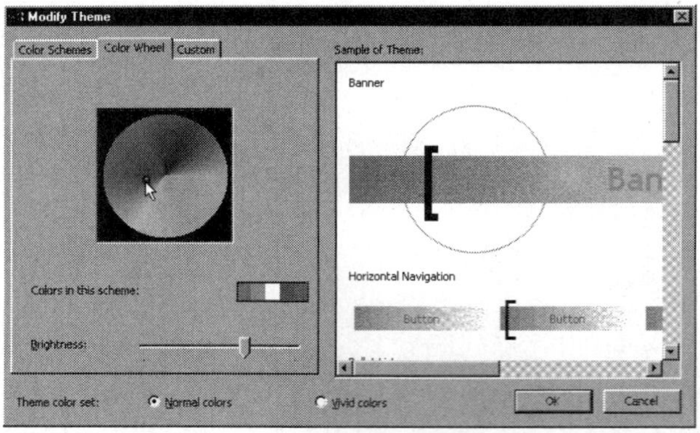

Figure 182.3 The Microsoft FrontPage Modify Theme dialog box, Color Wheel tab.

Place the mouse pointer over the small, clear bubble on the Color Wheel and hold down the left mouse button as you drag the mouse pointer and the bubble around the wheel. Whenever you release the left mouse button, FrontPage will display a color scheme defined by the bubble's position on the Color Wheel and the position of the Brightness slide below the Color Wheel.

By moving the bubble around the diameter of the Color Wheel, you can select the *hue*, or color value (i.e. the color resulting from a mix of various amounts of each of the primary colors) of the Normal Text color shown in the fourth box from the left in the Colors in this scheme field below the Color Wheel.

To control a hue's *saturation*, i.e. the purity of the colors used in the color mix, move the bubble along a radius of the Color Wheel. The closer you drag the bubble toward the center of the Color Wheel, the higher the saturation or purity of each of the primary colors used. Conversely, the further away from the center, the more neutral colors FrontPage adds to the primary colors in the mix to make the resulting color appear more pale or dull.

To control the color's brightness, use your mouse pointer to drag the Brightness bar toward the left (darker) or the right (brighter).

After you use the Color Wheel and Brightness slide to create the colors for the theme's Normal colors, click your mouse pointer on the Vivid colors radio button near the center at the bottom of the Modify Theme dialog box. Then repeat the current step (Step 6) to create a color set for the theme's Vivid colors.

Note: *You can only use the Color Wheel to set the Normal Text color (shown as the fourth color from the left in the Colors in this scheme field) for a theme. The third color from the left in the Colors in this scheme field is the background color—which you must set using the Custom tab. FrontPage, in turn, computes the other three colors for the theme based on the color you select as the Normal Text color.*

7. To select a color for each of the fourteen elements in a theme individually, click your mouse pointer on the Custom tab to expose the Item and Color fields shown in Figure 182.4.

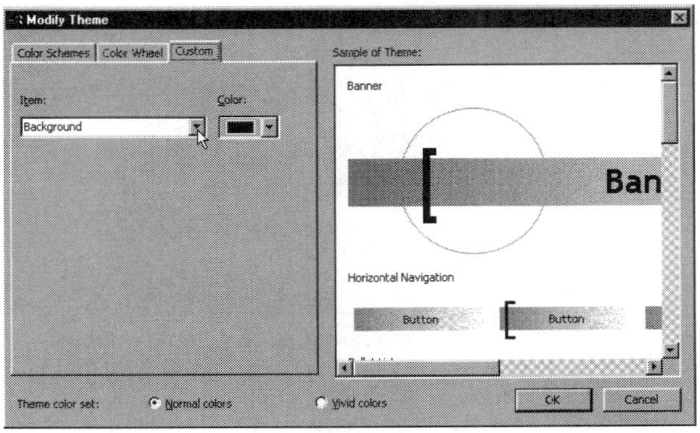

Figure 182.4 *The Microsoft FrontPage Modify Theme dialog box, Custom tab.*

8. Click your mouse pointer on the drop-down list button to the right of the Item field and select the item whose color you want to set. After you click your mouse pointer on an item in the drop-down list, FrontPage will display the item's current color in the Color field and the way the item will look on the Web page in the Sample of Theme display area. To change the item's color, click your mouse pointer on the drop-down list button to the right of the Color field, and then on one of the sixteen color swatches on the drop-down color pallet, or select More Colors at the bottom of the drop-down color pallet and create a custom color for the item.

Note: *Some of the items such as Background, Body, Heading (1 – 6), Hyperlinks, Hyperlink (Active), Hyperlink (Followed), and Table Border have both Normal colors and Vivid colors. Therefore, be sure to select (or create) a normal color for these items, and then click your mouse pointer on the Vivid colors radio button (at the bottom center of the Modify Theme dialog box) and select (or create) a Vivid color.*

9. Click your mouse pointer on the OK button near the lower right-hand corner of the Modify Theme dialog box. FrontPage, in turn, will return to the Themes dialog box.
10. Click your mouse pointer on the SAVE AS button near the lower right-hand corner of the Themes dialog box. FrontPage, in turn, will display a Save Theme dialog box similar to that shown in Figure 182.5.

Note: *Although you can overwrite one of the standard themes that come with FrontPage, there is no way to go back if you do so. Therefore, do not overwrite the standard themes. Instead, save each custom theme you create to new file, or overwrite a custom theme file you created previously.*

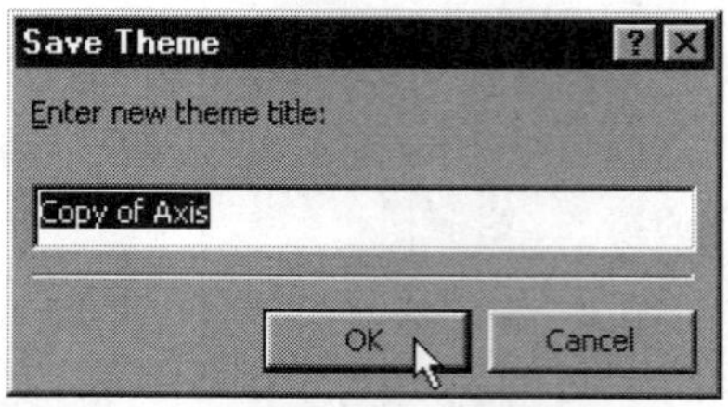

Figure 182.5 *The Microsoft FrontPage Save Theme dialog box.*

11. Into the Enter new theme title field, enter a descriptive name you can use to identify and select the theme later. If you modified the Axis theme, for example, enter a title such as **Axis – Custom** into the Enter new theme title field as the title of the custom theme you created.
12. Click your mouse pointer on the OK button near the center at the bottom of the Save Theme dialog box.

After you complete Step 12, FrontPage will save your custom theme to disk and add its title to the list of themes available for selection in the scroll box on the left-hand side of the Themes dialog box. To exit the Themes dialog box and return to the FrontPage application window, click your mouse pointer on the close button (the "X") in the upper right-hand corner of the dialog box.

The following two Tips will show you how to customize a theme's graphics and text fonts.

MODIFYING FRONTPAGE THEME GRAPHICS

If you like a theme's color scheme, but want to change its graphics elements, FrontPage lets you do just that. Changing a theme's graphics is similar to changing its color scheme in that both procedures involve selecting and then modifying a previously saved theme. However, unlike the procedure followed to change a theme's color scheme, in which you can create the colors you want to use while modifying the theme, when changing any of the theme's eleven graphics elements, you need to create or retrieve the new graphics image you want to use outside of the theme modification procedure.

The eleven theme graphics elements you can change are:

- **Background Picture** – the texture or other graphic image (such as a washed out picture) displayed in the background on each Web page to which the theme is applied.
- **Banner** – the normal and active picture displayed behind the banner text at the top of each Web page to which the theme is applied.
- **Bullet List** – the normal and active pictures used as the bullet characters for each of the three levels of bullets in a bulleted list.
- **Global Navigation Buttons** – the graphics image used for global navigation buttons.
- **Horizontal Navigation** – the normal and active pictures displayed as a default button, selected button, and hover button on a horizontal button bar.
- **Horizontal Rule** – the normal and active picture used as a horizontal line across the Web page.
- **Quick Back Button** – the normal and active graphics pictures used for the default Back button, selected Back button, and hover Back button.
- **Quick Home Button** – the normal and active graphics pictures used for the default Home button, selected Home button, and hover Home button.
- **Quick Next Button** – the normal and active graphics pictures used for the default Next button, selected Next button, and hover Next button.
- **Quick Up Button** – the normal and active graphics pictures used for the default Up button, selected Up button, and hover Up button.
- **Vertical Navigation** – the normal and active pictures displayed as a default button, selected button, and hover button on a vertical button bar.

Don't worry if your mind doesn't readily associate each of the graphics elements in a theme with its description in the forgoing bulleted list. When you work with the theme's graphics on the Picture tab in the Modify Theme dialog box, FrontPage will label the graphics element and show you how it currently appears in the Sample of Theme display area on the dialog box.

To change the graphics used in a FrontPage theme, perform the following steps:

1. Select the Format menu theme option. FrontPage, in turn, will display the Themes dialog box.
2. Select the theme you want to modify by clicking your mouse pointer on the theme's title in the scroll box on the left-hand side of the dialog box. For example, if you like the color scheme and font styles of the Blends theme, but want to change one or more of its graphics elements, click your mouse pointer on **Blends** in the themes scroll box on the left-hand side of the Themes dialog box. FrontPage, in turn, will display samples of the theme's graphics, text, and colors in the Sample of Theme display area of the Themes dialog box.
3. Click your mouse pointer on the MODIFY button below the lower left-hand corner of the Sample of Theme display area in the Themes dialog box to expose the additional buttons that let you modify the theme's colors, graphics, and text (see the Sample of Theme display area in Figure 182.1).
4. Click your mouse pointer on the GRAPHICS button. FrontPage, in turn, will display the Picture tab on a Modify Theme dialog box similar to that shown in Figure 183.

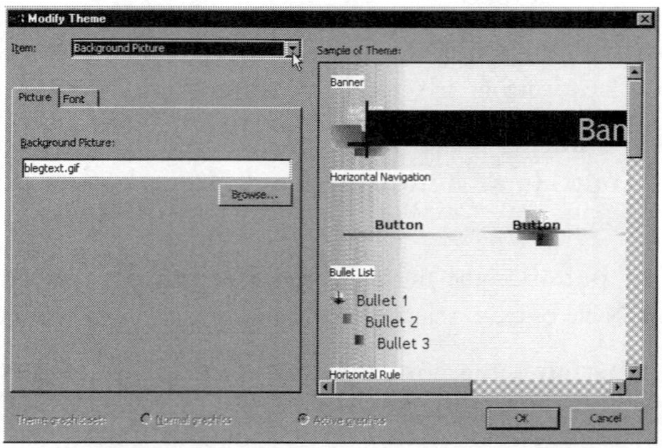

Figure 183 The Microsoft FrontPage Modify Theme dialog box, Picture tab.

5. Click your mouse pointer on the drop-down list button to the right of the Item field at the top of the dialog box, and select the theme graphics image you want to replace. For example, to replace the default graphics image used for a horizontal rule (i.e. a horizontal line), select **Horizontal Rule** from the drop-down list. FrontPage, in turn will display Horizontal Rule field on the Picture tab.

6. If you are substituting graphics images for theme graphics other than the Background Picture and the Global Navigation Buttons you must tell FrontPage whether you want to substitute the graphics image for either the graphic that is part of the theme's Normal graphics set or its Active graphics set. For consistency, if the graphic image you are planning to use is an animated GIF file, click your mouse pointer on the Active graphics radio button. Otherwise, click your mouse pointer on the Normal graphics button.
7. Enter the pathname of the graphics image you want to substitute for the theme graphic. Or, if you do not know its full pathname, click your mouse pointer on the BROWSE button to the right of the filename input file (the Horizontal Rule field for the current project). FrontPage, in turn, will display the Open File dialog box. Use the drop-down list button to the right of the Look in field and the folders below the field to navigate to the folder in which the graphics file you want is stored. When you see the filename of the graphics image you want to use in place of the theme graphic in the list box below the Look in field, click your mouse pointer on the filename, and then on the OPEN button near the lower right-hand corner of the Open File dialog box. FrontPage, in turn, will copy the graphic's filename to the filename input field (the Horizontal Rule field for the current project) on the Modify Theme dialog box Picture tab and display the graphics image in place of the original theme graphic in the Sample of Theme display area of the dialog box.

Note: *The names of the input field(s) and the number of fields displayed on the Picture tab depends on the theme graphic you selected in Step 5. For example, if you select Background Picture in Step 5, FrontPage will display the Background Picture field, so you can enter or navigate to the filename of the graphics image you want to use in place of the theme's background image (vs. the graphics image being used for horizontal rules). Similarly, if you select Horizontal Navigation in Step 5, FrontPage will display three input fields on the Pictures tab (Picture, Selected Picture, and Hover Picture), instead of a single field. In each case, enter the pathname of the graphics image you want to use in place of the original theme graphic, or use the BROWSE button to the right of the input field to navigate to the folder in which the graphics image is stored, and then click your mouse pointer on its filename to have FrontPage copy the file's name to the corresponding input field.*

8. If you want to change other theme graphics, repeat Steps 5 - 7. Otherwise, click your mouse pointer on the OK button near the lower right-hand corner of the Modify Theme dialog box to return to the Themes dialog box.

9. Click your mouse pointer on the SAVE AS button near the lower right-hand corner of the Themes dialog box. FrontPage, in turn, will display a Save Theme dialog box similar to the one you saw in Figure 182.5.
10. Into the Enter new theme title field, enter a descriptive name you can use to identify and select the theme later. If you modified the Blended theme, for example, enter a title such as **Blended – Custom** into the Enter new theme title field as the title of the custom theme you created.
11. Click your mouse pointer on the OK button near the center at the bottom of the Save Theme dialog box.

After you complete Step 11, FrontPage will save your custom theme to disk and add its title to the list of themes available for selection in the scroll box on the left-hand side of the Themes dialog box. To exit the Themes dialog box and return to the FrontPage application window, click your mouse pointer on the close button (the "X") in the upper right-hand corner of the dialog box.

The following Tip will show you how to customize a theme's text fonts.

MODIFYING THE APPEARANCE OF A THEME'S TEXT ELEMENTS

Like other Web page text, you can change the font, character size, and shading of text elements defined in a theme. Moreover, you can change the spacing around paragraphs and even draw borders around the theme's text. In short, any format changes you can make to Web page text, you can apply to text elements in a theme.

A theme's text elements include not only Body and Heading (1 - 6) text, but also the text on the theme's banner and buttons. To work with the Body and Heading (1 – 6) text elements, click your mouse pointer on the Text button in the Themes dialog box. Or, to work with the appearance of text on the theme's graphics elements (i.e., the appearance of text on the theme's banner and buttons), click your mouse pointer on the Graphics button.

To change the look of the text elements in a FrontPage theme, perform the following steps:

1. Select the Format menu theme option. FrontPage, in turn, will display the Themes dialog box.
2. Select the theme you want to modify by clicking your mouse pointer on the theme's title in the scroll box on the left-hand side of the dialog box. For example, if you want to work with the appearance of the text elements in the Barcode theme, click your mouse pointer on **Barcode** in the themes scroll box on the left-hand side of the Themes dialog

box. FrontPage, in turn, will display samples of the theme's graphics, text, and colors in the Sample of Theme display area of the Themes dialog box.

3. Click your mouse pointer on the MODIFY button below the lower left-hand corner of the Sample of Theme display area in the Themes dialog box to expose the additional buttons the that let you modify the theme's colors, graphics, and text (see the Sample of Theme display area in Figure 182.1).
4. If you want to change the appearance of the text on a theme's graphics images such as its:

- Banner (Normal graphics or Active graphics)
- Global Navigation Buttons
- Horizontal or Vertical Navigation Buttons (Normal graphics or Active graphics)
- Quick Back, Home, Next, or Up Buttons (Normal graphics or Active graphics)

click your mouse pointer on the GRAPHICS button near the bottom center of the Themes dialog box and continue with Step 5. If you want to change the appearance of the theme's text font skip steps 5 – 15 and continue at Step 16.

5. On the Modify Theme dialog box, click your mouse pointer on the Font tab.
6. Click your mouse pointer on the drop-down list button to the right of the Item field and select the graphic image whose text element you want to change. For example, to change the appearance of text on the theme's Banner, click your mouse pointer on the drop-down list button to the right of the Item field and select **Banner** from the drop-down list. FrontPage, in turn, will display the text font, style, size and alignment fields shown on the Font tab shown on the left-hand side of the Modify Theme dialog box in Figure 184.1.

Note: *If for a selected theme graphic the fields on the Font tab are grayed out, the theme graphic has no text whose appearance you can change. For example, the Background Picture, Bullet List (bullets), and Horizontal Rule theme graphics for the Barcode theme have no text for you to modify.*

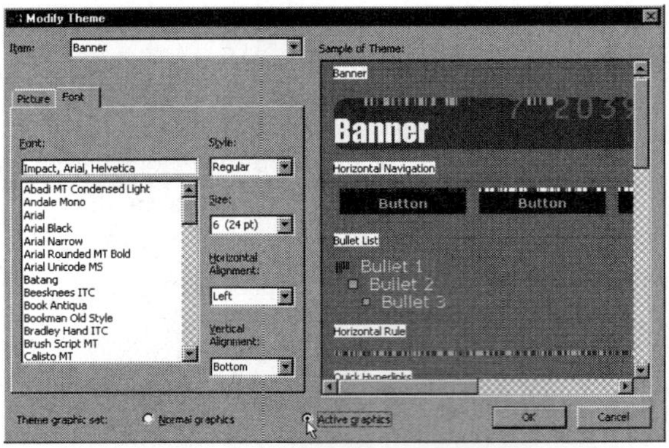

***Figure 184.1** The Microsoft FrontPage Modify Theme dialog box, Font tab.*

7. To modify the appearance of the text on the theme's Active graphics image, click your mouse pointer on the Active graphics radio button near the center at the bottom of the Modify Theme dialog box. If you have already modified the appearance of the text on the active graphics image, click your mouse pointer on the Normal graphics radio button to work with the look of the text on the Normal graphics image. [The Normal graphics and Active graphics radio buttons are grayed out (as not applicable) for the text on Global Navigation Buttons, so skip this Step if you selected Global Navigation Buttons in Step 6.]
8. Into the Font field, enter the names of the font(s) you want to use for text on the theme graphic you selected in Step 4. When you click your mouse pointer on the name of a font in the list box below the Font field, FrontPage copies the font's name into the Font field and applies the font to the text on the theme graphic, so you can see what the font looks like, in the Sample of Theme display area on the right-hand side of the dialog box. To get multiple fonts into the Font field, you must type the names of the fonts, separated by commas, instead of clicking your mouse pointer on the name of each font.

Note: *If you choose an unusual or custom font not installed on the visitor's computer, the Web browser will use its default font to display the text instead of the font you selected. By entering multiple fonts into the* Font *field, you increase your chances of selecting a font available on the visitor's computer. The Web browser will check to see if the system on which it is running has the first font listed in the* Font *field, and display the text using that font if it is available. If not, the browser will check for the second font, and then the third, and so on. If none of the fonts entered into the* Font *field are installed on the visitor's system, the Web browser uses its default font to display the text element.*

9. Click your mouse pointer on the drop-down list button to the right of the Style field and select Regular, Italic, Bold, or Bold Italic for the font's style from the drop-down list.
10. Click your mouse pointer on the drop-down list button to the right of the Size field to select the text's character size (from 8 – 36 pts).
11. Click your mouse pointer on the drop-down list button to the right of the Horizontal Alignment field and select Left, Right, or Center as the horizontal position of the text on the theme's graphics element.
12. Click your mouse pointer on the drop-down list button to the right of the Vertical Alignment field and select Top, Middle, or Bottom as the vertical position of the text on the theme's graphics element.
13. If you clicked your mouse pointer on the Active graphics radio button in Step 7 and now want to work with text on the graphic element (you selected in Step 4) in the theme's Normal graphics set (or vice versa), continue at Step 7.
14. If you want to change the appearance of the text on another graphics element, continue at Step 6.
15. Click your mouse pointer on the OK button near the lower right-hand corner of the Modify Theme dialog box. FrontPage, in turn, will return to the Themes dialog box.
16. If you want to change the appearance of Body or Heading (1 – 6) text, click your mouse pointer on the TEXT button just right of center near the bottom of the Themes dialog box. Otherwise, continue at Step 20.
17. Click your mouse pointer on the drop-down list button to the right of the Item field at the top of the Modify Theme dialog box, similar to that shown in Figure 184.2, and select the text element whose appearance you want to change from the drop-down list.

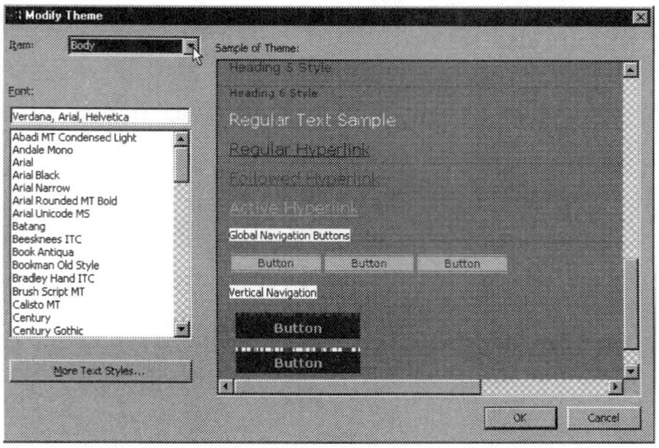

Figure 184.2 The Microsoft FrontPage Modify Theme (Text) dialog box.

18. Into the Font field, enter the character font(s) you want applied to the text element you selected in Step 17. When you click your mouse pointer on the name of a font in the list box below the Font field, FrontPage copies the font's name into the Font field and applies the font to the text displayed in the Sample of Theme display area to the right of the Font field. To get multiple fonts into the Font field, you must type the names of the fonts, separated by commas, instead of clicking your mouse pointer on the name of each font.
19. If you want to change the appearance of additional text elements, continue at Step 17.
20. Click your mouse pointer on the SAVE AS button near the lower right-hand corner of the Themes dialog box. FrontPage, in turn, will display a Save Theme dialog box similar to the one you saw in Figure 182.5.
21. Into the Enter new theme title field enter a descriptive name you can use to identify and select the theme later. If you modified the Barcode theme, for example, enter a title such as **Barcode – Custom** into the Enter new theme title field as the title of the custom theme you created.
22. Click your mouse pointer on the OK button near the center at the bottom of the Save Theme dialog box.

After you complete Step 22, FrontPage will save your custom theme to disk and add its title to the list of themes available for selection in the scroll box on the left-hand side of the Themes dialog box. To exit the Themes dialog box and return to the FrontPage application window, click your mouse pointer on the close button (the "X") in the upper right-hand corner of the dialog box.

USING THEME GRAPHICS FROM ONE THEME IN ANOTHER THEME

If you've read how to modify a theme's color scheme in the Tip entitled "Modifying the Colors of a FrontPage Theme," you saw how easy it is create a custom theme by applying the colors scheme from one theme to the elements of another theme. All you have to do is:

1. Select the Format menu Theme option.
2. Select the theme you want to modify by clicking your mouse pointer on the theme's title in the scroll box on the left-hand side of the dialog box.
3. Click your mouse pointer on the MODIFY button below the lower left-hand corner of the Sample of Theme display area in the Themes dialog box to expose the buttons you need to modify the theme.

4. Click your mouse pointer on the COLORS button to display the Modify Theme dialog box.
5. Click your mouse pointer on the title of the theme whose colors you wanted to apply to the theme you selected in Step 2.
6. Click your mouse pointer on the OK button near the lower right-hand corner of the Modify Theme dialog box to return to the Themes dialog box.
7. Click your mouse pointer on the SAVE AS button near the lower right-hand corner of the Themes dialog box to display the Save Theme dialog box.
8. Into the Enter new theme title field enter a descriptive name you can use to identify and select the theme later.
9. Click your mouse pointer on the OK button near the center at the bottom of the Save Theme dialog box.

Unfortunately, FrontPage does not make it quite so easy to copy graphics elements from one FrontPage theme into another. In fact, as described in a previous Tip entitled "Modifying FrontPage Theme Graphics," you must create or retrieve the graphics image you want to use in the theme outside the theme modification procedure. Moreover, FrontPage only lets you browse folders on disk and not other themes for the graphics you want to substitute for graphics elements in a theme. Fortunately, you can find the files for the graphics elements in the current theme in a subfolder of the C:\WINDOWS\TEMP\FRONTPAGETEMPDIR\MSTHEME folder.

To use graphics elements from one theme in another theme, perform the following steps:

1. If you currently have a FrontPage web open in the FrontPage application window, select the File menu Close Web option to close the web. (Be sure to save any changes you want to keep if prompted to do so.)
2. Create a single, blank Web page by clicking your mouse pointer on the Create a new normal page button (first button on the left with the blank page icon) on the Standard toolbar.
3. Select the Format menu Theme option. FrontPage, in turn, will display the Themes dialog box.
4. Select the theme whose graphics element(s) you want to use in another theme. For example, if you want to substitute the Nature theme's Horizontal Navigation buttons for the Horizontal Navigation buttons in the Expedition theme, click your mouse pointer on **Nature** in the themes scroll box on the left-hand side of the Themes dialog box.

5. Click your mouse pointer on the OK button near the bottom right-hand corner of the Themes dialog box. FrontPage, in turn, will apply the theme you selected in Step 4 to the blank Web page you created in Step 2, and copy the theme's graphics files into a subfolder in the C:\WINDOWS\TEMP\FRONTPAGETEMPDIR\MSTHEME folder.
6. Select the Format menu Theme option. FrontPage, in turn, will display the current theme (the Nature theme in the current example) in the Themes dialog box.
7. Click your mouse pointer on the MODIFY button below the lower left-hand corner of the Sample of Theme display area in the Themes dialog box to expose the additional buttons that let you modify the theme's colors, graphics, and text.
8. Click your mouse pointer on the GRAPHICS button. FrontPage, in turn, will display the Picture tab on a Modify Theme dialog box.
9. Click your mouse pointer on the drop-down list button to the right of the Item field at the top of the dialog box, and select the theme graphics image you want to use in the other theme. For the current example, select **Horizontal Navigation**.
10. Write down the names of the input fields and the filename of the graphics file in each of the fields on the Picture tab. Then, if not grayed out, click your mouse pointer on the Normal graphics radio button at bottom of the Modify Theme dialog box and write down the additional input field names and their graphics file name contents.
11. Click your mouse pointer on the CANCEL button at the lower right-hand corner of the Modify Theme dialog box.
12. Select the theme whose graphics element(s) you want to modify. For the current example, click your mouse pointer on **Expedition** in the themes scroll box on the left-hand side of the Themes dialog box.
13. Click your mouse pointer on the GRAPHICS button. FrontPage, in turn, will display the Picture tab on a Modify Theme dialog box.
14. Click your mouse pointer on the drop-down list button to the right of the Item field at the top of the dialog box, and select the theme graphics image you want to replace. For the current example, in which you are replacing the Horizontal Navigation buttons in the Expedition theme with those from the Nature theme, select **Horizontal Navigation** from the drop-down list. FrontPage, in turn will display the Picture, Selected Picture, and Hovered Picture fields on the Picture tab.
15. Click your mouse pointer on the BROWSE button to the right of the first field. FrontPage, in turn, will display the Open File dialog box.

16. Into the File name field at the bottom of the Open File dialog box enter **C:\Windows\Temp\FrontPageTempDir\MSTheme**. Then, click your mouse pointer on the OPEN button near the lower right-hand corner of the dialog box.
17. In the scroll box below the Look in field, double-click your mouse pointer on the folder in which FrontPage stored the graphics files for the current theme (i.e. the theme you most recently applied to a FrontPage web or to a Web page in the web). For the current example, double-click your mouse pointer on the **nature** folder.

Note: *When looking for the name of the folder, look for a form of the theme's title. For example, the* ***Nature*** *theme uses the "nature" folder; the* ***Expedition*** *theme uses the "expeditn" folder; and the* ***Geared Up Factory*** *theme stores its graphics in the "factory" folder.*

18. Double-click your mouse pointer on the filename of the graphics image from the theme whose graphic you want to use. In the current example, double-click your mouse pointer on **nahbs.gif**—the filename of the graphics image in the first field on the Pictures tab of the Modify Theme dialog box for the Nature theme.
19. Click your mouse pointer on the BROWSE button to the right of each of the remaining fields on the Pictures tab, and repeat Step 18 for each field. Each time you repeat Step 18, double-click the mouse pointer on the filename of the graphics file you wrote down in Step 10 that corresponds with the field whose BROWSE button clicked. Then, if not grayed out, click your mouse pointer on the Normal graphics radio button, and continue the process for the each of the additional fields displayed on the Picture tab.
20. Click your mouse pointer on the OK button near the lower right-hand corner of the Modify Theme dialog box. FrontPage, in turn, will return to the Themes dialog box.
21. Click your mouse pointer on the SAVE AS button near the lower right-hand corner of the Themes dialog box. FrontPage, in turn, will display the Save Theme dialog box.
22. Into the Enter new theme title field enter a descriptive name you can use to identify and select the theme later. If you modified the Expedition theme, for example, enter a title such as: **Expedition – Custom** into the Enter new theme title field as the title of the custom theme you created.
23. Click your mouse pointer on the OK button near the center at the bottom of the Save Theme dialog box.

After you complete Step 23, FrontPage will save your custom theme to disk and add its title to the list of themes available for selection in the scroll box on the left-hand side of the Themes dialog box. To exit the Themes dialog box and return to the FrontPage application window, click your mouse pointer on the close button (the "X") in the upper right-hand corner of the dialog box.

DISTRIBUTING FRONTPAGE THEMES TO OTHER COMPUTERS

If you installed your Microsoft Office programs to the default folders, you will find the standard themes that come with the FrontPage in subfolders at:

```
C:\Program Files\Common Files\Microsoft Shared\Themes
```

Each standard theme's subfolder normally has a name similar to the theme's title. For example, files for the Artsy theme are in the Artsy subfolder; files for the Expedition theme are in the Expeditn subfolder; and files for the Loose Gesture theme are in the loosegst subfolder.

When you create a new, custom theme, FrontPage uses the theme's title, (with spaces, if any, converted to dashes) to create a subfolder in which to store the theme's files at:

```
C:\Windows\Application Data\Microsoft\Themes
```

For example, FrontPage will store files for a custom theme titled zcustom in the zcustom subfolder; files for a custom theme called Barcode – Custom in the subfolder barcode-custom, and files for a custom theme title Copy of Loose Gesture in the subfolder copy-of-loose-gesture.

After you start the FrontPage application and select the Format menu Theme option for the first time during the current session, FrontPage goes through the subfolders in both the standard themes folder and the custom themes folder to build a single list of theme titles. FrontPage then displays the list of available themes, in alphabetical order by title, in the scroll box on the left-hand side of the Themes dialog box.

If you install or create a theme on one computer that is not (yet) available on another, you can make the theme available on the second system by copying the theme's subfolder (and its contents) to the appropriate folder on the other computer. For example, if you have the standard Artsy theme on your computer while the other computer does not, then save the Artsy subfolder (and its contents) to an intermediate location such as a floppy disk, shared folder on network drive, or an FTP site. Then, working at the target computer, copy the Artsy folder (and its contents) into the standard themes folder at **C:\Program Files\Common Files\Microsoft Shared\Themes**. Similarly, if you create a custom theme on your computer and want to make it available in the FrontPage application running on another computer, then copy the custom theme's subfolder (and its contents) from your machine to the custom themes folder at **C:\Windows\Application Data\Microsoft\Themes** on the other computer.

Instead of copying a theme's subfolder and its contents from one computer to another, you can make a new theme available on another system by transferring the theme as part of a FrontPage web. When you apply a theme to a web, FrontPage copies all of the theme's files into the web itself. If you open the web on a computer that does not have the web's theme installed, FrontPage will prompt you with a Download Theme message box similar to that shown in Figure 186 when you select the Format menu Theme option.

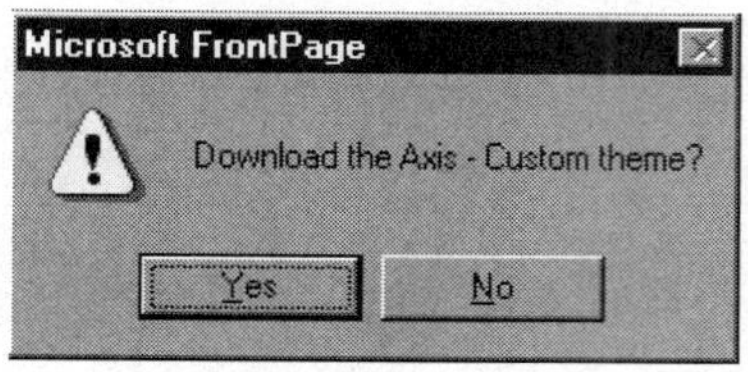

***Figure 186** The Microsoft FrontPage Download Theme message box.*

Click your mouse pointer on the YES button at the bottom of the message box. FrontPage, in turn, will create a subfolder in either the standard themes folder or in the custom themes folder (depending on whether the current web's theme is a standard FrontPage theme or a custom theme created from a standard theme), and copy the theme's files from the FrontPage web into the subfolder it creates. Thereafter, FrontPage will list the theme's title (in alphabetical order) in the scroll box on the left-hand side of the Themes dialog box along with the other themes available on the system.

SELECTING THE WEB PAGE BACKGROUND COLOR

Most themes you apply to a FrontPage web include a background image. While the theme's background image is a clipart graphics file, it is often called a "textured background" because the image is more like patterned wallpaper than a recognizable picture such as those in a photo album or comic strip. Although applying a theme is an easy way to add a background image (or texture) to a Web page, you do not need to apply a theme to create Web pages with something other than the default, white (or grey) background.

In the previous Tip entitled "Using a Background Image on a Web Page," you learned how use a graphics image as the background for a Web page. If you want to use a solid color instead of a background image as the Web page background, perform the following steps:

1. Open the Web page whose background you want to adjust on the Page view Normal tab.

2. Right-click your mouse pointer anywhere on the Web page and select Page Properties from the pop-up menu. (Or, select the File menu Properties option.) FrontPage, in turn, will display the Page Properties dialog box.
3. Click your mouse pointer on the Background tab to expose the fields used to specify the background settings for the current Web page, similar to those shown in Figure 187.1.

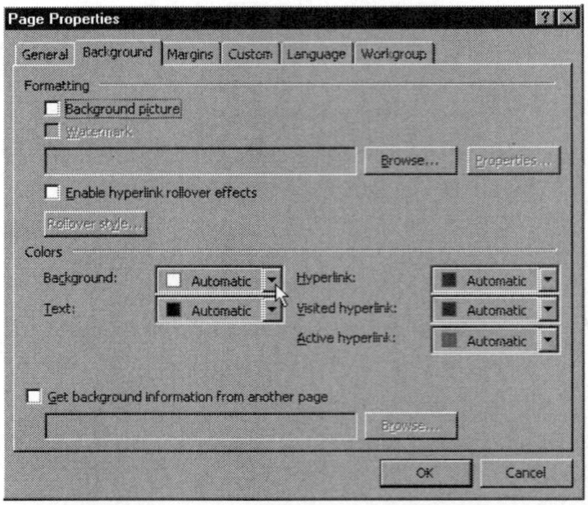

Figure 187.1 *The Microsoft FrontPage Page Properties dialog box, Background tab.*

Note: *If your Page Properties dialog box does not have a Background tab, you are working with a Web page to which a theme has been applied. FrontPage will not let you change the background color of a Web page formatted with a theme. To remove the theme, click your mouse pointer on the* CANCEL *button in the lower right-hand corner of the Page Properties dialog box. Next, select the Format menu Theme option to display the Themes dialog box. Select* **(No Theme)** *and click the mouse pointer on the OK button near the lower right-hand corner of the Themes dialog box to remove the theme from the current Web page. Then, continue at Step 2.*

4. Click your mouse pointer on the drop-down list button to the right of the Background field at the top of the Color section in the bottom half of the dialog box. FrontPage, in turn, will display a drop-down pallet with sixteen "browser safe" color swatches, swatches for colors you previously created and added to the Custom Colors list, and a More Colors option you can use to select or create additional colors not available for selection on the drop-down pallet.

***Note:** The sixteen colors displayed at the top of the drop-down pallet are "browser safe" because older browsers and all computer systems with standard color graphics cards can display them. If you create a color the visitor's browser, or display card, cannot render on the screen, the background will appear grainy as the system tries to translate the color you used into a color it can display through a process called dithering. Although, most desktop computers sold nowadays are able to display "millions of colors," there are still many laptops in use that can only display 256 colors at screen resolutions above 640x480. So, to be absolutely safe, use only one of the 16 "browser safe" colors. However, if you really have the need to use a custom color to make your Web pages "feel" just right, bear in mind that Web page background color may not look the same to all of your site's visitors.*

5. To select one of the 16 "browser safe" colors, click your mouse pointer on its color swatch and continue at Step 11. Otherwise, to select from the additional standard colors, or to mix your own custom color, select the More Colors option at the bottom of the drop-down pallet. FrontPage, in turn, will display a More Colors dialog box similar to that shown in Figure 187.2.

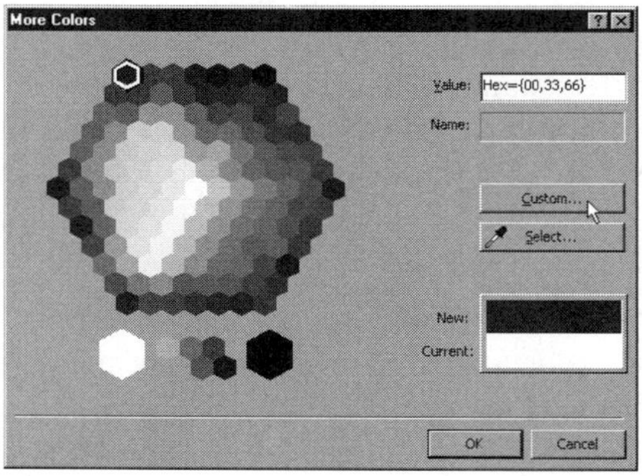

***Figure 187.2** The Microsoft FrontPage More Colors dialog box.*

6. To set the Web page background to one of the colors in the hexagon of colors on the left-hand side of the More Colors dialog box, click your mouse pointer on the color you want. FrontPage, in turn, will display the color you select in the New (color) field (above the Current color field) near the lower right-hand corner of the dialog box. If the color is what you want continue at Step 10, otherwise select another color until you find the right color. If none of the colors are right, you will want to mix your own custom color. To create your own custom color,

click your mouse pointer on the CUSTOM button near the middle at the right-hand side of the dialog box. FrontPage, in turn, will display a Color dialog box similar to that shown in Figure 187.3.

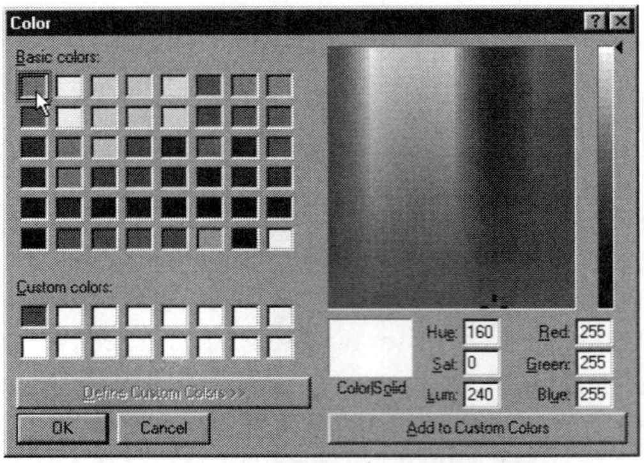

Figure 187.3 The Microsoft FrontPage (Custom) Color dialog box.

7. Click your mouse pointer on one of the Basic colors squares on the left-hand side of the dialog box or on the color you want in the rainbow of colors rectangle on the right-hand side of the dialog box. FrontPage, in turn, will display the color you selected in the Color|Solid rectangle below the rainbow of colors and show the color's RGB (Red, Green, Blue) and HSL (Hue, Saturation, and Luminosity) values in the fields at the lower right-hand corner of the dialog box.
8. If you want to adjust the color you selected in Step 7, either repeat Step 7 and click your mouse pointer on another point in the rainbow of colors rectangle, or change the values in the Hue, Sat, Lum, Red, Green, and Blue fields. FrontPage, in turn, will display the new color you select or define (with HSL or RGB values) in the Color Solid rectangle to the left of the color's HSL values.
9. To use the color you selected or mixed, click your mouse pointer on the OK button in the lower left-hand corner of the dialog box. Or, if you want to both select the color and make it available as a Custom Color swatch on the drop-down, click your mouse pointer on the ADD TO CUSTOM COLORS button in the right-hand corner of the dialog box. FrontPage, in turn, will return to the More Colors dialog box.
10. Click your mouse pointer on the OK button near the lower right-hand corner of the More Colors dialog box. FrontPage, in turn, will copy the color you selected or created from the New color field of the More Colors dialog box to the Background field in the Colors section of the Background tab, and return to the Page Properties dialog box.

11. Click your mouse pointer on the OK button near the lower right hand corner of the Page Properties dialog box.

After you complete Step 11, FrontPage will use the color you selected (or the custom color you created) as the solid color background of the current Web page. The next Tip will show you how to apply the same background to other Web pages without having to go through the custom color selection/creation process.

CREATING A COLOR MASTER TO ALLOW ONE WEB PAGE TO INHERIT THE COLORS AND BACKGROUND IMAGE FROM ANOTHER PAGE

FrontPage lets you change the appearance of one, some, or all of a Web site's pages by making a change to the background settings of a single page—the color master. Unlike a theme that sets a site's color scheme, text fonts, and graphics elements (including a background image), a color master controls only the Web page:

- Background Picture
- Background Color
- Text Color
- Unvisited Hyperlink Color
- Visited hyperlink color
- Active Hyperlink Color

Although you can use any one of the site's Web pages as a color master, for maximum flexibility, create a separate Web page used only as the color master instead. Remember, any changes you make to the color master's background color or picture or to its text or hyperlink colors will change the look of other Web pages, as well. Therefore, using one of the site's Web pages to serve as its color master prevents you from making changes to the color scheme and background image of that page alone—without changing the look of other pages on the Web site.

To create a color master, perform the following steps:

1. Click your mouse pointer on the Page button at the top of the Views Bar along the left-hand side of the FrontPage application window to go to Page view. (Or, select the View menu page option.)
2. Click your mouse pointer on the Create a new normal page button (first button on the left, with a blank page icon) on the Standard toolbar. FrontPage, in turn, will create a blank Web page and display it on the Page view Normal tab.

3. Right-click your mouse pointer anywhere on the blank Web page, and select Page properties from the pop-up menu. (Or, select the File menu Properties option.) FrontPage, in turn, will display the Page Properties dialog box.
4. Click your mouse pointer on the Background tab to expose the fields used to specify the Web page background image and color and its text and hyperlink colors, similar to that shown Figure 188.

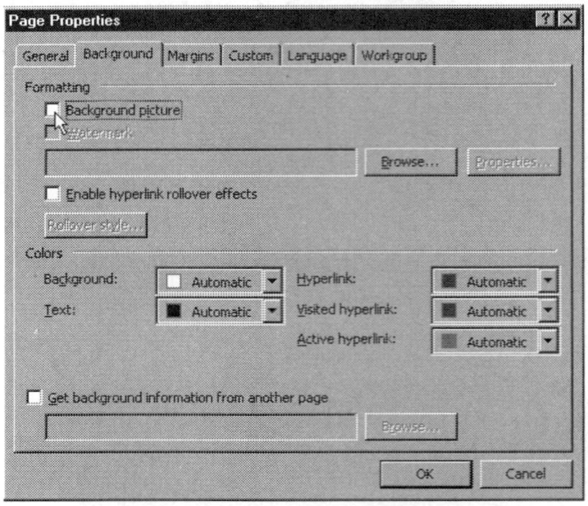

Figure 188 *The Microsoft FrontPage Page Properties dialog box, Background tab.*

5. If you want to use a picture or other graphics image (such as clip art drawing or textured background), click your mouse pointer on the Background picture checkbox until a checkmark appears. Otherwise, continue at Step 8.
6. If you want the background image to remain stationary as you scroll down (or up) through the content on a multiple screen Web page, click your mouse pointer on the Watermark checkbox until a checkmark appears. Conversely, if you want the background image to scroll along with the text and images on the Web page, clear the Watermark checkbox.
7. Into the field below the Watermark checkbox, enter the relative address of the image file you want to use as the Web page background. Or, click your mouse pointer on the BROWSE button to the right of the field to navigate to the folder in which the image file is stored using Select Background Picture dialog box. Then, double-click your mouse pointer on the picture's filename in the list box below the Look in field at the top of the dialog box.

8. To set the Web page background color, click your mouse pointer on the drop-down list button to the right of the Background field. Then, click the mouse pointer on one of the color swatches on the drop-down pallet displayed, or use the More Colors option at the bottom of the pallet to create and select a custom color.

Note: *If you elected to use a background image on the Web page, you will only see the background color if the background image you select is a transparent GIF. (To learn how to create a transparent GIF read the Tip entitled: "Creating a Transparent GIF".)*

9. To select the body (i.e., non-hyperlink) text color, click your mouse pointer on the drop-down list button to the right of the Text field. Then, click the mouse pointer on one of the color swatches on the drop-down pallet displayed, or use the More Colors option at the bottom of the pallet to create and select a custom color.
10. To select a color for the unvisited hyperlink anchor text, click your mouse pointer on the drop-down list button to the right of the Hyperlink field. Then, click your mouse pointer on one of the color swatches on the drop-down pallet displayed, or use the More Colors option at the bottom of the pallet to create and select a custom color.
11. To set the color of the visited hyperlink anchor text, click your mouse pointer on the drop-down list button to the right of the Visited hyperlink field. Then, click your mouse pointer on one of the color swatches on the drop-down pallet displayed, or use the More Colors option at the bottom of the pallet to create and select a custom color.
12. To select a color for the active hyperlink's anchor text, click your mouse pointer on the drop-down list button to the right of the Active hyperlink field. Then, click your mouse pointer on one of the color swatches on the drop-down pallet displayed, or use the More Colors option at the bottom of the pallet to create and select a custom color.
13. Click your mouse pointer on the OK button near the lower right-hand corner of the Page Properties dialog box.
14. Select the File menu Save As option. FrontPage, in turn, will display the Save As dialog box.
15. Use the drop-down list button to the right Save in field and the folders below the field to navigate to the folder you are using to store the current FrontPage web's HTML documents.
16. Click your mouse pointer on the CHANGE TITLE button right of center near the bottom of the dialog box. After you enter a descriptive title

(such as **Web Color Master**) into the Page title field on the Set Page Title dialog box, click your mouse pointer on the OK button near the bottom center of the dialog box.

17. Into the File name field near the bottom of the Save As dialog box, enter a descriptive filename (such as **ColorMaster**) for the color master Web page.
18. Click your mouse pointer on the SAVE button near the lower right-hand corner of the Save As dialog box.

After you save the color master to disk in Step 18, you can use it to insert a background image and set the background, body text and hyperlink colors of another Web page by performing the following steps:

1. Open the Web page that is to inherit its background, body text, and hyperlink color setting settings from the color master, and select the View menu Page option to display the page on the Page view Normal tab.
2. Right-click your mouse pointer anywhere on the Web page, and select Page properties from the pop-up menu. (Or, select the File menu Properties option.) FrontPage, in turn, will display the Page Properties dialog box.
3. Click your mouse pointer on the Background tab to expose the fields used to specify the Web page background settings.
4. Click your mouse pointer on the Get background information from another page checkbox near the bottom of the dialog box Background tab.
5. Into the field below the Get background information from another page checkbox, enter the relative address of color master Web page. Or, click your mouse pointer on the BROWSE button to the right of the field to use the Current Web dialog box to navigate to the folder in which you saved the color master Web page. Then, double-click your mouse pointer on the color master's filename in the scroll box below the Look in field at the top of the Current Web dialog box.
6. Click your mouse pointer on the SAVE button near the lower right-hand corner of the Save As dialog box.

After executing the preceding procedure on multiple Web pages, any changes you make to the background images or colors on the Background tab of the Page Properties dialog box for the color master Web page will automatically change the appearance of each Web page that gets its background information from the color master.

USING THE FONT DIALOG BOX TO CHANGE THE LOOK OF SELECTED TEXT

While themes and color masters let you change the font, style, size, color, and spacing of all of the hyperlinks and body text on the Web page at once, you sometimes only want to change the appearance of a specific word or group of words on a page. The Format menu Font option lets you change the way words and phrases look, so you can emphasize certain items on a Web page.

To change the appearance of one or more words on a Web page, perform the following steps:

1. Display the Web page with the text whose appearance you want to change on the Page view Normal tab.
2. Click and hold down the left mouse button as you drag the mouse pointer over the text whose font, color, or spacing you want to change. Then release the left mouse button.
3. Right-click the mouse pointer anywhere on the selected text, and then select Font from the pop-up menu. FrontPage, in turn, will display a Font Dialog box, similar to that shown in Figure 189.1.

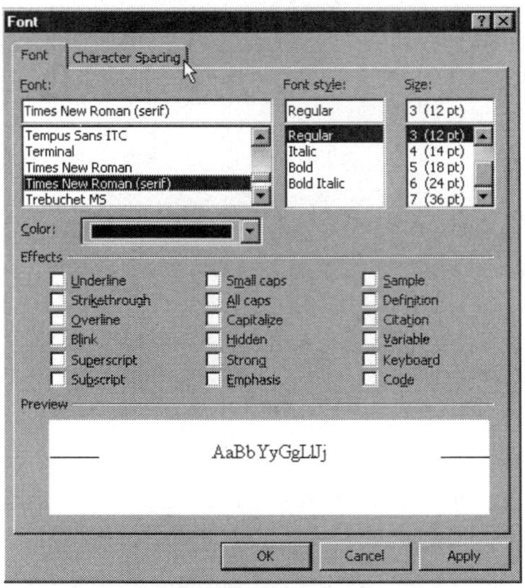

Figure 189.1 The Microsoft FrontPage Page Font dialog box, Font tab.

4. Use the Font, Font style, and Size scroll fields across the top of the Font tab to select the text's character font, style, and size. As you make your selections, FrontPage will use the Preview area at the bottom of the Font tab to show you what the text will look like based on the selections you make.

5. To change the color of the text you selected in Step 2, click your mouse pointer on the drop-down list button to the right of the Color field. Then, click the mouse pointer on one of the color swatches on the drop-down pallet displayed, or select the More Colors option at the bottom of the pallet to create and select a custom color.
6. To apply one or more of the text effects listed in the Effects area near the middle of the Font tab, click your mouse pointer on the checkbox to the left of each effect you want to apply until a checkmark appears. Conversely, to remove an effect, click your mouse pointer on the checkmark in the effect's checkbox to clear it.
7. Click your mouse pointer on the Character Spacing tab. FrontPage, in turn, will expose the fields used to adjust the amount of blank space between each character in the selected text, similar to those shown in Figure 189.2.

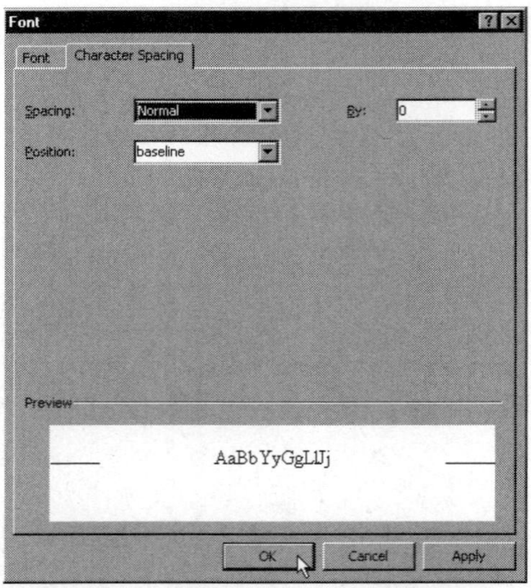

Figure 189.2 The Microsoft FrontPage Page Font dialog box, Character Spacing tab.

8. Use the drop-down list button to the right of the Spacing field to select **Normal**, **Expanded**, or **Condensed** spacing. Select **Normal** spacing if you do not want to change the character spacing of the selected text. To have the browser display the characters in the text further apart, select **Expanded** spacing. Conversely, to have the Web browser display the characters closer together, select **Condensed**.
9. If you select either **Expanded** or **Condensed** spacing in Step 9, into the By field, enter the change in the number of points of blank space between the letters in the selected text. For example, if you select

Expanded in Step 9 and enter a positive number into the By field, the Web browser will display the characters in the text further apart; enter a negative number into the field and the browser will display the text's characters closer together. Conversely, if you select **Condensed** in Step 9, a positive value in the By field tells the Web browser to display the letters closer together, while a negative value tells the browser to spread them out.

10. If you want the Web browser to change the position of the text as compared with the rest of the text on the same line, click your mouse pointer on the drop-down list button to the right of the Position field, and select one of the alignment options from the drop-down list.
11. Click your mouse pointer on the OK button near the lower right-hand corner of the Font dialog box. FrontPage, in turn, will apply the text format changes you specified to the text you selected in Step 2, and return to the Page view Normal tab.

The best rule of thumb when considering changes to the way text looks on a page is to use font, style, size, special effect and spacing changes sparingly. After all, if you bold all of the words on a Web page, none of them stands out.

Think twice before changing the color of hyperlinks or applying the underline effect to non-hyperlink text. If you change the hyperlink anchor text's color to something other than Automatic, the anchor text will remain the new color—even after the visitor has activated the hyperlink and expects the (now visited) hyperlink's color to change from its original color to the visited hyperlink color. Moreover, since hyperlinks on a Web page are underlined by default, if you apply the underline effect to text on a Web page with hyperlinks, the site visitor may have a hard time distinguishing between hyperlinks and underlined text.

PLACING A BULLETED LIST ON A WEB PAGE

To a Web browser, a bulleted list is a collection of paragraphs it must display with leading bullets. A *bullet* can be either a graphics image or a symbol (such as a solid or open circle, square, or diamond, a checkmark, or an arrow, to name a few). Use a bulleted list when you want to make each item in the list stand out from other text on the Web page and the order in which the items appear is unimportant.

To create a bulleted list, perform the following steps:

1. With the Web page displayed on the Page view Normal tab, type or paste the items in the bulleted list onto the page. Put each bullet (i.e. each item) in the list in a separate paragraph by pressing the ENTER key after the rightmost (last) letter in the bullet.

2. Click and hold down the left mouse button as you drag the mouse pointer over the bullets (items) in the list to select them. Then, release the left mouse button.
3. Click your mouse pointer on the Bullets button (sixth button from the right, with the three lines preceded by square bullets icon) on the Formatting toolbar. (If you do not see the Formatting toolbar, select the View menu Toolbars option and click your mouse pointer on Formatting to display the Formatting toolbar.) FrontPage, in turn, will turn the text you selected in Step 2 into a bulleted list using default bullet symbols or small graphics images (if you previously applied a theme to the Web page or the FrontPage web).

To add additional items to a bulleted list, click the mouse pointer to the right of the last letter in one of the bulleted items, press the ENTER key, and type the new item. (When you press the ENTER key, FrontPage moves the cursor to a new line starting with a bullet symbol (or graphic) on the Page view Normal tab by inserting <LI></LI> (line item) tags onto the Page view HTML tab.)

USING PICTURES IN PLACE OF BULLETS ON A BULLETED LIST

After you select and format Web page text into a bulleted list (which you learned how to do in the preceding Tip), you can change the bullet symbol to the left a single item on the bulleted list or the bullet symbols to the left of all items in the list at once.

To change the bullet symbol for a single item in a bulleted list, perform the following steps:

1. Right-click your mouse pointer on a point on the bullet list item whose bullet symbol you want to change, and select List Item Properties from the pop-up menu. FrontPage, in turn, will display the List Item Properties dialog box with only the Plain Bullets tab.
2. Click your mouse pointer on the rectangle with the plain bullet style you want to use, and then on the OK button near the lower right-hand corner of the dialog box.

Note: *For now, just ignore the STYLE button near the lower right-hand corner of the dialog box. Later in this book, you will learn how to create cascading style sheets (CSS) with character styles that let you select a bullet symbol other than one of the three plain bullet symbols by applying a user-defined style specification to the bullet text.*

If you change the bullet symbol of a single item in a bulleted list, FrontPage will no longer change that bullet symbol along with the others if, at some future point, you decide to change all the bullet symbols in the list at once. To get the bullet symbol to change when you tell FrontPage to change all bullet symbols in the list, repeat the preceding procedure and select the same bullet symbol used for the remaining items in the bulleted list in Step 2.

To change the bullet symbol, for all items in a bulleted list at once, perform the following steps:

1. Right-click your mouse pointer on any item or bullet symbol in the bulleted list, and select List Properties from the pop-up menu. FrontPage, in turn, will display a List Properties dialog box similar to that shown in Figure 191.1.

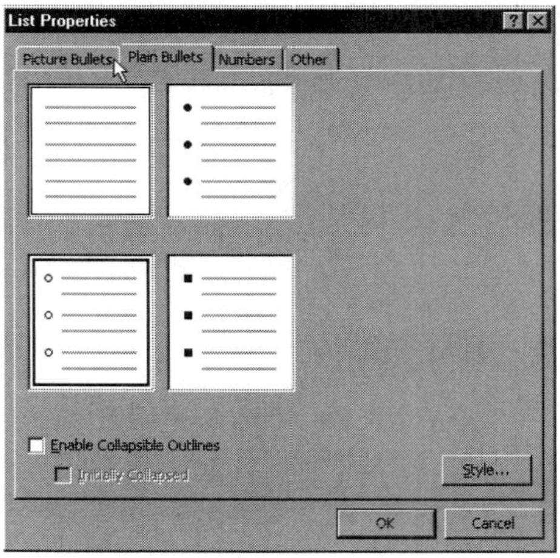

Figure 191.1 The Microsoft FrontPage List Properties dialog box, Plain Bullets tab.

2. To use one of the three plain bullet symbols in the bulleted list, click your mouse pointer on the Plain Bullets tab (if the tab is not already exposed). Then, click your mouse pointer on the rectangle with the bullet symbol you want to use, and continue at Step 6.
3. To use a graphics image instead of a symbol in front of each item in the bulleted list, click your mouse pointer on the Picture Bullets tab to expose the fields shown in Figure 191.2.

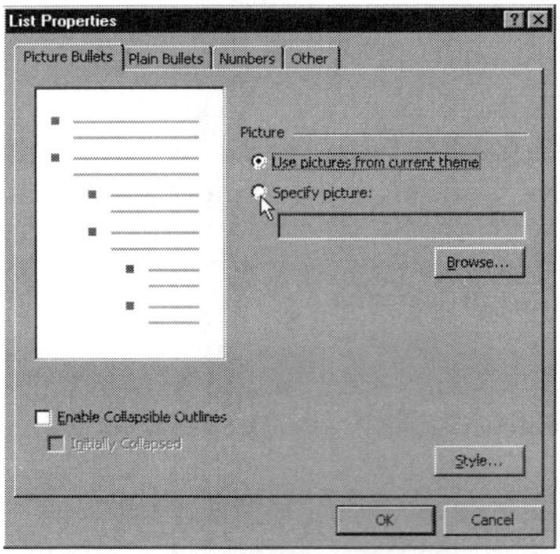

***Figure 191.2** The Microsoft FrontPage List Properties dialog box, Picture Bullets tab.*

4. Click your mouse pointer on the Specify picture radio button.
5. Into the field below the Specify picture radio button, enter the relative address or pathname of the graphics image you want to use as the bullet symbol, or click your mouse pointer on the BROWSE button below the field to use the Select Picture dialog box to search for and select the image file with the bullet picture you want to use.

***Note:** Make sure the graphics image you select for the "bullet symbol" is the appropriate size to be a bullet—about 15 pixels wide by 15 pixels high. If you only have a larger picture, reduce its size before using it as a bullet. Unlike other graphics images on a Web page, you cannot right-click your mouse pointer on a graphics bullet to change its properties—including its dimensions.*

To select one of the many clipart bullets available in the Clip Gallery, execute the procedure in the previous Tip entitled "Inserting Images From the Clip Gallery" to import the graphics image into the IMAGES folder in the current FrontPage web. Or, if you see a bullet graphic you like on a Web site, execute the procedure in the previous Tip entitled "Importing a Picture From a Web Site on the Internet Into the Current FrontPage Web," to import the picture into the IMAGES folder in the current FrontPage web. After you import the graphics bullet you want to use into the IMAGES folder, you can enter its relative address or use the BROWSE button to call the Select Picture dialog box to navigate to the IMAGES folder and select the graphics file.

6. Click your mouse pointer on the OK button near the lower right-hand corner of the List properties dialog box.

If you decide to change the default bullet symbol for some or all of the items in a bulleted list, bear in mind that some Web browsers only support bulleted lists that use the default bullet symbol (usually a small solid circle that looks like a dot). Web browsers that support bulleted lists that use of other (non-default) bullet symbols and graphics will display the bulleted list with the bullet symbols or images you specify; those that do not, will display the bulleted list using the default bullet symbol for all bullet items instead.

PLACING A NUMBERED LIST ON A WEB PAGE

A *numbered* list, like a bulleted list, consists of a group of related items. However, instead of a bullet symbol or graphics character, a number precedes each item in a numbered list. In fact, the items in a numbered (or ordered) list are numbered in ascending order. Therefore, you would use a numbered list (in place of a bulleted list) when the order of the items in the list matters. Numbered lists also make it easy to reference any particular item in the list (by its number) or to get a quick count of the number of items in the list (by looking at the ordinal value assigned to the last item in the list.)

To create a numbered list, perform the following steps:

1. With the Web page displayed on the Page view Normal tab, type or paste the items in the numbered list onto the page. Put each list item in a separate paragraph by pressing the ENTER key after the item's last (rightmost) letter.
2. Click and hold down the left mouse button as you drag the mouse pointer over the list (you copied or typed in Step 1) to select all of the items in the list. Then, release the left mouse button.
3. Click your mouse pointer on the Numbering button on the Formatting toolbar (seventh button from the right, with the three lines each of which starts with a number) on the Formatting toolbar. (If you do not see the Formatting toolbar, select the View menu Toolbars option and click your mouse pointer on Formatting to display the Formatting toolbar.) FrontPage, in turn, will convert text you selected in Step 2 into a numbered list.

To add additional items to a numbered list, click the mouse pointer to the right of the last letter in the item that precedes the place in the list where you want to add another item. Then, press the ENTER key. FrontPage, in turn, will insert a new line, numbered one higher than the preceding item and will increase the number of each of the succeeding items in the list. This is your prompt to enter the new item into the list by typing on the blank line.

Note: *You can convert a bulleted list into a numbered list by clicking your mouse pointer anywhere within the bulleted list, and then on the Numbering button on the Formatting toolbar.*

CHANGING THE NUMBERING STYLE OF A NUMBERED LIST

Rather than using "1,2,3,4,5,..." to number the items in a numbered list, you can use Roman Numerals or an ascending sequence of letters instead. Although you can change the numbering style of a single item in the list without changing the others, doing so will emphasize the item—as would using a different bullet symbol or graphics image for a single item in a bulleted list. Mixing numbering styles in the same numbered list only makes the numbering scheme more difficult to follow. Therefore, stick with a single numbering style for the entire numbered list, but feel free to replace the default, ordinal numbers with consecutive uppercase or lowercase letters or Roman Numerals.

To change the numbering style if a numeric list, perform the following steps:

1. Right-click your mouse pointer on any item or number in the numbered list, and select List Properties from the pop-up menu. FrontPage, in turn, will display a List Properties dialog box similar to that shown in Figure 193.

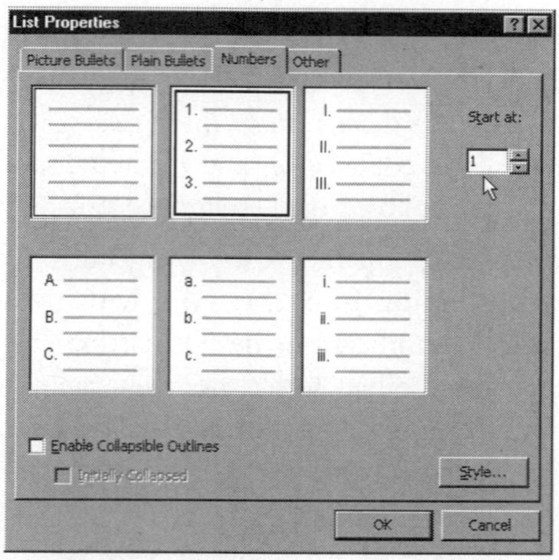

Figure 193 The Microsoft FrontPage List Properties dialog box, Numbers tab.

2. Click your mouse pointer on the rectangle with the numbering style you want to use.
3. Click your mouse pointer on the OK button near the lower right-hand corner of the List properties dialog box.

Although most numbered lists start with the first list item numbered as "1" ("I", "i", "A", or "a"), you can give the first item in the list an ordinal value greater than one, by changing the value in the Start at field near the top right-hand corner of the Numbers tab in the List Properties dialog box. For example, you would start the numbered list at a number other than "1" when the list is really a continuation of another numbered list that precedes it. Suppose, for example, that you were using the numbered list to order the steps in a procedure. If you detailed the first few steps in a numbered list and then inserted an illustration on the Web page, the first item in the (continuation) numbered list after the picture should start one number higher than the last item of the numbered list that precedes the image.

PLACING A DEFINITION LIST ON A WEB PAGE

As its name implies, a *definition* list lets you put a group of terms and their definitions on a Web page. FrontPage (like a Web browser viewing the defined list), puts the term being defined on one line and its definition, indented, on the next line. Therefore a definition list on a Web page will look something like:

```
bulleted list
       unordered list of items with each bullet item
       preceded by a symbol or graphics image
numbered list
       ordered list of items with each list item starting
       with a number or letter
definition list
       defined term followed by its definition on the next
       line
```

To create a defined list, perform the following steps:

1. With the Web page displayed on the Page view Normal tab, place the vertical blinking cursor where you want the defined list to begin.
2. Click your mouse pointer on the drop-down list button to the right of the Style field on the left-hand end of the Formatting toolbar, and select Defined Term from the drop-down menu. (If you do not see the Formatting toolbar, select the View menu Toolbars option and click your mouse pointer on Formatting to display the Formatting toolbar.)
3. Type the term, keyword, phrase, or sentence you want to associate with a definition or concept, and press the ENTER key. FrontPage, in turn, will move to the next line with the cursor indented to the right of the left margin.

4. Type the definition of the term or concept associated with the keyword, phrase or sentence entered in Step 3, and press the ENTER key. FrontPage, in turn, will move to the next line, placing the cursor at the left margin and wait for you to enter another defined term.

Note: *If you look at the HTML for a defined list (on the Page view HTML) tab, you will see that the list items (defined terms and definitions) are enclosed within <DL></DL> (defined list) tags. Each term entered in Step 3, is bracketed by <DT></DT> (definition title) tags, and each definition entered in Step 4, is enclosed by <DD></DD> (definition data) tags. Therefore, each item in a defined list consists of a definition title followed by its associated definition data.*

5. Repeat Steps 3 and 4 until you have entered all of the definition title and definition data items you want in the defined list.
6. Press the ENTER key (without entering a defined term, i.e. without entering a definition title). FrontPage, in turn, will change the style selection from Defined Term to Normal—thus ending the defined list so you can type normal (body text) onto the Web page.

FrontPage will automatically wrap the definition title (defined term) and definition data (definition) items at the right-hand margin. If you want to split a definition title or data item onto two lines prior to reaching the right-hand margin, press SHIFT-ENTER (i.e., hold down the SHIFT key while you press the ENTER key) to move from one line on the Web page to the next. FrontPage, in turn, will insert a <BR> line break into the Web page HTML instead of a </DT> or </DD> tag which would terminate the definition title or data item vs. just splitting its text across multiple lines.

PLACING A LIST WITHIN A LIST

For those times when you need to include bulleted items in a numbered list (or vice versa), FrontPage lets you place a list within a list. For example, while preparing to create a Web site on a new Web server, you might generate a numbered list of things to do such as:

```
1. Purchase the Web server hardware and software
2. Install software
3. Setup a permanent Internet connection through an ISP
4. Secure a domain name
5. Create and publish Web pages
```

The preceding numbered indicates the general sequence of events in the order in which you will need to carry them out. Now, suppose you want to add a bulleted list to show the items required to complete Step 1 and a numbered list showing the steps involved in completing Step 2. Your new, composite list will look something like the following:

```
1. Purchase the Web server hardware and software
       * Pentium Computer
       * Windows NT or 2000
       * Internet Information Server (IIS)
       * FrontPage Extensions
2. Install software
       1. Install Windows (NT or 2000)
       2. Install the IIS
       3. Install FrontPage extensions on IIS
3. Setup a permanent Internet connection through an ISP
4. Secure a domain name
5. Create and publish Web pages
```

To create a composite list (i.e. list which itself contains one or more lists), perform the following steps:

1. Open the Web page on which you wish to create the composite list and select the View menu Page option to display the page on the Page view Normal tab.
2. Create the list that is to contain the other list(s). For the current project, perform the procedure in the previous Tip titled "Placing a Numbered List on a Web Page" to create the first (numbered) list shown at the beginning of the current Tip. (If the top-level list were a bulleted list, you would perform the steps from the procedures found in the Tip titled "Placing a Bulleted List on a Web Page.")
3. Click your mouse pointer to the right of the last word on the line after which you want to insert another list. For the current project, click your mouse pointer to the right of the word **software** in Step 1 of the numbered list.
4. Press the ENTER key. FrontPage, in turn, will insert another numbered (or bulleted) item into the list.
5. Click your mouse pointer on the Increase Indent button (fourth button from the right) on the Formatting toolbar. FrontPage, in turn, will change the (bulleted or numbered) list item to a blank line and move the vertical cursor one level of indentation to the right.
6. If the list in which you are inserting another list is a numbered list, click your mouse pointer on the Bullets button (sixth button from the right) on the Formatting toolbar. Conversely, if you are inserting another list into a bulleted list, click your mouse pointer on the Numbering button (seventh button from the right) on the Formatting

toolbar. For the current project, click your mouse pointer on the Bullets button because you are inserting a list into a numbered list.

Note: *After you click your mouse pointer on the Formatting toolbar's Numbering or Bullets button to format the new, non-list type, indented item, FrontPage will format the item in a list type that* ***does not*** *match the list type of the button on which you clicked the mouse pointer. Therefore, if you click the mouse pointer on the Bullets button, FrontPage will format the new list as a numbered list. Conversely, if you click the mouse pointer on the Numbering button, FrontPage will format the new list as a bulleted list. At this point, do not worry about the list type of the list you are inserting. Just enter the items in the list for now (as called for in Step 7). You will be changing the inserted list's type in Step 8, if necessary.*

7. Type the items you want into the inserted list. Press the ENTER key after you type each item with the exception of the last item in the list. For the current project, enter the bullet list items shown in Step 1 of the example composite list at the beginning of the current Tip.
8. If the list you created in Steps 6 – 7 is not the type of list you want, (i.e. if FrontPage prompted you to insert a numbered list and you really want to insert a bulleted list, or vice versa) click your mouse pointer on any item in the list you inserted. Then, click the mouse pointer on the Bullets button on the Formatting toolbar to convert the list into a bulleted list, or on the Numbers button to convert it to a numbered list. For the current project, click your mouse pointer on the second item in the list you inserted and then on the Bullets button. FrontPage, in turn, will convert the numbered list you inserted (in Steps 6 – 7) into a bulleted list.
9. Repeat Steps 3 – 8 for each additional list you want to insert into the list you created in Step 2. For the current project repeat Steps 3 – 8 to insert the numbered list inserted in Step 2 of the example composite list at the beginning of the current Tip. In Step 3 (of the current procedure), click your mouse pointer to the right of the word **software** in Step 2 of the numbered list. In Step 7, enter the items shown in the numbered list inserted in the example composite list. Then, skip Step 8 because the second time through you want to insert a numbered list within another numbered list.

You are not constrained as to the type of list you place within another list. For example, you can place either a numbered list or a bulleted listed within a numbered list and vice versa.

Moreover, you can put a definition list within either a numbered or a bulleted list. So, feel free to combine lists as necessary to get the line spacing and indentation (i.e. the look and feel of the composite list), the way you want it to be.

ADDING A COLLAPSIBLE OUTLINE TO A WEB PAGE

A *collapsible outline* is a multilevel list, such as the numbered list with inserted bulleted and numbered lists you created in the preceding Tip. If a multilevel list is collapsible, you can click on an item at an upper level to display (expand) or hide (collapse) items subordinate to the item. The reason to use a collapsible outline (i.e. a collapsible list) is to put a large amount of information on one screen by displaying additional top-level items in place of hidden underlying detail until the visitor calls for it.

For example, look at the two lists at the beginning of the previous Tip. The first list takes up less space on the screen because it lists only the five (top-level) steps involved in setting up a Web site on a new Web server. Conversely, the second list takes up an additional seven lines on the screen because it exposes the "details" involved with completing each of the first two steps of the process.

In order for a list to be collapsible, it must have multiple levels. To create a multilevel list, you can either perform the procedure in the preceding Tip to insert one or more lists into another list, or perform the following steps to create a single multilevel list:

1. Open the Web page on which you wish to create a multilevel list, and select the View menu Page option, to display the page on the Page view Normal tab.
2. Move the FrontPage vertical cursor to the blank line on the page where you want to create the multilevel list.
3. To create a bulleted list, click your mouse pointer on the Bullets button (sixth button from the right) on the Formatting toolbar. Alternatively, to create a numbered list, click your mouse pointer on the Numbering button (seventh button from the right) on the Formatting toolbar. FrontPage, in turn, will indent the cursor and display the default bullet symbol (or item number) to prompt you to enter the list item. For the current project, click your mouse pointer on the Bullets button.
4. Enter the items (for all levels) in the list. Press the ENTER key after the last word in each item, and FrontPage will prompt you to enter the next. For the current project, enter:

```
Item one
Description of item 1
Item two
Description of item 2
Names of vendors that sell item 2
Address of vendors that sell item 2
Item three
Description of item 3
Definition of terms in the description of item 3
```

5. Increase the level of indentation of subordinate items by clicking your mouse pointer on an item and then on the Increase Indent button (fourth button from the right) on the Formatting toolbar. FrontPage, in turn, will indent the item and change its style to non-list text. For the current project, click your mouse pointer on one of the words in **Description of item 1** and then on the Increase Indent button to make "Description of item 1" subordinate to "Item one."
6. Convert the non-list text back to a list item by clicking your mouse pointer on either the Bullets or Numbering button on the Formatting toolbar—depending on the type of list you are creating. If you are creating a bulleted list, click your mouse pointer on the Numbering button. Conversely, if you are creating a numbered list, click your mouse pointer on the Bullets button. For the current project, click your mouse pointer on the Numbering button.
7. Repeat Steps 5 – 6 to adjust the level of indentation of the list items as necessary. An item indented further to the right of the item above it is subordinate to that item. For the current project increase the level of indentation such that the list shown in Step 4 appears as:

```
Item one
    Description of item 1
Item two
    Description of item 2
    Names of vendors that sell item 2
       Address of vendors that sell item 2
Item three
    Description of item 3
       Definition of terms in the description of item 3
```

To convert a multilevel list into a collapsible outline, perform the following steps:

1. Right-click your mouse pointer on the first item in the multilevel list and select List Properties from the pop-up menu. FrontPage, in turn, will display the List Properties dialog box.
2. Click your mouse pointer on the Enable Collapsible Outlines checkbox (near the lower left-hand corner of the exposed tab) until a checkmark appears. FrontPage, in turn, will enable (un-gray) the Initially Collapsed checkbox.
3. If you want the Web browser to hide the subordinate items when it first displays a Web page with a collapsible outline, click your mouse pointer on the Initially Collapsed checkbox until a checkmark appears.
4. Click your mouse pointer on the OK button near the lower right-hand corner of the List Properties dialog box.

Unlike hyperlinks (which are underlined and in a different color), there is nothing to distinguish an item with one or more collapsed (hidden) sub-items in a collapsible list from and an item without sub-items. Therefore, if you create a collapsible outline (especially one in which the detail (sub-items) are initially collapsed, and therefore hidden), be sure to place content on the Web page which informs site visitor that clicking on items in the list will display additional information. Alternatively, you might change the color (and perhaps underline) the list items that, when clicked, display or hide additional detail.

Note: *As of this writing, collapsible outlines only function on Web pages viewed using the Microsoft Internet Explorer (version 4 and above). Web browsers that do not support collapsible outlines will display a collapsible outline as a numbered or bulleted list (with all main items and sub-items displayed).*

PLACING A HEADING ON A WEB PAGE

Like headings in a newspaper, magazine or book, headings on a Web page are often used to denote the title of a page or story. In addition, headings on a Web page break up the text content on the page into smaller, more readable sections. Moreover, heading displayed in larger, boldface type, can make it easy to find specific information on the Web page by drawing the visitor's eye to section titles that give the viewer an idea of the content (in smaller non-bold type) that follows the heading in a particular area of the Web page.

To insert a Heading on a Web page, perform the following steps:

1. Open the Web page on which you wish to insert the heading and select the View menu Page option to display the page on the Page view Normal tab.
2. Type the text you want as the heading on a line without other text content, and then press the ENTER key.
3. Click your mouse pointer on any word in the heading text.
4. Click your mouse pointer on the drop-down list button to the right of the Style field (on the left-hand end) on the Formatting toolbar and then on the heading level you want. FrontPage, in turn, will apply the heading style (Heading 1, Heading 2, Heading 3, Heading 4, Heading 5, or Heading 6) you selected to the paragraph in which you placed the cursor in Step 3.

Note: *When you select a text style (including one of the heading styles) from the Style drop-down list on the Formatting toolbar, FrontPage applies the style to all of the text in the paragraph in which the cursor is located. Therefore, make sure you place the heading text in a paragraph by itself before selecting the heading style (1 – 6) you want to use.*

As show in Figure 197, HTML supports six levels of headings.

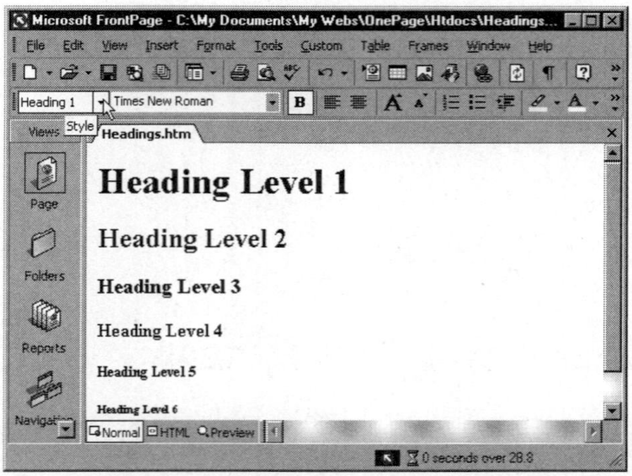

Figure 197 A Web page with examples of text styled using each of the six standard HTML heading types.

Viewing the heading styles from Heading 1 to Heading 6 in ascending order, notice that each of the six levels of headings uses a smaller point size for its characters than its predecessor. In fact, one could argue that Heading 5 and Heading 6 are only effective headings if used as titles for content whose character size is smaller than the size of normal, body text. (Heading 5 defaults to 10-point type, while Heading 6 defaults to 8-point type—both of which are smaller than the default "normal" 12-point type.)

USING AN FTP SERVER TO PUBLISH A WEB SITE

The most convenient way to copy a FrontPage web to a Web server is by selecting the File menu Publish Web option [or by clicking the mouse pointer on the Publish Web button (fifth button from the left) on the Standard toolbar]. As you learned in the previous Tip titled "Publishing a FrontPage Web to a Web Server with FrontPage Extensions," the FrontPage Publish Web Wizard not only copies new and updated Web pages to the Web server, but it also removes any pages and other support files from the server that you deleted from the copy of the FrontPage web on your local computer. In short, using the FrontPage Publish Web Wizard to publish a FrontPage web gives you an easy way to make the files on the Web site (i.e. on the web on the Web server) look exactly like the folder structure and files in the FrontPage web on your local computer.

However, in order to use the FrontPage Publish Web Wizard to publish a FrontPage web, the Internet Service Provider (ISP) hosting your Web site must install FrontPage Extensions on the Web server. Unfortunately, not all ISP's are willing to do so. If your Web site is hosted on a Web server without FrontPage Extensions installed, you must use the site's File Transport Protocol (FTP) server to copy the web's files from your computer to your Web site's folders on the Web server.

To publish a FrontPage web to a Web server without FrontPage Extensions installed, perform the following steps:

1. If you do not have a permanent (always on) connection to the Internet, use your modem to establish a dial-up connection to the Internet through your Internet Service Provider (ISP).
2. Start the FrontPage application and open the FrontPage web you want to publish to the Web server.
3. Select the File menu Publish Web option. FrontPage, in turn, will display a Publish Web dialog box similar to that shown in Figure 198.1.

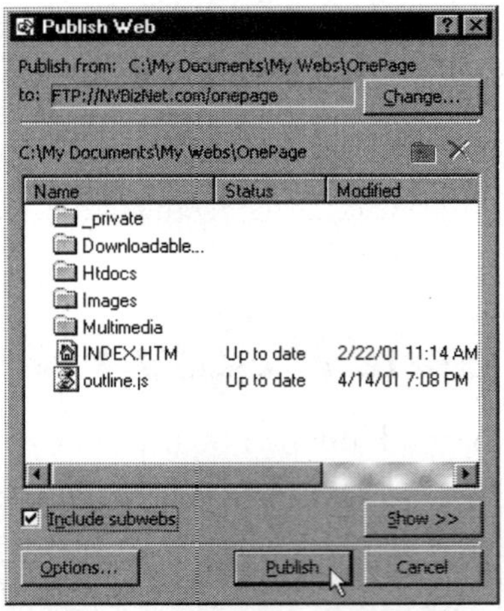

Figure 198.1 *The Microsoft FrontPage Publish Web dialog box.*

Note: *If you published a FrontPage web to an FTP server the last time you selected the File menu Publish Web option, FrontPage will prompt you to login to the FTP server by displaying a dialog box similar to that shown in Figure 198.4. If FrontPage prompts you with the Name and Password Required dialog box, either enter your username and password for the FTP server into the appropriate fields in the dialog box, and then click your mouse pointer on the OK button near its lower right-hand corner, or click your mouse pointer on its CANCEL button and continue at Step 5.*

4. If the Uniform Resource Locator (URL) in the to (publish destination) field at the top of the dialog box is not the one you want, click your mouse pointer on the CHANGE button to the right of the field. FrontPage, in turn, display a Publish Web dialog box similar to that shown in Figure 198.2. If the URL in the to field is the one you want, continue at Step 6.

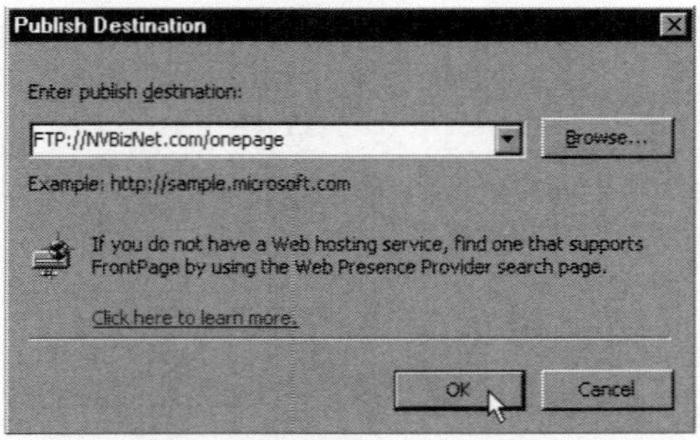

Figure 198.2 *The Microsoft FrontPage Publish Destination dialog box.*

5. Into the Enter publish destination field, enter the URL of your Web site's folder on the FTP server, and then click your mouse pointer on the OK button near the lower right-hand corner of the dialog box. The URL will typically be in the form:

```
FTP://<server name>/<path>
```

where:

- **<server name>** - is the domain name for the Internet Protocol (IP) address at which your ISP has installed the FTP server you are to use when publishing the Web site.
- **/path** - gives the FTP sever the address (i.e. the full pathname) of the folder that serves as the root directory for your Web site.

For example, to publish the FrontPage web OnePage to the OnePage folder on the NVBiznet.com Web server, you would enter **FTP://NVBiznet.com/OnePage** into the Enter publish destination field at the top of the Publish Destination dialog box, and then click the mouse pointer on the OK button near the lower right-hand corner of the dialog box.

Note: *Be sure to enter FTP:// vs. HTTP:// as the file transfer protocol in front of the server name. If you enter HTTP://, FrontPage will try to publish the web directly to the Web server (instead of going through the FTP server) and will display an error message box similar to that shown in Figure 198.3.*

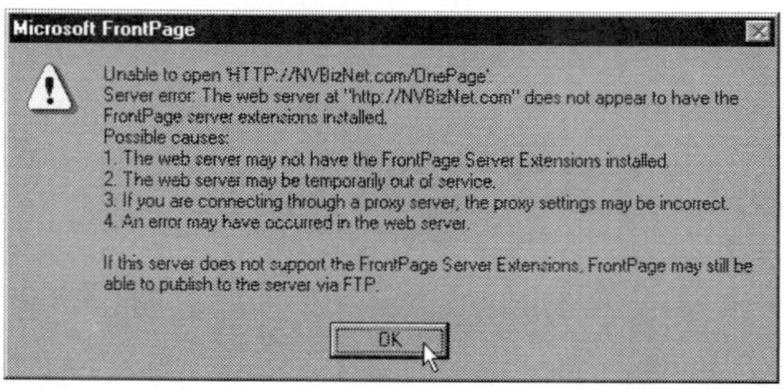

Figure 198.3 *The Microsoft FrontPage, FrontPage Extensions Not Installed on Server error message box.*

If FrontPage prompts you with the FrontPage Extensions Not Installed on Server message box, click your mouse pointer on its OK button, and then enter the correct URL for the site's FTP server as you repeat Step 5.

Note: Contact the ISP hosting your Web site to get the URL you must enter in order to use the site's FTP server to publish your FrontPage web to the Web server.

6. If you are not already logged into the FTP server for your Web site, FrontPage will display a Name and Password Required dialog box, similar to that shown in Figure 198.4, to prompt you to enter a valid username and password pair to login to the FTP server.

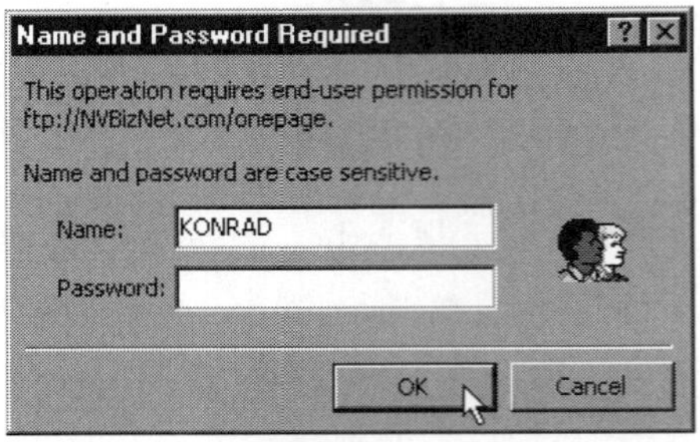

***Figure 198.4** The Microsoft FrontPage (FTP server) Name and Password Required dialog box.*

7. Into the Name field, enter your username on the FTP server, and into the Password field, enter the password assigned to the username you entered into the Name field. Then, click your mouse pointer on the OK button near the lower right-hand corner of the dialog box to login to the FTP server.

Note: If the path you entered in Step 5 does not exist, FrontPage will prompt you with message box asking if you want to create a new folder for the Web site's files. Verify the path's accuracy. If the path you entered is correct, click your mouse pointer on the OK button near the bottom center of the message box to have FrontPage create the folder(s) for your FrontPage web. Conversely, if the path is incorrect, click your mouse pointer on the CANCEL button, and continue at Step 5.

8. Tell FrontPage to publish any subwebs included in the current web by clicking your mouse pointer on the Include subwebs checkbox near the bottom of the Publish Web dialog box until a checkmark appears.
9. Click your mouse pointer on the PUBLISH button near the lower right-hand corner of the Publish Web dialog box to have the Publish Web Wizard starting using the FTP server to transmit the FrontPage web's files onto the computer running the Web server.

If your FrontPage web has any Web pages with features that only function if the Web server has FrontPage Extensions installed, FrontPage will prompt you to remove the features by displaying a message box similar to that shown in Figure 198.5. Make a nete of the items and the Web pages on which they are located, so you can remove the non-functioning components and republish the Web pages without them later. Then, click your mouse pointer on the CONTINUE button near the center at the bottom of the message box.

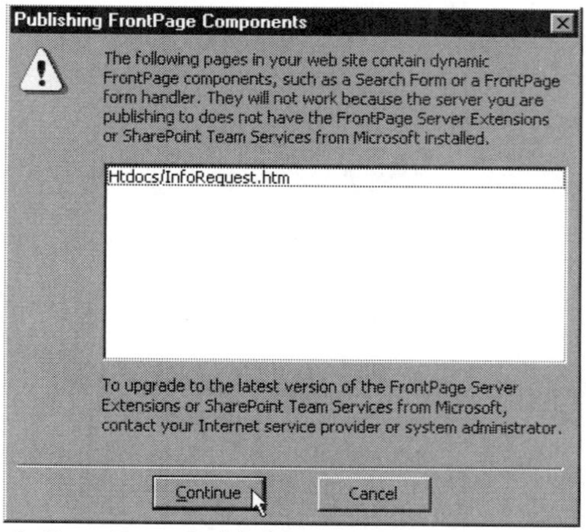

Figure 198.5 *The Microsoft FrontPage Publishing FrontPage Components message box.*

When you publish a FrontPage web to a Web server without FrontPage Extensions, you will not be able to use FrontPage to open and modify the web's pages directly on the Web server. Instead, you will have to make any modifications to the copy of the web stored locally, (i.e., on your hard drive or in a shared folder on the local area network), and then execute the preceding procedure to publish the updated web to the Web server.

PUBLISHING A FRONTPAGE WEB TO A FOLDER ON A LOCAL OR LAN DISK DRIVE

Prior to releasing your Web site to the public on the Internet, you may want to publish the FrontPage web to a workstation on your company's local area network (LAN). Those with access to the folder in which you publish the web can then use a Web browser to preview the site, test its capabilities, and make sure everything functions and looks the way it should before you put the site online on the Internet.

Note: *You do not need an Internet Service Provider or a Web server installed to publish a FrontPage web to a LAN drive, and then view its content with a Web browser.*

To publish a FrontPage web to a folder on your LAN, perform the following steps:

1. If your computer does not have a local drive mapped to the network drive on which you wish to publish the FrontPage web, right-click your mouse pointer on the Network Neighborhood icon on your Windows desktop and select Map Network Drive from the pop-up menu. Windows, in turn, will display a Map Network drive dialog box similar to that shown in Figure 199. If your computer already has a local drive mapped to the network drive on which you wish to publish the FrontPage web, continue at Step 5.

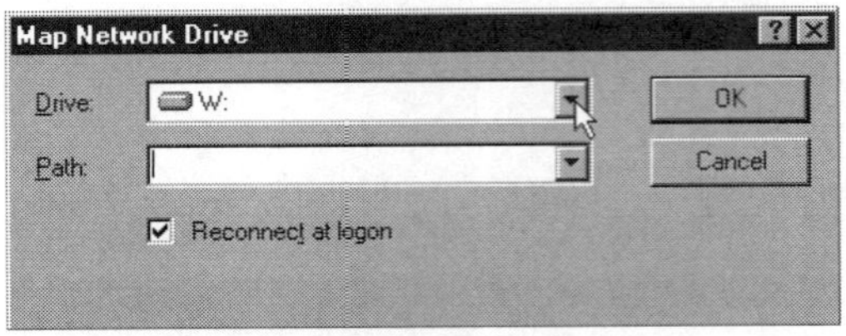

Figure 199 The Windows Map Network Drive dialog box.

2. Click your mouse pointer on the drop-down list to the right of the Drive field, and select a currently unused drive letter from the drop-down list.
3. Into the Path field, enter the name of the workstation and its shared drive as:

```
\\<workstation name>\<shared drive name>
```

   For example, to map the W: drive to a shared drive (or folder) called NVBizNet2_C on a LAN workstation named NVBizNet2, select the W: drive in Step 2 and enter **\\NVBiznet2\NVBiznet2_C** into the Path field. Windows, in turn, will establish a connection to the shared drive (or folder) on the LAN workstation as if it were (local) drive W: on your computer.
4. Click your mouse pointer on the OK button near the upper right-hand corner of the Map Network Drive dialog box.

Note: *Prior to publishing your FrontPage web to a shared folder on the LAN, contact your network administrator for the name of the workstation and shared drive (or folder) to which you can copy* *(i.e., publish) the web. Also, ask for the username and password you need to use, if the shared area on the workstation is password protected. Windows will prompt you to enter a username and password when you try to map a local drive letter to a password protected drive (or folder) on the LAN—unless you are already logged in on the workstation with a username that has the access rights copy files to the shared drive (or folder).*

5. Start the FrontPage application and open the FrontPage web that you want to publish to a shared drive (or folder) on the LAN.
6. Select the File menu Publish Web option. FrontPage, in turn, will display a Publish Web dialog box similar to the one you saw in Figure 198.1.

Note: *If FrontPage prompts you to enter the username and password for the Web or FTP server to which you last published the current FrontPage, click your mouse pointer on the* CANCEL *button and continue at Step 8.*

7. If the pathname in the publish destination field at the top of the dialog box is not the one you want, click your mouse pointer on the CHANGE button to the right of the field. FrontPage, in turn, will display a Publish Web dialog box similar to the one you saw in Figure 198.2. Otherwise, continue at Step 10.
8. Into the Enter publish destination field, enter the drive letter and folder to which you want to publish the FrontPage web. For example, to publish the current web to the OnePage folder on the W: drive [mapped to the shared drive (or folder) on the LAN workstation], enter **W:/OnePage** into the Enter publish destination field.

Note: *As an alternative to publishing the FrontPage web to a shared drive (or folder) on another workstation, you can publish the web to a shared folder on your own computer by entering the full pathname of the folder in which you wish to publish the FrontPage web into the Enter Publish Destination field. For example, to publish the web to the \TestWeb\OnePage folder on the local C: drive (on your computer), enter* ***C:/TestWeb/OnePage*** *into the Enter Publish Destination field. (Check with your network administrator for instruction if you do not know how to share a local drive with other workstations on your LAN.)*

9. Click your mouse pointer on the OK button near the lower right-hand corner of the Publish Destination dialog box.

Note: *If the path you entered in Step 8 does not exist, FrontPage will prompt you with message box asking if you want to create a new folder for the Web site's files. Verify the path's accuracy. If the path you entered is correct, click your mouse pointer on the OK button near the bottom center of the message box to have FrontPage create the folder(s) for your FrontPage web. Conversely, if the path is incorrect, click your mouse pointer on the* CANCEL *button, and continue at Step 8.*

10. Tell FrontPage to publish any subwebs included in the current web by clicking your mouse pointer on the Include subwebs checkbox near the bottom of the Publish Web dialog box until a checkmark.
11. Click your mouse pointer on the PUBLISH button near the lower right-hand corner of the Publish Web dialog box to have the Publish Web Wizard start copying the FrontPage web's files to a shared folder on the LAN.

After you complete Step 11, FrontPage will publish the current web to the folder you specified in Step 8, and then display a "Web site published successfully!" message box. When you see the message box, click the mouse pointer its DONE button.

To preview the Web site, start your Web browser and enter the pathname of the site's home page (INDEX.HTM or DEFAULT.HTM) into the browser's Address field. For example, if you published the FrontPage web to **W:/OnePage** enter **W:/OnePage/INDEX.HTM** into the Web browser's Address field and press the ENTER key to retrieve the site's homepage. Before network users can retrieve the Web site's home page, they must map a network drive (on their workstations) to the shared folder in which you published the FrontPage web. For example, after mapping a local drive letter, such as T: to the shared drive on which you published the Web site, the user would enter the address of the site's homepage as **T:/OnePage/INDEX.HTM** in the Web browser's Address field.

Bear in mind that as is the case when publishing a FrontPage web to a Web server without FrontPage Extensions installed, any components that require FrontPage Extensions will not function properly on Web pages published to a shared folder on local drive or workstation on the LAN. After all, Windows running on the workstation (or local computer) and not a Web server with FrontPage Extensions installed is "serving" the Web pages to the Web browsers that request them. As such, Web page components will not be able to call needed functions in the FrontPage Extensions installed on a Web server—since there is no Web server involved in sending the Web content to the Web browsers.

USING THE PUBLISH STATUS REPORT TO EXCLUDE UNFINISHED WEB PAGES FROM PUBLICATION

The two preceding Tips and a previous Tip titled: "Publishing a FrontPage Web to a Web Server with FrontPage Extensions" showed you how to use the FrontPage Publish Web Wizard to send all of a FrontPage web's content to a Web server or shared folder on a local area network (LAN) workstation. While the procedures in each of these Tips assumed that all of the FrontPage web's pages were ready for public consumption, this is not always the case. If you are working with a design team or must depend on department managers to supply content, some parts of the web will be ready before others. Moreover, you may be working on revisions to some pages on a previously published Web site and may not want Web pages containing "in-progress" changes copied to the Web site until you finish your work.

Fortunately, FrontPage lets you use the Publish Status report to tell the Publish Web Wizard which files the Wizard is not to send to the Web server, FTP server, or folder on the shared drive (or folder) on the LAN. To change the *publication* status of a Web page or other content file, perform the following steps:

1. Open the FrontPage web with the unfinished pages you do not want published.
2. To display the current web's Publish Status report, select the View menu Reports option; move your mouse pointer to Workflow and then select Publish Status. FrontPage, in turn, will display a Publish Status report similar to that shown in Figure 200.

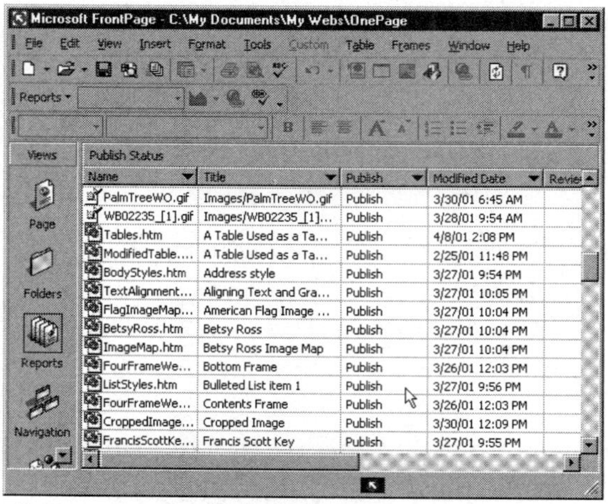

***Figure 200** The Microsoft FrontPage Publish Status report.*

3. Use the scroll bar along the right-hand side of the application window to move through the lines of the report until you see the Web page or file you do not want the FrontPage Publish Web Wizard to publish.
4. If the file whose publish status you want to change is not already highlighted (i.e. selected) on the report, click your mouse pointer in the Publish column of the report line for the file you do not want published. FrontPage, in turn, will highlight the line's columns to show you have selected it.

5. Click your mouse pointer on the Publish column in the highlighted (selected) line on the report. FrontPage, in turn, will display a drop-down list button to the right of file's publish column.
6. Click your mouse pointer on the drop-down list button (that FrontPage displayed in Step 5) and select **Don't Publish** from the drop-down list to prevent the Publish Web Wizard from publishing the file along with other files published the next time you use the Publish Web Wizard to publish the current web's to a server or shared folder on a LAN.
7. Click the mouse pointer on a column other than the publish column highlighted (selected) line on the report (or, click the mouse pointer on any column in another line on the report). FrontPage, in turn, will update the publish status of the file you selected in Step 4 to "Don't Publish" and mark the file's icon in the Name column with a white "X" on a red background.
8. Repeat Steps 3 – 7 for to change the publish status (as shown in the publish column) to Don't Publish for each of the files you do not want the FrontPage Publish Web Wizard to publish until you change the publish status back to Publish.

When a file you previously marked as Don't Publish is ready for publication, repeat the preceding procedure, only select Publish (instead of Don't Publish) from the drop-down list in Step 6.

Note: *You can sort any of the FrontPage reports (including the Publish Status report) by the values in a column by clicking your mouse pointer on the heading that the top of the column. As such, sort the lines on the Publish Status report according the file type and title by clicking your mouse pointer on the heading of the "Type" column. More often than not, you only want to prevent the Publish Web Wizard from publishing specific Web pages when you use the Wizard to publish a FrontPage web to a server or to shared folder on a LAN. Therefore, if you sort the Publish Status report by type, FrontPage will group all of the web's Web pages (i.e., files of type HTM or HTML) together on the report, which will make it easier to find the Web page(s) whose publish status you want to change—especially in a FrontPage web with a large mix of Web page and non-HTML content files.*

Similarly, when you are ready to change the publish status of some or all of the files you previously marked Don't Publish to Publish, click your mouse pointer on the heading at the top of the publish column. FrontPage, in turn, will sort all of the files with a Don't Publish status to the top of the list—which makes them easy to find, so you can select and change the publish status to Publish for those files you now want the Publish Web Wizard to send the Web server or shared folder on a LAN the next time you use the Wizard to publish the current FrontPage web.

CREATING AN IMAGE MAP

You learned how to anchor a hyperlink to a graphics image in a previous Tip titled "Using a Graphics Image as a Hyperlink." An *image map* is a graphics image used as the anchor for two or more hyperlinks. Instead of anchoring a single hyperlink to an entire picture, such that clicking the mouse pointer anywhere on the picture will activate the same hyperlink, when using an image map you map out areas called hotspots on the picture. You then anchor each hyperlink to one of the hotspots such that clicking the mouse pointer on different parts of the picture (or image map) activates a different hyperlink—the hyperlink anchored to the hotspot on which you clicked the mouse pointer. The process of mapping out or "drawing" the hotspots on an image is known as "creating an image map."

Often the hardest part of creating an image map is finding (or creating) the image you want to use. Although FrontPage lets you draw hotspots on any graphics image you want, the best image maps are those that require little to no explanation as to where to click the mouse pointer in order to activate a particular hyperlink. Suppose for example that a Web page at a geography Web site has a map of the world such as the one shown in Figure 201.1.

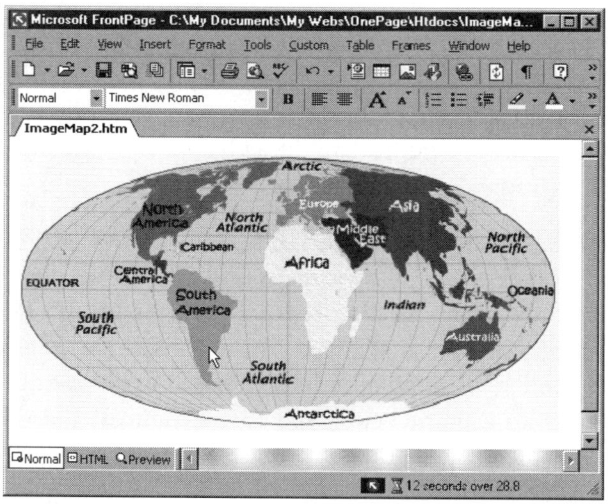

Figure 201.1 Web page with a world map used as the graphics image for an image map.

Due to the overall nature of the Web site's content, visitors to the site will infer that clicking the mouse pointer one of the continents on the world map will activate a hyperlink that displays a Web page with additional information on the continent selected. As an additional clue as to the world map's purpose, the site's authors might add a caption such as "Click on the name of a continent or ocean for more information and a detailed map."

To draw hotspots on a graphics image and then anchor hyperlinks to the hotspots, perform the following steps:

1. Open the Web page with the graphics picture you want to turn into an image map, and select the View menu Page option, to display the page on the Page view Normal tab.
2. Click your mouse pointer anywhere on the picture. FrontPage, in turn, will display the Pictures toolbar. (If FrontPage does not display the Pictures toolbar, select the Toolbars option, and click your mouse pointer on Pictures to display the toolbar.)
3. Click your mouse pointer on the Polygonal Hotspot, Circular Hotspot, or Rectangular Hotspot button (third, fourth, or fifth button from the left) on the Pictures toolbar—depending on the shape of the area that you want to map as a hotspot on the picture. After you click the mouse pointer on one of the three hotspot buttons (shown in Figure 201.2), FrontPage will change the arrow mouse pointer to a pencil whenever you move the mouse pointer onto the picture.

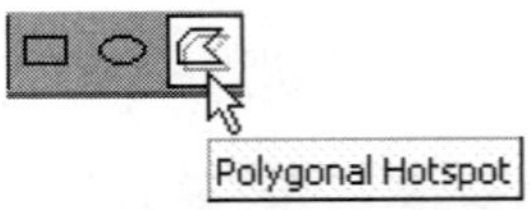

Figure 201.2 From left to right, the Rectangular Hotspot, Circular Hotspot, and Polygonal Hotspot buttons (third, fourth, and fifth buttons from the left) on the Pictures toolbar.

4. Use the pencil mouse pointer to "draw" a hotspot on the graphics image. For example:

- to draw a rectangle around "South Pacific" on a world map such as the one shown in Figure 201.1, click the mouse pointer on the Rectangular Hotspot button on the Pictures toolbar (in Step 3). Then, place the pencil mouse pointer above and to the left of the "S" in "South." Next, click and hold down the left mouse button as you drag the mouse pointer to a point below and to the right of the final "c" in "Pacific," and then release the left mouse button.
- to draw a circle around "South Atlantic" on a world map show as the one shown in Figure 201.1, click your mouse pointer on the Circular Hotspot button on the Pictures toolbar (in Step 3). Then, place the pencil mouse pointer at the center of the circle you plan to draw—in the center of the "South Atlantic" label for the current project. Next, click and hold down the left mouse button as you drag the mouse pointer outward until the circle expands to enclose both words in "South Atlantic," and then release the left mouse button.

- to draw a polygon around the South American continent on a world map such as the one shown in Figure 201.1, click your mouse pointer on the Polygonal Hotspot button on the Pictures toolbar (in Step 3). Move the pencil mouse pointer to a point on the continent's coast, and click (and release) the left mouse button. Move the pencil mouse pointer to another point on the coast, and click (and release) the left mouse button. As you move the pencil mouse pointer from point to point (along the coast), FrontPage will draw a straight line from the last point on which you clicked the mouse pointer to the next point at which you click the mouse pointer. Continue clicking the mouse pointer on points along the border of the area that you want to enclose as a hotspot on the graphics image—the more irregular the area, the more points on which you must click the mouse pointer. Be sure to click your mouse pointer on the point at which you started the polygon as the final point to close the polygon.

5. After you draw the hotspot on the graphics image (in Step 4), FrontPage will display an Insert Hyperlink dialog box similar to that shown in Figure 201.3. Into the Address field near the bottom of the dialog box, enter the address of the Web page to display (or the file to download) when the Web browser activates the hyperlinks anchored to the hotspot. Then, click your mouse pointer on the OK button near the lower right-hand corner of the dialog box.

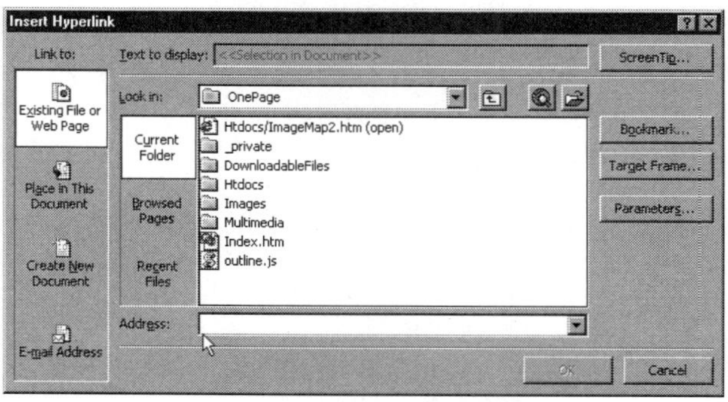

***Figure 201.3** The Microsoft FrontPage Insert Hyperlink dialog box.*

6. Repeat Steps 3 – 5 until you have defined all of the hotspots and hyperlinks you want on the image map.

After you complete Step 6, click your mouse pointer at a point on the current Web page outside the picture to return to the What-You-See-Is-What-You-Get (WYSIWYG) Web page editor on the Page view Normal tab.

ADJUSTING THE HOTSPOTS ON AN IMAGE MAP

If Web site visitors have difficulty activating the hyperlinks on an image map, you may want to change the size or location of its hotspots. Fortunately, FrontPage gives you a way to move and resize hotspots without deleting and redrawing them from scratch.

To edit the hotspots on an image map, perform the following steps:

1. Open the Web page with the image map whose hotspots you want to change, move, or delete, and select the View menu Page option to display the page on the Page view Normal tab.
2. Click your mouse pointer on the graphics image with the hotspots you want to adjust. FrontPage, in turn, will display the Pictures toolbar and the hotspots on the image map. (If FrontPage does not display the Pictures toolbar, select the View menu Toolbars option and click your mouse pointer on Pictures to display the toolbar.)
3. Click your mouse pointer on the Select button (sixth button from the right, with the arrow icon) on the Pictures toolbar.
4. Click your mouse pointer on the hotspot you want to adjust. FrontPage, in turn, will display sizing handles on the corners and sides of a rectangular hotspot, on the corners of a square enclosing a circular hotspot, or on each corner of a polygonal hotspot.
5. Move, resize, or delete the hotspot you selected in Step 4.

- **To move the hotspot** - place the mouse pointer on a point within the boundaries of the hotspot. Next, click and hold down the left mouse button as you drag the mouse pointer and the hotspot to its new location. Then, drop the hotspot into place by releasing the left mouse button.
- **To change the size and/or shape of the hotspot** - place the mouse pointer on one of the sizing handles on the hotspot. Next, click and hold down the left mouse button as you drag the mouse pointer and sizing handle either outward (away from the center of the hotspot) to expand it, or inward (toward the center the center of the hotspot) to make it smaller. After you have increased or decreased the size of the hotspot as desired, release the left mouse button.
- **To delete the hotspot** - press the DELETE or BACKSPACE key.

6. Repeat Steps 4 and 5 until you have adjusted and/or deleted the hotspots on the image map as desired. Then, click your mouse pointer

on a point on the Web page outside the image map to exit image editing and return to the What-You-See-Is-What-You-Get (WYSIWYG) Web page editor.

When adjusting the hotspots on a picture, make sure that you do not let the boundaries of adjacent hotspots overlap. If the site visitor clicks the mouse pointer on a hotspot whose border extends into the area defined for another hotspot, which of the two hyperlinks the Web browser will activate is unpredictable.

Remember, if necessary, you can repeatedly select the Edit menu Undo Edit Properties option to undo hotspot changes and deletions in the reverse order in which you made them.

CHANGING THE HYPERLINK ANCHORED TO A HOTSPOT ON AN IMAGE MAP

Even if the shape, size, and location of the hotspots on an image map are fine, you may have to change hotspot hyperlinks from time to time. This is especially true if the hotspots anchor hyperlinks to Web pages or downloadable files on other Web sites. After all, the site's owner may move or take the site offline or change the names of or delete one or more of the Web pages or files you hyperlinked.

To edit the hyperlink anchored to a hotspot on an image map, perform the following steps:

1. Open the Web page with the image map to which the hyperlink is anchored, and select the View menu Page option to display the page on the Page view Normal tab.
2. Right-click your mouse pointer on the hotspot to which the hyperlink is anchored, and select Picture Hotspot Properties from the pop-up menu. FrontPage, in turn, will display an Edit Hyperlink dialog box, similar to that shown in Figure 203.

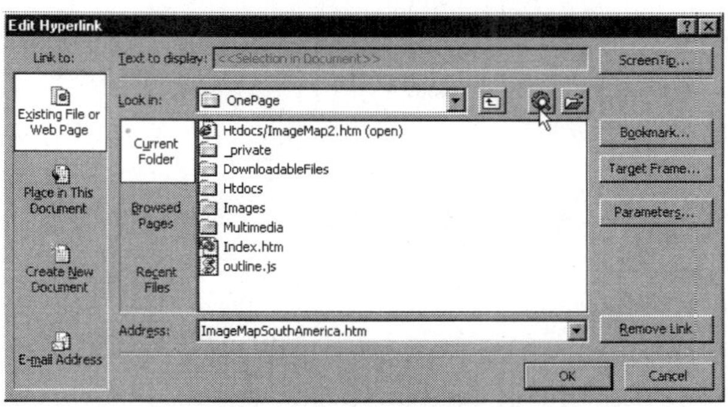

Figure 203 The Microsoft FrontPage Edit Hyperlink dialog box.

3. Into the Address field near the bottom of the dialog box, enter the new relative address of the hyperlink's target Web page or downloadable file. Alternatively, use the drop-down list button to the right of the Look in field near the top of the dialog box and the folders below the field to navigate to the folder with the hyperlink's new target. Then click the mouse pointer on the target file's name to have FrontPage copy its relative address to the Address field.

Note: *If the target file you want is an external file on the Internet, you can either enter its Uniform Resource Locator (URL) (i.e., its Web address) into the Address field at the bottom of the dialog box, or you can click your mouse pointer on the Search the Web button (with the globe an magnifying glass) to the right of the Look in field to navigate the Internet to the Web page you want. FrontPage, in turn, will tell Windows to start your Web browser. Use the Web browser to display the Web page you want the hyperlink to retrieve. Then, click your mouse pointer on the button for the FrontPage application on the Windows task bar. FrontPage, in turn, will copy the Web page URL from the Address field near the top of the Web browser's application window to the Address field near the bottom of the dialog box.*

4. Click your mouse pointer on the OK button near the lower right-hand corner of the Edit Hyperlink dialog box. FrontPage, in turn, will update the hyperlink's target address and return to editing the image map.
5. If the image map has more than one hyperlink whose target URL you need to change, repeat Steps 2 – 4 for each hyperlink you need to update. Then, click your mouse pointer on a point on the Web page outside the image map to exit image editing and return to the What-You-See-Is-What-You-get (WYSIWYG) Web page editor on the Page view Normal tab.

Note: *Be sure to run the Broken Hyperlinks report (by selecting the View menu Reports option, moving the mouse pointer to Problems and then selecting Broken Hyperlinks) every two weeks or so. The Broken Hyperlinks report will let you know if any of the Web site's hyperlinks (including those anchored to hotspots on image maps) point to target files that are no longer accessible.*

DISPLAYING A SCREENTIP WHEN THE MOUSE POINTER MOVES OVER A HOTSPOT ON AN IMAGE MAP

When the site visitor moves the mouse pointer over a hyperlink, including a hotspot on an image map, the Web browser displays the hyperlink target's uniform resource locator (URL) in the status bar at the bottom of the browser's application window. For each of the hotspots on an image map, you may also want to provide a *screen tip* that pops up and remains displayed as a label on the hotspot while the mouse pointer hovers over any point within the hotspot's boundaries. Screen tips are especially helpful in showing the site visitor where to click the mouse pointer to activate an image map's hyperlinks when the hotspots are close together or when their borders are not clearly defined by the picture's content.

To have the Web browser display a screen tip whenever the mouse pointer is over a hotspot on an image map, perform the following steps:

1. Open the Web page with the image map, and select the View menu Page option to display the page on the Page view Normal tab.
2. Right-click your mouse pointer on the image map, and select Picture Hotspot Properties from the pop-up menu. FrontPage, in turn, will display an Edit Hyperlink dialog box, similar to the one shown in Figure 203 of the preceding Tip.
3. Click your mouse pointer on the SCREENTIP button near the upper right-hand corner of the dialog box. FrontPage, in turn, will display the Set Hyperlink ScreenTip dialog box shown in Figure 204.

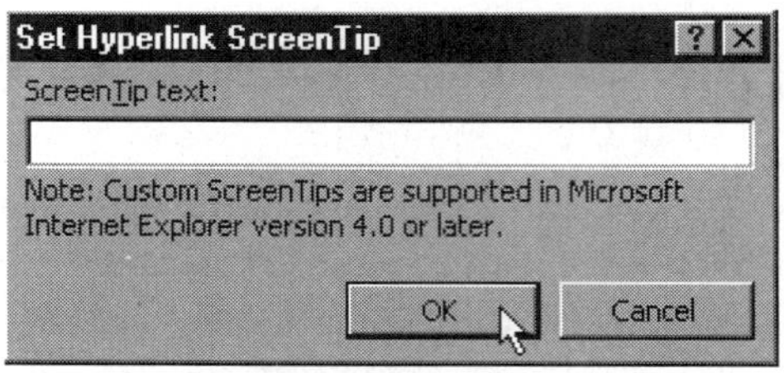

***Figure 204** The Microsoft FrontPage Set Hyperlink ScreenTip dialog box.*

4. Into the ScreenTip text field at the top of the dialog box, enter the text you want displayed while the mouse pointer hovers over any point within the boundaries of the hotspot on the image map. Then, click your mouse pointer on the OK button near the bottom right-hand corner of the Set Hyperlink ScreenTip dialog box.
5. Click your mouse pointer on the OK button near the lower right-hand corner of the Edit Hyperlink dialog box. FrontPage, in turn, will update the hyperlink's ScreenTip and return to editing the image map.
6. Repeat Steps 2 – 5 for each of the hotspots on the image map. Then, click your mouse pointer on a point on the Web page outside the image map to exit image editing and return to the What-You-See-Is-What-You-get (WYSIWYG) Web page editor on the Page view Normal tab.

If you create a screen tip for each of the hotspots on the image map, the site visitor will see a different pop-up label each time the visitor moves the mouse pointer from a non-hotspot area on the picture onto a hotspot. Since the screen tip changes as the site visitor drags the mouse pointer from hotspot to hotspot, the visitor will always know which hyperlink clicking the mouse pointer on a particular point on the image map will activate. Moreover, just displaying the screen tip itself provides a visual clue that the graphics image on the Web page is indeed an image map with hyperlinks the visitor can activate.

DEFINING A DEFAULT HYPERLINK FOR AN IMAGE MAP

As the final step in making an image map as easy to use as possible, you can provide a default hyperlink that the Web browser will activate if the visitor clicks the mouse pointer on any point outside one of the hotspots on an image map. Without a default hyperlink, clicking on a non-hotspot area on a graphics image has no effect—except perhaps to raise the visitor's frustration level because nothing happened. Using a default hyperlink, you can display a Web page that explains where on the image map to click the mouse pointer to activate the "hidden" hyperlinks anchored to its hotspots.

To create a default hyperlink for an image map, perform the following steps:

1. Open the Web page with the image map, and select the View menu Page option to display the page on the Page view Normal tab.
2. Right-click your mouse pointer on a non-hotspot area on the image map, and select Picture Properties from the pop-up menu. FrontPage, in turn, will display the Picture Properties dialog box. (If you see the Picture Hotspot Properties and not the Picture Properties selection on the pop-up menu, you right-clicked the mouse pointer on a hotspot, so move the mouse pointer to another point on the image map and repeat the current Step.)
3. If not already exposed, click your mouse pointer on the General tab of the Picture Properties dialog box to display the fields shown in Figure 205.
4. Into the Location field near the bottom of the dialog box, enter the relative address of the Web page you want the Web browser to display if the visitor clicks the mouse pointer on a non-hotspot area of the image map. For example, if you wanted the default hyperlink to retrieve a Web page named ImageMapInstructions.HTM which is in the same folder as the Web page that has the image map, enter **ImageMapInstructions** into the Location field.

Alternatively, you can click your mouse pointer on the BROWSE button to the right of the Location field to have FrontPage display an Edit Hyperlink dialog box (similar to the one you saw in Figure 203). You would then use the buttons and fields on the Edit Hyperlinks dialog box to navigate to and select a target Web page for the default hyperlink. After selecting the page you want, click the mouse pointer on the OK button near the bottom right-hand corner of the Edit Hyperlink dialog box to exit the dialog box and copy the relative address of the Web page selected from its Address field to the Location field on the Picture Properties dialog box.

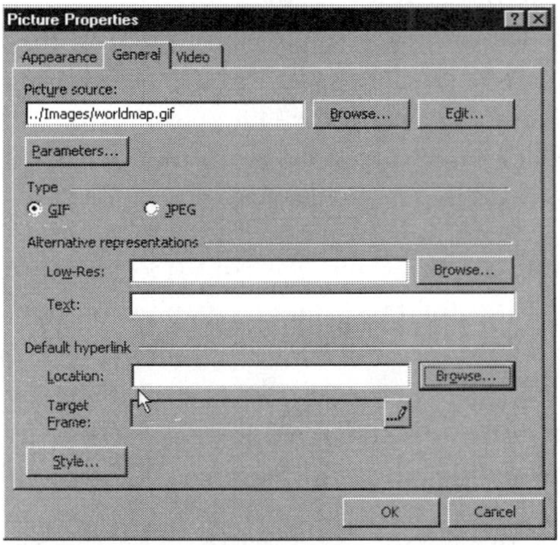

Figure 205 The Microsoft FrontPage Picture Properties dialog box, General tab.

5. Click your mouse pointer on the OK button near the lower right-hand corner of the Picture Properties dialog box. FrontPage, in turn, will update the picture's properties to include a default hyperlink to activate whenever the visitor's mouse click on the image map misses all of its hotspots and return to editing the image map.
6. Click your mouse pointer on a point on the Web page outside the image map to exit image editing and return to the What-You-See-Is-What-You-get (WYSIWYG) Web page editor on the Page view Normal tab.

If you use the default hyperlink to display a page of instructions about where to click the mouse pointer to activate the hotspots on the image map, be sure to include instructions on the Web to let the visitor how to get back to the image map itself. Either insert a hyperlink back to the Web page with the image map on the instructional page, or if you are using a generic page of instructions as the default hyperlink for several image maps, include a note that tells the visitor to click the mouse pointer on the Web browser's BACK button to return to previous Web page.

ADDING VIDEO TO A WEB PAGE FOR PLAYBACK BY INTERNET EXPLORER ONLY

Two companies, Microsoft and Netscape (now a part of America online), dominate the Web browser market. The term *market* is used loosely here to refer to only to the consumption (i.e. the buyer) side of the marketplace, since neither company *sells* its free browser. Because the two dominant players in the market give their feature-rich browsers away free of charge, the majority if the people that use a Web browser to surf the Internet, use either the Microsoft Internet Explorer or the Netscape Navigator. Therefore, to reach the widest audience with your Web page content, use FrontPage tools that generate HTML tags and attributes supported by *both* of the Internet's most popular Web browsers.

Fortunately, both the Internet Explorer and the Netscape Navigator support almost all of the same HTML tags and attributes for text content, graphic images, and animations using GIF files. Where the two differ, however is in their support for the playback of sound files and video clips. While the Microsoft Internet Explorer exploits ActiveX controls built into the Windows operating system for multimedia support, the Netscape Navigator looks for plug-ins—so called *helper programs*—that the browser runs to playback video clips and audio files.

A thorough discussion of ActiveX and plug-ins is beyond the scope of this book. However, you can think of an ActiveX control as a module or Dynamic Linked Library (DLL) with a .OCX extension. When the Internet Explorer needs to play a sound file or video clip, the browser sends the file to a module or subroutine (i.e. a DLL) in the Windows operating system for processing. Conversely, a plug-in, while also a DLL file, is an external application program that takes over a portion of the Web browser's application window and uses it to display the results of processing the contents of the multimedia file passed to it by the browser. While a system's DLL's and ActiveX controls are available to all applications running on the computer, plug-ins are available only to those programs in which they are explicitly installed—either by the plug-in or by the application program itself. (Many application programs, including the Netscape Navigator, search the hard drive for plug-ins they can use when you install the programs on the computer.) When the Netscape Navigator wants to playback a multimedia file, for example, the browser searches its plug-ins folder (usually **C:\Program Files\Netscape\Communicator\Program\PlugIns**) for the plug-in it needs, loads the helper program to extend the browser's capabilities, and then passes the multimedia file to the plug-in for processing.

Whether you make your Web site's sound files and video clips available for playback only to those that visit the site using the Microsoft Internet Explorer or to visitors using any Web browser that supports plug-ins is up to you. As you will learn in this Tip and the next, FrontPage gives you two different ways in which to insert a multimedia file. If you use the method explained in the current Tip to insert a video clip on a Web page, only site visitors running the Internet Explorer will be able to playback the video clip. Conversely, if you perform the procedure found in the next Tip, FrontPage will insert the file using HTML tags that make it available for playback by either Internet Explorer or Netscape Navigator.

To insert a video clip that will playback only when the Web page is viewed using Internet Explorer, perform the following steps:

1. Open the Web page on which you want to insert the video clip and select the View menu Page option to display the page on the Page view Normal tab.
2. Position the cursor on the Web page where you want the video clip to appear. Then, select the Insert menu Picture option and click your mouse pointer on Video. FrontPage, in turn, will display a Video dialog box (which looks and functions like the Picture dialog box you saw in a previous Tip titled "Using the Insert Menu Picture Option to Insert a Picture on a Web Page").
3. Use the drop-down list button the right of the Look in field at the top of the dialog box and the folders in the list box below the field to navigate to the folder with video clip you want to insert on the Web page. Then, click your mouse pointer on the video clip's filename in the list box below the Look in field. Alternatively, enter the uniform resource locator (URL) or relative address of the video clip into the File name field near the bottom of the dialog box.
4. Click your mouse pointer on the OPEN button near the lower right-hand corner of the Video dialog box. FrontPage, in turn, will use an <IMG> (image) tag to insert the video clip you selected in Step 3 onto the current Web page and return to the Page view Normal tab.

The Internet Explorer lets you insert a video clip as a graphics image [i.e. lets you use an <IMG> (image) tag in the Web page HTML to insert a video clip on the Web page] because Microsoft extended HTML by adding a DYNSRC (dynamic source) attribute to the <IMG> (image) tag. When the Internet Explorer sees the DYNSRC (dynamic source) attribute in an <IMG> (image) tag, the browser knows to pass the value assigned to the attribute (i.e., the address of a video clip) to the Windows ActiveX control that plays video clips. Other browsers that do not support ActiveX controls will display the graphics image given in the <IMG>

(image) tag's SRC (source) attribute. [If the <IMG> (image) tag has only a DYNSRC (dynamic source) and no SRC (source) attribute, the browsers will display a placeholder for a "missing" picture.]

ADDING VIDEO TO A WEB PAGE FOR PLAYBACK USING A PLUG-IN

In the preceding Tip, you learned that the Netscape Navigator would not take advantage the ActiveX controls installed on your system to playback a video clip inserted on a Web page using an <IMG> (image) tag. However, if you insert a video clip on the Web page as an *embedded* file [using the <EMBED> (embedded) tag] instead of as an image file [using the <IMG> (image) tag], both the Internet Explorer and the Netscape Navigator will play the video clip.

The reason for the difference is that a Web browser handles images (and text content) internally. Therefore, when the browser encounters an <IMG> (image) tag in the Web page HTML, it uses the tag's attributes to determine the way in which it is to display the graphics image. If the browser encounters an attribute it does not support in the <IMG> (image) tag (such as DYNSRC), the browser ignores the attribute. As mentioned in the preceding Tip, the DYNSRC attribute is a Microsoft specific extension of the <IMG> (image) tag's attributes. Since the Netscape Navigator does not recognize the DYNSRC attribute, it ignores it and will not play the source file (i.e., the video clip) stored at the address assigned to the attribute. The Internet Explorer, on the other hand, recognizes the DYNSRC attribute to mean it is to send the attribute's value to the Windows ActiveX control responsible for playing video and sound files.

When a Web browser encounters an <EMBED> (embedded) tag in the Web page HTML, the program does not try to handle the embedded file on its own. Instead, the browser checks its inventory of "helper programs" (i.e., the plug-ins installed in the program) for the plug-in it can use to process the embedded file's contents. The browser doesn't "know" that an embedded source file with an extension of .AVI, .ASF, .MOV, .MPG, .MPEG, or .QT is a video clip. All the Web browser does is check either an internal table or the Windows system table of file type associations to find the name of the plug-in it is to call to handle an embedded file with an extension such as the one it just encountered in the filename assigned to the <EMBED> (embedded) tag's SRC (source) attribute. After it finds the association in the table, the browser starts the helper application and passes the address of the source file (i.e. the video clip's relative pathname or uniform resource locator (URL)) to the plug-in for processing, and voila! you see the video clip playing in a portion of the browser's application window.

To embed a video clip on a Web page that will playback in browsers (such as the Netscape Navigator and the Internet Explorer) that support plug-ins, perform the following steps:

1. Open the Web page on which you want to insert the video clip and select the View menu Page option to display the page on the Page view Normal tab.
2. Position the cursor on the Web page where you want the video clip to appear and select the Insert menu Web Component option. FrontPage, in turn, will display an Insert Web Component dialog box similar to that shown in Figure 207.1.

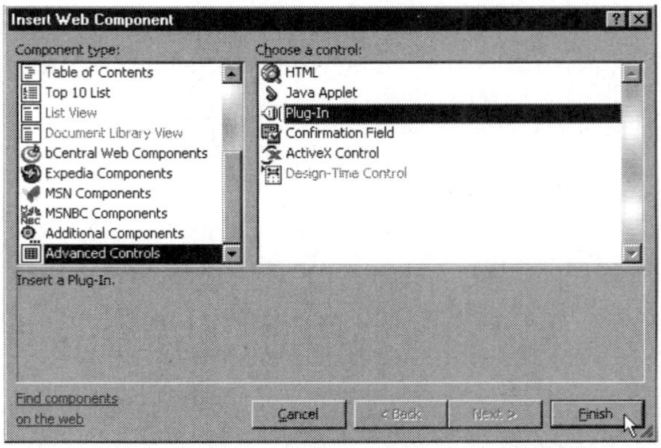

Figure 207.1 The Microsoft FrontPage Insert Web Component dialog box.

3. Click your mouse pointer on **Advanced Controls** in the Component type list box on the left-hand side of the dialog box, and then on **Plug-In** in the Choose a control list box on the right-hand side of the dialog box. Next, click your mouse pointer on the FINISH button in the lower right-hand corner of the Insert Web Component dialog box. FrontPage, in turn, will display a Plug-In Properties dialog box similar to that shown in Figure 207.2.

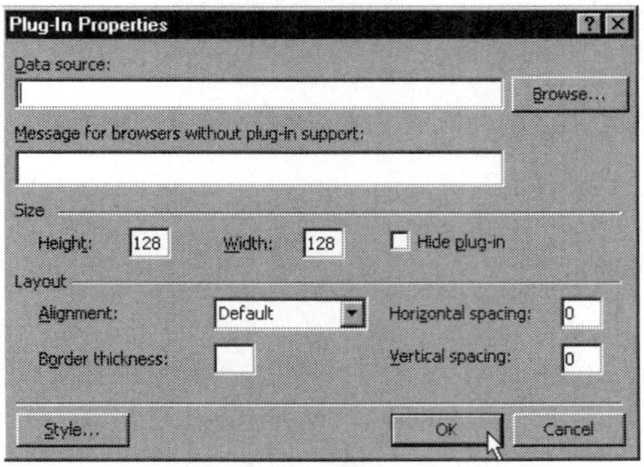

Figure 207.2 The Microsoft FrontPage Plug-In Properties dialog box.

4. Into the Data source field, enter the relative address or URL of the video clip. For example, if you wanted to embed the video file KOWLOON.AVI stored in the MULTIMEDIA folder in the current web onto a Web page stored in another subfolder of the current web's root, you would enter **\MULTIMEDIA\KOWLOON.AVI** into the Data source field. Alternatively, click your mouse pointer on the BROWSE button to the right of the Data source field and use the resources available on the Select Plug-In Data Source dialog box to navigate to and select the video clip file you want to insert.
5. Into the Message for browsers without plug-in support field, enter the text you want the Web browser to display in the video clip's placeholder on the Web page if the browser does not support the use of plug-ins (helper programs). For example, you might enter a message such as **Video clip viewer Plug-In not available** into the Message for browsers without plug-in support field.
6. Into the Height and Width fields, enter the dimensions (in pixels) of the area that you want the plug-in to take up on the Web page.

Note: *Most video clips look good when displayed at the default dimensions of 128 x 128 pixels. The plug-in that the Web browser calls to play the video clip will make the adjustments it needs to keep the aspect ratio of the image constant. For example, if you change the dimensions to 128x640 pixels, the plug-in will still display the video clip as a square image (if that is the way it was recorded) with extra blank (either white or black) space to the left and right of the image in the plug-in's area on the Web page. If you double both dimensions (i.e. specify a height and width of 256x256 pixels) and insert a video clip recorded with a screen size of 128 x 128 pixels, some plug-ins will increase the size of the image (and make it appear grainy), while other plug-ins will display the video clip at its recorded dimensions and fill the unused portion of the plug-in's area with a white or black border. The best method for setting the plug-in's dimensions is to accept the default, and then experiment by displaying the Web page using different browsers and adjusting the plug-in's dimensions such that the video clip looks best in relation to the page layout and the way it is displayed in the majority of the browsers.*

7. Normally, you will clear the Hide plug-in checkbox when you insert a video clip on a Web page. After all, the whole point is to let the site's visitors see the video clip. However, if you are using the plug-in to playback a multimedia file (such as an MPG, MPEG, or AVI file) which has both video and audio and you want only the audio portion, or if you are using the plug-in to play a sound file, click your mouse pointer on the Hide plug-in checkbox until a checkmark appears. When you click a checkmark into the Hide plug-in checkbox, the

browser will still call the plug-in to process the multimedia file, however, the Web browser does not let the plug-in display its output on the onscreen in a portion of the browser's application window.

8. Click the drop-down list button to the right of the Alignment field to select the way in which you want Web page text to flow around the video clip. You have the same options for text/video clip alignment that you learned about in a previous Tip titled "Understanding Picture/Text Alignment Options."
9. If you want a border around the video clip, enter the pixel width of the border into the Border thickness field. Conversely, to display the video clip without a border, leave the Border thickness field blank.
10. Into the Horizontal spacing field, enter the number of pixels of blank space you want the Web browser to leave between the video clip and Web page elements to the left and right of it on the Web page.
11. Into the Vertical spacing field, enter the number of pixels of blank space you want the Web browser to leave between the video clip and Web page elements above and below it on the Web page.
12. Click your mouse pointer on the OK button near the lower right-hand corner of the Plug-In Properties dialog box. FrontPage, in turn, will generate the HTML for the <EMBED> (embedded) tag on the Page view HTML tab, close the Plug-In Properties dialog box, and display the plug-in icon shown in Figure 207.3 on the current Web page at the location where you chose to embed the video clip (in Step 2).

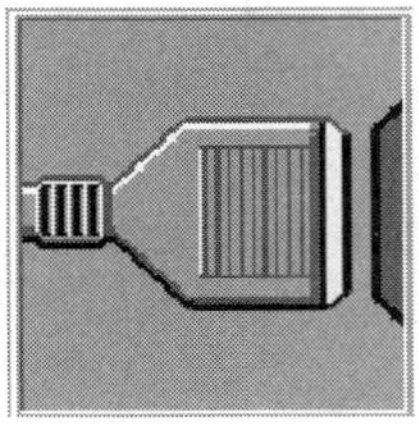

Figure 207.3 The placeholder for a Plug-In display area.

FrontPage will not play the video clip you inserted while on the Page view Normal tab. However, if you click your mouse pointer on the Preview tab, FrontPage will display the Web page as it will appear in a Web browser and play the video clip you inserted.

WORKING WITH VIDEO CLIP PROPERTIES

In the preceding Tip, you learned how to use the Plug-In Properties dialog box to embed a video clip on a Web page and how to control the size, borders, and alignment of the video clip's display area in the browser's application window. After, the Web browser passes the video clip to the plug-in, the browser's responsibilities for processing the video clip are finished. If you look at the HTML for the <EMBED> (embedded) tag that FrontPage generated when you inserted the video clip using the procedure in the preceding Tip, you will notice the lack of attributes that specify playback options.

For example, the attributes of a standard <EMBED> (embedded) tag such as:

```
<embed width="128" height="128"
       src="../MultiMedia/kowloon.avi">
       <noembed>Helicopter Tour of Kowloon</noembed>
```

include only the pixel width and height of the plug-in's display area, the address of the file that the browser is to pass to the plug-in for processing, and the text to display if the browser does not support plug-ins. If the plug-in's display area has a border, uses other than the default alignment with other text in the same paragraph, and is to be offset from other elements on the page by white space, the <EMBED> (embedded) tag will have ALIGN, BORDER, HSPACE, and VSPACE attributes, as well. However, control of the video clip's playback is left to the plug-in. Other than calling the plug-in and passing the video clip's address to it, the Web browser treats the embedded video clip as it would a graphics image—it creates a placeholder in which the rendering program (the browser's plug-in for video clip playback, in this case) will display its results.

Conversely, when you use the Insert menu Picture option to insert a video clip on a Web page (as you learned to do in a previous Tip titled "Adding Video to a Web Page for Playback by Internet Explorer Only"), the Web browser (Internet Explorer) controls not only the video clip's display area and alignment with other elements on the Web page, but also the playback of the video clip itself. For example, if you used the Insert menu Picture option to insert the same video clip embedded in a Web page by the procedure in the preceding Tip, FrontPage would generate the <IMG> (image) tag:

```
<img border="0" dynsrc="../MultiMedia/kowloon.avi"
     start="fileopen" width="128" height="128">
```

Notice that the preceding <IMG> (image) tag, contains not only dimension and border width attributes, but also tells the Web browser when to start the video clip—on "fileopen" (i.e. as soon as the browser retrieves the clip from the Web server), in the current example.

To work with the properties of a video clip inserted as an image on a Web page, perform the following steps:

1. Open the Web page with the video clip whose properties you want to change, and select the View menu Page option to display the page on the Page view Normal tab.
2. Right-click your mouse pointer on the video clip's placeholder on the Web page and select Picture Properties from the pop-up menu. FrontPage, in turn, will display the Picture Properties dialog box.
3. If not already exposed, click your mouse pointer on the Video tab to display video clip playback controls shown in Figure 208.

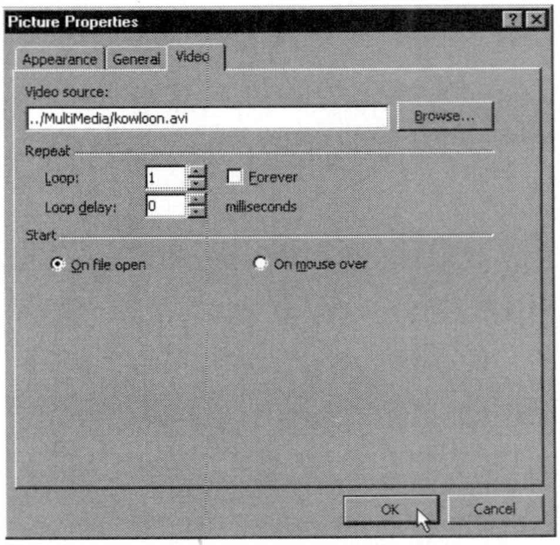

Figure 208 The Microsoft FrontPage Picture Properties dialog box, Video tab.

4. If you want to insert a different video clip on the Web page, enter the relative address of the new video clip into the Video source field at the top of the dialog box. Alternatively, click your mouse pointer on the BROWSE button to the right of the Video source field and use the resources available on the Video dialog box to navigate to and select the video clip you want.
5. If you want the Web browser to play the video clip continuously until the visitor tells it to stop or moves on to another Web page, click your mouse pointer on the Forever checkbox until a checkmark appears. Then, continue at Step 7. (If you tell the Web browser to play the video clip Forever, the site visitor can stop the playback by right-clicking the mouse pointer on the video clip in the Web browser's application window and selecting Stop from the pop-up menu.)
6. Into the Loop field, enter the number of times you want the Web browser to play the video clip.

7. If you entered a number greater than 1 into the Loop field or used the mouse pointer to click a checkmark into the Forever checkbox, and into the Loop delay field, enter the number of milliseconds you want the browser to wait after playing the video clip before repeating the video clip's playback from the beginning of the clip.
8. If you want the Web browser to start playing the video clip as soon as it retrieves clip from the Web server, click your mouse pointer on the On file open radio button. Otherwise, to have the Web browser display only the first frame of the video clip on the Web page and start the clip's playback only after the site visitor passes the mouse pointer over it, click your mouse pointer on the On mouse over radio button.
9. Click your mouse pointer on the OK button near the lower right-hand corner of the Picture Properties dialog box.

After you complete Step 9, FrontPage will update the <IMG> (image) tag's DYNSRC and START attributes and add LOOP and LOOPDELAY attributes as necessary to pass the specifications you entered in the fields of the Video tab on to the Web browser.

Note: *You already learned how the work with the Appearance and General tabs in the Picture Properties dialog box in previous Tips that dealt with working on graphics image properties. Remember, using the Insert menu Picture option to insert a video clip on a Web page tells FrontPage to use an <IMG> (image) tag to place the video clip on the page. As such, you control the dimensions of the video clip, how it aligns with other elements on the Web page, whether or not it has a border, and what to display if the video clip is unavailable by using the same procedures you used to work with these properties for a static graphics image.*

ADDING A SOUND FILE FOR PLAYBACK USING A PLUG-IN

As you might expect, embedding a sound file in a Web page is similar to embedding a video clip. After all, both video clips and digitally recorded sounds are stored in files (albeit in different formats), and as you learned previously, the Web browser simply passes the embedded file to the appropriate plug-in (i.e. helper file) for processing.

Unlike video clips, which require that you allocate an area on the Web page in which to view them, sound files need no display space when the plug-in plays them back for the site visitor. As such, when adding sound to your Web page, you can insert a visible set of buttons that let the site visitor control the sound file's playback, or (as you will learn how to do in the next Tip) you can hide the controls and have the browser play the sound file in the background while the visitor views the page.

To embed a sound file with playback controls visible on the Web page, perform the following steps:

1. On the Page view Normal tab, open the Web page on which you wish to insert the sound file.
2. Position the cursor on the Web page where you want the sound file's playback control buttons to appear, and then select the Insert menu Web Component option. FrontPage, in turn, will display an Insert Web Component dialog box (similar to that shown previously in Figure 207.1).
3. Click your mouse pointer on **Advanced Controls** in the Component type list box on the left-hand side of the dialog box, and then on **Plug-In** in the Chose a control list box on the right-hand side of the dialog box. Then, click your mouse pointer on the FINISH button in the lower right-hand corner of the Insert Web Component dialog box. FrontPage, in turn, will display a Plug-In Properties dialog box (similar to that shown previously in Figure 207.2).
4. Into the Data source field, enter the sound file's relative address or uniform resource locator (URL). For example, if you wanted to insert the sound file CANYON.MID stored in the MULTIMEDIA folder in the current web onto a Web page stored in another subfolder of the current web's root folder, you would enter the relative address **..\MULTIMEDIA\CANYON.MID** into the Data source field. Alternatively, click your mouse pointer on the BROWSE button to the right of the Data source field and use the resources available on the Select Plug-In Data Source dialog box to navigate to and select the sound file you want to insert.
5. Into the Message for browsers without plug-in support field, enter the text you want the Web browser to display instead of the sound file playback controls if the browser does not support the use of plug-ins (helper programs). For example, you might enter a message such as **Sound file player Plug-In not available** into the Message for browsers without plug-in support field.
6. Into the Height and Width fields, enter the dimensions (in pixels) of the area that you want the plug-in to take up on the Web page. Although the actual size of the playback controls depends on the plug-in installed to play sound files on the visitor's computer, entering 46 into the Height field and 146 into the Width field will display a set of sound file playback control buttons similar to one of those shown in Figure 209.

Sound File Playback Controls
46 x 146 (Pixel Height x Width)

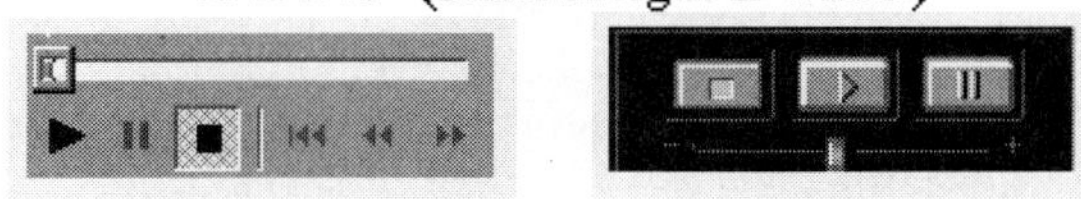

Internet Explorer **Netscape Navigator**

Figure 209 Sound file plug-in playback controls (dimensions: 46 x 146 pixels).

7. Clear the Hide plug-in checkbox, since you want the visitor to see and use the sound file plug-in's controls on the Web page.
8. Click the drop-down list button to the right of the Alignment field to select the way in which you want Web page text to flow around the sound file playback controls. You have the same options for text/playback control alignment that you learned about in a previous Tip titled "Understanding Picture/Text Alignment Options."
9. If you want the Web browser to draw a border around the sound file playback controls, enter the pixel width of the border into the Border thickness field. Conversely, to display the playback controls without a border, leave the Border thickness field blank.
10. Into the Horizontal spacing field, enter the number of pixels of blank space you want the Web browser to leave between the sound file playback controls and Web page elements to the left and right of it on the Web page.
11. Into the Vertical spacing field, enter the number of pixels of blank space you want the Web browser to leave between the sound file playback controls and Web page elements above and below it on the Web page.
12. Click your mouse pointer on the OK button near the lower right-hand corner of the Plug-In Properties dialog box. FrontPage, in turn, will generate the HTML for the <EMBED> (embedded) tag on the Page view HTML tab, close the Plug-In Properties dialog box, and display a plug-in icon (similar to that shown previously in Figure 207.3) on the current Web page at the location where you chose to insert the sound file in Step 2.

FrontPage will not display the sound file playback controls nor will it play the sound file while on the Page view Normal tab. However, if you click your mouse pointer on the Preview tab, FrontPage will display the Web page as it will appear in the Web browser and let you use the sound file playback controls to listen to the sound file you inserted on the Web page as often as you like.

ADDING BACKGROUND SOUNDS TO A WEB PAGE FOR PLAYBACK USING A PLUG-IN

In previous Tips, you learned how to use the tabs on the Page Properties dialog box to set the color of and/or select an image to act as the background of a Web page. The next Tip will show you how to use the fields on the Page Properties dialog box General tab to generate the HTML that tells the visitor's Web browser play a sound file in the background while displaying the Web page content. However, if you use the Page Properties dialog box to embed a background sound file on a Web page, only the Microsoft Internet Explorer will play the sound file.

As was the case with video clips, if you want a variety of Web browsers to play a background sound file, you must rely on a plug-in instead of using an ActiveX control. To insert a sound file on a Web page and hide its play back controls, such that the Web browser calls a plug-in to play the sound file automatically when the Web browser retrieves the Web page, perform the following steps:

1. On the Page view Normal tab, open the Web page on which you wish to insert the background sound file.
2. Position the cursor before the first element on the page and select the Insert menu Web Component option. FrontPage, in turn, will display an Insert Web Component dialog box (similar to that shown previously in Figure 207.1).

Note: *Although you can insert the background sound file anywhere on the Web page (since its controls will not be visible), put the file at the top of the page, so Web browsers will retrieve the sound file as the first non-text element on the page. When it finds the background sound file ahead of any other graphics images on the Web page, the visitor's browser will start playing the sound file before it retrieves the other pictures.*

3. Click your mouse pointer on **Advanced Controls** in the Component type list box on the left-hand side of the dialog box, and then on **Plug-In** in the Chose a control list box on the right-hand side of the dialog box. Then, click your mouse pointer on the FINISH button in the lower right-hand corner of the Insert Web Component dialog box. FrontPage, in turn, will display a Plug-In Properties dialog box (similar to that shown previously in Figure 207.2).
4. Into the Data source field, enter the relative address or uniform resource locator (URL) of the sound file. For example, if you wanted to insert the sound file SugarPlumFairyDance.MID stored in the

Multimedia folder in the current web onto a Web page stored in another subfolder of the current web's root folder, you would enter the relative address **..\Multimedia\SugarPlumFairyDance.MID** into the Data source field. Alternatively, click your mouse pointer on the BROWSE button to the right of the Data source field and use the resources available on the Select Plug-In Data Source dialog box to navigate to and select the sound file you want to insert.

5. Leave the Message for browsers without plug-in support field blank. (If the Web browser does not support plug-ins, you do not want the site visitor to know that there is a background sound file, since the browser will not play it.)
6. Enter a **1** into both the Height field and the Width field.
7. Click your mouse pointer on the Hide plug-in checkbox until a checkmark appears.
8. Click your mouse pointer on the OK button near the lower right-hand corner of the Plug-In Properties dialog box. FrontPage, in turn, will generate the HTML:

```
<embed width="1" height="1"
       src="../Multimedia/SugarPlumFairy.MID" hidden>
```

on the Page view HTML tab, close the Plug-In Properties dialog box, and display a small (barely recognizable) plug-in icon on the Page view Normal tab.

9. Click your mouse pointer on the HTML button do display the Web page HTML and find the <EMB> (embedded) tag generated in the preceding Step—you need to add the AUTOSTART attribute.
10. Move the cursor before the "h" in the HIDDEN attribute at the end of the <EMB> (embedded) tag for the background sound file, type: **autostart="true"** and then press the SPACEBAR. (Make sure you leave at least one space before **autostart** and at least one space after the close quotes in "**true**".)
11. Click your mouse pointer on the Normal tab.

To hear the sound file the Web browser's plug-in will play in the background while you view the Web page content, click your mouse pointer on the Preview tab. As an alternative, select the File menu Preview in Browser option. If you have more than one Web browser installed on your computer, FrontPage, in turn, will display a Preview in Browser dialog box similar to that shown in Figure 210.

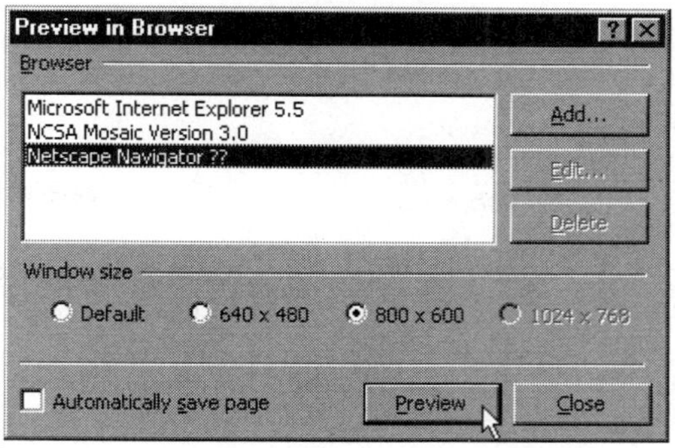

Figure 210 The Microsoft FrontPage Preview in Browser dialog box.

Click your mouse pointer on the Web browser in which you wish the preview the Web page content (while listening to the background sound file), and then on the PREVIEW button near the lower right-hand corner of the dialog box. FrontPage, in turn, will start the Web browser you selected and pass to it the current the Web page. Shortly thereafter you will hear your system's sound file plug-in (helper program) play the background sound file you inserted on the Web page.

When you are finished with the preview, click your mouse pointer on the close button (the "X") in the upper right-hand corner of the Web browser's application window, to close the browser and return the Page view Normal tab.

ADDING BACKGROUND SOUNDS TO A WEB PAGE FOR PLAYBACK BY INTERNET EXPLORER ONLY

As mentioned in the preceding Tip, FrontPage lets you use the General tab on the Page Properties dialog box to insert a sound file on the Web page background. The advantages of using the Page Properties dialog box to add background music to a Web page are that you can control the number of times the Web browser will play the sound file and the procedure for embedding the sound file into the Web page background is (slightly) simpler than the procedure in a previous Tip titled "Adding Background Sounds to a Web page for Playback Using a Plug-In."

However, if you use the Page Properties dialog box to insert a sound file onto the Web page background, only Microsoft's Internet Explorer will play the background sound file while displaying the page content. Therefore, only use the following method to add background music to a Web page if you are creating a site accessible only to those individuals using Internet Explorer. Otherwise, perform the procedure in the preceding Tip, so that everyone is able to enjoy the music you so meticulously selected—regardless of the browser used.

To insert a background sound file only the Microsoft Internet Explorer will play, perform the following steps:

1. On the Page view Normal tab, open the Web page on which you wish to insert the background sound file.
2. Right-click your mouse pointer anywhere on the Web page, and select Page Properties from the pop-up menu. FrontPage, in turn, will display the Page Properties dialog box.
3. If not already exposed, click your mouse pointer on the General tab.
4. Into the Location field in the Background sound section near the center of the General tab, enter the relative address or uniform resource locator (URL) of the sound file. For example, if you wanted to insert the sound file Anthem.MID stored in the Multimedia folder in the current web onto a Web page stored in another subfolder of the current web's root folder, you would enter the relative address **..\Multimedia\Anthem.MID** into the Data source field. Alternatively, click your mouse pointer on the BROWSE button to the right of the Location field and use the resources available on the Background Sound dialog box to navigate to and select the sound file you want to insert.
5. If you want the Web browser to play the sound file repeatedly (without end) while the visitor views the Web page, click your mouse pointer on the Forever checkbox to the right of the Loop field below the Location field. Otherwise, into the Loop field, enter the number of times you want the Web browser to repeat the sound file. (If you enter **0** into the Loop field, the Internet Explorer will play the background sound file one time.)
6. Click your mouse pointer on the OK button near the lower right-hand corner of the Page Properties dialog box. FrontPage, in turn, will close the Page Properties dialog box, insert the <bgsound> (background sound) tag:

```
<bgsound src="../Multimedia/Anthem.MID" loop="-1"
```

   the header section of the Web page HTML, and return to the Page view Normal tab.

Note: *FrontPage sets the value of the LOOP attribute to "-1" if you click a checkmark into the Forever checkbox to tell the Web browser to repeat the sound file an indefinite (unlimited) number of times. The Web browser will play the sound file once if LOOP attribute has a value of "0" and will play the sound file the number of times indicated in the attribute's value for LOOP values greater than "0."*

After you complete Step 6 of the preceding procedure, you will not notice anything different on the Web page because the background sound file does not add a visible element or content placeholder to the Web page body. Moreover, FrontPage, will not play the sound file while on the Page view Normal tab. To hear the sound playing in the background while you view the Web page content, click your mouse pointer on the Preview tab.

UNDERSTANDING TABLES

Each table on a Web page serves one of two purposes—it is either used to display related data values in tabular form (i.e. in rows of columns like a spreadsheet) or as a design tool to establish a grid of cells the developer can use to position text and graphics at specific locations on the page. HTML, the language used to create Web pages, was initially designed as a device independent way to share information between computers. Unfortunately, without knowing the display size, resolution, and graphics capability of the site visitor's computer, a Web page developer cannot specify that text and graphics images appear at specific x-y locations on the visitor's computer screen. In fact, standard HTML contains no positioning tags or attributes other than those the specify left, right, top, bottom, or center alignment of one element on a page in relation to another. Moreover, the original HTML specification did not include color attributes to allow people using computers with color graphics cards to share documents (unaltered) with those working on systems with monochrome screens.

Nowadays, it is hard to find a Web page without at least one color graphics image, and almost every computer used to surf the Internet is able to display at least 256 colors (with the majority of systems able to display millions of colors). As a result, color attributes have become a standard part of HTML tags, and all but a few of the oldest, legacy browsers support them. (Monochrome, text only Web browsers are like black and white television sets—you can still find and use them, but why would you?)

While every computer (for all practical purposes) can now display color graphics, physical screen display size and resolution settings still vary from system to system. As a result, standard HTML still excludes the tags and attributes necessary to place graphics and text at specific locations on a Web page (and by extension) at specific x-y coordinates on the site visitor's computer screen. Web browsers simply do not have the capability to translate coordinates, if specified in Web page HTML, into physical screen locations because the user can change the screen resolution settings and/or the size of the browser's application window at any time during a session.

Tables give the Web page developer a pseudo-absolute positioning capability. The Web browser draws a table without the benefit of knowing the desired x-y location of the table itself on the computer screen. However, the Web browser does know the exact dimensions of each of the table's cells and can therefore position elements (text and/or graphics) placed in a cell at a specific location relative to the cell's borders and the table's point of origin on the computer screen.

The next several Tips will show you how to create and use tables to display information in a tabular format (i.e. rows of individual data items arranged in columns with headings) and how to use tables as grids of cells to arrange graphics and text on a Web page. For now the important thing to know is that HTML lets you specify how text and graphics are to look on a Web page (i.e. the color, size, and font for text and the dimensions of graphics images) but not the location at which the browser is to display them. When you want to tell the Web browser *where* to put text and graphics, create a table to establish a grid of cells, and then tell the browser to put text and/or graphics items into specific cells within the table.

USING A TEMPLATE TO CREATE A TABLE

The easiest way to understanding how tables can help you with Web page layout is to select one of the 17 design templates that FrontPage provides on the Page Templates dialog box. (Although you will find more than 16 page templates on the General tab of the Page Templates dialog, only those that use tables for page layout are described here.)

FrontPage design templates that use tables to layout (or position) the elements on a page will let you create a Web page with one of the following looks:

- **Narrow, Left-aligned Body** – Web page with one column of text with lines that span up to 1/2 the width of the Web page, and the column of text is in the left-hand half of the page.
- **Narrow, Right-aligned Body** – Web page with one column of text with lines that span up to 1/2 the width of a Web page. Text content is in the right-hand half of the page.
- **One-column Body** – Web page with one column of text centered between the margins of the page.
- **One-column Body with Contents and Sidebar** – Web page with one column of text between a table of contents on the left and a sidebar on the right. (The sidebar might be a set of illustrations for the text content to its left, or perhaps a set of hyperlinks to related items or other pages on the Web site.)
- **One-column Body with Contents on Left** – Web page with a single column of text to the right of a table of contents along the left-hand side of the page.
- **One-column Body with Contents on Right** – Web page with a single column of text to the left of a table of contents along the right-hand side of the page.

- **One-column Body with Staggered Sidebar** – Web page with one column of text to the right of two columns of sidebar items. The sidebar items are staggered such that the first begins in the leftmost (first) sidebar column; then, the second item begins below the first in the rightmost (second) sidebar column; and the third item begins below the second in the leftmost (first) sidebar column, and so on.
- **One-column Body with Two Sidebars** – Web page with one column of text between a staggered sidebar along the left-hand margin of the Web page and a single (non-staggered) sidebar along the right-hand margin of the page.
- **One-column Body with Two-column Sidebar** – Web page with a single column of text to the left of two columns of sidebar items along the right-hand side of the page.
- **Three-column Body** – Web page with three columns of text.
- **Two-column Body** – Web page with two columns of text.
- **Two-column Body with Contents and Sidebar** – Web page with two columns of text between a table of contents along the left-hand side of the Web page and a sidebar along the right-hand side of the page.
- **Two-column Body with Contents on Left** – Web page with two columns of text to the right of a table of contents along the left-hand side of the page.
- **Two-column Staggered Body** – Web page with two columns of text arranged such that text items are staggered with the first item (idea or paragraph) is in the first (left-hand) column; the next item begins in the second (right-hand) column below the last line of the first item; then, the third item begins in the first (left-hand) column below the last line of the second item and so on.
- **Two-column Staggered Body with Contents and Sidebar** – Web page with two columns of staggered text to the right of a table of contents along the left-hand side of the Web page and a sidebar along the right-hand side of the page.
- **Wide Body with Headings** – Web page with a single column of text with preceded by a main heading and with individual concepts on the page separated by subheadings that act as titles for each new item.

To create a Web page from one of the FrontPage design templates that use tables for page layout, perform the following steps:

1. Select the File menu New option and click your mouse pointer on Page or Web. FrontPage, in turn, will display the New Page or Web menu along the right-hand side of the application window.
2. On the New Page or Web menu, click your mouse pointer on Page Templates under the New from template heading in the bottom half of the menu. FrontPage, in turn, will display a Page Templates dialog box similar to that shown in Figure 213.

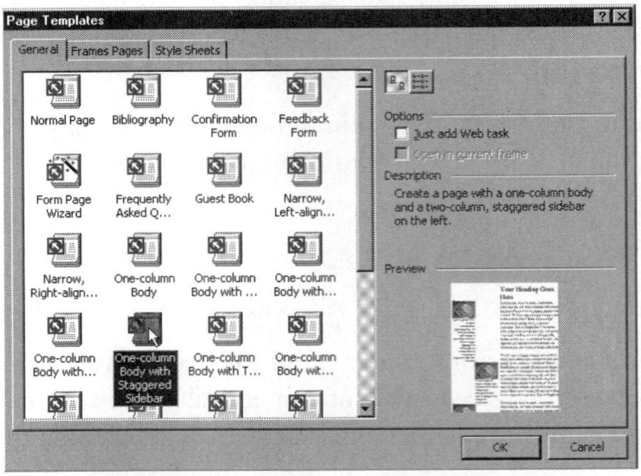

***Figure 213** The Microsoft FrontPage Page Templates dialog box, General tab.*

3. Click your mouse pointer on the template you want to use for the new Web page. (To see the different page layouts available, click your mouse pointer on template icons one at a time. FrontPage, in turn, will show you the template's "look" in the Preview section near the lower right-hand section of the dialog box.) For the current project, click your mouse pointer on the icon for the **One-column Body with Staggered Sidebar** template.
4. Click your mouse pointer on the OK button near the lower right-hand corner of the Page Templates dialog box. FrontPage, in turn, will use tables to create a new Web page with the layout you selected and display the page with "dummy" text and graphics images on the Page view Normal tab.

To create a web page with the content you want your site's visitors to see, replace the headings, graphics images, and "dummy" text used by FrontPage in the web page design template. FrontPage, in turn, will expand and contract the borders of the tables used to position elements on the Web page (shown as dotted lines in the Page view Normal tab) as you add and remove content.

To see what the Web page looks like (without the dotted borders along the edges of the hidden, positioning tables), click your mouse pointer on the Preview tab (near the lower left-hand corner of the Page view pane in the FrontPage application window. FrontPage, in turn, will display the Web page as it will appear in a visitor's Web browser. Although the tables are still there (holding text and graphics elements in place within their cells), the table borders are invisible, so you only see the Web page content arranged according to the template you selected.

USING THE MOUSE POINTER TO "DRAW" A TABLE ON A WEB PAGE

In addition to letting FrontPage generate tables for you by selecting a page layout (as you learned to do in the preceding Tip), you can use the mouse pointer to draw tables, one at a time, on a Web page. While the tables FrontPage generates when you use a design template to create a Web page with a specific layout always have hidden borders, all of the tables you draw on the Web page using the mouse pointer will (initially) have visible edges. After you draw the table you want, you can "hide" its border and the interior grid lines that surround its cells by changing the width of the borders to zero (0), so you can use the table for positioning Web page elements rather than as a visible table used to display tabular data.

To draw a table on a Web page, perform the following Steps:

1. Open the Web page on which you want to draw the table and select the View menu Page option to display the page on the Page view Normal tab.
2. Position the FrontPage vertical cursor in the Web page where you want to insert a table, and press the ENTER key as necessary to create a blank area on which to draw the new table. (Give yourself plenty of white space to draw the new table—you can select and remove blank lines you do not want later.)
3. Select the Table menu Draw Table option. FrontPage, in turn, will display the Tables toolbar and display the mouse pointer as a pencil (instead of an arrow).
4. Move the pencil mouse pointer to the point on the Web page at which you want the upper left-hand corner of the table to appear. Click and hold down the left mouse button as you drag the pencil mouse pointer down and to the right until it reaches the point at which you want the lower right-hand corner of the table to appear. Then, release the left mouse button. FrontPage, in turn, will draw a table with a single cell, similar to the one shown in Figure 214.1.

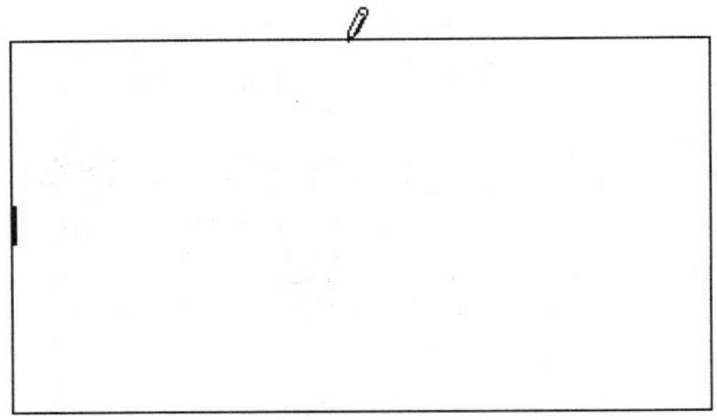

Figure 214.1 Table with a single cell.

5. To split a table column into two columns, move the pencil mouse pointer onto the border at the top of the table to the right of the table's left border (or to the right of another column's right-hand margin) at the width you want the new column have. Click and hold down the left mouse button as you drag the mouse pointer vertically down the length of the table (and the new column). FrontPage, in turn, will draw a dashed line showing where it will place the right-hand margin of the new column—extending the dashed line as you drag the pencil mouse pointer down the table. When the dashed line reaches the border at the bottom of the table, release the left mouse button. For the current project, "draw" a line vertically down the center of a table starting at a point similar to that shown in Figure 214.1, to split the single cell table created in Step 4, into two cells similar to that shown in Figure 214.2.

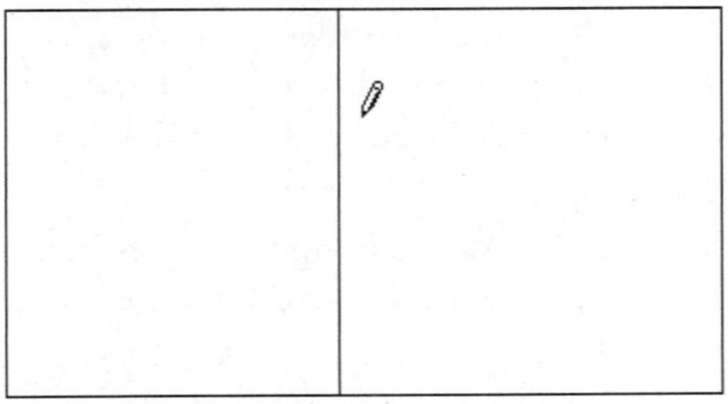

Figure 214.2 A table with two cells.

6. To split a table row into two rows, move the pencil mouse pointer to just right of the row's left-hand margin below the border at the top of the table or the below the bottom of the row above the new row at the

width you want the row to have. (If you move the pencil mouse pointer onto a vertical grid line in the interior of the table, FrontPage will change the mouse pointer to a double-headed arrow; move the mouse pointer a little to the right to change it back into a pencil.) Then, click and hold down the left mouse button as you drag the mouse pointer horizontally along the length of the new row. FrontPage, in turn, will draw a dashed line showing the bottom edge of the new row. When the dashed line reaches the new row's right-hand margin, release the left mouse button. For example, if you split the right-hand cell shown in figure 214.2 into five (approximately) equal rows, it will appear similar to that shown in Figure 214.3 just prior to the release of the left mouse button as you draw the line to split the fourth row in two—thereby creating the table's fifth row.

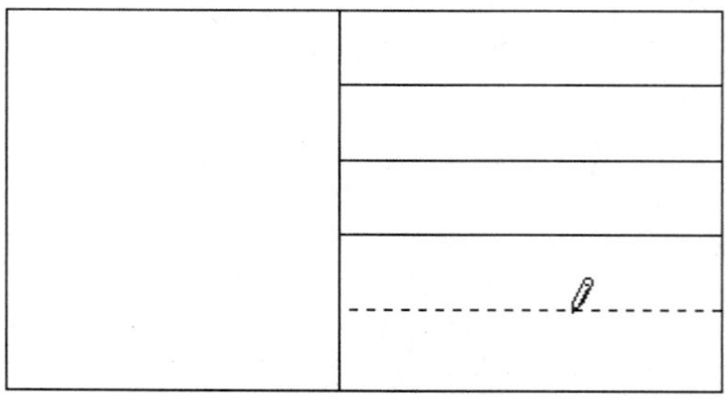

Figure 214.3 A table with two cells, with the right-hand cell split into five rows.

You can continue to split columns and rows as often as you like by repeating Steps 5 and 6. When you are finished drawing new columns and rows on the table, click your pencil mouse pointer at a point outside the table to leave table edit mode.

If you change your mind about splitting a row or column as you are splitting it, move the pencil mouse pointer back to the point at which you started the split. FrontPage, in turn, will shorten the length of the dashed line it draws as you drag the mouse pointer across the table. When the dashed line no longer spans the width of a row or column in the table, release the left mouse button. Alternatively, if you have already released the left mouse button and drawn a line on the table for a new set of rows or cells, select the Edit menu Undo Resize option to undo the row or column split and remove the new line from the table.

USING THE INSERT TABLE BUTTON TO INSERT A TABLE

In addition to "drawing" a table's border, and then using the mouse pointer to draw the interior gridlines that form the borders and margins of the table's rows and columns (as you learned to do in the preceding Tip), FrontPage also lets you create a table by clicking the mouse pointer on a button on the Standard toolbar. Not surprisingly, the button used to create a table, the Insert Table button (eighth button from the right) on the Standard toolbar, is labeled with a table icon.

To use the Insert Table button to insert a table on a Web page, perform the following steps:

1. Open the Web page on which you wish to insert a table and select the View menu Page option to display the page on the Page view Normal tab.
2. Position the FrontPage vertical cursor in the Web page where you want to insert the table.
3. Click your mouse pointer on the Insert Table button (eighth button from the right) on the Standard toolbar. FrontPage, in turn, will display a small drop-down grid of table cells, similar to that shown in Figure 215.

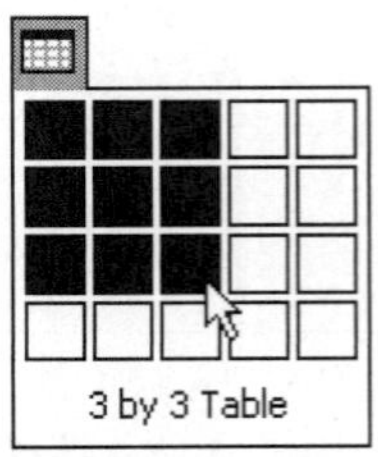

Figure 215 The Standard toolbar Insert Table button and drop-down grid of table cells.

4. Click and hold down the left mouse button as you drag your mouse pointer across the grid until FrontPage indicates it will draw the number of rows and columns you want. Drag the mouse pointer down, toward the bottom of the application window to increase the number of rows, or up to decrease the row count. Drag the mouse pointer to the right to increase the number of columns, or to the left to decrease the column count. (As you drag the mouse pointer toward an edge on the drop-down grid of table cells, FrontPage will increase the size of the grid, so you can insert a table with more than four rows of five columns each.)
5. After you highlight the number of columns and rows you want the new table to have in the Insert Table button's drop-down grid, release the left mouse button. (You can also see the number of rows and columns the new table will have by looking a the "X by Y Table" caption below the squares in the drop-down grid—where "X" is the number of rows and "Y" is the number of columns.)

After you release the left mouse button in Step 5, FrontPage, in turn, will insert a table with the number of rows and columns you selected from the drop-down grid on the Web page at the insertion point you set in Step 2. If you change your mind about inserting the new table as you are creating it, drag the mouse pointer to the left of the left-hand edge of the drop-down grid or to a point above the top of the grid, and then release the left mouse button. Alternatively, if you have already completed Step 5 to place the new table on the Web page, select the Edit menu Undo Insert option to remove the table you just inserted.

USING THE TABLE MENU INSERT TABLE OPTION TO CREATE A TABLE

Rather than using the mouse pointer to draw a new table on a Web page or creating a table by selecting the number of rows and columns from a drop-down grid, you can use the Insert Table dialog box to add a table to a Web page. In addition to specifying the number of rows and columns in the new table, the Insert Table dialog box also lets you specify the amount of space you want between the table's cells, the amount of space (in pixels) you want to leave between a cell's borders and its contents, the width of the border around the table, and the alignment of the table with other elements on the Web page.

To insert a table using the Insert Table dialog box, perform the following steps:

1. Open the Web page on which you wish to insert a table and select the View menu Page option to display the page on the Page view Normal tab.
2. Position the FrontPage vertical cursor in the Web page where you want to insert a table.
3. Select the Table menu Insert option and click your mouse pointer on Table. FrontPage, in turn, will display the Insert Table dialog box shown in Figure 216.

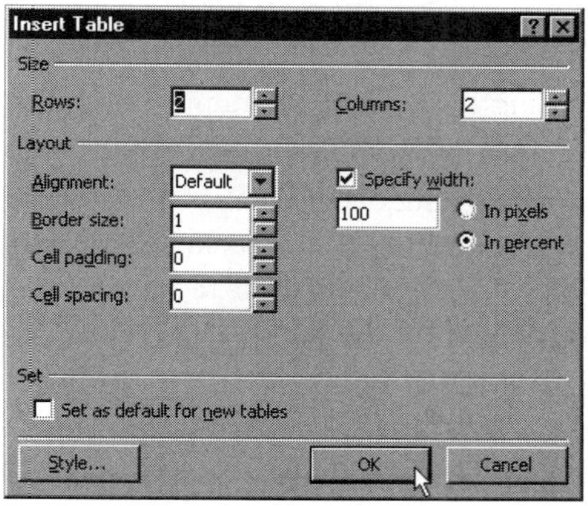

Figure 216 *The Microsoft FrontPage Insert Table dialog box.*

4. Into the Rows field in the Size area at the top of the dialog box, enter the number of rows you want the table to have, and into the Columns field, enter the number of columns. For example, to create a table with 5 rows (across the page) and 4 columns per row (down the page), enter a **5** into the Rows field and a **4** into the Columns field.
5. Click the drop-down list button to the right of the Alignment field and select the table's alignment on the Web page. Select **Left** to place the table's left-hand side flush with the left margin on the Web page; select **Right** to place the table's right-hand side flush with the right margin; select **Center** to center the table between the Web page's left and right margins; or select **Default** to place the left-hand side of the table where you placed the cursor in Step 2.
6. If you want the Web browser to adjust the table's width based on the sum of the widths of the widest objects you placed in its columns, clear the Specify width checkbox. Conversely, if you want the table to be a specific width, click your mouse pointer on the Specify width checkbox until a checkmark appears. Then, enter the table's width in pixels or as a percentage of the width of the Web browser's application window into the field below the Specify width checkbox. For example, to create a table that is half as wide as the Web browser's application window, click a checkmark into the Specify width checkbox, click your mouse pointer on the In percent radio button, and enter **50** into the field below the Specify width checkbox.
7. Into the Border size field, enter the width (in pixels) of the border around the outside of the table. Entering a width greater than (0) only sets the width of the border that encloses the table's cells. Conversely, if you enter zero (0) into the Border size field, the table will have neither visible borders nor visible interior grid lines.
8. Into the Cell padding field, enter the number of pixels of blank space the Web browser is to leave between each cell's margins and borders and the cell's contents.
9. Into the Cell spacing field, enter the number of pixels of blank space the Web browser is to leave between the margins of adjacent cells.
10. If you want to use the values you entered in the Layout section of the Insert Table dialog box as the defaults values FrontPage will use when you use the Table menu Insert option to create tables in the future, click your mouse pointer on the Set as default for new tables checkbox until a checkmark appears. Otherwise, clear the checkbox.
11. Click your mouser pointer on the OK button near the lower right-hand corner of the Insert Table dialog box.

After you complete Step 11, FrontPage will close the Insert Table dialog box, insert a new table on the Web page, and return to the Page view Normal tab. If you change your mind about inserting the table, select the Edit menu Undo Insert option.

INSERTING TEXT AND IMAGES INTO A TABLE

After you create a table, you will want to fill at least some (if not all) of its cells with content you want the Web site visitor to see and read. Placing text into a table cell is as simple as typing words onto a Web page. For example, to enter text into the third cell of the second row in a table, simply click the mouse pointer on the third cell in the second row to position the FrontPage vertical cursor (i.e. the insertion point). Then, type the text you want to see in that cell on the Web page. After you type text content into a cell, you can change its appearance by using the mouse pointer to select the text, and then work with the text's properties (i.e. its alignment, spacing, font, size, color, etc.), as you learned to do in previous Tips.

To insert a graphics image into a table, click your mouse pointer on the cell in which you wish to insert the image. Then, select the Insert menu Picture option and click your mouse pointer on Clip Art, From File, From Scanner or Camera, or Video—depending on the source of the image or video clip you want to insert. Next, perform the steps in the procedures you learned in previous Tips for inserting graphics images and video clips onto a Web page—only this time, insert the object into a cell in a table on the Web page instead of directly on the Web page itself. Do not worry about the size of a table cell relative to the size of the image or video clip you want to insert in the cell. As was the case with the (left and right) margins and (top and bottom) borders of a Web page, FrontPage will expand the dimensions of the cell into which you insert the graphics image or video clip such that it is large enough to accommodate the inserted object.

In short, FrontPage lets you work with the content within each of the table's cells as if the element you place within the cell were on a separate Web page. For example, you can use left, right, and center alignment to align text (or a graphics image) along the left, right, or at the center between the left-hand and right-hand margins (sides) of a cell in the table—just as you learned to align text and graphics images in relation to the left and right margins on a Web page in a previous Tip titled "Aligning Text." You can also select the background color for each cell in the table (independent of the background color of any other cell in the table) by working with the Color field in the Background section of the Cell Properties dialog box. (To display the Cell Properties dialog box, right-click the mouse pointer on the cell whose properties you want to change, and select Cell Properties from the pop-up menu.)

The next 20 Tips show you how to work with the appearance of a table, the appearance of content inserted into the table's cells, the alignment of text and graphics images placed in the same cell, and the alignment of the table itself in relation to the left and right margins of the Web page on which the table is inserted. In short, you will learn not only how to work with a table as an element (like text or a graphics image) on a Web page, but also how to work with a table as if it were a group of (little Web pages) held together by the table's interior gridlines. Each of the table's cells exhibits Webpage-like (text, image, and background) formatting and insertion capabilities.

ALIGNING CELL CONTENTS HORIZONTALLY

FrontPage lets you control both the horizontal and vertical alignment of the contents of each cell. By default, FrontPage aligns cell contents (horizontally) flush with the cell's left-hand margin and (vertically) centered between the top and bottom of the cell. To change the horizontal (left and right) alignment of a cell's contents, perform the following steps:

1. On the Page view Normal tab, open the Web page that contains the table with which you want to work.
2. Right-click your mouse pointer on the cell whose alignment you want to change and select Cell Properties from the pop-up menu. FrontPage, in turn, will display the Cell Properties dialog box.
3. Click your mouse pointer on the drop-down list button to the right of the Horizontal alignment field at the top of the dialog box, and select the alignment you want to use in aligning the cell's content between its left and right margins. Horizontal alignment options are **Default** (left), **Left**, **Right**, **Center**, and **Justify**.
4. Click your mouse pointer on the OK button near the center at the bottom of the Cell Properties dialog box to apply the alignment you selected in Step 3 to the cell you selected in Step 2 and return to the Page view Normal tab.

Figure 218 shows examples of a table whose cells were formatted using each of the five horizontal alignment options.

Instead of aligning cell contents one at a time, you can also select the cells whose alignments you want to change one row at a time or one column at a time. To select a column of cells, move your mouse pointer to the top edge of the column whose properties you want to change. When FrontPage changes the mouse pointer to a small black arrow (such as the one shown at the one shown above the word DEFAULT at the top of the table in Figure 218), click the left mouse button to select the column. Alternatively, click your mouse pointer on one of the cells in the column of table cells you want to select. Then, select the Table menu Select option and click your mouse pointer on Column.442

Similarly, to select a row of cells, move the mouse pointer to the left-hand border of the row you want to select, and click the left mouse button when FrontPage changes the mouse pointer to a small black arrow. Alternatively, click your mouse pointer on one of the cells in the row of table cells you want to select. Then, select the Table menu Select option and click your mouse pointer on Row.

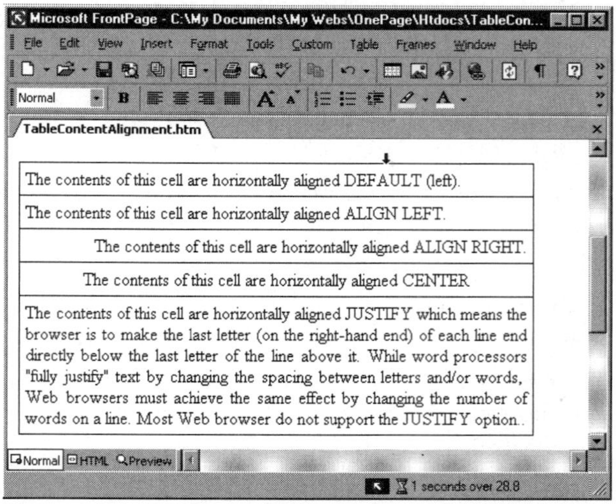

Figure 218 *Table with text aligned using each of the five horizontal alignment options.*

After you select the cells in the row or column you want, right-click your mouse pointer on any of the cells you selected. Then, select Cell Properties from the pop-up menu and continue at Step 3 of the procedure in this Tip.

Note: *When applying the Justify alignment to a cells text content, beware that most Web browsers either do not support Justify at all (and will therefore ignore the ALIGN attribute's value when you set it to justify) or do not support it very well. Justify implies that the text in the cell should be flush with the both the cell's left-hand and its right-hand margin. That is to say, the first and last letter on each line is to begin directly below the first and last letter (respectively) of the text on the line above it—thereby giving the text in the cell the appearance of starting and ending flush with both the cell's right-hand and left-hand margin. Word processors achieve the full justification effect by varying the spacing between letters in a word and between words on a line. Web browsers that support the Justify alignment option try to achieve the flush with both margins effect by moving a word (or two) from the end of one line to the beginning of the next. Unfortunately, if you apply Justify alignment to a cell's text content, the cell's text will appear fully justified when you view the Web page on the Page view Normal tab, but will appear Left justified (with a jagged right edge) when you use a Web browser (even the Microsoft Internet Explorer) to view the table.*

ALIGNING CELL CONTENTS VERTICALLY

You can align the contents of a cell vertically (i.e. relative to the top and bottom borders of the cell), as well as, horizontally between the cell's left and right margins, which you learned to do in the previous Tip. By default, FrontPage aligns cell contents (horizontally) flush with the cell's left-hand margin and (vertically) centered between the top and bottom of the cell.

To change the vertical (up and down) alignment of a cell's contents, perform the following steps:

1. On the Page view Normal tab, open the Web page that contains the table with which you want to work.
2. Right-click your mouse pointer on the cell whose vertical alignment you want to change, and select Cell Properties from the pop-up menu. FrontPage, in turn, will display the Cell Properties dialog box.
3. Click your mouse pointer on the drop-down list button to the right of the Vertical alignment field at the top of the dialog box, and select the alignment you want to use in adjusting the cell's content in relation to its top and bottom borders. Vertical alignment options are **Default** (middle), **Top**, **Middle**, **Baseline**, and **Bottom**.
4. Click your mouse pointer on the OK button near the center at the bottom of the Cell Properties dialog box to apply the alignment you selected in Step 3 to the cell you selected in Step 2 and return to the Page view Normal tab.

Figure 219 shows examples of a table whose cells were formatted using four of the five vertical alignment options.

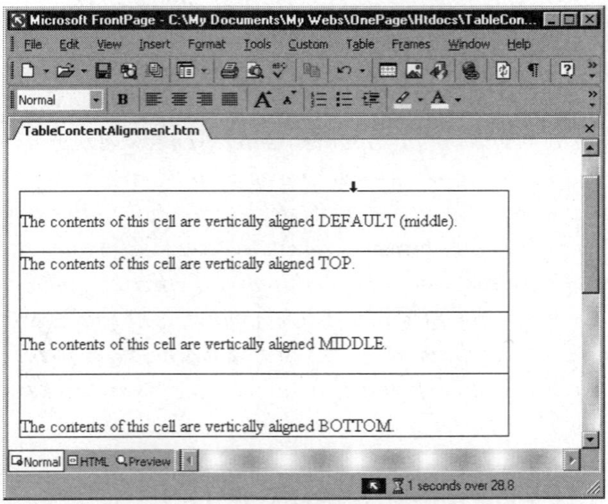

Figure 219 Table with text aligned using four of the five vertical alignment options.

Note: *Baseline and Middle alignment have essentially the same effect on text alignment. While Middle alignment centers the text between the top and bottom borders of the cell along an invisible line drawn through the center of the letters in the text, Baseline alignment uses an invisible line drawn along the bottom (vs. the center) of the text's letters. As such, Baseline alignment may give a slightly above vertical center appearance to the cell's text.*

Instead of aligning cell contents one at a time, you can also select the cells whose alignments you want to change one row at a time or one column at a time. To select a column of cells, move your mouse pointer to the top edge of the column whose properties you want to change. When FrontPage changes the mouse pointer to a small black arrow (such as the one shown at the one shown above the word DEFAULT at the top of the table in Figure 219), click the left mouse button to select the column. Alternatively, click your mouse pointer on one of the cells in the column of table cells you want to select. Then, select the Table menu Select option and click your mouse pointer on Column.

Similarly, to select a row of cells, move the mouse pointer to the left-hand border of the row you want to select, and click the left mouse button when FrontPage changes the mouse pointer to a small black arrow. Alternatively, click your mouse pointer on one of the cells in the row of table cells you want to select. Then, select the Table menu Select option and click your mouse pointer on Row.

After you select the row or column you want, right-click your mouse pointer on any of the cells you selected. Then, select Cell Properties from the pop-up menu and continue at Step 3 of the procedure in this Tip.

ADDING HEADINGS TO A TABLE

FrontPage lets you use the Header cell field on the Cell Properties dialog box to emphasize the contents of a row of cells, a column of cells, or even individual cells by telling the Web browser to change the bolding (i.e. the weight of the letters) and the alignment the text in the heading cell(s). When you are using a table to display items in tabular form, you often use the values in the columns across the first row (at the top) of the table to as the title or description of the items in the column of cells below the heading. As such, you may want to set off the first row's contents in some way to show that the contents of its columns are not data values but the headings that describe data values in the cells below the headings.

FrontPage lets you format table cells as table headings (using <TH> </TH> (table heading) tags) by performing the following steps:

1. On the Page view Normal tab, open the Web page that contains the table with which you want to work.

2. To select all of the cells in a row or column as headings, click your mouse pointer on one of the cells in the row or column of cells whose contents you want to use as column or row headings. Then, select the Table menu Select option, and click your mouse pointer on Row to select all of the cells in the same row as the cell on which you clicked the mouse pointer; or select the Table menu Select option and click your mouse pointer on Column to select all of the cells in the same column as the cell with the FrontPage vertical cursor.
3. Right-click your mouse pointer on one of the cells in the column or row you selected in Step 2, and select Cell Properties from the pop-up menu to work with the properties of all of the selected cells at once. If you skipped Step 2 because you want to designate an individual cell as a table heading, right-click the mouse pointer on the cell whose properties you want to change, and select Cell Properties from the pop-up menu.
4. Click your mouse pointer on the Header cell checkbox near the bottom of the layout section at the top of the Cell Properties dialog box until a checkmark appears.
5. Click your mouse pointer on the OK button near the center at the bottom of the Cell Properties dialog box.

FrontPage, in turn, will change the cell's tags in the Web page HTML from <TD></TD> (table data) to <TH></TH> (table heading), bold the text in the cell, and both vertically and horizontally center the cell's contents. FrontPage will also bold and center (both horizontally and vertically) any text you enter into an empty cell you format as a table heading or text you add to the existing contents of a heading cell.

If you later change your mind about a cell's "table heading" designation, you can convert a table heading cell back to a normal, table data cell by repeating the preceding procedure and clearing the Header cell checkbox in Step 4.

ADDING A CAPTION TO A TABLE

In addition to adding a row or column of heading cells that identify for the viewer what the values in the column or row represent (as you learned in the preceding Tip), you can add a *caption* as a title above the table or a footnote below the table. Although found within a table's <TABLE></TABLE> tags in the Web page HTML, a table's caption is not enclosed by the border (if any) around the table, nor does it take on the table's background color.

To add a caption as a title centered at the top of a table, perform the following steps:

1. Open the Web page with the table to which you want to add a caption, and select the View menu Page option to display the page on the Page view Normal tab.
2. Click your mouse pointer anywhere on the table on which you wish to place a caption.
3. Select the Table menu Insert option, and click your mouse pointer on Caption. FrontPage, in turn, will center its vertical cursor above the border at the top of the table.

Note: *If Caption is grayed out (as unavailable) on the list of selections FrontPage displays when you select the Table menu Insert option, then the table already has a caption. To edit an existing caption, click your mouse pointer on the caption (or in the area above the table where the caption should be), and make the changes you want. If you want to remove the caption altogether, click and hold down the left mouse button as you drag the mouse pointer across the words in the caption to select them. Then, press the BACKSPACE or DELETE key twice—once to remove the caption's text and the second time to delete the <CAPTION></CAPTION> tags from the Web page HTML.*

4. Enter the table's caption.

As you type the caption, FrontPage will center the text above the table. Since the caption can only extend the width of the table, FrontPage will split the caption onto multiple lines if the text you type would extend beyond the left and right sides of a table if displayed on a single line.

If you want to center the caption below the border at the bottom of the table (instead of above the border at the top of the table), perform the following steps:

1. Use the Page view Normal tab to display the Web page with the table that has the caption you want to move.
2. Right-click your mouse pointer on any word in the caption, and select Caption Properties from the pop-up menu. FrontPage, in turn, will display the Caption Properties dialog box shown in Figure 221.

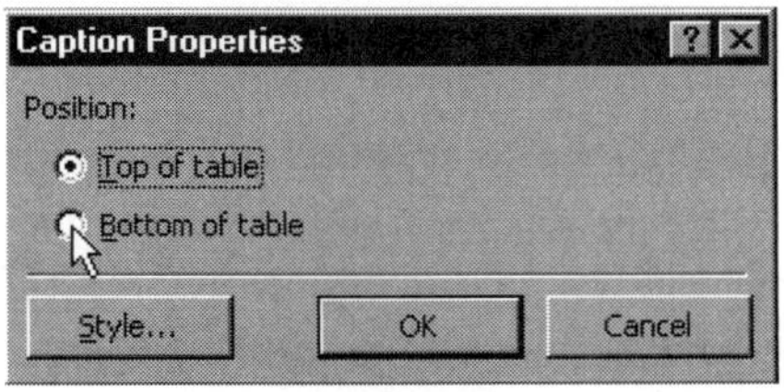

Figure 221 The Microsoft FrontPage Caption Properties dialog box.

3. To change the location of the caption such that it appears below the border at the bottom of the table, click your mouse pointer on the Bottom of table radio button.
4. Click your mouse pointer on the OK button near the bottom center of the Caption Properties dialog box.

After you complete Step 4, FrontPage will move the table caption from its location above the border at the top of the table to its new location below the border at the bottom of the table. If you later want to move the caption such that it appears above the table, repeat the preceding procedure and click your mouse pointer on the Top of table radio button (instead of the Bottom of table radio button) in Step 3.

CHANGING THE SIZE OF A TABLE

Although the size of a table's cells (and as a result, the size table itself) will expand and contract based on the size of content you put in them, you can specify the table's dimensions explicitly. However, when setting a table's height and width attributes, keep in mind that no matter what dimensions you specify, a table will always take at least the minimum amount of space required to display the contents of all of its cells. For example, if you specify that a table is to be 100 pixels wide and the table has contains three graphics images, each of which are 100 pixels in width, the table will be at least 300 pixels wide when the visitor's browser displays it.

After you insert a table on a Web page, you can specify its size (i.e. its height and width) by performing the following steps:

1. Open the Web page with the table whose size you want to set, and select the View menu Page option to display the page on the Page view Normal tab.
2. Right-click your mouse pointer anywhere on the table, and select Table Properties from the pop-up menu. FrontPage, in turn, will display a Table Properties dialog box similar to that shown in Figure 222.
3. To specify the table's minimum width, click your mouse pointer on the Specify width checkbox at the top of the Layout section at the top of the dialog box until a checkmark appears. On the other hand, if you want the Web browser to use the minimum width required to display table's borders, gridlines, and the contents of its cells, clear the Specify width checkbox and continue at Step 6.
4. If you want to specify the table's minimum width in pixels, click your mouse pointer on the In pixels radio button. Otherwise, to specify the

table's minimum width as a percentage of the width of the Web browser's application window, click your mouse pointer on the In percent radio button.

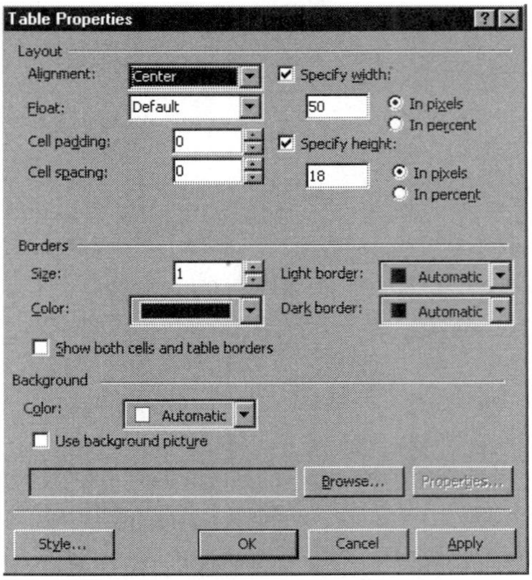

Figure 222 *The Microsoft FrontPage Table Properties dialog box.*

Note: *If you specify that the table is to be at least specific number of pixels in width and the table's width is wider than the Web browser's application window, the browser will display a horizontal scrollbar the site visitor can use to scroll the Web page horizontally to see the parts of the table that extend beyond the left and right sides of the browser's application window. Conversely, if you specify the table is to take up a percentage of the browser's application window, the width of the table will expand as the user increases the width of the browser's application window and contract if the visitor reduces the application window's width—up to a point. The table's width will only shrink to the minimum width required to display the contents of its cells. A cell with text content, for example, will only shrink to the width of the longest word in the cell; a cell with a graphics image will only shrink to the width of the graphics image. As such, it is possible for the visitor's Web browser to present a horizontal scroll bar when displaying a table even if you set the table's minimum width to be 100% (or less) of the width of the browser's application window.*

5. Into the field below the Specify width checkbox, enter the minimum number of pixels or percentage of the browser's application window the table is to occupy.
6. To specify the table's minimum height, click your mouse pointer on the Specify height checkbox near the bottom of the Layout section at the top of the dialog box until a checkmark appears. On the other

hand, if you want the Web browser to use the minimum height required to display the table's borders, interior gridlines, and the contents of its cells, clear the Specify height checkbox and continue at Step 9.

7. If you want to specify the table's minimum height in pixels, click your mouse pointer on the In pixels radio button. Otherwise, to specify the table's minimum height as a percentage of the height of the Web browser's application window, click your mouse pointer on the In percent radio button.

Note: *If you specify that the table is to be at least specific number of pixels in height and the table's height is greater than the height of the Web browser's application window, the browser will display a vertical scrollbar the site visitor can use to scroll the Web page vertically to see the part of the table that extends beyond the top or bottom of the browser's application window. Conversely, if you specify the table is to take up a percentage of the browser's application window, the height of the table will increase as the user increases the height the browser's application window and contract if the visitor reduces the application window's height—again, only up to a certain point. The table's height will only shrink to the minimum height required to display the contents of its cells. A cell with text content, for example, will only shrink to the height required to display the number of lines of text it contains; a cell with a graphics image will only shrink to the height of the graphics image. As such, it is possible for the visitor's Web browser to present a vertical scroll bar when displaying a table even if you set the table's minimum height to be 100% (or less) of the height of the browser's application window.*

8. Into the field below the Specify height checkbox, enter the minimum number of pixels or percentage of the browser's application window the table is to occupy.
9. Click your mouse pointer on the OK button near the bottom center of the Table Properties dialog box.

After you complete Step 9, FrontPage will update the table's definition in the Web page HTML and change its size based on the value(s) you entered into the Height and/or Width fields. If you specified the value(s) in the Height and/or Width fields as percentage (by clicking the mouse pointer on the In percent radio button), FrontPage will size the table as a percentage of the space available on the Page view Normal or Page view Preview tab.

WORKING WITH THE ALIGNMENT OF A TABLE ON A WEB PAGE

You learned how to align text and graphics images with the left and right margins on a Web page (or the left and right margin of a table cell) in a previous Tip titled "Understanding Picture/Text Alignment Options." If you create a table whose width is less than the 100%

the width of the Web page, you can align the table such that the Web browser will display the table flush against the left margin, flush against the right margin, or centered between the left and right margins on the Web page.

To change the alignment of a table relative to the margins on a Web page, perform the following steps:

1. Open the Web page with the table whose alignment you want to change, and select the View menu Page option to display the page on the Page view Normal tab.
2. Right-click your mouse pointer on the table whose alignment you want to modify, and select Table Properties from the pop-up menu. FrontPage, in turn, will display a Table Properties dialog box similar to the one in Figure 222.
3. Click your mouse pointer on the drop-down list button to the right of the Alignment field at the top of the Layout section at the top left-hand side of the dialog box. FrontPage, in turn, will display a drop-down list of alignment options below the Alignment field.
4. Click the mouse pointer on the alignment option you want in the drop-down list of alignment options displayed below the Alignment field. Select the **Left** or **Default** to place the table's left side flush with the left-hand margin on the Web page; select **Right** to place the table's right side flush with the right-hand margin on the Web page; or select **Center** to center the table between the left and right margins on the page.
5. Click your mouse pointer on the OK button near the bottom center of the Table Properties dialog box.

   After you complete Step 5, FrontPage will close the Table Properties dialog box and align the table you selected in Step 2 with the Web page margins as you specified in Step 4.

When selecting a table's alignment option, bear in mind that some older Web browsers (such as NCSA Mosaic) do not support the <CENTER></CENTER> tags used to center the table between the left and right margins on the Web page. If a visitor using an older Web browser views your page, the browser will ignore tags it does not understand (i.e. the <CENTER></CENTER> tags) and display the centered table flush against the Web page's left margin—which is the default placement for a table absent an alignment option.

Note: *Setting the table's alignment option only tells the Web browser where to display the table relative to the left and right margins on the Web page. The table's alignment with the Web page margins has no effect on the alignment of objects stored in the table relative to the right and left margins of the cell that holds each object.*

CREATING A FLOATING TABLE

A *floating* table does not hover above other content on a 3-dimensional Web page. To the contrary, so-called floating tables sit flat (against the background) on a Web page—just like all other tables. What turns an ordinary table into a floating table is the fact that text adjacent to a floating table wraps around the table's right or left side, similar to that shown in Figure 224. In an ordinary, non-floating table, text in the same paragraph with the table but outside its cells will appear above and below the table—not along either its left or right side.

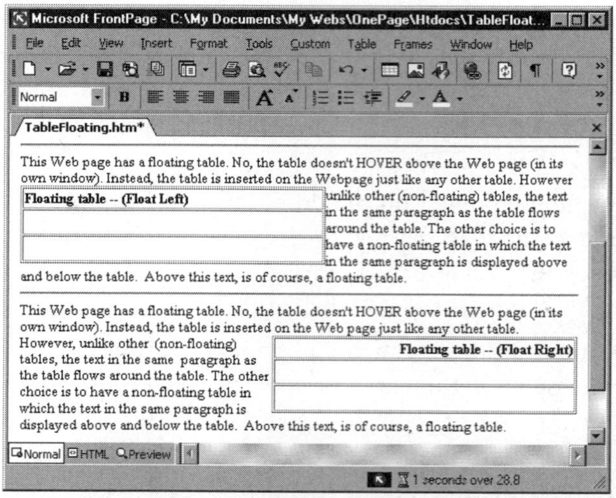

Figure 224 A Web page with two floating tables—the first aligned Left and the second aligned Right.

To create a floating table, perform the following steps:

1. Open the Web page with the table you want to float and select the View menu Page option to display the page on the Page view Normal tab.
2. Right-click your mouse pointer on ordinary table you want to change into a floating table, and select Table Properties from the pop-up menu. FrontPage, in turn, will display a Table Properties dialog box similar to the one you saw previously in Figure 222.
3. Click your mouse pointer on the drop-down list button to the right of the Float field near the top of the Layout section at the top of the dialog box. FrontPage, in turn, will display a drop-down list of float options below the Float field.

4. Decide whether you want text adjacent to the table to wrap around the left or right-hand side of the table. If you want to align the table with the right-hand margin on the Web page and wrap adjacent text down the left-hand side of the table, click the mouse pointer **Right** in the drop-down list below the Float field. Conversely, if you want to align the table with the left-hand margin on the Web page and warp adjacent text around the right-hand side of the table, click the mouse pointer on **Left**.
5. Click your mouser pointer on the OK button near the bottom center of the Table Properties dialog box.

After you complete Step 5, FrontPage will align the table with the Web page margin you specified in Step 4 and wrap any text that follows the table around the right-hand side of the table if you select **Left** in Step 4 (or around the left-hand side of the table if you selected **Right**).

If you change your mind and no longer want text to wrap around either side of a table, repeat the preceding procedure, only select **Default** in Step 4. FrontPage, in turn, will change the floating table back into a default (non-floating) table and move any text wrapped around the side of the previously floating table to a position below the table.

Note: *You can change a default (non-floating) table into a floating table before or after you add the text you want to wrap around the table. To float a (default) non-floating table on a Web page without any text following the table, perform the steps in the preceding procedure. After FrontPage aligns the table with either the right-hand or left-hand margin on the Web page (depending on the selection you made in Step 4), move the FrontPage vertical cursor to the corner at the top of the table on the side along which you want the text to appear and start typing the content you want.*

ADDING ROWS AND COLUMNS TO A TABLE

In a previous Tip titled: "Changing the Size of a Table," you learned how to change a table's dimensions. However, changing the width and/or height of a table only changes the size of its cells—not their number. FrontPage lets you add cells to the table one cell at a time (as you will learn in the next Tip) or several cells at once by adding one or more rows or columns to the table.

To increase the number of rows or columns in a table, perform the following steps:

1. On the Page view Normal tab, open the Web page with the table you want to modify.

2. If you plan to insert one or more columns of cells, click your mouse pointer in one of the cells in the table column where you want the new column(s) to appear. Otherwise, if you plan to insert one or more rows of cells, click your mouse pointer in one of the cells in the row of the table immediately above or below the point where you want to insert the new row(s).
3. Select the Table menu Insert option and click your mouse pointer Rows or Columns. FrontPage, in turn, will display the Insert Rows or Columns dialog box shown in Figure 225.

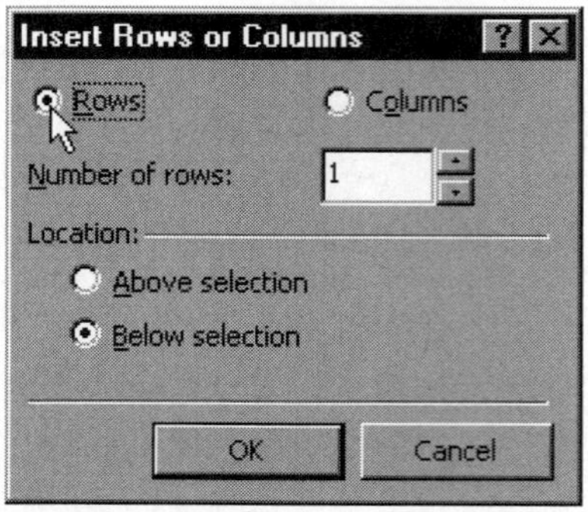

Figure 225 *The Microsoft FrontPage Insert Rows or Columns dialog box.*

4. If you want to insert one or more rows, click your mouse pointer on the Rows radio button. Otherwise, click your mouse pointer on the Columns radio button to insert one or more columns.

Note: *FrontPage will set the labels on the field and radio buttons below the Rows and Columns radio buttons based on whether you click the mouse pointer on the Rows radio button or on the Columns radio button in Step 4. If you click the mouse pointer on the Rows radio button, the field and radio button labels will be those shown in Figure 225. Conversely, if you click your mouse pointer on the Columns radio button, FrontPage will change the field label to Number of columns and change will change the labels of the radio buttons to Left of selection and Right of selection.*

5. If you clicked the mouse pointer on the Rows radio button in Step 4, into the Number of rows field, enter the number of rows you want to insert. Then, click the mouse pointer on the Above selection radio button to insert the new row(s) above the row in which you clicked the mouse pointer in Step 2; or click the mouse pointer on the Below selection radio button to insert the new row(s) below the row.

   Similarly, if you clicked the mouse pointer on the Columns radio button in Step 4, into the Number of columns field, enter the number of columns you want to insert. Then, click the mouse pointer on the Left of selection radio button to insert the new column(s) to the left of the column in which you clicked the mouse pointer on Step 2; or click the mouse pointer on the Right of selection radio button to insert the new column(s) to the right of the column.

6. Click your mouse pointer on the OK button near the bottom center of the Insert Rows or Columns dialog box. FrontPage, in turn, will insert the number of rows (or columns) you specified in Step 5 and return to the Page view Normal tab.

You can also use the Insert Rows button and the Insert Columns button on the Tables toolbar to insert rows and columns into a table. To do so, click the mouse pointer on the cell in the table where you want to insert the new row or column. FrontPage, in turn, will display the Tables toolbar. (If FrontPage does not display the Tables toolbar, select the View menu Toolbars option and click your mouse pointer on Tables to display the toolbar.) Each time you click the mouse pointer on the Insert Rows button (third button from the left on the Tables toolbar) FrontPage will insert a single row above the row with the cell in which you clicked the mouse pointer. Similarly, each time you click the mouse pointer on the Insert Columns button (fourth button from the left on the Tables toolbar), FrontPage will insert a column to the left of the column with the cell in which you clicked the mouse pointer.

ADDING A SINGLE CELL TO A TABLE

In addition to adding an entire row or column of cells to a table, FrontPage also lets you insert cells one cell at a time. Normally, you will only insert individual cells in a table used for page layout (vs. a table use to display tabular data). After all, if you insert a single cell in a table meant to display tabular data, you will either have a heading that has no data beneath it, or a data value with no heading that tells what it means.

To add a single cell to a table, perform the following steps:

1. Open the Web page with the table to which you want to add the additional cell, and select the View menu Page option to display the page on the Page view Normal tab.
2. Click your mouse pointer in the cell you want FrontPage to move to the right to make room for another cell.
3. Select the Table menu Insert option and click your mouse pointer on Cell. FrontPage, in turn, will add a new cell to the left of the cell in which you clicked the mouse pointer in Step 2.

When you insert individual cells to a table, the table will keep its rectangular shape—even if some of the rows or columns in the table have more cells than others. For example, if you perform the steps in the preceding procedure to add a cell to the table at the top of the Web page in Figure 226, the result will be a table similar to the one shown at the bottom of the figure.

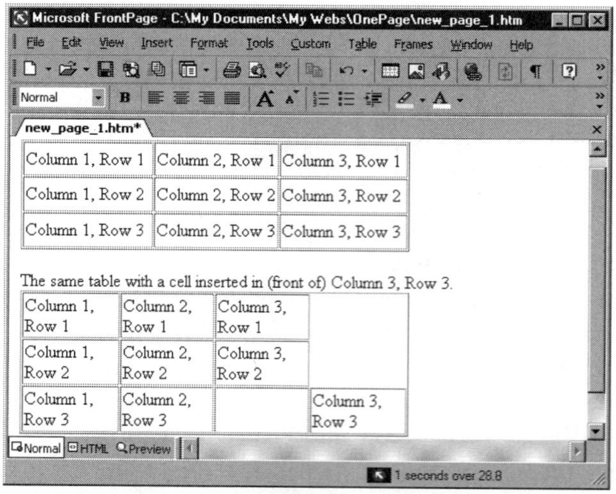

Figure 226 *A Web page showing the effects of adding a single cell to a 3-row by 3-column table.*

FrontPage maintains the table's rectangular shape by reducing the width of cells in the row to which you add a cell and padding rows with fewer cells with blank space that is neither a cell in the table nor blank space available for text or other Web page content. For example, in the current example, the table's width remains constant because FrontPage reduced the existing columns in the third row and padded the first two rows to keep the right-hand side of the table straight.

As shown by the current example, FrontPage will split single lines of text onto multiple lines (thereby increasing the height of the cells and the table) in an effort to keep the table's width constant. (FrontPage tries to accumulate the horizontal space it needs for the new column by reducing the width of existing column in the same row.) However, if the cells in the row to which you add the new cell contain graphics images that completely fill the cells or already have a single word of text per line, FrontPage will not be able to steal the space it needs for the new cell from other cells in the same row. When this happens, FrontPage will increase the width of the table by moving the table's right-hand side outward (to the right).

SPLITTING A SINGLE TABLE CELL INTO MULTIPLE CELLS

Rather than adding new cells to a table (either individually or a row or column at a time), you can increase the number of cells in a table by dividing a single cell into multiple cells. In effect, splitting a cell involves creating two or more rows or columns within a single cell. For example, Figure 227.1 shows the results of splitting the upper left-hand cell of a four-cell table into three columns and dividing the lower right-hand cell into three rows.

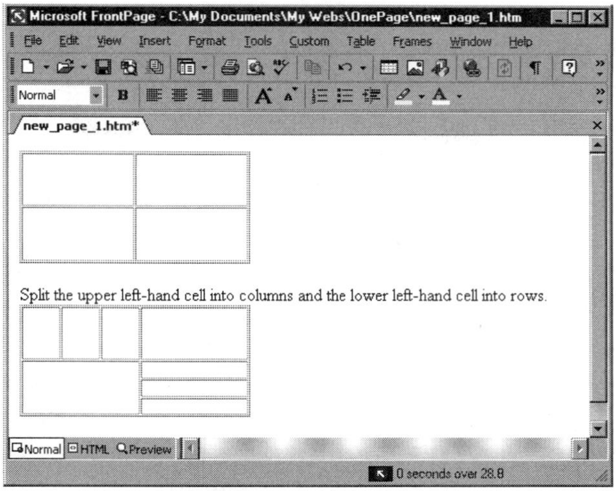

Figure 227.1 Two tables showing the effects of splitting cells into columns and rows.

To split a single cell in a table into multiple rows or columns, perform the following steps:

1. Open the Web page with the table you want to modify, and select the View menu Page option to display the page on the Page view Normal tab.
2. Right-click the mouse pointer on the cell you want to split into multiple columns or rows, and select Split Cells from the pop-up menu. FrontPage, in turn, will display the Split Cells dialog box shown in Figure 227.2.

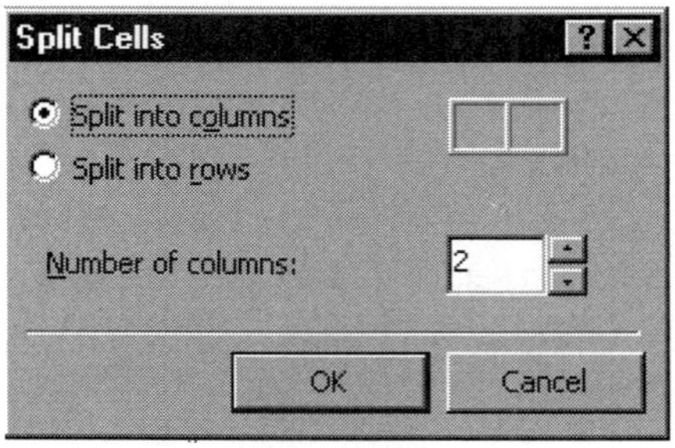

Figure 227.2 The Microsoft FrontPage Split Cells dialog box.

3. If you want to split the cell into multiple columns, click your mouse pointer on the Split into columns radio button. Conversely, if you want to split the cell into multiple rows, click the mouse pointer on the Split into rows radio button. FrontPage, in turn, will change the

graphic to the right of the radio buttons and the label of the field below the graphic to show rows or columns—depending on the radio button on which you clicked the mouse pointer.

4. If you click the mouse pointer on the Split into columns radio button (in Step 3), then into the Number of columns field, enter the number of columns into which you want to divide the cell you selected in Step 2. Conversely, if you click the mouse pointer on the Split into rows radio button, then into the Number of rows field, enter the number of rows into which you want to split the cell you selected in Step 2.
5. Click your mouse pointer on the OK button near the bottom center of the Split Cells dialog box. FrontPage, in turn, will split the cell in which you placed the cursor in Step 2 into the number of rows or columns you specified in Step 4.

If you want to split more than one cell into multiple rows or columns, click and hold down the left mouse button as you drag the mouse pointer across the cells you want to split in Step 2. Next, right-click your mouse pointer on any of the cells selected and then select Split Cells from the pop-up menu. Then, perform Steps 3 – 5 of the procedure in this Tip. When you complete Step 5, FrontPage will apply the Split (into rows or columns) you specified in Steps 3 – 4 to all of the columns you selected in Step 2.

MERGING MULTIPLE TABLE CELLS INTO A SINGLE CELL

In the preceding Tip, you learned how to split a single cell in a table into multiple rows or columns—thereby creating a set of smaller cells. FrontPage also lets you combine (or merge) multiple contiguous rows or columns of cells into a single, larger cell—i.e. reversing the process of splitting a cell into multiple rows or columns that you learned in the preceding Tip.

To merge two or more cells into a single larger cell, perform the following steps:

1. Open the Web page with the table with the cells you want to merge and select the View menu Page option to display the page on the Page view Normal tab.
2. Hold down the SHIFT key while you click your mouse pointer on the cells you want to combine into a single, larger cell. After you have selected you want to merge, release then release the SHIFT key.

Note: *Be sure to select only adjacent cells in either rows* **or** *columns. If you select noncontiguous cells or select both cells in rows* ***and*** *columns, FrontPage will not make the merge option available on the Table menu in the next Step.*

3. Select the Table menu Merge Cells option.

After you complete Step 3, FrontPage will remove the lines between the cells you selected in Step 2, and create a single, larger cell from the set of smaller cells.

NESTING TABLES WITHIN TABLES

As mentioned previously, the individual cells in a Table are like mini-Web pages. As such, you can insert just about any element into a cell that you can insert onto a Web page—including, text, a graphics image, bulleted list, numbered list, and even another table. *Nesting* (or inserting) a table in a cell within another table gives you a similar effect to splitting the cell into multiple rows and columns. However, unlike the splitting cells, inserting a table within another lets you set the cell spacing, cell padding, width of the border around, and the dimensions of the new cells created in the table—independent of the properties of the enclosing table.

To insert a table within another table, perform the following steps:

1. Open the Web page with the table into which you want to nest, or insert another table and select the View menu Page option to display the page on the Page view Normal tab.
2. Click your mouse pointer in the cell into which you want to create a nested table.
3. Nest the table in the column you selected in Step 2 by performing the steps in the table creation procedure you learned in a previous Tip titled "Using the Insert Table Button to Create a Table," or the steps of the procedure in the Tip titled "Using the Table Menu Insert Table Option."

If you insert a table within another table, the effect will be similar to that shown in Figure 229, which shows a nine-cell table inserted into the cell in the upper left-hand corner of a four-cell table.

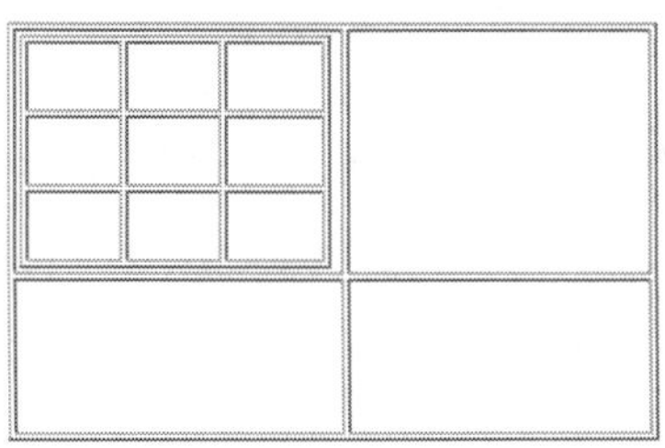

***Figure 229** A four-cell table with another table nested in its upper left-hand corner.*

Inserting tables into cells in other tables is a useful technique when you are using the tables for page layout, which you learn more about in the Tip titled "Using Tables for Page Layouts." In short, nesting a table within another lets you position elements on a Web page more precisely by increasing the number of cells in the grid and giving you greater control over the dimensions of individual cells and their positions on the Web page.

REMOVING ROWS, COLUMNS, AND CELLS FROM A TABLE

As you learned in a previous Tip titled "Merging Multiple Table Cells into a Single Cell," you can remove a column or row of cells from a table by deleting the lines between the cells to combine them into a single, larger cell. However, sometimes you may just want to remove individual cells or an entire column or row of cells altogether—without using them to create a new, larger cell.

To remove one or more cells from a table, perform the following steps:

1. On the Page view Normal tab, open the Web page with the table you want to modify.
2. Use your mouse pointer to select the cells you want to remove. For example, to select a single cell, click your mouse pointer in the cell you want to delete, then select the Table menu Select option and click your mouse pointer on Cell. To select all of the cells in a column, row, or table, click your mouse pointer on one of the cells you want to remove. Then select the Table menu Select option, and click your mouse pointer on Column, Row or Table. Alternatively, to select two or more individual cells, hold down the SHIFT key as you click the mouse pointer on the cells you want to select.
3. Select the Table menu Delete Cells option.

After you complete Step 3, FrontPage will remove not only the cells you selected, but also anything you inserted into the cells you deleted.

MAKING TABLE CELLS A UNIFORM WIDTH OR HEIGHT

If you have a table with several cells with various heights and widths, and you want to set some (or all) of the cells to a uniform height or width, there are three ways for doing so. You could:

- drag each cell's edges outward or inward as necessary.

- select the cells you want to modify, and use fields on the Cell Properties dialog box to specify the same pixel count or percentage width or height.
- select the cells you want to modify and use the Distribute Columns Evenly option or the Distribute Rows Evenly option on the Table menu. (Distribute Columns Evenly and Distribute Rows Evenly are also the sixth and seventh buttons from the right on the Tables toolbar.)

You will learn how to use the Cell Properties dialog box in the next Tip titled "Changing the Properties of Individual Cells." To give a set of cells a uniform (identical) height or width, perform the following steps:

1. Open the Web page with the table whose cell dimensions you want to change, and select the View menu Page option to display the page on the Page view Normal tab.
2. Use your mouse pointer to select the cells whose widths and heights you want to make a uniform size. For example, to select all of the cells in a column, row, or table, click your mouse pointer on one of the cells you whose dimensions you want to change. Then select the Table menu Select option, and click your mouse pointer on Column, Row or Table. Alternatively, to select two or more individual cells, hold down the SHIFT key as you click the mouse pointer on the cells you want to select.
3. If you want all of the cells you selected in Step 2 to have the same height, select the Table menu Distribute Rows Evenly option.
4. If you want all of the cells you selected in Step 2 to have an equal width, select the Table menu Distribute Columns Evenly option.

If you perform Step 3, FrontPage will resize all of the cells you selected in Step 2 such that each of them has the same height as the tallest cell in the group. Similarly, if you perform Step 4, FrontPage will change the dimensions of the cells you selected in Step 2 such that each of them has the same width as the widest cell in the group.

CHANGING THE PROPERTIES OF INDIVIDUAL CELLS

You can use the Cell Properties dialog box to control the characteristics shown in Table 232 for one or more cells in a table. After reviewing the settings available, you will see that FrontPage makes it easy to make each cell in a table unique in terms of its border color(s), background color and/or graphics image, dimensions, and the alignment of its contents.

Option	Description
Horizontal alignment	Set the horizontal alignment of the contents of a cell (i.e. the content's alignment between the cell's left and right walls). The available settings are: • **Left** or **Default** - flush with the cell's left-cell wall. • **Right** - flush with the cell's right-wall. • **Center** - centered between the cell's left and right walls. • **Justify** - flush against the cell's left-wall, with the right-most character of text on each line lined up directly below the last character of text on the line above it—as much as possible.
Vertical alignment	Set the vertical alignment of the contents of a cell (i.e. the alignment of the contents with respect to the top and bottom of a cell). The available settings are: • **Baseline, Default** or **Middle** - vertically centered between the top and bottom of the cell. • **Top** - flush against the top of the cell. • **Bottom** - flush against the bottom of the cell.
Specify width	Specify the width of a cell either as a number of pixels or as a percentage of the width of the table.
Specify height	Specify the height of a cell either as a number of pixels or as a percentage of the height of the table.
Rows spanned	Set the height of the cell by specifying the number of adjacent rows the left-hand or right-hand side of the cell is to span. (Row height X, the number of spanned rows = the height of the cell.)
Columns spanned	Set the width of the cell by specifying the number of adjacent columns the top or bottom of the cell is to span. (Column width X, the number of spanned columns = the width of the cell.)
Header cell	Center the cells text content and display it in the Table Header font—usually 12pt boldface Times New Roman.

Table 232 The cell properties one can set using the Microsoft FrontPage Cell Properties dialog box. *(Continued on next page)*

Option	Description
No wrap	Do not wrap text in a cell. For the cell's width to be wide enough to allow all text typed on a single line to be displayed as a single line.
(Border) Color	The single color border around the cell, or if you specify either the Light border color or the Dark border color, the setting of the Color becomes the Light border color if the Light border color is left as Automatic or the Dark border color if the Dark border color is left as Automatic.
Light border	Use Light and Dark Border colors to create 3-D borders around a cell. The Light border color will be the color of the bottom and right-hand side of the cell. Think of a flashlight held in the upper left-hand corner of the cell shining on the bottom and right-hand side of the cell.
Dark border	Use Light and Dark Border colors to create 3-D borders around a cell. The Dark border color will be the color of the left-hand side and top of the cell. Picture the light and shadows cast by a flashlight held in the upper left-hand corner of the cell—the left-hand side and top of the cell would cast a shadow into the cell.
(Background) Color	The color of the cell's background.
Use background picture	The graphics image to be displayed as the background for a cell. (Unlike placing a graphics image into a cell, if the graphics image used as the background picture is larger than the cell, the cell will not expand, and you will see only a portion of the background picture.)

Table 232 The cell properties one can set using the Microsoft FrontPage Cell Properties dialog box. (Continued from previous page)

To work with the properties of one or more cells, perform the steps in the following procedure:

1. Open the Web page with the table whose cell properties you want to set, and select the View menu Page option to display the page on the Page view Normal tab.
2. Use your mouse pointer to select the cells whose properties you want to change. For example, to select a single cell or all of the cells in a column, row, or table, click your mouse pointer on one of the cells

you want to remove. Then select the Table menu Select option, and click your mouse pointer on Cell, Column, Row or Table. Alternatively, to select two or more individual cells, hold down the SHIFT key as you click the mouse pointer on the cells you want to select.

3. Right-click the mouse pointer on any one of the cells you selected in Step 2, and select Cell Properties from the pop-up menu. FrontPage, in turn, will display a Cell Properties dialog box similar to that shown in Figure 232.

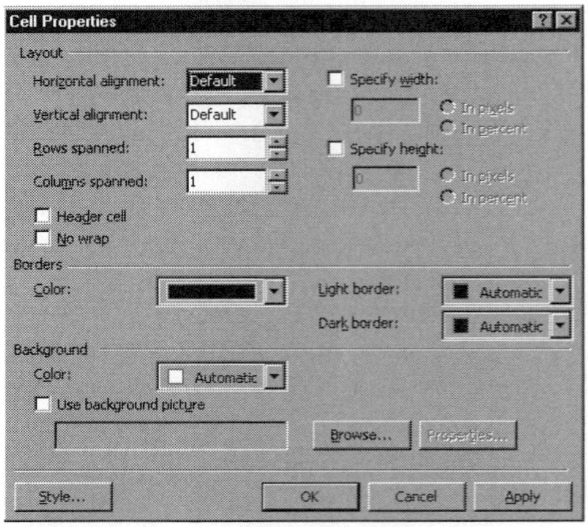

Figure 232 The Microsoft FrontPage Cell Properties dialog box.

4. Set the values of the fields in the Cell Properties dialog box as desired. (Please refer to Table 232 for a description of each field.)
5. Click your mouse pointer on the APPLY button to review your changes without leaving the Cell Properties dialog box. If you are not satisfied with the appearance of the cell(s), change the values of the fields and click the mouse pointer on the APPLY button again. After you are satisfied with the appearance of the selected cells, continue at Step 6.
6. Click your mouse pointer on the OK button near the bottom center of the Cell Properties dialog box. FrontPage, in turn, will make the adjustments you specified in Step 4 to the characteristics of the cell(s) you selected in Step 2.

Note: *If you use the Rows spanned or Columns spanned fields to set the column's width and height, FrontPage will shift columns around and create a padded area (if necessary) to maintain the table's rectangularity (similar to the effect you saw in a previous Tip titled "Adding a Single Cell to a Table"). Therefore, rather than use the Rows spanned and Columns spanned fields, perform the steps in the procedure in a previous Tip titled: "Merging Multiple Table Cells Into a Single Cell"* *when you want to create a single cell that spans the width of multiple columns or the height of multiple rows.*

Note: *If you specify the width of a cell as a percentage of the table's width, make sure that the sum of the cell width percentages for the cells in the same row does not exceed 100% or you will get unpredictable results. Similarly, if you specify the height of a cell as a percentage of the table's overall height, make sure that the sum of the height percentages for the cells in the same column does not exceed 100%.*

ADJUSTING A TABLE'S CELL PADDING, SPACING, AND BORDER WIDTH

Cell padding and cell spacing let you adjust the amount blank space the Web browser will insert into cells and between cells in a table. While *cell spacing* is the amount of space between the cells in a table, *cell padding* is the amount of space between a cell's content and its walls. Since a picture is worth a thousand words, please view Figure 233.1 for a further explanation of cell spacing and cell padding.

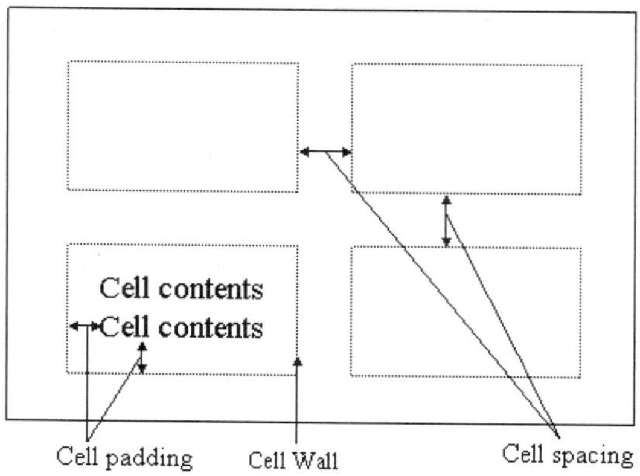

Figure 233.1 *Cell padding and spacing.*

When you tell FrontPage to create a table, the program sets both the cell spacing and cell padding to a width of one pixel. Figure 233.2 shows a four-cell table created using the default values for cell spacing, cell padding, and a (default) 1-pixel border around the table.

Row 1, Column 1	Row 1, Column 1
Row 1, Column 1	Row 1, Column 1

Figure 233.2 *A table with cell padding of one pixel, cell spacing of one pixel, and a 1-pixel wide border.*

To adjust the cell padding, cell spacing, and/or border width of a table, perform the following steps:

1. Open the Web page with the table whose blank space or border width you want to modify, and select the View menu Page option to display the page on the Page view Normal tab.
2. Right-click the mouse pointer anywhere within the table's border and select Table Properties from the pop-up menu. FrontPage, in turn, will display the Table Properties dialog box.
3. Into the Cell padding field, enter the amount of blank space (in pixels) that you want to leave between each cell's sides (between its walls) and its contents.
4. Into the Cell spacing field, enter the amount of blank space (in pixels) that you want to leave between the cells in the table.
5. Into the Size field at the top of the Borders section in the center of the dialog box, enter the number of pixels wide you want the border around the table to be.
6. Click your mouse pointer on the OK button near the bottom center of the Table Properties dialog box.

The table at the top of Figure 233.3 shows the table from Figure 233.2 with a cell padding (distance between each cell's contents and its walls) of 10 pixels, a cell spacing (distance between cells) of 20 pixels and a border with of 1 pixel.

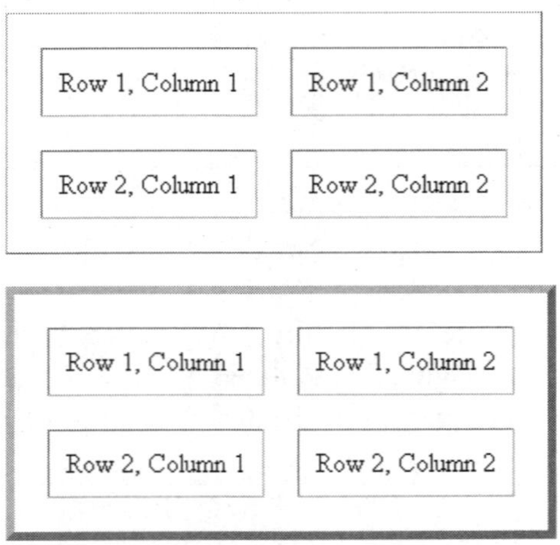

Figure 233.3 A table with cell padding of one pixel, cell spacing of one pixel, and a 1-pixel wide border.

The table at the bottom of Figure 233.3 has the same cell spacing and cell padding as the table at the top. However, its border is five pixels wide. Notice that setting the width of the table's border to a value greater than one has no effect on the 1-pixel width of the walls around each of the table's cells. In the Tip titled "Using Tables for Page Layouts" (found later in this book), you will learn how to hide the border around the table and the walls around its cells, so you can use the table as an invisible grid for positioning content on a Web page.

UNDERSTANDING TABLE PROPERTIES

In a previous Tip titled: "Changing the Properties of Individual Cells," you learned how to work with the appearance of a table's cells, the vertical and horizontal alignment of objects within each cell, and the color of the cell's background and its walls. In this Tip, you will learn how to use the Table Properties dialog box to set the overall appearance of the table itself.

Table 234 lists and describes the table properties you can set on the Table Properties dialog box. Some of the fields such as Alignment, Specify width, Specify height, (Border) Color, Light border, Dark border, (Background) Color, and Use background picture represent properties you can set both for the table overall and for particular cells in the table.

Where there is a conflict between an individual cell's setting and the table's overall setting for a particular property, the Web browser uses the cell's setting when rendering (drawing) the cell and its contents. Conversely, if a cell has no specific setting for a property or if the cell's property is set to Automatic, then the browser will use the table's setting for the property when rendering the cell. For example, if the background color for a particular cell is set to Automatic and you change the table's background color to blue, the cell's background color will change to blue, as well. Conversely, if you set the cell's background color to red, any changes you make to the table's background has no effect on the cell's background.

Option	Description
Alignment	If the table's width is less than 100% the width of the Web browser's application window, you can select: • **Default** or **Left** - to align the table with along the left-hand margin of the Web page, • **Right** - to align the table along the right-hand margin, or • **Center** - to center the table between the two margins on the page.

Table 234 The table properties one can set using the Microsoft FrontPage Table Properties dialog box. *(Continued on next page)*

Option	Description
Float	Select: • **Default** - to have the Web browser display Web page text that follows the table definition (i.e. the tables <TABLE></TABLE> tags) below the table itself. Alternatively, you can creating a floating table by selecting • **Left** - which tells the browser to display the table flush with the left-hand margin on the Web page and wrap text that follows the table's definition along the right-hand side of the table. If you select • **Right** - the browser will display the table flush with the right-hand side of the Web page and wrap text that follows the table's definition down the left-hand side of the table.
Cell padding	The number of pixels of blank space the Web browser is to insert between the walls of each cell and the cell's contents.
Cell spacing	The number of pixels of blank space the Web browser is to insert between the cells in the table, (i.e.the horizontal and vertical distance in pixels between the walls of adjacent cells).
Specify width	Specify the width of the table either as a number of pixels or as a percentage of the width of the Web browser's application window.
Specify height	Specify the height of the table either as a number of pixels or as a percentage of the Web browser's application window.
(Border) Size	The width (in pixels) of the border the Web browser is to draw around the outside of the table.
(Border) Color	The single color border around the cell. If you specify either the Light border color or the Dark border color, the setting of the (Border) Color becomes the Light border color if the Light border color is set to Automatic or the Dark border color if the Dark border color is set to Automatic.

Table 234 The table properties one can set using the Microsoft FrontPage Table Properties dialog box. *(Continued on next page)*

Option	Description
Light border	Use Light and Dark border colors to create 3-D borders around the table. The Light border color will be the color of the left-hand side and top of the table. Think of a flashlight held outside of the upper left-hand corner of the table shining on the top of the table and its left-hand side, thereby bathing the top and left sides of the cell in light.
Dark border	Use Dark and light border colors to create 3-D borders around a table. The Dark border color will be the color of the bottom and right-hand side of the table. Think of a flashlight held outside of the upper left-hand corner of the cell—the bottom and right-hand side of the table in the dark shadow below and to the right of the table.
Show both cells and table borders	When checked, the Web browser will draw a 1-pixel border (or wall) around each cell in the table. When unchecked, the Web browser will draw 1-pixel horizontal and vertical lines between each pair of cells in the table, and no lines (or borders) between the cells along the table's perimeter and its walls.
(Background) Color	Background color of the cells in a table that are set to Automatic.
Use background picture	The graphics image to be displayed as the background for the table. (If the graphics image used as the background picture is larger than the dimensions of the table, the Web browser will not expand the table, and you will see only a portion of the background picture.) Moreover, if a cell in the table has a background color setting other than Automatic or has a background picture of its own, the Web browser will display the cell's background (color or graphics image) over the table's background in the cell.

Table 234 The table properties one can set using the Microsoft FrontPage Table Properties dialog box. (Continued from previous page)

To work with a table's properties on the Table Properties dialog box, perform the steps in the following procedure:

1. Open the Web page with the table whose properties you want to set, and select the View menu Page option to display the page on the Page view Normal tab.

2. Right-click the mouse pointer anywhere within the table's borders and select Table Properties from the pop-up menu. FrontPage, in turn, will display a Table Properties dialog box similar to that shown in Figure 234.

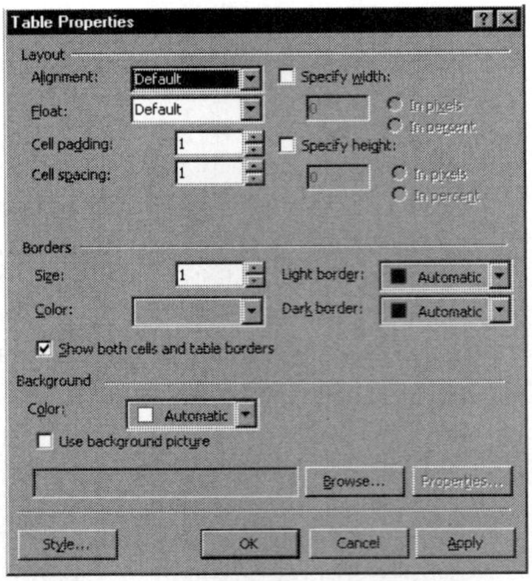

Figure 234 *The Microsoft FrontPage Table Properties dialog box.*

3. Set the values of the fields in the Table Properties dialog box as desired. (Please refer to Table 234 for a description of each field.)
4. Click your mouse pointer on the APPLY button to review your changes without leaving the Table Properties dialog box. If you are not satisfied with the appearance of the table, change the values of the fields, and click the mouse pointer on the APPLY button again. After you're satisfied with the appearance of the table, continue at Step 6.
5. Click your mouse pointer on the OK button near the bottom center of the Table Properties dialog box. FrontPage, in turn, will make the adjustments you specified in Step 3 to the table's characteristics and return to the display of the table with its new properties on the Page view Normal tab.

Note: *If you set the value of the Alignment field to Center, keep in mind that some Web browsers do not support the Center value for a table's alignment attribute. As a result, these Web browsers will use the default, Left alignment when positioning the table.*

Note: *If you set the width of a table's border (the value of the Size field in the Border section of the Table Properties dialog box) to* ***zero*** *pixels, Web browsers will not only display the table without a* *border, but also display its cells without walls. Conversely, if you set the border's width to* **one** *or more, Web browsers will display the table with a 1-pixel border around each cell and a border with a pixel width equal to the value of in Size field around the perimeter of the table.*

ADDING COLORS TO A TABLE

Tables, like Web pages, have a background whose color you can change. In fact, you can even use a different background color for each cell in the table.

When working with background colors, keep in mind that the Web browser will lay the table background over the Web page background and will lay the cell's background, in turn, over the table's background. Therefore, if you do not specify a background color for a table, the table will take on the Web page background color because the Web browser will not "paint" a color on the table's background when it display's the table's background on top of the Web page background. Similarly, if you do not specify a background color for a cell in a table, the cell will take on the table's background color because the Web browser will not fill in the cell's background with a color when it displays the cell's background on top of the table's background.

To set the background color of a table or the background color of an individual cell in the table, perform the following steps:

1. On the Page view Normal tab, open the Web page with the table whose background color(s) you want change.
2. If you want to change the background color of the entire table, right-click the mouse pointer anywhere within the table's borders and select Table Properties from the pop-up menu. FrontPage, in turn, will display the Table Properties dialog box. On the other hand, if you want to change the background color of an individual cell within the table, right-click the mouse pointer on the cell whose background color you want to change and select Cell Properties from the pop-up menu. FrontPage, in turn, will display the Cell Properties dialog box.

Note: *If you want to change the background color of several cells at once, you must first select the cells whose backgrounds you want to modify. After selecting the cells you want, right-click the mouse pointer in any one of them, and then select Cell Properties on the pop-up menu in Step 2. To select the cells whose backgrounds you want to change, click your mouse pointer one of the cells, select the Table menu Select option and click your mouse pointer on Cell, Column, Row or Table. Alternatively, to select two or more individual cells, hold down the SHIFT key as you click the mouse pointer on the cells you want to select.*

3. Click your mouse pointer on the drop-down list button to the right of the Color field at the top of the Background section near the bottom of the dialog box. FrontPage, in turn, will display a drop-down pallet with sixteen browser safe color swatches, swatches for colors you previously created and added to the Custom Colors list, and a More Colors option you can use to select or create additional colors not available for selection on the drop-down pallet.

Note: *The sixteen colors displayed at the top of the drop-down pallet are browser safe, because older browsers and all computer systems with standard color graphics cards can display them. If you create a color the visitor's browser, or display card, cannot render on the screen, the background will appear grainy as the system tries to translate the color you used into a color it can display through a process called dithering. Although, most desktop computers sold nowadays are able to display millions of colors, there are still many laptops in use that can only display 256 colors at screen resolutions above 640x480. So, to be absolutely safe, use only one of the 16 browser safe colors. However, if you really have the need to use a custom color for a table or an individual cell within a table, bear in mind that the table or cell's background color may not look the same to all of your site's visitors.*

4. To select one of the 16 browser safe colors, click your mouse pointer on its color swatch and continue at Step 10. Otherwise, to select from the additional standard colors, or to mix your own custom color, select the More Colors option at the bottom of the drop-down pallet. FrontPage, in turn, will display a More Colors dialog box similar to that shown in Figure 235.1.

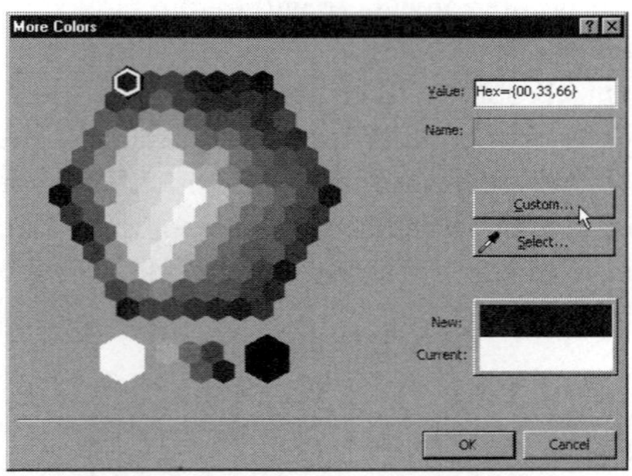

Figure 235.1 The Microsoft FrontPage More Colors dialog box.

5. To set the table or cell background to one of the colors in the hexagon of colors on the left-hand side of the More Colors dialog box, click your mouse pointer on the color you want. FrontPage, in turn, will

display the color you select in the New (color) field (above the Current (color) field) near the lower right-hand corner of the dialog box. If the color is what you want, continue at Step 10; otherwise click the mouse pointer on other colors until you find the right color. If none of the colors is right, you will want to mix your own custom color. To create your own custom color, click your mouse pointer on the CUSTOM button near the middle at the right-hand side of the dialog box. FrontPage, in turn, will display a Color dialog box similar to that shown in Figure 235.2.

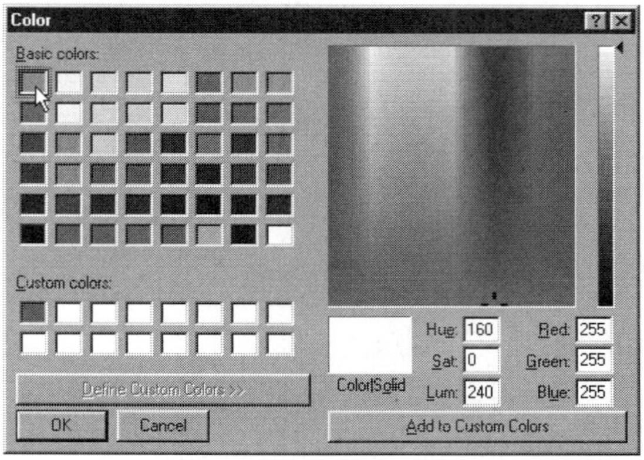

Figure 235.2 The Microsoft FrontPage (Custom) Color dialog box.

6. Click your mouse pointer on one of the Basic colors squares on the left-hand side of the dialog box or on the color you want in the rainbow of colors rectangle on the right-hand side of the dialog box. FrontPage, in turn, will display the color you selected in the Color|Solid rectangle below the rainbow of colors and show the color's RGB (Red, Green, Blue) and HSL (Hue, Saturation, and Luminosity) values in the fields at the lower right-hand corner of the dialog box.
7. If you want to adjust the color you selected in Step 6, either repeat Step 6 and click your mouse pointer on another point in the rainbow of colors rectangle, or change the values in the Hue, Sat, Lum, Red, Green, and Blue fields. FrontPage, in turn, will display the new color you select or define (with HSL or RGB values) in the Color Solid rectangle to the left of the color's HSL values.
8. To use the color you selected or mixed, click your mouse pointer on the OK button in the lower left-hand corner of the dialog box. Alternatively, if you want to both select the color and make it available as a Custom Color swatch on the drop-down, click your mouse pointer

on the ADD TO CUSTOM COLORS button in the right-hand corner of the dialog box. FrontPage, in turn, will return to the More Colors dialog box.

9. Click your mouse pointer on the OK button near the lower right-hand corner of the More Colors dialog box. FrontPage, in turn, will copy the color you selected or created from the New color field of the More Colors dialog box to the Background field in the Colors section of the Background tab, and return to the Page Properties dialog box.
10. Click your mouse pointer on the OK button near the lower right hand corner of the Page Properties dialog box.

After you complete Step 10, FrontPage will use the color you selected (or the custom color you created) as the solid color background of the table or the cell within the table you selected in Step 2 of the procedure in this Tip. The next Tip will show you how to change the color of the border (if any) the Web browser will draw around the perimeter of a table.

SETTING THE COLOR OF THE BORDER AROUND A TABLE AND THE WALLS AROUND ITS CELLS

You can choose up to two colors for the border around the perimeter of a table and either the same or a different pair of colors for the border (or wall) around each cell in the table. Similar to the selection of a table's background colors (which you learned about in the preceding Tip), changing the color(s) of the border around a table also changes the color(s) of the border (or wall) around each of the cells in the table—with the exception of those cells whose border colors you previously set to something other than Automatic. In other words, if you explicitly set the color(s) of the border around a cell, changing the color(s) of the border around the table has no effect on the color(s) of the cell wall.

By default, FrontPage sets the colors of the border around a table and the walls of its cells to light and dark gray. The program uses two colors for the table and cell borders to give the table a three-dimensional appearance. It makes the top and left-hand side of the table's border lighter than its bottom and right-hand side. Conversely, the program makes the top and left-hand side of each cell's border is darker than its bottom and right-hand side.

When changing the color(s) of the border around the table or the color(s) of the border around a cell, you can either select two new colors, or remove the three-dimensional effect by selecting a single color. To change the color(s) of a table's borders, perform the following steps:

1. Open the Web page with the table whose border colors you want to change, and select the View menu Page option to display the page on the Page view Normal tab.

2. If you want to change the color(s) of the border around the perimeter of the table, right-click your mouse pointer anywhere with the table's borders and select Table Properties from the pop-up menu. FrontPage, in turn, will display the Table Properties dialog box.

   On the other hand, if you want to change the color(s) of the wall around one or more cell in the table, right-click the mouse pointer on the cell(s) whose border color(s) you want to change and select Cell Properties on the pop-up menu. FrontPage, in turn, will display the Cell Properties dialog box.

Note: *If you want to set the border colors for several cells in the table at once, you must first select the cells whose borders you want to modify. After selecting the cells, right-click the mouse pointer in any of the cells selected, and then select Cell Properties on the pop-up. To select cells, click your mouse pointer on a cell and then select the Table menu Select option. Next, click your mouse pointer on Cell, Column, Row or Table. Alternatively, to select multiple cells one cell at a time, hold down the SHIFT key as you click the mouse pointer on the cells you want to select.*

3. If you want to set the color of the border around the table or the cell(s) you selected in Step 2 to a single color, click the mouse pointer on the drop-down list button to the right of the Color field in the Border section near the middle of the dialog box. Then, select the color you want by clicking the mouse pointer on one of the color swatches on the drop-down pallet of colors (or use the More Colors option at the bottom of the drop-down pallet to create and select a new, custom color).
4. If you want the table or its cells to have a three-dimensional appearance, select both light and dark colors for the border around the table and/or around each of its cells instead of selecting a single color border.

   First, click the mouse pointer on the drop-down list button to the right of the Light border field in the Border section near the middle of the dialog box. Then, select the color you want by clicking the mouse pointer on one of the color swatches on the drop-down pallet of colors (or use the More Colors option at the bottom of the drop-down pallet to create and select a new, custom color). Next, click the mouse pointer on the drop-down list button to the right of the Dark border field and repeat the color selection process.
5. Click the mouse pointer on the OK button near the bottom center of the dialog box.

If you elected to work with the table's border in Step 2, FrontPage will display the border around the outside of the table using either the single color you selected in Step 3, or the pair of colors you selected in Step 4.

Similarly, if you elected to work with one or more of the table's cells in Step 2, FrontPage will display the border (or wall) around each cell you selected using either the single color you chose in Step 3, or the pair of colors you selected in Step 4.

Note: *If you are using two-color borders (to create a three-dimensional effect for the table or its cells), the Web browser will use the Light border color for the top and left-hand side of the table and the Dark border color when drawing the table's bottom and right-hand side. Conversely, the Web browser will use the Dark border color for the top and left-hand side of the cell and the Light border color when drawing the cell's bottom and right-hand side.*

USING GRAPHICS IMAGES AS BACKGROUNDS IN A TABLE OR CELL

Instead of (or in addition to) selecting a background color for a table, you can tell FrontPage to place a graphics image on the table's background or on the background of one or more of its cells.

When working with background images, keep in mind that the Web browser will lay the table's background over the Web page background and will lay the cell's background, in turn, over the table's background. Therefore, if you do not insert a graphics image or specify a background color for a table, the Web browser will display the Web page background as the background behind the table's cells and in the blank area between its cells.

Similarly, if you do not specify a color or graphics image you want the browser to display on a cell's background, the Web browser will display the table's background as the background behind the text, graphics image(s), or other Web page elements placed in the cell.

Like the background image on a Web page, you can use a graphics image as wallpaper to cover the "glass" wall behind a table or the "glass" wall behind each of the cells in the table. Although you can use any picture you want as the background for a table or its cells, some images work better than others do. The key to selecting a background image is to choose one that does not interfere with the readability of the text content in the table's cells. When looking for a table or cell background picture, be sure to search the Microsoft Clip Gallery using the keyword wallpaper, background, or texture.

To use a graphics image as the background for a table or one or more of its cells, perform the following steps:

1. Open the Web page with the table whose appearance you want to modify, and select the View menu Page option to display the page on the Page view Normal tab.
2. If you want to place a graphics image in the table's background, right-click the mouse pointer anywhere within the table's borders and select Table Properties from the pop-up menu. FrontPage, in turn, will display the Table Properties dialog box.

   On the other hand, if you want to place a graphics image on the background of an individual cell within the table, right-click the mouse pointer on the cell whose background you want to change, and select Cell Properties from the pop-up menu. FrontPage, in turn, will display the Cell Properties dialog box.

Note: *If you want to place the same graphics image onto the backgrounds of several cells at once, you must first select the cells whose backgrounds you want to modify. After selecting the cells, right-click the mouse pointer in any of the cells selected, and then select Cell Properties on the pop-up. To select cells, click your mouse pointer on a cell and then select the Table menu Select option. Next, click your mouse pointer on Cell, Column, Row or Table. Alternatively, to select multiple cells one cell at a time, hold down the SHIFT key as you click the mouse pointer on the cells you want to select.*

3. Click your mouse pointer on the Use background picture checkbox (in the Background section at the bottom of the dialog box) until a checkmark appears.
4. Into the field below the Use background picture checkbox, enter the pathname of the picture you want to use as the background for the table or cell(s). (If you prefer, click your mouse pointer on the BROWSE button to the right of the field, and then use the Select Background Picture dialog box to search for and select the image file with the picture you want to use.)
5. Click your mouse pointer on the OK button near the bottom center of the dialog box. FrontPage, in turn, will close the dialog box and display the image you specified in Step 4 as the background (wallpaper) of the table or cell(s) you selected in Step 2.

If the picture you select is smaller than the dimensions of the table or cell for which you told FrontPage to use it as a background, the visitor's Web browser will tile the image (i.e. duplicate it as many times as necessary) to fill the background. Conversely, if the graphics image is larger than the dimensions table or cell background, the Web browser will only display the portion of the graphics image that falls within the borders of the table or cell.

REMOVING A TABLE FROM A WEB PAGE

While it make take you some time to create a table with the arrangement of columns and rows you need for the perfect arrangement of the content on a Web page, deleting a table (no matter how complex) takes only a moment.

If you want to delete a table while keeping the objects in its cells on the Web page, click your mouse pointer on the table you want to remove. Then, select the Table menu Convert option, and click the mouse pointer on Table to Text. FrontPage, in turn, will remove the code that defines the table from the Web page HTML while leaving in place the tags used to display the content that was in the table's cells. (FrontPage puts the content from each cell in a separate paragraph on the Web page.

On the other hand, if you want to remove both the table and its contents from the Web page, click your mouse pointer on the table you want to delete. Select the Table menu Select option, and click your mouse pointer on Table. Then, press the Backspace key on your keyboard to remove both the table and its contents from the Web page.

CREATING A 1-PIXEL TRANSPARENT GIF

In the two Tips following this one, you will need a 1-pixel transparent graphics image stored in the Graphics Interchange Format (GIF) you can use to position elements on a Web page. If you have an image editor (such as Microsoft Photo Editor, Photoshop, or Image Composer) installed on your computer, use the graphics program to create a single-pixel transparent image and store as a GIF file. Alternatively, you can use FrontPage to create a 1-pixel transparent GIF from one of the clips in the Clip Gallery by perform the following steps:

1. Click your mouse pointer on the Create a new normal page button (first button on the left, with the blank page icon) on the Standard toolbar.
2. Select the View menu Page option to display the new, blank Web page on the Page view Normal tab.
3. Select the Insert menu Picture option, and click the mouse pointer on Clip Art. FrontPage, in turn, will display the Insert Clip Art menu along the right-hand side of the application window.
4. Click the mouse pointer on the SEARCH button under the Search text field in the Search For section at the top of the Insert Clip Art menu. FrontPage, in turn, will display the thumbnails for several clips in the Clip Gallery.

5. Click the mouse pointer on the first thumbnail displayed to insert it onto the Web page. (Which clip art image you choose is inconsequential as you will have turned it into a 1-pixel transparent GIF by the time you complete the last step in this procedure.)
6. Right-click your mouse pointer on the picture you inserted (in Step 5), and select Picture Properties from the pop-up menu. FrontPage, in turn, will display a picture properties dialog box similar to that shown in Figure 239.1.

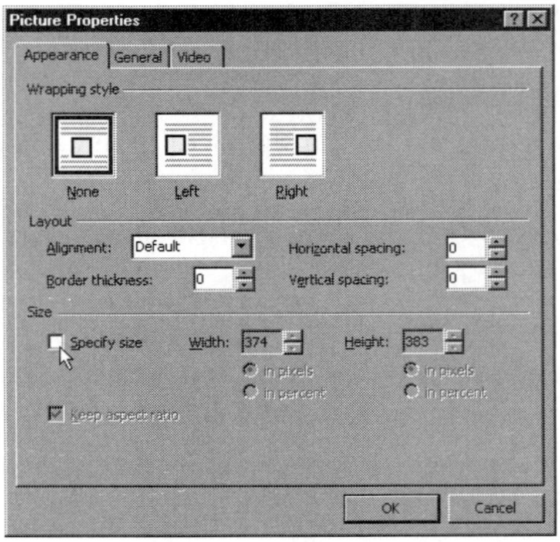

Figure 239.1 The Microsoft FrontPage Picture Properties dialog box.

7. If not exposed, click your mouse pointer on the Appearance tab.
8. Click your mouse pointer on the Specify size checkbox (in the Size section at the bottom of the dialog box) until a checkmark appears.
9. If the Keep aspect ratio checkbox is checked, clear it by clicking your mouse pointer on the checkbox until the checkmark disappears.
10. Delete the existing width specification in the Width field, and enter a **1**into the field. Then, click your mouse pointer on the in pixels radio button below the field.
11. Into the Height field, enter a **1**, and then click the mouse pointer on the in pixels radio button below the field.
12. Click the mouse pointer on the OK button near the lower right-hand corner of the Picture Properties dialog box.
13. Click your mouse pointer on the Resample button (seventh button from the right) on the Pictures toolbar.

14. Right-click the mouse pointer on the picture (it will look like a black square in the upper left-hand corner of the Web page and select Picture Properties from the pop-up menu.
15. Click the mouse pointer on the Specify size checkbox until a checkmark appears.
16. Into the Width field, enter **100**.
17. Click the mouse pointer the OK button near the lower right-hand side of the Picture Properties dialog box.
18. Click your mouse pointer on the Set Transparent Color button (tenth button from the right) on the Pictures toolbar and then on the picture you inserted (in Step 5).
19. Right-click the mouse pointer on the picture, and select Picture Properties from the pop-up menu.
20. Click the mouse pointer on the Specify size checkbox until a checkmark appears.
21. Into the Width field, enter **1**.
22. Click the mouse pointer the OK button near the lower right-hand corner of the Picture Properties dialog box.
23. Select the File menu Save As option. FrontPage, in turn, will display the Save As dialog box.
24. Into the File name field at the bottom of the dialog box, enter the pathname of the file in which you want to save the Web page temporarily. For example, enter **C:\MY DOCUMENTS\MY WEBS\TEMP.**
25. Click your mouse pointer on the SAVE button near the lower right-hand corner of the Save As dialog box. FrontPage, in turn, will display a Save Embedded Files dialog box similar to that shown in Figure 239.2.

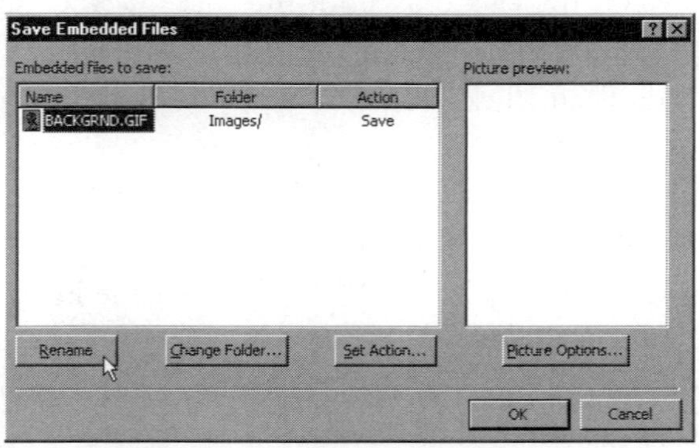

Figure 239.2 The Microsoft FrontPage Save Embedded Files dialog box.

26. Click your mouse pointer on the RENAME button near the lower left-hand corner of the dialog box and replace the filename at the top of the Name column with a name such as **Spacing.GIF**.
27. Click your mouse pointer on the OK button near the lower right-hand corner of the Save Embedded Files dialog box.

After you complete Step 27, FrontPage will store a transparent, 1-pixel by 1-pixel graphics image in a file name you entered in Step 26 (SPACING.GIF, in the current example) in the same folder you chose for the Web page in Step 24 (C:\MY DOCUMENTS\MY WEBS, in the current example).

Note: *The 1-pixel, transparent GIF you create by performing the steps in the preceding procedure will have a size of 422 bytes. Although the graphics image in the file consists of a single pixel (and therefore a single color), it is defined using a set of 8-bit values to specify the color from a 256-color palette. If you use an image program to create a 1-pixel, single bit (monochrome) image, you can create a 1-pixel transparent GIF that has a size of 43 bytes.*

USING A 1-PIXEL GIF TO CONTROL THE SPACE BETWEEN TABLE ELEMENTS PRECISELY

Standard HTML has no tags for positioning objects at specific x-y locations in the Web browser's application window. Because HTML tags only tell the Web browser the content to display and how it should look, Web browsers, for the most part, process the contents of an HTML document sequentially. As such, the browser reads and displays page elements on the screen as the browser comes across them (one after another sequentially) in the HTML that describes the Web page. Screen positioning, such as it is, occurs as the result of one object taking up space onscreen which moves the starting point available for the next (adjacent) object onscreen either to the right on the same line or on the next line flush with the left or right margin.

Tables, supported by almost all of the Web browsers in use today, provide a measure of control over the x-y location of objects on a Web page. Each table's HTML tags tell the Web browser to draw a set of rectangles (or cells) on the Web page and to display objects, one after another, at a starting point relative to the top and left-hand side of each of the cells.

A transparent GIF is an invisible graphics image you can use either with or without a table to effect the position of objects on a Web page. The site visitor will not see the transparent GIF on the computer screen, because the Web browser displays the GIF as if it were a pane of clear glass lying on the Web page background. Moreover, although you can see right through it, the GIF takes up space in the Web page foreground, and therefore, effects the starting point available for the next (adjacent) object onscreen.

Suppose, for example, that you want to create a Web page with a 150 pixel wide graphics menu down the left-hand side of the page and want to separate the menu from the remaining Web page content on the right-hand side of the page) with a 20 pixel wide "trough" of blank space. Assuming you have 590 pixels of horizontal screen space, the following steps will create a table for this page layout:

1. Select the View menu Page option to display the Page view Normal tab.
2. Click the mouse pointer on the Create a new normal page button (first button on the left, with the blank page icon) on the Standard toolbar to create a new, blank Web page.
3. Select the Table menu Insert option, and click the mouse pointer on Table to display the Insert Table dialog box.
4. Enter the number of rows and columns you want to table to have into the Rows and Columns fields in the Size section at the top of the dialog box. For the current project, into the Rows field, enter **1** and into the Columns field, enter **3**, to setup a table with one row and three columns.
5. Click the mouse pointer on the Specify width checkbox (in the Layout section at the center of the dialog box) until a checkmark appears.
6. Click the mouse pointer on the In pixels radio button and into the field below the Specify width checkbox, enter the number of pixels wide you want the table to be. For the current project enter **590** into the field below the Specify width checkbox to create a table which (at 590 pixels) will stretch completely across the area inside the Web browser's application window when displayed at a screen resolution of 800 x 600.
7. Since you only want to use the table for page layout purposes, hide the border around the table and the walls (or border) around its cells by entering a **0** into the Border size field.
8. Click the mouse pointer on the OK button near the lower right-hand corner of the Insert Table dialog box. FrontPage, in turn, will create a single row table with three columns of equal with and no borders at the top of the Page view Normal tab.

After you create the table, set the width of its columns by performing the steps in the following procedure:

1. Right-click your mouse pointer on the table's left-hand column, and select Cell Properties from the pop-up menu.

2. Click the mouse pointer on the Specify width checkbox (in the Layout section at the top of the dialog box) until a checkmark appears.
3. Click the mouse pointer on the In pixels radio button and into the field below the Specify width checkbox, enter the number of pixels wide you want the cell to be. For the current project, enter **150** into the field below the Specify width checkbox to make room in the cell for a 150-pixel wide menu bar.
4. Click the mouse pointer on the OK button near the bottom center of the Cell Properties dialog box. FrontPage, in turn, will adjust the width of the column you selected in Step 1 to the number of pixels you entered in Step 3 and return to the Page view Normal tab.

Next, repeat the steps in the procedure twice more to set the width of the remaining two columns. The second time through the procedure, right-click the mouse pointer on table's middle column in Step 1 and enter **20** into the field below the Specify width checkbox, to set the space between the menu along the left-hand side of the Web page and the content on the right to 20 pixels. Then, the third time through the procedure, right-click the mouse pointer on the table's rightmost column in Step 1 and enter **420** into the field below the Specify width checkbox, to set the page content's right-hand margin at 590 pixels (590 – 150 – 20 = 420).

Now, in a perfect world, you need only insert the menu graphic into the page layout table's left-hand column and add the content to its right-hand column. (FrontPage will expand the height of the table's columns you add content to its cells.) Unfortunately, while some Web browsers will display an empty cell (i.e. the middle column in the current example) with a fixed width as the specified number of pixels of blank space, others will "collapse" empty cells in an effort to display additional content onscreen. This is where the transparent GIF comes in.

To place a 1-pixel transparent GIF into a cell (or column) you are using to create blank space between objects on a Web page, perform the following steps:

1. Click the mouse pointer on the cell into which you wish to insert the transparent graphics image. For the current project, click the mouse pointer in the second column from the left in the 3-column page layout table.
2. Select the Insert menu Picture option, and click the mouse pointer on From File. FrontPage, in turn, will display the Picture dialog box.
3. Into the File name field near the bottom of the dialog box, enter the relative pathname of the GIF file (if you imported the GIF into the

current web previously) or the GIF file's full pathname (if the graphics image is not yet stored in a folder in the current web). For example, if you created the transparent GIF using the procedure in the preceding Tip, you would enter **C:\MY DOCUMENTS\MYWEBS\SPACING.GIF** into the File name field.

4. Click the mouse pointer on the INSERT button in the lower right-hand corner of the Pictures dialog box. FrontPage, in turn, will insert the graphics image (the 1-pixel transparent GIF file) into the cell you selected in Step 1.
5. Double-click your mouse pointer in the cell into which you inserted the picture in Step 4. FrontPage, in turn, will select the picture and display sizing handles on the picture's borders. (The sizing handles will be so close together that they will appear as a small square in the column.)
6. Right-click the mouse pointer on sizing handles on the graphics image (you inserted in Step 4), and select Picture Properties from the pop-up menu. FrontPage, in turn, will display the Picture Properties dialog box.
7. If not already exposed, click your mouse pointer on the Appearance tab.
8. Click the mouse pointer on the Specify size checkbox (in the Size section near the bottom of the dialog box) until a checkmark appears.
9. If there is a checkmark in the Keep aspect ratio checkbox, clear it by clicking your mouse pointer on the checkbox until the checkmark disappears.
10. Into the Width field, enter the number of pixels of blank space you want the 1-pixel transparent GIF to be, and then click the mouse pointer on the in pixels radio button below the field. For the current project, enter **20** into the Width field to fix the second column's width at 20 pixels.
11. Click the mouse pointer on the OK button near the lower right-hand corner of the Picture Properties dialog box.

That's it! By inserting a 1-pixel GIF with instructions to the Web browser that it is to display the transparent picture using the width (in pixels) you specified in Step 9, into the previously empty cell, you can prevent a Web browser from collapsing an (otherwise empty) cell and from reducing its width for any reason. As such, in the current example, your Web page will always have 20 pixels of blank space between the menu down the left-hand side of the page and the remaining Web content on the right-hand side.

USING A TRANSPARENT GIF TO POSITION ELEMENTS ON A WEB PAGE

A transparent *GIF file* is a graphics image (picture) stored in the Graphics Interchange Format—that is why it is called a GIF file. As you learned in a previous Tip titled "Creating a 1-Pixel Transparent GIF," you can create a 1-pixel transparent GIF by using a graphics image editor or even FrontPage itself to create a single-color graphics image with a 1-pixel height and width and setting the transparency attribute for the one color in the picture to TRUE (or on). Web developers (like yourself) use 1-pixel transparent GIF files to position elements on a Web page because of the picture's small file size (42 bytes if saved as a 1-bit, monochrome GIF), which does not increase the amount of time it takes to the Web browser to download and display a Web page.

Note: *Even if you use the same transparent GIF multiple times on several of the Web pages in a FrontPage web, the Web server sends the file to the visitor's computer one time per visit to the site. The operating system on the visitor's computer buffers graphics images it receives from a Web site in the C:\WINDOWS\TEMP or the C:\WINDOWS\TEMPORARY INTERNET FILES folder. As a result, if the site's pages reference the same 1-pixel transparent GIF multiple times, the Web browser retrieves the 42 byte file from the Web server once and uses the copy of the file stored on the local hard drive each time it needs to display the picture on a Web page.*

Moreover, the Web server always sends a 1-pixel picture—even if the <IMG> (image) tag tells the Web browser to use the transparent GIF to crate a 200-pixel-by-200-pixel blank area on the Web page. Remember, when you use the fields in the Size section of the FrontPage Picture Properties dialog box to increase the size of a picture and do not resample the graphics image, the picture's file size does not change. Instead of increasing the number of pixels in the graphics file, FrontPage increases the value of the WIDTH and HEIGHT attributes in the picture's <IMG> (image) tag in the Web page HTML. When the Web browser retrieves the Web page, the server sends the original (42 byte) 1-pixel transparent GIF, and the Web browser "stretches" the picture to the dimensions specified by the values of the <IMG> (image) tag's WIDTH and HEIGHT attributes.

In the preceding Tip, you learned how to use a transparent GIF to prevent a Web browser from "collapsing" an empty cell to guarantee the minimum width of a table column. You can also use transparent GIF files to:

- insert a precise amount of blank space between an object and the margins of a Web page or the sides of a cell in a table.
- insert a precise number of pixels of blank space between Web page elements in the same paragraph or within the same cell in a table.

- indent the first line in a paragraph.
- set the vertical space between adjacent paragraphs to something other than a multiple of the width of a single line. For example, you can set the space between paragraphs to the equivalent of 0.5 or 1.25 or 2.5 lines.

To use the transparent GIF for spacing purposes, simply insert it in the Web page content anywhere you want a space. Then, use the Picture Properties dialog box to adjust the (transparent) picture's dimensions to create the amount of blank space you need.

The most important thing to remember about a transparent GIF is that it interacts with other Web page elements just like any other graphics image you insert on the page. In short, the only difference between a transparent GIF and any other picture on the Web page is that the Web browser makes the transparent GIF invisible by displaying the page, table, or cell background through the transparent image—as if the picture were a pane of glass laying on the Web page.

USING TABLES FOR PAGE LAYOUT

As mentioned in previous Tips that dealt with placing graphics and text at specific locations on a Web page—HTML is one of the worst page layout description languages around. If you are looking for HTML tags that let you position objects at specific x-y coordinates on a page or that let you overlap one page element with another, save yourself some frustration and stop searching. To achieve the fancy page layouts you find on the Web—with banners, sidebars, and graphics mixed in with text—use tables and cells with invisible borders to setup a grid you can use to place things where you want them to appear on the Web page.

Note: *Later in this book, you will learn about positioning boxes and frames that let you layout the content on a Web. However, only the latest Web browsers support the <DIV></DIV> (division) container tag used to define a positioning box, and many browsers still do not support Web page frames. Because all but the very oldest, seldom used browsers, support tables, consider a table to be your primary page layout tool for now. Only use the other, more advanced tags if you cannot achieve the effect you want by using tables to create an invisible grid of cells that hold objects at specific locations on the Web page.*

The simplest way to use tables for page layout is to create a new Web page from one of the page templates on the General tab of the Page Templates dialog box—the steps for this procedure are described in a previous Tip titled: "Using a Template to Create a Table." After you select a template, FrontPage will create the tables you need to layout the Web page content as described by the template. Then, to prepare the Web page for use on your Web site, all you have to do is replace the generic text and graphics image placeholders supplied by the template with the pictures and text content you want on your Web page.

In addition to providing templates that generate page layout tables for you, FrontPage also provides tools that make it easy to create the tables from scratch. By adjusting the number of columns and rows and the dimensions of the cells in a table with zero-width borders, you can generate the grid of cells you need to layout the page content exactly the way you want it to look.

Therefore, when creating a new Web page, check the page layout templates FrontPage provides by executing the procedures from a previous Tip titled "Using a Template to Create a Table." If one of the design templates is close to the layout you want, tell FrontPage to create a new Web page based on the template. Then, use what you learned from previous Tips dealing with tables to modify the page layout tables and create the grid of cells you need to layout the page content as you want it to appear. Alternatively, if none of the design templates looks anything like the page you want to create, select the NORMAL PAGE template (from the template list box) on the Page Templates dialog box General tab to create a blank page, and then draw your own page layout tables on it.

The most important thing to remember when creating page layout tables is that you must set the value in the Size field in the Border section at the center of the Table Properties dialog box to zero (0). Entering zero (0) into the Size field of the Table Properties dialog box tells the Web browser not to display a border around the table and to hide the walls around its cells, as well, which gives you an *invisible* grid of cells so that you can position objects at specific locations relative to each other on a Web page.

USING POSITIONING BOXES TO LAYOUT WEB PAGE CONTENT

Both the Netscape Navigator and Microsoft's Internet Explorer let you use *positioning boxes* as containers for Web page content. After you place one or more page elements (such as text, tables, lists, graphics images, etc.) in a positioning box, you can move the positioning box (and its contents) to a specific location on the Web page. FrontPage encloses the contents of the positioning box (the Web page objects the Web browser will display onscreen) within <DIV></DIV> (division) tags in the Web page HTML. The positioning box's STYLE attribute tells the Web browser where to display the positioning box (and its contents) on the Web page.

Suppose, for example, that you want to position the text "JUGGLING CLOWNS FOR HIRE" in the center of a Web page; you could do so by performing the following steps to place the text in a positioning box and then placing the container at the center of the Web page:

1. On the Page view Normal tab, type the text you want to position at a specific location on the Web page. For the current project type JUGGLING CLOWNS FOR HIRE.

2. If not already displayed, select the View menu Toolbars option and click the mouse pointer on Positioning to display the Positioning toolbar.
3. Click the mouse pointer on one of the words in the text you want to position. For the current project, click the mouse pointer on the word "JUGGLING".
4. Click your mouse pointer on the Position Absolutely button (first button on the left) on the Positioning toolbar. FrontPage, in turn, will place the paragraph's text into a positioning box and display sizing handles on the positioning box's corners and at the middle of its sides.
5. Move you mouse pointer near one of the positioning box's sizing handles. When FrontPage changes the mouse pointer changes into a four-headed (positioning) cursor, like the one shown to the right and below the word "HIRE" in Figure 243, click and hold down the left mouse pointer as you drag the positioning box to the location on the Web page where you want its contents to appear. Then, release the left mouse button to drop the positioning box (and its contents) into place at its new location. For the current example drag the positioning box down toward the center of the Web page and then release the left mouse button.

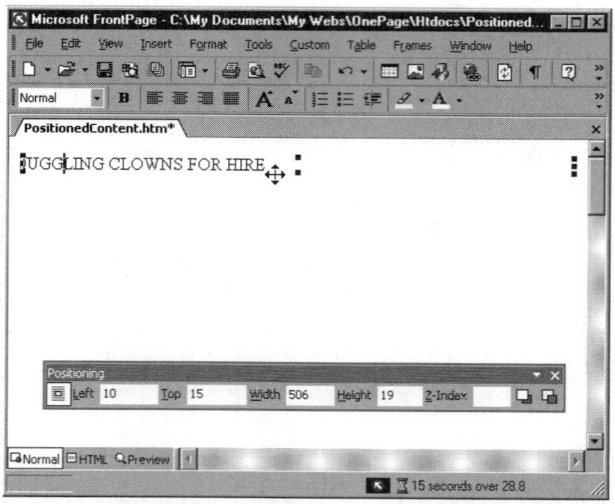

Figure 243 The Page view Normal tab with text enclosed in a positioning box at the top of the Web page and the positioning Toolbar near the bottom of the application window.

6. To hide the Positioning toolbar, click the mouse pointer on its close button (the "X") in the upper right-hand corner of the toolbar.
7. Click the mouse pointer on the Web page anywhere outside the borders of the positioning box to remove its sizing handles and the border around the container from view.

To see how where a Web browser will position the container's text on the Web page, click your mouse pointer on the Preview tab (near the lower left-hand corner of the application window. Then, take a look at the Web page HTML by clicking the mouse pointer on the HTML tab just left of the Preview tab. As mentioned at the beginning of this Tip, the positioning box is defined with <DIV></DIV> (division) tags on the Web page HTML. For the current example, the container's code on the HTML table will be similar to:

```
<div style="position: absolute; top: 135; left: 18;
    width: 506; height: 19">JUGGLING CLOWNS FOR HIRE</div>
```

Click the mouse pointer on the Normal tab to redisplay the Web page on the Page view Normal tab.

You can increase or reduce the size of the positioning box by using the mouse pointer to drag a sizing handle and the positioning box's side(s) either outward to expand the box, or inward to make it smaller. The positioning box will also expand as necessary to hold objects you insert into the positioning box—similar to the way a table cell expands to accommodate objects you place in it.

There are two important things to understanding about a positioning box. You can position content within the positioning box relative to the borders of the positioning box, and you can move the positioning box (and all of its contents) to a specific location on the Web page.

UNDERSTANDING THE POSITIONING TOOLBAR

As you learned in the preceding Tip, you can use the Position Absolutely button (first button on the left) on the Positioning toolbar (shown in Figure 244) to move an object from the Web page into a positioning box. Conversely, if you click the mouse pointer on a blank area inside the positioning box and then on the Position Absolutely button, FrontPage will move all of the objects inside the positioning box out of the container and back onto the Web page.

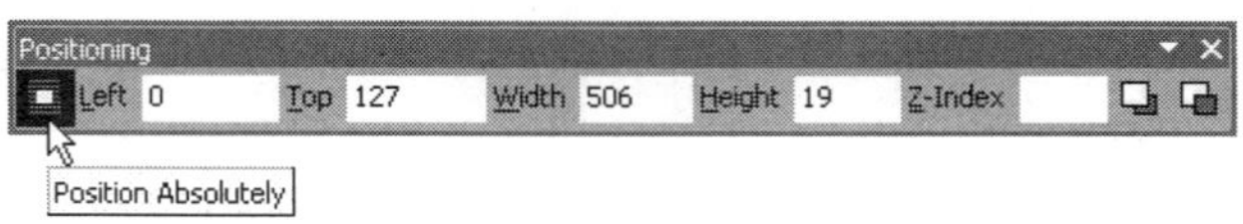

***Figure 244** The Microsoft FrontPage Positioning toolbar.*

From left to right, the buttons on the positioning toolbar are:

- **Position Absolutely** – move the currently selected item (or paragraph text) into (or out of) a positioning box.
- **Left** – the position of the left side of the positioning box relative to the left side of its container. If the positioning box is located on a Web page, the value in the Left field is the number of pixels the positioning

box is away from the left-hand side of the Web page. If the positioning box is itself within another positioning box, or container, the value in the Left field is the number of pixels the left side of the positioning box is away from the left side of the positioning box in which it is enclosed.

- **Top** – the position of the top of the positioning box relative to the top of its container. If the positioning box is located on a Web page, the value in the Top field is the number of pixels the positioning box is away from the top of the Web page. If the positioning box is itself within another positioning box, the value in the Top field is the number of pixels the top of the positioning box is away the top of the positioning box in which it is enclosed.
- **Width** – the width (in pixels) of the positioning box.
- **Height** – the height (in pixels) of the positioning box.
- **Z-Index** – controls the position of the positioning box on the z-axis. The Z-Index controls the behavior of overlapping containers. If two containers overlap, the Web browser will display the contents of the positioning box with the higher Z-Index value over those in the container with the lower Z-Index value. In general, the Web browser will display positioning box contents in ascending order by Z-Index. When two or more positioning boxes have the same Z-Index, the Web browser displays them in the order in which it finds their definitions in the Web page HTML. Therefore, if two overlapping containers have the same Z-Index, the Web browser will display the contents of the positioning box defined last (in the Web page HTML) in front.
- **Bring Forward** – increase the value of the container's Z-Index.
- **Send Backward** – decrease the value of the container's Z-Index

The Positioning toolbar bar buttons you will use most often are the Positioning Absolutely button (to move an element from the Web page into a new positioning boxing) and the Bring Forward and Send Backward buttons (to control which container's objects the Web browser displays when positioning boxes overlap).

CONTROLLING THE DISPLAY OF POSITIONING BOX CONTENT THAT OVERLAPS CONTENT ON A WEB PAGE OR IN ANOTHER POSITIONING BOX

If you use positioning boxes to control the location of elements on a Web page, you must decide how you want the Web browser to display the contents of a positioning box that overlaps another positioning box or content on the Web page itself.

When you move objects from a Web page into a positioning box, the objects no longer take up any space on the Web page itself. Suppose, for example, that you have a Web page (such as that shown in Figure 245.1) in which graphics images separate words of text.

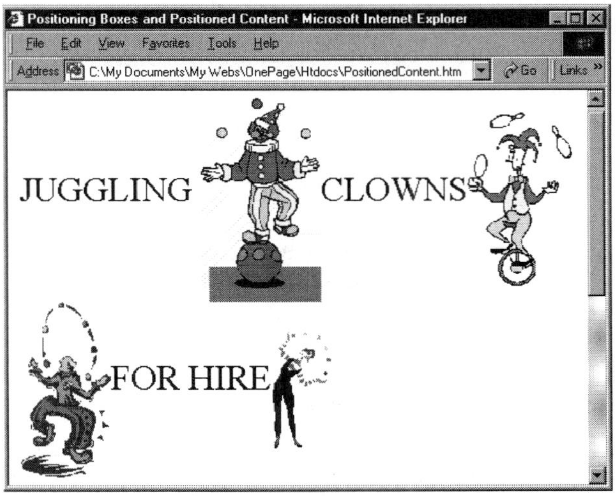

Figure 245.1 A Web page with words of text separated by graphics images.

If you click the mouse pointer on the graphics image inserted between the words "JUGGLING" and "CLOWNS" on the Web page, and then on the Position Absolutely button on the Positioning toolbar, FrontPage will move the picture of the clown into a positioning box. As a result, the clown will no longer take up space between the words on the Web page, and the Web browser will display the words "JUGGLING CLOWNS" together, behind the graphics image in the positioning box, similar to that shown in Figure 245.2.

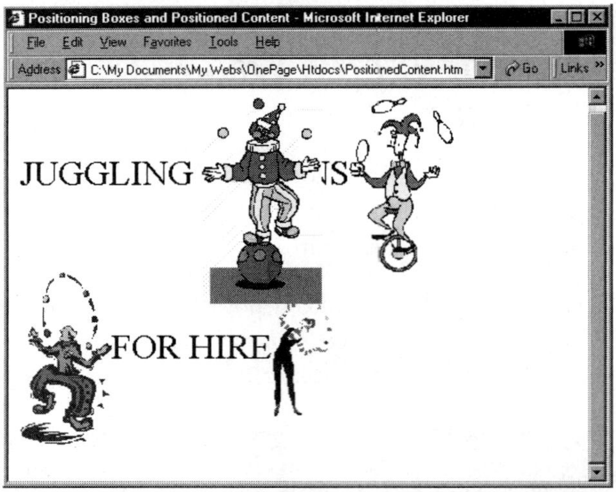

Figure 245.2 A Web page showing the effect of moving a graphics image that separated two words on Web page into a positioning container.

If you want the Web browser to display the contents of a positioning box (such as the picture of the clown in the current example) behind objects on the Web page, click the mouse pointer on blank space within the positioning box and enter a **-1** into the Z-Index field on the Positioning toolbar. (By default, all content inserted onto the Web page background or into the cells of a table on the Web page background has a Z-Index value of 0.)

Note: *While Microsoft's Internet Explorer correctly handles negative Z-Index values, Netscape Navigator (version 4.7) does not. As such, if you want Netscape Navigator to position a graphics image behind Web page text, you must first move the text into a positioning box. After you set the Z-Index value of the positioning box with the text to "2" and the Z-Index value of the positioning box with the graphics image to "1," Netscape Navigator (and Internet Explorer) will then display the graphics image behind the text. The Z-Index values "1" and "2" are used for illustrative purposes only. As long as both positioning boxes have a Z-Index value greater than zero (0), and the positioning box with the text has a higher positive Z-Index value than the positioning box with the graphics image, Netscape Navigator (and Internet Explorer) will display the graphics image behind the text.*

Similarly, if two positioning boxes overlap, click the mouse pointer on the one whose contents you want the Web browser to display in front of the contents of the other. Then click your mouse pointer on the Bring Forward button (second button from the right) on the Positioning toolbar until the value in the toolbar's Z-Index field is greater than the Z-Index of the other container. Conversely, if want to move one container behind another, click the mouse pointer on the container whose contents you want displayed behind the other container and then on the Send Backward button until the container's Z-Index value is less than the Z-Index value of the other container.

UNDERSTANDING THE INTERACTION BETWEEN POSITIONING BOX AND WEB PAGE CONTENT

The easiest way to understand the behavior of positioning boxes is to think of them as Post-It® notes stuck onto a Web page. After you move a graphics image or other content from a Web page into a positioning box, the object you moved no longer takes up any space on the Web page itself. As a result, the content that followed the object on the page moves up to fill the gap left by removing it. The object that was previously on the Web page now takes up space in its new container—the positioning box. The positioning box, in turn, sits on top of the Web page as if it were a Post-It® note affixed to a piece of paper. While the contents of the position box obscure the Web page content directly beneath it on the screen, the dimensions of the box and its content have no effect on the position of the text and graphics images on the Web page.

Although it may be a bit confusing at first, both position boxes and the Web page on which they sit are containers. After all, both Web pages and position boxes *contain* Web page elements such as tables, graphics images, text, lists, etc. When the Web browser reads through and processes the HTML file it receives from the Web server, the browser works with the tags that define each of the containers (and their contents) independently. As such, only the content in the Web page container effects the arrangement of the objects on the Web page. Similarly, only the content in a particular position box effects the arrangement of the objects in that position box.

The Web browser renders (or draws) the content in the containers it finds in the HTML file in the order of each container's Z-Index. By default, the Web page container has a Z-Index of zero. As a result, the Web browser will display the content in a positioning box with a Z-Index greater than zero after it displays the content in the Web page container, which has a Z-Index of zero. As the Web browser displays the content of one container after another, the content in the container it displays last always appears in front of the content in the container(s) the browser displayed onscreen previously. Thus, displaying containers on a Web page is like putting Post-It notes on a piece of paper—the writing or drawing on the Post-It note you stick on the paper last will be on top and hide any writing on the paper (and on other Post-It) notes beneath it.

Note: *If two containers have the same Z-Index value, the Web browser will display their content in the order in which the containers are defined in the HTML file. Since the definition of the Web page starts before the definition of any of the positioning boxes defined in the file, the Web browser will always display the contents of the Web page container before it displays the content in any other container with a Z-Index value of zero.*

As you learned in the preceding Tip titled: "Controlling the Display of Position Box Content that Overlaps Content on a Web Page or in Another Position Box," Microsoft's Internet

Explorer supports negative Z-Index values while Netscape Navigator does not. Therefore, Internet Explorer displays the contents of containers with Z-Index values less than zero before (and therefore, behind) the content in the Web page container. Conversely, Netscape Navigator treats containers with negative Z-Index values as if they have a Z-Index value of zero.

Therefore, when you want to display the contents of the Web page in front of the contents of a positioning box, move the Web page container's contents into a positioning box. Then, make sure the Z-Index of the positioning box with the Web page content is greater than the Z-Index of the container whose contents you want a browser to display behind the content from the Web page. For example, if you want to display a graphics image in a positioning box behind some text on a Web page, move the text into a positioning box with a Z-Index of two (2), and set the Z-Index of the positioning box with the graphics image to one (1).

UNDERSTANDING WEB PAGE FRAMES

Frames divide the Web browser's application window into multiple smaller windows, and the Web browser can (and usually does) display a different Web page in each frame. A frameset consists of a *frames page* and a set of *content* pages. The frames page contains HTML tags that define the position, dimensions, name, and the *frame source* for each of the windows (frames) the Web browser is to draw in its application window. A *frame source* is the name of Web page the Web browser is to retrieve from the Web server and display in a frame after it draws the frames defined by the HTML in the frames page.

In general, terms, when a Web browser requests the homepage from a Web site that uses frames, the Web server sends the frames page to the Web browser. Rather than display the contents of the frames page onscreen—as it would an ordinary Web (content) page—the Web browser uses the frames page HTML to divide the application window into multiple frames (windows) into which the browser displays the site's Web pages. After drawing the frames onscreen, the Web browser retrieves and displays in each frame the Web page named in the SRC (source) attribute of the <FRAME> tag that defines the frame. (The Web page that the Web browser loads into a frame after the browser draws the frame onscreen is called the frame's "frame source.")

For example, the Web page shown in Figure 247 has three frames (or windows):

- the frame at the top of the page—most likely used to display a banner.
- the frame along the left-hand side of the page—most likely used to display a menu or table of contents.
- the frame on the right-hand side of the page—most likely used to display a different Web page each time the visitor clicks a hyperlink in the menu or table of contents frame along the left-hand side of the application window.

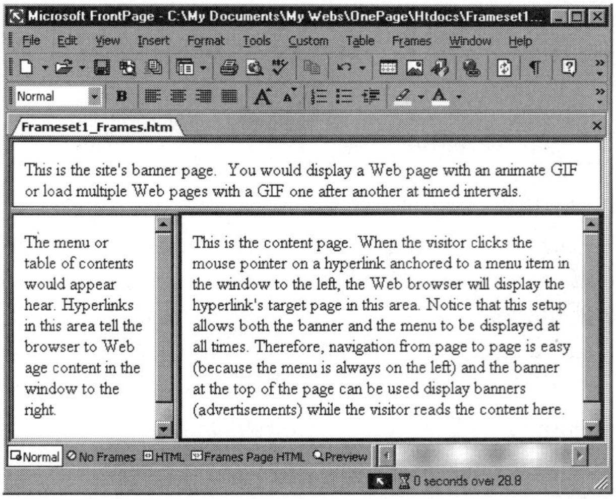

Figure 247 A Web page with three frames.

In the next few Tips, you will learn how to create and work with a frames page and how to display a hyperlink's destination page in any one of the frames or in a new window outside the browser's application window.

USING A FRAME TEMPLATE TO CREATE A FRAMES PAGE

The first (and perhaps most difficult) step in creating a framed Web site is deciding on the number and layout of the frames on the frames page. As you learned in the preceding Tip, the Web browser does not actually display the content of the Web page onscreen. Instead, it uses the frames page HTML to draw frames on a page and to retrieve and load an initial Web page (the frame source) into each frame.

Before you create the frames page, spend some time on its design. Make a rough sketch of the "framed" Web with its frames drawn to scale and arranged the way you want the site visitor to see them in the Web browser's application window. Decide whether the frames will have borders and which of them will have scrollbars. Next, choose the background image (if any) and decide on a color scheme or theme for each frame. Finally, create a set of temporary frame source Web pages—one page for each frame in the frameset. You will replace the temporary "placeholder" pages with the site's actual Web content pages later.

If you are not adding a frameset to an existing FrontPage web, you need to create a new web *before* you create the frameset's frames page. After you tell FrontPage to create the frames page and the Web pages you want the Web browser to display in its frames, you will save the frameset to a FrontPage Web.

For the current project, perform the following steps to create a new FrontPage web:

1. Select the File menu New option, and click the mouse pointer on Page or Web. FrontPage, in turn, will display the New Page or Web menu along the right-hand side of the application window.
2. Click the mouse pointer on Web Site Templates in the New from template section in the bottom half of the New Page or Web menu. FrontPage, in turn, will display the Web Site Templates dialog box.
3. Into the Specify the location of the new web field (in the Options section at the top of the right-hand side of the dialog box), enter the pathname of the folder in which you wish to create the new FrontPage web. For the current project, enter **C:\MY DOCUMENTS\MY WEBS\FramedWeb** into the Specify the location of the new web field.
4. Click your mouse pointer on the Empty Web icon in the list box to the left of the Options section.
5. Click the mouse pointer on the OK button near the lower right-hand corner of the Web Site Templates dialog box. FrontPage, in turn, will create a new FrontPage web in the folder you specified in Step 3 and take you to that Web page.

With your sketch of the frames page layout in hand, use one of the FrontPage templates to create the frames page by performing the following steps:

1. Select the File menu New option and click the mouse pointer on Page or Web. FrontPage, in turn, will display the New Page or Web menu along the right-hand side of the application window.
2. Click the mouse pointer on Page Templates in the New from template section in the bottom half of the New Page or Web menu. FrontPage, in turn, will display a Page Templates dialog box similar to that shown in Figure 248.1.
3. Click your mouse pointer on the Frames Pages tab.
4. Click the mouse pointer on the frames layout you want to use. Each time you click the mouse pointer on one of the layouts in the list box on the left-hand side of the Frames Pages tab, FrontPage will display a description of the layout in the Description area on the right-hand side of the Frames Pages tab and a picture of the layout in the Preview section below the description. For the current project, click the mouse pointer on the icon for the Banner and Contents template in the upper left-hand corner of the templates list box.

5. Click the mouse pointer on the OK button near the lower right-hand corner of the Page Templates dialog box. FrontPage, in turn, will display the frame layout you selected in the Page view Normal tab similar to that shown in Figure 248.2.

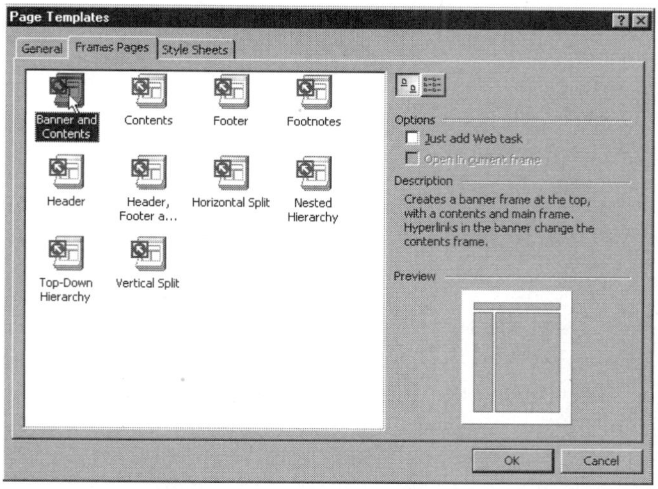

Figure 248.1 The Microsoft FrontPage Page Templates dialog box, Frames Page tab.

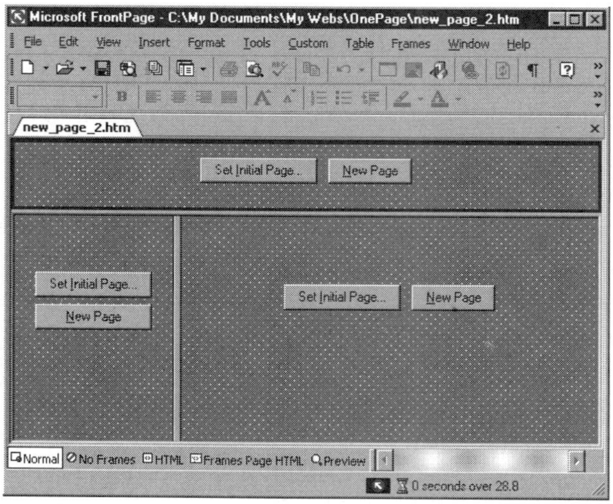

Figure 248.2 The frame layout of the Banner and Contents frames template displayed on the Page view Normal tab.

When you open or create a FrontPage web that uses frames, FrontPage adds two additional tabs to the Page view—the No Frames tab and the Frames Page HTML tab. Use the No Frames tab to create the Web page you want the site visitor's browser to display if the browser does not support frames. If you want to view the HTML tags on the frames page, which defines the site's frames and the initial Web page the browser is to display in each frame, click the mouse pointer on the Frames Page HTML tab.

In the next Tip, you will learn how to attach a blank Web page to each of the frames defined by the frames page. Each blank page you create will serve as a placeholder for the initial page you want the Web browser to display in one of the frames defined by the frames page.

ATTACHING A BLANK INITIAL PAGE TO A FRAME

After you perform the procedure in the preceding Tip to select a frames layout for your Web site, FrontPage will generate the frames page HTML. However, as you learned in previous Tips, the layout of the frames is only a part of the information the Web browser expects to see on the frames page. The frames page must also tell the Web browser the name of the Web page the browser is to display in each of the frames.

If you have already created the Web pages you want the Web browser to display after it draws the page frames, you can skip this Tip and go on to the Tip titled "Attaching a Default Web Page to a Frame." Otherwise, perform the following steps to attach a blank default (placeholder) page to each of the frames in the frameset:

1. If you have not done so already, execute the procedure in the preceding Tip titled "Using a Frame Template to Create Frames on a Web Page."
2. Click the mouse pointer on the NEW PAGE button in the frame for which you wish to create a blank default Web page. For the current project, click the mouse pointer on the NEW PAGE button in the banner frame across the top of the Web page. FrontPage, in turn, will display a blank Web page in the frame.
3. Enter a few words of text that describe the purpose of the frame's content. For example the current project, enter **This will be the Banner at the top of the page.**
4. Repeat Steps 2 – 3 for each of the other frames in the layout. For the current project, click the mouse pointer on the NEW PAGE button in the menu frame along the left-hand side of the Web page in Step 2 and enter **This will be a menu or the site's table of contents.** Then, the third time through the procedure, click the mouse pointer on the

NEW PAGE button in the main content frame on the right below the banner frame in Step 2 and enter **This will be the site's homepage and main content display area.**

Each time you complete Step 3 of the procedure, FrontPage will create a new Web page in memory and attach the page to a frame by placing its filename into the SRC attribute of the frame's <FRAME> tag. In the next Tip, you will learn how to save to disk the frames page and the frame source Web pages the frames page tells the Web browser to load into the frames in the frameset after the browser draws the frames onscreen.

UNDERSTANDING AND SAVING A FRAMESET

After you tell FrontPage to create a frames page (as you learned to do in a previous Tip titled "Using a Frame Template to Crate a Frames Page") and the initial Web pages you want the visitor's Web browser to load into the frames (as you learned to do in the preceding Tip), you need to save your work to disk. Remember, FrontPage stores any new Web pages you create (including content and frames pages) and any changes you make to those pages only in the computer's memory. To protect your work from loss due to such things as a power failure or computer lock-up *and* to make the Web pages available for retrieval and display by a Web browser, you must save your work to files on disk.

As mentioned in previous Tips, a *frameset* consists of a *frames page* and the *frame source* pages the Web browser loads into the frames defined in the frames page. That is, each *frame source* is the Web page you want the Web browser to load into a particular frame specified by the HTML tags in the *frames page*. For the current project, you created the frames page in the Tip titled "Using a Frame Template to Create a Frames Page," and you created the frame source pages in the preceding Tip titled "Attaching a Blank Initial Page to a Frame."

The first time you save a frameset (a frames page and its frame source pages), can be a bit confusing because you must save several Web pages, one after another. (Normally, when you select the File menu Save option to save a newly created Web page, FrontPage only prompts you with the Save As dialog box one time, since it only needs to save the current Web page to disk.)

To save a frameset to disk, perform the following steps:

1. Select the File menu Save option. FrontPage, in turn, will display a Save As dialog box (similar to that shown in Figure 250) prompting you to select a folder and enter a filename in which to store one of the frame source pages. FrontPage shows you which of the frame source pages it is prompting you to save by highlighting its frame in the frames page layout displayed along the right-hand side of the dialog

box. For example, Figure 250 shows a Save As dialog box similar to the one FrontPage displays when prompting you to save the frame source for the (banner) frame across the top of the framed Web page.

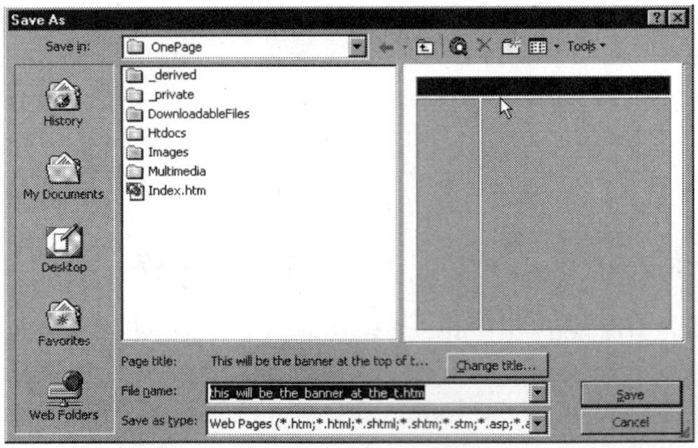

Figure 250 *The Microsoft FrontPage Save As dialog box.*

2. Use the drop-down list button to the right of the Save in field and the folders list below the field to navigate to the folder in the FrontPage web in which you wish to store the frame source Web page. For the current project, navigate to the C:\MY DOCUMENTS\MY WEBS\FramedWeb folder you created in a previous Tip titled "Using a Frame Template to Create a Frames Page."
3. Into the File name field near the bottom of the dialog box, enter a descriptive filename for the frame source Web page you are saving. For example, if you are saving the frame source page for the "banner" frame across the top of the Web page, enter a filename such as **Banner** into the File name field.

Note: *If your Web site has more then one frames page, you will want to include a one-word description of the frameset in the filenames you use for the frameset's frame source pages. For example, if you are saving a homepage with three frames (such as the one in the current project), you might use BANNER.HTM, SIDE.HTM, and MAIN.HTM as the filenames for frame source pages associated with the homepage frameset. If the site used the same three-frame layout for a framed "products" Web page, you would use filenames similar to PRODUCTS_BANNER.HTM, PRODUCTS_SIDE.HTM, and PRODUCTS_MAIN.HTM for the frame source pages in the "products" frameset.*

4. Click the mouse pointer on the CHANGE TITLE button above the File name field. FrontPage, in turn, will display the Set Page Title dialog box.

5. Into the Page title field, enter a short description of the frame source Web page. For the current project, enter **Homepage Banner** into the Page title field and click the mouse pointer on the OK button near the bottom center of the Set Page Title dialog box.
6. Click the mouse pointer on the SAVE button near the lower right-hand corner of the Save As dialog box. FrontPage, in turn, will save the frame source Web page for the frame highlighted in frames page layout displayed along the right-hand side of the dialog box.
7. Repeat Steps 2 – 6 to save each of the remaining frame source Web pages.

   For the current project, you will perform Steps 2 – 6 a total of three times because you are saving the three blank frame source pages you attached to the three-frame Web page when you executed the procedure in the preceding Tip. The second time through, FrontPage will prompt you to save the frame source page for the side (menu) frame. As such, enter **Side** into the File name field in Step 3, and **Homepage (Sidebar) Menu** into the Page title field in Step 5. The third (and final) time through Steps 2 - 6, FrontPage will prompt you to save the frame source page for the main document frame. As such, enter **Main** into the File name field in Step 3, and **Homepage Main Document** into the Page title field in Step 5.

After prompting you to save the frame source for each of the frames in the frameset, FrontPage will prompt you to save the frames page by highlighting the borders in the frame page layout displayed along the right-hand side of the Save As dialog box. (When saving the frame source for a particular frame in Steps 2 – 6, FrontPage highlighted the frame of the frame source it was saving.)

8. Into the File name field, enter a descriptive name for the frames page. For the current project, enter **Index** into the File name field to save the frames page as the sites homepage (INDEX.HTM).
9. Click the mouse pointer on the CHANGE TITLE button above the File name field. FrontPage, in turn, will display the Set Page Title dialog box.
10. Into the Page title field, enter a short description of the frames page. For the current project, enter **Framed Homepage** into the Page title field, and click the mouse pointer on the OK button near the bottom right-hand corner of the Set Page Title dialog box.
11. Click the mouse pointer on the SAVE button near the lower right-hand corner of the Save As dialog box. FrontPage, in turn, will save the frames page and return to the Page view Normal tab.

After you complete Step 11, you will have saved one frame source Web page for each of the frames in the frameset and the frames page which not only tells the Web browser how to split the application window into frames but also tells it which frame source to load into each frame.

Note: *If you are using placeholder Web pages for the frame source pages, you need to edit each of the Web frame source pages and fill it with the content you want the site visitor to see in the frames of the framed Web page before you publish the FrontPage web to the Web server.*

USING AN EXISTING WEB PAGE AS THE FRAME SOURCE FOR A FRAME IN A FRAMESET

In the two preceding Tips, you learned how to create and attach a new Web page to each of the frames in a frameset and how to save the frameset to disk. Moreover, in previous Tips about frames, you learned that the HTML tags and attributes in the frameset's frames page tell the Web browser how to layout the frames in the browser's application window. After drawing all of the frames in the frameset, the Web browser uses the value of the SRC (source) attribute in each of the <FRAME> tags in the frames page HTML to retrieve and display an initial Web page (the frame's frame source) in each frame.

The procedure in a previous Tip, titled "Attaching a Blank Initial Page to a Frame," had you create a new Web page as the frame source for each of the frames in the frameset. This Tip will show you how to use an existing Web page as a frame source.

Before you learn how to use existing Web pages as frame source pages for frames defined in the frames page, you need a FrontPage web and some existing Web pages to use when working the project. If you have not yet executed the procedures in the three preceding tips (starting with the Tip titled "Using a Frame Template to Create Frames on a Web page"), do so now to create the FrontPage web: "FramedWeb" in the C:\MY DOCUMENTS\MY WEBS folder on your C: drive.

Next, perform the following steps to create a set of "products" Web pages you will use as "existing" pages for the project later in this Tip:

1. Select the File menu Open Web option. FrontPage, in turn, will display the Open Web dialog box.
2. Into the Web name field (near the bottom of the dialog box), enter **C:\MY DOCUMENTS\MY WEBS\FramedWeb**, and click the mouse pointer on the OPEN button near the lower right-hand corner of the Open Web dialog box. FrontPage, in turn, will open the FrontPage web you created by executing the procedures in the three preceding Tips.

3. Select the View menu Page option to switch to Page view, and if you do not see the Folder List pane in the FrontPage application window, select the View menu Folder List option to display it.
4. Right-click your mouse pointer on the folder icon at the top of the Folder List pane (web's root folder). Select New from the pop-up menu and click your mouse pointer on Folder. FrontPage, in turn, will create a new (sub)folder in the current web and prompt you for its name.
5. Type **HTDocs**, and press the ENTER key on your keyboard to name the new folder you created in Step 4.
6. Click your mouse pointer on the Create a new normal page button (first button on the left, with the blank page icon) on the Standard toolbar. FrontPage, in turn, will create and display a new, blank Web page on the Page view Normal tab.
7. Onto the new Web page, type **Products Banner Page**.
8. Select the File menu Close option, and click the mouse pointer on the YES button when FrontPage prompts you with the Save changes message box. FrontPage, in turn, will display the Save As dialog box.
9. Into the File name field (at the bottom of the dialog box), enter **HTDOCS\Products_Banner**, and then click the mouse pointer on the SAVE button near the lower right-hand corner of the Save As dialog box.
10. Repeat Steps 6 – 9 four more times to create four additional Web pages to use as "existing" pages when you practice attaching existing Web pages to frames later in this Tip. Each time you repeat Steps 6 - 9, change the text you type onto the Web page and its filename when you save it, as follows:
    - first time through – type **Products List** on the new page in Step 7, and enter **Products_List** into the File name field in Step 9.
    - second time through – type **Information on Product 1** on the new page in Step 7, and enter **Product1** into the File name field in Step 9.
    - third time through – type **Information on Product 2** on the new page in Step 7, and enter **Product2** into the File name field in Step 9.
    - fourth time through – type **Information on Product 3** on the new page in Step 7, and enter **Product3** into the File name field in Step 9.

Now that you have a FrontPage web with existing Web pages, you can use as frame source pages you are ready to work the project for this Tip.

To use an existing Web page as the frame source for a frame in a frameset, perform the following steps:

1. Use a frames template to create the frames page for the frameset by executing the procedure in a previous Tip titled "Using a Frame Template to Create Frames on a Web Page." After executing the procedure, the Page view Normal tab in your FrontPage application window will appear similar to that shown in Figure 251.1.

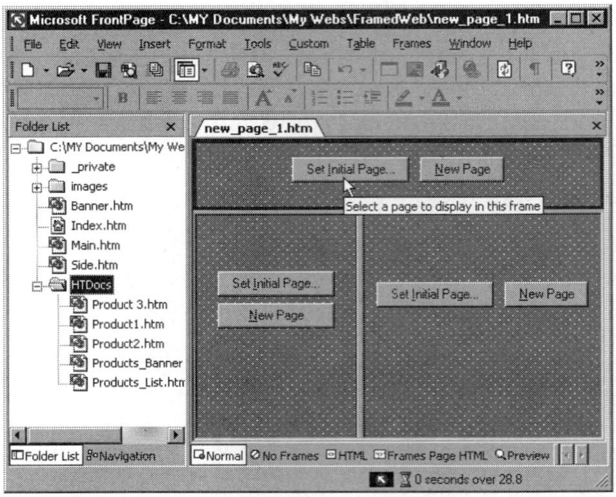

Figure 251.1 The Microsoft FrontPage Page view Normal tab with a three-frame frames page.

2. Click the mouse pointer on the SET INITIAL PAGE button in the frame for which you wish to use an existing Web page as the frame source. For the current project, click the mouse pointer on the SET INITIAL PAGE button in the banner frame across the top of the Web page. FrontPage, in turn, will display an Insert Hyperlink dialog box similar to that shown in Figure 251.2.

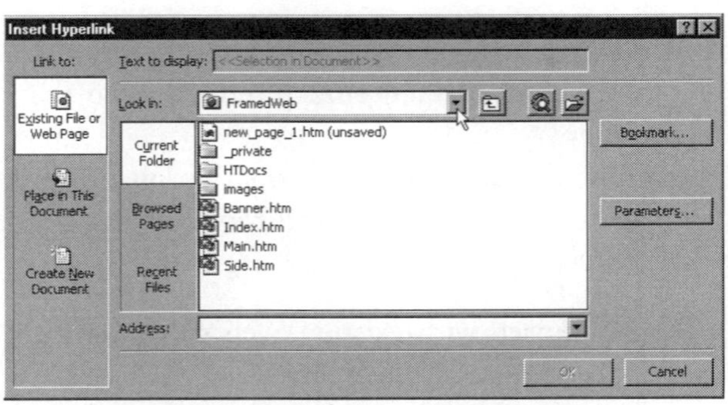

Figure 251.2 The Microsoft FrontPage Page Insert Hyperlink dialog box.

3. Use the drop-down list button to the right of the Look in field and the folders in the list box below the field to navigate to the folder that contains the Web page you want to use as the frame's frame source. For the current project, double-click the mouse pointer on the **HTDocs** folder in the folder list area below the Look in field, since the Web page you want to use is in the HTDOCS subfolder in the current web.

Note: *Although you are going to use a Web page in the current FrontPage web as the frame source for the current project, FrontPage also lets you attach a Web page located outside the current FrontPage web to a frame. If you want to use a Web page stored outside the current FrontPage web on your local hard drive or on another computer accessible on your local area network (LAN), use the Browse for File button (with the open file folder icon, to the right of the Look in field) to navigate to the folder in which the Web page is stored. Similarly, if you want to use a Web page on the Internet as the frame's frame source, use the Browse the Web button (with the globe icon, to the right of the Look in field) to navigate the Internet to the Web page you want to use.*

4. In the list box below the Look in field, click your mouse pointer on the name of the Web page you want to use as the frame's frame source. For the current project, click the mouse pointer on **Products_ Banner.htm**.
5. Click your mouse pointer on the OK button near the lower right-hand corner of the Insert Hyperlink list dialog box. FrontPage, in turn, will set the SRC (source) attribute for the frame you selected in Step 1 to the Web page you selected in Step 4 and display the frame source (Web page) in the frame.
6. Repeat Steps 2 – 5 for each of the other frames in the layout. For the current project, click the mouse pointer on the SET INITIAL PAGE button in the menu frame along the left-hand side of the Web page in Step 2 and then on **Products_List.htm** in Step 4. Then, the third time through the procedure, click the mouse pointer on the SET INITIAL PAGE button in the main content frame on the right below the banner frame in Step 2 and **Product1.htm** in Step 4.

Next, select the File menu Save option to save the frames page to disk by performing the following steps:

1. Select the file menu Save option. FrontPage, in turn, will display the Save As dialog box.
2. Use the drop-down list button to the right of the Save in field and the folders in the list box below the field to navigate to the folder in which

you want to store the frameset's frames page. For the current project, navigate to the HTDOCS folder.

3. Into the File name field (near the bottom of the dialog box), enter the name of the file in which you wish to store the frames page HTML. For the current project, enter **Products_Frames** into the File name field.
4. Click the mouse pointer on the CHANGE TITLE button above the right-hand corner of the File name field. FrontPage, in turn, will display the Set Page Title dialog box.
5. Into the Page title field at the top of the Page Title dialog box, enter a title for the frames page. For the current project enter **Products Frames Page** into the Page title field, and click the mouse pointer on the OK button near the lower right-hand side of the Set Page Title dialog box.
6. Click the mouse Pointer on the SAVE button near the lower right-hand corner of the Save As dialog box.

When you selected the File menu Save option to save the frameset in the preceding Tip, FrontPage prompted you to save each of the frame source pages, as well as, the frames page to disk. (FrontPage prompted you to save each of the frame source pages because all of them contained unsaved work.) When you selected the File menu Save option to save the frameset to disk in the current Tip, FrontPage only prompted you to save the frames page because was the only page in the frameset with work not yet saved to disk. Remember, you used existing (already saved) Web pages as the frame source pages for the frames you created in the current Tip.

CHANGING THE LAYOUT OF THE FRAMES ON A FRAMED WEB PAGE

When you want to divide a Web page into frames, so you can display multiple Web pages in the Web browser's application window at the same time, perform the procedure in a previous Tip titled "Using a Frame Template to Create Frames on a Web Page." Chances are good that one of the ten frames templates that come standard with FrontPage will have the exact frames page layout you want. However, if none of the layouts will do, select the frames template with frames arranged most closely to the way you want them and then resize, delete, and split frames as necessary.

Suppose, for example, that you execute the procedure in a previous Tip titled "Using a Frame Template to Create Frames on a Web Page" and use the Header, Footer and Contents template to display a frames page on the Page view Normal tab similar to that shown in Figure 252.1.

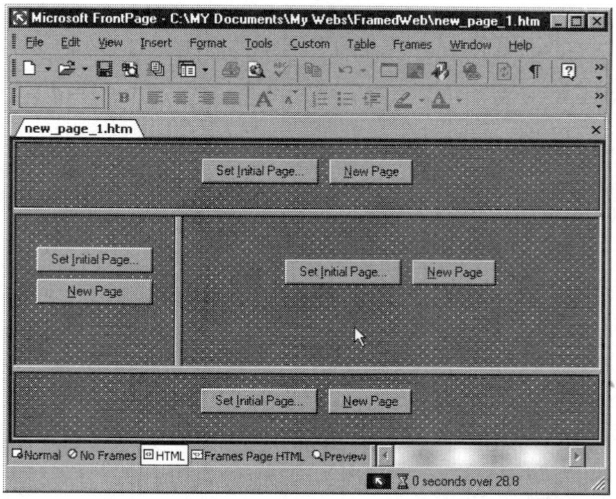

Figure 252.1 The Microsoft FrontPage Page view Normal tab with a four-frame frames page.

To split a frame in two, perform the following steps:

1. With the frames page displayed on the Page view Normal tab, click the mouse pointer on the frame you want to split. For the current project, click the mouse pointer on the center frame on the right-hand side.
2. Select the Frames menu Split frame option. FrontPage, in turn, will display the Split Frame dialog box shown in Figure 252.2.

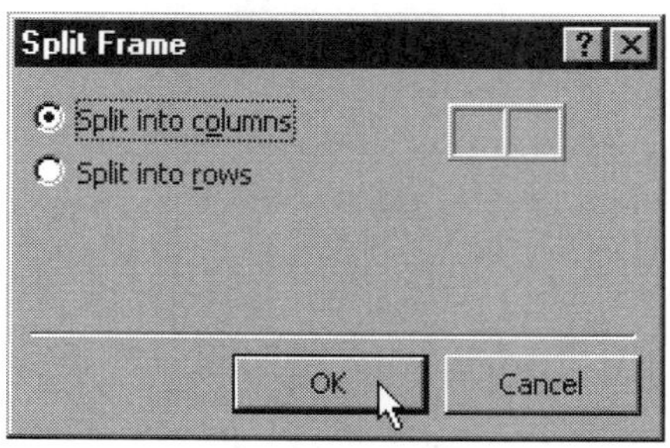

Figure 252.2 The Microsoft FrontPage Split Frame dialog box.

3. If you want to split the frame (you selected in Step 2) vertically, click the mouse pointer on the Split into columns radio button and then on the OK button at the bottom center of the dialog box. On the other hand, if you want to split the frame horizontally, click the mouse pointer on the Split into rows radio button and then on the OK button at the bottom of the Split Frame dialog box. For the current project,

click the mouse pointer on the Split into columns radio button and then on the OK button at the bottom of the dialog box to create a frames page layout similar to that shown in figure 252.3.

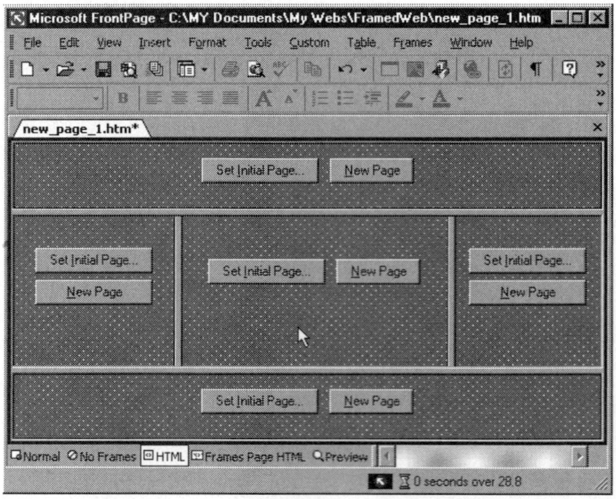

***Figure 252.3** The frames page from Figure 252.1 after splitting the middle frame on the right-hand side into columns (after splitting the frame vertically).*

***Note:** When you tell FrontPage to split one of the frames on the frames page, the program automatically adds buttons you can use to attach either a new Web page or an existing Web page to the frame as the frame's frame source.*

To delete a frame, perform the following steps:

1. With the frames page displayed on the Page view Normal tab, click the mouse pointer on the frame you want to delete. For the current project, click the mouse pointer on the frame shown in the center of the frames page on the Page view Normal tab in Figure 252.3.
2. Select the Frames menu Delete Frame option.

After you complete Step 2, FrontPage will remove the frame's definition from the frames page HTML and the adjoining frames will absorb the space previously used by the delete frame.

To change the size of a frame, move your mouse pointer over the border between the frames whose dimensions you want to change. When your FrontPage changes your mouse pointer into the double-headed arrow, click hand hold down the left mouse button as you drag the mouse pointer (and the side of the frame) either outward (to make the frame taller or wider) or inward (to make the frame shorter or narrower). When you are finishing moving the frame's border, release the left mouse button.

CHANGING THE CONTENT ON PAGES IN A FRAMESET

When you open a frames page on the Page view Normal tab, FrontPage reads the HTML in the frames page file (as a Web browser would) draws the frames as specified by the file's <FRAME> tags and loads the frame source (the initial Web page) into each frame. After FrontPage loads the frame source into the frame, you can edit the Web page in the frame as if the page were on its own Page view Normal tab (vs. inside a frame on the frames page). In short, the only difference between working on a Web page in a frame and working on the same page displayed by itself on the Page view Normal tab is the size of the editing area.

If you need more space to work on a Web page than is allowed by the frame in which it is displayed, right-click your mouse pointer in the frame, and select Open Page in New Window from the pop-up menu. FrontPage, in turn, will display the Web page in the frame source by itself on another Page view Normal tab. FrontPage will display any changes you make to the Web page either inside or outside its frame in both places.

When you are ready to save your work to disk, you can save the modified Web pages one frame at a time, or you can tell FrontPage to save all of them at once. To save the Web page in a single frame to disk, click the mouse pointer in the frame whose frame source you want to save, and then select the Frames menu Save Page option. If you want to save all modified frame source pages at once, select the File menu Save option.

The important thing to understand is that when you open and display a frames page on the Page view Normal tab, FrontPage draws the frames in the frameset and displays the frame source (the initial Web page the Web browser will load) in each of the frames. When working with a Web page in a frame on the frames page, you can make changes and set page properties as if you had opened the Web page itself (vs. loading the Web page into its frame on the frames page).

USING THE FRAME PROPERTIES DIALOG BOX TO SET A FRAME'S SIZE AND ITS SCROLL BARS AND RESIZE OPTIONS

As mentioned in previous Tips, the frames page contains the HTML tags that define the properties of each of the frames in a frameset. Although the properties settings for all of the frameset's frames are stored on the same frames page, you must adjust each frame's properties individually. Three of the properties you can set for each frame are the frame's dimensions, whether the frame has a vertical and/or a horizontal scrollbar, and whether the site visitor is allowed to change the frame's size in the Web browser's application window.

To change a frame's properties, perform the following steps:

1. With the frames page displayed on the Page view Normal tab, right-click the mouse pointer on the frame whose properties you want to change, and select Frame Properties from the pop-up menu. FrontPage, in turn, will display a Frame Properties dialog box similar to that shown in Figure 254.

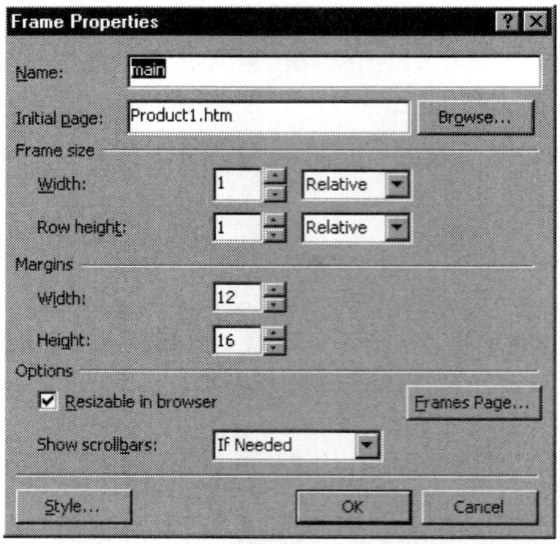

Figure 254 The Microsoft FrontPage Frame Properties dialog box.

2. Into the Width field, enter the frame's horizontal width as a number of pixels, percentage of the width of the application window, or set its width relative to the widths of the other columns of frames in the frameset.
3. Click the mouse pointer on the drop-down button on the right of the field next to the Width field and select Relative, Percent, or Pixels depending on how you want the Web browser to use the value you entered into the Width field.
   - Select **Percent** if you want the Web browser to set the frame's width as a percentage of the width of the browser's application window.
   - Select **Pixel** if you want to the Web browser to make the frame a specific number of pixels wide.
   - Select **Relative** if you want the Web browser to set the frame's width based on the widths of the other columns of frames in the frameset. For example, if you have a frameset with three columns of frames, and you elect to use the value in the Width as a relative measure of frame width, you can make the middle column twice as wide as the other two columns by setting the

value in its Width field to 2 and setting the value in the Width fields of each of the other two columns to 1. Similarly, if you want the middle column to have twice the width of the leftmost column and you want the rightmost column have twice the width of the middle column, set the value in the Width field of the leftmost column to 1, the value in the Width field of the center column to 2, and the value in the Width field of the rightmost column to 4.

4. Into the Row Height field, enter the frame's vertical height either as a number of pixels, as percentage of the height of the application window, or set its height relative to the heights of the other rows of frames in the frameset.
5. Click the mouse pointer on the drop-down button on the right of the field next to the Row Height field and select Relative, Percent, or Pixels depending on how you want the Web browser to use the value you entered into the Row Height field.
    - Select **Percent** if you want the Web browser to set the frame's height as a percentage of the height of the browser's application window.
    - Select **Pixel** if you want to the Web browser to make the frame a specific number of pixels tall.
    - Select **Relative** if you want the Web browser to set the frame's height based on the heights of the other frames in the frameset.
6. If you want to let the site visitor change the size of the frame when displayed in the Web browser's application window, click your mouse pointer on the Resizable in browser checkbox until a checkmark appears. On the other hand, if you do not want the visitor to be able to change the size of the frame, clear the Resizable in browser checkbox.

Note: *Whether or not you want the visitor to be able to change the dimensions of a frame depends on the frame's content and purpose. For example, if you create a frame across the top of the Web page and size the frame to width and height of a banner, you may not want the visitor to change the size of the frame. Conversely, if you have a menu along the left-hand side of the page and content in a frame to the right of the menu, you may want to let the visitor change the size of the content area by moving its left-hand side. By changing the size of the content frame, the visitor can display more of the content page onscreen (and less of the menu) after clicking the mouse pointer on a hyperlink in the menu frame to display retrieve and display the page in the content frame.*

7. Click the mouse pointer on the drop-down list button to the right of the Show scrollbars field and select:

- **If Needed** – to have the Web browser display horizontal and/or a vertical scroll on the side of the of the frame only if the frame is not large enough to display the entire Web page in the frame.
- **Never** – to prevent the Web browser from displaying scrollbars on the frame—even if all of the Web page content will not fit within the frame.
- **Always** – to have the Web browser display vertical and horizontal scrollbars on the frame whether the visitor will need them to scroll through the Web page content in the frame or not.

Note: *If you set the value of the Show scrollbars field to* **Never**, *you make sure that the all of the content on the Web page(s) you plan to display in the frame fits in the frame. Without scrollbars, the visitor will not be able to see any text or graphics images that fall outside the borders of the frame when the Web browser loads the Web page in the frame. For example, visitors using a 15" monitor will be somewhat annoyed when they can only see a portion of a word or picture because you set the Show scrollbars property to* **Never** *since the entire Web page fit inside the frame on your 21" monitor.*

8. Click the mouse pointer on the OK button near the bottom right-hand corner of the Frame Properties dialog box.

In general, when laying out the frames on a frames page, set the dimensions of the frames to give the Web page the "look and feel" you want the visitor to experience when the visitor first reaches the site. If you have a banner at the top of the Web page, and you always want it displayed, then by all means, clear the Resizable in browser checkbox for the frame with the banner. For all other frames, tell the Web browser display scrollbars "If Needed" and let the visitor change the dimensions of the frames in the Web browser as desired.

USING THE FRAME PROPERTIES DIALOG BOX TO SET FRAME MARGINS

Frame margins are to the content in a frame what cell padding is to the content in a table cell. While cell padding is the number of pixels of blank space been a cell wall and the content in the cell, a *frame margin* is the amount of blank space the Web browser will leave between the sides of a frame and the content on the Web page displayed in the frame.

To set the number of pixels the Web browser is to leave between the sides of a frame and its content, perform the following steps:

1. Open the frames page with the frame whose margins you want to change, and select the View menu Page option to display it on the Page view Normal tab.

2. Right-click the mouse pointer on the frame whose margin widths you want to change, and select Frame Properties from the pop-up menu. FrontPage, in turn, will display the Frame Properties dialog box.

Note: *If you right-click the mouse pointer on a frame without a frame source (without an initial Web page attached), FrontPage will display a* FRAME PROPERTIES *button instead of a pop-up menu. To display the Page Properties dialog box for a frame without a Web page, click the mouse pointer on the* FRAME PROPERTIES *button.*

3. Into the Width field in the Margins section at the center of the dialog box, enter the number of pixels of blank space you want the Web browser to leave between the left and right side of the frame and the left and right sides of the Web page displayed in the frame.
4. Into the Height field in the Margins section at the center of the dialog box, enter the number of pixels of blank space you want the Web browser to leave between the top and bottom of the frame and the top of the Web page and the last line of content displayed in the frame.
5. Click the mouse pointer on the OK button near the bottom right-hand corner of the Frame Properties dialog box.

By default, FrontPage sets the frame margins for each frame to 12 pixels of blank space between the vertical (left and right) sides of the frame and the Web page displayed in it, and 16 pixels of blank space between the horizontal sides (the top and bottom) of the frame and the first and last lines of content displayed in the frame. If you set the frame margin Width and Height fields to zero (0) for a frame, the Web browser will display its content flush against the sides of the frame—without any blank space between the sides of the frame and the content on the Web page in the frame.

USING THE PAGE PROPERTIES DIALOG BOX TO SET FRAMES PAGE PROPERTIES THAT APPLY TO ALL FRAMES IN THE FRAMESET

As you learned in the two preceding Tips, frame properties that can vary from frame to frame must be set one frame at a time using the Frame Properties dialog box for each frame. There are, however, two additional frame properties (Frame Spacing and Show Borders) that have the same value for every frame in the frameset. Since changing either of these values affects all of the frames on the frames page, you must use the Page Properties (vs. Frame Properties) dialog box to change them.

Frame spacing is the amount of space (in pixels) that the Web browser is to leave between the sides of the frames in the frameset. The default frame spacing is two pixels. While increasing cell spacing (the amount blank space between cells in a table) makes the cells appear to be further apart, increasing the number of pixels of frame spacing makes the border or wall between frames look thicker.

The reason for the difference in effect (between frame spacing and cell spacing) is that the Web browser shows the Web page background in the space between cells in a table while the browser displays the space between frames as a solid gray line—no matter what the background color of the frames page (or the background color of each of the frames in the frameset) may be. As a result, the visitor's mind interprets the gray space between frames as part of the border around the frames.

Unless turned off, *Frame borders* are always displayed as 1-pixel wide black lines along the top and left-hand side of each frame—no matter what the pixel width of the frame spacing may be.

To set the frames page Frame Spacing and Show Borders properties perform the following steps:

1. Open the frames page for the frameset whose properties you want to set, and select the View menu Page option to display the page on the Page view Normal tab.
2. Right-click the mouse pointer in any one of the frames on the page, and select Frame Properties from the pop-up menu. FrontPage, in turn, will display the Frame Properties dialog box.
3. Click your mouse pointer on the FRAMES PAGE button on the right-hand side of the Options section near the bottom of the dialog box. FrontPage, in turn, will display the Frames tab of the Page Properties dialog box, similar to that shown in Figure 256.

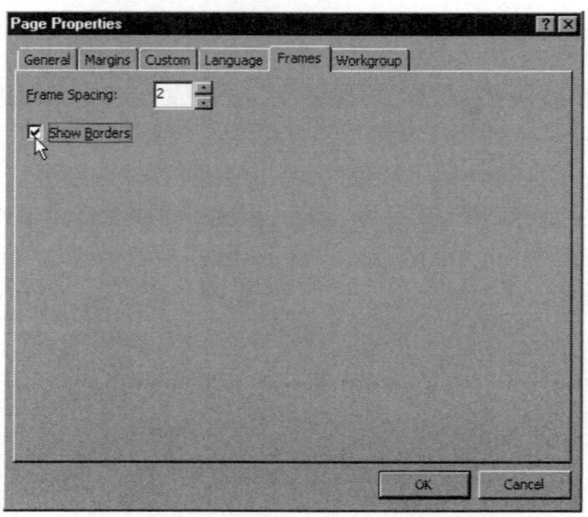

Figure 256 The Frames tab of the Microsoft FrontPage Page Properties dialog box.

4. Into the Frame Spacing field, enter the number of pixels of blank (gray) space the Web browser is to leave between the edges of the frames in the frameset.
5. If you want the Web browser to draw 1-pixel wide black lines along the top and left-hand side of each frame, click your mouse pointer on the Show Borders checkbox until a checkmark appears. Conversely, if you do not want the Web browser to draw the 1-pixel frame borders, clear the Show Borders checkbox.

Note: *If you click a checkmark into the Show Borders checkbox, the Web browser will leave at least a 1-pixel wide (gray) space between cells—even if you set the value in the Frame Spacing field to zero (0).*

6. Click your mouse pointer on the OK button near the bottom right-hand corner of the Page Properties dialog box. FrontPage, in turn, will return to the Frame Properties dialog box.
7. Click the mouse pointer on the OK button near the bottom right-hand corner of the Frame Properties dialog box. FrontPage, in turn, will return to the Page view Normal tab.

Each Web browser handles frame spacing and frame borders in a slightly different manner. Microsoft's Internet Explorer, for example, will show the space between frames and frame borders as described in this Tip. Netscape Navigator, on the other hand, does not draw the 1-pixel frame borders at all. Moreover, Netscape always displays a 1-pixel wide gray space between frames even if you set Frame Spacing to zero (0) and clear the Show Borders checkbox. Therefore, after you set the Frame Spacing and Show Borders properties, use the FrontPage File menu Preview in Browser option to display the frames page in the types of Web browsers visitors to your Web site will be using, so you can see how your framed Web page will look on their screens.

UNDERSTANDING TARGET FRAMES

A *target frame* is the frame in which the Web browser displays the Web page the browser retrieves from the Web server when you click your mouse pointer on a hyperlink. Said another way, a target frame is the frame in which the Web browser displays a hyperlink's target or destination page. When a Web page has several frames, any one of the frames in the frameset, including the frame with the activated hyperlink, can serve as the hyperlink's target frame.

When you tell FrontPage to use a Frames template to create a frames page, the program assigns a name to each frame it creates. You will find a frame's name assigned to the NAME attribute in the frame's <FRAME> tag in the frames page HTML. Suppose, for example, that you used the Header, Footer and Contents frames template to create a frames page similar to that shown in Figure 257.

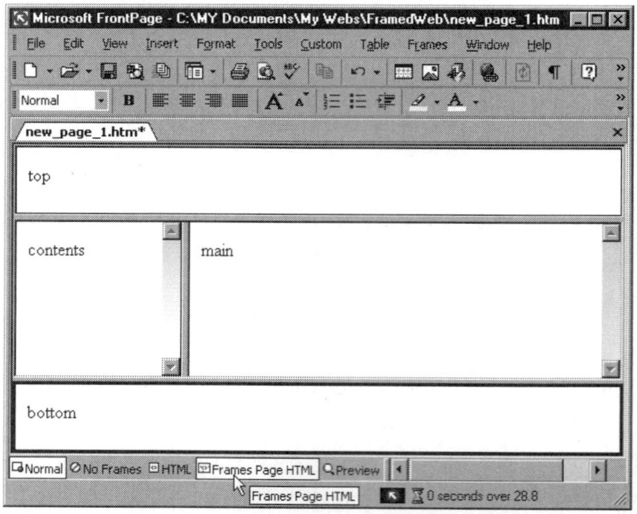

Figure 257 The Header, Footer, and Contents frame template frames page layout.

If you were to click your mouse pointer on the Page view Frames Page HTML tab, you would see the following code used to describe the frames in the frameset:

```
<frameset rows="64,*,64">
  <frame
       name="top" scrolling="no" noresize target="contents">

  <frameset cols="150,*">
    <frame name="contents" target="main">
    <frame name="main">
  </frameset>

  <frame
    name="bottom" scrolling="no" noresize target="contents">

  <noframes>
    <body>
    <p>This page uses frames, but your browser doesn't sup-
port them.</p>
    </body>
```

```
    </noframes>

  </frameset>
```

A review of the NAME attributes in the <FRAME> tags in the frames page HTML reveals that the names of the frames are:

- **top** – the name of the frame across the top of the frames page.
- **contents** – the name of the frame down the left-hand side of the page.
- **bottom** – the name of the frame along the bottom of the frames page.
- **main** – the frame to the right of the contents frame and between the top and bottom frames.

Once you know the names of each frame, the meaning of each frame's target attribute becomes clearer. For example, the contents value of the TARGET attribute in the <FRAME> tag for the top frame tells the Web browser to display in the contents frame, the Web page returned by activating a hyperlink anchored in the top frame. Similarly, the main value of the TARGET attribute in the <FRAME> tag for the contents frame tells the Web browser to display in the main frame, the Web page returned by activating a hyperlink anchored in the contents frame.

In short, the value of the NAME attribute in each <FRAME> tag identifies the frame, by name, to the Web browser. The TARGET in each frame attribute tells the Web browser the name of the frame in which to display Web pages retrieved in response to mouse clicks on hyperlinks in the frame.

If you want to change the default name FrontPage assigns to a frame, perform the following steps:

1. With the frames page displayed on the Page view Normal tab, right-click the mouse pointer on the frame whose name you want to change and select Frame Properties from the pop-up menu.
2. Into the Name field (at the top of the dialog box), enter the name you want to assign to the frame.
3. Click your mouse pointer on the OK button near the bottom right-hand corner of the Frame Properties dialog box.

Note: *If you change the name of a frame, you must also change (to the new name) any TARGET attributes that reference the name you changed.*

When deciding on the name for a frame, avoid using the names new, parent, self, and top, which have special meanings to the Web browser. Although not required by all Web browsers, use only lowercase letters and numbers in the name of a frame. Moreover, if you are inclined to separate words in a multiword name, use an underscore (_) or a dash (-) between words instead of a space.

MODIFYING TARGET FRAME SETTINGS FOR ALL HYPERLINKS ON A WEB PAGE

In the preceding Tip, you learned that the TARGET attribute in a <FRAME> tag tells the Web browser the name of the frame's target frame. You also learned that the Web browser displays in a frame's *target frame* any Web pages retrieved by activating hyperlinks located within the frame. For example, the <FRAME> tag:

```
<frame
        name="top" scrolling="no" noresize target="contents">
```

tells the Web browser to display in the frame named contents, Web pages retrieved by clicking the mouse pointer on hyperlinks in a frame named top. As such, referring to Figure 257 in the preceding Tip, anytime the visitor clicks the mouse pointer on a hyperlink in the frame named top (across the top of the page, in the current example), the Web browser will display the Web page retrieved in the frame named contents.

Note: *A frame without an explicit target frame, targets itself. In other words, if a frame's <FRAME> tag has no TARGET attribute, the Web browser will replace the Web page in the frame with the Web page it retrieves when the visitor clicks the mouse pointer on a hyperlink in the frame. For example, given the <FRAME> tag:*

```
<frame name="main">
```

the Web browser will display in the main frame any Web page retrieved by clicking the mouse pointer on a hyperlink in the main frame.

To override a frame's default target frame (the value of the <FRAME> tag's TARGET attribute), perform the following steps:

1. With the frames page displayed on the Page view Normal tab, right-click the mouse pointer in the frame whose target frame you want to change and select Page Properties from the pop-up menu. FrontPage, in turn, will display the Page Properties dialog box.

Note: *You must either create and attach a new Web page or attach an existing Web page to a frame, before you can override the frame's default target frame. As you will learn later in this Tip, FrontPage writes the <BASE> tag used to override the frame's default target frame in HTML of the Web page used as the frame's frame source. (As you already know, a frame's frame source is the Web page that the Web browser retrieves and displays in the frame after the browser draws the frameset's frames in its application window.)*

2. If not already exposed, click your mouse pointer on the General tab.
3. To change the default target frame, click the mouse pointer on the Change Target Frame button (with the three dots and pencil icon) to the right of the Default target name field near the middle of the General tab. FrontPage, in turn, will display a Target Frame dialog box similar to that shown in Figure 258.

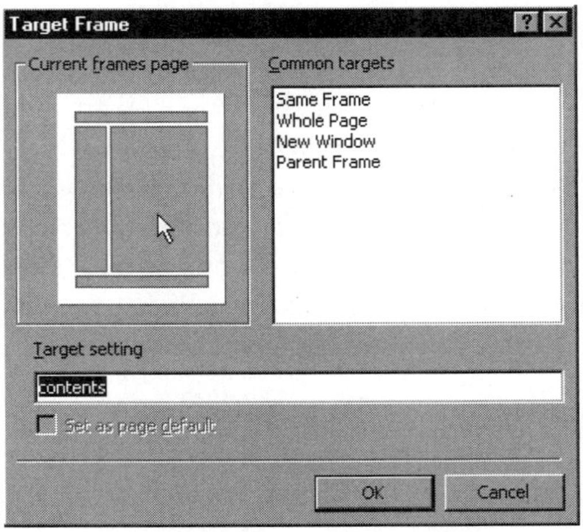

Figure 258 *The Microsoft FrontPage Target Frame dialog box.*

4. In the frameset layout, diagramed in the Current frames page section (on the upper left-hand side) of the dialog box, click the mouse pointer on the frame you want the Web browser to use as the default target frame for hyperlinks in the frame you selected in Step 1.
5. Click your mouse pointer on the OK button near the bottom right-hand corner of the Target Frame dialog box. FrontPage, in turn, will return to the Page Properties dialog box and enter the name of the target frame you selected into the Default target frame field.
6. Click the mouse pointer on the OK button near the bottom right-hand corner of the Page Properties dialog box.

If you click the mouse pointer on the Page view Frames Page HTML tab after you complete Step 6, you will see that the TARGET attribute (or lack thereof) for the frame you selected in Step 1 has not changed. As mentioned in the note following Step 1, FrontPage overrides a frame's default target frame by placing the name of the "new" default target frame into the TARGET attribute of a <BASE> tag in the HTML that defines the frame's frame source. Therefore, to display the HTML that overrides the frame's default target frame, click the mouse pointer on the Page view HTML tab, and look at the <BASE> tag's TARGET attribute in the HTML for the frame you select in Step 1.

In the next Tip you will learn that you can override both the TARGET attribute in a <BASE> tag and the TARGET attribute in a <FRAME> tag by adding a TARGET attribute to a hyperlink's <a> (anchor) tag.

CHANGING THE TARGET FRAME SETTING FOR AN INDIVIDUAL HYPERLINK ON A FRAME SOURCE WEB PAGE

In the two preceding Tips, you learned that the TARGET attribute in a frame's <FRAME> tag tells the Web browser the name of the target frame in which to display Web pages it retrieves when visitors activate hyperlinks in the frame. However, if the HTML for a frame's frame source has a <BASE> tag with a TARGET attribute that names a different target frame, the <BASE> tag's target frame setting overrides the one in the <FRAME> tag. For example, if you click your mouse pointer on a hyperlink in a Web page whose HTML contains the <BASE> tag:

```
<base target="bottom">
```

the Web browser will display the hyperlink's target page in the frame named "bottom."

If you want to set the target frame for a particular hyperlink in a frame, perform the following steps:

1. Open the frames page with the frame that has the hyperlink whose properties you want to change. Then, select the View menu Page option to display the frames page on the Page view Normal tab.
2. Right-click the mouse pointer on the hyperlink whose target frame you want to change and select Hyperlink Properties from the pop-up menu. FrontPage, in turn, will display the Edit Hyperlink dialog box.

3. Click your mouse pointer on the TARGET FRAME button near the center of the dialog box on its right-hand side. FrontPage, in turn, will display a Target Frame dialog box (similar to that shown previously in Figure 258).
4. In the frame layout diagram in the Current frames page section (on the upper left-hand side) of the dialog box, click the mouse pointer on the frame you want the Web browser to use as the target frame for the hyperlink you selected in Step 2.
5. If you want to use the target frame you selected in Step 7 as the default target frame for all hyperlinks on the Web page, click your mouse pointer on the SET AS PAGE DEFAULT checkbox until a checkmark appears.
6. Click your mouse pointer on the OK button near the bottom right-hand corner of the Target Frame dialog box. FrontPage, in turn, will return to the Edit Hyperlink dialog box.
7. Click the mouse pointer on the OK button near the bottom right-hand corner of the Edit Hyperlink dialog box.

In order to execute the procedure in this Tip, you must select a hyperlink from a Web page in a frame of a frameset displayed on the Page view Normal tab. If you select a hyperlink on a Web page not displayed in a frame, the Target Frame dialog box FrontPage displays after you perform Step 3 will not have a frameset diagram in its Current frames page section.

UNDERSTANDING SPECIAL TARGET FRAME OPTIONS

In the three preceding Tips, you learned how to select a named frame in a frameset to be the Web browser's target frame. As you now know, the visitor's Web browser will display the hyperlink's destination page (the hyperlink's target Web page) in the target frame.

When working with hyperlinks on frame source pages (the Web pages the Web browser loads into the frames of the frameset after it draws them), the Target Frame dialog box lets you select a target frame by clicking the mouse pointer in the target frame's area on the frameset diagram.

The Target Frame dialog box also contains a set of "special" target frame options listed in the Common targets list box in the upper-right-hand corner of the dialog box. Table 260 contains the name and a description of each of the target frame options available in the Common targets list box.

Common Target	Target Setting	Description
Page Defalt		target the frame in which the hyperlink is located. Equivalent to Same Frame.
Same Frame	_self	target the frame in which the hyperlink is located. The Web browser will replace the Web page in the current frame (the frame in which the hyperlink was activated) with the destination Web page.
Whole Page	_top	replace the framed Web page (the frames page) in the browser's application window with the hyperlink's destination page.
New Window	_blank	open a new browser application window and display the hyperlink's destination page in it. When the site visitor activates a hyperlink with a "_blank" or "_new" target frame setting, the Web browser tells Windows to open a new Web browser application window and display the destination page as it the visitor had started another Web browser session and typed the URL of the destination page into the browsers Address field. (See the next Tip for an explanation of how to use a "named" window if you want to have multiple hyperlinks display their destination pages in the same "new" window vs. having each one open yet another browser application window each time the visitor clicks the mouse pointer on the hyperlink.)
Parent Frame	_parent	if you are using nested frames (if one of the frames in a frameset has its own frames page and frameset), use the _parent target frame setting to replace the framed Web page (the frames page) in the frame in which the hyperlink is located. _top tells the Web browser to replace the top-level frames page with the hyperlink's destination page. _parent, meanwhile, tells the Web browser to replace only the frames page in the current frame with the hyperlink's destination page—which leaves the frames page in which you nested a frameset in control of the browser's application window.

Table 260 Target Frames available in the Common targets list box on the Target Frame dialog box.

To select one of the target frame options shown in Table 260 as the hyperlink's target frame, simply click the mouse pointer the target's name instead of on an area in the frameset diagram. FrontPage, in turn, will enter the target's setting in the Target setting field near the bottom of the dialog box and will use the setting as the value of the TARGET attribute in a <BASE> tag (if you are setting the default target frame for a Web page) or in an <A> (anchor) tag if you are setting the target frame for an individual hyperlink.

USING A NEW, NAMED BROWSER APPLICATION WINDOW AS A TARGET FRAME

When you click the mouse pointer on one of the items in the Common targets list box in the upper right-hand corner of the Target Frame dialog box, FrontPage, will write the target frame's setting into the Target setting field near the bottom of the dialog box. FrontPage also lets you type the setting or the name of the target frame into Target setting field, instead of clicking the mouse pointer on one of the items in the list box. Being able to type a target setting into the Target setting field also lets you tell the Web browser to display a hyperlink's destination page in a new, named application window.

If you click the mouse pointer on the New Window item in the Common Targets list box, FrontPage will enter either **_blank** or **_new** into the Target setting field. Either of these target frame settings is fine if you really want to have the Web browser start a new application window every time it displays the associated hyperlink's destination page. On the other hand, if you want to avoid opening multiple (secondary) browser application windows, you can tell the browser to create a named window (instead of the generic "_new" or "_blank" window).

To use a new, named window as the hyperlink's target frame, enter a name for the window (such as **new_window**, **product_list**, **addresses**, **any_old_text**, etc.) into the Target setting field and finish executing the procedure you started to assign a default target frame to the TARGET attribute of the <BASE> tag or the TARGET attribute in a hyperlink's <A> (anchor) tag.

When a hyperlink's target frame is a new, named window, each time the visitor clicks the mouse pointer on a hyperlink, the Web browser will display the hyperlink's target (destination) page in the one application window whose name is specified by the TARGET attribute in the hyperlink's <A> (anchor) or the Web page <BASE> tag. In other words, the Web browser will only open a new application window for the destination page if the named application window is not already open.

SPECIFYING TARGET FRAME SETTINGS FOR IMAGE MAPS

Several of the previous Tips that dealt with frames showed you how to display a hyperlink's target Web page (also known as the hyperlink's destination page) in a particular frame within the frameset (called the hyperlink's *target* frame). Although the Tips only discuss hyperlinks anchored to Web page text, you can also insert image maps (graphics images used to anchor hyperlinks) in one or more frames. Moreover, you can use each of the image map's hot spots (i.e. the areas on the graphics image to which a hyperlink is attached) to display the hot spot's target Web page in any of the frameset's frames.

To specify the target frame for a hyperlink anchored to a hot spot on an image map, perform the following steps:

1. Open the frames page with the frame in which the image map is displayed. If necessary, select the View menu Page option to display the frames page on the Page view Normal tab.
2. Double-click your mouse pointer on the hot spot (on the graphics image) to which the hyperlink whose target frame you want to change is anchored. FrontPage, in turn, will display the Edit Hyperlink dialog box.
3. Click your mouse pointer on the TARGET FRAME button on the right-hand side of the dialog box about halfway down from the top. FrontPage, in turn, will display a Target Frame dialog box (similar to that shown previously in Figure 258).
4. In the frame layout diagram in the Current frames page section (on the upper left-hand side) of the dialog box, click the mouse pointer on the frame you want the Web browser to use as the target frame for the hyperlink you selected in Step 2.
5. If you want to use the target frame you selected in Step 4 as the default target frame for all hyperlinks on this Web page (all of the hyperlinks within this frame), click your mouse pointer on the SET AS PAGE DEFAULT checkbox until a checkmark appears.
6. Click your mouse pointer on the OK button near the bottom right-hand corner of the Target Frame dialog box. FrontPage, in turn, will return to the Edit Hyperlink dialog box.
7. Click the mouse pointer on the OK button near the bottom right-hand corner of the Edit Hyperlink dialog box.

To check your work, click the mouse pointer on the Page view Preview tab and then on the hot spot with the hyperlink whose target frame you changed. FrontPage should display the hyperlink's target Web page in the frame you selected in Step 4. When you finish your test, click the mouse pointer on the Page view Normal tab to return to the What-You-See-Is-What-You-Get (WYSIWYG) Web page editor.

If you want to change the target frame for all of the image map's hyperlinks at once (vs. for an individual hyperlink), right-click the mouse pointer on the image outside all of its hot spots in Step 2. Select Picture Properties from the pop-up menu. (If you do not see the Picture Properties option on the pop-up menu, then you right-clicked the mouse pointer inside the borders of a hot spot, so press the ESC key and try again.) After you select Picture Properties from the pop-up menu, FrontPage will display the Picture Properties dialog box. In the Picture Properties dialog box, click the mouse pointer on the General tab and then on the Change Target Frame button to the right of the Target Frame field near the bottom of the General tab. Next, continue at Step 4 of the procedure in this Tip. In Step 7, click on the OK button near the lower right-hand side of the Picture Properties dialog box.

Note: *As is the case for hyperlinks anchored to text in a frame, any of the image map's hyperlinks whose <A> (anchor) tags do not contain a TARGET attribute will display their target Web page in the current frame's default target frame. The default target frame is defined either by the TARGET attribute in the <BASE> tag in the HTML for the Web page with the image map, or the TARGET attribute in the <FRAME> tag for the frame with the image map in the frameset's frames page HTML. If an image map is in a frame with no default target frame, each hyperlink on the image map that itself has no target frame, will display its target Web page in its own frame in place of the Web page with the image map.*

HANDLING VISITORS WITH BROWSERS THAT DO NOT SUPPORT FRAMES

Both Internet Explorer and Netscape Navigator support frames. As such, the majority of your site's visitors will have no problem viewing the content of your framed Web site. However, there are still a few people that use browsers without frames support. To accommodate visitors with browsers that will not display multiple Web pages (in frames) onscreen at the same time, add a No frames section to the frames page HTML. Browsers that do not support frames will ignore the <FRAMESET> and <FRAME> tags and all of the HTML code between the tags and process, instead, HTML between the <NOFRAMES></NOFRAMES> tags in the frames page HTML.

When you use a frames template to generate a frames page, FrontPage automatically adds the <NOFRAMES></NOFRAMES> tags to the frames page HTML to create a No frames section for browsers without frames support to display. However, FrontPage only insert a single line of text on the No frames Web page it generates. As such, if you do not replace the FrontPage generated content on the No frames page with your own, site visitor using browser that do not support frames will see the message:

```
This page uses frames, but your browser doesn't support them.
```

Rather than give visitors with frameless browsers the cold shoulder and preclude them from seeing your site's content, replace the text on the No frames page with hyperlinks that the visitors can use to access the content (non-frames) pages on your site.

To work with the No frames section on the frames page, open the frames page in Page View. Then, click your mouse pointer on the No Frames tab. FrontPage, in turn, will display the current No frames Web page on the No Frames tab, and you can edit its content as you would the content of a normal Web displayed on the Page view Normal tab.

In addition to creating a No frames Web page with hyperlinks to Web pages on your site, add a hyperlink that visitors can use to return to the original No frames page somewhere on each of these hyperlinked pages.

For example, if you create a three-frame Web page with the site's content menu in a frame along the left-hand side of the page, visitors with browsers that support frames do not need a way to re-display the menu after they activate one of its hyperlinks. After all, the Web browser will display the Web page it retrieves in a frame other than the one with the menu. As a result, the site's content menu will remain onscreen as the visitor activates its hyperlinks to display Web pages in another frame.

Conversely, when a visitor using a frameless browser activates a hyperlink on the site's menu, the menu disappears from view when the Web browser replaces the Web page (with the menu) in the No frames page in the browser's application window with the hyperlink's destination Web page. To use the menu to display another content page, the visitor must first redisplay the menu on the No frames page. If you provide a hyperlink back to the No frames page at the bottom of each of the Web pages targeted by hyperlinks on the No frames page, the visitor will not have to rely on the Web browser's Back button to navigate back to the site's content menu.

UNDERSTANDING WEB PAGE FORMS

In general, a form on a Web page consists of a set of labeled elements (such as text boxes, checkboxes, drop-down menus, and radio buttons) designed to get information from site visitors that take the time to fill out the form. Every element in a form has a name and a value. Each element's name is a unique identifier you can use internally (in the Web page

HTML) to refer to and work with a form element's current value while the visitor remains on the Web site.

In addition to form elements used to collect data from the visitor, forms also have at least two push button controls. Each form has a SUBMIT button or Picture Form Field that the visitor uses to send the form's data values and field names to the Web server for processing. Also, each form has a CANCEL or RESET button the visitor can use to set all of the form's elements back to their initial values.

When the visitor clicks the mouse pointer on the SUBMIT button or on the Picture Form field, the Web browser encodes the field names and their associated values as a long string of text in a file it sends to the Web server. What happens to the form data after it reaches the Web server depends on the form handler(s) activated by the form's SUBMIT button. A *form handler* is a program that runs on the Web server to process the form data (known as form results) sent to the Web server by the Web browser.

Depending on the type of form handler called by clicking the mouse pointer on the form's SUBMIT button, any number of things may happen to the form results. For example, the form handler might save the form results to a text file either with or without HTML formatting tags, add the form results to other form results already stored in a database, or format and send the form results in an e-mail message. In short, what a form handler can do with form results is limited only by the functions available within the programming language used to write the handler and the capability and imagination of the programmer that writes the application.

In the next several Tips, you will learn how to:

- create a form on a new Web page.
- how to create and insert a form on an existing Web page.
- use a form's elements to accept visitor input and selections.
- use FrontPage components to validate data entered into a form's text input fields.
- how to send form results to a form handler on the Web server for processing.
- how to send a Web page that confirms the server's receipt of the form results and thanks the visitor for taking the time to fill out the form.

For now, the most import thing to understand is that a form is a Web page object with named input fields, radio buttons, menus, and checkboxes (collectively called form elements) that the visitor can use to send information to the Web server for further processing.

USING THE FORM PAGE WIZARD TO CREATE A FORM

As is the case with most tasks that take more than a few keystrokes to perform, FrontPage provides a Wizard that will guide you through the process of creating a form. One important thing to understand before you use the Form Page Wizard to create a form is that the Wizard will create the form on a new Web page. After the Wizard creates the form, you can tell FrontPage to use the Windows clipboard to cut-and-paste (or to copy-and-paste) the form from the new Web page onto an existing page. However, the Form Page Wizard always creates a new Web page and puts the form it generates on that new page.

To use the Form Page Wizard to create a new form, perform the following steps:

1. Select the File menu New option, and click the mouse pointer on Page or Web. FrontPage, in turn, will display the New Page or Web menu along the right-hand side of the dialog box.
2. Click the mouse pointer on Page Templates in the New from template section near the middle of the New Page or Web menu. FrontPage, in turn, will display the Page Templates dialog box.
3. Click your mouse pointer on Form Page Wizard (in the list box section of the General tab) and then on the OK button near the lower right-hand corner of the dialog box. FrontPage, in turn, will start the Form Page Wizard, which, in turn, will display the initial Form Page Wizard message box that describes the Wizard.
4. Click the mouse pointer on the NEXT button near the bottom center of the message box. The wizard, in turn, will display the Add/Modify/Remove Form Questions dialog box shown in Figure 265.1.

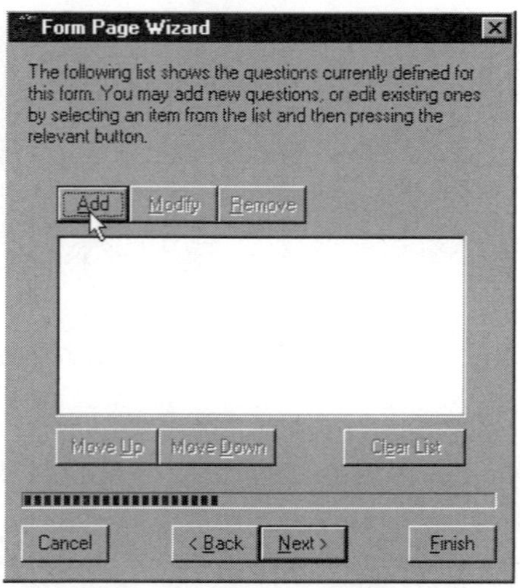

Figure 265.1 The Microsoft FrontPage Form Page Wizard, Add/Modify/Remove Form Questions dialog box.

5. Click the mouse pointer on the ADD button above the upper left-hand corner of the question list box. The Wizard, in turn, will display an Input Type dialog box similar to that shown in Figure 265.2.

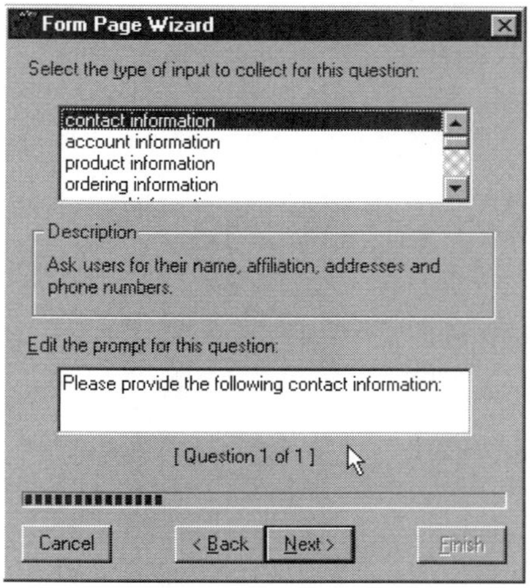

Figure 265.2 *The Microsoft FrontPage Form Page Wizard, Input Type dialog box.*

6. Click your mouse pointer on one of the input types listed in the scroll box at the top of the dialog box. For the current project, click the mouse pointer on contact information.
7. If you want to use text other than that generated by the wizard to prompt the visitor to enter data into the set of fields for the input type you selected in Step 6, enter the text you want displayed on the form into the Edit the prompt for this question textbox near the bottom of the dialog box. For the current project, replace the contents of the Edit the prompt for this question textbox with **Please provide the following in case we need to contact you.**
8. Click your mouse pointer on the NEXT button near the bottom center of the dialog box. The wizard, in turn, will display a Form Elements Selection dialog box similar to that shown in Figure 265.3.

Note: *The fields you can select on the Form Elements Selection dialog box will vary depending on which of the questions you selected in Step 6. For example, while the contact information question generates the fields shown in Figure 265.3, the account information question generates Username and Password fields. Similarly, the product information question generates a different set of form elements that ask for product name, model, version, and serial number data. The important thing to understand is that after you select an input type (in Step 6), the Form Page Wizard presents you with a set of form elements (fields) that relate to the type of information that you want the site visitor to provide.*

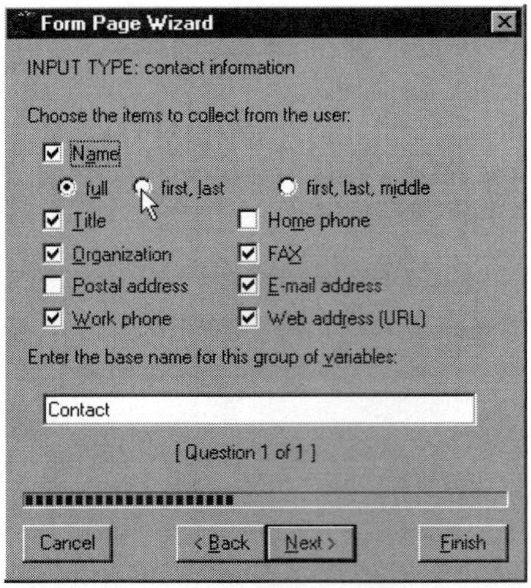

Figure 265.3 The Microsoft FrontPage Form Page Wizard, Form Elements Selection dialog box.

9. Use your mouse pointer to click a checkmark into the checkbox next to the form elements (fields) you want the Wizard to include on your form and click the mouse pointer on the radio buttons (if any) below the fields to select field options. For the current project, click the mouse pointer on the first, last radio button below the Name checkbox, clear the Organization checkbox, and click a checkmark into the Home phone checkbox and into the Postal address checkbox.
10. Into the Enter the base name for this group of variables field, enter the name you want to use when referring the values the visitor enters into current set of fields. For example, after the visitor enters data into the contact information fields (shown previously in Figure 265.3), code (written in scripting language such as JavaScript, PHP, or PERL) included elsewhere in the Web page HTML can refer to the contents of a field as <form name>.<base name>.<field name>. For the current project, accept the default value supplied by the wizard in the Enter the base name for this group of variables field.
11. Click the mouse pointer on the NEXT button near the bottom center of the dialog box. The wizard, in turn, will display the Add/Modify/Remove Form Questions dialog box again.
12. Repeat steps 5 – 11 as often as necessary to enter each of the questions and sets of form elements (fields) you want the wizard to include on the form. Use the MODIFY and REMOVE buttons to change and/or delete questions from the form as necessary. In addition, after you have two or more questions on the form, you can use the MOVE UP and MOVE DOWN buttons beneath the question list box to rearrange the

order of the questions (and form elements). After you have the list of questions you want to ask in the question list box, click your mouse pointer on the NEXT button near the bottom center of the Add/Modify/ Remove Form Questions dialog box. The Wizard, in turn, will display the Presentation Options dialog box shown in Figure 265.4.

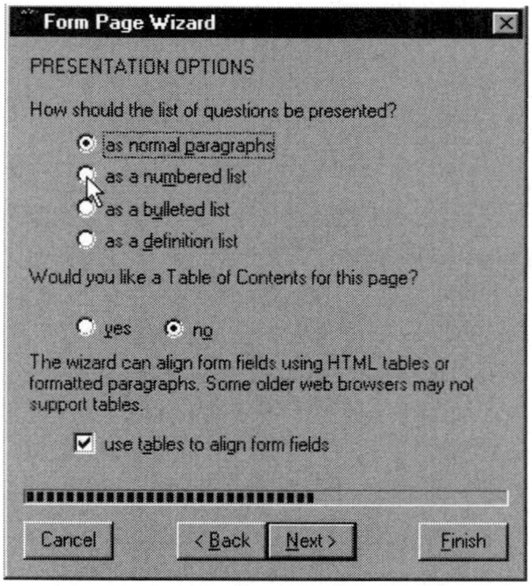

Figure 265.4 The Microsoft FrontPage Form Page Wizard, Presentation Options dialog box.

13. Click your mouse pointer on the radio buttons that describe the way in which you want the question(s) you selected in Step 5 to appear on your Web page. You can display each question as a paragraph or as an item in a list. For the current project, click the mouse pointer on the as normal paragraphs radio button, since the form will have only one question.

    If the form has many questions, you may want add a table of contents to the top of the form by clicking your mouse pointer on the yes radio button that follows the "Would you like a Table of Contents for this page?" question in the center or the dialog box. If you include a table of contents, the visitor will be able to click the mouse pointer on an entry in the table of contents to jump to the first form element for the question selected.

    Leave the use tables to align form fields checkbox checked unless you think the majority of the visitors to your site will not be using browsers that cannot handle tables. If you clear the use tables to align form fields checkbox, the Wizard will use the formatted text font for the form's text, so the Web browser will display sequences of repeating spaces it needs to align the data fields below each question in the form. Conversely, if you tell the Wizard to use a table for field alignment instead, you can apply any font you want to the labels next to each of the fields in the form.

14. Click your mouse pointer on the NEXT button near the bottom center of the dialog box. The Wizard, in turn, will display an Output Options dialog box similar to that shown in Figure 265.5.

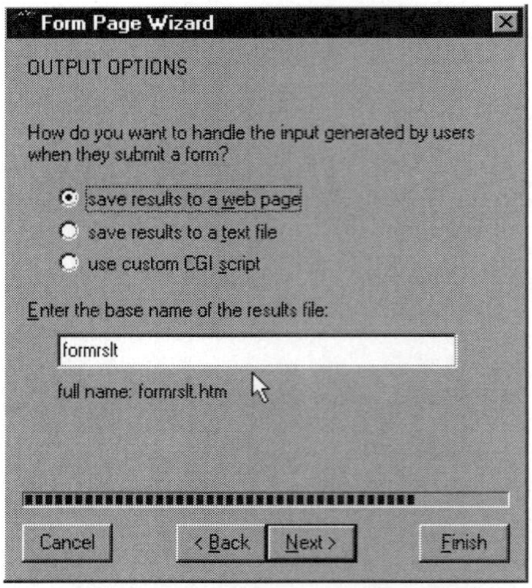

Figure 265.5 The Microsoft FrontPage Form Page Wizard, Output Options dialog box.

15. As mentioned in the preceding Tip, the purpose of a form is to collect data from the site visitor. After the visitor fills out the fields in a form, the Web browser needs to know what to tell the Web server to do with the form results. By clicking the mouse pointer on the corresponding radio button, you can have the Web browser send form data back to the Web server and tell the server to:
    - **save results to a web page** – the Web server will enclose the form results file it receives from the Web browser in <DL></DL> (definition list) tags and append the definition list to an HTML (Web page) file in the Web site's _PRIVATE folder. The name of the file will be the filename you enter in Step 16 with an .HTM extension. (If the Web page file does not exist when the server receives form results, the server will create it, and then add the form results to the file.) As the Web server processes the field name/field value pairs in the forms results file it received from the Web browser, the Web server encloses each field name in <DT></DT> (definition title) tags followed by the field's value enclosed in <DD></DD> (definition data) tags.

- **save results to a text file** - the Web server will take the form field name/value pairs in the form results file it receives from the Web browser and append them to a text file in the Web site's _PRIVATE folder. The name of the file will be the filename you enter in Step 16 with a .TXT extension. [If the text file does not exist when the server receives form results, the server will create it, insert the list of field names (each field name enclosed in quotes and separated by a tab), and then add the form results to the file.] As the Web server processes the field name/field value pairs in the form result file it received from the Web browser, the Web server encloses each field value in quotes and then appends a tab character followed by the quoted field value to the contents of the text file.
- **use custom CGI script** – the Web server will execute a program or script file, which will, in turn, process the field name/field value pairs the Web server receives from the Web browser. What the program or script file does with the form results depends on what it was programmed to do by the person that wrote it.

Note: *If you plan to use a Web browser to view the information, your site visitors submit through the form, select the save results to a Web page option. If you plan to use the form results as input for a program other than a Web browser, select the save results to a text file option.*

For the current project, click your mouse pointer on the save results to a Web page radio button.

16. If you clicked your mouse pointer on the save results to a Web page radio button in step 15, then into the Enter the base name of the results file field, enter the file name in which the Web server is to store the form results file it receives from the Web browser after the visitor clicks the mouse pointer on the form's SUBMIT button. The Wizard will append a .HTM extension onto the filename as indicated in the full name: *filename*.htm message below the file field.

    If you clicked your mouse pointer on the save results to a text file radio button in Step 15, then into the Enter the base name of the results file field, enter the file name in which the Web server is to store the form results file it receives from the Web browser after the visitor clicks the mouse pointer on the form's SUBMIT button. The wizard will append a .TXT extension onto the filename as indicated in the full name *filename*.htm message below the file field.

If you clicked your mouse pointer on the use custom CGI script radio button in Step 15, you will notice the Enter the base name of the results file field is grayed out so you cannot enter a filename, therefore, skip this step and continue at Step 17—the CGI script (or program) will decide what to do with the forms results.

17. For the current project use the default file name and click your mouse pointer on the NEXT button near the bottom center of the dialog box. The Form Page Wizard, in turn, will display a message box to let you know you have supplied all of the information it needs to generate the form.
18. Click your mouse pointer on the FINISH button in the lower right-hand corner of the message box. The Wizard, in turn, will generate the HTML needed to display the form on the Web page and add the code needed to tell the Web server call the appropriate form handler to process the form results data.

After you complete Step 18, the new Web page the Form Page Wizard created for the current project will look similar to that shown in Figure 265.6. Before you publish the Web page on the Web server, you will need to eliminate or change the New Page 1 title at the top of the page and the copyright information (not shown in the Figure) that the Wizard added to the bottom of the page.

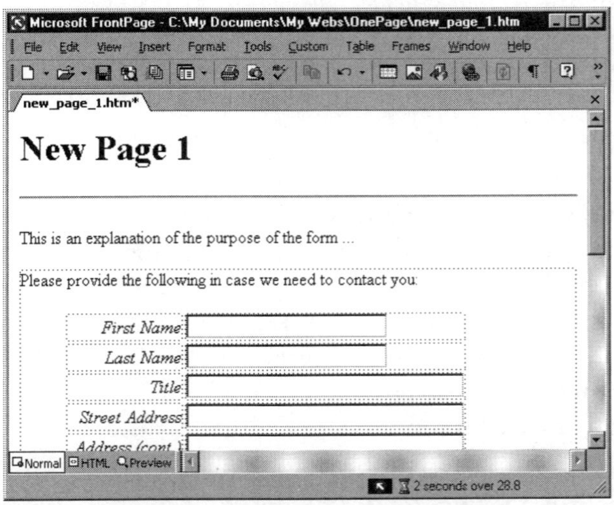

Figure 265.6 A Web page with a form, displayed on the Page view Normal tab.

Also, be sure to replace the "This is an explanation of the purpose of the form...", which the Form Page Wizard inserted above the top of the form, with a short message that asks the visitor to fill out the form and explains what you are going to do with the information provided.

Note: *If you click your mouse pointer on the Preview tab, you can use the Page view Preview tab to see what the form will look like and even enter data into the form's fields. However, the* SUBMIT *button at the bottom of the form will not function properly until use a Web browser to retrieve the Web page with the form from a Web server after publishing the form on the Web server with FrontPage Extensions installed.*

UNDERSTANDING THE FORM PAGE WIZARD INPUT TYPES

In the preceding Tip, you learned how to use the Form Page Wizard to create a form on a new Web page. The input type you selected in Step 6 of the procedure in the preceding Tip, told the Wizard what fields to present for your selection on the Form Elements Selection dialog box (shown previously in Figure 265.3) in Step 9 of the procedure.

Input types are the heart of the Form Page Wizard. After all, the form elements (text input fields, radio buttons, selection lists, checkboxes, etc.) determine the data that the site visitor will communicate to the Web server, and the input type you select, determines the form elements the Wizard lets you place on the form the Wizard creates.

Table 266 shows the 14 input types available for selection in the list box at the top of the Input Type dialog box (shown previously in Figure 265.2).

Input Type	Form Elements
contact information	Name (full or first, last or first, last, middle), Title, Home phone, Organization, FAX, Postal address, E-Mail address, Work phone, and Web address (URL).
account information	Username (as a single field or as first and last name fields). Password (require confirmation that you must type in twice or don't require conformation).
product information	Product name (select from menu or type it in), Model, Platform and version (for software products), Product code, and Serial number.

Table 266 List of Microsoft FrontPage Form Page Wizard input types and form elements for each input type. *(Continued on next page)*

Input Type	Form Elements
ordering information	List of products and quantities, Maximum number (of products per form), Billing information (purchase order), and Shipping Address.
personal information	Name (full or first, last or first, last, middle), Age (years old or date of birth), Sex, ID number, Height, Hair color, Weight, and Eye color.
one of several options	Enter the labels for the options, one on each line How should the user choose an answer? drop-down menu or radio buttons or list.
any of several options	Enter the labels for the options, one on each line. Use multiple columns to present the options. (checkbox)
boolean	How should the user provide an answer? (Checkbox or yes/no radio buttons or true/false radio buttons)
date	How should the user provide an answer? (mm/dd/yy or dd/mm/yy or free format)
time	How should the user provide an answer? (hh:mm:ss – am/pm or hh:mm:ss – 24 hour clock or free format)
range	How should the user provide an answer? (on a scale of 1 to 5 or bad, poor, average, fair, good or from 'disagree strongly to agree strongly) Choose for the following presentation options: mid-range choice is default or use drop-down menu instead of radio buttons).

Table 266 List of Microsoft FrontPage Form Page Wizard input types and form elements for each input type. *(Continued on next page)*

Input Type	Form Elements
number	This value will be collected from a text input box. (Set and/or eneter the maximum length)
string	This value will be collected from a text input box. (Set and/or eneter the maximum length)
paragraph	This value will be collected from a scrolling text box, with no length restrictions.

Table 266 List of Microsoft FrontPage Form Page Wizard input types and form elements for each input type. (Continued from previous page)

The next several Tips will teach you how to customize the generic form generated by the Form Page Wizard and how to create a new form from scratch (without using a Wizard). You will also learn how to use the Form Properties and the tabs on the Saving Results dialog box to change the form handler the Web executes when a visitor clicks the mouse pointer on the form's SUBMIT button.

INSERTING A FORM PAGE WIZARD GENERATED FORM IN AN EXISTING WEB PAGE

The Form Page Wizard always places the form it creates on a new Web page. Therefore, if you want to place a Wizard generated form and other content on the same Web page, you can perform the procedure in a previous Tip titled "Using the Form Page Wizard to Create a Form," and then add the additional content you want to the new Web page on which the Wizard generated the form. Alternatively, if you already have an existing Web page and want to insert a Wizard-generated form on that page, perform the following steps:

1. Open the Web page on which you wish to insert the form, and select the View menu Page option to display the Web page on the Page view Normal tab.
2. If you have not yet used the Form Page Wizard to create the form you want to insert, execute the procedure in the Tip titled "Using the Form Page Wizard to Create a Form." Alternatively, if you want to insert a previously created form, open the Web page with the form you want to insert and select the View menu Page option to display the page with the form on the Page view Normal tab.
3. To select the form and its elements, move your mouse pointer just above the upper left-hand corner of the dotted line border that en-

closes the form. Then, click and hold down the left mouse button as you drag the mouse pointer downward to just below the lower left-hand corner of the form. (As you drag the mouse down the side of the form, FrontPage will highlight the form's elements.). When your mouse pointer reaches a point just below the bottom of the form and you have highlighted (selected) all of the elements in the form (including the form's Submit Form and Reset Form buttons), release the left mouse button.

4. Right-click the mouse pointer anywhere within the form and select Copy from the pop-up menu.
5. Click the mouse pointer on the Page view tab with the Web page to which you wish to add the form.
6. Right-click your mouse pointer on the point in the Web page where you want to insert the form you copied to the Windows clipboard in Step 4, and select Paste from the pop-up menu.

After you complete Step 6, FrontPage will insert the form you copied to the Windows clipboard in Step 4, into the current Web page at the point below your mouse pointer.

In the next Tip, you will learn how to use the Insert menu Form option to create a form without using the Form Page Wizard.

USING THE INSERT MENU FORM OPTION TO CREATE A FORM

The preceding Tip shows how to use the Windows clipboard and the copy-and-paste procedure to get around the fact that the Form Page Wizard always puts the form it creates on a new Web page. Instead of calling on the Form Page Wizard to generate a form on a new Web page, you can use the Insert menu Form option to create a form on an existing page.

Suppose, for example, that you want each visitor to provide you with their first name, last name, and e-mail address. To use the Insert menu to create a new form on an existing Web page, perform the following steps:

1. Open the Web page on which you wish to create the form, and select the View menu Page option to display the page on the Page view Normal tab.
2. Position the cursor at the point on the page at which you want to insert the new form. Then, select the Insert menu Form option and

click your mouse pointer on the first element you want on the form. For the current project select the Insert menu Form option, and click the mouse pointer on Textbox. FrontPage, in turn, will create a new form with a textbox (which will accept a single line of text), a SUBMIT button, and a RESET button.

3. If you want to add an additional element to the form, position the cursor at the point in the form where you want the new element to appear. Then, select the Insert menu Form option, and click the mouse pointer on the element you want to add. For the current project, position the cursor to the left of the SUBMIT button, and press the ENTER key to move the button and the insert point onto the next line in the form. Next, select the Insert menu Form option, and click the mouse pointer on Textbox to add a second textbox to the form.
4. Repeat Step 3 until your form has all of the elements you want. For the current project, repeat Step 3 one time to add a third textbox to the form.
5. If you want the form's buttons to be on a line by themselves, move the cursor immediately to the left of the SUBMIT button, and press the ENTER key to move both the SUBMIT button and the RESET button to the line below the last element in the form.
6. Label each of the form's elements by placing the cursor to the left of the element and typing the text you want to see on the form. (If you want the label to follow the form element, simply place the cursor immediately to the right of the element before you type the label.) For the current project, place the cursor to the left of the first textbox and type **First Name:**. Then, to the left of the second textbox, type **Last Name:**. And finally, to the left of the third textbox, and type **E-mail Address:**. Although not required, leave a space between the colon at the end of each label and its textbox.

After you complete Step 6, your form will appear similar to that shown in Figure 268, which shows the results of executing the procedure in this Tip to create (and insert) a form between two paragraphs of existing text on a Web page.

Notice that FrontPage draws a dotted line, rectangular border around the perimeter of the form. As you add additional form elements to the form or insert other Web content inside the border around the form, FrontPage will automatically increase the size of the form to accommodate the items you add. Conversely, FrontPage will reduce the size of the form as you remove things from it.

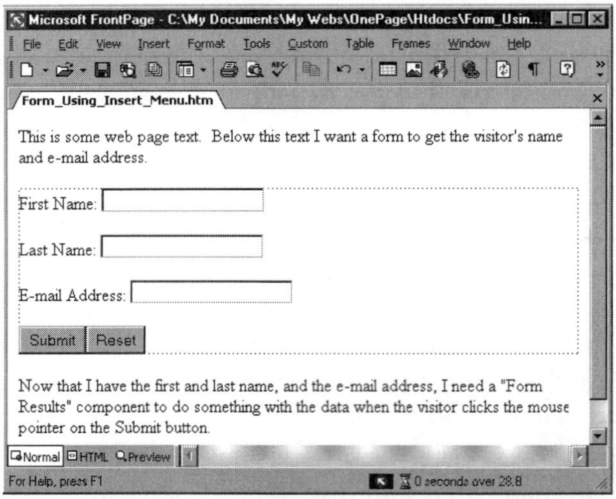

Figure 268 A Web page with a form inserted between two paragraphs of text.

To position content and form elements (such as buttons, input fields, selection menus, radio buttons, etc.) where you want them on the form, create a table with a zero (0) width (hidden) border (and hidden cell walls) within the borders of the form. Then, select the form elements and other objects one at a time, and use your mouse pointer to drag each item into the table cell at the location on the form where you want the item to appear. Moreover, when you add more items to the form, insert each one in the cell where you FrontPage to place the item on the form.

Note: *If you plan to use a page layout table (a table with a hidden border and hidden cell walls) to position items in a form, you may want to create the table before you add the items to the form. By placing the table in the form first, you can establish the grid of cells to use in positioning items on the form. With the layout grid is in place, you can place form elements and other content at specific locations on the form by inserting each item you add in the table cell located on the form where you want the form element or other content to appear.*

To add a table to a form before you add the first element, select the Insert menu Form option and click the mouse pointer on Form. FrontPage, in turn, will create a new form with only SUBMIT and RESET buttons. Then, use the Insert Table button on the Standard toolbar or the Insert menu Table option to insert a table inside the dotted line border around the form. FrontPage will automatically expand (or contract) the form's area as you adjust the size and count of cells in the table.

SAVING FORM RESULTS TO A TEXT FILE OR A WEB PAGE

Adding a form to a Web page only takes care of half of the communications process. After the site visitor uses the form's elements (its text boxes, checkboxes, radio buttons, and drop-down menus) to enter data into a form, the visitor's Web browser needs to send the form's data (results) to the Web server for processing. Therefore, the job of creating a form is not finished until after you program the form's SUBMIT button to tell the Web browser to *submit* (or send) the form results to the Web server.

To program the SUBMIT button to tell the Web server to execute a form handler that saves form results as either text or HTML code in a file on the Web server, perform the following steps:

1. Open the Web page with the form whose data you want saved to a file on the Web server, and select the View menu Page option to display the page on the Page view Normal tab.
2. Right-click the mouse pointer anywhere within the border around the form, and select Form Properties from the pop-up menu. FrontPage, in turn, will display a Form Properties dialog box similar to that shown in Figure 269.1.

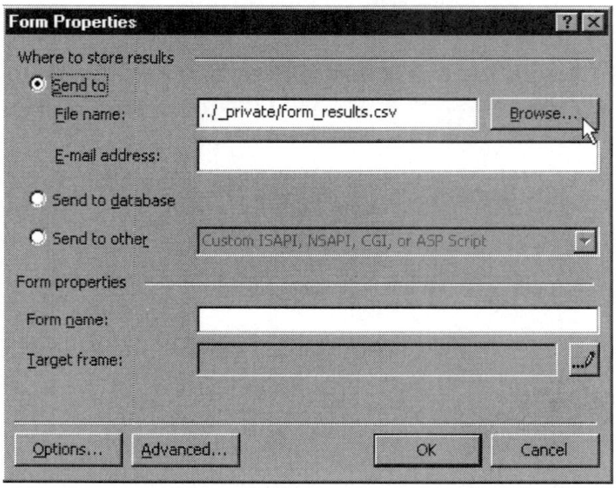

***Figure 269.1** The Microsoft FrontPage Form Properties dialog box.*

3. If not already selected, click your mouse pointer on the Send to radio button.
4. Into the File name field enter, the relative pathname of the file in which you want the form handler on the Web server to store the form results (the data that the visitor entered in the form). For the current project, enter **../_private/form_results.htm** into the File name field, so the form handler will store the form results in the FORM_RESULTS.HTM file in the _PRIVATE subfolder of the current FrontPage web. If you want the form handler to store results in an existing file, you can use the BROWSE button to the right of the File name field to navigate to and select the results file you want the handler to use.

Note: *When specifying a filename in which to store form results, it is very important that you use the correct three-letter extension for the type of data in the file. You can store the form's data as either Web page HTML, which you can then use a Web browser to view, or as text, which you will use as input to a program that will process the data in the file. If you plan to save the form results in a Web page (HTML) formatted file, make sure the filename you enter in Step 4 has a .HTM extension. On the other hand, if you plan to save the form results as text (without embedded HTML tags), give the filename a .TXT extension.*

5. Click the mouse pointer on the OPTIONS button in the lower left-hand corner of the Form Properties dialog box. FrontPage, in turn, will display a Saving Results dialog box similar to that shown in Figure 269.2

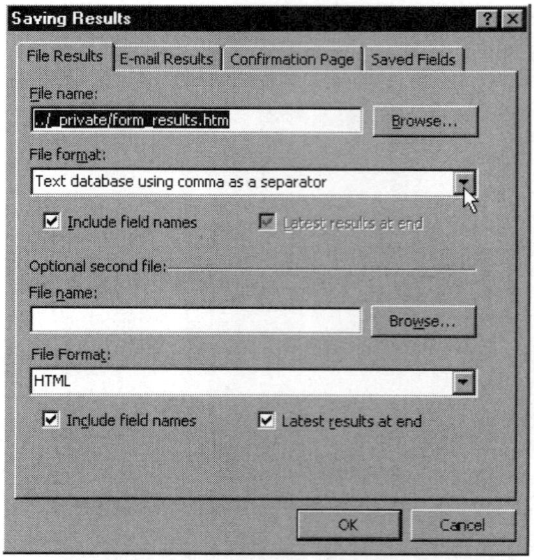

Figure 269.2 *The Microsoft FrontPage Saving Results dialog box.*

6. Click your mouse pointer on the drop-down list button to the right of the File format field, and select the format in which you want the Web server to store the form results. For the current project, select **HTML definition list**. (The next Tip in this book explains each of the eight available file formats.)
7. If you do not want the form handler to store the name of each of the form's fields (elements) in addition to its value, clear the Include field names checkbox.
8. If you want the form handler to append new form results onto the end existing data in the form results file, leave the Latest results at end checkbox checked. Conversely, if you want the form handler to insert

new form results in front of those already saved in the form results file (such that the newest form results are first in the file), clear the Latest results at end checkbox.

Note: *If you selected one of the four ASCII text file formats (vs. one of the four HTML Web page file formats) in Step 7, FrontPage will not let you clear the Latest results at end checkbox. The Web server's form handler always appends the latest set of form results onto the end of a non-HTML encoded ASCII text file.*

9. If you want the form handler to store form results in a second file (in addition to the form results file you specified in Step 4, into the File name field in the Optional second file section of the File Results tab, enter the relative pathname of the second form results file. For the current project enter: **../_private/form_results.txt** into the File name field.

Note: *Storing form results in two different files lets you save the data in two different file formats. If you store the data as HTML (Web Page) format in one file, you can then use a Web browser to view the form results formatted as paragraph or items in a list on a Web page. To format the form results as a Web page (HTML encoded) file, form handler inserts HTML tags in the form results it adds to the file. However, the tags get in the way if you want to use the form data stored in the form results file as input to another program. If you want the form results formatted both as a Web page and without HTML tags so you can use the data as input to a program other than a Web browser, tell the form handler to save two files. Then, select one of the four HTML formats for the first file and one of the four text formats (without HTML tags) for the second file.*

10. Click your mouse pointer on the drop-down list button to the right of the File format field, and select the format in which you want the Web server to store the form results. For the current project, select **Text database using comma as a separator.**
11. If you do not want the form handler to store the name of each of the form's fields (elements) in addition to its value, clear the Include field names checkbox.
12. If you want the form handler to append new form results onto the end existing data in the form results file, leave the Latest results at end checkbox checked. Conversely, if you want the form handler to insert new form results in front of those already saved in the form results file (such that the newest form results are first in the file), clear the Latest results at end checkbox.

Note: *If you selected one of the four ASCII text file formats (vs. one of the four HTML (Web page) file formats) in Step 7, FrontPage will not let you clear the Latest results at end checkbox. The Web server's form handler always appends the latest set of form results onto the end of a non-HTML encoded ASCII text file.*

13. Click your mouse pointer on the OK button near the lower right-hand corner of the Saving Results dialog box. FrontPage, in turn, will return to the Form Properties dialog box.
14. Click your mouse pointer on the OK button near the lower right-hand corner of the Form Properties dialog box. FrontPage, in turn, will update the <FORM> tag's ONSUBMIT attribute in the Web page HTML, and return to the Page view Normal tab.

One important thing to understand when saving form results to a file is that a program running on the Web server and not on the Web browser adds the form's data to the form results file. Therefore, in order to test the action of a form's SUBMIT button, you must first publish the Web page with the form to the Web server. Then, after you use a Web browser to retrieve the form from the Web server, you must fill out the form and click your mouse pointer on the form's SUBMIT button. Your Web browser, in turn, will send the form results back to the Web server for processing. The Web server, in turn, will execute a program called a form handler, which, in turn, adds the form results to the existing contents of the form results file in a folder on the server.

UNDERSTANDING FORM RESULTS FILE FORMATS

In the preceding Tip, you learned how to save form results to a file in a folder on the site's Web server. While storing the form's data completes the communication process, it is seldom (if ever) the last thing you want to do with the form results. After all, if you are not going to review the information gathered from site visitors or use the data as input to another program, then there is no reason to have visitors fill out the form in the first place.

FrontPage lets you select one of eight file formats for the form handler to use when storing form results in a file on the Web server. If you plan to use a Web browser to display the information submitted by your site's visitors via the form, select one of the four HTML (Web page) file formats. On the other hand, if you plan to use the form results as input for another program that or script executed by the Web server, select one of the four text (non-HTML) file formats.

The eight file formats a form handler running on the Web server can when storing form results data are:

- **HTML** – store each set of form results as a paragraph [inserted between <P></P> (paragraph) tags] in an HMTL Web page file. A

(line break) tag follows each of the field name/field value pairs, so each of them is displayed on a separate line, similar to that shown in Figure 270.1. (If you clear the Include field names checkbox, the field names will be omitted from the file.)

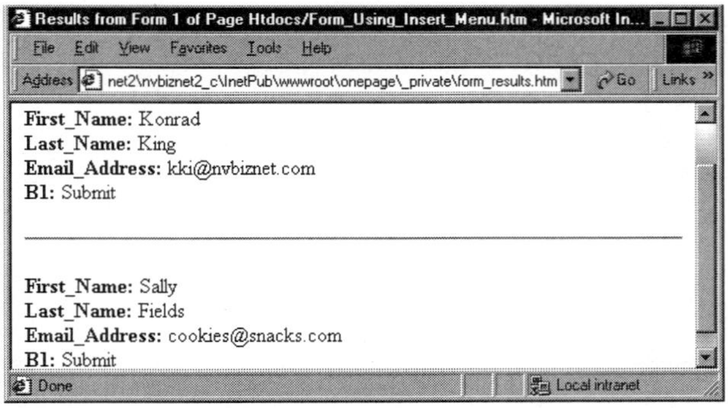

Figure 270.1 A Form Results file formatted as HTML paragraphs.

- **HTML definition list** – store each set of form results as a definition list [inserted between <DL></DL> (definition list) tags] in an HTML (Web page) file. Each field name is enclosed by <DT></DT> (definition title) tags and followed by its value inserted between <DD></DD> (definition data) tags. When viewed in a Web browser the form results appear similar to that shown in Figure 270.2. (If you clear the Include field names checkbox, the field names will be omitted from the file.)

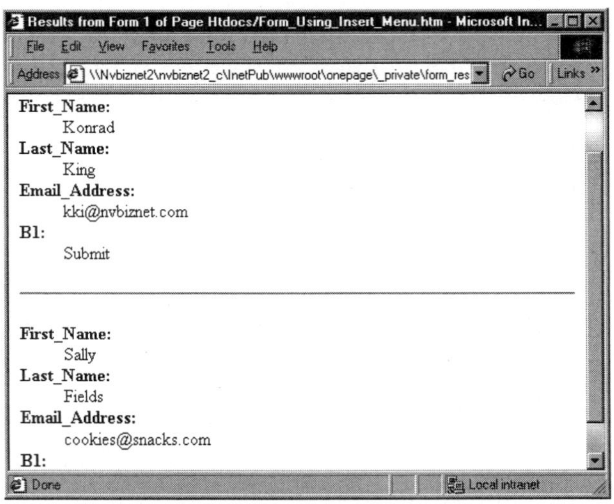

Figure 270.2 A Form Results file formatted as an HTML Definition List.

- **HTML bulleted list** – store each set of form results as a bulleted (unordered) list [inserted between <UL></UL> (unordered list) tags] in an HTML Web page file. Each field name/field value pair is enclosed by <LI></LI> (list item) tags. When viewed in a Web browser the form results appear similar to that shown in Figure 270.3. (If you clear the Include field names checkbox, the field names will be omitted from the file.)

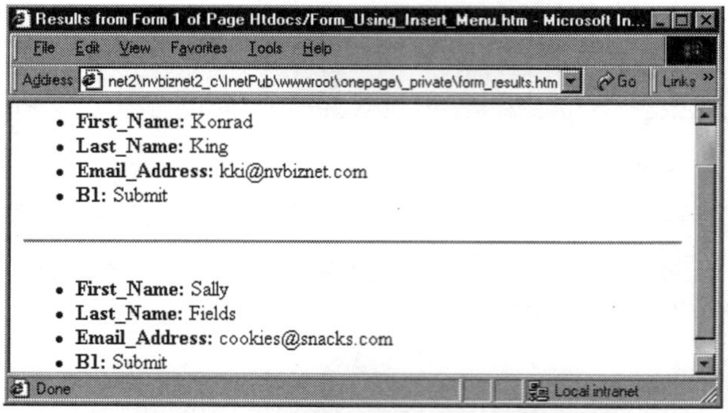

Figure 270.3 A Form Results file formatted as an HTML Bulleted List.

- **Formatted text within HTML** – store form results as formatted (monospaced) text [inserted between <PRE></PRE> (preformatted text) tags] in an HMTL Web page file. A line break (an ASCII carriage return/line feed pair) follows each of the field name/field value pairs, so each of them is displayed on a separate line, similar to that shown in Figure 270.1. (If you clear the Include field names checkbox, the field names will be omitted from the file.)

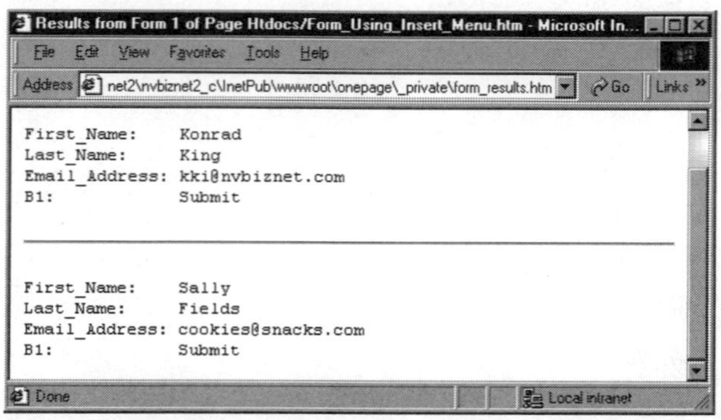

Figure 270.4 A Form Results file formatted as Formatted text within HTML.

- **Formatted text** – store form results in an ASCII text file (without HTML tags). For example, if you do not clear the Include field names checkbox, the Web server writes the field name/field value pair on separate lines in the file and separates one form results set from another with a line of asterisk (*) characters as:

```
************************************************************
First_Name:     Konrad
Last_Name:      King
Email_Address:  kki@nvbiznet.com
B1:             Submit
************************************************************
First_Name:     Sally
Last_Name:      Fields
Email_Address:  cookies@snacks.com
B1:             Submit
```

- **Text database using comma as a separator** – store form results as a single line in an ASCII text file with each of the field values enclosed in quotes ("") and separated from other values by a comma (,). For example, if you do not clear the Include field names checkbox, the Web server writes the names of the fields and the SUBMIT button's label as the first line in the file. It then writes the field values and button action on each of the subsequent lines in the file to format the file as:

```
"First_Name","Last_Name","Email_Address","B1"
"Konrad","King","kki@nvbiznet.com","Submit"
"Sally","Fields","cookies@snacks.com","Submit"
```

- **Text database using tab as a separator** - store form results as a single line in an ASCII text file with each of the field values enclosed in quotes ("") and separated from other values by a tab character. For example, if you do not clear the Include field names checkbox, the Web server writes the names of the fields and the SUBMIT button's label as the first line in the file. It then writes the field values and button action on each of the subsequent lines in the file to format the file as:

```
"First_Name"   "Last_Name" "Email_Address"     "B1"
"Konrad" "King"      "kki@nvbiznet.com"        "Submit"
"Sally"  "Fields"    "cookies@snacks.com"      "Submit"
```

- **Text database using space as a separator** - store form results as a single line in an ASCII text file with each of the field values enclosed in quotes ("") and separated from other values by a single space. For example, if you do not clear the Include field names checkbox, the Web server writes the names of the fields and the SUBMIT button's label as the first line in the file. It then writes the field values and button action on each of the subsequent lines in the file to format the file as:

```
"First_Name" "Last_Name" "Email_Address" "B1"
"Konrad" "King" "kki@nvbiznet.com" "Submit"
"Sally" "Fields" "cookies@snacks.com" "Submit"
```

As suggested at the beginning of this Tip, when specifying the way in which the form handler is to format data in the form results file, select the format that is most suitable for the manner in which you plan to use the data in the file. If you want to use a Web browser to display the form results onscreen, select the HTML file format that is most appealing to you. On the other hand, if you plan to use the form results as input to a program other than a Web browser select a (non-HTML) file format such as space, comma, or tab delimited text, so that the form handler will not add HTML (formatting) tags to the form results.

SENDING FORM RESULTS BY E-MAIL

Instead of (or in addition to) adding form results data to an ASCII text and/or HTML Web page file on the Web server, you can have the form handler send the form results to an e-mail address. Sending form results as e-mail messages is especially convenient with forms used to communicate customer inquiries or complaints. When you tell the Web server to save form results to a disk file, you must remember to check the form results file periodically to see if anyone filled out and submitted the form since you last checked the file's contents. However, if you tell the Web server to e-mail any new forms submissions to you. As a result, you avoid having to check the form results file because anytime a visitor to the Web site fills out and submits the form, the form results will appear automatically in your e-mail program's inbox.

Note: *Before you program the form's SUBMIT button to tell the Web server to send form results by e-mail, make sure that the Internet Service Provider (ISP) hosting your Web site has installed FrontPage Server Extensions on the Web server. Moreover, the ISP must not only install the FrontPage Server Extensions, but the ISP must also configure them to communicate with the site's SMTP (e-mail) server.*

To setup a form's SUBMIT button to send form results as an e-mail message, perform the following steps:

1. Open the Web page with the form whose data you want a form handler running on the Web server to send as an e-mail message, and select the View menu Page option to display the page on the Page view Normal tab.
2. Right-click the mouse pointer anywhere within the border around the form, and select Form Properties from the pop-up menu. FrontPage, in turn, will display a Form Properties dialog box (similar to that shown previously in Figure 269.1).
3. If not already selected, click your mouse pointer on the Send to radio button.
4. If you do not want to save form results to a file on the Web server (in addition to sending them as an e-mail message), clear the contents of the File name field.

Note: *You may want to both send an e-mail message and store the form results in a file on disk. While the e-mail message lets the visitor communicate the form's information to you immediately, storing the form results to a file (as well as sending the form data in an e-mail message) lets you accumulate the data for later analysis.*

5. Into the E-mail address field, enter the e-mail address of the person to whom the form handler is to e-mail the form results.
6. Click your mouse pointer on the OPTIONS button in the lower left-hand corner of the Form Properties dialog box. FrontPage, in turn, will display the Saving Results dialog box.

Note: *If you have not previously published the current FrontPage web to a Web server, or if you published the current web to a Web server on which the FrontPage Server extension have not been configured to send e-mail messages, FrontPage will display the message box shown in Figure 271.1.*

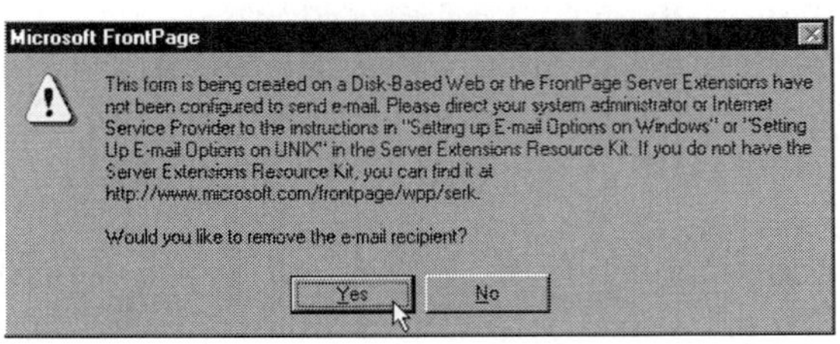

Figure 271.1 *The Microsoft FrontPage Server Extensions not configured to send e-mail message box.*

If you see the warning message, check with the ISP hosting your Web site to make sure that the host has not only installed FrontPage Server Extensions on the Web server, but has also configured the FrontPage Server Extensions to send e-mail messages.

If the ISP has done both things, click your mouse pointer on the NO button because you can ignore this warning. Conversely, if the Web server is unable to send form results by e-mail, click your mouse pointer on the YES button and remove the e-mail address from the E-mail Address field. Then, click your mouse pointer on the CANCEL button in the lower right-hand corner of the Form Properties dialog box, and skip the remaining steps in this procedure.

7. Click your mouse pointer on the E-mail Results tab of the Saving Results dialog box to expose the fields shown in Figure 271.2.

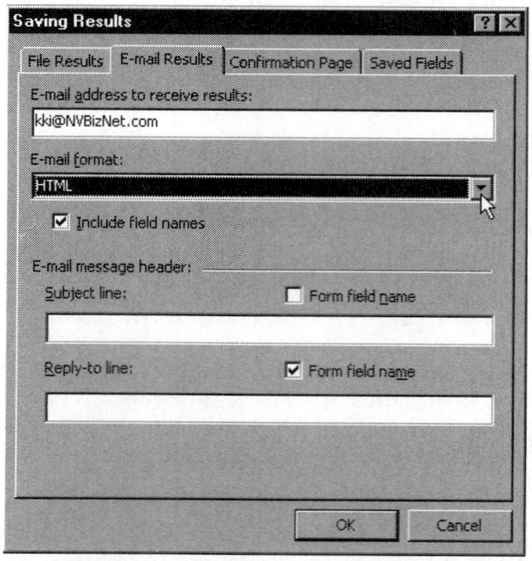

***Figure 271.2** The E-mail Results tab of the Microsoft FrontPage Saving Results dialog box.*

8. Click your mouse pointer on the drop-down list button to the right of the E-mail format field to select the format for the form results e-mail message.

***Note:** The form handler sends form results as the body of the e-mail message and not as an attachment. Moreover, you can format the e-mail message body using any of the eight form result file formats discussed in the preceding Tip. However, before you select one of the HTML formats, make sure that the recipient's e-mail program supports HTML formatted messages. If it does not, the e-mail program will display the HTML tags that the form handler inserted in the form results instead of using the tags to format the message displayed onscreen.*

9. If you do not want the form handler to e-mail the name of each of the form's fields (elements) in addition to its value, clear the Include field names checkbox.

10. Into the Subject line field, enter the text you want to appear as the "Subject:" line that precedes the body of an e-mail message. If you want the subject line to contain a constant (unchanging) text string that indicates the origin of the e-mail message, enter text such as **Results From a Customer Inquiry Form** into the Subject line field, and then clear the Form field name checkbox.

    Alternatively, if you want to subject line of the e-mail to contain the value in one of the form's elements (fields), click the mouse pointer on the Form field name checkbox until a checkmark appears. Then, into the Subject line field, enter the name of the form field whose value you want to appear in the subject line of the e-mail message.

11. Into the Reply-to line field, enter the e-mail address you want to appear in the e-mail message header's Reply-to field. If you enter an e-mail address in the Reply-to line field, be sure to clear the Form field name checkbox above the Reply-to line field, as well.

    Alternatively, if one of the form's fields asks for the visitor's e-mail address, you can tell the Web server use put the form respondent's e-mail address in the Reply-to to field in the form result e-mail's header. To copy the value in a form field into the e-mail message header's Reply-to field, click your mouse pointer on the Form field name checkbox until a checkmark appears. Then, into the Reply-to line field, enter the name of the form field that has the respondent's e-mail address.

12. Click your mouse pointer on the OK button near the lower right-hand corner of the Saving Results dialog box.

13. Click your mouse pointer on the OK button near the lower right-hand corner of the Form Properties dialog box.

After you complete Step 13, FrontPage will update the <FORM> tag's ONSUBMIT attribute (on the Page view HTML tab) and return to the Page view Normal tab.

USING A CUSTOM SCRIPT TO PROCESS FORM RESULTS

After you use the Form Properties dialog box to specify that the Web browser is to save form results to a file and/or to send the form results as an e-mail address, FrontPage adds code to the Web Page HTML that tells the Web browser to send form results to the Web server. The

Web server, in turn, passes the data from the form to a form handler called the Save Results component. [The Save Results component, by the way, is one of the application programs installed when the internet service provider (ISP) hosting your Web site installed FrontPage Server Extensions on the Web server.]

If your Web server does not have FrontPage Server Extensions installed, or if you want the Web server to process your form results in a way other than those provided by the installed FrontPage components, you can have the Web browser send the form results to other customer applications or scripts available on the Server. Unfortunately, if you are not a programmer, you may need to hire one if your Web host does not provide the form handler scripts you need. Still, check with your site's host before you hire someone. Most ISP's have a large library of standard form handlers (scripts) you can use free of charge.

To include code in the Web page HTML that tells the Web server to send form results to a custom script or application program running on the server, perform the following Steps:

1. Open the Web page with the form whose data you want the Web server to process using a custom script, and select the View menu Page option to display the page on the Page view Normal tab.
2. Right-click the mouse pointer anywhere within the border around the form, and select Form Properties from the pop-up menu. FrontPage, in turn, will display a Form Properties dialog box (similar to that shown previously in Figure 269.1).
3. Click your mouse pointer on the Send to other radio button near the center of the dialog box.
4. Click your mouse pointer on the drop-down list button to the right of the Send to other radio button, and select Custom ISAPI, NSAPI, or ASP Script from the drop-down menu.
5. Click your mouse button on the OPTIONS button in the lower left-hand corner of the Form Properties dialog box. FrontPage, in turn, will display the Options for Custom Form Handler dialog box shown in Figure 272.

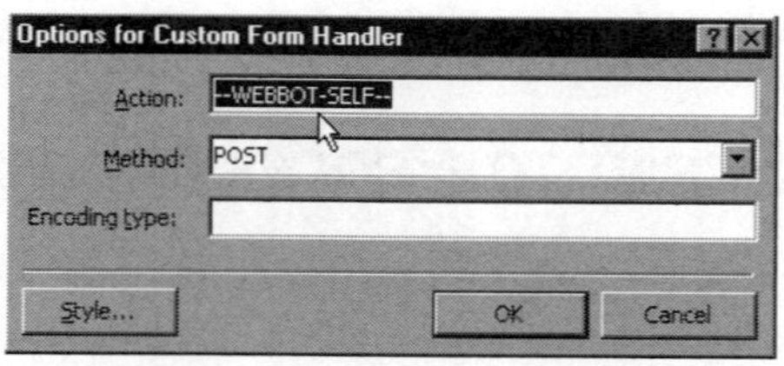

Figure 272 The Microsoft FrontPage Options for Custom Form Handler dialog box.

6. Into the Action field, enter the Uniform Resource Locator (URL), the relative address of the script or application program that is to process the form results. (If you do not know the form handler's URL, ask your Web host or system administrator.)
7. Click your mouse pointer on the drop-down list button to the right of the METHOD field and select POST from the drop-down list. Almost all Web browsers use the POST (vs. the GET) method to submit form results to scripts or programs through the Web server.
8. Unless otherwise directed by your Web host, leave the Encoding type field blank.
9. Click your mouse pointer on the OK button near the lower right-hand corner of the Options for Customer Form Handler dialog box.
10. Click your mouse pointer on the OK button near the lower right-hand corner of the Form Properties dialog box.

As was the case when you told FrontPage to include code that sent form results to the Save Results component, you will not see any changes on the form itself after you complete Step 10. However, if you click the mouse pointer on the HTML tab, you will find the URL of the script or application program to which the Web server will pass the form results for processing assigned to the <FORM> tag's ACTION attribute.

ASSIGNING A DESCRIPTIVE NAME TO EACH ELEMENT ON A FORM

Each form element (text input field, selection box, radio button, checkbox, button, etc.) on a form has two properties: a name and a value. When you use the Form Page Wizard to create a form, FrontPage automatically gives each field a descriptive name such as Contact_FirstName, Contact_LastName, Contact_WorkPhone, Contact_Email, etc. However, when you create a form from scratch or use the Insert menu Form option to add an element to an existing form, FrontPage assigns each element you add to the form a generic variable name such as S1, C1, T1, D1, or D2.

You can use either generic or descriptive element names to display the form's data values on the site's other Web pages and as the field name portion of the field name/field value pairs the Web browser sends to the form handler. However, as is the case when writing application programs, using descriptive names for the form's elements will make the Web page HTML and scripts that use form element names as variables easier to debug, understand, and maintain.

To assign a descriptive name to a form element or to view an element's name, perform the following Steps:

1. Open the Web page with the form element(s) on which you want to work, and select the View menu Page option to display the page on the Page view Normal tab.
2. Either double-click the mouse pointer on the form element whose name you want to view and/or change, or right-click the mouse pointer on the element, and select Form Field Properties from the pop-up menu. FrontPage, in turn, will display the element's *Properties* dialog box similar to the Text Box Properties dialog box shown in Figure 273.

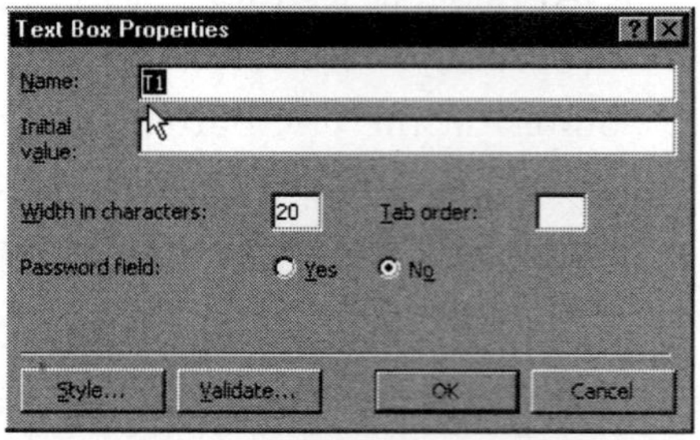

Figure 273 *The Microsoft FrontPage Text Box Properties dialog box.*

Note: *Each type of form element has a dialog box with a different set of properties fields. However, all of the Properties dialog boxes include a Name field.*

3. Into the Name field, enter a descriptive name for the form element. So you can use the form element name in the scripting language of your choice, start each name with a letter or underscore (_) and use only letters, digits, or underscores (_) in the rest of the name. If you want to use more than one word as an element's name, separate words with an underscore (_) rather than a space.
4. Make a note of the element's name in the Name field (by writing it own on paper or by typing it into a MS-Word document, for example). When you want to use the value of a form element in a script or elsewhere on the same Web page or on another page, you will use the element's name to refer to its value in the form.
5. Click your mouse pointer on the OK button near the lower right-hand corner of the dialog box.
6. Repeat Steps 2 – 5 for each of the other elements on the form. Do not forget to name and/or document the form's buttons, as well as, its other elements.

Naming the elements on a form only takes a few moments, and you will find it to be time well spent, when want to include the form's data values on the site's Web pages or on the form's confirmation page—as you will learn to do in the next Tip.

USING A TEMPLATE TO CREATE A CONFIRMATION PAGE

When a visitor clicks the mouse pointer on a form's SUBMIT button, the Web browser packages the form results and sends them to the form handler on the Web server for processing. However, unless the form handler tells the Web browser to display a page that confirms the receipt of the form results, the visitor will have no idea that *something* was done with the data entered and selections made on the form.

Fortunately, when a visitor submits form results to a FrontPage Save Results component, the Web server based form handler tells the Web browser to display a Web page that shows each of the field name/element name pairs it received. In other words, the Save Results component has the Web browser display the form results it received on a Web page to confirm (hence the name Confirmation page) that it received the form's data.

If you find the FrontPage generated confirmation page a bit too generic, you can use the Confirmation Form template to create a custom confirmation page by performing the following Steps:

1. Select the File menu New Page or Web option. FrontPage, in turn, will display the New Page or Web menu along the right-hand side of the application window.
2. Click your mouse pointer on Page Templates in the New from template section near the middle of the menu. FrontPage, in turn, will display the Page Templates dialog box.
3. Double-click the mouse pointer on the Confirmation Form icon, third from the left, in the first row of template icons in the templates list box on the General tab. FrontPage, in turn, will generate a new, confirmation page similar to that shown in Figure 274.1.
4. Replace the template-generated text with the content you want the site visitor to see on the confirmation page the Save Results component sends to the visitor.
5. Double-click the mouse pointer on each of the placeholders for a form element's value, and enter the name of the form element (field) whose value you want displayed in place of the placeholder. FrontPage, in turn, will display a Confirmation Field Properties dialog box similar to that shown in Figure 274.2.

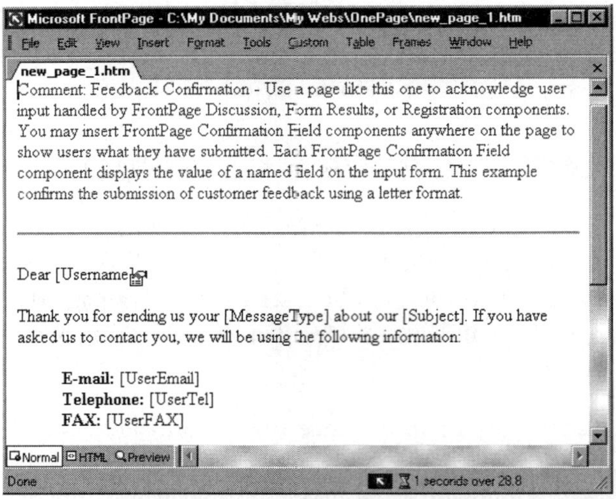

Figure 274.1 A confirmation page with template generated text and placeholders for form element data values.

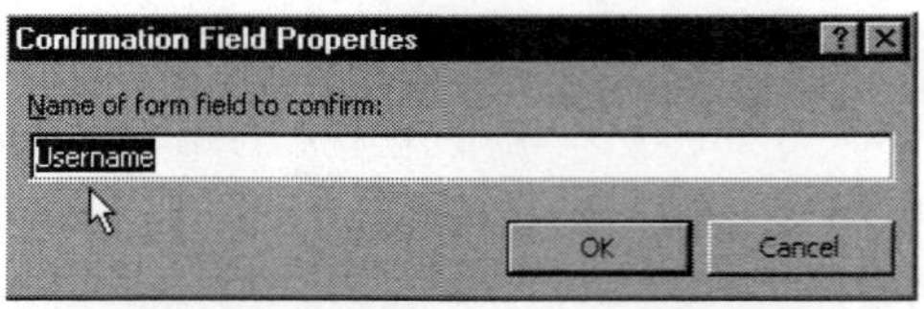

Figure 274.2 The Microsoft FrontPage Confirmation Field Properties dialog box.

Note: *Placeholders are displayed between brackets ([ ]). Moreover, when you move the mouse pointer over a placeholder, FrontPage displays the mouse pointer as a hand (holding a properties sheet), similar to that shown at the lower right-hand corner of the "[Username]" placeholder seen previously in Figure 274.1.*

6. Into the Name of form field to confirm field, enter the name of the form element whose value you want to display on the confirmation page in place of the placeholder you selected in Step 5. Suppose, for example, that you want to replace the [Username] template with the visitor's name, stored in the form element: First_and_Last_Name. Double-click the [Username] placeholder and type **First_and_Last_Name** into the Name of form field to confirm field.

Note: *Form element names are case sensitive. As such, make sure you type the name of the element (field) exactly as it appears in the Name field of the element's Properties dialog box. If you misspell the name or change the case of any of its letters, the Web browser will display the name you typed enclosed in brackets instead of the element's value on the confirmation page.*

7. Click your mouse pointer on the OK button near the lower right-hand corner of the Confirmation Field Properties dialog box. FrontPage, in turn, will display the form element's name in place of the text between the placeholder's brackets. ([ ])
8. If you need to remove a placeholder, click the mouse pointer on the placeholder, and select the Edit menu Delete option.
9. If you need an additional placeholder, right-click the mouse pointer on an existing placeholder, and select Copy from the pop-up menu. Move the cursor to the point in the confirmation Web page where you want a form element's value to appear and select the Edit menu Paste option. Then, continue at Step 5.
10. Select the File menu Save option to store the new confirmation page on disk. FrontPage, in turn, will display the Save As dialog box.
11. Click your mouse pointer on the CHANGE TITLE button. FrontPage, in turn, will display the Set Page Title dialog box.
12. Into the Page title field, enter a title for the confirmation page. For example, if the form is used to get the user's name and e-mail address, enter something like **Username & E-Mail Form Confirmation Page.**
13. Use the drop-down list button to the right of the Save in field and the folders below the field to navigate to the folder in which you wish to store the confirmation page.
14. Into the File name field near the bottom of the dialog box, enter a filename for the confirmation page.
15. Finally, click the mouse pointer on the SAVE button near the lower right-hand corner of the dialog box.

After you complete Step 15, which saves the new confirmation page to disk, you need to update the form to tell the Save Results component to use your custom confirmation page instead of the generic one it normal sends.

To setup the form to use an existing Web page as the confirmation page when a visitor clicks the mouse pointer on the form's SUBMIT button, perform the following steps:

1. Open the Web page with the form for which you have a new confirmation page, and select the View menu Page option to display the page on the Page view Normal tab.
2. Right-click the mouse pointer anywhere within the border around the form, and select Form Properties from the pop-up menu. FrontPage, in turn, will display a Form Properties dialog box (similar to that shown previously in Figure 269.1).

3. If not already selected, click your mouse pointer on the Send to radio button near the top left-hand corner of the Form Properties dialog box.
4. Click your mouse pointer on the OPTIONS button in the lower left-hand corner of the dialog box. FrontPage, in turn, will display the Saving Results dialog box.
5. Click your mouse pointer on the Confirmation Page tab to reveal the fields shown in Figure 274.3.

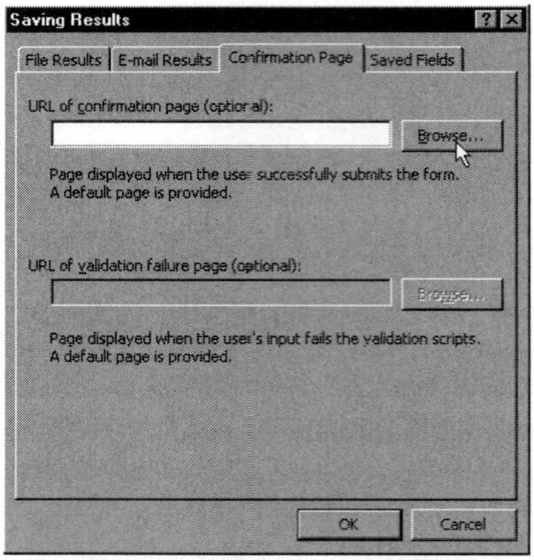

Figure 274.3 The Confirmation Page tab of the Microsoft FrontPage Saving Results dialog box.

6. Into the URL of confirmation page (optional) field, the relative pathname of the confirmation page you want the site visitor to see after submitting form results (data) to the Web server. Alternatively, click the mouse pointer on the BROWSE button to the right of the URL of confirmation page (optional) field. FrontPage, in turn, will display the Current Web dialog box. Use the drop-down list button to the right of the Look in field and the folders and files in the list box below the field to select the confirmation page. Then, click the mouse pointer on the OK button near the lower right-hand corner of the Current Web dialog box to return to the Saving Results dialog box and write the relative path for the confirmation page into the URL of confirmation page (optional) field at the top of the dialog box.
7. Click the mouse pointer on the OK button near the lower right-hand corner of the Save Result dialog box to return to the Form Properties dialog box.

8. Click the mouse pointer on the OK button near the lower right-hand corner of the Form Properties dialog box to return to the Page view Normal tab.

After you complete Step 8 and publish the confirmation page and the Web page with the update form properties to the Web server, the Form Result Component will tell the Web browser to display the new confirmation page whenever a visitor clicks the mouse pointer on the form's SUBMIT button.

USING AN EXISTING WEB PAGE AS A FORM'S CONFIRMATION PAGE

The preceding Tip teaches you to first use a template to create a new Web page and then to use the Form Properties dialog box to link the new page to a form as the form's confirmation page. However, you do not have to use the Confirmation Page Template to create a confirmation page. In fact, you can execute the second procedure in the preceding Tip to designate *any* Web page you want to be the form's confirmation page.

Although not required, a form's confirmation page normally displays the value in one or more of the form's elements (fields). By showing the visitor some (or all) of the form results on the confirmation page, you not only let the visitor know that the Web server received form data, but also that the data received was what the visitor entered on the form.

To insert confirmation fields (which display the value of form elements) on an existing Web page, perform the following steps:

1. Open the Web page to which you wish to add one or more confirmation fields, and select the View menu Page option to display the page on the Page view Normal tab.

Note: *In addition to using an existing Web page, you can also create a new Web page (with or without the use of a template) and add confirmation fields to the new page.*

2. Place the cursor at the point in the page where you want the form's data to appear (i.e. place the cursor where you want to insert the confirmation field).
3. Select the Insert menu Web component option. FrontPage, in turn, will display an Insert Web Component dialog box similar to that shown in Figure 275.

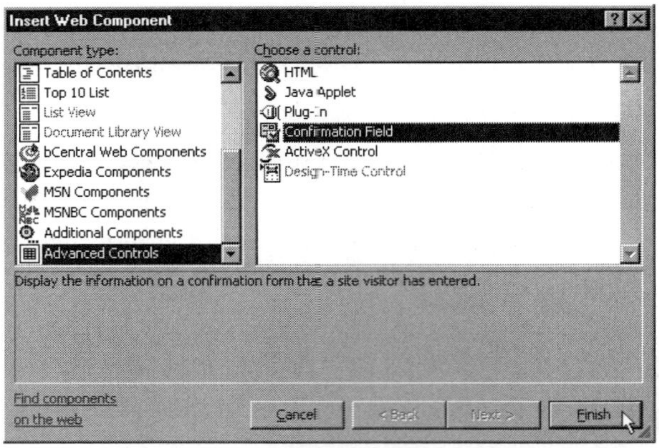

Figure 275 The Microsoft FrontPage Insert Web Component dialog box.

4. In the Component Type scroll box on the left-hand side of the dialog box, click your mouse pointer on the **Advanced Controls**. FrontPage, in turn, will display the available advanced controls in the Choose a control scroll box.
5. From the list of controls in the Choose a control scroll box on the right-hand side of the Insert Web Component dialog box, click your mouse pointer on **Confirmation Field**.
6. Click your mouse pointer on the FINISH button in the lower right-hand corner of the dialog box. FrontPage, in turn, will display a Confirmation Field Properties dialog box (similar to that shown previously in Figure 274.2).
7. Into the Name of form field to confirm field, enter the name of the form element (field) whose value you want to display on the confirmation page and then click the mouse pointer on the OK button near the lower right-hand corner of the Confirmation Field Properties dialog box. FrontPage, in turn, will display a placeholder [the form element's name enclosed by brackets ([ ])] at the insertion point on the confirmation page.

Note: *Form element names are case sensitive. As such, make sure you type the name of the element (field) exactly as it appears in the Name field of the element's Properties dialog box. If you misspell the name or change the case of any of its letters, the Web browser will display the name you typed, enclosed in bracket, instead of the element's value on the confirmation page.*

8. If you are finished adding confirmation fields to the Web page, skip the remaining steps in this procedure. Conversely, to add another con-

firmation field, right-click the mouse pointer the placeholder for a confirmation field you previously inserted on the Web page, and select Copy from the pop-up menu.

Note: *FrontPage makes it easy to tell the difference between text enclosed by brackets ([ ]) and a confirmation field placeholder. When you move your mouse pointer over bracketed text, nothing happens. Conversely, when you move the mouse pointer over the placeholder for a confirmation field, FrontPage changes your mouse pointer from an arrow into the Form Properties icon (a hand pointing to a form).*

9. Right-click the mouse pointer on the point at which you want to add another confirmation field, and select Paste from the pop-up menu.
10. Double-click the mouse pointer on the placeholder you inserted on the Web page in Step 9. FrontPage, in turn, will display the Confirmation Field Properties dialog box.
11. Continue at Step 7.

After you finishing adding all of the confirmation fields you want on the (confirmation) Web page, save your work to disk. Then, perform the second procedure in the preceding Tip to setup the form to display the Web page on which you inserted the confirmation fields in the procedure in the current Tip. Do not forget to publish both the Web page with the form and the confirmation page you created (in this Tip) to the Web server.

SELECTING THE FORM ELEMENTS AND OTHER DATA YOU WANT TO INCLUDE IN THE FORM RESULTS

By default, the Web browser will send only (and all of) the values of the form's elements to the Web server for processing as form results. However, FrontPage not only lets you tell the Web browser which of the form's elements to include in the form results, but also lets you add additional information about the visitor and the date and time the visitor submitted the form.

To work with the makeup of the form results, perform the following steps:

1. Open the Web page with the form whose form results you want to adjust, and select the View menu Page option to display the page on the Page view Normal tab.
2. Right-click the mouse pointer anywhere within the border around the form, and select Form Properties from the pop-up menu. FrontPage, in turn, will display the Form Properties dialog box.

3. Click your mouse pointer on the OPTIONS button in the lower left-hand corner of the Form Properties dialog box. FrontPage, in turn, will display the Saving Results dialog box.
4. Click your mouse pointer on the Saved Fields tab to expose the fields shown in Figure 276.

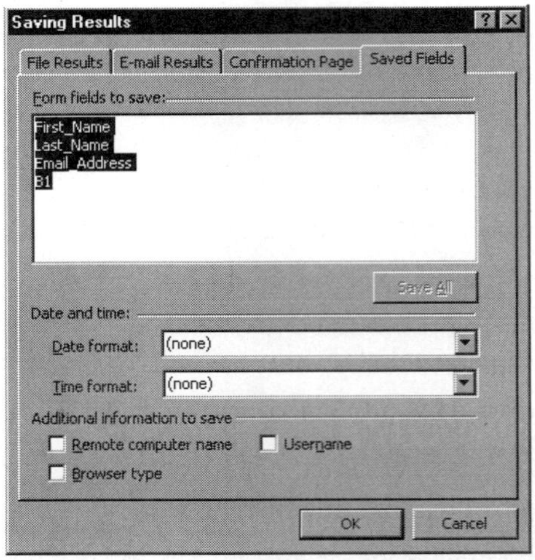

Figure 276 The Saved Fields tab of the Microsoft FrontPage Saving Results dialog box.

5. Use the Form fields to save list box the top of the dialog box to select form elements whose values you want to send to the Web browser as part of the form results. To prevent the Web browser from sending a form element's value to the Web server, use your mouse pointer to highlight (select) the name of the form element you want to remove from the form results, and then press the DELETE key on your keyboard.

Note: *If you later change your mind, you can either re-enter the form elements you deleted or click your mouse pointer on the SAVE ALL button below the lower right-hand corner of the scroll box to list the names of all of the form's elements in the Form fields to save list box.*

Note: *The form element selections you make in Step 5 only affect the form results sent to the form handler on the Web server. The confirmation page will still display a form element's value after you remove the element's name from the Form fields to save list box.*

6. If you want the Web browser to include the date on which the visitor submitted the form results, click your mouse pointer on the drop-down list button to the right of the Data format field, and select a date format from the drop-down list.
7. If you want the Web browser to include the time at which the visitor submitted the form results, click your mouse pointer on the drop-down list button to the right of the Time format field, and select a time format from the drop-down list.
8. In the Additional information to save area at the bottom of the dialog box, click a checkmark in to the checkboxes for the additional information about the visitor that you want the Web browser to include in the results set. The items you can select are:
    - **Remote computer name** – Internet Protocol (IP) address of the computer from which the visitor submitted the form.
    - **Username** – username that the visitor used to login to the Web site. (Only available on a restricted access Web, which requires visitors to login prior to accessing the Web's content.)
    - **Browser type** – the type of browser being used to access the Web site, as specified by the browser.
9. Click your mouse pointer on the OK button near the lower right-hand corner of the Saving Results dialog box. FrontPage, in turn, will return to the Form Properties dialog box.
10. Click your mouse pointer on the OK button near the lower right-hand corner of the Form Properties dialog box to return to the Page view Normal tab.

After you complete Step 10, save and publish (to the Web server) the Web page with the form whose properties you changed.

ACCEPTING INPUT THROUGH A SINGLE-LINE TEXTBOX

There are five types of form elements you can use to gather information from your site visitors. The next five Tips will discuss each of the element types in detail—starting with the single-line textbox in this Tip.

When you want the site visitor to enter a short string of text, insert a single-line textbox on the form. For example, if you want to capture the visitor's first name, last name, and e-mail address, you would insert three, single-line textboxes on the form similar to those shown on the form in Figure 277.1.

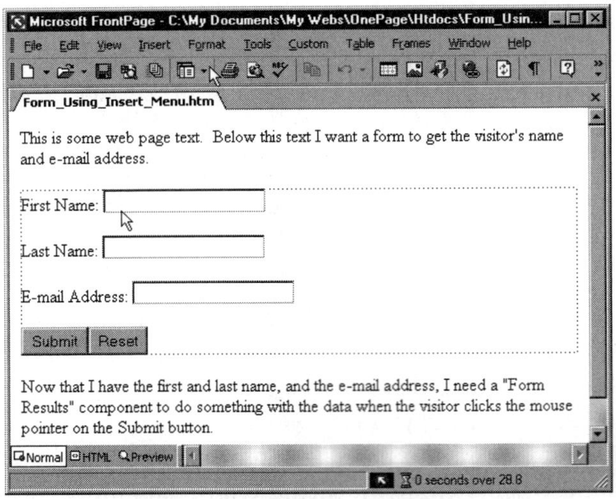

Figure 277.1 A form with three single-line textboxes.

To insert a single-line textbox on a form, perform the following steps:

1. Open the Web page with the form you want to modify (or a page on which you wish to create a new form), and select the View menu Page option to display the Web page on the Page view Normal tab.
2. To add a single-line textbox to an existing form, position the cursor inside the form at the point where you want the single-line textbox to appear. Conversely, if you want to create a new form and place a single-line textbox in it, position the cursor on the Web page where you want to place the new form. As long as you place the cursor outside the borders around any existing forms, FrontPage will put the single-line textbox on a new form when you complete the next step.
3. Select the Insert menu Form option, and click the mouse pointer on Textbox. FrontPage, in turn, will insert a textbox on the form at the cursor position.

After you add a single-line textbox to an existing form or create a new form with only a textbox and SUBMIT and RESET buttons you will want to adjust the form element's properties. If nothing else, each element on a form must have a unique name, so you can easily identify its value in the form results.

To adjust the properties of a single-line textbox, perform the following steps:

1. Double-click the mouse pointer on the single-line textbox (or right-click the mouse pointer on the textbox and select Form Field Properties from the pop-up menu). FrontPage, in turn, will display a Text Box Properties dialog box similar to that shown in Figure 277.2.

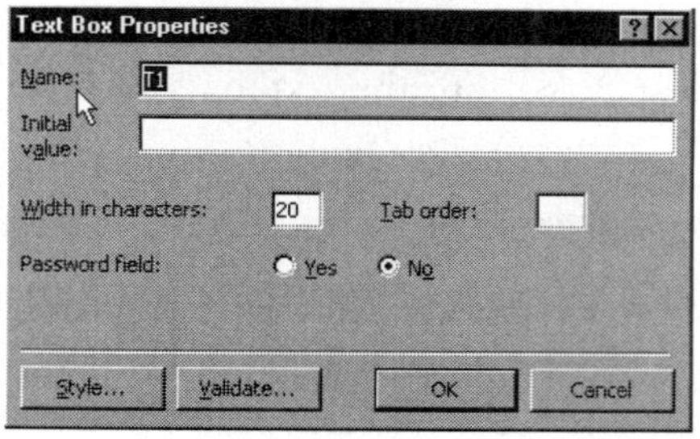

Figure 277.2 The Microsoft FrontPage Text Box Properties dialog box.

2. Into the Name field, enter a descriptive name for the single-line textbox. So you can use the name as a variable that refers to the value in the textbox in the scripting language of your choice, start each name with a letter or underscore (_). Moreover, use only letters, digits, or underscores (_) in the rest of the name. If you want to use more than one word in an element's name, separate words with an underscore (_) rather than a space.
3. If you want the single-line textbox to have an initial value, into the Initial Value field, enter the text you want the Web browser to put in the textbox when it draws the form and each time the visitor clicks the mouse pointer on the form's SUBMIT or RESET button.
4. Into the Width in characters field, enter the number of characters of text you want the visitor to see in the textbox at one time. The visitor will be able to enter more characters into the textbox than the number you enter into the Width in characters field. As the visitor types characters into the textbox that extend the text string beyond the width you specify, some of the initial characters entered will be hidden "beneath" the left side of the textbox as the Web browser scrolls text in the textbox to the left to make room for more characters..

Note: *To make the form's text input fields easy to use, you should size them based on the length of the data visitors will normally enter. If you are asking for a three-letter abbreviation, for example, then enter **3** into the Width in characters field. Similarly, if you are asking for a phone number formatted as: (xxx)-xxx-xxxx then set the element's Width in characters field to **14**. If you do not know the exact number of characters the visitor will enter (as is the case when requesting a name or an e-mail address), size the element such that most visitors will be able to see everything they type into the field without having the scroll its contents.*

5. If you are using the single-line textbox to collect data you do not want displayed onscreen, click the mouse pointer on the Password Field Yes

radio button. With the password option selected, the Web browser will display any text typed into the textbox as a string of asterisks (*).

6. Click the mouse pointer on the OK button near the lower right-hand corner of the dialog box.

That is all there is to it! After you complete Step 6, your form will have a single-line textbox in which visitors can enter a single line of text. If the number of characters entered exceeds the width of the textbox, the Web browser will scroll the contents of textbox "under" the left-hand side of the textbox as the visitor inserts additional characters.

ACCEPTING INPUT THROUGH A MULTI-LINE, SCROLLING TEXTBOX

As you learned in the preceding Tip, you will use a single-line textbox on a form whenever you want to visitor to enter a short, single line of text. Although a single-line textbox will let the visitor type several hundred characters, using a single-line textbox to gather more than about 70 characters of text is inconvenient because visitors will not be able to see everything they type into the textbox at once. Therefore, when you want your visitors to enter a long text string, accept the input as several lines of text by using a multi-line, scrolling textbox (such as that shown in Figure 278.1) on the form.

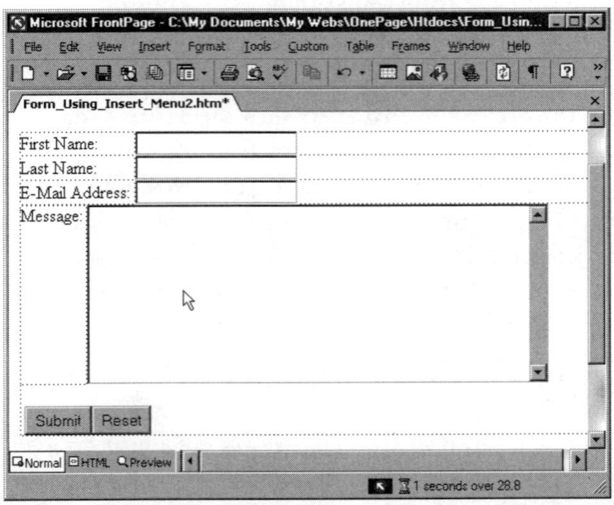

Figure 278.1 A form with three single-line textboxes and a multi-line, scrolling textbox labeled "Message:".

To insert a multi-line, scrolling textbox on a form, perform the following steps:

1. Open the Web page with the form you want to modify (or a page on which you wish to create a new form) and select the View menu Page option to display the Web page on the Page view Normal tab.
2. To add a multi-line textbox to an existing form, position the cursor inside the form at the point where you want the textbox to appear. Conversely, if you want to create a new form and place the multi-line textbox in it, position the cursor on the Web page where you want to insert the new form. As long as you place the cursor outside the borders around any existing forms, FrontPage will put the textbox on a new form when you complete the next step.
3. Select the Insert menu Form option, and click the mouse pointer on Text Area. FrontPage, in turn, will insert a multi-line, scrollable textbox at the cursor on the form position.

After you add a multi-line textbox to an existing form or create a new form with only a textbox and SUBMIT and RESET buttons, you will want to adjust the form element's properties. If nothing else, each element on a form must have a unique name, so you can easily identify its value in the form results.

To adjust the properties of a multi-line textbox, perform the following Steps:

1. Double-click the mouse pointer on the multi-line textbox (or right-click the mouse pointer on the textbox and select Form Field Properties from the pop-up menu). FrontPage, in turn, will display a TextArea Box Properties dialog box similar to that shown in Figure 278.2.

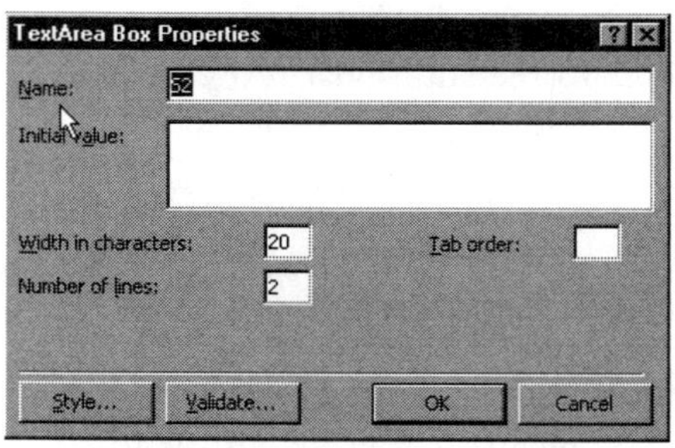

***Figure 278.2** The Microsoft FrontPage TextArea Box Properties dialog box.*

2. Into the Name field, enter a descriptive name for the multi-line textbox. So you can use the name as a variable that refers to the value in the textbox in the scripting language of your choice, start each name with

a letter or underscore (_). Moreover, use only letters, digits, or underscores (_) in the rest of the name. If you want to use more than one word in an element's name, separate words with an underscore (_) rather than a space.

3. If you want the multi-line textbox to have an initial value, into the Initial Value field, enter the text you want the Web browser to put in the textbox when it draws the form and each time the visitor clicks the mouse pointer on the form's SUBMIT or RESET button.
4. Into the Width in characters field, enter the number of characters you want the Web browser to display on each line of the multi-line textbox.
5. Into the Number of lines field, enter the number of lines of text you want the Web browser to display at once in the scrollable textbox.

Note: *As was the case with a single-line textbox, you want to make a multi-line textbox user friendly by sizing the textbox such that the product of the number of characters per line and the number of lines in the textbox is large enough to display everything the visitor types into the textbox at once. If the visitor enters more text than can be displayed within the multi-line textbox, the Web browser will continue to accept input into the textbox and activate the scrollbar along its right-hand side.*

6. Click the mouse pointer on the OK button near the lower right-hand corner of the dialog box.

After you complete Step 5, your form will have a multi-line, scrollable textbox in which visitors can enter several paragraphs of text. If the number of characters entered exceeds the number entered into the Width in characters field (in Step 4) times the number entered into the Number of lines field (in Step 5), the Web browser will activate the scrollbar along the right-hand side of the textbox. To see additional text that exceeds the capacity of the textbox to display onscreen at once, the visitor can click the mouse pointer on the scrollbar to scroll backwards and forwards through its contents one or several lines at a time.

ACCEPTING VISITOR RESPONSES THROUGH CHECKBOXES

While the textboxes described in the two preceding Tips let you retrieve strings of text from site visitors, checkboxes are a convenient way for visitor to select one or more items from a predefined list. Although normally used in groups (such as the group of six checkboxes shown above the Message textbox in Figure 279), each checkbox is independent. When checked, the form results data contains the value of the checkbox, when unchecked, the element's value is returned as a zero length (blank) string.

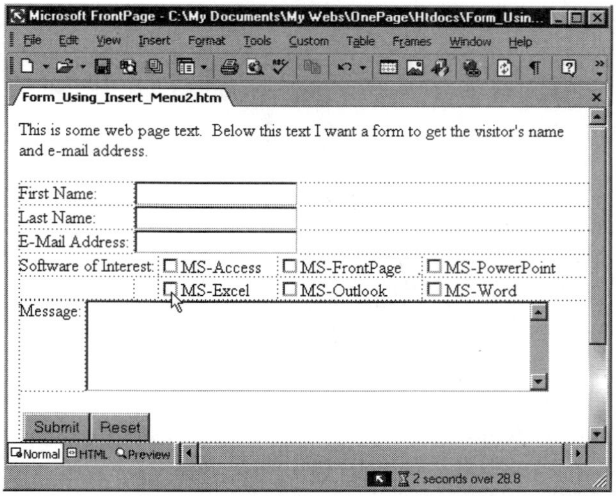

Figure 279.1 A group of six checkboxes between text elements on a form.

To insert a checkbox on a form, perform the following steps:

1. Open the Web page with the form you want to modify (or a page on which you wish to create a new form), and select the View menu Page option to display the Web page on the Page view Normal tab.
2. To add a checkbox to an existing form, position the cursor inside the form at the point where you want the checkbox to appear. Conversely, if you want to create a new form and place the checkbox in it, position the cursor on the Web page where you want to place the new form. As long as you place the cursor outside the borders around any existing forms, FrontPage will put the checkbox on a new form when you complete the next step.
3. Select the Insert menu Form option and click the mouse pointer on Checkbox. FrontPage, in turn, will insert a checkbox at the cursor position on the form.

After you repeat Steps 2 and 3 to add each of the several checkboxes that you want to appear as a group on the form, you will want to adjust the properties of each checkbox. If nothing else, each checkbox must have a unique name and a unique value, so you can easily determine if the visitor clicked a checkmark into the checkbox or cleared it before submitting the form's data for processing.

To adjust the properties of a checkbox, perform the following steps:

1. Double-click the mouse pointer on the checkbox (or right-click the mouse pointer on the checkbox, and select Form Field Properties from the pop-up menu). FrontPage, in turn, will display a Check Box Properties dialog box similar to that shown in Figure 279.2.

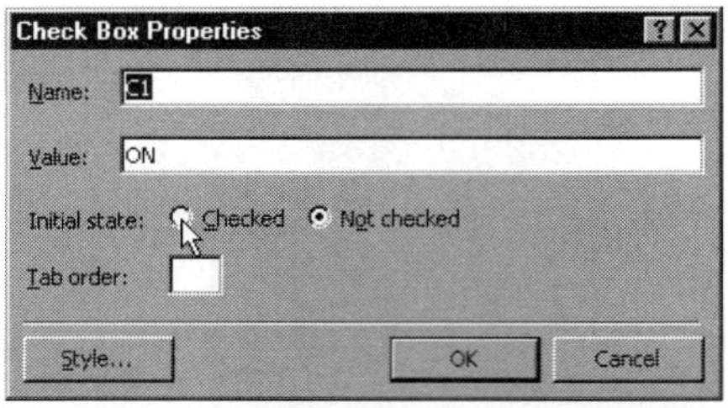

Figure 279.2 The Microsoft FrontPage Check Box Properties dialog box.

2. Into the Name field, enter a descriptive name for the checkbox. So you can use the name as a variable that refers to the value of the checkbox (if checked) or blank (if unchecked) in the scripting language of your choice, start each name with a letter or underscore (_). Moreover, use only letters, digits, or underscores (_) in the rest of the name. If you want to use more than one word in an element's name, separate words with an underscore (_) rather than a space.
3. Into the Value field, enter the value you want the browser to put into the form results if the visitor clicks a checkmark into the checkbox.
4. Click your mouse pointer on the Initial state Checked radio button if you want the Web browser to check the checkbox when it draws the form and each time the visitor clicks the mouse pointer on the form's SUBMIT or RESET button. Conversely, if you want the checkbox left unchecked (unselected) each time the Web browser draws the form, click your mouse pointer on the Initial state Not checked radio button.
5. Click the mouse pointer on the OK button near the corner of the dialog box.

Repeat Steps 1 – 5 for each checkbox in the group of checkboxes you added to the form will executing the first procedure in this Tip. As was mentioned at the beginning of the Tip, each checkbox is independent of the others. Therefore, the visitor can use the mouse pointer to click a checkmark into one, some, all, or none of the checkboxes. If you only want the visitor to make a single selection from a group of choices, use radio buttons instead of checkboxes when presenting the choices to the visitor. (You will learn how to use radio buttons in the next Tip.)

ACCEPTING VISITOR RESPONSES THROUGH RADIO BUTTONS

In the preceding Tip you learned how to use checkboxes to let a visitor select zero, one or more items from a predefined list. Sometimes, however, you only want the visitor to select a single item from a group of choices. To allow the visitor to select only one choice, present the set of choices as radio buttons in a group. In each group of radio buttons (such as the two groups of radio buttons shown below the Message box in Figure 280.1), a visitor can select only a single choice. If the visitor clicks the mouse pointer on a second radio button in a group, the Web browser automatically clears the previous radio button selected.

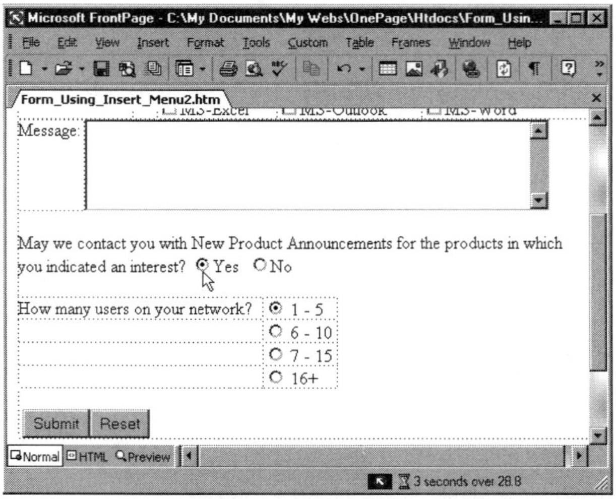

Figure 280.1 A form with two groups of radio buttons: Yes/No and network user counts.

To insert a radio button on a form, perform the following steps:

1. Open the Web page with the form you want to modify (or a page on which you wish to create a new form), and select the View menu Page option to display the Web page on the Page view Normal tab.
2. To add a radio button to an existing form, position the cursor inside the form at the point where you want the radio button to appear. Conversely, if you want to create a new form and place the radio button in it, position the cursor on the Web page where you want to place the new form. As long as you place the cursor outside the borders around any existing forms, FrontPage will put the radio button on a new form when you complete the next step.
3. Select the Insert menu Form option, and click the mouse pointer on Option Button. FrontPage, in turn, will insert a radio (option) button at the cursor position.

Whether you repeat Step 3 to add additional radio buttons to the same group, or repeat Steps 2 and 3 to add additional radio button groups, be sure to adjust the properties of each radio button. If nothing else, you must give each radio button in the group the same Group name and a unique value, so you can determine which of the group's radio buttons the visitor selected when you process the form results.

Because the Web browser must prevent a visitor from selecting more than one of the radio buttons in a group, radio buttons, unlike checkboxes, must be related. In the preceding Tip, you learned that checkboxes are only visually related while being truly independent of each other. As a result, the Web browser will let a visitor select (click a checkmark into) one, some, or all of the checkboxes in the visual group. Radio buttons, on the other hand, are grouped by Group name (which you will learn how to set in the next procedure), and the visitor can only select a single radio button from among those in the same group.

To adjust the properties of a radio button, perform the following steps:

1. Double-click the mouse pointer on the radio button (or right-click the mouse pointer on the radio button and select Form Field Properties from the pop-up menu). FrontPage, in turn, will display an Option Button Properties dialog box similar to that shown in Figure 280.2.

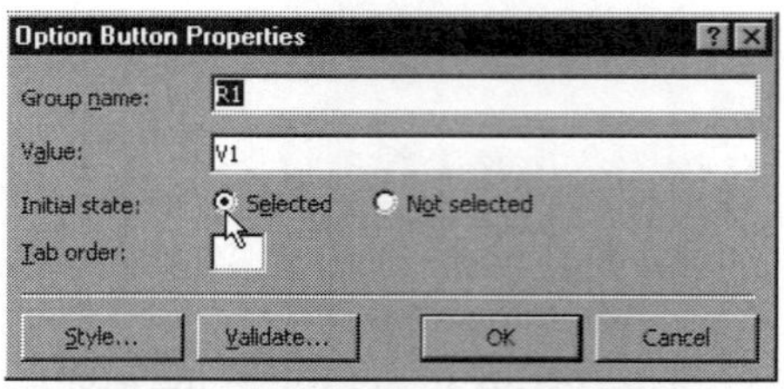

Figure 280.2 The Microsoft FrontPage Option Button Properties dialog box.

2. Into the Group Name field, enter a descriptive name for the group in which the radio button belongs. For example, referring back to the two groups of radio buttons in Figure 280.1, you might enter **Contact_OK** in the Group Name field for each of the two radio buttons (Yes and No) in the first group. Similarly, you might enter **Network_User_Count** into the Group Name field for each of the four radio buttons (1 – 5, 6 – 10, 7 – 15, and 16+) in the second group of radio buttons.

Note: *So you can use the name you assign to the group of radio buttons as a variable that refers to the value of the radio button selected in the scripting language of your choice, start each group name with a letter or underscore (_). Moreover, use only letters, digits, or underscores (_) in the rest of the group* *name. If you want to use more than one word as a radio button group's name, separate words with an underscore (_) rather than a space.*

3. Into the Value field, enter the value you want the browser to associate with the group name in the form results if the visitor clicks on the radio button you selected in Step 1. For example, given the radio buttons in the first group of radio buttons shown on the form in Figure 280.1, you might enter **YES** into the Value field for the first radio button and **NO** into the Value field for the second radio button in the group. Similarly, given the second set of radio buttons in the Figure, you might enter you might enter **1-5** into the Value field for the first radio button, **6-10** into the Value field for the second radio button, **7-15** into the Value field for the third radio button, and **6-10** into the Value field for the fourth (and final) button in the group of radio buttons.

Note: *The form results will contain the Group name assigned to the group of radio buttons (as entered in the Group name field of the Option Button Properties dialog box) followed by the Value of the radio button the visitor selected (as entered into the radio button's Value field).*

4. Click your mouse pointer on the Initial state Selected radio button, if you want the Web browser to select the radio when it draws the form and each time the visitor clicks the mouse pointer on the form's SUBMIT or RESET button. Conversely, if you want the radio left unselected each time the Web browser draws the form, click your mouse pointer on the Initial state Not checked radio button.
5. Click the mouse pointer on the OK button near the corner of the dialog box.

Repeat Steps 1 – 5 for each radio button in the group of radio buttons you added to the form while executing the first procedure in this Tip. As was mentioned at the beginning of the Tip, radio buttons in the same group (those radio buttons with the same text in the Group name field) are interrelated. The Web browser will only let the site visitor select one of the radio buttons with the same group name. Moreover, for any group of radio buttons, the form results will contain the Group name for the radio buttons and the value of the one radio button the visitor selected.

ACCEPTING VISITOR SELECTIONS FROM A DROP-DOWN MENU

A drop-down menu, as its name implies, is a menu whose choices may remain hidden until the visitor clicks the mouse pointer on the menu's drop-down list button to display them.

Unlike a traditional drop-down menu that displays only one menu choice or all menu choices, you can control the number of menu choices displayed by the drop-down menu on your form. For example, the drop-down menu shown on the bottom left of Figure 281.1 has five choices, yet the Web browser displays only one until the visitor clicks the mouse pointer on the drop-down list button to the right of the menu. Meanwhile, the drop-down menu on the bottom right of Figure 281.1 has six choices, five of which are displayed at a time. The scrollbar along the right-hand side of the menu lets the visitor scroll through the menu choices available. However, because of the menu's properties, only five choices will appear onscreen at once.

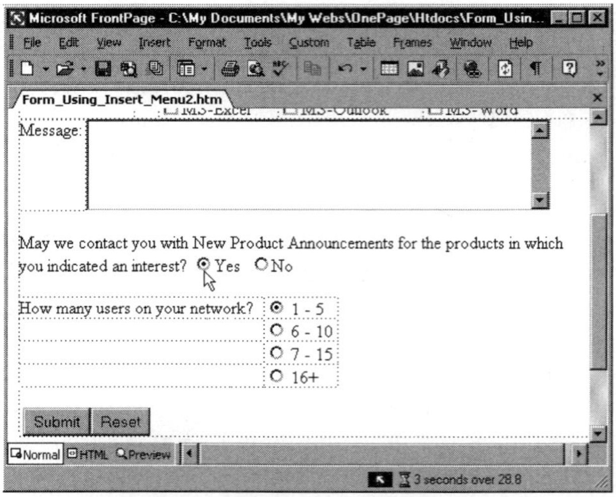

Figure 281.1 A form with two drop-down menus above the form's SUBMIT *and* RESET *buttons.*

In addition to specifying the number of options the drop-down menu is to display onscreen at one time, you can also specify whether the menu's choices are to be treated as a group of checkboxes or as a group of radio buttons. If you specify that the drop-down menu is to allow multiple selections, then its choices behave like a group of check boxes by allowing the visitor to select more than one choice. Conversely, if you specify that the drop-down menu is to allow only a single selection, then its choices behave like a group of radio buttons by allowing the visitor to select only one of them.

To insert a drop-down menu on a form, perform the following steps:

1. Open the Web page with the form you want to modify (or a page on which you wish to create a new form), and select the View menu Page option to display the Web page on the Page view Normal tab.
2. To add a drop-down menu to an existing form, position the cursor inside the form at the point where you want the drop-down menu to

appear. Conversely, if you want to create a new form and place the drop-down menu in it, position the cursor on the Web page where you want to place the new form. As long as you place the cursor outside the borders around any existing forms, FrontPage will put the drop-down menu on a new form when you complete the next step.

3. Select the Insert menu Form option and click the mouse pointer on Drop-Down Box. FrontPage, in turn, will insert a drop-down menu at the cursor position.

Unlike the form element described in the four preceding Tips, the drop-down menu (form element) is non-functional immediately after you add it to a form. After all, the only thing in the element is a drop-down list button—until you add the menu choices.

To add menu choices to a drop-down menu and/or set its height and multiple selections allowed properties, perform the following steps:

1. Double-click the mouse pointer on the drop-down menu (or right-click the mouse pointer on the drop-down menu, and select Form Field Properties from the pop-up menu). FrontPage, in turn, will display a Drop-Down Box Properties dialog box similar to that shown in Figure 281.2.

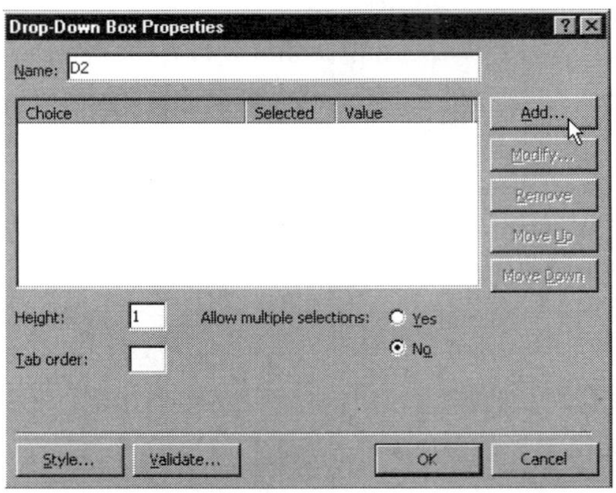

Figure 281.2 The Microsoft FrontPage Drop-Down Box Properties dialog box.

2. Into the Name field, enter a descriptive name for the drop-down menu. So you can use the name as a variable that refers to the value of the drop-down menu items selected or blank (if unselected) in the scripting language of your choice, start each name with a letter or underscore (_). Moreover, use only letters, digits, or underscores (_) in the rest of the name. If you want to use more than one word in an element's

name, separate words with an underscore (_) rather than a space. For example, if you were creating a drop-down menu for the company type (similar to that shown at the bottom left in Figure 281.1), you might enter **Company_Type** into the Name field.

3. To add a choice to the drop-down menu, click the mouse pointer on the Add button at the top of the buttons along the right-hand side of the Drop-Down Box Properties dialog box. FrontPage, in turn, will display an Add Choice dialog box similar to that shown in Figure 281.3.

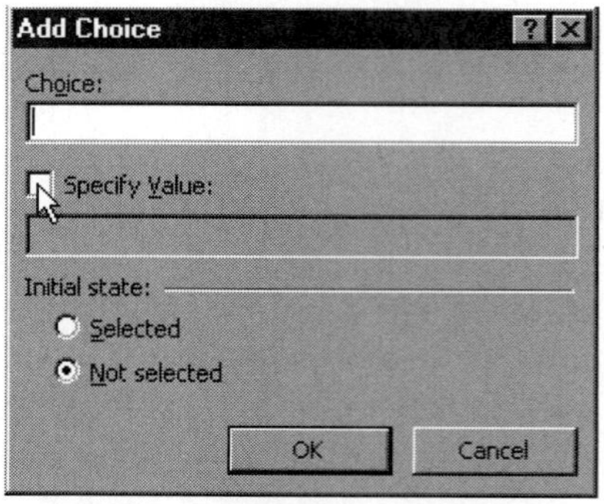

Figure 281.3 The Microsoft FrontPage Add Choice dialog box.

4. Into the Choice field at the top of the dialog box, enter the text you want the visitor to see as the menu choice on the drop-down menu.
5. If you want the Save Results component to pass something other than the text you entered into the Choice field as the value of the menu choice in the form results data, click the mouse pointer on the Specify Value checkbox until a checkmark appears. Conversely, if you want the Save Results component to pass the text you entered in Step 4 as the value of the drop-down menu choice in the form results data, clear the Specify Value checkbox and continue at Step 7.
6. Into the field below the Specify Value checkbox, enter the text you want passed as the value of the drop-down menu selection when the visitor selects the mouse pointer on the menu choice you are adding.
7. Click your mouse pointer on the Initial state Selected radio button, if you want the Web browser to select the menu choice you are adding when it draws the form and each time the visitor clicks the mouse pointer on the form's SUBMIT or RESET button. Conversely, if you want the Web browser to leave the menu choice unselected each time it draws the form, click your mouse pointer on the Initial state Not selected radio button.

8. Click your mouse pointer on the OK button near the bottom center of the Add Choice dialog box. FrontPage, in turn, will add the menu choice to the drop-down list menu and show it in the list of menu choices in the scroll box below the Name field on the Drop-Down Box Properties dialog box.
9. Repeat Steps 3 – 8 until you have added all of the menu choices you want in the drop-down menu.

   If you need to modify a menu choice, either double-click the mouse pointer on the menu choice, or click the mouse pointer on the choice and then on the MODIFY button on the right-hand side of the dialog box. FrontPage, in turn, will display the current properties of the menu choice you selected. As such, continue at Step 4 and adjust the menu choice properties as desired.

   To remove a choice, click the mouse pointer on the choice you want to remove and then on the REMOVE button.

   Finally, to arrange the menu choices in the order in which you want them to appear on the drop-down menu, click your mouse pointer on the menu choice you want to move to a new location on the menu. Then, click the mouse pointer on the MOVE UP button to move the menu choice toward the top of the drop-down menu, or on the MOVE DOWN button to move the choice toward the bottom of the menu.
10. Into the Height field, enter the number of drop-down menu choices you want displayed onscreen at one time.

Note: *If you enter a number greater than 1 (i.e., 2 – 99) into the Height field, the Web browser will always display the number of choices specified by the value you enter into the Height field. For example, if you enter a 5 into the Height field and the menu has only three choices, the Web browser will display the drop-down menu with the text of the three choices available followed by two blank choices. Similarly, if the drop-down menu has ten choices and you enter a 5 into the Height field, the Web browser will display the drop-down menu with the text for five choices onscreen and a scrollbar along its left-hand side so the visitor can scroll through the remaining choices. However, the browser will only display five choices onscreen at any one time.*

If you enter a 1 into the Height field, the drop-down menu on the form will act like a traditional menu—displaying all of its choices when the visitor clicks the mouse pointer on the menu's drop-down list button—unless you allow the visitor to make multiple selections. If you click your mouse pointer on the Allow multiple selections: Yes radio button in the next Step, the Web browser will display a scrollbar along the left-hand side of the drop-down menu and display onscreen at one time only the number of choices you enter into the Height field.

11. If you want the Web browser to allow the visitor to select multiple choices from the drop-down menu, click your mouse pointer on the Allow multiple selections: Yes radio button. Otherwise, to limit the visitor to making only a single choice from the drop-down menu, click the mouse pointer on the Allow multiple selections: No radio button.
12. Click the mouse pointer on the OK button near the corner of the dialog box.

After you complete Step 12, FrontPage will return to the Page view Normal tab and display the drop-down menu similar to the way it will appear to the site visitor. However, to check the behavior of the drop-down menu in response to mouse clicks on its menu choices and drop-down button or scrollbar, you will need to click the mouse pointer on the Preview tab and work with the form on the Page view Preview tab.

As is the case with all form elements, to see what the form results look like for a drop-down menu, you will need to save the form with the drop-down menu to disk an then publish the form the Web server. After you use a Web browser to retrieve the Web page with the form from the Web server and fill out the form's field (including making selections from the form's drop-down menus), you can view the value(s) saved to the form results file by the Save Results component on the Web server.

PLACING TEXT IN FRONT OF OR AFTER A FORM ELEMENT

The procedures for adding elements to forms in the five preceding Tips made no mention of placing text labels next to the elements once they are on the form. As a result, if you simply followed the procedures you may have asked, "What gives?" when the forms you created did not look like those in the Figures. Unlike the forms in the Figures, your forms have only textboxes, checkboxes, radio buttons, drop down menus—and no labels. Obviously, a form with elements without labels is to say the least very user unfriendly—and actually, downright unusable. So, be sure to add descriptive text to label each of the form's elements.

Fortunately, labeling an element is as simple as placing the cursor either before or after the element (depending on where you want the label to appear relative to the element) and typing the text you want to see on the form. For example, to label two radio buttons you insert on a form to get a Yes/No answer perform the following steps:

1. Open the Web page with the form you want to modify (or a page on which you wish to create a new form), and select the View menu Page option to display the Web page on the Page view Normal tab.

2. Execute the procedures in a previous tip titled "Accepting Visitor Selections Through Radio Buttons" to add a radio button to a form.
3. Position the cursor just to the left of the radio button and type the text of the yes/no question, and then press the SPACEBAR to separate the question from the radio button with a single space. For example, you might type **May we contact you with New Product Announcements for the products in which you expressed an interest?** and then press the SPACEBAR.
4. To label the radio button (with text the follows it), move the cursor immediately to the right of the radio button, press the Spacebar and enter the radio button's label text, such as **Yes**, for example.
5. Press the SPACEBAR a couple of times for spacing, and repeat Step 2 to add a second radio button. Then, continue at Step 6.
6. Position the cursor to the right of the second radio button, press the SPACEBAR and type the text **No**, and then press the ENTER key on your keyboard.

After you complete Step 6, your form will look similar to that shown in Figure 282.1.

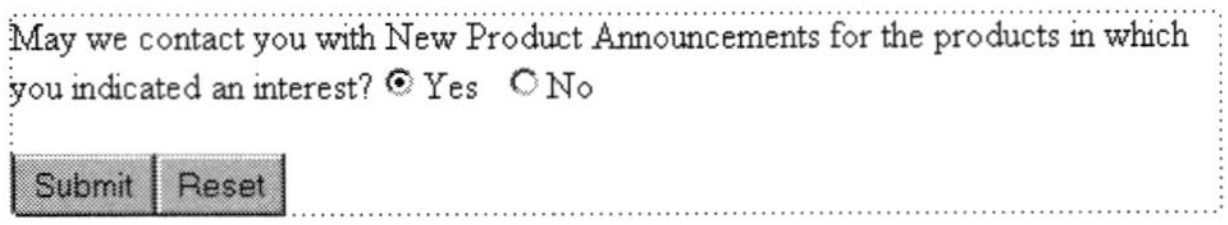

***Figure 282.1** A form with a Yes/No question answered using radio buttons labeled Yes and No.*

The most important thing to understand when labeling form elements is that text and form elements interact on a form the same way in which text and graphics images interact on a Web page. By default, the Web browser will align the label (i.e. the text typed next to a form element) such that the bottom of the text lines-up with the bottom of the form element. This behavior is fine for single-line elements such as radio buttons and checkboxes. However, if you want to label a group or radio buttons or checkboxes or a multi-line textbox on a form, you may need to put both the label and the form element into a table to align the two the way in which you want.

For example, if you execute the procedures in a previous Tip titled "Accepting Input Through a Multi-Line, Scrolling Textbox" to create a 50 character wide by 10 line high textbox and then type the text "Message:" as the label to is left, your form will appear similar to that shown in Figure 282.2.

Figure 282.2 A form with a multi-line textbox and a label aligned along the bottom of the form element.

If you want the label to appear next to the top left-hand corner of the textbox, as shown in Figure 282.3, you must place the textbox and its label into separate cells in a table.

Figure 282.3 A form with a multi-line textbox and a label aligned along the bottom of the form element.

After you create a table with one row and two columns, you can place the form element's label in the left-hand cell and the textbox in the table's right-hand cell. Next, to align the text with the top of the form element (the textbox, in the current example), set the alignment of the left-hand cell's contents at the "Top" of the cell (as you learned to do in a previous Tip titled "Aligning Cell Contents Vertically."

(You will, of course, want to set the table's border width to 0, as you learned to do in a previous Tip titled: "Adjusting a Table's Cell Padding, Spacing, and Border Width," so the border around the table and the border around each of its cells are hidden from view.)

UNDERSTANDING FRONTPAGE FORMS VALIDATION

Traditionally, you had to write (or hire a programmer to write) a custom script to perform forms validation. A typical forms validation process proceeds as follows. After the visitor clicks the form's SUBMIT button, the Web browser sends the form results to the Web server, which in turn, runs the validation script on the form results. If all of the form's data is ok, the server passes the form results on to a form handler (such as the Save Results component of the FrontPage Server Extensions) for processing and the form handler sends the visitor a confirmation page. Conversely, if the validation script finds an error in the form data, it sends a correction page back to the visitor's Web browser explaining what was wrong with one or more entries on the form. The visitor then corrects the errors on the form and starts the validation process again by resubmitting the form for processing.

FrontPage supports both server-side (traditional) and client-side forms validation. As was outlined in the preceding paragraph, server-side validation requires the Web browser to send form results to the Web server for validation. Moreover, a script running on the server generates the error page and sends it to the Web browser for display. In client-side forms validation, on the other hand, the script used to validate data in each field of a form runs on the Web browser as part of the Web page HTML.

The advantage of using client-side vs. server-side validation is speed. If the visitor enters data into a form element that violates the element's validity rules, the Web *browser* will display a dialog box that prompts the visitor to correct the entry after the visitor clicks the mouse pointer on the form's SUBMIT button. Therefore, the validation process finishes more quickly because it does not involve sending the form's data to the Web server, applying the rules to the data, and then sending a page of error messages back to the Web browser. Instead, the Web browser validates the form's data before submitting the form results to the Web server, which means the Web browser only sends validated data across the Internet.

The disadvantage of using client-side vs. server-side validation is that some Web browsers may not support the scripting language in which the validation script embedded in the Web page HTML is written. If the Web browser does not support the scripting language, or if the visitor has turned off the browser's ability to execute embedded scripts, the browser will not validate the form data. Then, since the Web server assumes that the Web browser already validated the form results, the Web server may pass on invalid form data to the form handler for processing.

You will have to decide whether the need for speed outweighs the need to be sure of the validity of the form results. FrontPage lets you select either client-side or server-side validation and will generate the script necessary to perform either one. If you tell FrontPage to store data rules in the Web page HTML (to perform client-side validation), the program will call on the Script Wizard to generate the validation script and add it to the Web page file. Conversely, if you tell FrontPage to store data validity rules on the Web server (i.e. to perform server-side validation), the program still adds the data rules to the Web page HTML. However, additional code in the Web page file tells the Web server to call on the Validation component of the FrontPage Server Extensions on the Web server to check on the form results data after the visitor clicks the form's SUBMIT button.

By default, FrontPage will generate forms that use client-side validation. To have the program generate code that calls for server-side validation instead, perform the following steps:

1. Select the File menu Open Web option and open the FrontPage Web whose form validation option you want to set.
2. Select the Tools menu Web Settings option. FrontPage, in turn, will display the Web Settings dialog box.
3. Click the mouse pointer Advanced tab to expose the fields shown in Figure 283.

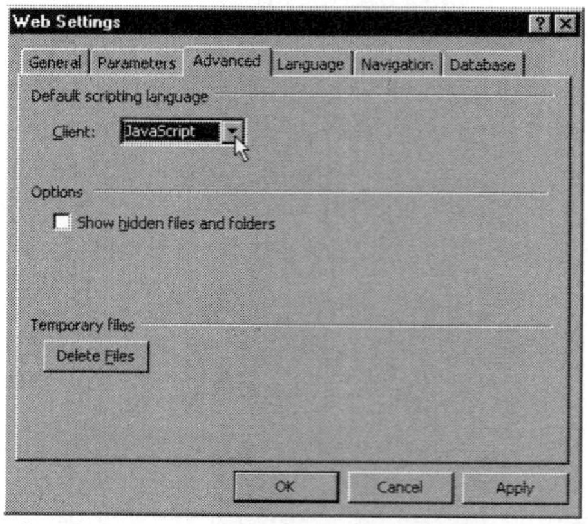

Figure 283 *The Advanced tab of the Microsoft FrontPage Web Settings dialog box.*

4. To use server-side validation, click the mouse pointer on the drop-down list button to the right of the Client field (in the Default scripting language section at the top of the Advanced tab), and select <None> from the drop-down list.
5. Click your mouse pointer on the OK button near the bottom center of the Web Settings dialog box.

After you complete Step 5, FrontPage will prompt you with the "Recalculate the Web now?" message box if you changed from client-side to server-side validation on a form with elements for which you have previously selected validation options. If presented with the Recalculate Web message box, click your mouse pointer on its OK button. FrontPage, in turn, will update the Web hyperlinks, text indexes, and form validation scripts to tell the Web server to use its Validation component to validate form results before sending the form results on to the form handler (the Save Results component) for processing. (If none of the form's elements have validation scripts when you complete Step 5, FrontPage will see there are no validation scripts to change, so the program will not prompt you with the Recalculate Web dialog box.)

Selecting server-side form validation may be a little slower than client-side validation because the Web server must allocate some of its resources to run the form results through the Validation component running on the server. Moreover, both the form's data and the error page must be sent across the Internet—perhaps multiple times. However, server-side validation is safer than client-side validation because the Web server makes sure that all form results are validated against the form's data regardless of the script execution capabilities or settings of the Web browser.

SELECTING THE FORMS VALIDATION SCRIPTING LANGUAGE

By default FrontPage adds code to the Web page HTML that tells the Web browser perform client-side form results validation. As you will learn in the next four Tips, you can choose whether FrontPage writes the client-side form results validation script in VBScript or JavaScript.

To select the scripting language FrontPage will use to write client-side form element validation scripts (or to switch back from server-side to client-side validation), perform the following steps:

1. Select the File menu Open Web option, and open the FrontPage Web whose form validation option you want to set.
2. Select the Tools menu Web Settings option. FrontPage, in turn, will display the Web Settings dialog box.
3. Click the mouse pointer Advanced tab to expose its fields (shown previously in Figure 283).
4. To use client-side validation, click the mouse pointer on the drop-down list button to the right of the Client field (in the Default scripting language section at the top of the Advanced tab), and select either VBScript or JavaScript from the drop-down menu. For the current project, select JavaScript.

Note: *In client-side validation, the Web browser runs a script (validation programming code) embedded in the Web page HTML. FrontPage defaults to writing the data validation code (the validation script) using the JavaScript language because both Netscape Navigator and Internet explorer support JavaScript. VBScript, loosely based on Microsoft's Visual Basic programming language, is supported mainly by Internet Explorer and few other Web browsers. Remember, if a Web browser does not support the scripting language used, the browser ignores the client-side forms validation code. Therefore, unless you 1) are familiar with Visual Basic, 2) know that all of your site visitors will be using Internet Explorer, and 3) plan to "tweak" the validation script FrontPage generates, select JavaScript in Step 4.*

5. Click your mouse pointer on the OK button near the bottom center of the Web Settings dialog box.

After you complete Step 5, FrontPage will prompt you with the "Recalculate the Web now?" message box if you have changed the validation from client- to server-side or vice-versa. Click your mouse pointer on the OK button near the bottom center of the message box. FrontPage, in turn, will update the Web hyperlinks, text indexes, and form validation scripts to tell the Web browser to validate data entered and selections made on the form after the visitor clicks the mouse pointer on the form's SUBMIT button.

In the next four Tips, you will learn how to specify the rules that define what is and what is not a valid entry or selection for a form element.

CREATING RULES TO VALIDATE DATA INPUT INTO FORMS TEXTBOXES

Both single-line and multi-line textboxes let site visitors enter a mixture of alphanumeric characters and special symbols. Therefore, a textbox is useful when you need to gather data such as a name, street addresses, zip code, phone number, comment, question, complaint, etc. However, the very versatility of a textbox increases the likelihood that some visitors will enter an invalid string of text. Unfortunately, the textbox itself does nothing to restrict what the visitor types into the form element. Therefore, you might ask for a phone number, for example, and the visitor (being a stickler for privacy) might enter xxx-xxx-xxxx. Similarly, if you need a zip code to generate a valid shipping label for a product purchased online, you want to make sure that the site visitor does not leave the zip code textbox on the order form blank.

Fortunately, FrontPage will generate code for either the Web browser or the Web server to use to validate what the visitor entered (or failed to enter) into a textbox. While the textbox itself still accepts whatever the visitor enters, if you tell FrontPage to create a validation script, you can have the Web browser or the Validation component on the Web server check the data in the textbox for errors after the visitor clicks the mouse pointer on the form's SUBMIT button.

To create a validation script for a textbox, perform the following steps:

1. Open the Web page with the form with the textbox whose data you want to validate, and select the View menu Page option to display the Web page on the Page view Normal tab.
2. Double-click the mouse pointer on the single-line or multi-line textbox for which you want FrontPage to create a validation script (or right-click the mouse pointer on the textbox and select Form Field Properties from the pop-up menu). FrontPage, in turn, will display the Text Box Properties dialog box if you selected a single-line textbox, or the TextArea Box Properties dialog box if you select a multi-line textbox.

3. Click your mouse pointer on the VALIDATE button near the lower left-hand corner of the dialog box. FrontPage, in turn, will display a Textbox Validation dialog box similar to that shown in Figure 285.1.

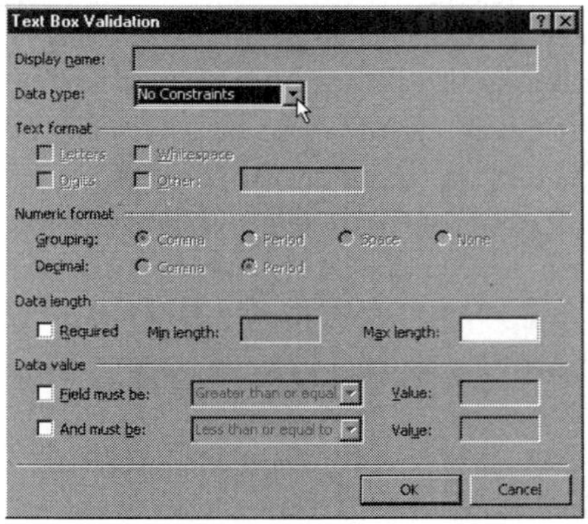

Figure 285.1 The Microsoft FrontPage Textbox Validation dialog box.

4. Click your mouse pointer on the drop-down list button to the right of the Data type field, and select the type of data you want the visitor to enter into the textbox. The available selections are:
    - **No Constraints** – the visitor can enter any characters (numbers, letters, and special symbols) without constraint. (This is the default).
    - **Text** – the visitor can enter any characters (numbers, letters, and special symbols) except those you specify in Step 5.
    - **Integers** – the visitor can entry only a whole number (a number without a decimal point and fractional portion) into the textbox.
    - **Numbers** – the visitor may enter only numeric data (a whole number or a decimal) into the textbox.
5. If you selected **Text** in Step 4, FrontPage will make the checkboxes and Other field in the Text format section of the dialog box available. (If you selected No Constraints, Integers, or Numbers in Step 4, the fields in this section are grayed out as inapplicable, then continue at Step 6.) The Text format options are:
    - **Letters** – click a checkmark into the Letters checkbox to allow the visitor to enter alphabetic characters into the textbox.
    - **Whitespace** – click a checkmark into the Whitespace checkbox to allow the visitor to enter one or more spaces into the textbox.
    - **Digits** – click a checkmark into the Digits checkbox to allow the visitor to enter numbers into the textbox.

- **Other** – if you want to let the visitor enter non-alphanumeric characters into the textbox, click a checkmark into the Other checkbox and into the field to the right of the checkbox, enter the list of symbols [such parenthesis (()), comma (,), period (.), pound sign (#), etc.] the visitor is allowed to enter.

6. If you selected **Integers** or **Numbers** in Step 4, use the Grouping radio buttons in the Numeric Format section of the dialog box to specify how the visitor is to group each set of three digits in he numeric data entered into the textbox. (If you selected No Constraints or Text, the fields in the Numeric format section are grayed out at inapplicable, then continue at Step 8.) The Grouping options are:
   - **Comma** – click the mouse pointer on the Comma radio button if you want the visitor to enter a comma (,) between each set of three digits in the whole number of decimal entered in the textbox. For example: 123,456,789.
   - **Period** - click the mouse pointer on the Period radio button if you want the visitor to enter a period (.) between each set of three digits in the whole number of decimal entered in the textbox For example: 123.456.789.
   - **Space** - click the mouse pointer on the Space radio button if you want the visitor to enter a space between each set of three digits in the whole number of decimal entered in the textbox. For example: 123 456 789.
   - **None** - click the mouse pointer on the None radio button if you want the visitor to type only the digits in the whole number of decimal entered in the textbox. For example: 123456789.

7. If you selected **Numbers** in Step 4, use the Decimal radio buttons in the Numeric Format section of the dialog box to specify how the visitor is to separate the decimal portion from the whole number part of the number entered into the textbox. (If you selected No Constraints, Text, or Integers the Decimal radio buttons are grayed out at inapplicable, then continue at Step 8.) The Decimal options are:
   - **Comma** – click the mouse pointer on the Comma radio button if you want the visitor to enter a comma (,) between the whole number and the decimal portion of the number entered in the textbox. For example: 1234,567. [You cannot use a comma (,) to separate the whole number from the decimal portion of the number if you selected comma (,) separation for the three number groups in Step 6.]

- **Period** - click the mouse pointer on the Period radio button if you want the visitor to enter a period (.) between the whole number and the decimal portion of the number entered in the textbox. For example: 1234.567. [You cannot use a period (.) to separate the whole number from the decimal portion of the number if you selected period (.) separation for the three number groups in Step 6.]

8. To require that the visitor enter something into the textbox (to prevent the visitor from leaving the textbox blank), click your mouse pointer on the Required checkbox until a checkmark appears.
9. If you clicked a checkmark into the Required checkbox in Step 8, into the Min length field, enter the minimum number of characters the visitor must enter into textbox.
10. If you want to limit the length of visitor's entry in the textbox, into the Max length field, enter the maximum number of characters the visitor is allowed to enter.
11. If you want to place additional restrictive conditions on the content in the textbox, use your mouse pointer to click a checkmark into the Field must be checkbox and/or the And must be checkbox, select a condition from the drop-down condition list next to the checkbox, and enter a value into the Value field. For example, if you want to limit numeric data to the range 5 – 999, then:
    - Click the mouse pointer on the Field must be checkbox until a checkmark appears.
    - Select **Greater than or equal to** from the conditions drop-down list box to the right of the Field must be checkbox.
    - Enter **5** into the Value field on the same line.
    - Click the mouse pointer on the And must be checkbox until a checkmark appears.
    - Select **Less than or equal to** from the conditions drop-down list box to the right of the And must be checkbox.
    - Enter **999** into the Value field on the same line.
12. If you specified any of the textbox validation rules, into the Display name field (at the top of the dialog box), enter the text you want the Web browser to display in the error message box if the visitor submits a form with invalid data in the textbox. Suppose, for example, that you enter **Number of Widgets** into the Display name field for a textbox for which you clicked a checkmark into the Required checkbox in

Step 8. The Web browser will prompt the visitor to correct the data entered into the textbox with the message box shown in Figure 285.2 if the visitor fails to enter something into the textbox prior to clicking the mouse pointer on the form's SUBMIT button. (If the Display name field is grayed out as unavailable, you have not specified any validation rules for the textbox.)

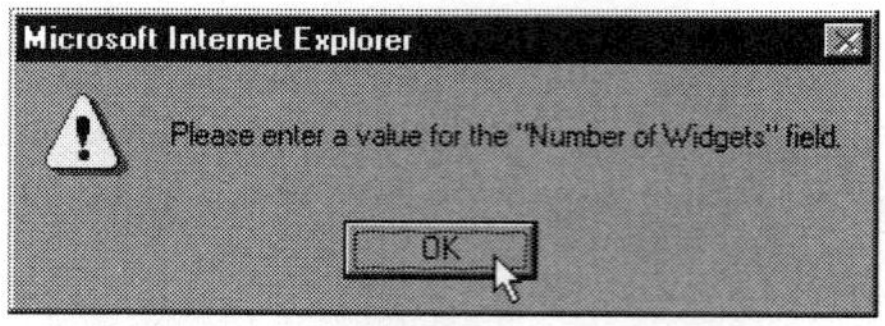

Figure 285.2 An Invalid Form Data message box.

13. Click your mouse pointer on the OK button near the lower right-hand corner of the Text Box Validation dialog box. FrontPage, in turn, will return to the Text Box Properties dialog box or to the TextArea Box Properties dialog box.
14. Click the mouse pointer on the OK button near the lower right-hand corner of the dialog box to return to the Page view Normal tab.

After you save the updated Web page to disk and then publish it to the Web server, textbox validation will be in effect.

If you tell FrontPage that you want to perform client-side forms validation, the Web browser will execute the FrontPage generated validation script in the Web page HTML to check the visitor's entry in the textbox against the a set of rules after the visitor clicks the mouse pointer on the form's SUBMIT button. If the textbox contents violate one or more of the rules that define "valid" data, the Web browsers will prompt the visitor to correct that information in the textbox and will not send the form results to the Web server until the Web browser finds all of the form results are valid.

Similarly, if you tell FrontPage that you want to perform server-side forms validation, the Web server will pass the FrontPage generated validation scripts in the Web page HTML along with the (un-validated) form results it receives from the Web browser to the Validation component of the FrontPage Server Extensions installed on the Web server. The Validation component, in turn, will use the validation scripts to check the validity of the data in the form's elements (including any textboxes). If the data in one or more of the form's elements violates at least one of the rules that define "valid" data, the Validation component will create a Form Results Error Web page with the list of problems it found in the forms data. The Web server, in turn, will send the Form Results Error Web page to the Web browser for display, so the visitor knows what needs to be done to fix the errors in the form element(s) before resubmitting the form to the Web server for processing.

CREATING RULES TO VALIDATE DATA INPUT FROM RADIO BUTTONS

As you learned in a previous Tip titled "Accepting Visitor Responses Through Radio Buttons," the Web browser only lets the site visitor select one of the radio buttons in a group of radio buttons. In the same Tip, you also learned that the text (i.e. the name) entered in the Group name field on the radio button's Option Button Properties dialog box specifies the group to which a radio button belongs. Radio buttons with identical values in the Group name field are in the same group.

The Web browser ensures that the visitor can select at most one radio button in a particular group of radio buttons by de-selecting the previous selection (if any) when the visitor clicks the mouse pointer on a second radio button in the same group. However, the browser does not ensure that the visitor will click the mouse pointer on at least one of the radio buttons in a group.

To require the visitor to select at least one of the radio buttons in a group of radio buttons, perform the following steps:

1. Open the Web page with the group of radio buttons in which you want to ensure that the visitor makes a selection. Then, select the View menu Page option to display the Web page on the Page view Normal tab.
2. Double-click the mouse pointer on one of the radio buttons in the group (or right-click the mouse pointer on one of the group's radio buttons and select Form Field Properties from the pop-up menu). FrontPage, in turn, will display the Option Button Properties dialog box.
3. Click your mouse pointer on the VALIDATE button near the lower left-hand corner of the dialog box. FrontPage, in turn, will display an Option Button Validation dialog box similar to that shown in Figure 286.1.

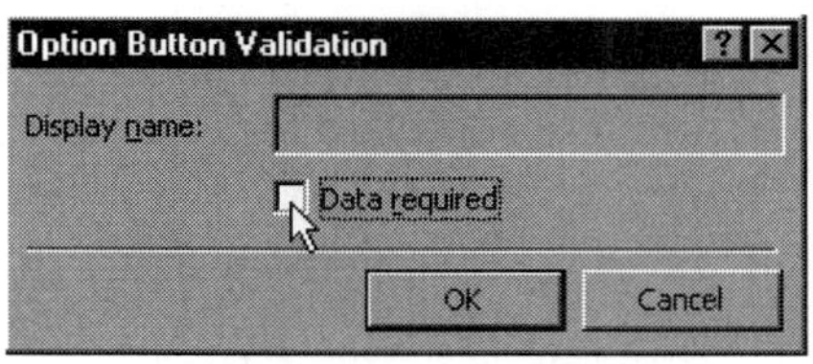

Figure 286.1 The Microsoft FrontPage Option Button Validation dialog box.

4. Click your mouse pointer on the Data required checkbox until a checkmark appears.

5. Into the Display name field (at the top of the dialog box), enter the text you want the Web browser to display in the error message box if the visitor fails to click the mouse pointer on one of the radio buttons on the group. For example, if you enter **User Count** into the Display name field for one of the radio buttons in the Network_User_Count group, the Web browser will prompt the visitor with the message box show in Figure 286.2, if the user submits the form without selecting one of the radio buttons in the group.

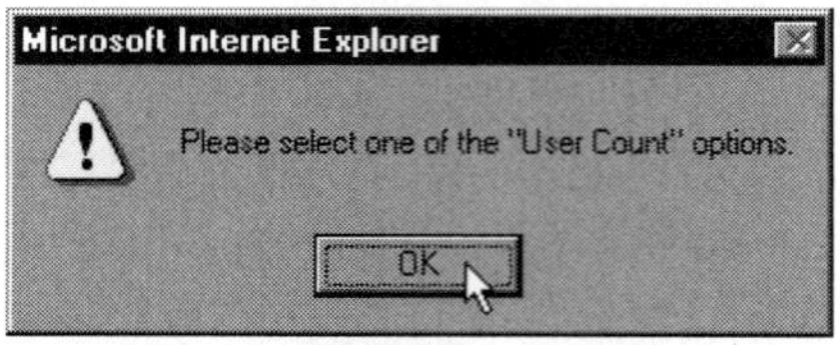

Figure 286.2 A Failed to Select Radio Button message box.

6. Click the mouse pointer on the OK button near the bottom center of the Option Button Validation dialog box.
7. Click the mouse pointer on the OK button near the lower right-hand corner of the Option Button Properties dialog box.

After you save the updated Web page to disk and then publish it to the Web server, the Web browser or the Web server (depending on whether you tell FrontPage to generate a client-side or server-side validation script) will ensure that the visitor selects one of the radio buttons in the radio button group you selected in Step 2.

One important thing to understand when setting up radio button validation is that the validation process only works if you make sure that the Initial state on the Option Button Properties dialog box is set to Not selected for all of the radio buttons in the group. After all, if you tell the Web browser to select one of the radio buttons by default when it draws the form, you will not know if the visitor clicked the mouse pointer on the default radio button, or if the visitor failed to select one of the radio buttons in the group before submitting the form.

Therefore, if you want to make sure the visitor really selects one of the group's radio buttons vs. just accepting the default selection, look at your form on the Page view Normal tab. If you see one of the radio buttons in the group is selected, double-click the mouse pointer on the selected radio button (i.e. the one with the black "dot") and change its Initial state to Not selected (as you learned to do in a previous Tip titled "Accepting Visitor Responses Through Radio Buttons").

VALIDATING DROP-DOWN MENU SELECTIONS

Validating drop-down menu selections is similar to validating radio button selections. Since any selection is, by default, valid, the validation process simply involves making sure that the visitor has made at least one selection.

If you require the visitor to select at least one of the choices from a drop-down menu (the visitor is to select one and only one of the drop-down menu choices), then make the first selection on the menu read something like "— Select One —". If the visitor is to make one or more selections of the drop-down menu choices, then make the first selection on the menu read something like "— Select One or More —". Since every drop-down menu displays at least its first choice onscreen, the visitor will see the prompt to make a selection—even if the remainder of the drop-down menu's options are hidden from view.

To require the visitor to select at least one of the choices on a drop-down menu, perform the following steps:

1. Open the Web page with the drop-down menu from which you want to ensure that the visitor makes at least one selection. Then, select the View menu Page option to display the Web page on the Page view Normal tab.
2. Double-click the mouse pointer on the drop-down menu (or right-click the mouse pointer on the drop-down menu, and select Form Field Properties from the pop-up menu). FrontPage, in turn, will display the Drop-Down Box Properties dialog box.
3. Click your mouse pointer on the VALIDATE button near the lower left-hand corner of the dialog box. FrontPage, in turn, will display a Drop-Down Box Validation dialog box similar to that shown in Figure 287.1.

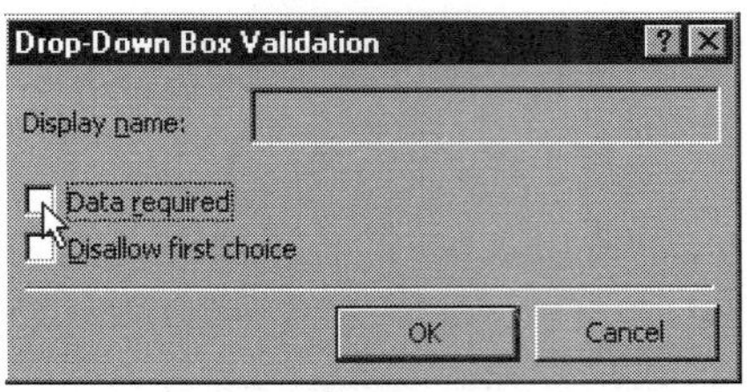

***Figure 287.1** The Microsoft FrontPage Drop-Down Box Validation dialog box.*

4. Click your mouse pointer on the Data required checkbox until a checkmark appears.

5. If you inserted a prompt such as "—— Select One ——" as the first choice in the drop-down menu, click your mouse pointer on the Disallow first choice textbox until a checkmark appears. Conversely, if the first choice on the drop-down menu is an actual menu choice (vs. a prompt to make a menu choice), clear the Disallow first choice textbox.
6. Into the Display name field (at the top of the dialog box), enter the text you want the Web browser to display in the error message box if the visitor fails to select one or more of the items in the drop-down menu before submitting the form. For example, if you enter **Company Type** into the Display name field, the Web browser will prompt the visitor with the message box shown in Figure 287.2, if the visitor clicks the mouser pointer on the form's SUBMIT button without having selected at least one of the choices on the drop-down menu.

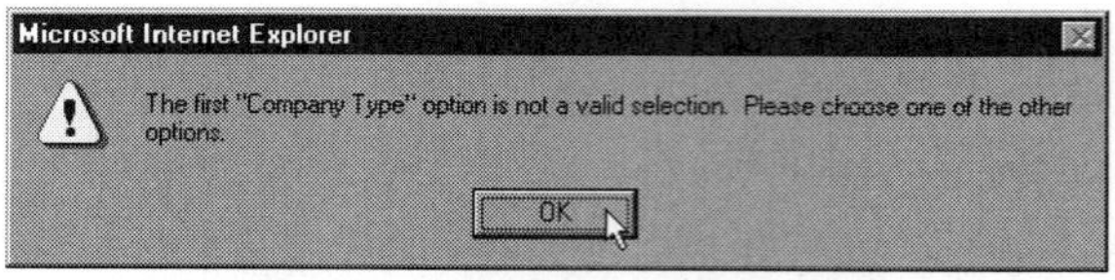

***Figure 287.2** A Failed to Make Selection from Drop-Down Menu message box.*

7. Click the mouse pointer on the OK button near the bottom center of the Drop-Down Box Validation dialog box.
8. Click the mouse pointer on the OK button near the lower right-hand corner of the Drop-Down Box Properties dialog box.

After you save the updated Web page to disk and then publish it to the Web server, the Web browser or the Web server (depending on whether you tell FrontPage to generate a client-side or server-side validation script) will ensure that the visitor selects at least one of the items on the drop-down list you selected in Step 2.

One important thing to understand when setting up drop-down menu validation is that the validation process only works if you make sure that the Selected value for each item on the Drop-Down Box Properties dialog box is set to No. After all, if you tell the Web browser to select one or more of the drop-down menu items by default when it draws the form, you will not know if the visitor selected the default menu choice(s) or if the visitor failed to select an item from the drop-down menu submitting the form.

Therefore, if you want to make sure the visitor really selects one or more of the items on the drop-down menu vs. just accepting the default selection(s), turn off all default selections on a drop-down menu by performing the following steps:

1. Double-click the mouse pointer on the drop-down menu (or right-click the mouse pointer on the drop-down menu and select Form Field Properties from the pop-up menu). FrontPage, in turn, will display the Drop-Down Box Properties dialog box.
2. Look at the values in the Selected column. If none of the values is Yes, continue at Step 7.
3. Double-click your mouse pointer on the first Yes you see in the Selected column (or click the mouse pointer on the first Yes, and then on the MODIFY button in the button list along the right-hand side of the dialog box). FrontPage, in turn, will display a Modify Choice dialog box similar to that shown in Figure 287.3.

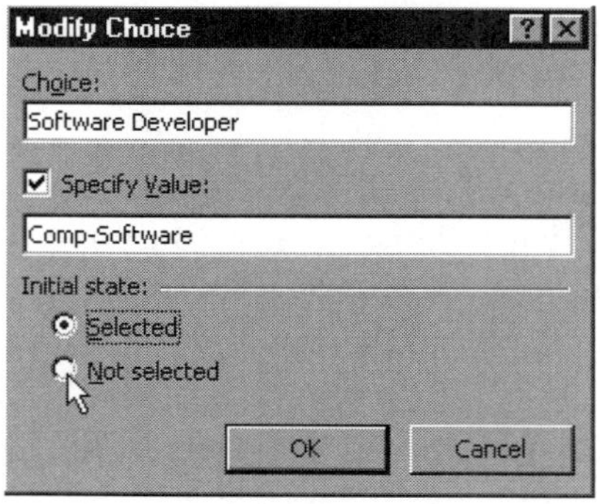

Figure 287.3 The Microsoft FrontPage Modify Choice dialog box.

4. Click your mouse pointer on the Not selected radio button just above the buttons at the bottom of the dialog box.
5. Click the mouse pointer on the OK button near the bottom center of the Modify Choice dialog box.
6. Continue at Step 2 if any other of the values in the Selected column are Yes, otherwise, continue at Step 7.
7. Click the mouse pointer on the OK button near the lower right-hand corner of the Drop-Down Box Properties dialog box.

After you eliminate any default drop-down menu item selections, the Web browser or Web server will be able to determine accurately whether the visitor made at least one selection from the drop-down menu.

UNDERSTANDING HIDDEN FIELDS

While its name and value are included in the form results, a *hidden field* does not appear anywhere on a form—hence the word "hidden" in its name. However, the word "field" in *hidden field* is misleading because it implies that a hidden field can some accept input of one type or another when this is not the case. Rather, adding one or more hidden fields to a form's definition is a way to insert Name/Value pairs into the form results in addition to those produced by the visitor's data entry and selections on a form.

Hidden fields are useful if you are accumulating data from two or more different forms or more than one version of a single form into the same form results file on the Web server. By adding one or more hidden fields to a form, you can insert text (i.e. Name/Value pairs) in the form results file that identifies the source of the form results and/or gives special processing instructions to a custom script you are running on the Web server to process the form.

To add a hidden field to a form, perform the following steps:

1. Open the Web page with the form you want to modify, and select the View menu Page option to display the Web page on the Page view Normal tab.
2. Right-click your mouse pointer anywhere within the border around the form, and select Form Properties from the pop-up menu. FrontPage, in turn, will display the Form Properties dialog box.
3. Click your mouse pointer on the Advanced button near the lower left-hand corner of the dialog box. FrontPage, in turn, will display an Advanced Form Properties dialog box similar to that shown in Figure 288.1.

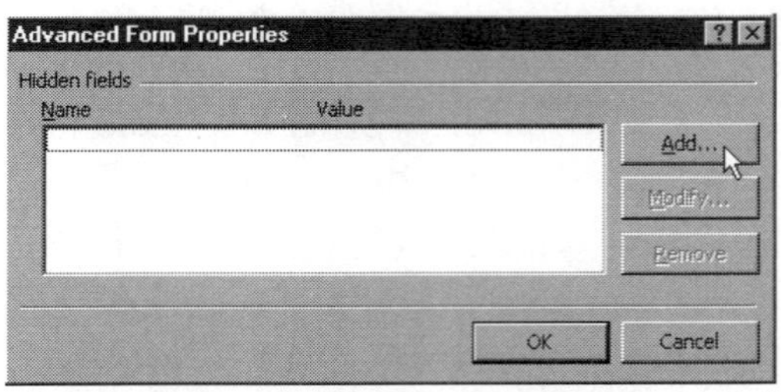

Figure 288.1 The Microsoft FrontPage Advanced Form Properties dialog box.

4. Click your mouse pointer on the ADD button. FrontPage, in turn, will display the Name/Value pair dialog box shown in Figure 288.2.

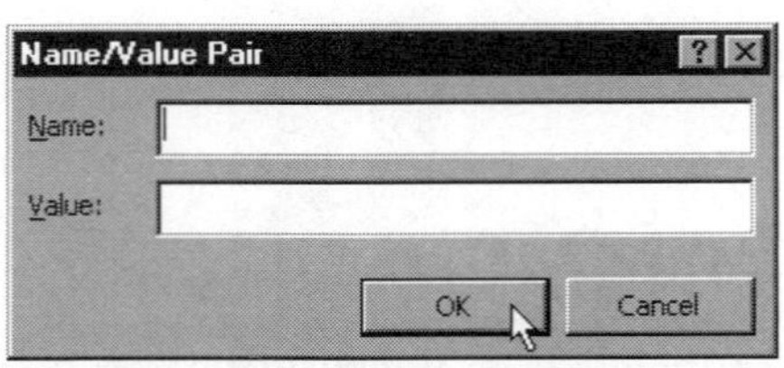

Figure 288.2 The Microsoft FrontPage Name/Value Pair dialog box.

5. Into the Name field, enter a descriptive name for the text string you want the Web browser to send along with the hidden field's data value (which you will enter in the next step). So you can refer to it in the scripting language of your choice, start each name with a letter or underscore (_). Moreover, use only letters, digits, or underscores (_) in the rest of the name. If you want to use more than one word in a name, separate words with an underscore (_) rather than a space.
6. Into the Value field, enter the text string that you want the Web browser to insert in the form results before sending the form to the Web server after the visitor clicks the mouse pointer on the form's SUBMIT button.
7. Click your mouse pointer on the OK button near the bottom center of the Name/Value Pair dialog box. FrontPage, in turn, will add the name (you entered in Step 5) and text string (you entered in Step 6) to the list of hidden fields in the hidden fields list box in on the Advanced Form Properties dialog box.
8. If you have additional Name/Value pairs (hidden fields) you want to add to the form results file, continue at Step 4.
9. If you want to remove a hidden field, click your mouse pointer on the Name or on the Value column in the row with the Name/Value pair you want to remove and then on the REMOVE button. (Repeat this step for each hidden field you want to remove.)
10. If you want to change the name and/or value of a Name/Value pair, click your mouse pointer on the Name or on the Value column of the row with the Name/Value pair you want to change and then on the MODIFY button. After FrontPage displays the Name/Value Pair dialog box, continue at Step 5. (Repeat this Step for each Name/Value pair you want to change.)
11. Click your mouse pointer on the OK button near the lower right-hand corner of the Advanced Form Properties dialog box to return to the Form Properties dialog box.
12. Click your mouse pointer on the OK button near the lower right-hand corner Form Properties dialog box to return to the Page view Normal tab.

After you complete Step 12, you will not see any changes in your form on the Page view Normal tab. However, FrontPage added to the Web page HTML (shown on the Page view HTML tab) an <INPUT> tag with its TYPE attribute set to hidden for each of the hidden fields you added by performing Steps 4 – 7. Moreover, the NAME and VALUE attributes in each of the <INPUT> tags are set to the text you entered into the Name and Value fields in Steps 5 and 6, respectively.

Although the FrontPage places all hidden fields at the end for the form definition (just before the form's closing </FORM> tag), you can use the procedure you learned in a previous Tip titled "Selecting the Form Elements and Other Data You Want to Include in the Form Results" to put the hidden field Name/Value pairs where you want them to appear in the form results. When executing the procedure in the tip, delete the name of the hidden field from its default location near the bottom of the list of fields in the Form fields to save list box on the Save Fields tab of the Saving Results dialog box. Then, insert the hidden field's name where you want the hidden field's Name/Value pair to appear in the form results (relative to the other Name/Value pairs being saved), and press the ENTER key.

Note: *While hidden field Name/Value pairs are not displayed on the form, the visitor can see the hidden fields by telling the Web browser to display Web page source (HTML code) file. Moreover, if you are using the form handler's default confirmation page, the visitor will see the hidden field Name/Value pairs along with the other form results on the confirmation page. Therefore, do not place any confidential or sensitive information in a form's hidden fields.*

ADDING A SUBMIT BUTTON TO A FORM

Whenever you create a new form (either by using the Form Page Wizard or by inserting a form element on a Web page outside the borders around any existing forms), FrontPage inserts a SUBMIT button and a RESET button at the bottom of the form. If you want to add an additional SUBMIT button (so your form has more than one) or if you want to replace a SUBMIT button you previously removed from the form, perform the following steps:

1. Open the Web page with the form you want to modify, and select the View menu Page option to display the Web page on the Page view Normal tab.
2. Click your mouse pointer at the point in the form where you want the SUBMIT button to appear.
3. Select the Insert menu Form option, and click your mouse pointer on Push Button. FrontPage, in turn, will insert a button (labeled Button) at the point on the form where you placed the cursor in Step 2.
4. Right-click your mouse pointer on the button you created in Step 3, and select Form Field Properties from the pop-up menu. FrontPage, in turn, will display a Push Button Properties dialog box similar to that shown in Figure 289.

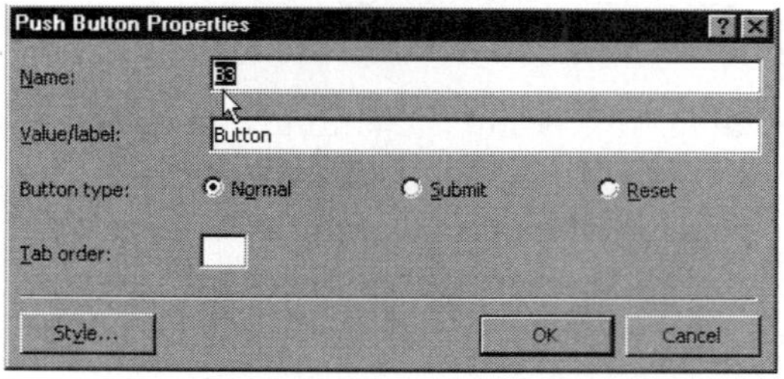

***Figure 289** The Microsoft FrontPage Push Button Properties dialog box.*

5. Into the Name field, enter a descriptive name for the SUBMIT button. So you can refer to it in the scripting language of your choice, start each button name with a letter or underscore (_). Moreover, use only letters, digits, or underscores (_) in the rest of the name. If you want to use more than one word in a name, separate words with an underscore (_) rather than a space.

   If you are planning to insert multiple SUBMIT buttons on the form, give each of them a unique name. The Web browser includes the SUBMIT button's name (and value, which you will enter in the next step) in the form results it sends to the Web server. Therefore, if you give each SUBMIT button on the form a unique name, you can determine which one of them the visitor activated to submit the form data to the Web server by looking at the SUBMIT button's name in the form results file.
6. Into the Value/label field, enter the text you want to appear as the label on the SUBMIT button. Normally, you will enter a value/label such as **Send** or **Transmit** or **Submit** or **Submit Form**. (In addition to placing the text you enter using the Value/label field as the label on top of the SUBMIT button, the Web browsers also sends text to the Web server as the Value portion of a Name/Value pair if the visitor clicks the mouse pointer on the button to submit the form.
7. Click your mouse pointer on the Submit radio button.
8. Click your mouse pointer on the OK button near the lower right-hand corner of the Push Button Properties dialog box.

Normally, you will only place a single SUBMIT button somewhere near the bottom of a form. However, if you have a long form that takes several screens to display and you want let the visitor submit partially completed forms, you might add a SUBMIT button at the bottom of each page onscreen. If you put a SUBMIT button at the bottom of each page, the visitor will not have to scroll all the way to the bottom of the form to submit the data entered and selections made up to that point.

ADDING A RESET BUTTON TO A FORM

As mentioned in the preceding Tip, FrontPage automatically inserts both a RESET button and a SUBMIT button on new forms you create with the Form Page Wizard or by inserting a form element on a Web page outside the borders around any existing forms. If you want to add an additional RESET button (so your form has more than one) or if you want to replace a RESET button you previously removed from the form, perform the following steps:

1. Open the Web page with the form you want to modify, and select the View menu Page option to display the Web page on the Page view Normal tab.
2. Click your mouse pointer at the point in the form where you want the RESET button to appear.
3. Select the Insert menu Form and click your mouse pointer on Push Button. FrontPage, in turn, will insert a button (labeled Button) at the point on the form where you placed the cursor in Step 2.
4. Right-click your mouse pointer on the button you inserted in Step 3, and select Form Field Properties from the pop-up menu. FrontPage, in turn, will display a Push Button Properties dialog box (similar to that shown previously in Figure 289).
5. Into the Value/label field, enter the text you want to appear as the label on the RESET button. Normally, you will enter a label such as **Clear Form** or **Reset** or **Start Over**.
6. Click your mouse pointer on the Reset radio button.
7. Click your mouse pointer on the OK button near the lower right-hand corner of the Push Button Properties dialog box.

When a visitor clicks the mouse pointer on a RESET button, the Web browser will clear text entered and selections made on the form by the visitor. Moreover, the Web browser will reset the value of each textbox and the selected/checked state of each radio button, menu item, and checkbox to the default value you entered in the Initial value field or selected in Initial state section on the element's Properties dialog box. Unfortunately, the Web browser does not move the cursor (to the form's focus) back to the first field on the form when the visitor clicks the mouse pointer on the RESET button.

USING AN IMAGE AS A SUBMIT BUTTON ON A FORM

If you are not satisfied with the standard gray SUBMIT button on a form, you can replace it with a graphics image. Although not required, select a graphics image that makes its purpose on the form obvious, such as a picture finger pressing a button, or perhaps a red button labeled Press Here. After you find the image you want, import it into the IMAGES folder in the current FrontPage Web.

Note: *The Microsoft Design Gallery Live Web site, the Clip Gallery on your computer, and forms that use graphical buttons on other Web sites are all excellent places to search for the graphic image that is just right for your form's submit button. Follow the procedures in previous Tips on graphics to import the graphics image you want into the current FrontPage web. For example, if you want to use a non-copyrighted image from a Web site on the Internet, execute the procedure in a previous Tip titled "Importing a Picture From a Web Site on the Internet Into the Current FrontPage Web" to copy the submit button graphic to the IMAGES folder in the current FrontPage web.*

After you import the graphics image you want into the current FrontPage web, perform the following steps to use the picture as the submit button on a form:

1. Open the Web page with the form you want to modify, and select the View menu Page option to display the Web page on the Page view Normal tab.
2. Click your mouse pointer at the point in the form where you want the graphical submit button to appear.
3. Select the Insert menu Form and click your mouse pointer on Picture. FrontPage, in turn, will display the Picture dialog box.
4. Use the drop-down list button to the right of the Look in field and the folders below the field to navigate to the folder in which you stored the graphics image you want to use as a submit button on the form.
5. Click your mouse pointer on the name of the graphics image you want to use as a submit button and then on the INSERT button near the lower right-hand corner of the Picture dialog box. FrontPage, in turn, will insert the graphics image at the point on the form where you placed the cursor in Step 2.
6. Right-click your mouse pointer on the graphics image you inserted in Step 5, and select Form Field Properties from the pop-up menu. FrontPage, in turn, will display a Picture Properties dialog box similar to that shown in Figure 291.
7. Into the Name field, enter a descriptive name for the graphical submit button. So you can refer to it in the scripting language of your choice, start the name with a letter or underscore (_). Moreover, use only letters, digits, or underscores (_) in the rest of the name. If you want to use more than one word in a name, separate words with an underscore (_) rather than a space.

   If you are planning to insert multiple graphical submit buttons on the form, give each of them a unique name. The Web browser includes the submit button's name in the form results it sends to the Web server. Therefore, if you give each graphical submit button on the form a unique name, you can determine which one of them the visitor activated to submit the form data to the Web server by looking at the submit button's name in the form results file.

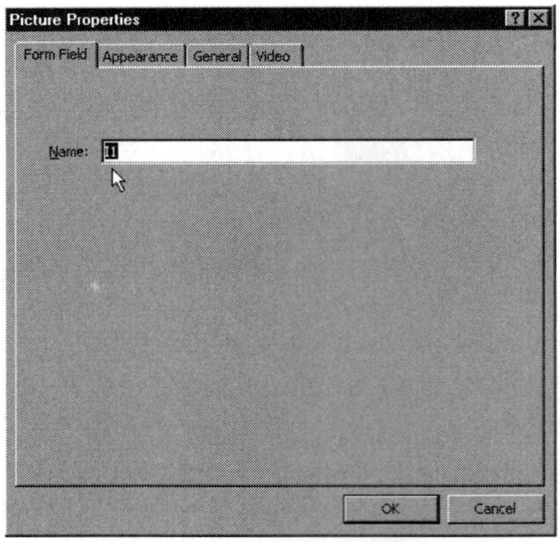

Figure 291 The Form Field tab on the Microsoft FrontPage Picture Properties Push Button Properties dialog box.

Note: *The name you enter in Step 7 will not appear as a label on the submit button, so you will not see the name displayed on the form. Instead, the Web browser uses the name to label the x,y coordinates it sends to the Save Results Wizard for inclusion in the form results file if the visitor clicks the mouse pointer on the graphics submit button. For example, if you enter* ***Submit*** *into the Name field, the Web browser will insert text such as Submit.x,47,Submit.y, 28 to indicate the x,y coordinates in pixels (relative to the upper left-hand corner of the submit button) at which the visitor clicked the mouse pointer to submit the form.*

8. Click your mouse pointer on the OK button near the lower right-hand corner of the Picture Properties dialog box.

Note: *Do not be concerned that your graphic image does not have the same HTML tag or the same Form Field Properties dialog box as does the generic gray SUBMIT button. For although a picture inserted on the form looks the same as a picture used as a submit button, you can tell the difference from the pop-up menu you see when you right-click the mouse pointer on a picture vs. on a picture used as a submit button. When you right-click the mouse pointer on a picture (vs. a graphics submit button), you do not see the Form Field Properties choice on the pop-up menu.*

Also, if you look at the Web page HTML, you will see that a graphics image inserted in a form is inside an <IMG> (image) tag while a graphics submit button uses an <INPUT> tag.

After you insert the graphics image you want to use as a submit button on your form, you may need to re-size it. If you do, click your mouse pointer on the picture to have FrontPage display sizing handles you can then drag outward (away from the center of the picture) to increase the picture's size or inward (toward the center of the picture) to make it smaller. If you decrease the size of the picture, be sure to click the mouse pointer on the Resample button (seventh button from the right) on the Pictures toolbar. (You learned how to use the Resample button to decrease the file size of a graphics image in a previous Tip titled: "Creating a 1-Pixel Transparent GIF."

FrontPage only supports using graphic images as SUBMIT buttons. Therefore, your form's RESET button(s) must remain the generic gray. If you want to use graphics buttons to perform other tasks, you will have to link the graphics you insert on the form to custom scripts (written in a scripting language such as JavaScript, VBScript, Perl, etc.). Unfortunately, learning how to write custom scripts and using them for forms processing is beyond the scope of this book, so check with the Internet Service Provider (ISP) hosting your site if you need help writing scripts.

ADDING A FILE UPLOAD CONTROL TO A FORM

In addition to accepting information through textboxes, radio buttons, and checkboxes, you can also use a form to let visitors upload files to your Web site. Using a file upload control on a form is a convenient alternative to sending and receiving large files as attachments on e-mail messages for several reasons. First, not all Internet service providers (ISP's) allow customers to send and/or receive large file attachments on e-mail messages. Second, some ISP's that do allow large e-mail attachments have a complicated procedure for attaching files or saving attachments received to disk files. Third, and perhaps most importantly, not everyone has a high-speed, unlimited access Internet connection, and the last thing you want to see when you establish a 33.6Kb dial-up connection to your ISP is an e-mail with a 5-megabyte file attached.

To allow visitors to upload files to a folder on your Web site, perform the following steps:

1. Open the Web page with the form to which you wish to add a file upload control (or a page on which you wish to create a new form with a file upload control), and select the View menu Page option to display the Web page on the Page view Normal tab.
2. To add a file upload control to an existing form, position the cursor inside the form at the point where you want the control appear. Conversely, if you want to create a new form and place a file upload control in it, position the cursor on the Web page where you want to

place the new form. As long as you place the cursor outside the borders around any existing forms, FrontPage will put the file upload control on a new form when you complete the next step.

3. Select the Insert menu Form option, and click the mouse pointer on File Upload. FrontPage, in turn, will insert the file upload control as a single-line textbox and a BROWSE button at the cursor location on the form.

After you add the file upload control to the form, you need to create a new folder or select an existing folder in the current FrontPage web to which the file upload control will save the file the visitor wants to send to the Web site. If you already have a file upload folder in the current web, skip the following procedure. Otherwise, create a new folder at the root of the current FrontPage Web by performing the following steps:

1. In the Folder List pane (along the left-hand side of the FrontPage application window), right-click your mouse pointer on the current web's root folder. (If you do not see the Folder List pane in the application window, select the File menu Folder List option to display it, and then right-click the mouse pointer on the current web's root folder in the Folder List pane.)
2. On the pop-up menu displayed when you complete Step 1, select the New option and click your mouse pointer on Folder. FrontPage, in turn, will create a new folder at the root of the current FrontPage web.
3. Type a name for the new folder, and then press the ENTER key. For example, you might type a name such as **Files_Submitted**.

Next, perform the following steps to work with the form's properties to set the form upload control's target folder:

1. Right-click the mouse pointer anywhere within the border around the form with the file upload control, and select Form Properties from the pop-up menu. FrontPage, in turn, will display the Form Properties dialog box.
2. Click the mouse pointer on the OPTIONS button in the lower left-hand corner of the Form Properties dialog box. FrontPage, in turn, will display the Saving Results dialog box.
3. Click your mouse pointer on the File Upload tab to expose the fields shown in Figure 292.1

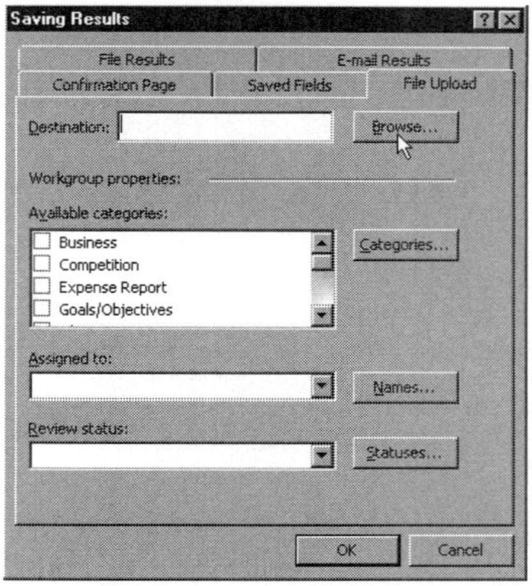

Figure 292.1 The File Upload tab of the Microsoft FrontPage Saving Results dialog box.

4. Click your mouse pointer on the BROWSE button to the right of the Destination field. FrontPage, in turn, will display the Current Web dialog box. Use the drop-down list button to the right of the Look in field and folders in the list box below the field to navigate to the folder with the file upload folder (**Files_Submitted** in the current example).
5. Click your mouse pointer on the file upload (target) folder and then on the OK button near the lower right-hand corner of the Current Web dialog box. FrontPage, in turn, will return to the Saving Results dialog box and copy the folder name (you selected in Step 4) followed by a forward slash (/) to the Destination field on the File Upload tab.
6. Click your mouse pointer on the OK button near the lower right-hand corner of the Saving Results dialog box. FrontPage, in turn, will return to the Form Properties dialog box.
7. Click the mouse pointer on the OK button near the lower right-hand corner of the Form Properties dialog box to return to the Page view Normal tab.
8. To adjust the size of the textbox into which the visitor enters the name of the file to upload, double-click your mouse pointer on the textbox to the left of the file upload control's BROWSE button. (Alternatively, right-click your mouse pointer on the textbox and select Form Field Properties from the pop-up menu.)

As the final step before publishing the form with the file upload control to the Web server, perform the steps in the following procedure to set the control's properties:

1. Double-click the mouse pointer on the file upload control's textbox. Alternatively, right-click the mouse pointer on the textbox, and select Form Field Properties from the pop-up menu. FrontPage, in turn, will display a File Upload Properties dialog box similar to that shown in Figure 292.2.

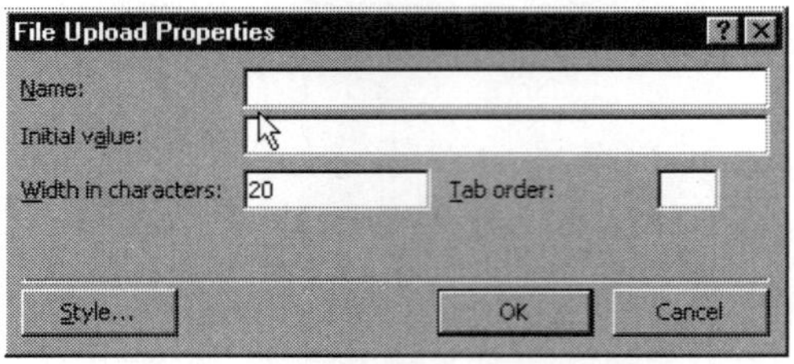

***Figure 292.2** The Microsoft FrontPage File Upload Properties dialog box.*

2. Into the Name field, enter a descriptive name for the file upload control's textbox. While not displayed on the form, the Web browser includes the name in the form results, and the Save Results component includes it on the default confirmation page. So you can refer to it in the scripting language of your choice, start each name with a letter or an underscore (_). Moreover, use only letters, digits, or underscores (_) in the rest of the name. If you want to use more than one word in a name, separate words with an underscore (_) rather than a space. For example, you might enter a name such as **File_Submitted** into the Name field.
3. If the files visitors submit start with the same text or end with the same extension, into the Initial value field, enter the text normally found in filenames visitors upload. If there is no common text, then leave the Initial value field blank.
4. Into the Width in characters field, enter the number of characters you want displayed in the textbox at one time. Try to set the textbox width to the number of characters most often entered by visitors when specifying the full pathname of the files they want to upload to the target folder on the Web site.
5. Click your mouse pointer on the OK button near the bottom center of the File Upload Properties dialog box.

Next, save the Web page with the upload control to disk, and then publish it to the Web server. Remember, the upload control, like other FrontPage forms, will only function properly if your ISP has installed FrontPage Server Extensions on the Web server.

When you publish a form with an upload control to a Web server, FrontPage will create the target (file upload) folder if it does not exist. If you created a new folder (vs. selecting an existing folder as the file upload control's target folder), perform the following steps to work with the new folder's properties on the Web server:

1. Select the File menu Open Web option. FrontPage, in turn, will display the Open Web dialog box.
2. Into the Web name field at the bottom of the dialog box, enter your site's .com address and subweb name if applicable. For example, if you were working with the ONEPAGE subweb on NVBIZNET2.COM, you would enter **HTTP://NVBizNet2.com/OnePage** into the Web name field.
3. Click your mouse pointer on the OK button near the lower right-hand corner of the Open Web dialog box. FrontPage, in turn, will connect to the Web server and prompt you to enter your username and password on the server if you are not already logged in.
4. In the Folder List pane along the left-hand side of the dialog box, right-click the mouse pointer on the file upload (target) folder. (If you do not see the Folder List pane, select the View menu Folder List option to display it, and then right-click the mouse pointer on the target folder.) Then, select Properties from the pop-up menu. FrontPage, in turn, will display an upload folder properties dialog box similar to that shown in Figure 292.3.

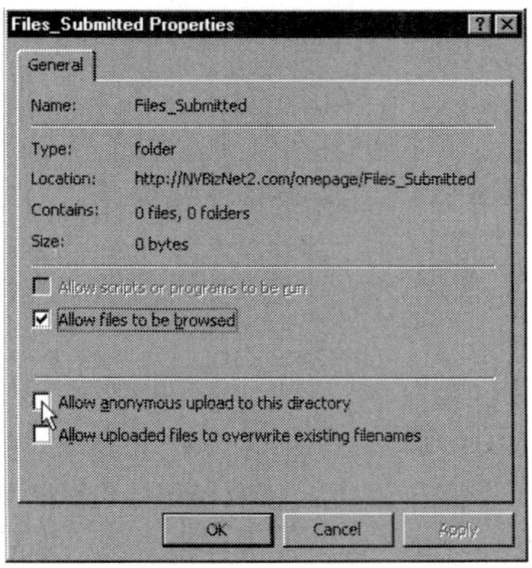

Figure 292.3 A folder properties dialog box.

5. Click your mouse pointer on the Allow anonymous upload to this directory checkbox until a checkmark appears.
6. If you want to let visitors overwrite an existing file with the same name as the file they are uploading, click your mouse pointer on the Allow uploaded files to overwrite existing filenames checkbox until a checkmark appears. Otherwise, clear the checkbox to allow site visitors to upload only files with filenames not already present in the upload folder.
7. Click your mouse pointer on the OK button near the bottom center of the dialog box.

After you complete Step 7, startup your Web browser and test your form on the Web server. If the ISP has installed FrontPage Server Extensions and you still have difficulty uploading files to the Web server, check with the ISP for additional privileges the ISP may need to assign to the Web server to allow file uploads.

USING LABELS TO ALLOW A VISITOR TO NAVIGATE TO FORM ELEMENTS

In a previous Tip titled "Placing Text in Front of or After a Form Element," you learned how to place text labels next to elements on a form. Text labels are especially important when the form includes textboxes, checkboxes, and radio buttons. Without a label, the visitor will not be able to distinguish one radio button or checkbox from another. Similarly, a text label tells the visitor what to enter a textboxes on a form.

When you type text on a form, the label is only "visually" linked to the form element next to, above, or below it. If you want to let visitors use the underlined letter or number in a label as a keyboard shortcut, you must associate the descriptive text with a form element by making it a part of the form element's HTML.

To let visitors navigate from one textbox to another or to select checkboxes and radio buttons by holding down the ALT key and pressing the underlined letter in the label, perform the following steps:

1. Open the Web page with the form you want to modify, and select the View menu Page option to display the Web page on the Page view Normal tab.

2. Use your mouse pointer to select both the descriptive text and the form element with which you want to associate the text.
3. Select the Insert menu Form option, and click your mouse pointer on Label.

Note: *If the form element you want to label is in a table, the descriptive text you want to use as its label must be in the same cell. If you select text in one cell and a form element in another, or if you do not select both text and a form element before selecting the Insert menu Form option and clicking the mouse pointer on Label, FrontPage will display the warning message box shown in Figure 293.*

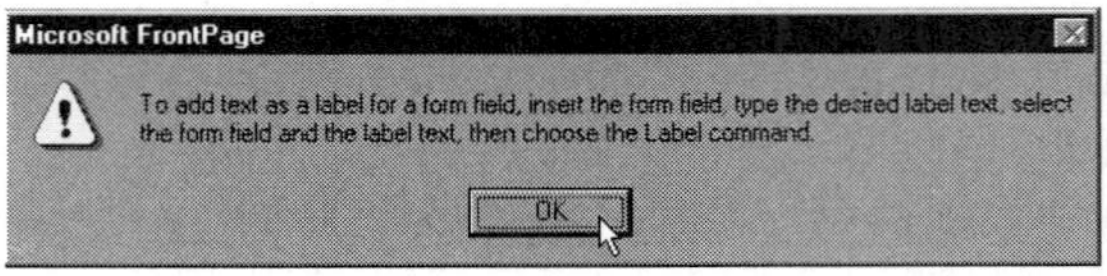

Figure 293 *The Microsoft FrontPage Failed to Select Text and Element for Label message box.*

If you see the message box, click your mouse pointer on its OK button and try your selection again. If the problem is that the text and form element are not in the same table cell, move both to the same cell before repeating Steps 2 – 3.

4. To designate the label's shortcut letter or number, use your mouse pointer or keyboard to select one of the letters or numbers in the label's text and press CTRL+U on your keyboard.
5. Repeat Steps 2 – 4 for each label you want to associate with an element on the form.

After you complete Step 5, save the updated form to disk and then publish it to the Web server. Bear in mind that many Web browsers do not support keyboard shortcuts on form elements. For example, while Internet Explorer supports the shortcuts, Netscape Navigator (through version 4.7) does not.

USING A GROUP BOX TO LABEL A GROUP OF ELEMENTS ON A FORM

When you want to draw a labeled box around a group of elements on a form, such as that around the Software Products in the form shown in Figure 294.1, insert the elements into a Group Box.

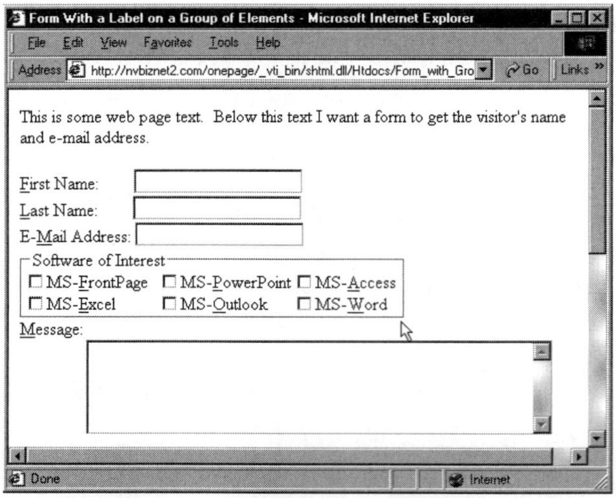

Figure 294.1 A Web page with a group of elements enclosed in a Group Box.

The easiest way to "draw" a labeled box around a group of elements on a form is to insert the Group Box on the form first and then insert form elements in the box. (If the form elements you want to "group" are already on the form, insert the Group Box, and then drag-and-drop the form elements you want into the group box.)

To insert a Group Box on a form, perform the following steps:

1. Open the Web page with the form to which you wish to add a Group Box (or a page on which you wish to create a new form with a Group Box), and select the View menu Page option to display the Web page on the Page view Normal tab.
2. To add a Group Box an existing form, position the cursor inside the form at the point where you want the box to appear. Conversely, if you want to create a new form and place Group Box in it, position the cursor on the Web page where you want to place the new form. As long as you place the cursor outside the borders around any existing forms, FrontPage will put the Group Box on a new form when you complete the next step.
3. Select the Insert menu Form option, and click the mouse pointer on Group Box. FrontPage, in turn, will insert a Group Box at the cursor location on the form.

After you insert it on the form, insert into the Group Box container the form elements you want to group together visually. As is the case when you want to position elements at specific locations on a form, to position form elements in a Group Box precisely, insert a table (with a zero width border) in the Group Box, and then insert the form elements in the table's cells.

To change the text of the Group Box label (from the default Group box), perform the following steps:

1. Right-click your mouse pointer anywhere with the Group Box, and select Group Box Properties from the pop-up menu. FrontPage, in turn, will display a Group Box Properties dialog box similar to that shown in Figure 294.2.

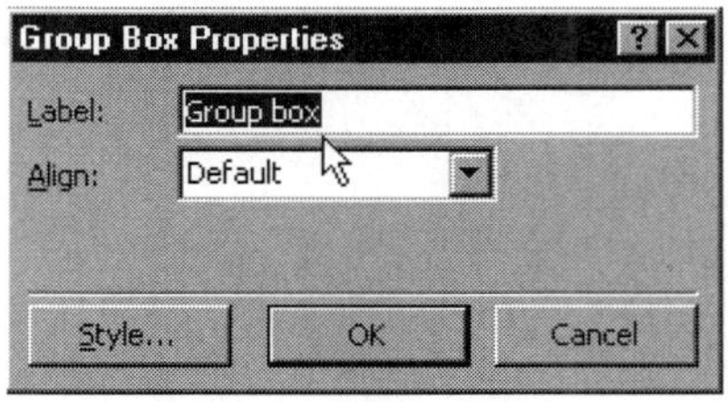

Figure 294.2 The Microsoft FrontPage Group Box Properties dialog box.

2. Into the Label field, enter the label you want displayed on the Group Box.
3. Click your mouse pointer on the drop-down list button to the right of the Align field, and select the location of the text label from the drop-down list. Select Default or Left to place the Group Box label in the upper left-hand corner of the Group Box; select Right to place the label in the upper right-hand corner of the Group Box; or select Center to center the text label along the top of the Group Box.
4. Click your mouse pointer on the OK button at the bottom center of the Group Box Properties dialog box.

When you insert a Group Box in a form, FrontPage draws the box such that it spans the width of the Web page. If you want a Group Box that is narrower than the width of the Web Page, place the Group Box inside a table cell that has the width you want.

USING FRAMES TO DISPLAY FORM RESULTS

By default, a Web browser replaces the form displayed in its application window with a confirmation page that shows the form results after the visitor submits the form by clicking the mouse pointer on the form's SUBMIT button. However, if your Web site uses frames (and the visitor's Web browser supports them), you can keep the form onscreen by displaying the form results in a frame other than the one with the form.

To select a frame in which to display form results, perform the following steps:

1. Open the frames page for the frameset that includes the Web page with the form, and select the View menu Page option to display the Web pages in the frameset on the Page view Normal tab.
2. Right-click your mouse pointer anywhere with in the border around the form, and select Form Properties from the pop-up menu. FrontPage, in turn, will display a Form Properties dialog box similar to that shown in Figure 295.1.

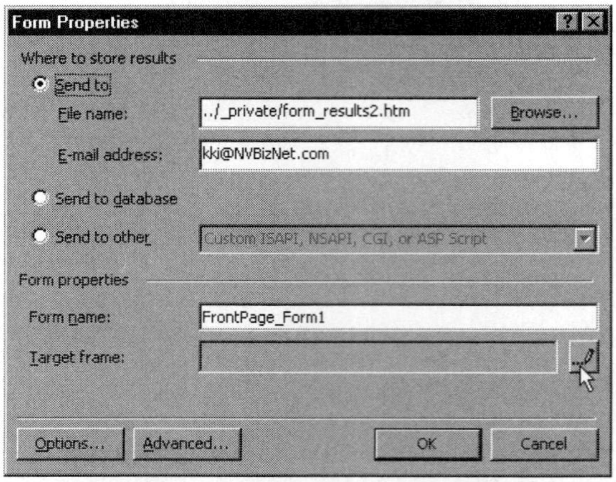

Figure 295.1 The Microsoft FrontPage Form Properties dialog box.

3. Click your mouse pointer on the browse button to the right of the Target frame field. FrontPage, in turn, will display a Target Frame dialog box similar to that shown in Figure 295.2.

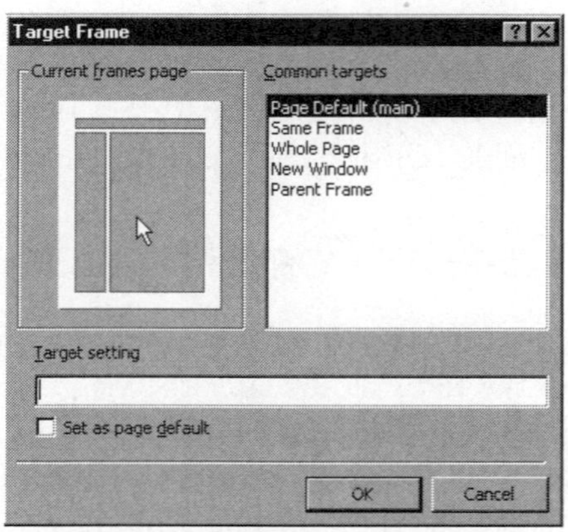

Figure 295.2 The Microsoft FrontPage Target Frame dialog box.

4. Click your mouse pointer on the frame in which you want the Web browser to display form results in the Current frames page section in the upper left-hand corner of the dialog box. Alternatively, click the mouse pointer on one of the targets listed in the Common targets list box on the right-hand side of the dialog box. For example, if you want the Web browser to display the form results (the confirmation page) in a new application window, click your mouse pointer on New Window in the Common targets list box.
5. Click your mouse pointer on the OK button near the lower right-hand corner of the Target Frame dialog box
6. Click your mouse pointer on the OK button near the lower right-hand corner of the Form Properties box.

Displaying form results in a frame other than the one with the form is often used to display search form results—with the form used to specify the search parameters in one frame and the results of the search displayed in another frame. Similarly, if you have visitors fill in a multi-line textbox for a guestbook, you might display the guestbook's updated contents as the form results in a second frame.

PLACING A BANNER ON A WEB PAGE

As you surf the Web you will undoubtedly see horizontal banners across the top and/or vertical banners along the side(s) of the Web pages at many of the Web sites you visit. Banners on Web pages serve the same function as billboards on interstate highways and busy streets around town. However, unlike billboards whose advertisements remain unchanged during the billboard's rental period, the graphics images on billboard-like Web page banners typically change every few seconds. Although sometimes a nuisance (like commercials on television) banner advertisements are designed to defray the cost of development and the ongoing cost of keeping Web sites "open for business" without having to charge visitors to use the site's services.

If you find sponsors that want to place banner ads on your Web page(s), FrontPage lets you add a rotating banner ad (a banner with graphics images that change automatically) to a Web page by performing the following steps:

1. Open the Web page on which you wish to insert a banner ad, and select the View menu Page option to display the Web page on the Page view Normal tab.
2. Place the cursor where you want the banner ad to appear on the Web page. Then, select the Insert menu Web Component option. FrontPage,

in turn, will display an Insert Web Component dialog box similar to that shown in Figure 296.1.

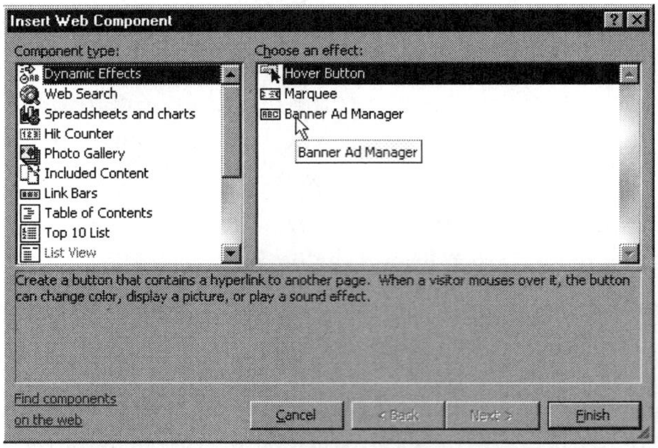

Figure 296.1 The Microsoft FrontPage Insert Web Component dialog box.

3. In the Component type list box, click your mouse pointer on Dynamic Effects. Then, click your mouse pointer on Banner Ad Manager in the Choose an effect list box.
4. Click your mouse pointer on the FINISH button in the lower right-hand corner of the Insert Web Component dialog box. FrontPage, in turn, will display the Banner Ad Manager Properties dialog box shown in Figure 296.2.

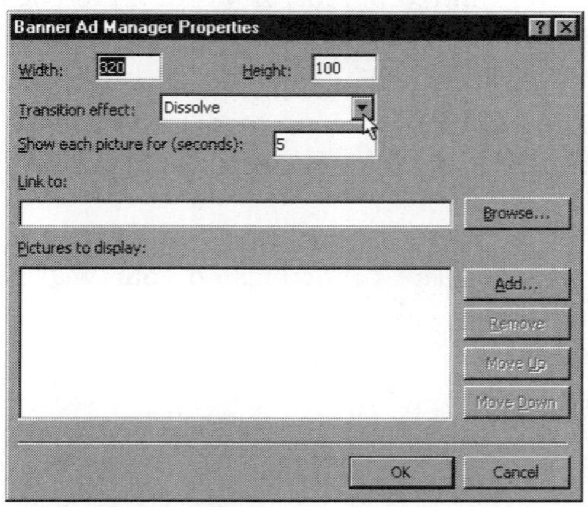

Figure 296.2 The Microsoft FrontPage Banner Ad Manager Properties dialog box.

5. Into the Height and Width fields, enter the height and with of the graphics images you want displayed in the banner ad on your Web page.

Note: *The graphics images you use for the banner ads must all have the same dimensions. If a graphics image is larger than the rectangular area you specify in Step 5, the Web browsers will only display the portion of the graphics image that fits into the banner ad's display area. Conversely, if the image is too small, the Web browser will display the banner ad's gray background in the portion of the banner ad's rectangular area not taken up by the picture displayed.*

Typical banner ad dimensions are 468 pixels by 60 pixels when displaying a banner ad horizontally across the top of a Web page, and 220 pixels by 50 pixels when displaying a vertically oriented banner add.

6. Click your mouse pointer on the drop-down list button to the right of the Transition effect field and select the visual effects you want FrontPage to use when changing graphics images in the banner. The possible effects are:
    - **None** – no visual effect, just display the next graphics image.
    - **Blinds Horizontal** – display portions of the next graphics image on horizontal rectangular strips that widen until they completely fill the banner add display area with the new graphics image.
    - **Blinds Vertical** – display portions of the next graphics image on vertical rectangular strips that widen until they completely fill the banner add display with the new graphics image.
    - **Dissolve** – the current graphics image dissolves (gets blurry) and then "clears up" to reveal another graphics image.
    - **Box In** – the Web browsers appears to draw the next graphics image inward (toward the center) from the four sides of the border around the banner ad.
    - **Box Out** – the Web browsers appears to draw the next graphics image outward (toward the four sides of the border around the banner ad) from its center.
7. Into the Show each picture for (seconds) field, enter the number of seconds that you want the Web browser to display each graphics image onscreen.
8. If you want to display another Web page when the visitor clicks the mouse pointer on the banner into the Link to field enter the URL (the Web address) of the Web page to display.

Note: *Even if you rotate through ads from several different sponsors, you can only let the site visitor click through to a single Web page—regardless of which ad is on display when the visitor clicks the mouse pointer on the banner.*

9. To add a graphics image to the banner ad rotation, click your mouse pointer on the Add button to the right of the Pictures to display list box. FrontPage, in turn, will display the Add Picture for Banner Ad dialog box.
10. Use the drop-down button to the right of the Look in field and the folders below the field to navigate to the folder in which the banner ad graphics image is stored.
11. Click your mouse pointer on the graphics image you want displayed as one of the images in the banner ad and then on the OPEN button near the bottom right-hand corner of the Add Picture for Banner Ad dialog box.
12. FrontPage, in turn, will return to the Banner Ad Manager Properties dialog box and add relative address of the graphics image you selected in Step 11 to the list of graphics images you previously added to the banner ad rotation in the Pictures to display list box.
13. If you want to remove a graphics image from the rotation, click your mouse pointer on the relative address of the graphics image you want to remove from the Pictures to display list box and then on the REMOVE button to the right of the list box.
14. If you want to change the order in which the Web browser displays graphics images in the banner ad, click your mouse pointer on one of the relative addresses in the Pictures to display list box. Then click the mouse pointer on the MOVE UP button to display the picture earlier in the banner ad rotation or on the MOVE DOWN button to display the picture later. Repeat this step as often as necessary (selecting a different graphics image each time, of course) until you have arranged the graphics images to appear in the order you want them to appear in the banner ad rotation.
15. If you want to add additional graphics images to the rotation, continue at Step 9.
16. Click your mouse pointer on the OK button near the lower right-hand corner of the Banner Ad Manager Properties dialog box. FrontPage, in turn, will return to the Page view Normal tab and display the first graphics image of the banner ad rotation in a rectangular area (whose dimensions you specified in Step 5) at the location where you placed the cursor in Step 2.

FrontPage adds to the Web page HTML code for a Java applet that maps out a rectangular area within which to display the graphics images listed in the applet's definition in the Web browser's application window. To run the applet (and watch the rotation of the graphics images in the banner ad), you need to publish the Web page with the banner add to the Web server and then use your Web browser to retrieve and display the page from the Web server.

If you want to change the banner ad's properties (after you have had a chance to see it in operation), return to the FrontPage application window. Then, right-click your mouse pointer anywhere on the banner ad on the Page view Normal tab and select Banner Ad Manager Properties from the pop-up menu. Then, continue at Step 5 in the preceding procedure.

ADDING A HIT COUNTER TO A WEB PAGE

A *hit counter* is an odometer-like row of numbers on a Web page that shows the number of times Web browsers have requested the page from the Web server. Each time a Web browser requests a Web page that has a hit counter on it, the Web server's hit counter component registers the page view (or *hit*) by incrementing the hit counter's value. Given that most visitors access your site's Web pages through its homepage, placing a hit counter on the homepage will give you an idea as to the number of visitors that have found your site and lets you display the visitor count for all to see.

Note: *A hit counter does not give you a unique visitor count. It only tells you the number of times Web browsers have retrieved a particular Web page. For example, if one person visits the same Web page five times, the Web server will have increased the value of the hit counter on the page by five (and not by 1). Similarly, each time a site visitor tells the Web browser to refresh (or reload) a Web page, the Web server increments the hit counter's value before sending the page to the Web browser for display.*

To add a hit counter to a Web page, perform the following steps:

1. Open the Web page on which you wish to insert a hit counter, and select the View menu Page option to display the Web page on the Page view Normal tab.
2. Place the cursor where you want the hit counter to appear on the Web page. Then, select the Insert menu Web Component option. FrontPage, in turn, will display an Insert Web Component dialog box (similar to that shown previously in Figure 296.1).
3. In the Component type list box, click your mouse pointer on Hit Counter.
4. Click your mouse pointer on the FINISH button in the lower right-hand corner of the Insert Web Component dialog box. FrontPage, in turn, will display the Hit Counter Properties dialog box shown in Figure 297.

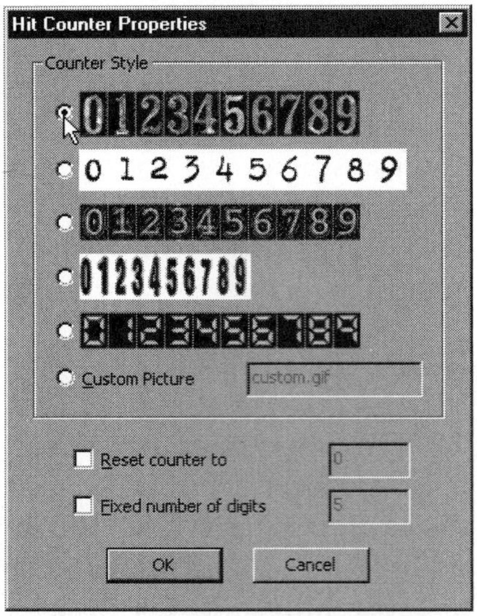

Figure 297 *The Microsoft FrontPage Hit Counter Properties dialog box.*

5. Click the mouse pointer on the radio button next to the hit counter graphics style you want to display on your Web page.
6. To set the hit counter's starting value, click the mouse pointer on the Reset counter to checkbox, and enter the starting value in the field to the right of the label that follows the checkbox.
7. If you want the hit counter to always have at least a certain number of digits, click your mouse pointer on the Fixed number of digits checkbox until a checkmark appears. Then, enter the number of digits into the field to the right of the checkbox. If you clear the checkbox, the Web browser will display the hit counter using the number of digits necessary to display the number of hits. For example, if you use your mouse pointer to click a checkmark into the Fixed number of digits checkbox and enter a **5** into the field following the checkbox, the Web browser will display a hit count of 25 using five digits as 00025. Conversely, if you clear the checkbox, the Web browser will display the same hit count using two digits as 25.
8. Click your mouse pointer on the OK button near the lower left-hand corner of the Hit Counter Properties dialog box.

After you complete Step 8, FrontPage will return to the Page view Normal tab and display a placeholder for the hit counter as [**Hit Counter**] at the location on Web page where you placed the cursor in Step 2. To see the actual hit counter graphic (with the page view/hit count), you must save the Web page with the hit counter to disk and publish it to the Web server. Then, start your Web browser and retrieve the Web page from the Web server. When the Web server receives the Web page request from the Web browser, the Web server increments the hit counter that the Web browser, in turn, will display on the Web page in place of the [**Hit Counter**] placeholder you saw on the Page view Normal tab.

If you later want to change the hit counter graphic, reset the counter, or change its minimum number of digits, double-click the mouse pointer on the hit counter's placeholder ([**Hit Counter**]). (Alternatively, you can right-click the mouse pointer on the placeholder and select FrontPage Component Properties from the pop-up menu.) FrontPage, in turn, will display the Hit Counter Properties dialog box, so you can work with the hit counter's properties by performing Steps 5 – 8 of the procedure in this Tip.

Hit counters, while popular, are not very useful for compiling the site traffic information advertisers want to know when determining the amount to pay for placing banner ads on your Web site. Commercial sponsors are generally interested in the number of unique visitors a Web page receive, vs. its total page views. Still, hit counters are a "fun" feature you can add to a Web page for bragging rights or to get a feel for how often Web browsers retrieve a particular Web page on your site.

CREATING A CUSTOM HIT COUNTER GRAPHIC

If you do not want to use one of the five hit counter graphics supplied with FrontPage, you can create your own hit counter using the graphics editor of your choice to generate a GIF file that contains the numbers 0 through 9. The numbers in the hit counter graphic can be either "text" (such as those in the first image in Figure 298), or "graphics" (such as those shown in the second image the Figure).

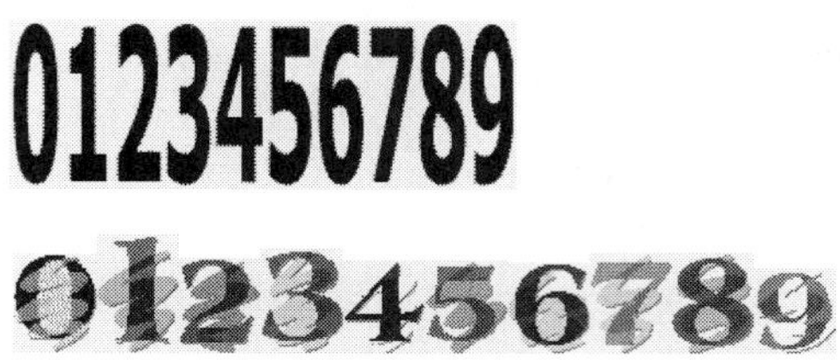

Figure 298 Two examples of hit counter graphics.

In fact, you can use any ten graphics images you want to compose the hit counter's "number" in the GIF file. The only restriction is that each of the numbers in the hit counter graphic must take up 10% of the graphic's width. In other words, each of the digits in the counter must be the same width.

After you create a hit counter graphic and save it to a folder (such as IMAGES) in the current FrontPage web (or import a graphic hit counter from the Internet), perform the following steps to use the new graphics image as the hit counter on a Web page:

1. Open the Web page on which you wish to insert a hit counter, and select the View menu Page option to display the Web page on the Page view Normal tab.
2. Place the cursor where you want the hit counter to appear on the Web page. Then, select the Insert menu Web Component option. FrontPage, in turn, will display an Insert Web Component dialog box (similar to that shown previously in Figure 296.1).
3. In the Component type list box, click your mouse pointer on Hit Counter.
4. Click your mouse pointer on the FINISH button in the lower right-hand corner of the Insert Web Component dialog box. FrontPage, in turn, will display the Hit Counter Properties dialog box (shown previously in Figure 297).
5. Click the mouse pointer on the Custom Picture radio button, and enter the pathname of the hit counter graphics file relative to the root of the FrontPage web. For example, if you want to use the GIF file HITCOUNTER.GIF that you previously stored the IMAGES subfolder in the current Web's root folder, enter **IMAGES/HITCOUNTER.GIF** into the field to the right of the Custom Picture radio button.
6. To set the hit counter's starting value, click the mouse pointer on the Reset counter to checkbox and enter the starting value in the field to the right of the label that follows the checkbox.
7. If you want the hit counter to always have at least a specific number of digits, click your mouse pointer on the Fixed number of digits checkbox until a checkmark appears. Then, enter the number of digits into the field to the right of the label after the checkbox. If you leave the checkbox blank, the Web browser will display the hit counter using the number of digits necessary to display the number of hits. For example, if you use your mouse pointer to click a checkmark into the Fixed number of digits checkbox and enter a **5** into the field following the checkbox label, the Web browser will display a hit count of 25 using five digits as "00025". Conversely, if you clear the checkbox, the Web browser will display the same hit count using two digits as 25.
8. Click your mouse pointer on the OK button near the lower left-hand corner of the Hit Counter Properties dialog box.

After you complete Step 8, FrontPage will return to the Page view Normal tab and display a placeholder for the hit counter as [**Hit Counter**] at the location on Web page where you placed the cursor in Step 2. To see the actual hit counter graphic (with the page view/hit count), you must save the Web page with the hit counter to disk and publish it to the Web server. Then, start your Web browser and retrieve the Web page from the Web server. When the Web server receives the Web page request from the Web browser, the Web server increments the hit counter that the Web browser, in turn, will display on the Web page in place of the [**Hit Counter**] placeholder you saw on the Page view Normal tab.

The most important things to remember when creating custom hit counter graphics are to:

- place ten equal width digits in a single GIF file. (Remember each digit can be either an actual number you type by pressing a numeric key on your keyboard or a graphics image that represents a number.)
- arrange the digits in the hit counter GIF file in ascending order (0 through 9) from left to right.
- when enter the pathname of the hit counter graphics file, make sure to specify it relative to the root of the current FrontPage web and NOT relative to the document on which you insert the hit counter.

If you later want to change the hit counter graphic, reset the counter, or change its minimum number of digits, double-click the mouse pointer on the hit counter's placeholder ([**Hit Counter**]). (Alternatively, you can right-click the mouse pointer on the hit counter placeholder, and select FrontPage Component Properties from the pop-up menu.) FrontPage, in turn, will display the Hit Counter Properties dialog box, and you can work with the hit counter's properties by performing Steps 5 – 8 of the procedure in this Tip or Steps 5 – 8 of the procedure in the preceding Tip.

USING A RECTANGULAR HOVER BUTTON TO CREATE A MOUSEOVER EFFECT

Clicking the mouse pointer on a hover button activates its hyperlink just like clicking the mouse pointer on hyperlinked text or an image map activates the hyperlink anchored to those Web page objects. However, unlike image maps and hyperlinked text, a hover button changes color or perhaps displays a graphics image when the visitor passes the mouse pointer over the button. In other words, a hover button is an animated hyperlink, and the Web browser "plays the animation" whenever the site visitor moves the mouse pointer over the button.

By default, FrontPage creates hover buttons as rectangular boxes that change color when the mouse pointer moves over them (hence, the term *mouseover effect*). However, as you will learn in the next Tip, you can use the FrontPage Hover Button component to convert any graphics image into a hover button. Moreover, if you want to go beyond using a color change as the mouseover effect, you can specify a second graphic that is to appear and/or a sound file to be played when the site visitor moves the mouse pointer over a hover button.

To create a rectangular hover button, perform the following steps:

1. Open the Web page on which you wish to insert a hover button, and select the View menu Page option to display the Web page on the Page view Normal tab.
2. Place the cursor where you want the hover button to appear on the Web page. Then, select the Insert menu Web Component option. FrontPage, in turn, will display an Insert Web Component dialog box (similar to that shown previously in Figure 296.1).
3. In the Component type list box, click your mouse pointer on Dynamic Effects.
4. In the Chose an effect list box, click your mouse pointer on Hover Button.
5. Click your mouse pointer on the FINISH button in the lower right-hand corner of the Insert Web Component dialog box. FrontPage, in turn, will display the Hover Button Properties dialog box shown in Figure 299.1.

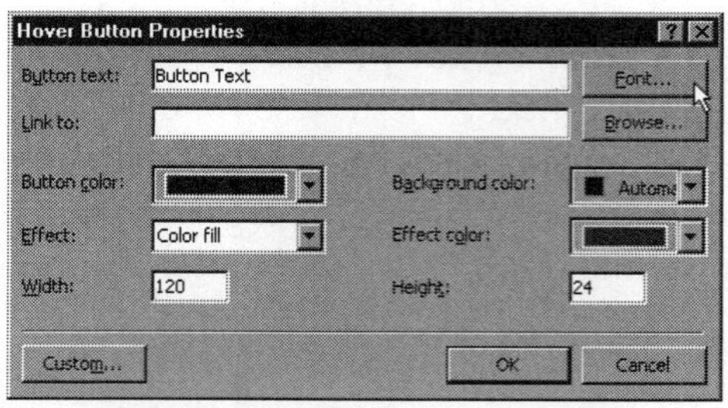

Figure 299.1 The Microsoft FrontPage Hover Button Properties dialog box.

6. Replace the default text (Button Text) FrontPage places in the Button text field with the text you want to appear as the label on top of the hover button. The text label should describe the action the Web browser will take when the visitor clicks the mouse pointer on the hover button to activate its hyperlink. For example, if you are using the hover button as part of a menu to display Web pages on your Web site, you might enter **FAQ** into the Button text field if clicking the mouse pointer on the hover button tells the Web browser to display the site's Frequently Asked Questions page.
7. If you want to change the font, font style, size, and/or color of the label on the hover button, click your mouse pointer on the Font button to the right of the Button text field. FrontPage, in turn, will display the Font dialog box you can use to change the appearance of the label on the hover button. After you use the Font dialog box to make

the adjustments you want to the button's text label, click the mouse pointer on the OK button near the bottom center of the dialog box to return to the Hover Button Properties dialog box.

8. Into the Link to field, enter the relative address of the file or Web page the Web browser is to retrieve when the visitor clicks the mouse pointer on the hover button. Alternatively, you can use the BROWSE button to the right of the Link to field to navigate to, and select the file or Web page you want to hyperlink to the hover button.
9. Set color in the Button color field to the color you want the hover button to be while the mouse pointer is not hovering over the button. To select the button's normal color, click your mouse pointer on the drop-down list button to the right of the Button color field. Then, click the mouse pointer on one of the color swatches on the drop-down pallet displayed, or use the More Colors option at the bottom of the pallet to create and select a custom color. If you select Automatic, the hover button will be the same color as the background color of the Web page or table cell on which you inserted the hover button (the hover button will be "invisible" until the mouse pointer passes over it, at which time the *mouseover effect* will appear).
10. Click your mouse pointer on the drop-down list button to the right of the Effect field and select the mouseover effect you want from the drop-down list. The mouseover effects available on the drop-down list are:
    - **Color fill** – replace the button color you selected in Step 9 with the Effect color you will select in Step 11.
    - **Color average** – replace the button color you selected in Step 9 with the average of the red, green, blue (RGB) components of the button color you selected in Step 9 and the Effect color you will select in Step 11.
    - **Glow** – replace the color in the center of the button with the Effect color you will select in Step 11 while the left and right edges of the button remain the button color you selected in Step 9.
    - **Reverse glow** – replace the color of the left and right edges of the button with the Effect color you will select in Step 11 while the center of the button remains the color you selected in Step 9.
    - **Light glow** – replace the color in the center of the button with a "washed out," lighter tint of the button color you selected in Step 9 while the color of the left and right edges of the button remains unchanged.

- **Bevel out** – lighten the top and left edges of the button while darkening the button's bottom and right edges, and move the button's label slightly up and to the left.
- **Bevel in** – darken the top and left edges of the button while lightening the button's bottom and right edges, and move the button's label slightly down and to the right.

11. Set color in the Effect color field to the color you want the Web browser to use for the hover button's mouseover effect (which you selected in Step 10). To select the color of the "mouseover" effect, click your mouse pointer on the drop-down list button to the right of the Effect color field. Then, click the mouse pointer on one of the color swatches on the drop-down pallet displayed, or use the More Colors option at the bottom of the pallet to create and select a custom color..
12. Into the Width and Height fields, enter the button's width and height in terms of pixels.
13. If you want to play a sound file when the visitor moves the mouse pointer over the hover button and/or clicks the mouse pointer on the button, continue at Step 13. Otherwise, continue at Step 16.
14. Click your mouse pointer on the CUSTOM button near the lower left-hand corner of the Hover Button Properties dialog box. FrontPage, in turn, will display a Custom dialog box similar to that shown in Figure 299.2.

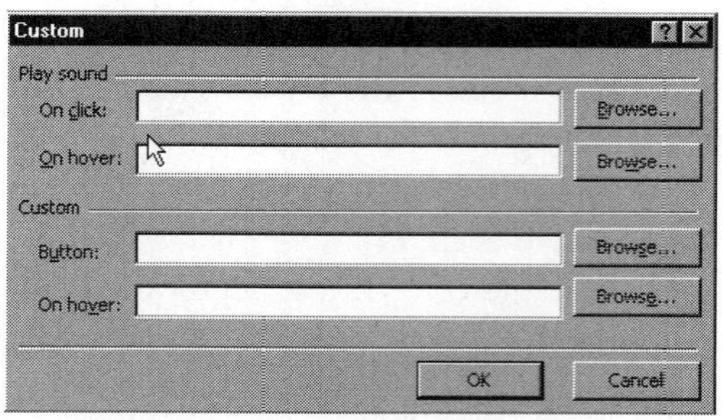

Figure 299.2 The Microsoft FrontPage Custom dialog box.

15. If you want to play a sound file when the visitor clicks the mouse pointer on the hover button, into the On click field, enter the relative address of the sound file you want to play. Otherwise, clear the On click field.

16. If you want to play a sound file when the visitor moves the mouse pointer over the hover button, into the On hover field, enter the relative address of the sound file you want to play. Otherwise, clear the On hover field.
17. Click your mouse pointer on the OK button near the lower right-hand corner of the Custom dialog box.
18. Click your mouse pointer on the OK button near the lower right-hand corner of the Hover Button Properties dialog box.

After you complete Step 18, FrontPage will add a Java applet to the Web page HTML. Although the hover button you insert is visible on the Page view Normal tab, you must preview the Web page in a Web browser that supports Java to see the full effects of the hover button.

USING A GRAPHICS HOVER BUTTON TO CREATE A MOUSEOVER EFFECT

In the preceding Tip, you learned how to create a rectangular hover button. As you now know, a *hover button* is an animated hyperlink that changes its appearance when the mouse pointer hovers over it. Moreover, the hover button reverts to its initial look when the mouse pointer moves on to hover over another object on the Web page or its background.

For rectangular hover buttons, the mouseover effect (the animation started by moving the mouse pointer over a hover button) is normally a change in the button's background color. However, you can have a graphics image replace the rectangular hover button instead of just changing its color as a mouseover effect. Actually, you do not have to start with a rectangular hover button at all. Instead, you can use a graphics image as a hover button and then have one graphics image replace another as the hover button's mouseover effect.

To use a graphics image as a hover button, perform the following steps:

1. Open the Web page on which you wish to insert the graphics hover button, and select the View menu Page option to display the Web page on the Page view Normal tab.
2. Place the cursor where you want the hover button's graphics image to appear on the Web page. Then, select the Insert menu Web Component option. FrontPage, in turn, will display an Insert Web Component dialog box (similar to that shown previously in Figure 296.1).
3. In the Component type list box, click your mouse pointer on Dynamic Effects.

4. In the Choose an effect list box, click your mouse pointer on Hover Button.
5. Click your mouse pointer on the FINISH button in the lower right-hand corner of the Insert Web Component dialog box. FrontPage, in turn, will display the Hover Button Properties dialog box (shown previously in Figure 299.1).
6. Replace the default text (Button Text) FrontPage placed in the Button text field with the text you want to appear as the label on top of the graphics image you plan to use as a hover button.

   If the graphics image is self-explanatory as to its function, clear the Button text field to display the hover button as a graphics image with a text label written on it. Then, continue at Step 8.

   Conversely, if the graphics image, like the rectangular hover button, requires an explanation as to its function, into the Button text field, enter the text you want to appear across the center of the graphics image. The text label should describe the action the Web browser will take when the visitor clicks the mouse pointer on the graphics hover button. For example, if you are using the graphics hover button as part of a menu to display Web pages on your Web site, you might enter: **FAQ** into the Button text field if clicking the mouse pointer on graphics image tells the Web browser to display the site's Frequently Asked Questions Web page.
7. If you want to change the font, font style, size, and/or color of the label on the graphics image you are using as a hover button, click your mouse pointer on the Font button to the right of the Button text field. FrontPage, in turn, will display the Font dialog box you can use to change the appearance of the label on the button's graphics image. After you use the Font dialog box to make the adjustments you want to the button's text label, click the mouse pointer on the OK button near the bottom center of the dialog box to return to the Hover Button Properties dialog box.
8. Into the Link to field, enter the relative address of the file or Web page the Web browser is to retrieve when the visitor clicks the mouse pointer on the graphics hover button. Alternatively, you can use the BROWSE button to the right of the Link to field to navigate to and select the file or Web page you want to hyperlink to the graphics image.
9. Set color in the Background color field to the color you want to use as the color of the background behind the graphics image on the hover button. Unless the graphics image that you plan to use is smaller than dimensions of the hover button (which you will specify in the next

step), you will not see the background color because the picture will cover the entire hover button. Select Automatic as the Background color, so the graphics image will appear without a color border along its right-hand side and bottom if the picture is smaller than the size of the hover button.

10. Into the Height and Width fields, enter the dimensions of the graphics hover button in pixels.

Note: *When using a picture as a hover button, make sure the hover button's initial graphics image and the one you want displayed as a mouseover effect fit into the rectangle defined by pixel height and width you enter in this step. If the graphics image is larger than the hover button's dimensions, the Web browser will only display the portion of the graphics image that fits within the hover button's borders. Conversely, if the graphics image is much smaller than the hover button, the Web browser will display the background color you selected in Step 9 to the right and blow the graphics image.*

11. Click your mouse pointer on the CUSTOM button near the lower left-hand corner of the Hover Button Properties dialog box. FrontPage, in turn, will display a Custom dialog box (similar to that shown previously in Figure 299.2).
12. If you want to play a sound file when the visitor clicks the mouse pointer on the graphics hover button, into the On click field, enter the relative address of the sound file you want to play. Otherwise, clear the On click field.
13. If you want to play a sound file when the visitor moves the mouse pointer over the graphics hover button into the On hover field, enter the relative address of the sound file you want to play. Otherwise, clear the On hover field.
14. Into the Button field, enter the relative address of the graphics image you want displayed as the hover button when the mouse pointer is not "hovering" over the button.
15. Into the On hover field, enter the relative address of the graphics image you want displayed as the mouseover effect when the visitor moves the mouse pointer over the graphics hover button.
16. Click your mouse pointer on the OK button near the lower right-hand corner of the Custom dialog box.
17. Click your mouse pointer on the OK button near the lower right-hand corner of the Hover Button Properties dialog box.

After you complete Step 17, FrontPage will add a Java applet to the Web page HTML. Although the graphics image you select as the hover button in Step 14 is visible on the Page view Normal tab, you must preview the Web page in a Web browser that supports Java to see the full effects of the hover button (including the switch of graphics images when you place the mouse pointer over the graphics hover button).

Using the Substitution Component to Update Text on Multiple Web pages

If you find yourself typing the same text on several of your site's Web pages, consider using the substitution component instead. Although using the substitution component is no easier than typing the text initially, if you later have to change the information, the substitution component lets you make the change once, then let FrontPage propagate the updated text throughout the site's Web pages.

For example, if you show the names and e-mail address of key employees at the bottom of each Web page, changing the contact information as employees are replaced becomes tedious (and time consuming) if you have make the same change on many pages, one page at a time. However, if you use substitution components to place employee names and e-mail address the site's Web pages, you only need to make a change to the employee name and/or e-mail address once, and the substitution component will replicate the change throughout the Web site's pages.

The substitution component works its magic with Web page text by replacing named *web parameters* with their values. As installed, FrontPage has four predefined, named web parameters that it maintains:

- **Author** – the username of the person that created the Web page.
- **Description** – text entered into the Comments scroll box on the Summary tab of the Web page's Properties dialog box. (To access the Description in the Comments scroll box, right-click the mouse pointer on the Web page filename in the Folder List pane, select Properties from the pop-up menu, and then click the mouse pointer on the Summary tab.)
- **Modified By** – the username of the person that last updated the Web page.
- **Page URL** – the Uniform Resource Locator (URL), the Web address from which the Web browser loaded the Web page.

To add additional web parameters you can use to place text on the site's Web pages, perform the following steps:

1. Select the Tools menu Web Settings option. FrontPage, in turn, will display the Web settings dialog box.
2. Click your mouse pointer on the Parameters tab to expose the web parameters list box and buttons shown in Figure 301.1.

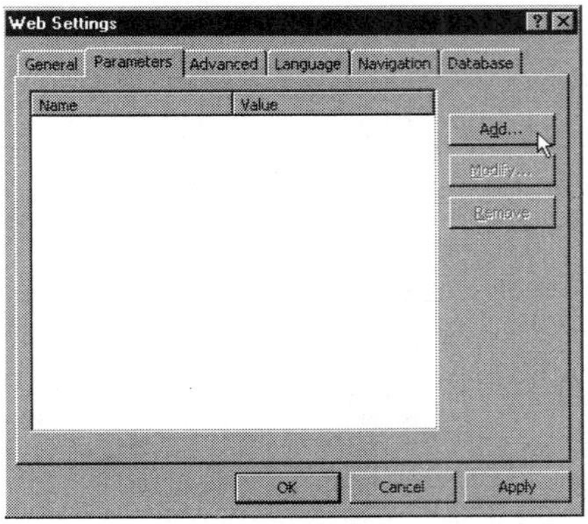

Figure 301.1 The Parameters tab of the Microsoft FrontPage Web Settings dialog box.

3. To add a new named web parameter, click your mouse pointer on the Add button near the upper right-hand corner of the Parameters tab. FrontPage, in turn, will display the Add Name and Value dialog box shown in Figure 301.2.

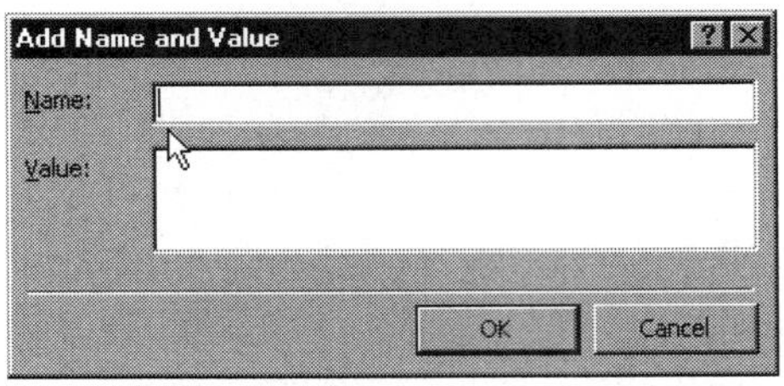

Figure 301.2 The Microsoft FrontPage Add Name and Value dialog box.

4. Into the Name field, enter the web parameters name. For example, if you want to display the marketing department manager's name on several Web pages, you might enter **Marketing Manager** into the Name field.
5. Into the Value field, enter the text you want to display each time you insert the web parameter with the name you entered in Step 4 on a Web page. For example, to substitute the actual marketing department manager's name for the Marketing Manager web parameter,

you would enter the manager's name such as **Konrad King** into the Value field.

6. Click your mouse pointer on the OK button near the lower right-hand corner of the dialog box. FrontPage, in turn, will add the web parameter name and value to the other web parameter names and values shown in the list box on the parameters tab.
7. If you want to remove a web parameter, click your mouse pointer on the web parameter's name or on its value and then on the REMOVE button.
8. To change a web parameter's name and/or its value, click your mouse pointer on the name or value of the web parameter you want to change and then on the MODIFY button. After FrontPage displays the web parameter's current name and value in the Modify Name and Value dialog box, continue at Step 4.
9. Repeat Steps 4 – 6 for each web parameter name and value you want to use on Web pages in the current FrontPage web, and then click your mouse pointer on the OK button near the bottom center of the Web Settings dialog box.

After you execute the preceding procedure to create web parameters, you can use the substitution component to display a web parameter's value on your Web pages by performing the following steps:

1. Open the Web page on which you wish to insert the web parameter text (the web parameter's value), and select the View menu Page option to display the Web page on the Page view Normal tab.
2. Place the cursor where you want the text to appear on the Web page. Then, select the Insert menu Web Component option. FrontPage, in turn, will display an Insert Web Component dialog box (similar to that shown previously in Figure 296.1).
3. In the Component type list box, click your mouse pointer on Included Content.
4. In the Choose a type of content list box, click your mouse pointer on Substitution.
5. Click your mouse pointer on the FINISH button in the lower right-hand corner of the Insert Web Component dialog box. FrontPage, in turn, will display the Substitution Properties dialog box shown in Figure 301.3.

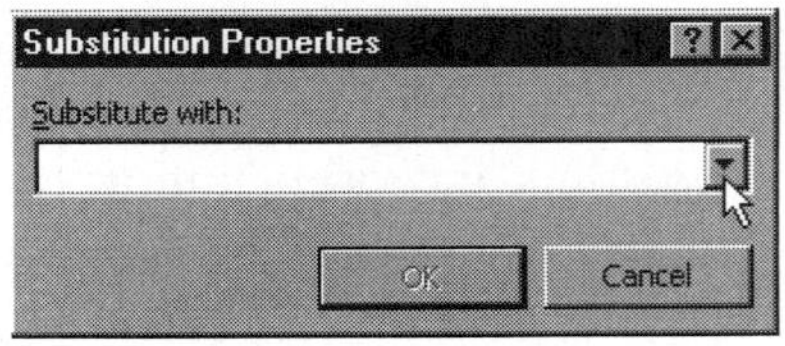

Figure 301.3 The Microsoft FrontPage Substitution Properties dialog box.

6. Click your mouse pointer on the drop-down list button to the right of the Substitute with field, and select the name web parameter whose value you want displayed on the Web page where you placed the cursor in Step 2. For example, to display the marketing department manager's name (which you added as a Web parameter in this Tip's first procedure) on the Web page, select **Marketing Manager** from the drop-down list.
7. Click your mouse pointer on the OK button near the bottom center of the Substitution Properties dialog box. FrontPage, in turn, will return to the Page view Normal tab and display the value of the web parameter you selected in Step 6 on the Web page.

By inserting substitution components that display web parameter values on the site's Web pages, you can use the Tools menu Web Settings option to change a web parameter value once and have the change reflected automatically on all the Web pages that display the web parameter's value. For example, if your company hires a new marketing department manager named Sally Fields, you can update all Web pages on the Web site to reflect the change by executing the first procedure in this Tip one time. Instead of adding a new web parameter in Step 3, change the web parameter's value by clicking the mouse pointer on **Marketing Manager** and then on the MODIFY button. In Step 5, enter the new web parameter's value (the name of the new marketing manger) **Sally Fields**, into the Value field.

After you publish the FrontPage web to the Web server, Web pages, on which you used the substitution component to display the value of the Marketing Manager web parameter, will display the name of the new marketing department manager.

ADDING A SEARCH FORM TO ALLOW VISITORS TO SEARCH YOUR WEB SITE

By inserting a web search component on a Web page within the current FrontPage web, you can provide your Web site visitors a convenient way to search the site's pages for content of interest. After entering a keyword or phrase into the search form's textbox, the visitor can click the mouse pointer on the form's START SEARCH button, to display a list of the site's Web pages on which the keyword or phrase appears. Moreover, each of the Web page titles listed on the search results page is actually a hyperlink the visitor can activate to retrieve and display the associated Web page with the keyword or search phrase.

To insert a search form on a Web page, perform the following steps:

1. Open the Web page on which you wish to insert the search form, and select the View menu Page option to display the Web page on the Page view Normal tab.
2. Place the cursor where you want the search form to appear on the Web page. Then, select the Insert menu Web Component option. FrontPage, in turn, will display an Insert Web Component dialog box (similar to that shown previously in Figure 296.1).
3. In the Component type list box, click your mouse pointer on Web Search.
4. In the Choose a type of search list box, click your mouse pointer on Current Web.
5. Click your mouse pointer on the FINISH button in the lower right-hand corner of the Insert Web Component dialog box. FrontPage, in turn, will display the Search Form Properties dialog box shown in Figure 302.1.

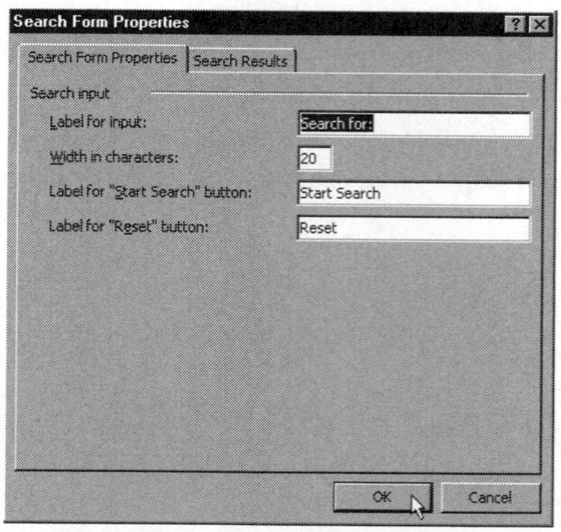

Figure 302.1 The Search Form Properties tab of the Microsoft FrontPage Search Form Properties dialog box.

6. Click your mouse pointer on the OK button near the lower right-hand corner of the Search Form Properties dialog box to accept FrontPage default values for the search page setup.

After you complete Step 6, FrontPage will add a search form similar to that shown in Figure 302.2 on the Web page where you placed the cursor in Step 2.

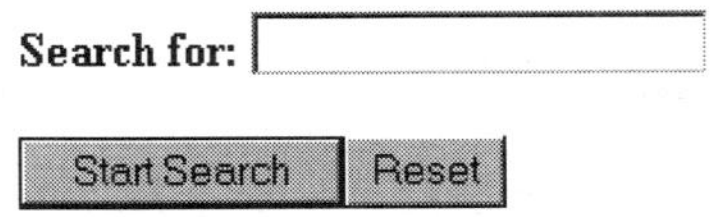

Figure 302.2 The basic/default search form.

If you inserted the search form on a Web page with other content, you need only publish the Web page with the search form to the Web server. Conversely, if you inserted the search form on a new Web page, then either before and/or after the form, add text that explains the scope of the search (that this is a search of the current Web site only) and give examples of keywords to enter into the form's Search for textbox.

After entering the keyword or text string for which to search into the search form's Search for textbox, the visitor will click the mouse pointer on the Start Search button in the lower left-hand corner of the form. The Web browser, in turn, submits the form results [i.e. the keyword(s) in the Search for textbox] to the Web server for processing. The Web server, in turn, passes the form results on to a text search component of the FrontPage Server Extensions. The text search component searches a FrontPage maintained text index on the Web server and returns the search results on a Web page similar to that shown in Figure 302.3.

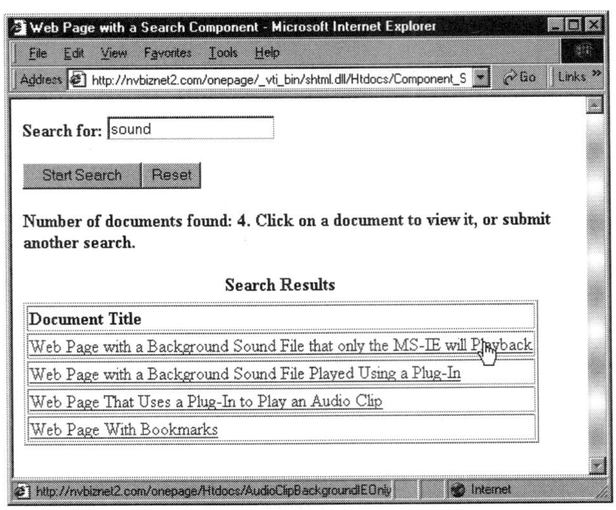

Figure 302.3 A Web page with a search form and a set of Search Results.

The site visitor can click the mouse pointer any of the Web page titles in the Search Results table displayed immediately after the search form on the Web page to display the content on a Web page returned by the search component.

USING AN INCLUDE PAGE TO DISPLAY STANDARD HEADERS, FOOTERS, AND MENUS

In a previous Tip titled "Using the Substitution Component to Update Text on Multiple Web Pages," you learned how to create web parameters whose values the FrontPage substitution component would display on Web pages throughout the Web site. Unfortunately, the process of creating and inserting web parameters can become quite tedious when you have a lot of data items you want to display on several of your site's pages. After all, you must create a web parameter/value pair for each data item, and then you must insert a substitution component for each of the web parameter values you want to display. Moreover, the substitution component cannot handle graphics images (such as a company logo or banner you want you to place on each of the Web site's pages). (Web parameter values are text only.)

Fortunately, the include page component lets you insert the content of one Web page on another. By placing a banner graphic, a menu, or a footer on a Web page by itself and then using the include page component to insert the Web page on other Web pages, you can display graphics images and many lines of text content on multiple Web pages quickly and easily. Moreover, if you change the content on an "included" Web page, the include page component will update the content on all of the Web pages that display the page.

To use the include page component to insert one Web page in another, perform the following steps:

1. Open the Web page on which you wish to insert another page, and select the View menu Page option to display the Web page on the Page view Normal tab.
2. Place the cursor at the location in the Web page where you want the inserted page content to appear. Then, select the Insert menu Web Component option. FrontPage, in turn, will display an Insert Web Component dialog box (similar to that shown previously in Figure 296.1).
3. In the Component type list box, click your mouse pointer on Included Content.
4. In the Choose a type of content list box, click your mouse pointer on Page.
5. Click your mouse pointer on the FINISH button in the lower right-hand corner of the Insert Web Component dialog box. FrontPage, in turn, will display the Include Page Properties dialog box shown in Figure 303.

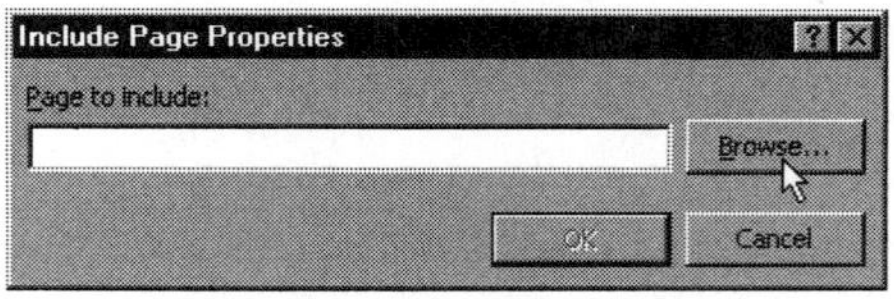

Figure 303 The Microsoft FrontPage Include Page Properties dialog box.

6. Into the Page to include field, enter the relative address of the Web page whose content you want to insert at the cursor location in the current page. Alternatively, click your mouse pointer on the BROWSE button to the right of the Page to include field and use the Current Web dialog box to search for and select the Web page to insert.
7. Click your mouse pointer on the OK button near the lower right-hand corner of the Include Page Properties dialog box.

After you complete Step 7, FrontPage will return to the Page view Normal tab and display the content on the Web page you told the include page component to insert on the current Web Page in Step 6. If you have additional Web pages whose content you want to insert on the current page, repeat Steps 2 – 7 of the procedure. Remember, you can use page layout tables (i.e. tables with zero width borders) to position objects where you want them to appear on the Web page—this includes include page components that display the content from other Web pages.

Note: *In the preceding Tip, you learned how to create a search form that lets site visitors search the text in the Web site's pages based on a keyword or phrase. Since, the Web pages you include in other pages are normally just fragments of information not meant to be displayed independent of the Web pages that include them, you need to hide the included Web pages from the Web server's text search component. If you do not, the text search component will present hyperlinks to the included Web pages along with hyperlinks to the site's regular Web pages on the search results page.*

To prevent the text search component from searching the text on included Web pages, put the included page files in the site's _PRIVATE folder. FrontPage does not index the text in files stored in the _PRIVATE folder or for that matter, in any folder whose name starts with an underscore (_). As a result, the text search component, which searches only the site's text index for the names of Web pages that include the keyword or phrases entered in the search form's Search for field, will not find any of the included Web pages—because their names will never exist within the text index.

When you need to change the content on a Web page you have included in other Web pages, open the included Web page on the Page view Normal tab and make the changes you want. After you save the page and re-publish the site to the Web server, the updated information will appear on the site's Web pages that include the Web page you changed.

Although you cannot directly edit the content of the included page on the Web page in which you used the include page component to insert it, you can use the included content as a shortcut to opening the inserted page. To open the included Web page on the Page view Normal tab, simply right-click your mouse pointer on the included content and select the Open Page in New Window from the pop-up menu.

Note: *FrontPage actually updates the included content whenever it recalculates the site's hyperlinks—which it does each time you publish the Web site to the Web server. If you want to recalculate the site's hyperlinks (thereby refreshing included content on the site's Web pages) without publishing the site to the Web server, select the Tools menu Recalculate Hyperlinks option.*

SCHEDULING INCLUDE PAGES TO APPEAR WITHIN A CERTAIN DATE RANGE AND TIME PERIOD

The scheduled include page component, like the include page component that you learned about in the preceding Tip, lets you insert the contents of one Web page on another web page. However, the scheduled include page component also lets you specify the time period during which the included page content is to appear. Therefore, the scheduled include page component provides a convenient way to display a different Welcome message on the Web page based on the time of day. You can also use the component to display news of an upcoming event or a customer special, and then have the notice disappear from the Web page after the event or the offer's expiration date.

To use the scheduled include page component to insert one Web page in another within a specific time period and date range, perform the following steps:

1. Open the Web page on which you wish to insert another page, and select the View menu Page option to display the Web page on the Page view Normal tab.
2. Place the cursor at the location in the Web page where you want the inserted page content to appear. Then, select the Insert menu Web Component option. FrontPage, in turn, will display an Insert Web Component dialog box (similar to that shown previously in Figure 296.1).
3. In the Component type list box, click your mouse pointer on Included Content.
4. In the Choose a type of content list box, click your mouse pointer on Page Based on Schedule.
5. Click your mouse pointer on the FINISH button in the lower right-hand corner of the Insert Web Component dialog box. FrontPage, in turn, will display the Scheduled Include Page Properties dialog box shown in Figure 304.

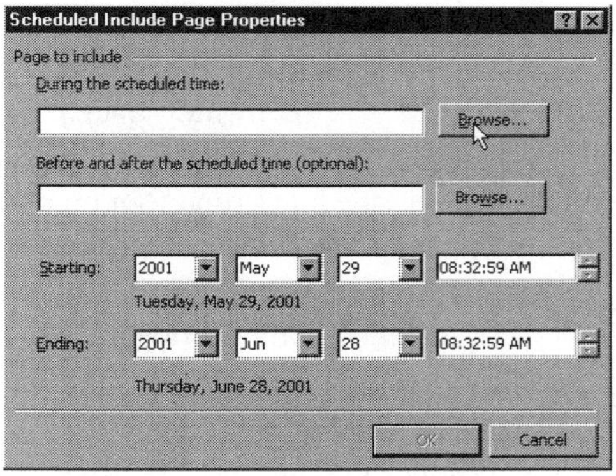

Figure 304 *The Microsoft FrontPage Scheduled Include Page Properties dialog box.*

6. Into the During the scheduled time field, enter the relative address of the Web page whose content you want to insert at the cursor location in the current page during the date range or time period you will specify in Steps 8 - 9. Alternatively, click your mouse pointer on the BROWSE button to the right of the field, and use the Current Web dialog box to search for and select the Web page to insert.
7. Into the Before and after the scheduled time (optional) field, enter the relative address of the Web page whose content you want inserted at the cursor location of the current page when the scheduled include page component is not inserted into the Web page specified in Step 6. Alternatively, click your mouse pointer on the BROWSE button to the right of the field and use the Current Web dialog box to search for and select the Web page to insert.

Note: *If you just want the included content to go away after the specific time period, leave the Before and after the scheduled time (optional) field blank. Conversely, if you insert the scheduled include page component in a table cell and the absence of content in the cell leaves a blank spot in the middle of your Web page, be sure to supply an alternate Web page the scheduled include page component can use to fill in the gap at the expiration of the time period.*

8. Into the Starting fields, enter the year, month, day, and time at which you want the scheduled include page component insert into the Web page specified in Step 6 in the Web page you opened in Step 1. [If you entered the relative address of a Web page into the Before and after the scheduled time (optional) field in Step 7, the scheduled include page component will insert that page at the cursor location in the current Web page if you enter a future date and time.] To display the included content immediately, enter a date in the past.

9. Into the Ending fields, enter the year, month, day, and time after which you no longer want the scheduled include page component inserted into the Web page specified in Step 6 in the Web page you opened in Step 1. [If you entered the relative address of a Web page into the Before and after the scheduled time (optional) field in Step 7, the scheduled include page component will insert that page at the cursor location in the current Web page if you enter a date and time in the past.] To display the included content indefinitely, enter a date far into the future.
10. Click your mouse pointer on the OK button near the lower right-hand corner of the Scheduled Include Page Properties dialog box.

After you complete Step 10, FrontPage will return to the Page view Normal tab and display the content you told the scheduled include page component to insert on the current Web Page in Step 6—in accordance with the date and time you specified in Steps 8 – 9. If the current date and time is outside the period specified in Steps 8 - 9, FrontPage will display the content of the Web page you specified in Step 7, or if you left the alternate Web page blank, FrontPage will display [**Scheduled Include Page**] or [**Expired Scheduled Include Page**] on the Page view Normal tab instead. (The placeholder text will only be visible on the Page view Normal tab and not displayed by a Web browser that retrieves the Web page with the future or expired scheduled include page.)

Unfortunately, there is a slight (or perhaps major) glitch in the way in which FrontPage handles the scheduled include page component. Because the scheduled included page component only updates its content when you recalculate the web's hyperlinks, the included content will not appear or disappear according to the schedule unless you recalculate the FrontPage web's hyperlinks on a daily basis. Therefore, in order for the scheduled include page component to function properly, you must either update and publish (to the Web server) a Web page with hyperlinks each day or use FrontPage to open the web **on the Web server** and then use the Tool menu Recalculate Hyperlinks to recalculate hyperlinks on the Web on a daily basis.

SCHEDULING A GRAPHICS IMAGE TO APPEAR WITHIN A CERTAIN DATE RANGE AND TIME PERIOD

Like the scheduled include page component that you learned about in the preceding Tip, the scheduled picture component lets you insert content on a Web page for a specific period of time. However, while the scheduled include page component lets you insert an entire Web page, the scheduled picture component only lets you insert a graphics image on the target page.

You can use the scheduled picture component to do such things as tag new additions to your Web site or to the company's product list by placing a small picture emblazoned with the word **NEW** next to the new item. Of course, a new product or Web site feature (by definition) cannot be new forever. As such, the scheduled picture component provides a convenient way to make those new tags disappear after a week or two. Similarly, if you like to dress up your company logo or banner for the holidays, you can use the scheduled picture component to display a holiday logo or banner during the holidays, and the normal, holiday-neutral logo or banner during the rest of the year.

To use the scheduled picture component to insert an image on a Web page for a specific period of time, perform the following steps:

1. Open the Web page on which you wish to insert the graphics image, and select the View menu Page option to display the Web page on the Page view Normal tab.
2. Place the cursor at the location in the Web page where you want the picture to appear. Then, select the Insert menu Web Component option. FrontPage, in turn, will display an Insert Web Component dialog box (similar to that shown previously in Figure 296.1).
3. In the Component type list box, click your mouse pointer on Included Content.
4. In the Choose a type of content list box, click your mouse pointer on Picture Based on Schedule.
5. Click your mouse pointer on the FINISH button in the lower right-hand corner of the Insert Web Component dialog box. FrontPage, in turn, will display the Scheduled Picture Properties dialog box shown in Figure 305.

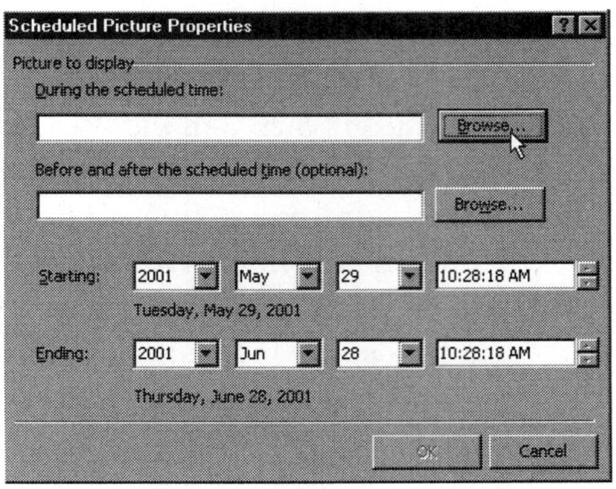

Figure 305 The Microsoft FrontPage Scheduled Picture Properties dialog box.

6. Into the During the scheduled time field, enter the relative address of the graphics image you want displayed at the cursor location in the current page during the date range or time period you will specify in Steps 8 - 9. Alternatively, click your mouse pointer on the BROWSE button to the right of the field and use the Picture dialog box to search for and select the graphics image to insert.
7. Into the Before and after the scheduled time (optional) field, enter the relative address of the picture want to display at the cursor location in the current page when the scheduled picture component no longer inserts the graphics image specified in Step 6. Alternatively, click your mouse pointer on the BROWSE button to the right of the field and use the Picture dialog box to search for and select the graphics image to insert.

Note: *If you just want the graphics image to disappear after the specified time period, leave the Before and after the scheduled time (optional) field blank. Conversely, if you insert the scheduled picture component in a table cell and the absence of the picture in the cell will leave a blank spot in the middle of your Web page, be sure to supply an alternate graphics image to display so the scheduled picture component can use it to fill in the gap at the expiration of the time period.*

8. Into the Starting fields, enter the year, month, day, and time at which you want the scheduled picture component to insert the graphics image you specified in Step 6 in the Web page you opened in Step 1. [If you entered the relative address of a graphics image into the Before and after the scheduled time (optional) field in Step 7, the scheduled picture component will insert that graphics image at the cursor location in the current Web page if you enter a future date and time.] To display the graphics image immediately, enter a date in the past.
9. Into the Ending fields, enter the year, month, day, and time after which you no longer want the scheduled picture component to insert the graphics image you specified in Step 6 in the Web page you opened in Step 1. [If you entered the relative address of a graphics image into the Before and after the scheduled time (optional) field in Step 7, the scheduled picture component will insert that picture at the cursor location in the current Web page if you enter a date and time in the past.] To display the graphics image indefinitely, enter a date far into the future.
10. Click your mouse pointer on the OK button near the lower right-hand corner of the Scheduled Include Page Properties dialog box.

After you complete Step 10, FrontPage will return to the Page view Normal tab and display the graphics image you told the scheduled picture component to insert on the current Web Page in Step 6—unless the current date and time is outside (i.e., before or after) the period specified in Steps 8 – 9. If the current date and time is outside the period specified in Steps 8 - 9, FrontPage will display the graphics image you specified in Step 7, or if you left the alternate picture field blank, FrontPage will display [**Scheduled Picture**] or [**Expired Scheduled Picture**] on the Page view Normal tab instead. (The placeholder text will only be visible on the Page view Normal tab and not displayed by a Web browser that retrieves the Web page with the future or expired scheduled image.)

Unfortunately, the schedule picture component suffers from the same flaw as the scheduled include page component. Because the scheduled picture component only updates its content when FrontPage recalculates web's hyperlinks, the included picture will not appear or disappear according to schedule unless you recalculate the FrontPage web's hyperlinks on a daily basis. Therefore, in order for the scheduled picture component to function properly, you must either update and publish (to the Web server) a Web page with hyperlinks each day or use FrontPage to open the web **on the Web server** and then use the Tool menu Recalculate Hyperlinks to recalculate hyperlinks on the Web on a daily basis.

PLACING A "LAST UPDATE" DATE AND TIME ON A WEB PAGE

Many Web sites let visitors know when the web site was last updated by displaying a "last update" date and time on the site's homepage. Financial and news sites use the last update date and time to let you know they are providing the latest news stories and stock market quotes available. You may want to display the date and time of your site's most recent changes, so people visiting your home page will browse the site's pages if you have updated the site's content since their last visit.

To insert a FrontPage component that automatically keeps track of the date and/or time a Web page was last updated, perform the following steps:

1. Open the Web page on which you wish to display the date (and time) of the last update, and select the View menu Page option to display the Web page on the Page view Normal tab.
2. Place the cursor where you want the date (and time) to appear on the Web page. Then, type a text label for the last updated information, such as **This page last updated:**
3. Press the SPACEBAR (leave one space between the label and the last update date (and time), and then select the Insert menu Date and Time option. FrontPage, in turn, will display a Date and Time dialog box similar to that shown in Figure 306.

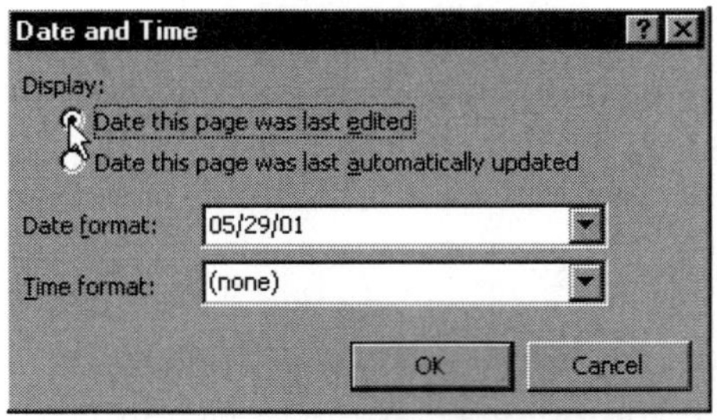

Figure 306 The Microsoft FrontPage Date and Time dialog box.

4. If you want to display the date the (and time) the content on the current Web page was changed manually, click your mouse pointer on the Date this page was last edited radio button. When you select this option, the last update date (and time) will not reflect the date (and time) of automated changes in *included content* or *web parameter values*. The last update date and time only changes when someone makes changes directly on the Web page and uses FrontPage to save the updated Web page to disk.

   If you want to display the date (and time) the content on the current Web page was changed either manually or automatically, click your mouse pointer on the Date this page was last automatically updated radio button. When you select this option, the last update date (and time) will reflect the date (and time) changes made directly on the Web page, as well, as any changes in *included content* or *web parameter values*.
5. Click your mouse pointer on the drop-down list button to the right of the Date format field, and select from the drop-down list, the format in which you want the last update date displayed. If you only want to display the last update time (and omit the date), select **none** from the drop-down list.
6. Click your mouse pointer on the drop-down list button to the right of the Time format field and select from the drop-down list, the format in which you want the last update time displayed. If you only want to display the last update date (and omit the time), select **none** from the drop-down list.

Note: *TZ in the Time format field stands for Time Zone. That is, FrontPage will automatically display the update time with an offset for the number of hours your time zone is ahead or behind Greenwich Mean Time (GMT). For example, if you live in the Central European Time (CET) zone, and you choose a time format that includes TZ, then your time display on the Web page will* *show the update time and +0100 (i.e., 1 hour ahead of GMT) during the period CET is on standard time and +0200 (i.e., 2 hours ahead of GMT) when CET is on daylight savings time. Similarly, if you live in the Pacific Time zone, then your time display on the Web page will show the update time and -0800 (i.e., 8 hours behind GMT) during the period the Pacific Time zone is on standard time and -0700 when daylight savings time is active.*

7. Click your mouse pointer on the OK button near the bottom center of the Date and Time dialog box.

After you complete Step 7, FrontPage will display the current date and/or time on the Page view Normal tab. Then, depending on the on the last update option you selected in Step 4, FrontPage will update the date and/or time displayed on the page each time someone changes content on the Web page and whenever FrontPage automatically changes included content or web parameter values (if you clicked the mouse pointer on the Date this page was last automatically updated radio button in Step 4).

INDEX